The Field and the Forge

The Field and the Forge

*Population, Production, and Power
in the Pre-industrial West*

JOHN LANDERS

OXFORD
UNIVERSITY PRESS

OXFORD
UNIVERSITY PRESS

Great Clarendon Street, Oxford OX2 6DP

Oxford University Press is a department of the University of Oxford.
It furthers the University's objective of excellence in research, scholarship,
and education by publishing worldwide in

Oxford New York

Auckland Cape Town Dar es Salaam Hong Kong Karachi Kuala Lumpur
Madrid Melbourne Mexico City Nairobi New Delhi Shanghai Taipei Toronto

With offices in

Argentina Austria Brazil Chile Czech Republic France Greece
Guatemala Hungary Italy Japan Poland Portugal
Singapore South Korea Switzerland Thailand Turkey Ukraine Vietnam

Oxford is a registered trade mark of Oxford University Press
in the UK and in certain other countries

Published in the United States
by Oxford University Press Inc., New York

© John Landers 2003

The moral rights of the author have been asserted

Database right Oxford University Press (maker)

First published 2003

First published in paperback 2005

All rights reserved. No part of this publication may be reproduced,
stored in a retrieval system, or transmitted, in any form or by any means,
without the prior permission in writing of Oxford University Press,
or as expressly permitted by law, or under terms agreed with the appropriate
reprographics rights organization. Enquiries concerning reproduction
outside the scope of the above should be sent to the Rights Department,
Oxford University Press, at the address above

You must not circulate this book in any other binding or cover
and you must impose this same condition on any acquirer

British Library Cataloguing in Publication Data

Data available

Library of Congress Cataloging in Publication Data

Data available

ISBN 0-19-924916-4
ISBN 0-19-927957-8 (pbk.)

1 3 5 7 9 10 8 6 4 2

Typeset by Kolam Information Service Pvt. Ltd, Pondicherry, India
Printed in Great Britain
on acid-free paper by
Biddles Ltd, King's Lynn, Norfolk

To Diana

Acknowledgements

I AM VERY grateful to all the people who helped me in the course of the work for this book. Charles Tilly provided very helpful comments on an earlier draft and I am grateful to him, and to Robert Franklin and Diana Parker for their essential help in the final revision. Professors Sir Michael Howard, Sir Tony Wrigley, Bob O'Neill, and Jan de Vries read draft chapters and I benefited greatly from their comments. Sir Michael Howard also provided crucial help and encouragement from an early stage of the project for which I am extremely grateful. I have benefited from conversations with many friends and colleagues in Oxford, among whom I should particularly like to thank Robin Briggs for sharing his compendious knowledge of the naval history and many other aspects of early modern Europe, and Jim Adams, Jane Lightfoot, and Simon Swain, for their patient guidance among the complexities of the ancient world. I am grateful to the AHRB for funding a term's research leave which facilitated the completion of this work.

I should like to thank Clifford Rogers for pointing out some errors and infelicities in the original which I have endeavoured to rectify in this paperback edition. Any remaining errors are of course entirely my own responsibility.

J.L.

Contents

List of Figures   xi
List of Tables   xii

1. Introduction: Time, Space, and Population   1

PART I: THE ORGANIC ECONOMY AND DEMOGRAPHIC SPACE

2. Population Dynamics   19
3. Production and Technology   47
4. The Means of Transport   72
5. Trade and Traffic   98

PART II: MILITARY TECHNOLOGY

6. Battlefields before Gunpowder   127
7. The Gunpowder Revolution   153
8. Military Capital: Oars, Sails, Walls, and Guns   176

PART III: FORCE, POWER, AND SPACE

9. War and the Organic Economy   202
10. Power and Space I: Expanding Control   227
11. Power and Space II: Maintaining Control   250

PART IV: WAR, POPULATION, AND RESOURCES

12. The Cost of War: Manpower and Resources — 282

13. Population, Power, and Technology — 309

14. The Cost of War: Mortality and Population Loss — 334

15. Spending, Taxing, and Borrowing — 355

16. Conclusion — 378

Appendix I: *Metropolitan Provisioning: Economic and Administrative Maxima* — 383
Appendix II: *Army Strengths and Casualties* — 386
References — 404
Index — 429

List of Figures

2.1.	Long-term population growth in Europe	24
2.2.	The classical model of diminishing returns to labour	37
4.1.	The cost of carrying wheat to London from within southern and eastern England *c*.1300	92
13.1.	Sauvy's model of the 'power optimum' population	311
13.2.	Military power as a function of force size and troop quality (on assumptions (A))	328
	(*a*) Effectiveness curves	328
	(*b*) Values of M for forces of quality grades I–IV and size categories A–D (A < B < C < D)	328
13.3.	'Imperial' and 'barbarian' forces: military power and escalation dominance	329
13.4.	Military power as a function of force size and troop quality (on assumptions (B))	330

List of Tables

2.1.	European population in the age of the Antonines	21
2.2.	Population of selected European countries in millions, 1500–1900	25
2.3.	European urbanization	41
	(*a*) Growth ratios of the urban percentage and the total population	41
	(*b*) The urban percentage of total population	41
2.4.	Estimated English population by sector	42
3.1.	Energy costs of activity in kilojoules per hour	48
3.2.	Productivity in arable agriculture	59
	(*a*) Seed–yield ratios	59
	(*b*) Yields per acre in England	59
4.1.	Duration of voyages, 1609–1611	80
4.2.	Estimated load capacity for pack animals	81
4.3.	Average speeds of draught animals	83
4.4.	The costs of bulk transport	87
	(*a*) Wheat Transport costs relative to initial values: overland haulage	87
	(*b*) Freight cost ratios (per ton mile)	88
4.5.	Doubling distances for agricultural commodities in mid-nineteenth-century Germany	89
7.1.	Army strengths in battle	170
7.2.	Infantry organization	172
	(*a*) Authorized company strengths	172
	(*b*) Actual strengths	172
	(*c*) Infantry formations (authorized strength)	172
8.1.	Sieges and assaults: attackers' casualties	187
8.2.	Garrison size	189
9.1.	Gun crews and capacities: sixteenth-century French royal army	206
12.1.	Some military wage differentials	292
13.1.	Estimated east Roman and Byzantine troop strengths	317
13.2.	Total troop strengths	321

14.1.	Total wartime troop losses	337
14.2.	Total combat deaths (killed in action and died of wounds)	338
14.3.	Battle casualties by period	339
14.4.	Estimates of wartime disease mortality among troops	341

CHAPTER ONE

Introduction: Time, Space, and Population

THIS BOOK IS concerned with the effects that western economies' reliance on organic sources of energy and raw material had on the spatial organization of human activities over the lengthy period between the transition to settled cultivation and the industrial revolution. Time and space are intimately related in the world of human affairs no less than in the world of modern physics. 'The past', claimed the writer L. P. Hartley, 'is another country. They do things differently there.' If this claim is true then we might expect that the sense of difference should increase proportionately the further we go back into the past. As historical novelists know very well, this is not always true. The ancient world can seem strangely familiar, and the currents of historical change do not flow at a constant rate. Sometimes it is as if they were dammed or diverted into side channels and backwaters until something happens that clears the obstruction, when events seem to surge forward with a rapid and almost purposeful movement.

The industrial revolution in western Europe and the wider Atlantic world was one of these 'great unstoppings'. At its heart was a transformation in the sources of energy and raw material inputs to production that the historian E. A. Wrigley has described as a movement from 'organic' to 'mineral' economies. We are concerned with the nature of the limits that organic economies imposed on the societies they supported, and particularly in respect of what is usually termed 'spatial integration' and refers to the co-ordination of activities across geographical distances. The geographical coverage of this book is restricted to the 'west', which is, like 'Europe' itself, a fuzzily defined but real historical entity. Its boundaries were never clearly drawn and its centre of gravity shifted over time; from south-west Asia to the Mediterranean basin and then northward into Europe. It was nonetheless a zone whose social, economic, and political structures were clearly distinct from those of the peoples ringing it to the north, east, and south. On its fourth side it was bounded first by open sea and then by the newly discovered lands of America. These drew its centre of gravity westwards again, as the 'Atlantic World' came to play a prominent, and eventually a predominant, role, but for most of the time with which we are concerned America was either unknown to the people whose history is our subject matter or was a frontier zone. Within this area of geographical space the events and processes with which we are concerned unfolded on a number of distinct time scales.

1.1. TIME AND STRUCTURE

The longest time scale is that of the so-called *longue durée*, a term which is associated with the work of the French historian Fernand Braudel and conventionally imported into English without translation. Less a period than a chronological frame of reference, these 'expanses of slow-moving history' as Braudel calls them (1980: 33) are defined by the persistence of long-term underlying relationships or 'structures' that constrain the course of 'surface' events and the processes that immediately give rise to them. The *longue durée* with which we are concerned is defined by three sets of structures in this sense of the term, or, perhaps more accurately, three sets of consequences of a single structural constraint. This was the almost exclusive reliance on organic, as opposed to mineral, inputs in the spheres of production, transport, communications, and more broadly any activity that required raw materials or energy. Wood, vegetable fibres, and animal products accounted for the great majority of raw material inputs. Heat-intensive processes were usually fuelled by wood, but the largest direct contribution to the energy budget came from muscle power, and most of the muscle was human. Animal traction had an important secondary role in some economies, but, in either case, muscle power needed fuel and, like supplies of firewood, this depended ultimately on the production of the land.

This reliance on organic sources of both energy and raw materials was the foundation, the central fact, of economic life before the industrial revolution and is the basis for Wrigley's term 'the organic economy'. The reliance on organic sources restricted energy inputs, and thus productivity per head, to a low level. Low productivity meant that most people could afford only the means of subsistence, and the resulting conditions of mass poverty further limited the expansion of production through a failure of demand. Low productivity restricted the division of labour because a large majority of the workforce was needed to produce food for the minority of non-food producers. This restriction impeded social differentiation in general, and the development and transmission of society's 'stock of knowledge' was rarely the province of specialized institutions. Technical knowledge in particular was transmitted orally, through informal networks often based on kinship or affinity, and various institutionalized forms of 'learning by doing'. These modes of transmission favoured a conservative particularism in technology, which often associated the perpetuation of existing practices with respect for tradition in general and even with the maintenance of ethnic or other forms of collective identity.

Military technology made greater use of metals—almost a monopoly use in some instances—but until the sixteenth century it was muscle power which 'drove' military activity both on and off the battlefield. At this point there was a bifurcation. Military transport and communications continued to rely on muscle power, and military logistics on the productivity of an organic economy, but the technology of violence itself witnessed an unprecedented transformation as muscle power gave way to the chemical energy of gunpowder. In this respect the military *longue durée* ended with the sixteenth century. In other respects it persisted into the nineteenth and even early twentieth centuries and the transition to 'mineral economies' based on coal and iron. The intervening period was one in which two 'energetic regimes' coexisted. It witnessed unusual strains because the new technology of violence allowed, or even required, commitment of resources on a scale that tested the productive and logistical limits of an organic economy.

A demographic *longue durée* also ended in late nineteenth-century Europe. This was less a question of population growth, though it too broke through existing limits, than of the underlying 'vital processes' of fertility and mortality and the structures that had previously constrained them. With only late and limited exceptions, potentially fatal diseases were incurable, specific preventive measures absent, and the underlying mechanisms of infection unknown. On the fertility side, there was no safe, reliable, and unintrusive means of blocking the path from coition to conception and thence to birth. The deliberate premature termination of births to sexually cohabiting couples was unknown on any demographically significant scale before the end of the eighteenth century, and then only in France. Birth and death rates were correspondingly higher than they were to be for most of the twentieth century, but they varied over space and time. The constraints on fertility and mortality were not rigid determinants, and both of them varied in response to a diversity of influences. These influences acted through sets of underlying relationships between demographic and other variables that are conventionally termed 'vital regimes' and the long-term persistence of which defined a demographic *longue durée*.

1.2. CYCLES AND SEASONS

The structures of the *longue durée* defined a set of outer limits but economic and demographic life was anything but static within these. Significant movements occurred in both the medium and short term. In the medium term, the population of Europe and the Mediterranean fluctuated substantially in a series of wavelike cycles of advance and retreat. Some kind of estimation is possible for roughly two thousand years before the later eighteenth century, during which three of these cycles of advance and recession seem to have succeeded each other. Conventionally labelled the 'ancient', 'medieval', and 'early modern' demographic cycles, each consisted of a long wave of sustained growth followed by an era of stagnation or absolute decline. These two successive phases, which we shall call the 'A' and 'B' phases for brevity, witnessed corresponding movements in economic activity, prices, and the geography of settlement. The B phase of the early modern cycle extended beyond 1750 when it gave way to an unprecedented wave of growth. This 'modern rise of population', as it has been termed, endured well into the twentieth century, but its first decades were nonetheless a product of the old demographic regime. From the 1860s things changed. The curve of population growth continued outwardly the same, but its underlying structures were transformed. Mortality and fertility both declined and outward migration rose to unprecedented peaks.

Individual and collective experience was also shaped by temporal structures beneath the levels of the *longue durée* and the economic-demographic conjuncture. The most important of these was the rhythm of the agricultural year imposed by the growing seasons for crops and pasture. Freezing weather and short days also restricted working hours in sectors outside agriculture, and the availability of many raw material inputs varied with the seasons. Seasonal weather conditions blocked roads, froze rivers, and for many centuries limited the 'sailing season' to summer and late spring. Geographical horizons shrank as communications deteriorated. For cultivators and artisans the northern world was a smaller place in winter, and became intractably large for rulers, merchants, and anyone else whose business concerned the disposition of resources in space. Changing weather and activity patterns also advanced or retarded the opportunities for pathogens to infect human hosts, as it did the opportunities for human and animal procreation. Births and deaths displayed characteristic seasonal patterns, varying in space and time and interacting in complex ways.

The economic historians Ad van der Woude and Jan de Vries have used the term 'time frontier' in talking of seasonal disruptions to inland navigation (de Vries and van der Woude 1997). The image of the time frontier has its limitations, like any metaphor, but it is a very powerful one with a broad range of reference. Temporal zones of relative inactivity, whether imposed by climate or other limiting factors such as a shortage of raw materials, were as much a feature of the pre-industrial world as were spatial frontiers, and they had much in common. Characteristically contested and ambiguous, frontiers were zones of shifting alliance and unstable identity. Just as the spatial frontier was *terra nullius* to an imperial power and fit only for colonization, so the time frontier was a zone of worthless indolence in the eyes of moral reformer and capitalist alike. But to its inhabitants it was one in which economic activity yielded to an intensity of social life, of informal gatherings that reworked the multitude of networks and alliances on which life in small-scale communities depended.

As in space, so in time, there were also 'internal frontiers', sanctified religious holidays and feast days on which no work was done, and others like 'St Monday' that were merely workless by tradition. Capital eventually colonized the time frontier, banishing workless days, and it was this, far more than the lengthening of the working day itself, that was responsible for expanding eighteenth-century English productivity (Voth 2000). But the time frontier too was a zone of shifting alliance and identity for as long as it endured. The cultivator, cling as he might to traditional patterns of sociability, often welcomed paid employment for himself and, still more, his animals in slack agricultural seasons when labour and carriage might thereby be obtained greatly 'below cost'. The practice of secondary or 'by-employments' provided another alternative as cultivators metamorphosed into artisans or tradesmen, literally, for a season. Elsewhere winter turned farmers into raiding warriors, and where organized states bordered transhumant pastoralists as in twelfth-century Asia Minor, the geography of political control itself could fluctuate with the seasonal passage of flocks from upland to lowland pasture (Hendy 1985: 117).

1.3. ENERGY AND DEMOGRAPHIC SPACE

The elements of economic and demographic life are situated in space as well as time. Processes such as the growth of trade, the integration of regional and supra-regional markets, or the spread of infectious disease only become comprehensible when the spatial organization of human activities is taken into account. But if space is a central concept in both economic and demographic history, it is not a straightforward one. Defined by the *Concise Oxford Dictionary* as 'continuous extension', space is at once a familiar and an elusive reality. To exist at all is to exist in space as well as time, and space is the medium through which interaction of any kind occurs. Yet, as R. D. Sack points out, the very 'entanglement of space and thing and space's infusion into every realm of thought' makes it that much harder to pin down exactly what constitutes 'spatiality' as a specific property of objects or events (Sack 1980: 4). The spatial character of economic and demographic phenomena is bound up with the processes that sustain them and with the consumption of energy, and it was this which gave the spatial organization of organic economies their characteristic form.

Space can be conceptualized in very different ways. For most purposes geographical space, the physical space of the earth's surface, can be thought of in Newtonian or 'absolute' terms. Absolute space complies with the rules of three-dimensional Euclidean geometry and has a timeless and immaterial existence that is both real and independent of the bodies occupying it. Twentieth-century physical scientists were, however, forced to abandon this conceptualization in favour of a relativistic approach which treats space 'as merely a relation between events or an aspect of events, and thus bound to time and process' (Blaut 1961: 1). Economic and demographic interactions occur in a space of just this kind, as we can see if we consider the example of economic transactions between sets of individuals, settlements, or distinct regions. Any sensible measure of the relative 'closeness' of these transactors for economic purposes has to be based on the time or costs involved in moving goods between them, rather than the physical distance in a straight line, but measures of this kind are neither timeless nor absolute. They vary with the nature of the transportation system, the commodities involved, and sometimes with the season of the year, and they do not obey the laws of Euclidean geometry (see below, Chapter 4).

The spatial character of economic and demographic interactions therefore differs greatly from that of geographic space. Their elements are located within geographic space, but the interrelationships between them constitute a spatial reality of a different order, which we shall term for convenience 'demographic space' and whose configuration is bound to the processes through which demographic and economic structures persist and are reproduced. All of these processes require the consumption of energy. Energy is consumed by the physiological processes that sustain and reproduce life and by the economic processes through which goods and services are produced and consumed. Increased energy inputs are generally needed if there are to be major increases in labour productivity, and since increased productivity is a prerequisite for the long-term differentiation of social structures, the process of social differentiation itself rests ultimately on increases in energy consumption.

The processes of production, consumption, and social differentiation through which demographic space is produced and reproduced all require energy to be consumed. As economic and social processes become more complex and elaborated so the energy requirement increases, but the relationship between energy and space goes beyond the reproduction of demographic or economic structures taken in isolation and extends to their spatial organization, the disposition of economic and demographic elements in geographic space. As this spatial organization becomes more complex so the necessary consumption of energy increases. At its simplest, different geographical distributions of production and consumption activities require different levels and patterns of transport and communications if the economy is to keep going. Where everyone lives close by their place of employment far fewer energy inputs are needed to maintain the distribution of settlement and economic activity than where the average journey to work is many miles per day. What is true of labour is true of other inputs to production, and the more differentiated economies and societies become, the more complex their spatial organization is likely to be, and the larger the energy input that is required to maintain it.

1.4. THE FIELD AND THE FORGE

The historical nexus between energy and space in organic economies can be depicted in a pair of concrete symbols or 'metonyms': the field and the forge. Until very recently, in historical terms, the energy required to reproduce demographic space derived, either directly or indirectly, from the produce of the land. The geography of production in the organic economy was, above all, a geography of fields. In concrete terms, industrial raw materials like energy and food supplies were overwhelmingly derived from the products of cultivation or pasturage. The products of woodland and waste might make an important secondary contribution, but it was a contribution whose limits were set by the requirements of cultivation. Like pasturage, they competed with cultivation for the available supply of land, and the cycles of population growth and decline in western Europe can be traced in the shifting balance between arable agriculture and other forms of land use.

The geography of organic economies was also a geography of fields in a more abstract sense. Whereas mining or factory production are effectively located at points in geographical space, activities like cultivation or stock-rearing are dispersed across the landscape and so have an 'areal' rather than a 'punctiform' distribution. The areal geography of production imposed a corresponding pattern on the geography of consumption in organic economies. As long as haulage depended on muscle power there were severe constraints on the distances high-bulk, low-value commodities, such as staple foods, could be transported by land. Most people thus had to live very close to where their food was grown, and many industrial workers had to live close to their raw material supplies. Both production and consumption were thus dispersed over a landscape of fields and pastures, woods and small-scale settlements. Across such a landscape, the traffic in subsistence products, which accounted for the great bulk of production, was overwhelmingly small scale and short distance. The rarity of major, clearly defined, points of production, consumption, or exchange meant that the volume of traffic on any given route was kept too low to provide an economic rationale for large investment in infrastructure. The geography of land transport was thus, for the most part, dominated by the capillary-like mesh of small-scale routeways which served to integrate the economic life of subregional blocks of territory.

Alongside the economy of the field, and the space to which it gave rise, existed another—the economy of the forge. The forge is a metonym for the world of metalworking, and above all ironworking, and for heat-intensive production generally. It was the antithesis of the field in terms of its energy, its geography, and its political economy. In energy terms, although muscle power long remained a necessary factor in ironworking from its first appearance in the second millennium BC, it played a secondary role to heat, and the practicability of the process depended as much on supplies of fuel as it did on the availability of ore itself. Geographically, heat-intensive production always occurred at specific points in space. These points might be broadly scattered as small-scale units serving their local communities, or else dispersed across economically specialized regions such as the early modern English Weald, but as the scale of production increased the result was the formation of larger units, or denser aggregations, rather than ever-broader productive fields. The punctiform geography of the forge, allied to the value of its products and its voracious appetite for fuel, allowed the development of long-range transport networks for raw materials and products long before cross-country haulage of food supplies became possible on a comparable scale.

In principle, field and forge were synergistic. Ceramics and metal tools had a place in production and consumption across the organic economy, but the scarcity of energy placed heat-intensive products out of the reach of poor men and women, on any substantial scale, until the eve of the industrial revolution. The world of the forge was bound up with the world of wealth and political power. In particular, the technology of iron was a technology of war, and control of the means of coercion depended, above all, on control of the forge and its products. For rulers to exert effective power, of course, required more than just control over the means of coercion. It was also necessary to exercise control, whether by coercion or other means, over the population and the resources on which it depended. In other words it was necessary to exercise control over the elements of demographic space. In those contexts both the 'space' and the 'demographic' need to be emphasized. The exercise of control was in part a matter of geography, requiring control over settlements and communications, and thus was subject to the same sorts of constraints as those affecting the geography of production and consumption, although these operated in a distinctive fashion. The 'demographic' also requires emphasis, however, for the exercise of power rested much more on control over demographic space—population, resources, and networks of communications—than it did simply over territory, geographic space, as such. Indeed, the institutions and ideologies of rulership were often defined in these terms.

The geographies of long-distance trade and politico-military power were both characteristically expressed in terms of spatial inequality and the formation of what have been termed 'core–periphery' relations. Raw materials, including mineral ores and valuable organic products, as well as manpower in the form of mercenaries or slaves, moved from the non-, or only weakly, monetarized periphery to the core, whilst manufactured luxuries moved the other way. The relative roles of political and economic differentials varied. In early modern Europe the relationships were largely mediated through the market and the tendency of prices to be lower in peripheral regions than they were in the core. In the ancient world the opposition of core and periphery more often coincided with that between the zone of organized states and stateless 'barbarian' societies, and trade was mediated through non-market channels. In the absence of formal political structures, barbarian political leadership characteristically rested on social status gained through the acquisition and redistribution of prestige goods, success in war, or both. The manipulation of trading links with the core was one route to political leadership. Raiding was another route and one which ensured that relationships between the barbarian periphery and the 'civilized' core were rarely stable in the long term.

1.5. WAR AND THE ORGANIC ECONOMY

The balance of power between core and periphery depended in the first instance on the relative military effectiveness of their inhabitants which itself depended very much on the military technology at their command. Major changes in military technology occurred throughout the period, just as in the economic sphere we can recognize a military *longue durée* defined by the virtually exclusive reliance on muscle power as an energy source. Unlike the economic or demographic spheres, however, the *longue durée* in military technology came to an end in the sixteenth century with the general diffusion of firearms. This 'gunpowder revolution', as it can fairly be called, was a historically unique phenomenon since it was the first time that muscle power had been supplanted by chemical energy as the primary power source in a major area of human activity. From the beginning of the sixteenth century the tactical capabilities of European armies were increasingly defined by the characteristics of gunpowder weapons—even though elements of the old world long persisted into the new. Cavalry troopers carried lances and swords into the early battles of the First World War and the second saw Soviet cavalrymen sabre German Panzer Grenadiers on occasions, but these events were now historical curiosities to all but their participants. The military limits of the possible were set by trucks, tanks, and aircraft.

The gunpowder revolution liberated the technology of fighting from the limitations of muscle power, but at another level the military *longue durée* endured into the twentieth century in the shape of a reliance on animal power for transportation.[1] In a broader sense, the persistence of the civilian organic economy also constrained the development of military power by restricting its material foundations. The chronological mismatch between energy revolutions in these different spheres did more than complicate the delineation of historical periods; it affected the substance of history itself. The problem lay in the ambiguous relationship between political power, armed force, and the economy on the one hand and the changing contribution of manpower and capital resources to military effectiveness on the other. Political power can be defined as the ability to subjugate others' will to one's own and requires access to the means of organized violence—or military force—if it is to be sustainable in the long term.

Force is therefore a necessary condition for the exercise of power even if it is rarely sufficient in itself as an instrument of effective government. If military force is the foundation of political power, it is equally true that access to resources is the foundation of an effective military force. Without access to force to protect it this foundation is unlikely to be preserved for long, but if the deployment is too massive the foundations themselves collapse and the whole structure comes crashing down. Organic economies imposed limitations on transport and supply, and so constrained the conduct of military operations, but they also restricted the volume of available resources that could be devoted to warfare. This restriction always mattered, but its effects were partly offset by the nature of muscle-powered military technology which curtailed the scope for gaining greater effectiveness merely by increasing numbers. Often a qualitative superiority made up for a deficiency in numbers.

The consequences of the gunpowder revolution are part of the story of the west's organic economies as a result of the demographic and economic burdens

---

[1] During the First World War the British military animal herd peaked at a total of 870,000 in 1917. At this time some 300,000 animals were used on the western front to bring supplies forward the final 5 miles or so from the advance collection points to the trench lines themselves. By 1939 the British military had dispensed with horses other than for ceremonial purposes, but they continued to play a major role as transport animals in continental armies. The German forces facing Russia disposed of 625,000 horses at the opening of the invasion in 1941 and the total military herd reached 1.2 million in February 1945. The military exploitation of horsepower on this scale had serious implications for the civilian economy. The Soviet horse herd is estimated to have fallen from 21 million to only 7.8 million between 1940 and 1943, and 7 million of 16.1 million horses in the occupied territories are estimated to have been either killed or removed (DiNardo and Bay 1988).

that they imposed. These were substantial because the gunpowder revolution made it easier to use large forces effectively and more difficult to set quality against quantity. Larger forces were correspondingly more expensive and resources remained scarce. If Europe's rulers had been willing and able to fight within their means this might not have mattered, but it was military and political priorities that chiefly decided the scale of military effort and these strongly favoured long-term increases. War became more expensive and destructive as a result. For the first hundred and fifty years or so of the gunpowder era much of the increased cost was born by the inhabitants of the war zones themselves, but as military and administrative institutions became more elaborate the costs were increasingly transferred to the public treasuries.

This transfer of costs reduced the economic and demographic destructiveness of war, but it greatly increased the fiscal burden, and things were made worse by the fact that the new military technology, unlike its predecessors, imposed a ratio of manpower to capital commitments which was out of keeping with the demographic cycle. In the short term, the growing quantity and sophistication of public credit enabled war to be financed by an ever-expanding debt, but ultimately debts had to be paid, or at least serviced, and by the end of the eighteenth century the states of Europe were perilously close to financial collapse. As it happened, the first major power to collapse was France, whose real wealth and demographic resources made it a potential military giant. The successor regimes went on to realize this potential. Their methods looked backwards to the older style of predatory warfare at least as much as they foreshadowed the coming age of militarized nationalism, but they were the fruit of political revolution and England's economic revolution was their nemesis.

1.6. THE NATURE OF LIMITS

The nineteenth century saw the end of a *longue durée* in European demographic and economic history. Population grew, but production expanded still more, so that living standards eventually rose after an uncertain start. Political structures changed too. States became both more centralized and more significant in terms of their bureaucratic agencies and the impact that these had on their subjects' daily lives. Some also expanded geographically, and by the end of the nineteenth century a number had expanded their tentacles to embrace the globe in world-spanning empires just as steam power and the electric telegraph had begun to weave together a global economy. The eighteenth and nineteenth centuries saw population growth, economic expansion, and the co-ordination of human activity across ever greater distances. In each sphere events moved forward in such tightly choreographed lock-step that the hypothesis of some close and necessary causal connection between them appears irresistible. This is even more the case if we move back through the two preceding centuries of institutional change to the geographically fragmented Europe of the later Middle Ages. In this chronological perspective, the unavoidable conclusion seems to be that spatial integration depended on demographic and economic growth of a distinctively 'modern' kind, but the picture looks very different if we move the time horizon further back. Some of the largest political units that Europe and the Mediterranean basin have seen existed in antiquity, and elsewhere in the world some very large states persisted into the early modern period. On the economic plane, a degree of large-scale spatial integration in the form of far-flung trading networks pre-dated the working of iron, let alone the coming of coal-powered industry.

There is a paradox here, because that link between spatial integration and economic growth that characterized the end of the nineteenth century is not just a matter of observation after the event, it also rests on a priori analytical foundations. At the root of the matter is the very severe restriction on energy availability that characterized organic economies. This restriction constrained the scope for spatial integration as much as it did population dynamics and the expansion of production. Economic integration involved the co-ordination of production and the exchange of products over a distance. Political integration involved the systematic exercise of coercion at a distance from the power centre and thus the projection of power over space. The two forms of integration were distinct, but they were related to each other and they both required energy inputs. The production of goods, the means of transport, and the means of coercion all involved the consumption of energy at one or more stages in the process, as did the formation of highly specialized skills whether these were economic, administrative, or military. Time is limited and specialists in any of these spheres could not produce all of their own food and other subsistence requirements. Specialists therefore had to be supported by other people, who needed to produce correspondingly more than would otherwise have been the case. Productivity gains of this kind often required additional energy inputs, and the consequent transportation and distribution always did so.

The solution to the paradox of large-scale spatial integration in the ancient world lies in the crucial but easily overlooked fact that constraints are not determinants. Rather they specify an envelope of possibilities within which activities attract differential costs in such a way as to make some developments easier and more likely than others. In consequence two kinds of limit existed. The first kind were the 'hard' limits which marked the outer edge of what was possible given a reliance on organic resources. This outer edge was rarely if ever reached because within it lay another envelope of 'soft' limits which were set by the institutional arrangements in any given society and the efficiency of the technology to which it had access. The effectiveness of marketing or administrative structures, the degree of physical security, and the state of transport and communications all set immediate limits to the progress of spatial integration, but the hard limits of an organic economy encompassed substantial variation in all these respects and so in the longer term this inner envelope was a permeable one.

The extent of the gap between the hard and soft limits varied greatly over space and time, but it was often substantial. A major reason for this was the way in which poverty depressed demand, so discouraging investment in greater productivity and promoting a widespread underutilization of resources. The prevalence of technological bottlenecks had similar consequences, just as the areal geography of an organic economy discouraged investment in transport infrastructure. In consequence there was substantial scope for the mobilization of underemployed resources, particularly man and animal power, by rulers who were sufficiently efficient, ingenious, or ruthless and whose goals were political rather than economic. Paradoxically, as economic processes became more efficient and resources were more fully utilized it became more expensive to mobilize them for the pursuit of non-economic goals.

In the ancient world spatial integration was largely driven by military or political imperatives, and one manifestation of this was that, where large-scale communications systems were constructed, they catered to the needs of soldiers, couriers, or administrators rather than heavy freight. The administrative structures of medieval and early modern states were too weak to duplicate these achievements, but a growing economic sophistication saw the emergence of regional and supra-regional markets. When early modern rulers sought to mobilize manpower on a large scale they made considerable use of market relationships, by contracting with mercenary brokers and other middlemen, in addition to or in place of administrative structures. Their efforts were constrained by the inadequacy of the prevailing fiscal systems, which acted as a soft limit by preventing resources which were physically available from being mobilized for political ends.

From the later Middle Ages large-scale borrowing provided a means of circumventing this limit by exploiting the growing sophistication of economic institutions. In the short term it allowed much greater military efforts to be mounted than could have been paid for from taxation, but in the longer term it merely added interest payments to those which had to be made to soldiers and contractors. By the late eighteenth century the European powers were in a state of potential collapse financially and the wars that followed the actual collapse of Bourbon France resolved themselves into a struggle between two sharply contrasted systems of resource mobilization. The French system broke through the soft limits of *ancien régime* finance by means of administrative coercion. Young men were forced to become soldiers in exchange for wages that were too low to induce them to volunteer, and the resulting armies were used to extract resources from enemies and nominal allies alike. The British sustained the war against France with a new system of finance which broke through the soft limits of the old fiscal regime, but at the same time the hard limits of the organic economy were themselves beginning to give way.

1.7. SCHEME OF PARTS

The book falls into four parts. The first part considers the relationships between population, production, and transportation before the industrial revolution and the ways in which these advanced or retarded the integration of space. Part II is concerned with military technology and the consequences of the gunpowder revolution which ended its exclusive reliance on muscle power by introducing chemical energy to warfare. Part III considers the political integration of space through the coercive power of armed force and the ways in which this process was limited by the constrained structures of an organic civilian economy and a muscle-powered military technology. Part IV brings together the economic, demographic, and military spheres with a consideration of the ways in which resources were mobilized for military and political goals, the costs that this process imposed, and the ways in which it was affected by changes in military technology.

PART I

The Organic Economy and Demographic Space

Introduction

THE DYNAMICS OF population and productivity growth in organic economies were intimately bound up with changes in the organization of what we have called demographic space, or the geographical arrangement of population and resources. The scope for variations in either space or time was constrained by the organic economies' reliance on the productivity of the land for sources of raw materials and energy. Ultimately everything depended on the efficiency of plant photosynthesis and the energy conversion of biological 'engines', and both are low by mechanical standards. Maize, the most efficient photosynthesizer in 1950s North America, converted no more than 3 per cent of radiant energy into theoretically available calories, whilst the human body converts only one fifth of dietary calories into usable energy, so that the best-nourished worker can expend no more than about 600 calories through physical exertion (Cottrell 1955: 16–18). The fact that workers could bring so little energy to bear meant that productivity was correspondingly low, and low productivity made for general scarcity, which condemned the majority of the population to poverty and ensured that the demand for non-subsistence goods remained weak. The weakness of demand in its turn meant that there were few inducements to expand output per head through technological innovation, and under these circumstances, as population grew and labour supplies increased, so the productivity of labour tended to decline. Low productivity, combined with seasonal and other bottlenecks in the production process, meant that all too often general scarcity coexisted with a chronic under-employment of labour and other productive resources.

Regional specialization was one possible route to productivity growth, but it was one which was impeded by the nature of the resource base and its spatial organization. The establishment of regional and inter-regional economic units required the co-ordination of activities at increasing distances from each other and the development of systematic patterns of geographical movement on the part of goods and people. The scope for spatial integration of this kind depended on the level of productivity obtained in the agrarian economy and on the efficiency of transport and communications. Prior productivity levels were important because they determined how many specialist traders and transport workers the economy could afford to feed, whilst the efficiency of transportation set a limit to how big a volume of commodities could be moved and how far. Land transportation depended mainly on muscle power, whose inefficiency as a prime mover meant that the long-distance land haulage of cheap, bulky commodities was rarely a practical economic proposition because draught or pack animals consumed fodder equal to the value of their cargo in a matter of days.

The diffuse—or 'areal'—geography of organic production also confined most physical movement of commodities to short distances at low traffic densities, which provided little incentive for expensive investment in major roads and other transport infrastructure.

The organic economies' heavy reliance on agrarian produce impeded large-scale spatial integration. It also made it more difficult to maintain productivity as population expanded. The fact that the land was the main source of food, energy inputs, and industrial raw materials meant that their supply was difficult to expand and that they were likely to come into competition for the available land as population and output grew. Population growth was also bound up with spatial structure and its dynamics. Growth brought characteristic patterns of geographical redistribution away from richer, longer-settled agricultural districts towards less productive woodlands, hills, and especially towns and cities. Movement of this kind also affected mortality by altering levels of exposure to infection, just as greater spatial integration could introduce new infectious agents.

CHAPTER TWO

Population Dynamics

THE ENERGY INPUTS available to organic economies were very limited and overall productivity was consequently low. Demographic patterns were consequently constrained in ways which themselves had economic implications. Economic and demographic patterns were bound to be very closely related as long as human labour was the main variable factor of production and subsistence needs formed the main element of consumption. The transition to mineral economies in nineteenth-century Europe also coincided with the beginning of what demographers call the 'demographic transition', which saw fertility and mortality fall to hitherto unprecedented levels. Before these two transitions low productivity had ensured the prevalence of mass poverty and all that this implied in terms of low-quality housing, diet, clothing, and sanitation. Poverty of this kind provided pathogenic micro-organisms with ideal opportunities to multiply and infect human beings, leading to death rates that were high even by the standards of the twentieth-century Third World. Even the favoured few who were wealthy suffered in this way because they were rarely able to isolate themselves from their social inferiors and the epidemiological hazards that they represented. Birth rates were correspondingly high in the absence of systematic control over marital fertility, but pre-transitional population patterns were neither static nor uniform.

Population in Europe and elsewhere displayed a long-term cyclical pattern in which phases of sustained growth alternated with stagnation or absolute decline. Substantial regional differences also existed in the underlying demographic determinants of growth. Levels of fertility within marriage varied geographically, for reasons that are still not fully understood, but the principal demographic regulator was variation in the age at, and incidence of, marriage itself. The west European marriage pattern, which combined delayed female marriage with substantial proportions remaining permanently single, seems to have been unique before the twentieth century and reduced birth rates below the levels prevailing elsewhere. The consequences apparently extended to generally lower mortality and higher living standards in the region, as well as a birth rate that responded to changing economic conditions as these advanced or retarded the prospects for marriage. The consequences of this marriage pattern ameliorated the impact of the organic economy's underlying constraints, but it could not remove them, and when population grew the conditions of life for the mass of the population deteriorated.

2.1. CYCLES OF POPULATION GROWTH

Malthus likened the material prospects for human societies to an endless race between the hare of population growth and the tortoise of agricultural production.[1] The history of pre-nineteenth-century European population growth is shrouded in varying degrees of obscurity, but it is quite clear that the hare's performance was as inconsistent as its fabulous predecessor's, with periods of rapid exertion and prolonged inactivity alternating in a wave-like demographic trajectory. Demographers recognize three major cycles of population growth, which are conventionally termed 'ancient', 'medieval', and 'early modern', before the onset of the so-called 'modern rise of population' in the later eighteenth century. Each cycle consisted of successive movements of advance and retreat, which can most conveniently be labelled 'A' and 'B' phases respectively. Our knowledge and understanding of these movements is necessarily patchy because the statistical apparatus of census-taking and civil registration of births and deaths was not established across most of Europe before the nineteenth century.

Some reasonably reliable information is available for early modern populations, but the quality and quantity of demographic evidence both decline as we move back into the medieval period and with them the extent of consensus among demographic historians.[2] Though there are few certainties where medieval numbers are concerned, there is at least broad agreement as to the trend of population after AD 1000. The preceding period is, by contrast, a true demographic Dark Age, and our understanding of ancient population levels is mainly based on 'intelligent guesswork' using a mixture of logical deduction and inferences from archaeological finds, literary accounts, and fragmentary documents relating particularly to taxation or counts of sub-groups within the various populations. The period's economic history is rather better understood, and its political history much more so, but there is little consensus as to what, if any, demographic inferences can legitimately be drawn from this understanding.

---

[1] Malthus developed his ideas through successive editions of his *Essay on the Principle of Population* (see for instance Malthus 1970, 1989) and his *Principles of Political Economy* (Malthus 1989). For a brief introduction to Malthus' ideas see Winch (1987), and for demographic aspects the various contributions to Coleman and Schofield (1986) and Dupâquier, Fauve-Chamoux, and Grebenik (1983). The recent reassessment of his standing as an analyst of population dynamics in an organic economy is largely due to the forceful advocacy of Wrigley; see for instance Wrigley (1983, 1986, 1987b).

[2] See Hollingsworth (1976) for a general survey of sources for population history and Flinn (1981) for a more recent discussion of early modern Europe. The relatively abundant material for early modern England is discussed in Wrigley, Davies, et al. (1997); for early modern France see Dupâquier (1988a). For the medieval period in Europe see inter alia Russell (1972), Pounds (1979, 1994), and Livi-Bacci (1999); for England see Hatcher and Bailey (2001), Hatcher (1977) and Smith (1991), and for France Dupâquier (1988b). Estimated population levels in the Roman Empire still depend heavily on the 19th-century work of Julius Beloch but valuable surveys of current thinking are to be found in Parkin (1992) and the relevant chapters of the second edition of *The Cambridge Ancient History*. The articles by Durand and Biraben on long-term trends are necessarily speculative but have been influential (Biraben 1979; Durand 1977, 1967). The estimates collected in McEvedy and Jones (1978) have been widely cited in the literature although, as these authors freely admit, their evidential base is variable in quality and sometimes very flimsy.

2.1.1. THE ANCIENT DEMOGRAPHIC CYCLE

The only thing we can say with certainty about the ancient demographic cycle is that it occurred. We know this because the total population that Europe could have supported before the transition to agriculture is far below the plausible minimum for Roman Italy alone (Hassan 1981). We can also be fairly confident that, at least in some parts of Europe, there were fewer people c. AD 700 than there had been when Rome was at its height (Ward-Perkins 2000a; Hodges and Whitehouse 1983: 52–3). We can therefore say that long-term population growth certainly occurred in the last millennia of the pre-Christian era and that it was subsequently reversed, but we cannot say very much about either the chronology of these movements or the relative contribution of birth and death rates. The demographic consequences of the disruptions accompanying Europe's Iron Age are a particularly murky topic (Sherratt 1998; Cunliffe 1988, 1997), but once these had settled down growth is likely to have resumed until at least the early second century AD, when the population of the Roman Empire is thought to have lain in the fifty to seventy million range. Europe probably accounted for rather more than half of this total (Pounds 1973: 110–16; Frier 2000) and the Empire itself certainly contained the great majority of a European population whose contemporary centre of gravity lay towards the western Mediterranean (see Table 2.1).

The middle of the second century is conventionally seen as a turning point in the demographic fortunes of the Empire. There is little direct evidence for this, but a number of pieces of indirect evidence point forcefully towards the cessation of population growth and are often interpreted as signs of absolute decline. The first of these was a large-scale episode of epidemic disease which seems to have

Table 2.1 *European population in the age of the Antonines*

	Range of population estimates	
	Population in millions	Density per sq mile
Roman Empire in Europe		
Italy	6.0–9.0	52–78
Sicily	0.6–1.0	60–104
Sardinia and Corsica	0.3–0.6	23–47
Gaul	6.0–10.0	26–44
Spain	7.0–12.0	31–52
Britain	1.0–2.5	18–52
Danubian provinces	3.0–6.0	44–88
Balkan provinces	3.0–6.0	16–31
Rest of Europe		
Germany	3.0–5.0	16–26
Eastern Europe	1.0–3.0	3–8
Northern Europe	0.5–1.5	less than 3–5

Source: Pounds (1973: table 3.1).

persisted for more than two decades after breaking out on Rome's eastern frontier in the winter of AD 165/6. Traditionally referred to as 'plague', it is more likely to have been an airborne infection such as smallpox and has been credited with an overall mortality rate of 7–10 per cent in the initial outbreak (Gilliam 1961; Littman and Littman 1973). Losses on this scale could easily have been recouped in a generation under 'normal' conditions, but conditions ceased being normal shortly thereafter and the third century was one of recurrent political and military crises. There are signs that depopulation may have become established as a continuing problem from at least its central decades. The main documentary evidence is the growing proportion of land classified as derelict for tax purposes, but the introduction of forced recruitment to the army and the binding of cultivators to the land suggest a serious manpower shortage in both the civil and military spheres (Brunt 1987; Southern and Dixon 1996: 67–9; Boak 1955; Whittaker 1982). Archaeological surveys in a number of regions have also revealed a decline in the number of settlement sites that does not seem to be offset by increases in their size (Greene 1986).

The balance of probability, taking the evidence as a whole, seems to favour the existence of depopulation, but no single piece of evidence is entirely convincing in its own right, and each is capable of some other interpretation.[3] Shortages of military manpower may have arisen because the army's demands increased at a time when population was standing still, and the burden of a heavy and inequitable land tax may have forced a withdrawal from less fertile soils. But whether population merely stagnated or actually declined, it remains the case that either the birth rate fell or higher death rates persisted even after the immediate epidemic waves of the mid-second century had subsided. There is no direct evidence on either birth or death rates, but a major fall in the former seems unlikely on a priori grounds.[4] Analogies with the better-documented experience of the early modern period suggests that mortality might well have risen during the military crises of the third century. Certainly these would have provided ideal conditions for the diffusion of infectious disease, and the balance of probability seems to lie with increased mortality and consequent demographic stagnation if not actual decline.

---

[3] The case for continuing depopulation was advanced by Boak (1955), and its weaknesses scrutinized by Finley (1958). Parkin is cautiously sympathetic to the argument (1992: 62) whilst Whittaker, who queries the extent of land abandonment, is somewhat more sceptical (Whittaker and Garnsey 1998). There seems to be more agreement that depopulation accompanied the 3rd-century crises than there is with the claim that it continued thereafter. A recent survey by Cameron summarizes current understandings thus: 'Though it is notoriously hard to demonstrate that there had been a population fall in the third century, this still seems probable in general terms for the western provinces. In contrast, there is evidence to suggest a considerable population rise in the east from the end of the fourth century and especially in the fifth. However, by the fifth century, political conditions in the west were very different, and did not conduce to a similar rise' (Cameron 1993: 114).

[4] The reason for this is that large changes in the birth rate require a change either in nuptiality or in fertility within marriage. The large-scale practice of delayed marriage is not, however, thought to pre-date the medieval period at the earliest whilst deliberate regulation of marital fertility is generally assumed to be more modern still (Knodel and Van de Walle 1979). Patlagean has, however, argued for significant birth rate declines in some sections of early Byzantine society (Patlagean 1969).

The fifth century in the west is likely to have seen an accentuation of the fourth-century demographic trends, but there is evidence of substantial recovery in the Empire's eastern provinces (Patlagean 1977; Ward-Perkins 2000a). Population and prosperity both apparently peaked in the hundred years after AD 450, although the toll of subsistence and other crises may already have been worsening by the early decades of the sixth century. Certainly, the earlier upward trend was devastatingly reversed by the appearance of bubonic plague in 541. Constantinople lost at least half of its population in 541/2, and there were widespread outbreaks in the provinces (Allen 1979; Biraben and Goff 1969; Sarris 2002). The scale of the death toll for the Eastern Empire at large is unknown, but it was clearly very considerable and may have approached that of the 1340s. Plague recurred at intervals of roughly fifteen years over the following century and sporadically for another century after that. The western Mediterranean suffered less than the east, but it too is likely to have reached its lowest demographic point in the later sixth century. Plague does not seem to have reached northern Europe, other than the British Isles which were affected in the mid-seventh century (Maddicott 1997), and it was probably around this time that the continent's demographic centre of gravity started to shift away from the Mediterranean basin.

2.1.2. THE MEDIEVAL DEMOGRAPHIC CYCLE

We do not know the trend of population between the seventh and tenth centuries. There may have been a limited recovery around AD 800, the time of the Emperor Charlemagne, that was subsequently reversed during the Viking invasions of the later ninth and tenth centuries, but there is no real evidence either for or against this possibility. There are, however, clear signs of renewed growth across much of western Europe by the eleventh century (Russell 1972; Pounds 1994: 145–50; Duby 1968: 65 f.) and Fig. 2.1 depicts a broadly accepted picture of the subsequent trend. The main issues of contention are just when growth came to an end and whether numbers had already fallen before the onset of bubonic plague in the 1340s. The contemporary evidence consists mainly of documented changes in the area under cultivation, along with records of taxation and feudal dues of various sorts and other sources that provide local household counts (Pounds 1994: 125–30). These can be used to track trends, but it is difficult to estimate absolute numbers without knowing household size and we do not have this. Nonetheless, Europe's total population is thought to have passed the Roman peak soon after AD 1000 and by the early fourteenth century it had probably grown to at least twice that size. By this time it may have approached the hundred million mark, and rural densities were above eighty, or even 100, people per square mile in parts of western Europe.

The nature of the sources makes it very difficult to construct estimates for individual countries, even relatively well-documented France, but it is clear that the continental balance was shifting northwards. The widely cited estimates of

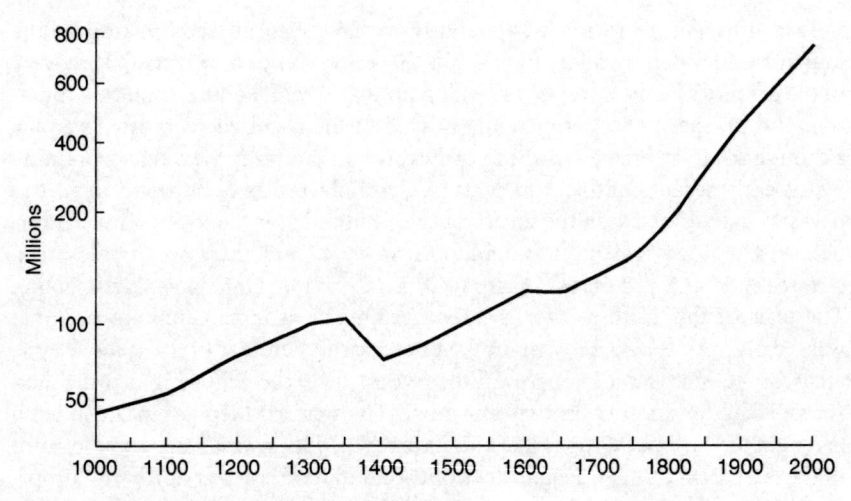

FIG. 2.1. Long-term population growth in Europe.
Source: Livi-Bacci (1999).

Beloch and Russell both attribute around a third of western Europe's medieval peak population to Iberia and Italy jointly. This equates to around a quarter of the continental total (Pounds 1973: 328). At the second-century peak the proportion was probably above 40 per cent. Western Europe was hit by a very destructive series of famines in the decades around 1300. Although there were geographical differences, many regional populations seem to have been pressing against the limits of what the contemporary economy could support (Hatcher and Bailey 2001: 30 f.; Bois 1984: 277 f.; Campbell 1991). Growth had almost certainly ceased by the second quarter of the century, and may already have gone into reverse, but it was the 'Black Death'—the catastrophic reappearance of plague in 1347–8—that decisively reversed the earlier trend. In two years stagnation turned into a dramatic decline of 20 per cent or more whilst the regular recurrence of plague evidently held Europe's population at an even lower level for some decades after this (Pounds 1994: 150 f.).

2.1.3. THE EARLY MODERN DEMOGRAPHIC CYCLE

Precisely when the demographic recession troughed remains unclear, but the 'A' phase of the ensuing early modern cycle was certainly under way by 1500. Estimates for Europe as a whole suggest the 'B' phase began a century later when total population was probably a bit above 110 million (Livi-Bacci 1999: 7–12). After fifty years of stagnation, slower growth resumed after 1650, and Europe's population was around 150 million when the modern cycle commenced in the latter part of the eighteenth century. The early modern cycle is better documented than its predecessors, particularly in the parish registers that become available for England after 1541 and for some other parts of Europe from the seventeenth century onwards.[5] This evidence shows the continental estimates to be misleading guides to national trends, which diverged after 1550 (see Table 2.2). France experienced demographic stagnation in the century following 1550, with very modest growth thereafter. Italy and Germany both experienced setbacks in the first half of the seventeenth century, followed by limited 'catch-up' growth after 1650.

This growth continued through the early eighteenth century in Italy, when the Spanish population also experienced modest expansion, having remained virtually static through the seventeenth century. The Netherlands and England both expanded rapidly until the middle of the seventeenth century followed by a hundred years of little or no growth. France is estimated to have contained about a fifth of Europe's population in 1150, with Italy and Spain together accounting for a slightly smaller share. The demographic balance of north and south changed little during the early modern cycle, but a marked eastward shift occurred as cultivators displaced pastoralists on the eastern European grasslands from the later seventeenth century. By 1700 Russia and Poland together accounted for between 20 and 25 per cent of Europe's population, around twice their probable share at the pre-plague peak. The shift continued after 1700, so that Russia alone accounted for nearly half of total European population growth from 1700 to 1750, bringing its share to around 17 per cent of the total.

Table 2.2 *Population of selected European countries in millions, 1500–1900*

	1500	1550	1600	1650	1700	1750	1800	1850	1900
Ireland	—	—	—	—	2.5	3.2	5.3	6.6	4.5
England	—	3.1	4.2	5.3	5.2	5.9	8.7	16.7	30.4
Norway	—	—	—	—	0.5	0.6	0.9	1.4	2.24
Sweden	—	—	—	—	1.4	1.8	2.4	3.5	5.14
The Netherlands	1.0	1.3	1.5	1.9	1.9	1.9	2.1	3.1	5.1
France	15.5	19.5	19.6	20.3	22.6	24.6	29.3	36.3	40.6
Germany	9.0	11.6	16.2	10.0	16.0	17.0	24.5	35.4	56.4
Russia	6.0		11.0	14.5	19.5	28.0	40.0	60.0	109.7
Italy	9.0	11.5	13.5	11.7	13.6	15.8	18.3	24.7	33.8
Spain	—	5.3	6.7	7.0	7.4	8.6	10.6	14.8	18.6
Europe	84.0	97.0	111.0	112.0	125.0	146.0	195.0	288.0	422.0

Sources: Livi-Bacci (1999: table 1.1); except for Germany pre-1700 (Pfister 1996), England (Wrigley, Davies, et al. 1997), Russia pre-1800 (Clark 1967), and France 1500 (Wrigley 1985b).

---

[5] Helleiner's classic survey (1967) remains a useful starting point for this period. Flinn's coverage of more recent work (1981) is invaluable but has little to say about overall population totals. For England see Wrigley, Davies, et al. (1997); supplemented by Houston (1992) for Britain as a whole. For France see Dupâquier (1988c), for Germany Pfister (1996), for the Netherlands de Vries and van der Woude (1997: 46 f.), and for Italy Livi-Bacci (1977, 1978).

2.1.4. THE MODERN DEMOGRAPHIC CYCLE

The modern cycle of population growth began across most of Europe in the latter decades of the eighteenth century and differed from earlier cycles in two important respects. The first is that European population growth was now only one element in a much broader and historically unprecedented episode of global expansion. The second difference is that, unlike all earlier cycles, when the 'A' phase came to an end it did so because of the spread of fertility control within marriage. European population is thought to have reached around 200 million by 1800, with more robust estimates of 288 and 422 million in 1850 and 1900 respectively. The period saw a continuing eastward shift in population, so that by 1900 Russia held more than a quarter of the continental total, whilst the contribution of Italy and Spain had fallen to around 12 per cent and France to below 10. Germany, which overtook France in the later nineteenth century, accounted for around 13 per cent of the total by 1900. The largest increase, however, was in England, where population rose from around 4 per cent of Europe's total in 1750 to an estimated 7.2 per cent in 1900. Birth rate declines became established in an increasing number of countries from the last quarter of the nineteenth century and more than offset the very large, and equally unprecedented, contemporary decline in mortality. Emigration also acted as an important brake on population growth in some regions.

2.2. POPULATION: VITAL PROCESSES AND VITAL REGIMES

The size and structure of any population are determined in the first instance by two factors: migration and 'natural increase', the balance of births and deaths whose relative importance usually depends on geographical scale. Small districts are often affected more by migration than anything else, whereas the size and structure of national and, before the twentieth century, of regional populations normally reflects the pattern of natural increase. The technical theory of demographic analysis was developed with reference to so-called 'closed' populations with zero migration of any kind. Since actual populations nearly always experience some level of migration, the theory has to be generalized to take account of this where necessary, but in practice it is often possible to treat large populations as if they were closed without distorting the results very much, and this is particularly true in historical demography, where levels of migration were generally much lower than they were to become in the course of the nineteenth century.

Demographers are interested in why population size and structure should vary over time and space and what implications this has for other aspects of social and economic life. Answering these questions depends first of all on understanding differing patterns of migration and natural increase. The latter respond to a wide diversity of influences and, in order to make this amenable to analysis, demographers deploy a conceptual abstraction, treating the so-called 'vital events' of birth and death as tangible manifestations of underlying 'vital processes' that are not themselves directly observable. The vital processes of 'fertility' and 'mortality' represent, in an abstract form, all the things 'going on' in a population that make its members more or less likely to experience associated vital events. Since the great majority of births have, historically speaking, taken place within formally recognized unions, overall fertility variations can be broken down into one component due to differences in 'marital fertility' and another due to differences in 'nuptiality', which is the process underlying the vital event of marriage.

The appearance of 'modern' demographic information, based on civil registration and regular censuses, dates only from the nineteenth century in most of Europe, and before this we have to rely primarily on parish registers for our evidence. Surviving registers are unevenly distributed geographically, and few of them date from before the seventeenth century, but there is enough English material to form a reasonable national picture from the later sixteenth century. Elsewhere only France and Sweden have yielded comparable pre-nineteenth-century data, and these only become available around the middle of the eighteenth century. Local data are, however, more plentiful, and most parts of north-western Europe are represented by surviving parish registers from at least the eighteenth century, with patchier coverage of the central and south-western regions. Good national-level fertility and mortality estimates are available for England from the later sixteenth century, and for Sweden and France from the middle of the eighteenth.

2.2.1. FERTILITY AND NUPTIALITY

The results of these studies show very little long-term change in marital fertility before the onset of the sustained decline accompanying the demographic transition.[6] Levels nonetheless varied greatly between regions with the so-called Total Marital Fertility Rate (or TMFR) ranging between values of around six and ten.[7] Demographers still disagree on the reasons for this variation, but it evidently arose from differences in intervals between successive births rather than differences in the age at which women ceased childbearing. The age structure of marital fertility therefore corresponded to what is termed 'natural fertility', in which married women continue reproduction for as long as they are physiologically capable, and many demographers believe observed regional variations to have reflected the physiological consequences of differing infant feeding regimes rather than any systematic attempt to restrict childbearing within this interval (Landers 1990*b*; Knodel 1988).

---

[6] Fertility fell sharply in times of food shortage, but the relative contribution of physiological, psychological, and social factors to these falls remains controversial (Ladurie 1979; Menken, Trissell, and Watkins 1981).

[7] This rate is equal to the average number of children born to a hypothetical woman who marries at 15 and remains married to age 50 and so it excludes the direct effects of changing mortality and nuptiality (Hinde 1998).

The prevalence of natural fertility within marriage meant that changing marriage patterns were mainly responsible for changes in overall fertility, and western Europe's marriage patterns seem to have been unique in this from at least the close of the Middle Ages until the twentieth century (Hajnal 1965; Landers 1995). Their distinguishing factor was that women delayed marriage by an average of as much as ten years beyond puberty, with substantial numbers remaining permanently unmarried, so that overall fertility levels were apparently much below those prevailing among populations elsewhere. The historical origins of this behaviour remain obscure but its sociological foundations lay in the region's pattern of household structure and formation which was based on the nuclear family and 'neo-local' residence (Hajnal 1983). This meant that couples had to establish their own structurally independent household at marriage, rather than joining an already existing one, and to do this they had to have accumulated a certain body of skills and petty capital. Since the time required to achieve this varied with economic and demographic circumstances, west European birth rates were not only relatively low but also potentially responsive to changing conditions. This phenomenon has been credited with a variety of benign economic and demographic consequences. In particular, living standards seem, on the whole, to have been higher, mortality less severe, and the proportion of dependent children lower than could be the case where marriage was tied to physiological maturity (Wrigley 1986, 1987a). Historical demographers conventionally refer to these two sets of circumstances respectively as high- and low-pressure demographic regimes.

2.2.2. THE OLD MORTALITY REGIME

The century after 1870 saw unprecedented changes in the mortality as well as the fertility of western populations (Chesnais 1992; Schofield, Reher, and Bideau 1991; Preston 1976). The average expectation of life at birth, which had rarely been much above forty years and was often much less, almost doubled, and the structure of mortality rates by age and cause of death was transformed. Previously some 20 to 30 per cent of live-born babies in most populations had died before their first birthday, and the proportion surviving to age 15 was rarely outside the range of 35 to 50 per cent. By the 1970s mortality risks had all but disappeared from infancy and childhood, and younger adult levels had declined dramatically. At the same time, degenerative and other non-infectious diseases replaced infectious diseases as the major causes of death in the population at large.

Pre-transitional mortality regimes were all dominated by early death from infectious disease but they were far from uniform in other respects. Overall mortality levels fluctuated considerably, in both the long and short term, and there was a great deal of spatial variation. English life expectation stood at a little over forty years on the eve of the transition, having apparently fluctuated between the ages of roughly thirty and forty over the preceding three centuries. Mid-eighteenth-century Swedish mortality was somewhat below the English level, and

French mortality substantially above it, both having declined considerably since the middle of the eighteenth century. For other comparisons we have to fall back on local data. These suggest that English communities on the whole enjoyed mortality advantages over their early modern continental neighbours, most of whose life expectancies are likely to have ranged from the high twenties to the mid-thirties. Geographical and temporal variations were substantial and are important, both in their own right and for what they can tell us about factors underlying mortality as a whole. Geographically, the main contrast was between large towns and cities and smaller settlements elsewhere which generally had much lower mortality, the exceptions mostly occurring where there were specific rural health hazards such as malarial infestation or polluted groundwater (Dobson 1997; Van Poppel 1989).

There seems to have been a series of long-term cycles of mortality change although only the last is clearly documented, and even the existence of the first cannot be established beyond doubt. Belief in its existence is based on a widely assumed increase in the severity of infectious disease mortality, beginning with the 'Antonine' epidemics in the second-century Roman Empire, reinforced by the crises accompanying collapse in the fifth-century west, and culminating in the disastrous plague pandemic of the 540s AD.[8] If, as is often assumed, changes in population growth tracked changing life expectation over the medieval centuries, then the tenth and eleventh centuries saw sustained improvement. Mortality levels certainly rose disastrously with the reappearance of plague in the 1340s, and it is likely that they had deteriorated over the preceding decades, but we do not have the evidence needed to translate this into changes in life expectation (Hatcher and Bailey 2001; Hatcher 1977; Grigg 1980: 64–82). The English national series compiled by Wrigley and Schofield captures the ensuing recovery phase together with the whole of the early modern cycle that followed it. The series shows life expectancy to have improved rapidly in the second half of the sixteenth century, interrupted by some major crises, and then to have deteriorated in the course of the seventeenth, remaining at a relatively low level after 1760 when it recovered. Mortality in western and central Europe probably shared common trends with some regional differences in timing and amplitude.

2.2.2.1. *Mortality crises*

Mortality levels were much higher before the transition than after it but they were also much more given to short-term variation. On the shortest time scale, seasonal weather conditions interacted with modes of infection to produce distinctive patterns of seasonal mortality that varied between diseases and localities (Landers and Mouzas 1988). Respiratory infections were usually worst in the winter and

---

[8] There can be little doubt that population declined at this time, and that mortality had a large share in this. What is at issue is whether there was a systematic rise in infectious disease mortality over the period as a whole, or whether the losses were due to a disconnected series of major crises between which 'normal' levels remained more or less the same.

fly-borne diseases in the late summer, whilst droplet infections like smallpox spread more readily in dry conditions. Infants are particularly vulnerable to seasonal extremes of temperature, and in some populations pre-harvest food shortages, and the need of mothers to wean their babies before going into the fields, boosted mortality at that time of year (Breschi and Bacci 1997). Superimposed on this fairly regular and predictable pattern of seasonal variation was one of jagged, and potentially very destructive, year-on-year fluctuations. The worst of these so-called 'mortality crises' could see normal death rates more than treble with 10 to 15 per cent of a regional population losing their lives, whilst bubonic plague may sometimes have killed as many as half of some local populations in a matter of weeks (Flinn 1981; Charbonneau and Larose 1979; Landers 1993: 14 f.).

Historical demographers have devoted a great deal of attention to mortality crises and we consequently know more about them than we do about any other aspect of European population dynamics before the nineteenth century. The reason is partly one of practical convenience. Census-like material is rare for this period, but burial registers are relatively abundant, so we can often count the numbers of deaths occurring in a population without knowing how big it was. This prevents us from measuring absolute levels of mortality, but lets us track their short-term movements fairly accurately on the usually reasonable assumption that these closely follow the movements in recorded burial totals. Mortality crises were also central to a very influential theoretical interpretation of long-term mortality change. This 'crisis theory' assumed that there was a clear qualitative distinction to be drawn between crisis mortality and the so-called 'background' mortality of non-crisis years which was thought to vary little in time or space. Differences in overall mortality levels therefore stemmed from differences in the incidence and severity of crises. The first stage of mortality transition was accordingly thought to have occurred because crises diminished in frequency and severity. This process, termed the 'stabilization of mortality', was conventionally dated to some time in the late seventeenth or eighteenth centuries, a hundred years or more before background levels began their systematic decline.

Subsequent research has shown that relationships between absolute mortality levels and their short-term stability were much more complex than were allowed for in this schematic formulation. Background mortality itself varied considerably because of differences in the incidence of deaths from endemic or small-scale epidemic causes, and parts of Europe experienced severe crises well into the nineteenth century even if they were rarer than in some earlier centuries. But even if crisis theory is no longer sustainable in its original form, mortality crises themselves remain historically important and theoretically illuminating. This latter quality arises paradoxically from the fact that background and crisis mortality were not qualitatively distinct and that crises often stemmed from the quantitative exacerbation of factors at work in 'normal' non-crisis years. Since these factors became more visible as mortality heightened, the study of crises can elucidate the mechanisms underlying normal mortality and their long-term variations.

Work of this kind has required a change in the analytical framework used to study crises. Initially crisis theory treated these events as the result of external 'shocks', such as when normal social or economic conditions broke down following harvest failure or when some mortality factor not usually present, such as bubonic plague, intruded into a population. Consequently, the approach adopted was typological and based on a classification of precipitating shocks. 'Subsistence crises', due to harvest failures, were distinguished from 'military crises', resulting from war or social disorder, and from 'pure' epidemics, and a residual category of 'mixed' crises. This approach has proved to be both too rigid and too static. Whatever the precipitating cause, the great majority of crisis deaths were immediately due to epidemic disease, which relegated the event to the residual category of 'mixed' crises, were the typology to be retained. It also proved relatively rare for 'pure' epidemics to drop as if from a clear sky. More often some prior social or economic disruption fostered the spread of disease through its effects on migration or overcrowding. Even after major harvest failures, relatively few casualties succumbed to infections recovery from which depended on nutritional factors (Post 1985, 1990; Dupâquier 1989). When prices reached crisis levels many people took to the road in search of food or crowded into inadequate accommodation to save money on rent and fuel. The resulting conditions of overcrowding and sanitary breakdown were ideal for the spread of epidemic dysentery and other 'crowd diseases' which seem to have caused most of the additional deaths. This group of diseases also accounted for a very large share of non-crisis mortality, and it is in this respect that years of unusually severe mortality resemble the quantitative intensification of 'normal' conditions rather than the eruption of something wholly new.

2.2.2.2. *Epidemiological regimes: exposure and resistance*

Mortality crises were generally triggered by violent increases in levels of exposure to infection, and there are good reasons for thinking that this variable also underlay much of the spatial and historical variation in pre-transitional mortality. This, as we have seen, was due mainly to the effects of infectious disease and so its overall level reflected the balance between a population's exposure and resistance to infectious micro-organisms (or 'pathogens') (Johansson, S. R. and Mosk, C. M. 1987). Since many infections generate an immune response among those who catch them and survive, exposure and resistance were strongly correlated in the short term, but beyond this relationship levels of resistance primarily reflected the effects of nutrition. In a low-productivity organic economy most changes in living standards were realized in terms of changes in the quality and quantity of food consumed, and so it is reasonable to expect a close relationship to exist between living standards as measured by the buying power of wages (or 'real wage' level) and nutritionally based resistance to infection. If changing resistance was the key to long-term mortality change we should therefore expect to see a strong link between that change and variations in living standards, but this is not the case before the nineteenth century in western Europe.

The demographic trough following the bubonic plague pandemic of the 1340s saw living standards rise for the mass of the population, but mortality seems to have remained very high for a century or so. Similarly, real wages in early modern England, for which we have much better data, were relatively high in the period 1670–1750, but life expectancy remained below that observed in other periods during which living standards were under pressure. The most powerful evidence against nutritional determinism, however, is the fact that well-fed social elites enjoyed no systematic mortality advantage over the general population (Livi-Bacci 1991: 63–9). The life expectation of the British peerage remained close to or actually below that of the English population at large until the middle of the eighteenth century, a striking anomaly which remains to be fully explained but was almost certainly due to a high level of exposure to infection. This in turn was probably due to patterns of sociability and domestic architecture that kept elites in cities and brought them into relatively close contact with the general population, allied to a long-persisting cultural tolerance of dirt which extended to those with the wherewithal to keep themselves clean (Kunitz 1987; Razzell 1974; Woods and Williams 1995).

The fact that changes in nutritionally based resistance cannot explain pre-transitional mortality change in western Europe means that something else must have been responsible.[9] The identity of this 'something' remains controversial, but it clearly acted through its effects on exposure to infection, and one very influential theory attributes responsibility to climatic variations or biological changes in the relevant pathogens. This theory of the so-called 'autonomous death rate' (Chambers 1972) cannot be either confirmed or refuted because we do not have the necessary evidence, but not all of the changes which are likely to have occurred in the pathogenic environment afflicting pre-transitional populations require to be explained in such terms. Many of them can be attributed to larger-scale versions of the mechanisms which have been shown to underlie mortality crises.

Geographical studies have thrown a valuable light on these mechanisms which mainly turned on the relationship between exposure and the development of immunity to infectious agents. Systematic differences in the factors affecting this relationship caused corresponding differences in the configuration of mortality

---

[9] An important note of dissent to this conclusion has been entered by the economic historian R. W. Fogel, who argues that 'nearly all of the decline in mortality rates between 1750 and 1875 appears to be explained by marked improvements in anthropometric measures of malnutrition' (Fogel 1992: 271). The difficulties with Fogel's argument are twofold. First, for adult mortality, it mainly relies on recent observations of the relationship between stature, body mass, and mortality in populations with a very different cause of death structure from those prevailing before the transition. Secondly, the improvements in stature to which Fogel refers arose from improvements in the balance between calories consumed and calories expended. Since, as Fogel concedes, exposure to infectious disease itself represents a major energy drain on the body, it is unclear how much of the increase in heights can be attributed to better diet as opposed to a declining prevalence of infection.

levels and their short-run stability. These varying configurations are sometimes termed 'epidemiological regimes'. Where exposure is continuous and severe, mortality is likely to be high and concentrated in the early years of life, but those who survive will have a high level of immunity. Conversely, where it is intermittent and moderate, mortality will be lower but so will the overall level of immunity, so that the population will be vulnerable to recurrent epidemics affecting people across a wide range of ages. Mary Dobson has provided an illuminating comparative analysis showing how these relationships worked themselves out in south-eastern England, the New England settlements, and the Chesapeake Bay area during the seventeenth century (Dobson 1989).

In the first of these regions, the increasing density of settlement and communications raised levels of exposure to infection, much of it spreading out of London. Overall mortality went up as a result, but, precisely because levels of exposure were so high, a large proportion of adults carried antibodies to a wide range of potentially fatal pathogens. As a result of this there were relatively few susceptible individuals present at one time, most of them children and recent immigrants from more isolated areas. The scope for large-scale epidemics was correspondingly low, and regional mortality rates varied only moderately from year to year, because most deaths were due to endemic infections, or small-scale local epidemics. In New England, where settlements were dispersed and relatively inaccessible, the pattern was very different. Virulent, immunizing pathogens were unable to persist locally, and introductions from outside were rare. Long-term levels of exposure to infection were consequently low, but so were levels of immunity, and the occasional introduction of new and virulent strains of pathogen triggered severe epidemics on a regional scale.

The New England epidemiological regime combined relatively high expectations of life with a short-run pattern closely resembling the traditional dichotomy of crisis and background mortality. Conditions in Old and New England both contrast starkly with the very unhealthy Chesapeake Bay region, where the physical conditions allowed Old World pathogens to persist to a degree very unusual outside metropolitan populations. Mortality was very high, and population numbers only maintained by recurrent immigration of other susceptible individuals, leading to a short-run pattern of recurrent, violent instability. Metropolitan populations characteristically displayed a fourth pattern, of the kind exemplified by eighteenth-century London. Constant movement to and from the outside world combined with poor housing and inadequate hygiene and sanitation to produce very high levels of exposure to infection. Overall mortality was severe, particularly in childhood and adolescence, but there was little scope for epidemics since even smallpox was permanently present in the population. London's political and economic centrality also buffered it against the effects of harvest failures, and there was little year-on-year change in the numbers of burials.

Some of these epidemiological divergences were due to differences in physical geography, but they chiefly reflected variations in patterns of settlement, trade, and migration. The importance of these latter influences meant that economic change could influence mortality patterns through its effects on variables other than nutrition and the standard of living. In sixteenth- and early seventeenth-century England there was a clear distinction between what Andrew Appleby termed 'the two Englands': the lowland south and east and the upland north and west (Walter and Schofield 1989*a*: 21 f.; Appleby 1973). The uplands were only weakly integrated into the national economy, and their communications network was poorly developed. This exposed them to the risk of severe subsistence crises, while giving them a degree of protection from the large-scale epidemics afflicting the contemporary lowlands. The latter's relatively dense settlement and communications networks promoted both the spread of pathogens and a degree of economic integration which buffered markets within the region against the effect of harvest failures. From the early seventeenth century, major subsistence crises ceased to play a significant role in lowland mortality patterns. This regional contrast disappeared in the course of the seventeenth century as integrated national markets developed. Harvest fluctuations were relegated to secondary importance in both zones, at the price of growing exposure to infectious diseases and a corresponding increase in epidemic mortality.

2.2.2.3. *Larger-scale effects*

The work we have looked at so far was mainly concerned with variations on a regional or national scale, but long-term mortality change on a much larger scale may be explicable in similar terms. Kunitz has advanced such an explanation in the context of the European mortality transition (Kunitz 1983). To begin with, he argues, Europe's weak economic integration and poor communications meant that epidemics of infectious disease struck at intervals and affected substantial numbers of adults with relatively high case fatality rates. This condition persisted into the eighteenth century in much of the continent, but subsequent growth in marketing and communication networks created a sufficient density of interaction for many pathogens to persist in local populations causing endemic diseases of childhood with lower case fatality rates and a reduction in both the level and instability of mortality. This argument might also explain the otherwise puzzling fact that a clear socio-economic gradient in mortality began to emerge just as overall levels were declining. Kunitz attributes this to the fact that the first diseases to decline were epidemic conditions little affected by nutritional factors, whilst those replacing them in the nineteenth century, mainly respiratory tuberculosis and the so-called 'pneumonia-diarrhoea complex', were nutritionally sensitive and so richer, better-fed, individuals now enjoyed correspondingly lower mortality.

Earlier waves of mortality change may also reflect the epidemiological consequences of large-scale political, military, and economic changes. Arguments of this kind are necessarily speculative, but an early influential contribution by Durand drew attention to the remarkable parallelism of population growth around the world from the sixteenth century onwards (Durand 1967). Durand suggested that the European voyages of exploration and conquest had led to the diffusion of diseases around the globe, so that regional populations were exposed to new infections against which they had no immunities, and mortality had risen accordingly. Following this a phase of adaptation had occurred whose effects were reinforced by the diffusion of new food crops with consequent improvements in diet and hence resistance to infection, all of which ushered in a new phase of declining mortality and demographic expansion.

William McNeill developed this line of reasoning on a larger scale in his book *Plagues and Peoples* (McNeill 1977), arguing that the adoption of a sedentary way of life with the transition to agriculture, followed by urbanization, had led to the formation of distinct regional pools of infection, to which populations developed a certain level of adaptation, both culturally and immunologically. Over time, political, military, and economic developments led to the formation of linkages between regions, and consequent transfer of pathogens, so that populations became exposed to infections to which they had neither immunity nor cultural means of adaptation. In his words this led initially to a 'die off', or a period of increased mortality followed by a decline as adaptations were developed. The precise quantitative dimensions of this phenomenon cannot be reconstructed for lack of data and because of the intrinsic complexity of the processes involved, but it seems likely that the emergence of spatial integration through the development of economic linkages and the projection of military power played a predominant role in driving large-scale mortality change prior to the mortality transition of the nineteenth century.[10]

2.3. MODELS OF PRE-INDUSTRIAL POPULATION AND ECONOMY

Agricultural production in Europe's organic economies evidently had to cope with fluctuations of at least 20 to 30 per cent between the peaks and troughs of the demographic cycle. We know so little about absolute population levels across most of the continent that it would be vain to hope for robust estimates of growth rates, but the English data are relatively informative and show early modern growth to have peaked in the late sixteenth century at an annual rate of around 1.1 per cent (Wrigley, Davies, et al., 1997). This equates to a doubling of population in

---

[10] Specifically, McNeill attributes the first period of increased mortality, in the later Roman period, to the emergence of the 'crowd diseases', as urban populations passed the threshold at which these could be maintained in the long term, followed by the exchange of pathogens between China and the west with the establishment of trading links across inner Asia. The medieval plague pandemic can also be attributed to movement in this region, in this case to the wars associated with the establishment and dissolution of the Mongol Empire which spread the disease from its initial reservoir in the Himalayan foothills of south-west China. McNeill follows Durand in explaining the early modern mortality increase as an indirect consequence of the 'expansion of Europe'. Le Roy Ladurie, in his article 'The Unification of the Globe by Disease', developed a similar argument with particular reference to the consequences of pathogenic diffusion for mortality in the Pacific basin (Ladurie 1981a).

roughly sixty years and is close to the peak 'industrial revolution' growth of the decade 1811–20. This level may be modest by the standards of twentieth-century Third World demography but it posed a formidable challenge to the very limited productive capacity of pre-industrial agriculture. In fact the main 'growth' problem posed by the 'A' phase of pre-industrial demographic cycles, far from expanding output per head, was simply to increase aggregate output fast enough to keep per capita levels steady. Like Lewis Carroll's Red Queen, agriculture had to run just to stand still, and various combinations of extensive and intensive growth occurred as a result. We shall examine their technological basis in the next chapter, but at this point our concern is with their outcomes and what these implied for the long-term social and economic consequences of population growth. These consequences have been analysed in terms of a number of schematic abstractions which we shall label respectively the 'classical', 'hearth', and 'ecological' models.

2.3.1. THE CLASSICAL MODEL

The first model is based on the ideas of the classical economists and particularly on what they believed was the tendency of per capita productivity to decline as the labour force expanded beyond a certain point. Its elements are set out in Fig. 2.2, which is based on the simplifying assumptions that the size of the labour force reflects changing population size in a simple and direct manner and that average living standards are set by average productivity per head.[11] The upper panel tracks the effects of population size on both the marginal and the average productivity of labour. The first of these quantities is equal to the output of a hypothetical additional labourer, so if there are N workers at a given point the marginal productivity of labour equals the output of an N+1th. Where population is low and labour scarce, the initial consequences of growth are positive because a certain amount of work has to be undertaken in order to clear the ground and organize production in an efficient manner. Marginal productivity therefore rises as far as P(0), the point at which shortages of other factors of production block the efficient deployment of further labour and it begins to fall.

Average productivity continues to rise for some time until a maximum is reached at point P(1) which is the economic optimum population size. Any further growth will bring down average productivity and erode the general standard of living until, at P(2), it falls to the level of bare subsistence. Labour force growth in commercial agriculture will cease at this point, because additional labourers would have to be paid more than the value of their output in order to survive, and so any further population growth beyond this point has to be absorbed outside agriculture or goes to swell the ranks of the wholly destitute.

[11] The term 'classical' is preferable to the more widely used 'Malthusian' label because the model's underlying assumptions were widely held among Malthus' peers. Ironically in view of his reputation as a prophet of doom, Malthus' own views on long-term living standards were relatively optimistic by contemporary criteria; see Wrigley (1987b).

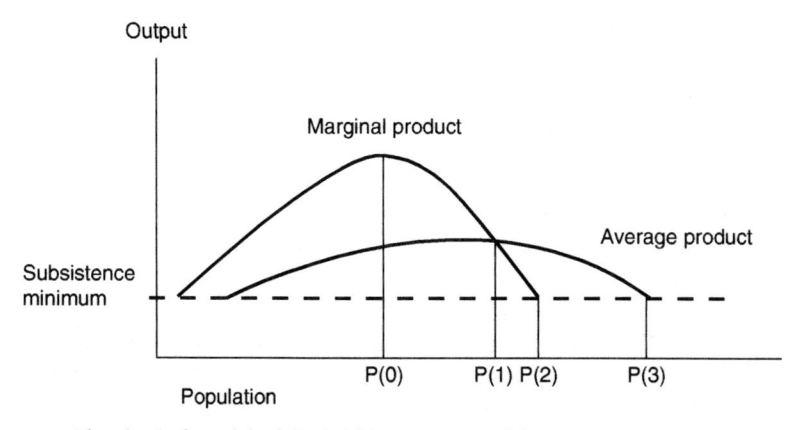

FIG. 2.2. The classical model of diminishing returns to labour.

Where agriculture is family based as in many peasant societies and labour markets are weak or absent the position may be rather different, because an overriding priority may be attached simply to keeping the family on the farm as an economic unit rather than maximizing its net income. If this is so then labour will be retained in agriculture until the equivalent of point P(3) is reached, where average output per head is only equal to the subsistence minimum and starvation looms.

Regardless of whether agricultural organization is commercial or familial the long-term prospect is bleak. In the commercial case population growth beyond P(2) renders increasing numbers unemployed and destitute, whilst in a family-based economy the population remains economically active on the land but in an increasingly wretched condition until they are pushed to the very margin of survival. Such models are condemned by their very nature to oversimplify a complex reality, and this one in particular neglects some potential benefits of population growth. But the available evidence does largely bear out its expectations, even in the schematic terms outlined above. In England, wage, price, and population movements can be tracked with some confidence from the middle of the sixteenth century, and here the buying power of wages seems to have declined whenever population growth exceeded a sustained annual rate of about a half of 1 per cent (Wrigley 1983; Wrigley and Schofield 1981: 407–12). This was apparently the highest rate at which sustainable labour demand could be expanded before the end of the eighteenth century, and it is unlikely that, outside Holland, other European economies were able to match even this modest accomplishment (de Vries 1985; de Vries and van der Woude 1997; Allen 2001).

The available data do not allow long-term analysis of this kind to be replicated in other places and periods, but what is available does suggest that living standards fell as population pressure intensified in the medieval and early modern 'A' phases (Bath 1963: 112 f.). Fortunately there is another prediction from the classical model which is much easier to test since it is based on the movement of relative prices alone. If population growth creates an imbalance between food production and food requirements then, in monetarized economies with markets, the price of staple foods will rise faster than money wages. The mass of consumers will then be forced to shift expenditure towards these and away from other commodities, and then increasingly to 'trade down' within the basket of staples. At the same time, labour is likely to be shifted to staple food production and away from other sectors where marginal productivity is likely to remain relatively high. The consequence of all this should be that the prices of essential subsistence goods rise relative to non-essentials and those of the cheapest grains rise most steeply of all. The available evidence suggests that this is exactly what happened to commodity prices in both the medieval and early modern cycles. Food prices rose by more than those for non-food items, grains by more than animal products, and the less favoured grains more rapidly than wheat (Bois 1984: 88–90; Bath 1963: 112–24; Clay 1984: 29–32).

The economic consequences of medieval and early modern population growth seem to bear out the predictions of the classical model, but the picture is more complicated where its demographic expectations are concerned. We need to consider two distinct sets of circumstances. In one of them the level of fertility is high and inflexible. Under these conditions population growth will force down living standards to a point where mortality begins to deteriorate and the death rate eventually rises to equal the birth rate at P(3). This outcome, with high birth and death rates and living standards barely sufficient to keep body and soul together, corresponds to the familiar 'Malthusian' prophecy of inevitable gloom and doom. Malthus envisaged such an outcome as a result of rising death rates through the mechanism that he termed the 'positive check' to population, but he was also aware of a more benign possibility which he referred to as the 'preventive check'. In this instance the birth rate is itself flexible in the face of falling living standards and so pre-empts the action of the positive check, with population growth terminating at a point where mortality remains moderate and living standards relatively high.

The positive check seems, as we have seen, to have played at most a secondary role in western Europe's long-term demographic evolution from the fourteenth century onwards, and this suggests that the region's distinctive marriage pattern acted as an effective preventive check. There is much more evidence for short-term relationships between living standards and mortality, with violent upswings in food prices triggering recurrent crises, but even these were variable in their incidence. In England the effect was substantially weakened at the end of the early modern 'A' phase in the mid-seventeenth century, although it persisted for longer in France and elsewhere in continental Europe (Galloway 1988). Even in these cases, however, the changing incidence of harvest-related crises cannot explain the longer-term shifts which occurred in mortality levels. The fact that economically sensitive marriage behaviour seems not to have existed in other regions, and possibly not in western Europe before the late Middle Ages, suggests that the preventive check was absent in these cases. If this suggestion is correct then the role of the positive check must have been correspondingly greater, leading to a prevalence of 'high pressure' regimes in which life expectation and average living standards were both relatively low (Wrigley 1987a; Krause 1959).

2.3.2. THE HEARTH MODEL

The classical model is a valuable guide to the consequences of population growth in organic economies, but it is not a complete one. The model assumes that labour and produce are both exchanged for cash in market transactions and has very little to say about questions of population structure. These are important limitations because large-scale commercial organization was relatively unusual, taking the period of organic economies as a whole, and successive waves of demographic expansion changed the structure of populations as well as their size. The changes were both geographical and socio-economic and many of them affected the level and security of living standards. Geographical shifts of population occurred within and between regions. On the largest scale, the continent's demographic 'centre of gravity' migrated from southern Europe and the Mediterranean first towards the north and west and then eastwards, but substantial changes also occurred on a smaller scale.

These changes reflected an important general property of the relationship between any population's growth rate and its overall composition. Whenever growth occurs its products are usually distributed unevenly between the various categories of any given variable such as age or social class so that changes in a population's size lead to corresponding changes in its structure or 'shape'. Some of these structural shifts arise directly from demographic processes, as in the case of age structure, but others reflect economic or social interrelationships. For instance, good-quality arable land was usually well settled relatively early in the 'A' phase of the demographic cycle, so that later additions to the population had to seek their livelihoods in 'marginal' areas elsewhere, in pastoral districts, woodlands, or uplands, and in urban populations (Grigg 1980). But much more than just geographical redistribution was involved. The balance between social categories could alter profoundly and wholly new categories emerge.

The simplest way of approaching this question is in terms of inheritance and what has been called 'heirship' (Wrigley 1978). In many contexts, including much of early modern Europe, the organization of production and reproduction can usefully be thought of in terms of a model based on family labour within households. This 'hearth model' as it is sometimes termed sees both agricultural and non-agricultural production as organized around small parcels of productive capital (or 'hearths') exploited primarily by family labour, and transmitted as indivisible units through so-called 'impartible' inheritance[12]. The consequ-

---

[12] The hearth model was originally developed in the context of theories of population control associated with the north-west European marriage pattern. Its proponents argued that, where marriage required access to hearths that could only be gained through inheritance, a relatively rigid form of demographic homeostasis would develop because changes in mortality would trigger offsetting movements in the age at marriage (Lee 1973, 1977; Scott Smith 1977; Ohlin 1961). The model does not fit

ence of such a pattern, given a relatively inelastic supply of hearths, was an economic-demographic system that resembled a system of ecological niches in which even moderate sustained population growth can have far-reaching consequences.

Let us suppose that, in a given population, livelihoods are inherited through the male line and numbers expand by 10 per cent in a generation, equivalent to a modest 0.3 per cent annually. The number of adult males will grow to exceed the number of hearths by a margin of around 9 per cent. If they are not to become destitute some additional livelihoods must be created for these 'surplus sons' as we shall call them. In practice a surplus of this kind could probably be accommodated without much difficulty in family farms and workshops, but the position alters significantly if population growth rates double in the next generation. This produces a very small acceleration in overall growth, to a level about 9 per cent higher than it would have been at the earlier lower rate, but the number of surplus sons has doubled, even though the annual rate of population growth is barely more than a half of 1 per cent.

Where the economy was organized around such a family-based structure the surplus population had to eke out a living on its margins by whatever means they could, but the lesson of this simple example applies more broadly. Wherever a relatively fixed supply of socially valued goods was transmitted through impartible inheritance, sustained population growth necessarily had a potentially destabilizing effect because of the disproportionate expansion in the number of people denied access to them. This consequence bore on social elites no less than farmers or artisans. Where high-ranking positions were transmitted through primogeniture, or were otherwise limited in number, even marginal falls in mortality generated surplus sons for whom no appropriate position was available. Consequently a form of 'overpopulation' could arise among the elite even if the general balance of population and material resources remained favourable (Goldstone 1991).

Depending on their social position and native abilities, and on the structure of economic opportunities, surplus sons went to swell the ranks of wage labourers, artisans, mercenary soldiers, or beggars. Towns and cities formed a natural magnet for the members of this 'marginal' social category, and urban populations grew disproportionately during the 'A' phases of the medieval and early modern cycles. Reasonably reliable estimates of medieval urban populations are hard to come by, but de Vries has assembled a very valuable set of figures for the larger European cities in the period 1500–1800 (see Table 2.3). These show an overall increase in the percentage of urban dwellers, using de Vries's criterion, from 5.6 in

---

the data from England, where the role of labour markets was substantial, though it performs better in France (Smith 1981; Dupâquier 1988*d*; Wrigley 1985*a*), but the schematic classical model also has difficulty with the full range of English nuptiality change (Weir 1984). Goldstone has attempted a synthesis based on the concept of a two-sector system, one with some 'hearth-like' properties and the other based on wage labour (Goldstone 1986). This provides a relatively good fit to the demographic data though its underlying assumptions have been questioned (Schofield 1989).

Table 2.3 *European Urbanization*
(a) *Growth ratios of the urban percentage and the total population* (urban percentage/total population)

	1550/1500	1600/1550	1650/1600	1700/1650	1750/1700	1800/1750
North and west Europe	1.1/1.2	1.1/1.2	1.3/1.3	1.2/1.1	1.0/1.1	1.1/1.4
Central Europe	1.1/1.2	1.3/1.1	1.2/0.9	1.2/1.1	1.1/1.1	0.9/1.3
Mediterranean Europe	1.2/1.1	1.2/1.1	0.9/0.9	0.9/1.2	1.0/1.2	1.1/1.2
Eastern Europe	1.1/1.1	1.2/1.2	1.2/0.9	1.5/1.0	1.3/1.3	1.2/1.3
The Netherlands	1.0/1.3	1.6/1.2	1.3/1.3	1.1/1.0	0.9/1.0	0.9/1.1
Belgium	1.1/1.2	0.8/1.0	1.1/1.3	1.1/1.0	0.8/1.1	1.0/1.3
Northern Italy		1.1/1.1	0.9/0.8	1.0/1.3	1.0/1.1	1.0/1.1
Central Italy		1.1/1.2	1.1/0.9	1.0/1.0	1.0/1.1	0.9/1.2
Southern Italy		1.3/1.1	0.9/0.9	0.9/1.1	1.1/1.2	1.1/1.2

(b) *The urban percentage of total population*

	1500	1550	1600	1650	1700	1750	1800
North and west Europe	6.6	7.2	8.2	10.9	13.1	13.6	14.9
Central Europe	3.7	4.0	5.0	6.0	7.1	7.5	7.1
Mediterranean Europe	9.5	11.4	13.7	12.5	11.7	11.8	12.9
Eastern Europe	1.1	1.2	1.4	1.7	2.6	3.5	4.2
The Netherlands	15.8	15.3	24.3	31.7	33.6	30.5	28.8
Belgium	21.1	22.7	18.8	20.8	23.9	19.6	18.9
Northern Italy		15.1	16.6	14.3	13.6	14.2	14.3
Central Italy	12.4	11.4	12.5	14.2	14.3	14.5	13.6
Southern Italy		11.9	14.9	13.5	12.2	13.8	15.3

Source: de Vries (1984: tables 3.6, 3.7).

1500 to 8.3 in 1650. Generally speaking, much larger proportionate increases occurred where town dwellers initially formed a low percentage of the population, but the relatively urbanized Netherlands also experienced a doubling in the proportion, from 15.7 to 31.6 per cent.

The relationship between population growth and urbanization was, however, neither simple nor mechanical. Towns might also expand in response to a broader range of economic and other stimuli, whilst in continental Europe the early stages of the modern rise of population saw only modest urban growth because, de Vries argues, rural economic expansion generated sufficient non-agricultural employment to retain much of the surplus labour in the countryside. Wrigley has provided some data on a similar expansion in England, albeit one which in that instance proved compatible with urban growth (see Table 2.4). Sixteenth-century urbanization was not therefore a simple product of population growth but also stemmed from the relative rigidity of the contemporary rural economy.

Table 2.4 *Estimated English population by sector* (millions)

	Total	Urban	Rural Agricultural	Rural Non-agricultural
1520	2.40	0.13	1.82	0.45
1600	4.11	0.34	2.87	0.90
1670	4.98	0.68	3.01	1.29
1700	5.06	0.85	2.78	1.43
1750	5.77	1.22	2.64	1.91
1801	8.66	2.38	3.14	3.14

Sources: Wrigley (1987c: table 7.4).

In areas whose economic organization resembled that of the hearth model, population growth swelled the ranks of surplus sons who had to find employment away from the family plot. Where wage labour or non-agricultural work was unavailable locally, then emigration to the city or to marginal agricultural districts elsewhere might be the only alternative. Where tenurial arrangements were less rigid the result was generally a reduction in the average size of holdings as small plots proliferated, sometimes in conjunction with the formation of a small number of very large farms. The extent of this phenomenon can be seen in some detailed local evidence from early modern England. In Chippenham, Cambridgeshire, the number of farms of more than 90 acres rose from two to nine between 1544 and 1712, whilst the number of landless households increased from twenty-one to thirty-one, and other landholding households declined in numbers (Spufford 1974: 65–84).

In North Arden 40 per cent of later seventeenth-century households were too poor to pay the hearth tax (Skipp 1978: 78–9). This suggests that the landless numbered over 1,000 people, roughly equivalent to the total population growth of the previous hundred years. On a much larger scale, in England as a whole, the work of Gregory King furnishes some idea of the social transformation that had been wrought during this period of population growth. Writing at the end of the seventeenth century King asserted that over half of English households belonged to the category of paupers, labourers, or 'cottagers', who were unable to survive without wages or welfare payments (Glass 1965; Laslett 1973, 1985). It would be rash to accept King's figures at face value, but the very fact that a well-informed contemporary believed such an assertion to be plausible shows how much things had changed from the early sixteenth century, when the great majority of English households are likely to have been composed of self-sufficient agricultural producers.

2.3.3. THE ECOLOGICAL MODEL

Population pressure affected the security of livelihoods at least as much as their overall level and the consequences could seriously aggravate the risks of subsistence crises. The classical model predicts that population pressure and deteriorating living standards should do this by eroding the 'cushion' of accumulated resources that households need in order to see them through the normal range of fluctuations in harvest yields. This effect could be very important but the origins of increased crisis vulnerability were more complex and rooted in a range of structural consequences of population growth. These are captured in what we shall term the 'ecological' model of population growth because it is based on an analysis of the ways that rural agricultural communities characteristically responded to increasing food needs and the implications that these had for their relationship to the land.

These responses included expanding the area under cultivation at the expense of commons, woodland, or waste, increasing arable at the expense of pasture, and substituting food crops for non-foods. Within the basket of food crops itself there was likely to be a growing concentration on a narrower range of high-yielding species and varieties. These measures might provide a workable solution to the Red Queen problem for an extended period, but they carried substantial risks. The expansion of ploughland reduced the scope for pastoral agriculture and, with it, the potential availability of animal power, fertilizer, and animal products generally. The narrowing of the crop base increased the risk of harvest failure due to blight or bad weather, whilst the loss of commons and woodland reduced the cultivators' ability to fall back on a collecting economy and survive on wild foods should crops fail (Grigg 1980).

The risks of subsistence failure were aggravated by changes in the socio-economic structure of village communities that stemmed from the deteriorating ratio of land to labour as population pressure intensified. The immediate effects depended on tenurial arrangements and other legal or social structural factors. If these imposed a regime of impartible inheritance the results were those depicted by the hearth model, but in other circumstances they could be a multiplication of marginal holdings which barely sufficed to support their incumbents when harvests were normal. This development often gave rise to a second phase of consolidation, as marginal landholders were forced to abandon their plots, leading to the polarization of village society and the emergence of a small number of large holdings. In either case the result was a disproportionate increase in the marginal or wholly landless households, and empirical studies have repeatedly found the victims of subsistence crises to have been drawn primarily from these 'famine vulnerable' strata.

When crops are deficient, it is the holders of marginal plots who are particularly badly hit, and demand for agricultural wage labour falls with declining harvest volumes. The producers of non-essential goods and services also have to confront sky-rocketing food prices just as local demand for their own output collapses due to the redirection of expenditure towards essentials (Sen 1981; Watkins and Menken 1985; Wrigley 1969: 66–8). Pierre Goubert demonstrated the consequences of this vulnerability at the community level in a study of the Beauvais region of northern France during the wave of bad harvests in the 1690s (Goubert 1960;

Wrigley 1969: 64–9). Villages relying on cereal monoculture suffered more than did those with access to pasture, but the worst impact was felt in the districts that specialized in small-scale handicraft production. Socio-economic factors also led to differences in famine vulnerability within communities. The landless households risked starvation in the absence of relief. Marginal landholders might survive by selling, or mortgaging, whatever they possessed and thereby would sink to the ranks of the famine-vulnerable landless, or debt-ridden.

The consequences of this process were starkly depicted in a study of the fourteenth-century manor of Halesowen undertaken by Zvi Razi. The recurrent pre-plague subsistence crises hit the poorest peasants disproportionately (Razi 1980: 34–45), but things were very different at the other end of the spectrum.

Well-to-do peasants suffered losses along with everyone else in the village when the harvests failed, but they were able to sustain these losses better than other villagers. During these crises they not only succeeded in feeding their families, but were even able to lend money and corn to their poorer neighbours and to buy and lease their lands. (Razi 1980: 87)

The poorer households died out or emigrated, their lands passing to the better-off, whose younger sons were thereby able to start households of their own. But these were poorly resourced, and so the ranks of the poor were replenished. In other circumstances, smallholders were forced down into the ranks of the landless or even slaves, whilst wealth was concentrated in an ever-smaller number of hands, or passed to outsiders such as urban merchants or absentee landlords. In this way a vicious circle developed as recurrent subsistence crises multiplied the numbers of the famine vulnerable even as it thinned their ranks in the short term.

2.3.4. SUMMARY: THREE FORMS OF OVERPOPULATION

The consequences of population growth can be viewed in terms of output levels per head of the labour force, the transmission of productive assets between generations, or changing patterns of land use. These three sets of consequences are ultimately interrelated, but for analytical convenience they can be described by three distinct models which we have called 'classical', 'hearth', and 'ecological'. Each of these depicts the consequences of population pressure in its own specific terms, but the classical model differs from the other two in describing a form of under- as well as 'overpopulation'. This arises because labour force growth, even in these schematic terms, had benefits as well as costs. More people meant more economic activity, and more opportunity for specialization, along with extra labour for 'overhead' tasks, like clearing land for cultivation, and forming capital and infrastructure such as mills, roads, or bridges that allowed labour to be employed more efficiently.[13]

---

[13] Some 20th-century writers have taken this argument further and questioned the validity of the classical model by pointing to ways in which increased population could itself promote longer-term output growth. Where labour was initially underutilized, population pressure might stimulate technological innovations allowing more hours to be worked and overall output per head to increase, even

We can therefore define underpopulation on the classical criterion (or 'classical underpopulation') as existing where population size falls in the zone of increasing marginal output as depicted in Fig. 2.2, just as classical overpopulation exists where it is above the point of decreasing average output. Overpopulation on the criterion of the hearth model occurs where the supply of 'sons' exceeds that of socio-economic niches or 'hearths' to accommodate them and may, as Goldstone has shown, occur among elite groups as well as the general population. We shall therefore refer to this as 'Goldstone overpopulation'. The third form, 'ecological overpopulation', occurred where patterns of land allocation and use led to fluctuations in harvest yields on a scale that exceeded the coping ability of a substantial proportion of households. This could occur even where long-term average living standards remained adequate if cultivation was heavily dependent on a narrow range of failure-prone crops.

2.4. CONCLUSION

Population patterns in the era of organic economies were characterized by birth and death rates which were much higher than those that prevailed from the later nineteenth century, when the European demographic transition got under way. Pre-transitional demography was, however, neither static nor uniform. Birth rate variations were principally determined by differences in the age at and incidence of female marriage. In this respect the main contrast, from the close of the Middle Ages at the latest, was one between western Europe where marriage was delayed and appreciable proportions of women remained unmarried, and other regions where marriage seems to have been early and universal. The demographic consequence of the west European marriage pattern was a set of birth rates which were relatively low but which also varied over time as the likelihood of marriage altered with changing economic and demographic circumstances.

Death rates also varied over time, but the causes of this variation are still not fully understood. At least from the fourteenth century onwards, mortality was if anything worse in periods when living standards were relatively high, just as the social elite apparently experienced mortality levels that were no better than those of the general population. These observations seem to rule out nutrition as the main factor in long-term mortality change and suggest that differences in exposure to infection were responsible. Geographical studies have shown how physical environments, settlement patterns, and networks of trade and migration affected

---

where the returns to each hour of work were falling. More speculatively, increases in the size and number of urban settlements might foster intellectual and with it technological progress by increasing the density of social interactions. The best-known exponents of this view have been Esther Boserup (1965, 1981) and Julian Simon (1977); but see also Clark (1967), Sauvy (1969), and Lee (1986). The evidence for long-term changes in pre-industrial European wages and prices, however, suggests that any benefits of this kind were eventually outweighed by the deleterious consequences of population growth.

levels of exposure, and English regional mortality patterns were transformed in the seventeenth century as the formation of a national market integrated hitherto isolated regions into a broader system that was epidemiological as well as economic. A similar process may have affected wider areas of continental Europe a century later although the lack of adequate data means that this possibility must remain a matter of speculation.

Short-term movements in mortality occurred in response to a range of factors including food-price fluctuations, and could be very violent. The strength of the short-term price–mortality relationship itself varied in space and time, and in England it seems to have weakened significantly in the course of the seventeenth century. Harvest failures were not the only cause of mortality crises. Sometimes they followed very closely on each other, but this does not seem to have been due to the physiological consequences of acute malnutrition. What happened instead was that very high prices caused social dislocation and this in turn greatly increased the levels of exposure to a number of diseases that were also present in the population and caused a large proportion of the deaths in non-crisis years. Crisis mortality was therefore a quantitatively exaggerated form of 'normal' mortality, and the study of crises can throw valuable light on why the latter should have varied over time even though long-term mortality change cannot itself be explained by changes in the incidence and severity of crises. Changes in birth and death rates in turn altered the rate of population growth, leading to waves of demographic expansion and recession which put substantial pressure on the productive capacity of organic economies. The consequences of the west European marriage pattern provided the region's population with a degree of protection under these circumstances, and probably explain the lack of a strong positive relationship between prices and mortality, but this could not prevent the symptoms of overpopulation from manifesting themselves in the long term. These symptoms included the erosion of output, and therefore of living standards, per head, the proliferation of men and women for whom there was no 'niche' in the traditional household-based socio-economic structure, and the emergence of increasingly risk-prone patterns of land use.

CHAPTER THREE

Production and Technology

The history of organic economies was never quite a 'history that stood still' in Leroy Ladurie's memorable phrase, but it was a history in which movement was generally slow, constrained, and asymptotic in form.[1] The limits of the possible were the limits of productivity growth, and of agricultural productivity above all. In this chapter we shall be concerned with what these limits were, how they operated in agricultural production, and to what extent they could be stretched through innovations in technology. The limits were set by the restricted quantity of energy obtainable from organic sources, which gives the technology of energy and its applications a particular priority, but it was in agriculture that the implications of these limits were most far-reaching. The chronically low level of agricultural productivity in organic economies made poverty ubiquitous, and the mass of the population endured standards of living that were very meagre by the standards of an industrial economy. In monetarized economies expenditure was almost wholly devoted to subsistence goods.

Quantitative data on consumers' expenditure are very rare before the nineteenth century, but what is available suggests that at least three-quarters of most families' expenditure went on food and that staples accounted for most of this proportion (Wrigley 1989: 247; Cipolla 1976: 27–35). Most adults in pre-industrial Europe are likely to have needed between 2,000 and 3,000 dietary calories per day to sustain their normal activities, depending on what these were (see Table 3.1 for estimated energy costs of manual work), and this quantity could be provided by about 2 pounds of bread or other equivalent staple.[2] Data on diets are not much easier to come by than are those on household expenditure, but the evidence

---

[1] The phrase translates *L'Histoire immobile*, which was the original title of Ladurie's 1973 inaugural lecture to the Collège de France and described a history in which 'a peasant population lived and reproduced itself over twelve or thirteen generations, between 1300 and 1720, in conditions determined by a strait-jacket of numerical possibilities, characterized by certain inexorable constraints' (Ladurie 1981b: 10–11). Exponential and asymptotic growth are two contrasting forms of increase over time. In the first, characteristic of industrial economies and biological populations, a constant rate of proportional increase leads to ever-greater absolute increments and an upward-bending growth curve. Asymptotic growth curves, by contrast, flatten off as an upper limit, or asymptote, is approached. Curves of this shape arise where a quantity increases by a constant absolute increment, and thus a declining proportional rate, in each time interval.

[2] Energy needs vary with body mass and levels of physical activity. Clark (1967: 127–30) estimated requirements for adult males aged 20–29 years, in selected Third World populations, at around 1,800–2,000 calories per sedentary day, plus c.150–170 for each daily hour worked. Taking Clark's figure of 3.2 calories per gram of cereal consumed, an intake of one kilogram would provide 3,200

Table 3.1 *Energy costs of activity in kilojoules per hour*

Activity	kJ/h
Log-carrying	840
Planting groundnuts	920
Hoeing	1050–1470
Weeding	1340
Clearing bush	1700
Tree-felling	2000

Note: 1 kJ = 4.2 calories.

Source: Harrison, Weiner, et al. (1977: 490) based on Passmore and Durnin (1955).

assembled by Livi-Bacci (1991) suggests that this requirement was generally met from the fourteenth century onwards—at least by the 'settled' members of rural communities in the absence of major harvest shortfalls, although many of the very poor may have been malnourished.[3] The position with regard to meat and other animal products is less clear. These were much more expensive to produce in energy terms and it is likely that they played at best a minor role in the diet of most agricultural populations. Even this was reduced when food prices increased relative to incomes as they did, in the short term, when harvests were deficient, and when population pressure eroded living standards in the long term during periods of demographic expansion.

Technological innovation provided a route to productivity growth, although contemporaries paid it relatively little attention. The classical economists saw occupational or regional specialization as the main route to productivity growth, but organic economies were caught in a vicious circle in this respect. Specialization boosted productivity, but the limits of agricultural productivity themselves limited the progress of occupational or regional differentiation. Both processes required increases in the relative numbers of non-agricultural producers or providers of services such as transport and communications, and since these people still had to eat, each remaining agricultural producer had to grow more in order to feed them. Most forms of specialization also required continuing capital investment, in whatever form, and even where the necessary capital existed, it was unlikely to be forthcoming where a scarcity of staple foods depressed demand for all other commodities.[4]

---

calories, sufficient for at least seven hours' work. It should be borne in mind that wastage in transport, storage, and processing can rarely have amounted to much less than a quarter of a crop's initial energy value (see also Campbell, Galloway, et al. 1993: 31–45; Livi-Bacci 1991: 23–32).

[3] Fogel believes that malnourishment was a serious problem among the very poor in 18th-century England, and still more so in France (Fogel 1992). His argument is ingenious but relies on a number of debatable assumptions; for a detailed critique see Voth (2000: 161–75).

[4] This point is made particularly by de Vries (1976: 176–209). On the production side, small-scale and diffuse organization also limited the demand for 'lumpy' capital items such as industrial watermills (Holt 1997).

Technology has a special priority in this context because of its rare ability to deliver what economists term 'free lunches', or increases in output that are disproportionate to the costs involved.[5] By boosting agricultural productivity it raised the limits on specialization as a growth-promoting process as well as enhancing productivity directly. Innovation in other sectors also 'fed back' into enhanced agricultural productivity by providing workers with more efficient tools or services, but technology's historical role is as enigmatic as it was potentially significant. Technology is a complicated phenomenon both to understand and to define. Instantiated in physical artefacts from digging sticks to digital processors, it is nonetheless not identical to them, because such devices are only one element in a broader system that incorporates accumulations of knowledge or practice that are incarnated in skilled practitioners.

The economic historian Joel Mokyr provides a very general definition of technology as 'the application of information to the production process in such a way as to increase efficiency' (Mokyr 1990: 6). This is valuable because it captures a sense of technology as something that stands between the classical factors of production, or acts as a mode of their coming together in order to attain desired outcomes, but general as the definition is, it is still too narrow for our purposes in two respects. First, a great deal of the technology with which we are concerned lay outside the sphere of production narrowly defined. Some involved activities like transport, or even consumption, whilst much else, like military technology, was ostensibly non-economic. The reference to efficiency is also problematic because innovation did not necessarily boost the return per unit of a given input. Sometimes total output was increased by allowing more of a given factor, such as labour, to be applied productively at lower unit returns. Such 'Red Queen' innovation was common in pre-industrial agriculture because demand pressure often made it necessary to raise total production at the price of declining returns.

We need therefore to stretch Mokyr's formulation even further and define technology as 'any application of information to a recurrent activity in such a way as to enhance desired outcomes'. Technology defined in these terms always involves a trinity of three distinct elements which we shall term 'hardware', 'procedure', and 'personnel'. The first embraces the non-human physical objects involved, whether inanimate tools and machinery or agricultural crops and animals. Employing the hardware effectively required an appropriate body of procedure (termed 'doctrine' in recent military contexts), consisting of relevant knowledge and practice that might be derived entirely from experience or contain a significant theoretical component. This in turn requires to be applied by practitioners with whatever training and experience is necessary, and this body of 'personnel' makes up the third element of any technological system.

---

[5] For a discussion of the 'free lunch' phenomenon and a demonstration of why, contrary to received wisdom, such things do exist, see Mokyr (1990).

3.1. ENERGY AND POWER

The main constraint on activity in organic economies was the limited supply of energy, which was derived almost entirely from primary plant production, whether directly or indirectly, and so was constrained by the level of sunlight falling on a given land area and the efficiency with which this was photosynthesized. Since the latter approximates a half of 1 per cent, the amount of energy such a source could supply for human use was correspondingly restricted. Fernand Braudel estimated total energy inputs for late eighteenth-century Europe as follows (in million horsepower): draught animals, 10.0; wood, 4.0–5.0; watermills, 1.5–3.0; manpower, 0.9; non-military sail-power, up to 0.23; and windmills, 0.4–1.0 (Braudel 1981: 371). Braudel's estimates imply a total power input barely twenty times that of unaided human muscle — compared with several hundred times in industrial economies (Grigg 1992, p. 50) — and the consequence was low productivity throughout the economy.

Much of the technological innovation that occurred was aimed at using human muscle power more efficiently, or letting more of it be brought to bear on a given task. Less often it provided supplementary or replacement energy sources such as animal power or combustible fuel. These were useful in most areas of production, but in agriculture and, above all, in metallurgy they were often essential if the activity was to be performed at all. The context of technological development differed greatly as between agricultural and non-agricultural (or 'industrial') production. Innovations in agricultural technology generally involved improved crop varieties and rotations, qualitative and quantitative improvements in the domestic animal herd, and more and better tools. Cultivation, at least in northern Europe, also relied heavily on the muscle power of animals. Industrial technology was more often concerned with improving the efficiency of human effort, although metallurgy always stood out from other sectors because of its reliance on combustible energy sources for essential heat-intensive processes.

Processes requiring large amounts of heat, in metallurgy, ceramic production, or elsewhere, normally relied on fuel wood, and on Braudel's estimates this accounted for a quarter of total European energy inputs by the end of the eighteenth century. Animal power was the primary supplement to human labour elsewhere in the economy and Braudel credits it with a share of rather over half the total energy supply. Supplies of fuel wood and fodder both depended on the productivity of the land, and it was this which, more than anything, gave organic economies their 'organic' character and constrained their capacity for expansion. A sustainable annual supply of fuel wood requires between a half and one acre of land for each ton, for an energy yield only half that available from the same weight of coal (Wrigley 1988: 54–5). Coal and peat were both more efficient heat sources than wood. Peat made an important contribution in the early modern Netherlands and some authors credit its local abundance with much of that country's ability to sustain urbanization and economic growth (de Vries and van der Woude 1997: 37–40; Unger 1984). London was unusual in consuming substantial quantities of coal. By the early eighteenth century it was accounting for about a sixth of English national production, and the capital's coal imports were employing half of the country's merchant marine tonnage (Wrigley 1967). A hundred years later consumption reached a million tons annually, a volume with an energy content equivalent to the yield of about a million acres of woodland (Wrigley 1988: 54–5). At this time Paris accounted for more than two million tons of wood and charcoal annually (Braudel 1981: 367).

The problem of energy was most severe in ferrous metal production, where very high temperatures were required. Even when furnaces capable of producing wrought iron became available, sustainable output was strictly limited if deforestation was not to eliminate readily accessible energy supplies. Each ton of product required approximately 10 acres of timber, so a single forge could consume as much fuel as a small town in order to produce, by the eighteenth century, some 100–50 tons of iron per year (Wrigley 1988: 80). As a result, before the nineteenth century, production was generally scattered in small-scale units and the resulting product was correspondingly expensive. What was true of iron was generally true of materials requiring heat-intensive processing. Near fourteenth-century Dijon, for instance, six furnaces producing terracotta tiles employed 423 woodcutters and 334 drovers to procure and transport fuel (Braudel 1981: 364). The energy costs of production, processing, and transport kept the economic uses of mineral raw materials to a low level. Iron proliferated in military equipment from the early Middle Ages, and military demand was responsible for much of what geographical concentration there was in early modern ferrous metal production. By contrast the civilian world of pre-industrial Europe long remained a world of wood; a set of iron tyres could multiply the value of a fourteenth-century English peasant's cart by a factor of ten or more, and a plough's iron fittings could raise its value from almost nothing to 3–4 shillings (Dyer 1989: 171).

Water power provided one important supplement to muscle power as a source of kinetic energy. Waterwheels were potentially useful wherever anything had to be cut, ground, or beaten and were used in antiquity. Roman engineers invented the vertical form of the wheel but despite this the less efficient horizontal turbine-style wheels predominated, and their use was generally confined to grinding grain and lifting water. The early Middle Ages saw the diffusion of the vertical wheel and the substitution of the overshot for the undershot design with a more than threefold gain in efficiency. By 1086 Domesday Book listed nearly 6,000 water-mills in southern England. With the addition of the crank the following century saw a proliferation of industrial applications such as sawmills, fulling mills, trip hammers, and water-powered bellows.[6]

Watermills proliferated through the early modern period, so that the Paris basin alone eventually boasted some 1,200, and the total for Europe as a whole has been estimated at 500,000–600,000 (Braudel 1981: 356–8). Since the average

---

[6] Industrial mills certainly existed by the 12th century, but their frequency is another matter. Whereas Mokyr asserts that 'medieval men and women were surrounded by water-driven machines doing the more arduous work for them', Holt believes that all but fulling mills were rare and the latter were only constructed once local cornmill requirements had been met (Mokyr 1990: 34; Holt 1997: 150).

watermill had a capacity five times that of a two-man hand mill, their presence in these numbers represented an energy gain in the range of 1.5–3 million horsepower. But water power was not a panacea. Watermills' power transmission relied on wooden components for everything except the drive shaft, until cast iron became available in the eighteenth century, and this greatly restricted their capacity (Holt 1997). Moreover, they needed suitable locations, and their proliferation itself restricted the scope for river transport. By the 1690s the fortress of Metz had to be provisioned by land, at considerable expense, since the numerous millraces of Lorraine ruined any grain transported by barge (Braudel 1988: 344–5). Furthermore, once local energy demands had been met, any subsequent increases in efficiency would be pointless since there was no means of transmitting energy to regions deprived of water power because of their terrain or hydrology.

Mills could be turned by animal or human muscle power in regions that were too flat or dry for watermills, but the most important large-scale alternative was wind power.[7] Windmills were operating in Iran by the ninth century and had reached Christian Spain by the tenth. They were sufficiently familiar for a papal tithe to be imposed by 1195, and by 1300 England probably held some 3,000, as against some 9,000 watermills (Holt 1997). The Christian mill developed into a more sophisticated device than its eastern progenitor, gaining in efficiency with the substitution of a vertical wheel for the horizontal original. Windmills, like watermills, were restricted to suitable terrain, and here the Netherlands, with strong and reliable westerlies, enjoyed a substantial advantage. By the sixteenth century Dutch engineers had refined the initial 'post-mill' design to produce the more efficient tower mill. Beyond flour-grinding these mills were widely employed in industrial processing and production, and in drainage. By 1731 nearly 600 windmills were employed in the industries of the Zaan region, whilst 43 were constructed to reclaim some 17,000 acres in the North Holland Beemser Polder. Windmills were more powerful than watermills, but they were also more complex. This made them more expensive to build, maintain, and operate per unit of output, and so, their regional importance notwithstanding, they could not provide a general solution to the energy problem. On Braudel's estimates, watermills may have provided close to 15 per cent of European energy inputs by the end of the eighteenth century whereas windmills are unlikely to have contributed as much as 5 per cent.

3.2. AGRICULTURAL PRODUCTION

The level and responsiveness of agricultural productivity constrained the possibilities for per capita output growth elsewhere in the economy and so overall

---

[7] The relatively small size of horse mills suited them for domestic use. They have left little direct evidence, but Holt believes they were widespread in medieval England and that this explains the lack of popular interest in watermills, in apparent contrast to northern Italy (Holt 1997; Squatriti 1997). If this explanation is correct then it is a further reflection of the superior access to horsepower enjoyed by the English peasantry relative to their continental peers (Langdon 1986, 1984).

growth depended very much on the progress of productivity in this one sector. In practice, however, the most pressing problem facing pre-industrial agriculture was often one of merely keeping per capita output roughly constant in order to expand total production more or less in line with population growth. It was the different degrees of success with which economies resolved this version of the Red Queen problem that accounted for much of the variation in pre-industrial living standards. 'Red Queen growth' in total output was obtained in a number of ways, the simplest of which was to extend the land under cultivation. Europe's demographic cycles witnessed a corresponding ebb and flow in the area of ploughland, but substantial labour inputs were usually required to achieve growth of land under cultivation so there was little prospect of maintaining output per head. Extensive growth also threatened the overall productivity of the land, as cultivation spread to poorer-quality soils, and reduced the land available for animals and non-food crops, driving up their price and curtailing demand; something that affected inputs to a wide range of productive sectors in an organic economy. The agricultural Red Queen problem was never fully resolved before the nineteenth century, though western Europe's post-Roman economies held their ground to a remarkable extent through various combinations of extensive growth and technological innovation. Increasing longer-term levels of production was not, however, the only problem facing the cultivator.

The agriculturalists' reliance on cultivation for the means of subsistence created a basic tension between two often incompatible goals: increasing average output in the long term and minimizing short-term fluctuations with all the risks that these entailed. The essence of cultivation is to produce artificial increases in the density of a restricted number of species or varieties in a given environment, and this has both positive and negative consequences when compared with the older regime of hunting and gathering. The amount of normally available food can be increased substantially and a much larger population supported, albeit within limits, but the artificial ecological simplicity of farmed environments increases the risk of actual yields falling dangerously below the average. Hunter-gatherers generally exploit 'climax' ecosystems, which are buffered against the effects of climatic fluctuations or intrusive micro-organisms by their very complexity (Howell 1976; Lee and DeVore 1986; Sahlins 1972). Agriculturalists have their eggs in a much smaller number of baskets, and the risks that necessarily follow from this are compounded where holdings are small, soil productivity low, and crop species derive from other climatic regions. All of these conditions held for many European farmers.

3.2.1. TECHNOLOGICAL CHANGE

The first agriculturalists are thought to have entered the continent from the south-east some 10,000 years ago, bringing with them domesticated varieties of wheat, barley, flax, and a range of legumes from the Near East (Bender 1975; Hodder 1990; Whittle 1985). By the beginning of the first millennium BC cultivation had spread to the edge of the northern forests, and the range of cultivars had expanded. In the south, cereal cultivation was supplemented by two planted crops, the vine and the olive, which along with wheat constituted the 'Mediterranean triad' (Sallares 1991). In northern Europe two further cereals, oats and rye, were domesticated, whilst millet was grown in many parts of the continent from at least the beginning of the first millennium BC.

The nature of this crop mix made it difficult to reconcile short-term risk reduction with long-term increases in productivity. Risk was most readily reduced by broadening the crop base, and particularly by including a range of crops with different climatic requirements and sensitivities, but the simplest way of increasing output was to concentrate on the highest yielding varieties and abandon the others. Furthermore, the most productive crops were not necessarily the most weather-resistant and this became an increasingly serious problem as cultivation moved further north. Of the two original cereals, wheat is nutritionally superior to barley and has generally had higher status, but barley is more resilient. Millet by contrast is low yielding and nutritionally inferior, but its short growing season and general robustness made it an excellent choice for the purposes of risk reduction. The principal climatic risk in the Mediterranean region was spring drought. Around Athens rainfall may have been inadequate for a normal wheat crop as often as one year in four (Garnsey 1988: 9–13). Droughts were much less of a problem further north, and the higher levels of normal early-summer rainfall made spring-sown cereals much more productive, but harsh winters and late frosts were a serious threat. Winter wheat was particularly vulnerable in this respect, but any cereal crop could be ruined by unusually heavy rain in the weeks leading up to harvest.

Long-term increases in agricultural productivity usually required improvements in technological 'hardware'. Tools and machinery played a secondary role in this process for most of the period with which we are concerned. The cultivator's basic kit of hand tools, including the hoe, sickle, and scythe, was assembled before the end of the Iron Age, and the heavy wheeled plough and the lighter Mediterranean 'scratch' plough were both known in classical antiquity. There are reports of a horse-drawn mechanical reaping machine being used in the north of Roman Gaul, but it was unsuited to southern conditions and appears, in any case, to have had a high spoilage rate (Greene 2000). The main developments concerned changes in the crop base and in the use of draught animals. The discovery of the Americas in the early modern period brought an influx of new crops which famously included the potato (Crosby 1972), but long before this the Mediterranean crop base had already been widened through transfers including rice and durum wheat from the east and from sub-Saharan Africa (Duby 1972).

Progress occurred by broadening the crop base and changing the way its elements were combined so as to protect soil quality. If bad weather was the farmer's greatest short-term worry, in the longer term his most serious problem was the depletion of soil nitrates as a result of cereal growth. In Mediterranean environments the low initial level of soil moisture and consequent desiccation compounded the problem, and without substantial irrigation it necessitated a biennial fallow, during which repeated cultivation was needed to prevent weed growth and consequent moisture loss.[8] Further north a range of solutions was possible. At one extreme the soil could just be left uncultivated for long periods. This technique required a pattern of extensive land use ranging up to the shifting cultivation attributed to the ancient Germanic peoples and the early medieval Slavs. Alternatively, shorter periods of fallow could be incorporated into a rotational pattern of land use, although for best results this required sufficient livestock to manure the soil whilst the fallow was grazed. A system of this kind was developed in the early medieval period in northern Europe and went some way to meeting the additional food needs of a growing population. At the same time there was extensive growth in arable farming. The cultivated area was expanded externally through colonization, particularly on Germany's eastern frontier, and internally through the 'assarting' of woodland and waste around existing villages (Duby 1972, 1968; Bath 1963: 151–60; Abel 1980: 25–8; Hatcher and Bailey 2001: 33–8).

The basis of the new agricultural system was a pattern of large, communally managed, open fields with first a two-course and then a three-course rotation. This allowed the land to be fallowed and fodder crops grown for the animals that provided both manure and draught power. The system relied on a new combination of hardware and an associated form of social and economic organization. Under the two-course rotation animals could browse on the fallow and their manure boosted soil fertility, but from the Carolingian period there developed a further refinement in the form of a three-course rotation. In this system, along with the fallow, a spring sowing of oats and legumes complemented the winter sowing of wheat, rye, or barley (Duby 1972). The two sowings provided a hedge against crop failure as well as a more even distribution of labour input across the year, and this system greatly increased labour productivity in those areas where climate and soil fertility allowed its implementation.

The key to the system was the heavy wheeled plough furnished with coulter and mould board (White 1962) which had a number of advantages in heavy soils. Unlike the Mediterranean plough the mould board turned the furrow, thereby eliminating the need for cross-ploughing and reducing labour requirements whilst improving drainage. The increased friction it created necessitated a much larger plough team, and unlike the pair of oxen that often sufficed for the scratch plough, the wheeled version needed as many as eight animals to pull it. This was too expensive for a single peasant household and so the necessary support was obtained by pooling the resources of a number of households, each of which was allocated strips in the large open fields. Even so some households were too poor to afford even a share in a team. These had to rely on hoe

---

[8] This, at least, is the traditional view, but it may underestimate the importance of intensive mixed farming in ancient Greece (Sallares 1991). Roman authors discussed systems of crop rotation, although the extent of actual practice remains unclear. Certainly inter-cultivation of wheat with planted crops seems to have been important (White 1963, 1965).

cultivation by hand, whilst a richer stratum eventually emerged who could afford a team of their own. This distinction between those the French termed respectively *manouvriers* and *laboureurs* marked the emergence of a rural socio-economic differentiation that was to persist into the modern era.

Horses began to supplant oxen as draught animals in parts of northern Europe from the twelfth century. Oxen had some advantages as prime movers because they yielded a higher power/weight ratio than horses and converted dietary protein more efficiently, but horses moved faster and generated more actual power. They could do double the daily work in a large field and were more manoeuvrable on small plots or rough ground (Langdon 1986), but realizing their potential required a series of changes in harness design. The ancient world employed draught animals in yoked pairs with a throat and girth harness originally designed for oxen. Horses, however, lack the bony ridges that hold an ox harness in place on the animal's back, and they exert traction from their hind legs, which gives them a higher angle of draught. As a result, the older form of harness cut into a horse's windpipe when it exerted full traction, effectively choking it and forfeiting perhaps as much as 80 per cent of the animal's superior power output (Greene 2000; Burford 1960; White 1984). The solution was a new form of harness (Langdon 1986, 1984; White 1962). This initially took the form of the breast-strap, which probably appeared in Europe in the sixth century, and then the horse-collar, which arrived two to three hundred years later and had been generally adopted by the eleventh century. At the same time, nailed horseshoes, known in antiquity but apparently abandoned subsequently, reappeared around the ninth century and were in general use by the eleventh. The yoke was increasingly replaced by rope and leather traces. The introduction of the whippletree—small wooden bars linking the traces to the plough or vehicle itself—increased manoeuvrability and permitted the use of odd-numbered teams. Power-efficiency was also increased by the adoption of file-harnessing in place of the line-abreast system, which seems to have prevailed in antiquity.[9]

Unlike oxen, horses required feeding on grain, preferably oats, in order to work efficiently. The three-course rotation met this requirement in northern Europe, but most southern summer rains were inadequate to support a spring sowing and oxen generally retained their place in southern agriculture, being supplemented by water buffalo in Italy. North Italian agriculture also compensated for the lack of spring sowing with a network of irrigation canals and through the introduction of new crops. By the end of the fifteenth century sorghum, durum wheat, and rice were all in cultivation, as was a range of new horticultural produce (Duby 1972). The intensification of production generally required capital investment and in most regions played a secondary role to extension of the cultivated area. The early

---

[9] The dating of each of these innovations, and whether they were in fact innovations in the medieval period, has been a matter of some controversy. As Langdon argues, however, what mattered in this period was not any single development in itself, but rather 'a whole series of improvements, some of them known in Roman times and before, which gradually coalesced into a new system or systems of traction' (Langdon 1986: 16).

centuries of expansion seem to have brought qualitative improvements in the diet of many regions as millet production declined, and wheat supplemented barley or rye in the more developed areas.

By the 1250s, however, the tide was beginning to turn. Extensive growth was slowing or had stopped in most regions, probably because of deteriorating land quality. Population pressure led to three-course rotations being extended to unsuitable soils, further reducing yields, and continuing growth led to unmistakable signs of crisis appearing by the beginning of the fourteenth century. Harvest failures became more frequent, with a catastrophic famine after 1315 (Jordan 1996), and the 'A' phase of demographic expansion seems to have come to an end shortly afterwards. The gathering crisis reflected the underlying technological limitations of contemporary agriculture when confronted with population growth. In the long run, the number of domestic animals, and thus the volume of available manure, seems to have been inadequate to maintain the level of soil fertility. Duby goes so far as to claim:

The continual exhausting of under-manured, overworked, and under-rested arable land seems to have been an inherent feature of the agrarian system of medieval Europe ... From agronomical necessities alone, the medieval peasant was a coloniser. (Duby 1972: 198)

The extension of cultivation to indifferent terrain and the overextension of three-course rotations contributed to the crisis, but social and institutional factors were also involved. Technological innovations that might have been possible apparently failed to materialize because of inadequate investment by feudal landholders, in contrast to the experience of some urbanized regions, particularly in Flanders and northern Italy, where investment in intensified production and land improvements allowed economic and population growth to be maintained in parallel. In these cases urban markets stimulated demand for non-staple pastoral and horticultural products which further encouraged investment. Comparable development occurred in the English region of East Anglia, where investment in a cluster of innovations known as the 'new husbandry' permitted substantial increases in labour inputs per acre (Campbell 1983a, 1983b). Animals were stall-fed and their manure transported to the fields, thereby maintaining soil productivity, but at least in England this seems to have required a disproportionate labour input so that output per head declined (Hatcher and Bailey 2001: 38–9). Extensive growth in cultivation, more intensive use of labour, better crop rotations, and regional specialization also enabled substantial 'Red Queen growth' to occur during England's early modern 'A' phase (Kussmaul 1990; Overton 1996). Fallow was eliminated from the most developed areas whilst new fodder crops allowed more intensive stall-feeding and the replenishment of soil nitrates, but these innovations fended off disaster rather than impoverishment. In Campbell and Overton's words:

So long as food requirements could only be met by extending cultivation to inferior soils and intensifying methods of production through the application of increased labour, the inevitable tendency of population growth was to drive down the marginal productivity of labour in agriculture. (Campbell and Overton 1991: 2)

3.2.2. A BASIC CONTINUITY

Crops and production techniques varied across the era of organic economies, but the problem of energy inputs provided a basic continuity. Levels of agricultural production were energy sensitive in the same way as any other economic sector, and although the ensuing constraints were less acutely visible than they were in heat-intensive metallurgy or ceramics, they existed and their implications were profound. Pre-industrial agriculture was relatively efficient as an energy system. The ratio of dietary calories yielded to those invested in the production, processing, and distribution of food compared well with those prevailing in the late twentieth century (Wrigley 1987b: 41), but the very limited amounts of energy available from organic sources kept the productivity of land and labour correspondingly low. Animal power was the major supplement to human muscle power, and it was essential if European arable was to yield substantially more calories than those expended by the cultivator.

An ox could furnish five times as much power as a man, and a horse eight times or more, as well as providing valuable fertilizer. Variations in the availability of draught animals explain much of the overall variation in the productivity of arable agriculture, but animal power was far from being a 'free lunch', and there were constraints on its exploitation. The most important was that domestic animals' fodder requirements competed with human food needs for land that was a potentially scarce resource. Contemporaries estimated that in England around 1800 a horse required 5 acres of land for its support (Wrigley 1993: 6). In the London region in the early fourteenth century around a quarter of net grain output was devoted to livestock (Campbell, Galloway, et al. 1993: 42–3). Other potential boosters to soil productivity, such as marling, carried similar energy penalties. It has been estimated that marling 100 acres of farmland might require 30,000 ton-miles of haulage, 'fuelled' by around 70 tons of grain—the net production of some 160 acres of arable land (Wrigley 1988: 43).

3.2.2.1. Arable productivity and harvest failure

Arable productivity can be measured in terms of output per unit of land, or per head of the workforce, but in many periods the most readily available indicators are the so-called 'yield ratios' that relate the number of grains yielded to those planted as seed (see Table 3.2 for a range of estimated values for these measures). This is unfortunate in one way, because yield ratios cannot tell us how much food was grown in any given area, but in another way the ratios are a very appropriate measure because it was their meagre level that underlay the endemic problem of low and insecure living standards. Ratios varied geographically and in some areas they rose towards the close of the period, but they were normally in single figures. In the late Republican period, the ratio may have reached eight in Roman Sicily, but the contemporary writer Columella believed four would be an unusually high figure in mainland Italy (White 1963: 208, 1970; Greene 2000, 1986). In the early

Table 3.2 *Productivity in arable agriculture*
(a) *Seed–yield ratios*

		\multicolumn{4}{c}{Seed–yield ratios}		
		Wheat		Barley	
Country	Century	Mean	N	Mean	N
England	13th	3.8	24	3.6	28
	14th	3.8	35	3.2	44
	15th	4.6	26	3.5	15
	16th	5.5	2	4.7	2
	17th	10.5	20	7.7	26
The Netherlands	16th	13.6	3	7.5	3
France	18th	6.6	5	20.0	1
Germany	16th	4.7	12	4.1	2
	17th	4.4	12	3.6	20
	18th	6.5	6	3.9	8

(b) *Yields per acre in England* (bushels)

	Lincolnshire		Norfolk and Suffolk		Hertfordshire	Hampshire
	Wheat	WACY	Wheat	WACY	Wheat	Wheat
1300			14.9	11.5		10.8
1550	9.5	8.0			9.0	
1600	11.7	9.9	12.0	8.5	12.2	11.0
1650	15.8	10.0	14.5	9.3	16.0	12.9
1700	15.6	10.7	16.0	9.2	17.0	
1750	20.0	13.5	20.0			
1800	21.0	15.8	22.4		24.0	21.0

Note: WACY = yields for wheat, rye, oats, and barley weighted by crop proportions and price relative to wheat.
Source: Bath (1963: tables II and III); Overton (1996: table 3.7).

modern period, ratios were generally higher in northern Europe, particularly in England and the Netherlands, than they were elsewhere. For the decades 1650–99 Slicher Van Bath estimates an average yield ratio of 9.3 for grains in England and the Netherlands, compared with 6.2 for contemporary France, Spain, and Italy, and 4.1 for Germany, Switzerland, and Scandinavia (Bath 1963: tables II and III; Grigg 1992: 34). In the relatively advanced London region wheat yielded only a fourfold return, net of seed, around the peak of the medieval 'A' phase, and a wheat yield ratio of no more than four and an areal yield of some 10 bushels per acre are probably reasonable estimates for much of pre-industrial European agriculture.

Low as these ratios are many of them give a misleadingly optimistic impression of how many people contemporary agriculture could support with a reasonable degree of security. There were two basic problems. The first was that where seed–yield ratios were low, a relatively large proportion of gross production had to be kept back for the following year's planting. With a gross yield of five, 20 per cent of the harvest was needed for seed, so the net yield was only four. Grain also had to be retained for human and animal consumption on the farm itself, and Wrigley has examined the implications of these requirements in the context of early modern north-west European agriculture (Wrigley 1989). If farming households consumed 75 annual bushels of wheat, with another bushel per acre for animal feed, then gross returns of 10 bushels per acre and a yield ratio of four imply that 11.5 acres of land would be needed to support the household and its animals in a normal year. Market production would be confined to holdings above this size and only these could produce subsistence for a non-agricultural population. For instance, a 20-acre plot would furnish a normal surplus equal to about three-quarters of household consumption.

The second problem, however, was that conditions were often not normal. Actual yields fluctuated from year to year, and the security of livelihoods depended more on the frequency of bad harvests than on long-term average volumes. The problem was exacerbated where normal yields were low, because the amount needed for seed was independent of the yield obtained in a given year and could represent a very large proportion of a poor harvest. As an example, where normal gross yield ratios were only four a holding producing a hundred units of grain needed twenty-five of them for seed. If another twenty-five units were needed for on-farm consumption, a 25 per cent shortfall in gross harvest yields would actually halve the net surplus from fifty to only twenty-five units. If, by contrast, the normal gross yield ratio was as high as ten then the normal surplus would be sixty-five per hundred units and it would fall by only 38 per cent.

The risks of harvest failure therefore increased disproportionately as the level of the normal yield declined, but it was also linked to holding size. Subsistence-level holdings were much more vulnerable than larger plots, whilst large-scale commercial farmers could profit from poor harvests. Wrigley's calculations show that the 20-acre plot in his example would go into grain deficit if harvest volumes fell to 70 per cent of the norm. A 100-acre holding, by contrast, would normally yield 575 surplus bushels only half of which would be wiped out by a 70 per cent harvest, and the remainder's cash value might be greater than normal because market prices rose disproportionately when yields fell. Bad harvests therefore brutally distinguished the fates of large and small producers, the latter having insufficient grain to feed themselves and their dependants whilst large farmers survived if they did not actually profit.

3.2.2.2. *The problem of over- and underpopulation*

The relationship between population growth, holding size, and harvest vulnerability where productivity was low underlay the condition of endemic food insecurity which we termed in the last chapter 'ecological overpopulation', but this condition also arose from circumstances other than population growth.

'Induced overpopulation', as we shall term it, could be caused by changes in the crop base and a switch from lower- to higher-risk varieties. Switches of this kind occurred because weather-resistant crops were often less valuable or prestigious than more sensitive alternatives. Where cultivators needed cash to pay rents or taxes, or if the crop mix was dictated by landowners who were not going to starve if the harvest failed, the result might be a cropping pattern yielding higher returns under normal conditions at the price of increased risk of failure.[10] Under these circumstances the incidence of subsistence crises increases in a way characteristic of ecological overpopulation despite a notional improvement in average living standards.

Population pressure was a recurrent problem in organic economies, but it would be wrong to infer that the central problem of pre-industrial economic demography was always and everywhere one of overpopulation. The inference may provide a reasonable guide to much of what happened in western Europe after the twelfth century, but as a general proposition it owes more to post-Malthusian 'folk demography' than to the economic and demographic realities it purports to describe (Ardener 1974). The equation of poverty and famine-proneness with the symptoms of population growth both ignores the possibility of induced overpopulation and fails to recognize that these can also be symptoms of classical underpopulation which, as we saw in the last chapter, occurs where population size falls in the classical model's region of increasing marginal returns. Where numbers were low and labour scarce the consequences could be severe, because fixed amounts of labour were required to clear land for cultivation regardless of the numbers who were then going to cultivate it, and small numbers impeded capital formation and the division of labour.

Population in western Europe may have literally outgrown the benefits of larger numbers in its medieval and early modern 'A' phases, but this does not mean the benefits did not exist, or that their absence was not felt in low-density populations elsewhere and at other times. The problem was exacerbated by the prevalence of low seed–yield ratios. These widened the gap between gross harvest volumes and the net amount of grain actually available for consumption once allowance had been made for the following year's seed and other necessary non-food uses. As a result, the net amount of food a labour force of any given size could produce was equal to the gross production of a substantially smaller number of workers, rather as if the horizontal axis on the classical population model we considered in the previous chapter had been shifted to the right. The potential consequences of this shift were very important because the threshold

---

[10] North-eastern England in the early Norman period provides an example of such a conflict of interest. The first wave of Norman landholders required fine wheaten bread as an accoutrement of their social position, but wheat was a very insecure crop across much of the region. The peasant cultivators preferred to grow oats which were more suited to the climate but had a low social status. Norman settlement on the 'wrong' side of the so-called oat bread line was therefore confined to districts which had been devastated during the Conquest and whose condition allowed a manorial organization to be imposed in which the lord dictated which crop was grown (Kapelle 1979: 183–90, 223–5).

population size at which the marginal net productivity of labour began to decline could be much higher than the threshold for declining gross productivity, and it was net productivity which determined how much food was actually available to be eaten.

Wrigley's calculations provide a simple demonstration of how this affected grain production at the level of a single 100-acre farm (Wrigley 1989). He begins by assuming that the holding is worked by ten men and that diminishing gross marginal returns to labour have already set in, so that the gross marginal output has fallen to the level of the average output per head. Under these circumstances any further increase in the labour force will reduce the average gross amount of grain produced by each worker, but the position is very different if we consider the net volumes available for disposal off the farm once the necessary deductions have been made for seed and on-farm consumption. Using the assumptions outlined in our earlier discussion of his example, Wrigley showed that net grain production per head would continue to rise with increases in the labour force until this numbered fourteen workers. When the labour force reached a size of sixteen workers, gross output per head would be 13 per cent less than it was with the original ten-man force, but the net average output of the larger force would still be equal to the initial gross average.

The distinction between gross and net output is likely to have been particularly important in two sets of circumstances. The first occurred in regions whose poor soils or rudimentary techniques of cultivation kept seed–yield ratios low. The dangers of extrapolation from micro- to macro-levels are well known, but Wrigley's example shows clearly how labour shortages may have occurred in these circumstances. The lower the yield ratio, the further population growth has to proceed beyond the point of diminishing gross marginal productivity before net levels begin to decline and the population leaves the zone of classical under-population. This raises the possibility of what is termed a 'low-level equilibrium trap' in which labour shortages keep output and living standards low, leading to high mortality or emigration which in turn perpetuates the shortage of labour. The implied association between poor soils, backward technology, and under-population is counter-intuitive, but it may well have prevailed in much of ancient and early medieval barbarian Europe where there is evidence for labour shortages as well as poverty and famine-proneness.[11]

---

[11] This argument would fall if it were the case that diminishing gross marginal returns set in very much earlier, relatively speaking, where the gross yield ratios were themselves low. There is no direct evidence for or against this possibility, but the widespread evidence for manpower shortages in barbarian societies suggests that it is unlikely to have been the case. This evidence consists mainly of the characteristic hunger for additional manpower, whether through slave raiding or the absorption of conquered groups. In the later Roman period at least, barbarians' slaves were widely used as agricultural labourers (Mathews 1989: 316; Wolfram 1997: 41). It may also be relevant that the German tribes are said to have disapproved of the practice of infant abandonment, an attitude which contrasted sharply with that of the Romans and is unlikely to have arisen from a greater delicacy of feeling on their part (Harris 1980).

The second set of circumstances corresponds to what can be termed 'induced underpopulation' and might prevail, even where yields were relatively high, if output were subject to a heavy fixed charge in the form of rent or taxation. Charges of this kind widen the gap between gross and net output in the same way as would a decline in seed yields and might convert declining gross marginal returns into rising net ones. If such charges were heavy enough, and sufficiently insensitive to variations in gross output, the labour force might become too small for a commercially viable agriculture, or even for subsistence cultivation to persist. Less fertile land would then pass out of cultivation whilst activity intensified in more favoured regions to offset the decline in total output. Something like this may well have happened in the later Roman period, with the growing burden of inequitable land taxation forcing the abandonment of marginal tracts whilst the hoarding of labour on better land triggered endemic manpower conflicts between the state and the agricultural sector.

3.3. INDUSTRIAL PRODUCTION

The development of civilian technology reflected the structure of economic demand, and so non-agricultural innovations were concentrated in the areas of food-processing, textiles, and construction.[12] This technology was overwhelmingly one of tools which were designed to make better use of muscle power or allow more of it to be brought to bear. The Greeks knew of five so-called 'simple machines' for transmitting and transforming power but made little civilian use of them other than in transportation. The crank was added to the wheel, screw, cam, ratchet, and pulley some time before the middle of the ninth century and allowed the transformation of reciprocating motion into continuous rotary motion. This was a development with far-reaching potential, but for hundreds of years its use was confined to the grindstone and the hurdy-gurdy.

3.3.1. METALLURGY AND MINING

The great exception to the rule of muscle power lay in heat-intensive processing which was concentrated in metallurgy but extended to brewing and ceramic manufacture. Metallurgical technology was correspondingly distinct from that found elsewhere, and it enjoyed a particular priority because the scarcity of metal artefacts limited what could be achieved in other sectors (White 1984: 120–6; Smith and Forbes 1956; Forbes 1957; Tylecote 1992). Metallurgy was itself

---

[12] See Mokyr (1990) for a thought-provoking discussion of technology in the context of economic history. The contributions to the standard survey edited by Singer et al (Singer, Holmyard, Hall, and Williams 1957, 1956) focus more on the development of technique. Useful general surveys of pre-modern engineering are to be found in Hill (1984) and Landels (1978). The standard work on the classical period is White (1984). The contributions to Brady (1997) revise some older views on medieval technology with an eye to issues in economic history. See Kellenbenz (1974) and White (1972) for brief introductions to the early modern and medieval periods respectively.

subdivided into the working of precious and base metals. The technological requirements for the two categories differed because precious metals required much lower temperatures, and the production of pure metal was often an end in itself. By contrast, the processing of base metals, and especially iron, was highly energy intensive and was generally undertaken as an initial step in the manufacture of artefacts.[13]

Whatever the metal involved, however, the first requirement was to obtain the ore, and so the extent of metalworking of all kinds was limited by the state of mining technology. The chief difficulty here was one of physically getting to the ore. Before the development of blasting with explosives this too relied on muscle power, and muscle power was also used to bring the ore to the surface and stop the galleries from flooding. Mining probably saw less progress than did any other sector in the ancient and medieval periods. It was unpleasant and dangerous work, and it was work performed in a fundamentally alien environment. As Mumford noted, mines were the first 'completely inorganic environment to be created and lived in by man', and they were often invested with supernatural as well as physical dangers (Mumford 1946: 67). Mine labour accordingly had very low status and was generally enforced. Indeed, Mumford goes so far as to assert that:

no one entered the mine in civilised states until relatively modern times except as a prisoner of war, a criminal, a slave. Mining was not regarded as a humane art: it was a form of punishment. (Mumford 1946: 69)

The stigmatization of mine labour itself impeded technological progress. The Romans' engineering skill allowed their mine-slaves to move around and work in an upright position, unlike the Greeks', but as long as workers could be replaced cheaply, mine operators could freely engage in hazardous procedures such as ventilation by fire-setting and generally disregard their health or safety (White 1984). Some problems, such as flooding, nonetheless posed threats that went beyond the lives of the workforce and had to be addressed. Roman hydraulic expertise yielded a range of pumps and other devices enabling workings to descend some 200 yards below the water table (Greene 2000). The medieval world, however, made no improvement on Roman methods if they even retained them. Flooding remained a serious problem, especially in the mining of precious metals, and the flooding or working out of older veins in the Harz mountains contributed to the pervasive currency shortages of the later Middle Ages (Spufford 1987). The conjunction of falling supply and rising demand for silver coinage did however act as a spur to innovation, and from the later fifteenth century substantial progress was made through the application of water and animal power, as well as gunpowder. Mining eventually emerged as a 'leading edge' technology some of whose elements, including the use of rails for haulage and eventually

---

[13] Iron may have enjoyed a brief career as a precious metal early in the first millennium BC when bar iron has been excavated from Near Eastern palace treasuries. It was evidently used in jewellery at this time, if not actually as a store of value (Tylecote 1992: 47).

steam power, were to have far-reaching applications elsewhere. At the same time, the mode of transmission of mining procedure acquired a distinctively 'modern' form. Printed treatises appeared, and whilst they may have had very limited circulation or influence, the fact that the transmission of expertise was now free of the constraints of personal networks was a major development in itself.

Once the ore had been got out of the ground it had to be processed. Precious metals could sometimes be found in pure 'native' form in veins of quartz, but ores generally consisted of metallic compounds, sometimes with an admixture of impurities. Whilst gold could be purified by 'cupellation' at relatively low temperatures, large-scale processing required substantial quantities of mechanical energy and water in order to separate the 'overburden' from the ore itself. The Roman gold mines at Las Medullas in Spain were served by three aqueducts delivering nearly seven million gallons per day over a distance of 15 miles, whilst Pliny described crushing machines incorporating 150-pound weights (White 1984: 119). Gold and silver derived their precious status from their physical and chemical qualities, which fitted them as a medium for skilled craftsmanship and as a store of value, but also from their scarcity. Medieval Europe's gold stock apparently derived from Roman-era accumulations supplemented by some North African imports, but the metal was too valuable for general use before the late Middle Ages and its scarcity, unlike that of silver which was the main medium of commercial exchange, does not seem to have constrained economic life.

The first of the non-precious metals to be smelted was copper. It requires a relatively low temperature of 700–800°, and it is likely that the process originated with the kiln firing of copper-glazed ceramics in the Neolithic period. The casting of molten copper, by contrast, requires temperatures approaching 1100° and was developed in the 'copper age' cultures of south-eastern Europe around 4500 BC. Bronze, an alloy of copper and tin which was smelted in the eastern Mediterranean from around 3000 BC, was the first metal to be made sufficiently hard for everyday use, and the Greeks' main metallurgical contributions lay in bronze-working and -casting. The Romans furthered the technology of copper-processing by developing methods for the large-scale exploitation of the more abundant sulphide ores, but in other respects there was little progress in non-ferrous metallurgy until the modern period.

Iron ore was relatively abundant, compared with copper, and iron supplanted bronze as Europe's utilitarian metal during the first millennium BC. Iron can be smelted at 1150 °C, but much higher temperatures are needed to produce the molten pig iron required for casting. Chinese smiths developed the necessary techniques very soon after ironworking first appeared, but Roman furnaces, which were unable to reach the necessary temperature, yielded a spongy and impure 'bloom' needing extensive hammering and reheating if it was to be of any use. Despite their skill in hydraulic engineering, the Romans failed to develop water-powered bellows or hammers for this purpose, and the output of their ironworks was low and very variable in quality. The application of water-powered bellows at the end of the fifteenth century allowed temperatures to be reached which enabled the production of molten pig iron, a product that could be either cast or wrought. The results were cheaper and more abundant than were those of the older 'bloomeries', and as blast furnaces grew larger and more efficient so iron became more widely available in Europe. Iron production was still bound by the energy constraints of the organic economy, however, and the metal was correspondingly expensive. For this reason the major centres of European iron production were usually associated with armaments manufacturing until the eighteenth century and civilian technology continued to rely on wood. The introduction of printing with movable type was one consequence of the new ferrous metallurgy,[14] but wood persisted as a material even for precision mechanisms and continued in clockmaking well into the eighteenth century (Landes 1983: 310).

3.3.2. MANUFACTURE AND ENGINEERING

The medieval elite's fondness for building cathedrals and castles fostered the development of heavy lifting machinery. Some of this found its way onto docksides but designs in this area were only limited refinements of those known in antiquity. A very different state of affairs prevailed in the world of tools for production. Much if not most of the innovation occurred in the textile sector, where the introduction of new hardware substantially boosted the productivity of labour (Usher 1954: 267–84). From the twelfth century, the use of flywheels allowed the development of the spinning wheel, and in the sixteenth century the introduction of the treadle marked a further improvement. Labour productivity in weaving was more than trebled from the eleventh century through the replacement of the ancient world's horizontal loom by the vertical form. At the end of the sixteenth century these two devices were joined by the stocking frame, a machine for knitting.

The introduction of the verge-and-foliot escapement at the end of the thirteenth century allowed the development of weight-driven clocks and so the accurate measurement of time in all weathers (Usher 1954: 193–210). This was revolutionary in itself, but the progressive refinement of escapements encouraged further developments in instrument-making and the construction of control and governing mechanisms as well as increasingly accurate mechanical clocks (Landes 1983; Usher 1954: 304–31). The application of the flywheel and crank to the lathe in the sixteenth century was an important step forward in precision engineering, allied to the Renaissance development of instrument-making, although the development of true high-precision machine tools awaited the later eighteenth century (Usher 1954: 360–74).

---

[14] Progress in ferrous metal technology was necessary because, whilst it was theoretically possible to use wooden movable type, it was prohibitively expensive in practice, and very hard punches were needed to produce type of a quality that could compete on what was initially still a luxury market. The success of printing also required the availability of oil-based inks and an abundance of paper (Usher 1954: 238–57).

The greatest technological legacy of the fifteenth century in Europe was undoubtedly the combination of printing with movable type and the development of power-driven papermills. From the 1450s when Gutenberg perfected the technique, printing presses spread rapidly, helped by exemptions from taxation and guild restrictions, so that by the end of the century there were over a thousand public presses in Germany alone. The cultural implications were profound and far-reaching. The written word now assumed a priority over oral tradition and customary authority, and could either subvert or support established social and political hierarchies.[15] Moreover printing was a new kind of activity. In Mumford's words it was 'a completely mechanical achievement. Not merely that: it was the type for all future instruments of reproduction: for the printed sheet, even before the military uniform, was the first completely standardised product' (Mumford 1946: 135).

3.4. INNOVATION AND OUTPUT GROWTH

Technological progress could arise from improvements in any or all of its three constituent elements, but it was the hardware that set the long-term limits to what could be achieved, and progress in this sphere set the pace for technological progress overall. It generally occurred in two stages because new or improved hardware had first to be conceived of as a physical or mental model before it could be applied in practice. The two stages are conventionally termed 'invention' and 'innovation', and the factors responsible for promoting either of them remain something of a mystery. It is clear nonetheless that the two responded to different stimuli and that, historically speaking, invention outpaced innovation for many centuries in the west, at least where non-agricultural technology was concerned. The ancients' knowledge of mechanical devices, or of principles allowing their construction, far exceeded their application to the problems of production, whilst the widespread application of the crank, an early medieval invention of fundamental importance, was delayed for several centuries. The chronology of invention itself is also hard to understand, and there is no apparent correlation between a society's level of political organization, or any other index of 'civilization', and the degree of inventiveness it displayed. The Romans were completely outclassed in this regard by their 'barbarian' Gallic neighbours, whilst the invention of the humble wheelbarrow awaited the supposed retrogression of the post-Roman 'Dark Ages'.

---

[15] The potential of writing to subvert traditional forms of knowledge and the social arrangements that they underpinned is widely recognized; in the words of Goody, 'alphabetic literacy made it possible to scrutinise discourse in a different kind of way by giving oral communication a semi-permanent form: this scrutiny favoured the increase in scope of critical activity, and hence of rationality, scepticism and logic' (Goody 1977: 37). There is no doubt that printing could greatly accelerate the formation and transmission of new knowledge, but it did not necessarily do so and could have the reverse effect. Mark argues that the early proliferation of printed architectural treatises actually reduced experimentation by entrenching the hegemony of classical models and design rules (Mark 1997).

The puzzles of long-term technological change are often approached using biological metaphors. These are potentially very useful, but like all metaphors they have their limitations which it is important to keep in mind. The major limitation springs from the fact that biological systems reproduce themselves, whereas technology is produced by human agents. The process is constrained by the availability of existing hardware, procedures, and personnel in ways which give biological metaphors their utility, but there is no direct equivalent of the genetic continuity linking successive generations of reproducing organisms. The production of technology has also to be explained with reference to the conscious intentions of those who produce it, whereas modern evolutionary theory holds that the process is devoid of intention or purpose.

Evolutionary theory has concerned itself with changes of three kinds, of which only two are recognized by current neo-Darwinian orthodoxy. The least problematic, and the least theoretically interesting, of these three is the continuous long-term development of a trait, or complex of traits, in a given direction such as increased size or functional specialization. This 'phyletic' evolution as it is called is familiar from the fossil record and is easy to explain by the action of natural selection. Of greater theoretical difficulty, and much greater theoretical importance, is what is termed 'speciation', the splitting off of one or more new species from a single ancestral population. Neo-Darwinian theory contends that speciation occurs by the same mechanism as phyletic evolution. Small adaptive changes (or 'micro-mutations') accumulate slowly over long periods and cause local populations of a single species to diverge until they eventually constitute distinct reproductive units. Other variants of post-Darwinian theory reject this concept of so-called 'phyletic gradualism', contending instead that speciation occurs rapidly through a sudden 'burst' of natural selection acting on an existing pool of variation, or because of a single massive change in the genetic composition of an individual (termed variously a 'macro-mutation' or 'saltation').

The history of technology provides many instances of a phenomenon akin to phyletic evolution, episodes in which technology developed through the accumulation of small incremental refinements built on existing hardware or procedures by a process of 'learning from experience'. There is also no doubt, whatever may be the case in biological evolution, that saltation-like events can and do occur in the history of technology even if they were very rare throughout the period of organic economies. A further pursuit of the biological metaphor can illuminate the processes and problems involved. The evolutionary geneticist Sewell Wright—one of the co-founders of neo-Darwinian theory—developed a model of genetic change in populations which represents the possible states of a population's gene pool as points on a two-dimensional surface whilst a third, vertical, dimension represents the Darwinian 'selective value', or 'fitness', of the state concerned. As a population evolves its gene frequencies change, and so it traverses the surface, moving through the horizontal dimensions, X and Y, and rising or falling on the vertical dimension, Z, according to the changes in its mean fitness. Defined in these terms the surface resembles a hilly landscape of adaptive peaks and troughs, and since it is a defining tenet of neo-Darwinism that natural selection maximizes fitness, a selective pressure will automatically propel a population situated on a slope upwards towards the nearest summit.

The technological analogue of 'directional selection' is the process of 'learning from experience' by making incremental changes to existing technologies and keeping those that are seen to work. But technology is not restricted to phyletic evolution. The production of technology by conscious agents—and the absence of reproductive continuity between generations—allows human ingenuity to make breaks in technological development or to introduce entirely new systems by extrapolation from experience or the exercise of creative imagination. Technological saltations of this kind initiate renewed episodes of phyletic development as the new system is incrementally refined in the light of experience, leading to the 'stepwise' pattern so characteristic of invention in organic economies. Fundamentally new ideas appeared at extended and irregular intervals followed by a process of diversification. There was thus a distinctive early medieval 'burst' of new inventions, but this had more or less run its course by the fifteenth century, and from then until well into the eighteenth such hardware development as occurred consisted mainly of the improvement and elaboration of existing devices.

A major reason for the scarcity of technological saltations was the long separation of practical invention from the process of abstract scientific enquiry. The development of both hardware and procedure chiefly relied on observation and practical experience, rather than on the application of theoretical principles or other abstractions to concrete instances. This was a good basis on which to refine existing technologies, but it was much harder to make a radical extrapolation from past experience or to conjure up something wholly new by this means.[16] This strongly empirical flavour was itself a consequence of the constraints that organic economies' low productivity imposed on the accumulation and transmission of specialized knowledge, and therefore on the 'personnel' component of technology. If it is indeed true that 'those who can do, and those who can't teach', organic economies could afford neither to support many of the latter, nor to produce large quantities of written training materials at a price affordable by any artisans or craftsmen who might be literate. For this reason it was rare for existing practice, skills, or technological knowledge to be transmitted within a formal institutional matrix distinct from the practice itself. Such

---

[16] The conservative implications of this constraint were felt particularly in the case of shipbuilding, where there was no means of determining the seaworthiness of a new vessel before it was actually put in the water and so any radical design innovation was intrinsically risky (Unger 1980: 24–5). In principle this constraint should have been eased by the development of increasingly accurate scale models in the early modern period and then by the refinement of hydrodynamic theory in the eighteenth century, but it is doubtful how far this happened in practice. Gardiner argues that the relevant hydrodynamic calculations took so long to carry out that they were of little practical use and warship design remained essentially empirical. Even the elaborate ship models produced for the British Navy Board were, in his view, primarily for display purposes and were sometimes constructed after the vessel had been launched (Gardiner 1992: 119–20).

knowledge was instead passed on orally and through observation of actual practice. It relied heavily on varieties of learning by doing of which apprenticeship was a formalized instance.

The reliance on observation and learning by doing had important implications for the transmission of specialized knowledge across time and space. Transmission over time depended on a chain of intergenerational linkages and thus on the unbroken continuity of the practice in question. Where this was disrupted, as it was in parts of the post-Roman west, then technical knowledge might be lost as a result (Ward-Perkins 2000b: 361). Spatial transmission was affected because the formation of skills and the exchange of expertise between skilled practitioners both depended on personal networks that were established on such bases as kinship, propinquity, or forms of religious and ethnic solidarity. Under these circumstances innovation and best practice both diffused slowly, and network boundaries could become effective barriers to the spread of knowledge. One result of this was a form of conservative technological particularism manifested in what can be termed 'ethnic technologies'. These were technological variants, or styles, whose occurrence was restricted to certain populations, whether defined on linguistic, geographical, religious, or some other ground. Sometimes, as in the case of 'Damask steel', this restriction was imposed consciously, in order to retain a military or economic advantage.[17] Elsewhere, regional patriotism seems to have been responsible, so that the vertical waterwheel diffused through northern France but failed to penetrate the south (Bloch 1967; Planhol and Claval 1994: 130–1). In other cases deeper issues of cultural identity were involved, particularly those that divided the Christian and Islamic worlds (Mokyr 1990: 39–45, 189).

3.5. CONCLUSION

The energy inputs available in organic economies were very restricted and this lowered productivity in all sectors. The consequences were most far-reaching in the agricultural sector, because low agricultural productivity restricted what could be achieved elsewhere in the economy, but they were most visible in sectors such as metallurgy that required heat-intensive processing. The reliance on fuel wood in these cases severely limited output as compared with coal or, to a lesser extent, peat. Low productivity meant that living standards were also low and the resulting poverty constrained both the accumulation of capital and the incentives to invest it productively. Technological development occurred, subject to these constraints, in both agricultural and non-agricultural production.

---

[17] 'Damask steel', as it was known in the Christian west, was a highly carbonized crucible-forged steel used in the Islamic world to produce lightweight blades of great strength and sharpness. The material is thought to have originated in India and was already known to the Romans via the Axumites of Abyssinia who apparently misrepresented its origins as Chinese (Braudel 1981: 376–7; Forbes 1957: 57).

In agriculture this took the form of new crop mixes and the more efficient exploitation of animal muscle power. These helped raise output in line with population growth, although the extension of arable cultivation probably made a larger contribution and output per head nonetheless fell in both the medieval and early modern cycles. Soil productivity, as measured by seed–yield ratios, remained low and this led to a gap between gross and net arable yields which could be very large and had implications on both the small and large scales. On the small scale, it aggravated subsistence cultivators' vulnerability to the normal range of fluctuations in harvest volumes of a kind that could enrich larger commercial farmers. On a larger scale, it opened the possibility of underpopulation in particularly unproductive regions by raising the point at which net marginal returns to labour began to decline. Barbarian societies in ancient and early medieval Europe may have experienced endemic labour shortages as a result of this phenomenon, which could also be induced by a heavy flat-rate charge on the land of the kind levied in the later Roman period.

Technological developments elsewhere enabled more efficient furnaces to be built, allowing greater output of ferrous metals whose scarcity impeded the diffusion of efficient tools and machinery throughout the period. Wind and water power were also exploited, but a great deal of non-agricultural technology was devoted to the more efficient exploitation of muscle power through devices such as the pulley, crank, or wheelbarrow. The chronology of these inventions is puzzling since it does not coincide with the advance of civilization as generally conceived. The classical world produced surprisingly little in the way of production technology whereas the ensuing centuries were relatively fecund. One distinctive feature of technological development was that it was predominantly incremental and based on learning from experience rather than applying abstract conceptual knowledge. This probably accounts for the scarcity of radical innovation in technology and itself reflected the energy limitations of an organic economy through the ensuing constraints on the development of social differentiation. Specialized institutions for forming and transmitting skills were virtually absent and the process depended heavily on informal networks, observation, and learning by doing, all of which hampered the spatial diffusion of technological knowledge and endangered intergenerational transmission should the continuity of specialized production be disrupted.

CHAPTER FOUR

The Means of Transport

Spatial integration was a prerequisite for both economic growth and political centralization and its practicability depended on the state of transport and communications. Consumption in pure subsistence economies might be restricted to the products of local resources, but economic differentiation required inputs from different localities to be combined, and regional specialization was a vital contributor to productivity growth. The elaboration of formal political structures also involved the extension of control over space, the transfer of information and material resources, and the efficient delivery of the means of coercion. Both these political and economic forms of spatial integration required the co-ordination of activities at distant locations, and reasonably effective transport and communication networks were essential if this was to be possible. Organic economies imposed as many constraints in this sphere as they did in production and it is essential to understand how these operated if the economic and political geography of the period as a whole is to make any sense.

The basic constraint was the same one that affected production: a heavy reliance on organic sources of raw materials and energy. Just as with production, transport and communications technology depended primarily on muscle power and wood, with the important addition of wind power to supplement or replace muscle when moving over water. This gave shipping a significant energetic advantage, but shipping also had its limitations. Ships were slow and had to be loaded and unloaded, and there were limits to the size of wooden hulls. Sailing ships needed a fair wind and shipping of all sorts was vulnerable to bad weather if not piracy, so land carriage was the usual mode of choice for high-value, low-bulk luxury goods. Bulk cargoes, such as staple foods, might go more cheaply by land over short distances, but the cost of feeding transport animals made this prohibitively expensive after a few days' journey time, and shipping enjoyed an effective monopoly of long-range bulk transport wherever the choice was governed by economic criteria.

The technology of transportation, like production technology, underwent progressive refinement. Road-building saw little advance from classical standards until the close of the period, but substantial progress occurred in the design of inland waterways and their locks. Developments also occurred in the sphere of vehicles and prime movers. Horses were substituted for oxen, and vehicles replaced pack animals in suitable terrain. Goods vehicles themselves acquired greater manoeuvrability and endurance and so became more effective load carriers. Carriages and other passenger vehicles also emerged as luxury items towards the close of the period, but the main developments occurred in shipping and particularly in the design of sails and rigging. Sailing ships became faster, more manoeuvrable, and less vulnerable to contrary winds, which allowed them to displace oared vessels even as carriers of luxury goods. By the eighteenth century the full-rigged ship had developed into the most sophisticated technology known to the pre-industrial world.

The overall relationship between transport costs and economic growth was nonetheless complex and in some respects perverse. Low-productivity economies characteristically made very inefficient use of labour, which was often virtually unemployed during the 'slack' seasons of the agricultural year, and at these times many rural areas contained pools of men and animals that could be hired very cheaply as hauliers or muleteers. As productivity grew and labour was used more efficiently, haulage became the prerogative of full-time specialists who were correspondingly more expensive, but long journey times and high costs per mile were not the only obstacles to the progress of trade and spatial integration. The uncertainty as to when, or even whether, a cargo would arrive and how much its journey would cost could cause even more problems. Inland waterways offered advantages in this respect, and the uncertainties of land transport were reduced by both technological progress and the provision of greater security by governments. Long sea voyages remained intrinsically risky propositions well into the nineteenth century, but many of the disincentives that this provided to marine commerce were removed by the development of more sophisticated financial institutions and particularly by insurance that translated the uncertainties of risk into a fixed premium that could be determined in advance.[1]

4.1. TRANSPORT TECHNOLOGY

The fundamental problem for transport technology was one of applying energy to overcome the effects of friction or gravity. This gave water transport an intrinsic advantage for the movement of heavy loads and allowed wind energy to be exploited. Bulk goods could always be moved more cheaply by sea than by land, and inland waterways were also cheaper over long distances. Wind was, however, an unreliable energy source, and though muscle power could be faster over short distances it could not be used effectively on long voyages. Sea transport was therefore slow, and the hazards of bad weather or contrary winds meant that it was also unpredictable. Land transport relied for its hardware on a combination of up to three components. There always had to be a prime mover which might be

---

[1] Roman merchants were able to offset some of the risk of maritime commerce through a legal provision that loans taken out to support ventures of this kind were only repayable when the ship arrived safely in harbour. Such loans were judged so risky for the lender that trustees were forbidden from undertaking them on the part of their trusts (Goldsmith 1987: 27).

human or, more often, animal. A rider or runner could carry light goods over long distance, and porters could carry heavier loads a shorter way, but efficient bulk transport required vehicles, and to be effective these also needed the third component—an infrastructure of firm surfaces. Development occurred across the range of transport technologies, but it was limited by the energetic capacities of wind and muscle, and the structural properties of wood.

4.1.1. SEA TRANSPORT

The efficiency, and with it the cost, of maritime transport was limited by the maximum tonnage carried per crew member and per unit of capital bound up in the vessel. Operationally, it also depended on the frequency and distance of voyages undertaken in any period, and the proportion of cargoes that were lost at sea. In the nineteenth century steam power and iron hulls revolutionized shipping and freight costs fell dramatically (Grigg 1992). Until then ships were made of wood and relied on wind or muscle power for propulsion. This always imposed limitations on their cargo capacity and operational abilities, but substantial progress was made in the design of hulls and rigging, and the last generation of wooden sailing ships were probably the most complex technological systems ever constructed in the pre-industrial world.

4.1.1.1. *Oars and sails*

Seagoing ships used oars, sails, or a combination of the two for motive power, and from antiquity the hull shapes of larger vessels divided into two. As their name suggests, 'longships' or galleys were long and narrow, with a ratio of length to beam that rose as high as 10 : 1 in some Greek triremes (Casson 1971: 82). They had a relatively low freeboard, which meant the deck was close to the waterline, and they could move under oar power alone when needed. 'Roundships' were much broader, with a length-to-beam ratio as low as 3 : 1 (Unger 1980: 36), and rode higher in the water. Smaller vessels of this kind sometimes carried a few oars for manoeuvring or emergencies, but sails were their primary energy source. Oar power by contrast allowed ships to manoeuvre regardless of wind speed or direction, which was an important military advantage and allowed commercial galleys to manoeuvre into port or round a headland while sailing ships were waiting for the wind to change. But there were limits to how long oarsmen could keep up a useful speed, and larger galleys normally relied on sails to cruise in open waters, though these might be of secondary importance on smaller ships.

Their tactical strengths made galleys the vessel of choice for traders for whom piracy posed a serious threat, or opportunity, as it often did in the ancient world.[2] Oared ships could also hold their own commercially against roundships in coastal

---

[2] See Snodgrass (1983) for oared vessels as traders; de Souza (1999) provides an extended review of ancient piracy, its context and implications.

luxury trades, but they had serious disadvantages as cargo carriers. Their low freeboard made them vulnerable to heavy seas, limiting their ability to operate in open waters, particularly in northern Europe where they were limited to coastal navigation outside the summer season. The range of galleys was also restricted because the food, and particularly the water, requirements of their large crews forced them to keep close to shore. Above all, the basic galley design made for a very inefficient bulk carrier because there was so little available space on board. More space could be made available by dispensing with sleeping accommodation, but this further restricted their range because the crew had to go ashore each night. The tonnage per crew member was too low to justify the carriage of anything but high-value, low-bulk luxuries. Fifteenth-century Venetian 'Great Galleys', specifically built to rival roundships, raised freight capacity to 2 tons per crewman, but their sail-powered competition managed from 5 to 8 tons (Unger 1980: 178; Pryor 1988: 43–4).

If the performance of a galley was limited by the muscular endurance of its rowing gang, a sailing ship was only as good as its rigging. Pre-modern rigging divided into two categories: 'square rigging' and 'fore and aft'.[3] Square rigging was simpler and faster with a following wind and the sail—which might be just a rectangular piece of cloth—set at 90 degrees to the prevailing wind. Square-rigged ships needed smaller crews but were heavily dependent on wind speed and direction. If the wind failed altogether, no rigging was of any use, but fore-and-aft systems could exploit contrary winds with varying degrees of efficiency. By setting sails parallel to the wind direction, vessels were able to sail 'closer to the wind' and make headway where square-rigged ships were becalmed. The system was evidently known in antiquity, but square rigging seems to have been more widely used on larger ships. The fore-and-aft system was widely diffused during the early Middle Ages, in the form of the 'lateen' sail, and led to the growing exploitation of wind power at sea. Fore-and-aft rigs improved manoeuvrability, and cut the sailing time lost through contrary winds, but there was a price. They needed larger crews than square-rigged ships, and incorporated spars of a length that could be difficult to procure when very large vessels were being constructed. Once this price was paid, however, it cost little more to add some square sails and obtain the combined benefits of the two systems. The first such 'full-rigged' designs appeared at the close of the Middle Ages and were progressively elaborated into the nineteenth century with gains in both speed and manoeuvrability (Chappelle 1968).

4.1.1.2. *Hull types*

Improvements in rigging increased the operational efficiency of sailing ships, but the cargo capacity of any wooden vessel was constrained by limitations on the size

---

[3] Casson (1971) provides an extensive analysis of ancient systems; for the medieval period see Unger (1980).

of hulls. These limitations had a potentially serious effect on costs because larger ships were, in principle, cheaper and more efficient freight carriers. Per ton of cargo capacity, they needed less wood for their hulls. This was a significant consideration given the frequency of timber shortages among medieval and early modern shipbuilding regions, but it was often outweighed in practice by the difficulty of finding individual timbers big enough for the masts and spars of large ships, particularly once fore-and-aft rigging came into general use (Unger 1980; Horden and Purcell 2000). Larger ships were more efficient operationally because the ratio of tonnage to crew size rose with hull size, which was important since crewing accounted for a large share of total operational costs, and it became more so as the growing complexity of rigging increased overall manpower requirements.[4]

Always provided that they could be sailed effectively, big ships offered economies in the carriage of low-value bulk freight, and they had a greater range and endurance. They were also more efficient in terms of so-called 'security costs'. Before the advent of effective shipborne artillery, the larger the ship the greater was its security from attack, and the threat of piracy continued into the gunpowder era. In some waters it required ships to carry much larger crews than were needed just for sailing and the disproportion was all the greater the smaller the vessel.[5] These advantages of scale did, however, have to be balanced against some operational disadvantages if trade volumes were low and distances short. Smaller ships had advantages in these circumstances because less time was wasted in loading or in waiting for a full cargo, and so they could make more trips over any given period.

The upper limits to the size of wooden hulls were approached relatively early in historical terms. As Fernand Braudel observed:

the art of shipbuilding had already produced its record tonnages a good century before the Invincible Armada... The use of iron made larger hulls possible only in about 1840. A hull of 200 tons had until then been the general rule, one of 500 an exception, one of 1000 to 2000 an object of curiosity. (Braudel 1981: 423)

The capacity of ancient shipping was comparable with anything achieved before the nineteenth century.[6] Many Hellenistic vessels ranged from 350 to 500 tons, and freighters between 1,700 and 1,900 tons were built at Syracuse. The Roman grain carriers on the Alexandria–Ostia run apparently had a standard capacity of 340 tons, but some were much bigger. The *Isis*, subject of a detailed

---

[4] The relative efficiency of larger ships seems to have increased dramatically around the middle of the 18th century with space-saving improvements in hull design. Among merchant ships entering London from Jamaica, the average tons per man rose from 10.5 for vessels in the 100–49 ton class to 16.0 in those over 300 tons. In the Baltic trades the equivalent ratios were 11.4 and 21.9 (Davis 1962).

[5] The early modern Mediterranean was especially dangerous, and merchant ships on the lucrative Levant trade rated only 4.5–5 tons per crewman at a time when ratios elsewhere often ran into double figures (Unger 1980).

[6] For ancient ships and shipbuilding see Casson (1971); for the medieval period in general see Unger (1980), and Pryor (1988) for the Mediterranean.

literary description when it was blown off course and into the Pirrhaeus, has been estimated at 1,200 tons (Casson 1971: 184-8). Roman hulls were built like furniture on a system of mortise and tenon joints that produced a very strong weight-bearing outer shell. This was watertight without caulking, and, like Roman roads, required very little maintenance. Like their roads, Roman hulls were 'overbuilt' in the sense that their construction took up much more time and effort than was necessary to produce a seaworthy vessel.

'Clinker building', by contrast, formed the shell from a series of overlapped planks. The resulting hull needed continual maintenance but was cheap and relatively easy to construct. The clinker building technique spread through northern Europe in the early Middle Ages along with the use of sails as a power source. By AD 700 sails were entering general use in Scandinavia, and two types of northern roundship, the 'hulk' and 'cog', were established in open and inshore waters respectively. Both types progressively increased in size, and converged in design, so that by the fifteenth century the terms were interchangeable (Unger 1980: 169). The cog had a very high freeboard. This allowed missile-armed troops to fire down into attacking longships, and commercial vessels of this kind could defend themselves very effectively against pirate attacks. With the further addition of fighting platforms (or 'castles') at either end they could be pressed into service as warships (Runyan 1993: 83-7; Friel 1994: 814; Unger 1980: 140). Although galley construction continued in northern Europe, by the close of the Middle Ages they were restricted to inland and coastal waters. They held on longer in the Mediterranean, where the technologically conservative Venetians sent their Great Galleys north to Flanders as late as the 1530s, but even in these waters northern roundships commanded a growing share of maritime trade from the late sixteenth century.

Clinker-built hulls were light, flexible, and highly seaworthy, and their virtues were forcefully demonstrated by generations of Scandinavian sea-raiders and colonists, but the technique had its limitations. Heavier vessels rode through, rather than over, the water and needed stronger hulls than clinkering could provide, as did ships carrying gunpowder artillery. The solution lay in the technique of 'carvel' building, in which planks are laid edge to edge and the strain taken by the hull's internal skeleton rather than its shell. Carvel building was used by Mediterranean shipwrights before the eleventh century, and its spread to northern Europe permitted the region's shipbuilders to construct substantially larger hulls. Some fourteenth-century carvel-built cogs displaced 150-200 tons or more, and before the end of the century they were superseded by the faster fore-and-aft rigged caravels, most of which were of this size.

The caravel was the west's first truly oceanic vessel, and two of them accompanied Christopher Columbus' *Santa María* in 1492. Caravels appear to have been much liked by their sailors but they were too small for the growing number of long-range voyages. Particularly after the 1540s, when the discovery of Andean silver stimulated increased transatlantic migration and trade, there was a demand for ocean-going bulk freighters which was met by adapting a Mediterranean type of vessel, the 'carrack'. Sixteenth-century carracks were big ships. Some displaced over 2,000 tons and had the largest all-wooden hulls ever built,[7] but they were too big to make effective ocean sailers and had an indifferent record for seaworthiness and handling (Parry 1967: 201). Following this unwieldy giganticism two distinctive design philosophies arose and civilian and military ship types diverged as a result.

The first galleons, a style rather than a specific type of ship, were launched in the 1550s and strongly influenced subsequent warship design until the age of steam and iron (Unger 1980; Cipolla 1965; Naish 1957). Narrower than earlier roundships and lacking their high castles, galleons were faster and more manoeuvrable than carracks. The largest examples ranged up to 1,000 tons, but more were between 500 and 800 and some as small as 100 tons. The lower castles were a disadvantage in close combat but were offset by powerful broadside artillery mounted in a dedicated gun deck and a strengthened hull. This arrangement reduced the available cargo space, and though early galleons served as merchant vessels in particularly dangerous waters, their future lay as specialized warships growing progressively larger and more heavily armed and manned.

As this process of specialization unfolded, the design of merchant shipping followed a contrary direction under Dutch influence. Dutch design philosophy developed in the sixteenth century and culminated in the 1590s with the so-called *fluyt* (Unger 1980, 1978). Smaller than most galleons, *fluyts* were relatively long and shallow with a length-to-beam ratio ranging up to 6 : 1, but their distinctive feature was a remorseless pursuit of operational efficiency. Like much Dutch technology this was built around a central principle of labour-saving, so that speed was sacrificed for a simpler rigging. This, along with their boxy hulls and light superstructure, gave the *fluyts* a capacity of up to 20 tons per man, enabling them to offer freight rates 30–50 per cent below those of English competitors (Parry 1967: 212). Design efficiency on this scale meant that ships could also be built smaller, to gain the operational advantages of a smaller hold, and the optimum proved to be in the 300- to 500-ton range. *Fluyts* were originally designed as civilian ships for northern waters where capacity could be enhanced by dispensing with defensive armament. In Mediterranean and oceanic sailing the problem of piracy made this impracticable and also necessitated larger crews and a heavier build. Here, as in slave trading, security requirements prevented the Dutch realizing the full potential of their labour-saving technology and the English were better able to compete. The *fluyt*'s influence was nonetheless pervasive, and few cargo carriers in the last century of wooden ships ranged above 200–500 tons (Parry 1967: 212; Naish 1957).

4.1.1.3. Navigation

Sea transport offered unparalleled economies for bulk cargoes such as grain, and access to the sea shaped the geography of major metropolitan centres,

---

[7] Wooden ships over 2,000 tons were built in the 19th century but their hulls were braced with iron. Without this support very large wooden hulls tended to bend in the middle, or 'hog', unless they rose so far out of the water as to compromise their seaworthiness (Gardiner 1992).

but sea transport was not a panacea. Luxury goods that risked spoilage often had to go by land. Above all, water transport of any kind was unsuitable where speedy delivery was required. The duration of sea voyages is a paradoxical topic because ships, under ideal conditions, could be the fastest means of travel, but they were often the slowest. Journey times were even more variable than those by land and long sea voyages remained an icon of dangerous unpredictability into the nineteenth century. The larger galleys of the ancient and early modern worlds could probably manage 6 knots under oars, and up to 8 or more in short bursts, but normally cruised under sail. Figures collected by Casson (1971: 292–6) suggest that ancient Mediterranean shipping normally covered around 100 to 150 nautical miles per day with favourable winds and about half this with the wind against them. At this time navigation depended largely on sighting known landmarks, and so limited visibility, as much as winter storms, restricted the Mediterranean sailing season to the period from late spring to early autumn. The pattern of prevailing northerlies during these months meant that north–south voyages took around half as long as the return journey. In the ancient world, the Rome–Alexandria grain transports apparently aimed at three return trips for every two seasons, a schedule that put a high premium on dockside efficiency (Casson 1971: 297–9).[8]

By the end of the sixteenth century the compass and other improvements in navigation had extended the sailing season throughout the year, although summer voyages were still apparently faster. The maximum cruising speed of a well-manned galley under ideal conditions was around 150 nautical miles per day, but the more abundant documentation available for this period gives a striking indication of how variable actual journey times could be. Braudel suggests that north–south voyages across the Mediterranean normally took one to two weeks, and a voyage from east to west around two to three months. This may have been the general pattern but a Venetian roundship took only a month from Crete to Cadiz in 1561, whilst a few years later a pair of galleys needed more than ten weeks to get from Algiers to Constantinople. Some figures assembled by Braudel from the port of Livorno allow this variation to be quantified in a little more detail (see Table 4.1).

Advances in rigging and shipbuilding techniques, together with the replacement of the steering oar by the stern-post rudder and the introduction of the keel, allowed true ocean-going vessels to be constructed from the fifteenth century onwards. Undertaking a voyage on this scale also required the development of an effective means of navigation. The Scandinavians had been able to make accurate landfall after voyages of some length, but how they did this remains mysterious, and even they were prone to become lost on the high seas (Leighton 1972: 148–51). The development of the magnetic compass, first mentioned in the west at the end

---

[8] The expense of feeding and housing the ships' slave crews during their lengthy periods of enforced idleness outside the sailing season must also have substantially increased the costs of the operation.

Table 4.1 *Duration of voyages, 1609–1611*

Cartagena/Alicante–Livorno (duration in days)	Alexandria–Livorno (duration in days)
7	23
9	26
9	29
10	32
15	56
25	
30	
49	
Median duration 12.5	29.0

Source: Braudel (1972: 363).

of the twelfth century and in general use by the fifteenth, allowed deep-water Mediterranean navigation to continue through the winter months when cloud cover made it difficult to take sightings. Northern mariners, hugging the continental shelf, could make greater use of soundings, but the compass came into its own when they ventured into deeper waters such as the Bay of Biscay (Lane 1963).

Oceanic navigation required a means of establishing a vessel's position as well as its direction. Much of the movement in the earlier voyages of discovery was north–south so that the first priority was the determination of latitude (Parry 1974). In temperate waters this could be done by direct star sighting and in the tropics by determining the sun's meridian through indirect observation. The relevant instruments, quadrant and astrolabe respectively, were in use by the later fifteenth century, but they used an artificial horizon and needed to be kept perpendicular, which made them difficult to use on a moving ship. The sixteenth-century introduction of the cross-staff and back-staff eliminated this requirement and made sighting much easier. Observation and experiment was a sufficient basis for developing instruments of this kind, but using their readings to calculate an actual latitude posed challenges of a different order, particularly in the tropics, where the navigator had to know the angle of solar declination on any given day of the year. The problem was solved in the 1480s when a panel of mathematical experts drew up simplified tables and rules of procedure at the behest of the Portuguese monarchy. This kind of politically directed application of abstract science to practical issues was still rare, but the fact that it happened at all was a sign of changing times. Nonetheless, the accurate determination of longitude resisted such initiatives until well into the eighteenth century (Yeates 2001).

4.1.2. LAND TRANSPORT

Land transport relied on human or animal muscle power. Porterage could play a role in difficult terrain and over short distances but goods were usually carried by pack or draught animals. The efficiency of the process depended on the nature of the animal, the vehicle if any, and the surface over which it moved.

4.1.2.1. Pack carriage

Most pack animals were equines—horses, mules, or donkeys—but oxen were sometimes used, and pack camels were invaluable in arid landscapes. Pack animals had pride of place in the ancient world, retaining much of their importance in Mediterranean Europe well into the modern period. Sixteenth-century Spain was said to hold 400,000 pack mules, and their breeding caused fears for the supply of warhorses (Braudel 1972: 285; Stradling 1984). Pack animals' main advantage was their ability to cross rough terrain, which made them less reliant on the state of the roads than were draught animals. They were generally faster than carts or wagons and mules, able to work for very long hours, and could cover 50 miles a day under favourable conditions. Camels seem to have been domesticated in the late Roman period and by the early Middle Ages had displaced draught animals on the desert margins of the Mediterranean and south-west Asia (Bulliet 1975). They were successfully introduced into the Iberian peninsula and early medieval Gaul but played no other role in Europe itself.

Pack animals' cross-country abilities were offset by their inferior load capacity which ranged from 150 pounds to 400 pounds depending on the species (see Table 4.2). The load had to be divisible into two roughly equal halves in order to balance it, so not all commodities were readily transportable in this way. The animals also needed to be unloaded every evening so that they could rest and roll over, whereas vehicle loads could be left in place throughout the journey where security permitted. Draught haulage was generally more efficient and its use increased over the medieval centuries. By the early modern period pack animals played a secondary role in northern Europe, and in England they were restricted to light loads and short distances (Chartres 1977a, 1977b).

Table 4.2 *Estimated load capacity for pack animals*

Donkey with panniers	150–200 lb
Mule with panniers	300 lb
Horse with panniers	400 lb
Bullock	400 lb
Camel	400–500 lb +

Sources: White (1984: 129); for camel: Bulliet (1975: 20 n. 34).

4.1.2.2. *Draught haulage*

Substantial improvements in both vehicle and harness design promoted the expansion of draught haulage. Fragmentary Roman data suggest that contemporary goods vehicles were very inefficient, with the Theodosian Code specifying a 1000-pound upper limit on their loads (Burford 1960; White 1984: 127–40). Oxen were then the main source of draught power and the substitution of horses was one route to greater efficiency. Horse haulage was known in antiquity, but its efficiency was impaired by the retention of ox harness. The introduction of 'modern' shoulder harness and tandem harnessing, together with the readoption of nailed horseshoes, increased efficiency, whilst the introduction of dual shafts and the whipple-tree gave horse-drawn vehicles a manoeuvrability they had not had before.

Early fourteenth-century English demesne accounts show some 75 per cent of haulage being undertaken by horses, as opposed to oxen, with horses accounting for a comparable proportion of the peasant-owned draught herd (Langdon 1984). There were also improvements in the design of vehicles themselves, with lighter, spoked wheels and friction-reducing bearings. Pivoting front axles did not appear until the end of the Middle Ages, restricting very heavy vehicles to a single axle if they were to be at all manoeuvrable. This made them too heavy for draught horses and kept them to the speed of the plodding ox team. The ancient and medieval worlds judged horseback riding the only proper way for elite males to get about, but vehicle travel became more acceptable for gentlemen at the beginning of the early modern period. New, more comfortable, forms of passenger vehicle emerged; iron-bound wheels and leather suspension straps appeared on late sixteenth-century German carriages along with the turning-front carriage—a 'fifth wheel' that allowed the vehicle to pivot (Parry 1967). These became increasingly common in the following century and their improved wheel and axle systems spread to carts and wagons with consequent gains in efficiency. The capacity of the freight-wagon bed itself was expanded but at the end of the eighteenth century a four-horse wagon was still limited to a capacity of little more than a ton.

Goods vehicles needed to move on firm surfaces, and the quality of a heavy-vehicle route from A to B was only as good as its poorest section. Road quality had to be consistent because a single bad stretch could break a wagon wheel or bog it down and block the route to all other traffic. Pack animals also did better on firm surfaces, and so the overall efficiency of goods transport depended as much on the infrastructure of routeways and bridges as it did on vehicles and prime movers. The history of pre-eighteenth-century roads is often portrayed as a long dark age illuminated only by the glorious light of Rome but the reality is more complex. Roman roads, impressive as engineering achievements, were built to serve military and political, rather than commercial, needs, to which they were poorly adapted. Their hard surfaces, narrow bridges, steep gradients, and preference for commanding high ground made them unsuitable for heavy vehicles, which may have run along the verges rather than along the roadways themselves (White 1984: 94–7).

Roman roads could go without maintenance for up to a century, but they wasted labour and materials in the building of unnecessary foundations. Medieval roads were much simpler in design. In their construction, of broken stone or cobbles laid on sand, they were closer to the modern method of allowing the subsoil to bear the weight of traffic. Their surfaces were also better suited to wheeled vehicles and shod hooves, and they were more resistant to frost (Leighton 1972: 58–9). The shortcomings of medieval and early modern roads were real enough, however, and they have generated a richly anecdotal literature. Roads were often unmarked and so finding one and keeping to it required local knowledge, and the chance appearance of a local guide could be greeted as a providential, if not angelic, intervention (Maczak 1994: 11). Once on the road, surfaces were still hard and uneven enough to play havoc with wheels and axles, particularly on vehicles without suspension. Lacking weatherproof surfaces, many roads quickly degenerated into a morass in wet weather. In the words of one historian of early modern travel: 'all forms of European road traffic in those days took place to the sound of wheels breaking and axles snapping' (Maczak 1994: 7).

4.1.2.3. *Journey times*

The frequency of such accidents makes it difficult to gauge actual journey times. In principle, draught horses could manage 3–3.5 miles per hour for eight hours or so, and oxen about two-thirds of this (see Table 4.3). These rates allowed goods vehicles a daily journey of 15 and 20 miles respectively, and were obtained in practice over good surfaces in the absence of breakdowns and other delays. Nonetheless the most striking feature of what information we have on actual journey times is their variability. In fourteenth-century Northamptonshire carriers averaged 22 miles per day and managed 31 miles on one occasion, but their colleagues in Essex achieved only 10 to 14 miles and were correspondingly expensive (Masschaele 1993). Le Goff credits medieval merchants and their pack trains with

Table 4.3 *Average speeds of draught animals*

Animal	Speed (mph)
Horses	3–3.5
Mules	3–3.5
Bullocks	2–2.5
Camels	3

Source: See Elton (1996: table 5, p. 293).

from 25 to 60 kilometres per day according to the nature of the ground. It took two weeks to go from Bologna to Avignon, 22 days from the Fairs of Champagne to Nîmes, eleven to twelve days to go from Florence to Naples. (Le Goff 1988: 136–78)

Unladen travellers could move much faster than goods, but they did not always do so. English coaches could manage an average of 6 miles an hour by 1800, with the Oxford to London 'flying coach' covering the distance in a day. This is likely to have been as good a performance as horse-drawn travel ever managed. It reflected the good state of the roads as much as the efficiency of vehicle design, but even in eighteenth-century Britain coach journeys could be disrupted by accidents of travel. James Boswell took from 15 to 19 November 1762 to travel from Edinburgh to London, suffering a broken wheel and an overturn en route (Boswell 1950). In really difficult terrain things could be spectacularly worse. In 1583 the Polish cleric Stanislaw Reszka accompanied future Cardinal Andrziy Batory to Rome via the Tyrol. South-west of Prague their vehicle broke apart.

They bought a new one. Below Nitterau in Bavaria the wheels broke, in Landshut— the carriage itself. In Munich all the wagons were adapted to make them suitable for the mountain passes but, as was soon evident, with no greater success. Near Partenkirchen the wagons had to be repaired again, then each day after they had passed Innsbruck… On the Italian slopes things were slightly better. Reszka made a note of repairs after six days at Borghetto, after eleven at Merinengo and after nineteen at Piacenza. (Maczak 1994: 7)

In France, as late as 1800, an inspector of roads had his carriage overturned six times in a 300-mile tour, and was towed out of the mud by oxen on eleven occasions (Braudel 1988). In earlier periods most travellers who could afford the necessary costs rode on horseback, and their daily progress also varied with the weather and the state of the roads. For sixteenth-century horsemen:

the *gouvernement* of Picardy, a territory of roughly 10,000 sq km, was two days' journey from east–west. The routes given by Charles Estienne in 1552 indicate that most places along the Somme were two and two-and-a-half days from Paris but it took another three-and-a-half days to get to Calais from Amiens, a journey of 31 leagues by much less satisfactory roads. Nicholas Carew in 1529 took seven days for his journey from Calais to Paris via Amiens and even the common route through Clermont and Luzarches took three overnight stops at seven leagues a day. Ten leagues were possible though only for a traveller in a hurry. (Potter 1993: 19)

King's messengers in fourteenth-century England probably averaged little more than 20 miles a day, but on one occasion a horseman covered the 190 miles from London to York in under five summer days (Stenton 1936).

4.1.3. INLAND WATER TRANSPORT

Inland water transport presented fewer technological challenges than did sea transport in many respects and fewer practical problems than overland haulage. There was little danger of getting lost on rivers or canals, and animals could haul boats where suitable towpaths existed. Very light vessels could be pressed into service since hulls did not have to be heavily weatherproofed, and timber could be rafted downstream without the need for any vessel at all.[9] There was no need to worry about getting bogged down on bad roads and little friction to overcome on inland waterways, but their utility was limited by both geography and climate. Some locations were inaccessible by water, and navigable waterways did not necessarily interconnect. France was fortunate in having navigable rivers that interconnected to form a virtual network, but the position could be very different elsewhere. The major Iberian rivers followed separate courses to the sea, and most flowed north and west into the Atlantic and away from the main direction of traffic. Spain, furthermore, had only two stretches of river that were passable by large seagoing vessels, the lower Guadalquivir and Ebro (Ringrose 1970: 3).

Existing waterways could be improved, or new ones constructed, where natural access was inadequate, but this was subject to technical and operational difficulties and could be formidably expensive. There were three main problems. The first was finding the labour to carry out the necessary excavation or embankment. This usually required central direction since the spatial structure of organic economies meant that there was rarely sufficient local demand for any major spontaneous initiatives to occur at this level. The Roman authorities were sometimes able to do this, generally for military purposes, but their achievements were modest, and their medieval successors found the task beyond them (Leighton 1972; Roth 1999). Gradients posed the second problem, affecting both canals and natural waterways, whose currents might be strong enough to make movement upstream difficult.

Effective locks presented the technical solution, coming into use at the end of the sixteenth century, but operational difficulties remained. Early locks were particularly time consuming to negotiate (Dyos and Aldcroft 1974), and the delays they imposed could be substantial given the large numbers required in difficult terrain. The Briase canal had forty-one locks over a stretch of 21 leagues and the Languedoc canal 119 in 148 miles (Braudel 1982: 359; Parry 1967: 215). The third problem was that the use of existing waterways for transportation, and especially their 'improvement', was prone to create serious conflicts with local communities who were likely to see 'their' watercourses primarily as fisheries and millstreams. Even purpose-built canals could be subject to obstruction and exactions by local landowners keen to seize on the chance of some additional income. The construction of commercially effective canal networks therefore required public authorities capable of protecting traffic as well as sufficient demand to justify the investment.[10]

[9] This was an important advantage given the high costs of cross-country haulage, and timber-exporting regions depended heavily on river transport (Parry 1967: 179–80).
[10] The construction of the Dutch passenger canal network offers a spectacular instance of public authority and commercial interest working together in this way (de Vries 1978). Where canal-building was politically driven, as in Spain, it was prone to the same economic shortcomings as centrally directed highway construction. In the Spanish case an over-lavish specification drove up building costs and imposed crippling delays. In particular 'none of the critical junctions was ever made, with the result that for economic purposes the canals began nowhere and ended nowhere' (Ringrose 1970).

Where these difficulties could be overcome, canal journeys were the most predictable of all forms of travel, but they were never rapid. Horse-drawn Dutch passenger barges averaged only 3 miles an hour, but they impressed seventeenth-century travellers by their regularity as well as by the availability of night-boats. Where towpaths were unavailable river boats were at the mercy of the winds, and strong currents could hamper movement upstream. Early medieval journeys from Lyons to Avignon took between two and five days down the Rhône by flatboat, but it took nearly a month to get back again, towed upstream by ox teams. By the seventeenth century horse-drawn barges made the downstream journey in a day, but it could still take six weeks for grain to get upstream from Provence (Leighton 1972: 126; Braudel 1982: 357). The installation of effective locks dealt with the problem of currents but imposed other delays; the journey from Hamburg to Lübeck took three weeks because of the numerous locks (Braudel 1982: 357–9). Finally, inland navigation could be interrupted by harsh winter weather. The Thames downstream of London was liable to freeze under these conditions, as it did in the winters of 1740/1 and 1813/14, interrupting food and fuel supplies and seriously disrupting the capital's economic life (Schwarz 1992; Beattie 1986). In France, the Seine could be unusable for two-thirds of the year (Braudel 1990: 470).

4.2. TIME AND COST

The economic feasibility of long-distance trade, or any form of transaction involving physical movement of goods, depends in the first and last instances on the cost of transport relative to the value of the cargo. Transport costs were made up of a number of elements on top of the basic freight charge per mile (or 'mileage cost') and were closely related to journey times because the longer this took, the more fodder or food was consumed and the greater the cost of carriage. Longer journey times also increased wage bills and reduced the number of cargoes that could be transported. This depressed the return on the capital tied up in the means of transport and, other things being equal, increased the charge to the customer. Longer intervals between the purchase and resale of traded commodities also increased the interest charges payable by the merchant.

The relative inefficiency of muscle-powered transport, and the bulky 'fuel' on which it depended, were responsible for a substantial fraction of total mileage costs. Energy constraints restricted the practicability of bulk transport, especially by land, but they were not always as restrictive in practice as they appear in principle. The very nature of biological 'engines', and the characteristic inefficiency of resource use in organic economies, offered possibilities that were absent where more 'efficient' mechanical and economic systems prevailed. The existence of the 'time frontier', as we termed those lengthy periods of underemployment that were so common, could be exploited to obtain transport services at prices below the total cost to the producer. Other costs were more difficult to evade in this way. On top of the basic mileage costs, which were based on journey times under 'average' conditions, was a second set of costs that reflected the less predictable hazards of loss, damage, or theft of cargoes. Sea transport, otherwise much cheaper than the alternatives, was particularly vulnerable in these respects and the costs that resulted from this could form a significant fraction of the total costs of maritime commerce (Menard 1991).

4.2.1. RELATIVE MILEAGE COSTS

The relationship between commodity values and transport costs per ton mile is conveniently summarized in the 'doubling distance', which is the distance a commodity can be moved before transport costs rise to equal the initial purchase price.[11] Studies of doubling distances in organic economies are dominated by two findings: the prohibitive costs of hauling bulky, low-value commodities long distances over land, and the relative advantages of water transport. Price data are scarce before the eve of the railway age, and the fragmentary material available often presents serious difficulties of interpretation, particularly for the ancient world, but the small sample of figures in Table 4.4 bears out both findings at first sight. Four of the doubling distances, by land, fall roughly in the range 150–300 miles, and two are substantially less than 100. River transport, by contrast, is much cheaper and sea transport even more so. More tellingly, the costs incurred by 50 miles of land haulage are never less than 20 per cent of the initial price. If consumers had to spend as much as 60 per cent of their income on staples even where these were available from local production—and sometimes they had to spend more than this—a price increase of 20 per cent due to transport costs would absorb more than a quarter of the income they had left. In practice it is

Table 4.4 *The costs of bulk transport*
(a) *Wheat transport costs relative to initial values: overland haulage*

Location	Doubling distance (English miles)	Cost multiplier per 50 miles	Source
Rome c.200 BC	60	1.83	(1)
Late Roman Empire	196	1.25	(2)
14th-century England	250	1.20	(3)
18th-century England	143	1.35	(3)
18th-century Spain	238	1.21	(4)
19th-century Germany	66	1.76	(5)
15th/16th-century England		1.13	(6)

[11] The final delivered price at this point will normally be more than twice the purchase price since, profits apart, other costs will also be incurred. Transport costs made up about half of the approximately 125% price increase sustained by early modern Sicilian grain exports to Spain. Export fees and insurance accounted for the rest (Parry 1967: 157–8).

Table 4.4 *The costs of bulk transport (continued)*
(b) *Freight cost ratios* (per ton mile)

Location	Sea	River	Land	Source
Greece, 4th century BC	1		17.9	(1)[a]
Late Roman Empire	1	4.9	42	(2)[b]
14th-century England	1	4.0	8	(3)
Early 18th-century England	1	4.7	22.6	(2)
Roman Empire	1	5.9	62.5	(7)

[a] The land figure is for carriage by ox carts; for pack-camel it is only 34.
[b] For transport of terracotta tiles.

Sources: (1): Yeo (1946); (2): Duncan-Jones (1974: 366–9); (3): Masschaele (1993); (4): Ringrose (1970); (5): See Grigg (1992: fig. 6.2); (6): Bowden (1967: 612); (7): J. Künow, *Negotiator et Vectura: Händler und Transport im freien Germanien* (1980), quoted Greene (1986: 40).

likely that increases of more than 30 per cent above the initial cost would have priced staple foods out of most commercial markets.[12]

4.2.1.1. Overland

Land haulage suffered from the problems of inadequate roads, and other infrastructure, but above all from the 'Von Thünen problem', the fact that transport animals consumed quantities of fodder that were both large and costly relative to their load capacity if this consisted of a staple food such as wheat. Wheat was moreover a fairly 'transport efficient' staple because it was relatively expensive and, like other grains, filled almost all the space it was contained in.[13] The doubling distance for cheaper or bulkier commodities was much shorter (see Table 4.5). The constraints that followed from this were genuine and severe, but the economics of land haulage were more complex than can be conveyed simply by Von Thünen's ratio. The implied costs in Table 4.5 are far from uniform, and they noticeably fail to bear out the expectation that long-term technological progress should have made land haulage less expensive.

This is partly because the figures have different origins, and some of them are based on very flimsy evidence. The land figures from Republican Rome come from a statement by the Elder Cato on how much it cost him to transport an olive press, something that may reflect unusual local circumstances and concerns a peculiarly heavy and time-consuming item.[14] The late Imperial figures are the official maxima set out in the Emperor Diocletian's Price Edicts, and they present

---

[12] The prevalence of subsidies and other interventions by municipal authorities makes it important to stress the adjective *commercial* in this context.

[13] Moskoff cites corresponding proportions of only 35–60% and 35–80% for cabbages and potatoes respectively (Moskoff 1990: 96 n. 11).

[14] This point is made by Laurence who suggests that later authors may have adopted an unduly pessimistic attitude to the role of land transport as a result of one unrepresentative instance. He also attributes a more important economic role to Roman roads than do most other authors (Laurence 1998).

Table 4.5 *Doubling distances for agricultural commodities in mid-nineteenth-century Germany*

Commodity	Distance (miles)
Mangolds	4
Sugar beet	6
Potatoes	10
Hay	13
Fresh fruit	26
Milk	26
Rye, barley, oats	50
Wheat	66
Live animals	400
Cheese	400
Butter	660

Source: See Grigg (1992: fig. 6.2).

serious interpretative problems (Corcoran 2000; Duncan-Jones 1974). Diocletian's purpose was to reduce the prices then prevailing, so the maxima are presumably below what was actually being charged in the Empire's markets. The implied sea distance is remarkably long, and this may reflect the inflated grain prices current in the eastern cities where the Edicts were proclaimed. If this is so then the land doubling distances will be too great as well. The eighteenth-century English land distances are also based on judicial norms and so probably understate market prices, but the fourteenth-century data reflect actual expenditure by the county sheriffs provisioning English forces.

4.2.1.2. *Inland water*

Water transport was generally cheaper than land haulage for reasons we have already discussed. In seventeenth-century France, Vauban believed that six men with a four-horse team could move as much by barge as could 200 men by road, and on the eve of the railway age the tonnage of waterborne freight equalled some 10 per cent of what was moved on French roads. Water transport's cost advantages could be cancelled out over short distances by the fixed costs of loading and unloading, which made the shipment of grain by water from eighteenth-century Rouen to Paris as costly as land haulage (Braudel 1982: 352). Heavy cargo boats were, moreover, specialized pieces of equipment and not something peasant households were likely to need for their normal activities. Small craft were ubiquitous on the rivers and streams of medieval Europe, but anyone needing to move a large cargo would probably have to pay the full cost of carriage.[15]

---

[15] Draught animals could also be found to haul river boats at low cost in the off season. During Russian winters peasant muscle power could be even cheaper than that of animals (Symons and White 1972: p. xvi).

4.2.1.3. Time, cost, and space

The constraints on transport and the different ways in which they affected different media had far-reaching implications for the configuration of demographic space if we think of this as a medium in which the proximity of different points is governed by the time or cost required to travel between them. We can see this if we consider three settlements A, B, and C. They exist in physical space and can be represented straightforwardly as points on a two-dimensional map. Their spatial relationships in physical space are timeless and obey the familiar rules of Euclidean geometry, because the linear distances AB and AC will be the same on any two dates within historical time, and if we know these and the angle between them we can calculate the third distance BC precisely. Furthermore, AB and BA are identical by definition.

This simplicity rapidly breaks down, however, if we think of space as a medium of interaction which imposes greater or lesser resistance to interactions between pairs of points according to their relative proximity. In an economic or demographic context this proximity is most appropriately measured by the time or cost involved in moving between the two, and linear distance is only one of many influences on these quantities. A and B for instance might be separated by a mountain range, whilst A is connected to C by a good road, even though the distance in a straight line is twice as great. The shortest travel distance between each pair of settlements would clearly be a more useful measure than linear distance, but if we use these the rules of Euclidean geometry break down, because there is now no necessary relationship between the three distances, except that BC cannot exceed AB + AC, and each settlement effectively generates its own map. Travel distances can also change greatly over time, as roads are constructed or fall into disrepair, whilst their practicability may vary with the seasons.

Travel distances are a more realistic indicator of proximity than are linear distances, but in themselves they tell us nothing about the nature of the routes concerned, and the ease or difficulty of travel. A better course would be to take the minimum journey time between each pair of points, but this introduces fresh complexities because journey times are relative to the mode of transport adopted. Faster modes are likely to be more expensive, and so the effective proximities of different settlements are likely to vary between rich and poor travellers, even if their relative proximities are not very different. Furthermore, the geometry of journey-time maps deviates even further from Euclidean rules, because AB and BA may differ. Where journeys involved river transport, the difference between the time needed to travel up- or downstream could be substantial.[16]

---

[16] The costs involved could also be vastly different. An early Chinese attempt to settle the region of the Ordos loop on the exposed north-western frontier failed because the settlements had to be provisioned by convoys moving against the current of the Yellow River, and nearly all the allocated supplies seem to have been consumed in the process of transportation. A later effort is known to have required labour gangs numbering tens of thousands of men to tow the barges (Lattimore 1962: 111–12).

Journey times form a sensible basis for measuring proximities where we are interested in the movement of people, or information, but if we want to analyse other kinds of economic relationships then transport costs may be of more relevance. Fig. 4.1 shows the costs of grain transport to medieval London plotted as 'isopleths'—lines of equal cost—on a geographical map of the region. The figure formed by the isopleths is clearly oriented along the axis of the river Thames. This is just what we would expect given the relative cheapness of water transport, but if it was cheap it was also slow, and a comparable map based on journey times would yield quite different results. Nor was water transport suited for all forms of traffic. Luxury goods usually went by land, and so a map based on the costs of luxury transport would have yet another shape.

4.2.2. TRANSPORT COSTS AND THE TIME FRONTIER

As transport technology became more efficient, and a specialized haulage sector developed, the cost to the customer should have come down. Other things being equal this was no doubt the case, but other things were rarely equal and the reality was more complex. In particular, the final price charged to the customer cannot be simply extrapolated from the fodder and other expenses that were borne by the haulier. The main reason for this is that transport animals are not machines and so do not consume fuel only when they are working. Animals have to be fed even if they are doing nothing and the cost of the extra fodder consumed in transporting a load may be relatively small. Furthermore, whilst agricultural machinery and modern heavy goods vehicles are too specialized to be capable of mutual substitution in most circumstances, a peasant cart could take crops to market, or between markets, as easily as it could move them around the farm.[17] This ability came into its own during the many slack periods of the agricultural year when there was little farm work to be done, and the countryside held a reserve of underemployed vehicles and muscle power.

The cultivator's interest at such times was to find work for himself and his animals even if he received less than the total cost of the fodder consumed in the process. What mattered was that he received more than the cost of the extra feed the animals needed in order to do the work. As wagons, carts, and draught teams proliferated on the peasant holdings of medieval northern Europe, a pool of transport capacity emerged that could sometimes be hired at below cost price. This was not new. The heavy materials for public works such as temple-building in ancient Greece had been transported in the off season by contractors using local farm animals. Stone blocks weighing up to 8 tons were moved more than 20 miles to the temple at Eleusis by this means. The costs varied considerably, evidently in response to differences in local conditions and the extent of seasonal underemployment (Burford 1960). David Ringrose's study of Spain on the eve of

---

[17] This may not have been strictly true of all medieval carts, some of which were confined to farm work for lack of iron tyres (Dyer 1989: 171).

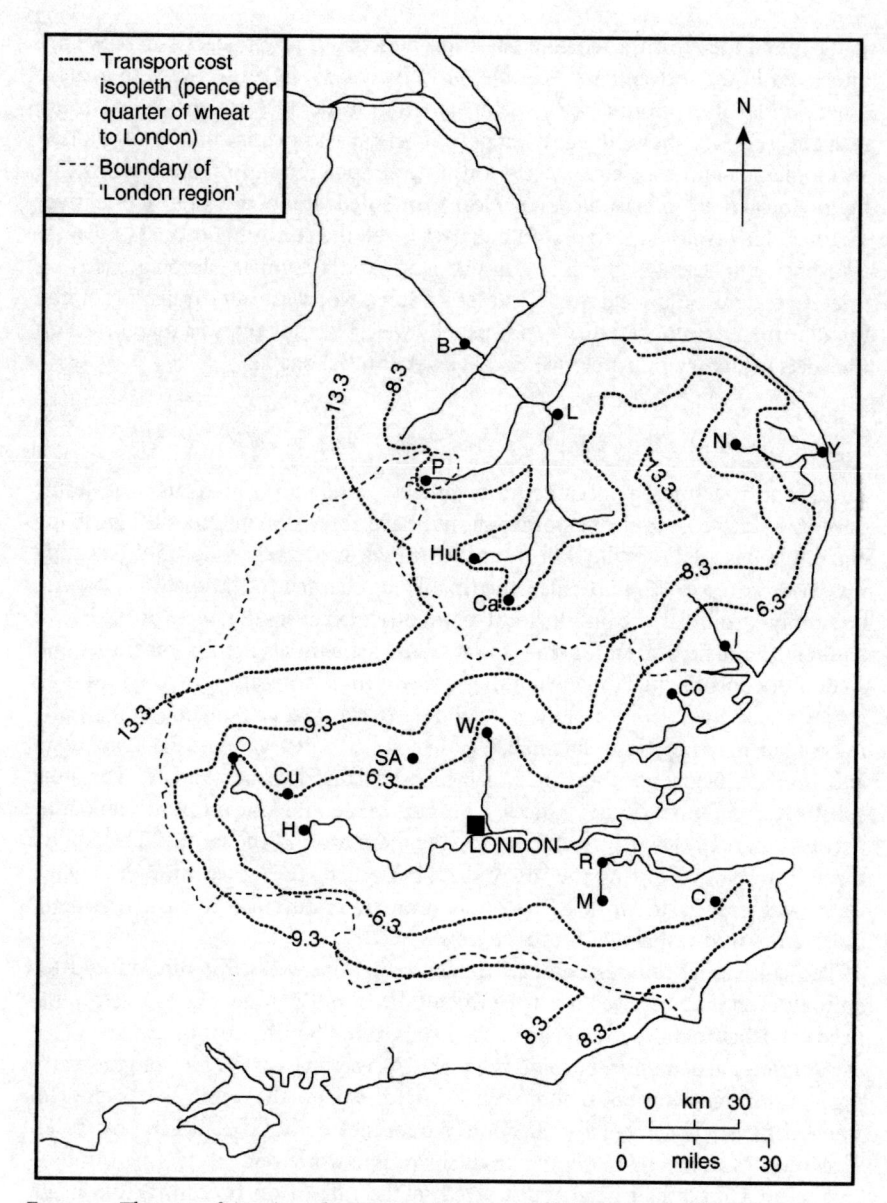

FIG. 4.1. The cost of carrying wheat to London from within southern and eastern England c.1300

Note: B=Boston; C=Canterbury; Co=Colchester; Cu=Cuxham; H=Henley-on-Thames; Hu=Huntingdon; I=Ipswich; L=Lynn; M=Maidstone; N=Norwich; O=Oxford; P=Peterborough; R=Rochester; SA=St Albans; W=Ware; Y=Yarmouth.
Source: Campbell Galloway et al. (1993:61).

the railway age shows just how economically important carrying could be as a seasonal 'by-employment' (Ringrose 1970). The contemporary Spanish interior contained an estimated 140,000 or more pack beasts. Primarily employed in farming, these animals were switched to transportation in the lengthy late summer and autumn season when agricultural activity ground to a halt. Crisscrossing the countryside on a dense network of local *caminos* this underemployed reserve column enabled regional economic specialization to proceed in spite of the difficult terrain and the absence of a trade-oriented highway network.

Growth in agricultural productivity and occupational specialization had a perverse effect on transport costs in these circumstances. If productivity rose then grain prices would fall, other things being equal, but as assets were used more efficiently and carriage became the preserve of full-time specialists, customers had to meet a larger proportion of total costs and haulage prices rose despite the fall in fodder costs. The result was an appreciable fall in the doubling distance for staple foods. The reverse logic also holds, and this probably explains the seeming efficiency of medieval, relative to eighteenth-century, haulage. Medieval England's expanding draught herd provided increased capacity, whilst population pressure raised both underemployment and grain prices. Doubling distances are likely to have lengthened as a result, but by the later eighteenth century agricultural improvement had reduced rural underemployment and increased grain output, leading to a contraction in the distances, despite an overall increase in efficiency.[18]

Organic economies were prone to endemic inefficiencies, but these sometimes made land haulage more rather than less economic by ameliorating the Von Thünen problem. Large, heavy cargoes were hauled in appreciable quantities in the pre-industrial period and sometimes they were hauled over considerable distances. The funerary and other monuments of the ancient world are evidence of this, but substantial volumes of less spectacular commodities were also transported under seemingly unpropitious circumstances. Other factors helped to make this possible. Not all heavy commodities were cheap, and the high initial value of a cargo such as metal-rich ore or fine marble could make its long-range haulage costs acceptable. Tin was transported over 300 miles by pack mule, to the mouth of the Rhône, in the first century BC, and iron ore carried 600 yards up hill tracks to a suitable smelting site (Planhol and Claval 1994: 30; Snodgrass 1983). Valuable artefacts could also be transported overland if need be. In 1367 an alabaster table was carried from Northampton to St George's Chapel in Windsor by eight-horse carts, a journey that took seventeen days (Stenton 1936).

It is important to distinguish what lay within the calculus of economical rationality from what was physically possible once economic criteria had been set aside. Political or religious authorities sometimes obtained services without payment by offering other kinds of rewards to those under their sway. The haulage requirements for large-scale public works in Greek city states could be

---

[18] This assumes that the size of the herd was not reduced due to pressure on pasture as the human population grew. Fourteenth-century England apparently escaped the worst effects of such land-use conflicts, although they did become a problem in 19th-century Spain (Ringrose 1970: 128).

provided by wealthy citizens in exchange for civic honours, whilst in medieval Europe cathedral-building prelates invoked notions of pious duty to obtain portage, sometimes from members of the elite in person, at no financial cost to themselves. The first column for the Basilica at Monte Cassino, transported from the ruins of Rome, was carried to the summit by local people as an act of devotion (Leighton 1972: 37). Where such inducements failed, coercion might be an alternative. Unfree tenants in early medieval Europe owed labour obligations including message- and load-carrying, although they were later commuted to money payments, and many states exerted forced labour obligations from their peasantry. Labour obtained under customary obligations of this kind often had to be fed or rewarded in some way, and so was not necessarily a 'free good' for the recipient, although the resources required might be realized by taxation or the imposition of other customary obligations. In a crisis military commanders could simply coerce local inhabitants to work at their own expense.

The constraints on transport formed a series of obstacles requiring successively greater resource inputs to overcome them before any rigid limits were encountered. Where the governing criteria were political or military, the mass mobilization of labour and other resources might be undertaken to a level well past the point of diminishing returns. In thinly populated or uncultivated areas, provisioning regular large-scale movements of troops or materials from the surrounding countryside might present serious difficulties, but even in such unpromising circumstances rulers with the administrative capacity and the power to do so might be able to organize networks of feeding stations, or a 'one-off' convoy, should a sufficiently high priority be assigned to the task. Military operations aside, political or religious authorities could transport monumental materials very long distances for reasons that were 'expressive' rather than instrumental. The 276-ton monolith which capped Theodoric's mausoleum was transported overland from Istria to Ravenna (Leighton 1972: 37).

4.2.3. THE COST OF UNCERTAINTY

Journey times depended on the properties of the prime mover and vehicle, the surface over which it was moving, and the incidence of obstruction, breakdowns, bandit attacks, or other 'incidents of travel'. The frequency of such incidents affected the variability of journey times as well as their average length and created an unpredictability which was, as Braudel argues, a *structural* feature of the era of organic economies. Distances themselves 'were not invariable, fixed once and for all. There might be ten or a hundred different distances, and one could never be sure in advance, before setting out or making decisions, what timetable fate would impose' (Braudel 1972: 360).

The uncertainties of travel and transport presented two kinds of problem which did as much as the length of the journey times to limit the contribution that long-distance movements could make to the life of pre-industrial economies. The first kind of problem sprang from the existence of uncertainty itself, reflected in anecdotal catalogues of misfortune of the kind recounted by Maczak (1994) and others. In one sense such catalogues contain a serious and potentially misleading bias, because the private journals or correspondence on which they largely depend—and still more authors who abstract from them—are much more likely to record unusual occurrences than the sort of thing that contemporaries would take for granted. They are consequently unreliable guides to the normal and the average, but they do serve to indicate what *could* happen and evidently *did* happen often enough to form part of the spectrum of reasonably foreseeable possibilities. Incidents such as mechanical breakdown or contrary winds extended journey times by a degree that might be tolerable in itself, but whose very unpredictability impeded planning and co-ordination of the kind essential to so many political or mercantile enterprises. The need for planning and co-ordination meant that predictability might be more important than average speed, and this gave efficiently operated inland waterways like the Dutch *Trekvaart* a substantial advantage. Speeds were low but varied very little, and the network seems to have been the first to provide passenger and freight movements according to a regular published timetable (de Vries 1978).

Ocean voyages were at the other end of the spectrum and retained an element of dangerous unpredictability throughout most of the period. Improvements in rigging and navigational instruments allowed early modern captains to make headway in the sort of conditions that had defeated their predecessors and this made travel times less variable, but the second kind of problem remained. This was the possibility of an outcome that was seriously damaging or unacceptable in itself such as the loss of a ship and cargo due to accident or piracy. Technological limitations heightened the vulnerability of shipping in both respects for much of the period. European mariners rarely ventured far from land before the modern period, exposing them to the depredations of predatory littoral communities and dangerous shorelines, whilst Mediterranean currents confined navigation to a network of routes studded with vulnerable choke points.

The problem here lay with the nature of the possible outcome, rather than the fact of uncertainty itself, but the level of uncertainty is nonetheless important because we can make a qualitative distinction between two levels of uncertainty which affected human activity in different ways. In the first case, the level of uncertainty is so high as to leave the envelope of possibilities virtually undefined: the frequency of negative outcomes cannot be foreseen and the worst possible outcome is simply as bad as anything that can be imagined. This state of 'chaotic uncertainty' (or simply 'chaos'[19]), in which virtually anything bad can happen at any time, should be distinguished from one of mere 'hazardous uncertainty' (or hazard). In the latter case, the outcome of any given venture remains unpredictable, but it is possible to form a reasonable assessment of the

---

[19] This usage of the term 'chaos' in this context refers to the everyday definition of a state of extreme confusion and has no connection at all with the mathematical theory of that name.

likely magnitude and frequency of unfavourable outcomes and the forms that they might take.

The importance of this distinction lies in the fact that the rational response to the two conditions is very different. In a condition of chaos, circumstances are so unstable that planning is pointless in all but the shortest term and all one can do is reduce exposure to danger by such means as the abandonment of trade or flight from threatened territories. The main sources of chaotic uncertainty were threats to physical security of the kind represented by piracy, bandit attack, or invasion, and conditions of this kind apparently prevailed over much of west and northern Europe in the late Roman and Viking periods. In these circumstances, or those that prevailed at times in parts of inner Asia, conditions were too disturbed for trade to be possible on any substantial scale. In other circumstances chaos could be reduced to hazard and hazard progressively ameliorated by investment in security and other relevant measures.

Public authorities could sometimes achieve this, as they did in much of medieval Europe, but outside the borders of organized states, or on the high seas, private action was often necessary. Ships could be armed and made more seaworthy at a price, and overland caravans provided with armed escorts, whilst local chiefs might be bribed. The significance of the transition from chaos to hazard was that it allowed a rational balancing of potential costs and benefits and investment in the reduction of identifiable risks, even if these remained high. The risks of early modern long-distance trade remained substantial, but they could be balanced against the even greater rewards of success. The development of gunpowder artillery gave Europeans an increasing advantage in distant waters, leading to a longer-term reduction in uncertainty through the establishment of fixed bases and local territorial control. At the same time, growing institutional sophistication and the rise of marine insurance transformed uncertainty into the measurable accounting quantity known as actuarial risk (North 1991). The danger of an unacceptable outcome like the total loss of a cargo could then be commuted into a tolerable monetary cost, fixed in advance.

4.3. CONCLUSION

Land transport relied on muscle power in all organic economies and muscle power needed fuel in the form of bulky food or fodder. Water transport could exploit the additional energy of wind power and in some circumstances the power of currents. This ability made sailing ships cheaper load carriers than draught or pack animals. Sailing ships were also cheaper and more robust than galleys and they had a significantly longer range, but they were slow and subject to unfavourable winds. Substantial progress had to be made in the design of sails and rigging before they could compete with galleys in the luxury trades, but they were always the most economic bulk carriers over anything but short distances. Progress was made in land transport technology but it was always subject to the basic limitations of its energy source and remained an uneconomic means of bulk transport over distances of more than 50–60 miles. It is very important, however, to distinguish between what was economically sustainable and what was physically possible. Staple foods could be moved a long way overland if economic criteria were overridden by political or military imperatives, and heavy cargoes could be carried economically if they were sufficiently valuable, but landlocked populations generally had to rely on local sources for bulk raw materials and staple foods.

Restricted energy inputs limited what could be achieved, but they did not determine what was actually achieved within these limits, and low productivity sometimes facilitated transportation by providing a pool of underemployed men and animals available for hire at rates below full cost. Other economic and political factors made for substantial variation in the extent and effectiveness of transport and communication networks. This was especially true where high-value, low-bulk goods were concerned. Goods of this kind, including information, could travel at ten times or more the daily rate of bulk commodities, but effective security had to be provided if the possibilities that this offered were to be exploited. Political authorities could sometimes enforce security on land, but this was much harder to establish on the open sea, and 'security costs' could form a substantial element of maritime transport's total costs. They were never wholly eliminated, but as financial institutions became more sophisticated the growth of marine insurance made them more tractable.

CHAPTER FIVE

Trade and Traffic

The growth of output and the formation of centralized political structures in organic economies both involved the co-ordination of activities across growing distances, or 'spatial integration'. Economic growth did this by promoting trade and regional specialization, whilst centralized power is, by definition, exercised over geographical space. Both forms of spatial integration were linked to the emergence of towns and cities as centres of exchange, co-ordination, and, more rarely, specialized production. Very large cities usually emerged for political rather than economic reasons, but their very size could also act as a stimulus to economic integration. The underlying structure of organic economies nonetheless constrained the process of spatial integration just as much as they did those processes involved in production. The constraints arose in part from the restricted energy inputs available in transportation, but they also reflected the basic geography of economic activity.

Organic economies derived their energy and raw material inputs almost entirely from the produce of the land, and this gave them a characteristic spatial structure because the bulk of the population had to live close to the land that provided their food, raw material, and employment. The primary geography of population and economic activity was one of areal dispersion; it was a geography of fields in both the concrete and the abstract senses of the term. Subsistence production and consumption were not, however, the whole of the economy in any but the least developed regions. Alongside or superimposed upon it was a second level of activity based on the production, consumption, and exchange of luxury goods and possessing its own distinct geographical pattern. Where the first-level spatial structure was one of territorial fields and their central settlements, the second was a structure of links and nodes.

The primary level was oriented around the movement of 'low-level' traffic, the short-distance transport of mainly bulk subsistence commodities over the mesh of minor routeways that connected rural settlements with their markets and thereby integrated local territorial units. On this was superimposed the second level of spatial structure formed by long-distance transport and communication networks carrying high-value, low-bulk luxuries and, sometimes, the lightest and potentially most valuable commodity of all, information. The notorious deficiency of many contemporary roads reflected this two-level economy rather than any lack of engineering skills. The volume and value of low-level traffic on any single local route was too low to stimulate major infrastructure investment, and it was difficult to translate the needs of long-distance trade into effective demand. Under these circumstances the building of long-range road networks, in the rare cases where this occurred, reflected a political rather than an economic logic and direction.

This two-level spatial structure was reflected in a division between two kinds of urban system. The first was organized around a hierarchy of so-called 'central place' settlements oriented to the requirements of cultivators, their supporting specialists, and local masters, the second was a network of nodal trading centres oriented to regional and supra-regional elites. Flows of human migration and mobility moved between the two levels in complex patterns that varied greatly over time, but in other respects they were related only weakly if at all for very long periods. The agrarian economy was localized, its market structures too weak to promote integration at regional or higher levels, and long-range trading networks had little to offer it. The formation of centralized political structures on a large scale reflected a different logic of spatial integration. Oriented around cities as foci of power, they required effective networks for the transmission of information and force, and the means of extracting resources from the agrarian economy. The concentration of wealth and power turned successful political centres into luxury trading nodes, but the sheer size of some of them created a volume of subsistence needs too great for local resources to satisfy. Where this occurred a long distance inter-regional trade in bulk agrarian produce developed and the two spatial systems merged.

5.1. TRAFFIC AND INFRASTRUCTURE

The development of spatial integration in organic economies was hindered by the endemic inadequacy of their transport infrastructure. There were two problems. The first was the poor physical state of so many roads, which we touched on in the last chapter. This was not due simply, if at all, to any failure of engineering knowledge or experience. Road-building of a kind had been practised in Europe from prehistoric times, and the ancient Greeks knew how to build roads of a high standard even though they very rarely did so; most Greek roads were very bad (Burford 1960: 12). The organic economy's spatial structure—the geographical pattern of production and consumption, and the kind of transportation demand that it generated—lay at the root of the problem. It also underlay the second problem, which was the general absence of co-ordinated long-range route networks oriented around major economic centres.

In their place there proliferated dense meshes of minor routeways oriented around local centres, often with multiple redundancies. These met the needs of an economic life dominated by the consumption of locally produced goods. It was the density of local production and consumption that underlay the fundamental distinction between what Braudel terms 'high-level traffic' and 'low-level traffic'

(Braudel 1990: 461).[1] The first of these was long range and, at least relatively, rapid whilst the second was local and slow. In the metaphor used by Braudel, this was a distinction between capillaries and arteries, the difference being that the capillaries carried the staple foods and raw materials which made up the lifeblood of daily life, whilst the arteries were more concerned with luxuries and with the flow of information that enabled the political integration of space.

5.1.1. LOW-LEVEL TRAFFIC

The predominance of low-level traffic stemmed from the organic economy's low productivity and the endemic poverty that ensued. Poverty restricted the bulk of consumption to the subsistence needs of humans and their animals, ensuring that the geography of consumption matched a population geography which was mostly one of dispersed or small-scale settlements. The geography of production was also one of dispersal across fields, forests, or plantations, in marked contrast to the mineral economy's punctiform geography of mines and factories, and almost all of it was locally consumed. The pattern was established in the ancient world, where Roman Britain already possessed a network of market centres serving hinterlands some 10 miles in diameter (Hodder and Hassall 1971), and it persisted throughout the era of organic economies. In eighteenth-century Languedoc less than 15 per cent of total produce was consumed away from its point of production (Braudel 1990: 488–9), and in the following century Calvados had forty-five weekly markets with a catchment area some 7 miles in diameter, whilst the contemporary fairs of western Brittany served a hinterland equal to the distance a herd could travel in two to three hours (Planhol and Claval 1994: 206–7).

The persisting localism of economic life shaped the pattern of investment in transport infrastructure wherever this followed economic criteria, and in this light the supposed retrogression of transport and communications in the post-Roman 'Dark Ages' takes on a very different appearance. Constructed to move armies that no longer existed between points that had lost their importance, such Roman roads as endured were mostly an impressive irrelevance.[2] The medieval road network arose from local initiatives, used local resources, particularly labour, and expressed the continuing vitality of small-scale local traffic in an era of political fragmentation, whilst economic recession, insecurity, and the multiplication of tolls sent long-range traffic into eclipse. In LeGoff's words:

---

[1] We have preferred the English word 'traffic' to that of 'circulation' as used by Braudel's translator since it seems to provide a more appropriate combination of the senses of commerce and physical movement.

[2] Or even a liability; for, as Lopez points out, good roads 'would offer an easier passage for armies, but it was not always clear whether the armies would be friends or enemies' (Lopez 1956: 24). As late as the mid-16th century, Charles V's French invasions failed more because of the country's poor roads than the strength of its armed resistance (Braudel 1988: 110).

For this race of walkers and riders, whose freight was carried on the backs of pack animals or on archaic carts, and who were unhurried... the straight paved Roman road, designed for soldiers and civil servants, had no advantage. Medieval people travelled along paths and lanes, through a network of diverse routes which rambled about between certain fixed points: towns where fairs were held, places of pilgrimage, bridges, fords, and mountain passes. (Le Goff 1988: 137)

The primacy of this local network persisted into the modern era. Eighteenth-century Spain was poorly furnished with long-distance transport, but 'the rural economy of the interior was served by a network of primitive roadways and trails which crisscrossed the country in all directions, connecting most towns, reaching into every valley, and crossing every mountain pass' (Ringrose 1970: 17). The network of French 'royal roads' had expanded to around 21,000 miles by the 1830s, supplemented by a secondary *departmental* network of some 22,500 miles, but the network of local *chemins* comprised some 480,000 miles. In 1828 the volume of goods travelling on royal roads was estimated at 10.4 million tons compared with 30.9 million on the minor roads (Braudel 1990: 464–5).

5.1.2. HIGH-LEVEL TRAFFIC

Low-level traffic in substance goods moving short distances over tracks and minor routeways made up the great bulk of physical movement in organic economies, but it coexisted with longer-range flows of people and goods over distinct networks with their own links and nodes. These 'high-level' flows were of two kinds. Their mainstay was the long-distance movement of valuable goods, but as centralized political structures developed there arose a corresponding need for communications networks to transmit information and, where necessary, military force.

5.1.2.1. Long-distance trade

Material exchange over long distances emerged as early as the Bronze Age and before regional agrarian economies were sufficiently integrated to support substantial central place settlements. There were two preconditions for trade to develop on this geographical scale. First, there had to be long- or short-term regional variations in the supply of the relevant commodities. Differences in natural resource endowments could produce these, as some minerals, plants, or animal products were simply not available in certain regions, but differences in factors such as access to water could also create big cost differentials. In addition, geographical differences in technological knowledge restricted the production of some goods, particularly in the pre-industrial world, and fostered substantial regional differences of costs or quality. Finally, regional crop failures could create short-term variations in food availability, as serious shortages in some areas coincided with surpluses elsewhere.

If regional variations of this kind were to stimulate the growth of inter-regional trade in a commodity, then it was also necessary that the ratio of transport cost to initial value be low enough to prevent it being priced out of distant markets. In other cases, such as governmental provisioning of metropolitan centres, political considerations might take priority over profits, but basic logistical constraints still applied. The large-scale long-distance movement of cheap bulky commodities usually required sea transport. Costly lightweight goods such as the generic 'spices' of medieval Europe were a very different matter. Where the value of the commodity was such as to make the transport costs acceptable such goods could be, and were, transported very long distances over regular networks, sometimes on an intercontinental scale. The commodities involved in long-distance exchanges can be divided into three main categories.

5.1.2.1.1. Luxuries

The first and generally the most important of these three categories was that of high-value, low-bulk luxury goods. These were often transported by land, and usually consisted of manufactured or processed items such as jewellery or silks, although plant products such as spices were prominent in intercontinental trade. Luxury goods were of high value by definition, and they were usually low in bulk, but this was not necessarily the case. Wine was exported in substantial volumes from Italy, to Gaul and elsewhere, from the time of the Roman Republic, and large quantities of olive oil were exported substantial distances from Roman Spain (Harris 2000). The direction of such movement in the ancient and early medieval worlds was, for the most part, from the developed 'core' regions of Europe and the Mediterranean basin towards the barbarian 'periphery'. Such goods also moved by means other than trade. Barbarian leaders accumulated luxuries, and other prestige items, through the payment of bribes of various kinds by the rulers of organized states, and as loot from raids or larger-scale incursions.

The Roman world also received luxury imports, particularly silks, overland from east Asia. This trade continued into the Middle Ages and was increasingly supplemented by the trade in spices from south Asia and the south-west Pacific. Initially in the hands of Asiatic maritime powers, this trade fell increasingly under European control from the fifteenth century onwards (Tracy 1993). Luxury items were usually transported by land wherever possible, and luxury imports arrived in Europe and the Mediterranean basin overland from elsewhere in the Old World until European maritime activity expanded and sea routes to the 'Indies' were opened up in the fifteenth century. Before this, well-established caravan routes had connected China with the west through Turkestan and central Asia, and had connected the eastern Mediterranean littoral with the Red Sea termini of the Arabian Sea routes (Parry 1967; Rossabi 1993). These operations presented formidable technical difficulties, in respect of provisioning and navigation, but the political and military problems could be even greater. Trading caravans were a tempting target for raiders. Hired guards or bribery could be used to improve the chances of safely getting across lawless or potentially hostile areas, but in practice the regular operation of long-distance routes, like the central Asian 'Silk Road', required the presence of political authorities willing and able to maintain order. Control over routes of this kind was a potentially very lucrative asset, and the rise and decline of Eurasian trade was bound up with the rise and decline of imperial dynasties among the steppe nomads (Rossabi 1993; Christian 1998).

5.1.2.1.2. Raw materials

The second major category of commodities involved in long-distance transport was that of raw materials. These generally moved in the reverse direction, from the periphery to the core. Metallic ores, for example, were probably exported from northern and western Europe towards the Mediterranean basin from early in the first millennium BC (Planhol and Claval 1994; Sherratt 1998; Cunliffe 1988), and gold and hides crossed the Sahara at intervals throughout the period (Abulafia 1987). The western world in turn re-exported gold to pay for luxury imports from the east, both from the eastern Mediterranean and further afield. In the later Middle Ages the growing consumption of textiles, allied to the reduced demand for grain, stimulated the development of an international market in wool which was exported from England via the Calais 'staple' (Power 1969; Bowden 1962; Carus-Wilson 1987). A special case of the trade in 'raw materials' was the slave trade. Slave labour was an important factor of production in the Greek and Roman worlds and large numbers were generated by their wars of conquest and by piracy (de Souza 1999). Subsequent campaigns along the borders generated additional supplies, as did abortive barbarian incursions, but there also developed a long-range trade from northern and eastern Europe which persisted through the early Middle Ages, as well as a trans-Saharan trade (Harris 1980; Abulafia 1987).

5.1.2.1.3. Subsistence goods

The third category of long-range movement involved subsistence goods, primarily grain. This was very unusual in the world of organic economies where regional specialization rarely progressed far enough to make a long-distance grain trade profitable. Where it occurred the trade was usually politically driven, even if it was not directly organized by government, and reflected the growth of metropolitan centres that were too big to be provisioned from their immediate hinterland. In the ancient world, Attica is estimated to have relied on imports for as much as half its grain consumption in normal years.[3] The major cities of the Roman world, particularly Rome itself, and later Constantinople, drew on large volumes of grain shipped from Egypt and North Africa as well as from the islands of the

---

[3] This estimate is due to Whitby (1998) who defends the traditional view of Athenian import-dependence against Garnsey's (1988) sceptical reassessment.

western Mediterranean.[4] Transfers of this kind declined with the recession of urban life from late antiquity, but in the later medieval and early modern periods substantial volumes of Baltic grain reached the cities of northwestern Europe and especially the Netherlands (de Vries 1976).

The early modern period saw some examples of regional specialization on a scale sufficient to promote an inter-regional trade in food. Certain regions developed so-called 'proto-industrial' characteristics, with household-based non-agricultural production growing to a level that required food imports from commercially oriented agricultural regions elsewhere (Ogilvie 1993; Kriedte, Medick, and Schlumbohm 1981; Levine 1977). The boundary between necessities and luxuries shifted over time as rising incomes increased the demand for clothing and other manufactured items, and exports developed from proto-industrial regions across regional and national boundaries. Inter-regional trade in food was also stimulated by regional harvest failures of a kind that became increasingly common during the expansionary 'A' phase of the early modern demographic cycle. A large proportion of the Mediterranean basin's estimated 50,000 ton annual grain surplus was traded in this way during the sixteenth century (Parry 1967). The importing regions were not necessarily specialized non-food producers, but the trade required the development of ports and other entrepôts which implied a degree of spatial economic differentiation.

5.1.2.1.4. The implications of long-distance trade

The development of high-volume long-distance trade was necessary for the development of regional economic specialization or the emergence of very big cities, but inter-regional trade did not have to attain high volumes in order to bring about substantial changes in the participating communities. This was because the availability of luxury commodities had a political as well as an economic significance, particularly in stateless societies where leadership might rest on control over the influx and distribution of these and other prestige goods. The social position and followings that this could bring contributed to the early stages of state formation, and in this way trading contacts with the core stimulated the emergence of social, and sometimes political, hierarchy on the periphery. Rulers in early medieval Europe also sought to enhance their position through control of long-distance trade flows, and even when such attempts had been abandoned, tolls and similar revenues might transform a ruler's financial position and provide an economic basis for the further centralization of power.

Long-range trade stimulated the growth of entrepôts and, where sea transport was involved, of ports and shipyards. Servicing, if not actually constructing, trading vessels could become a major source of economic activity in itself if volumes reached the required threshold. This activity generated employment for

---

[4] Garnsey estimates peak annual consumption at around 200,000 tons, as much as half of which may have come from North Africa (Garnsey 1983: 118–21); for a standard account of Roman grain supply see Rickman (1980).

a range of specialists whose expenditure went on to create further demand. High-value transactions could, however, stimulate specialization even if the physical volumes involved remained low. Once exchanges passed beyond the level of barter, such trade fostered the rise of specialized financial institutions and credit instruments. Traders repatriating profits from distant markets rarely wanted to carry large sums in gold or silver and negotiable securities such as bills of exchange provided a means of avoiding this. Instruments of this kind developed in the early modern period along with networks of mercantile correspondents who were able to issue or discount them (Bernard 1972; Parker 1974; Braudel 1981: 470–8). These networks emerged from the process of trade itself but in time they took on banking functions by channelling capital, usually generated by trade, to borrowers in need of funds. Many of the latter were private individuals, but rulers often found themselves needing to borrow against future income. They represented a generally better risk than did their subjects, but lending money to men who could throw their creditors in jail carried special risks of its own. Prudence required the successful lender to have as much information as possible about the policies and personalities of the court and so mercantile correspondents became intelligence as well as credit agents.[5]

5.1.2.2. *Communication and information*

Heavy goods travelled slowly by land or water. Commodities light enough to be carried by a man on horseback could move much faster, and the lightest of all commodities was information. Successful rulers from Sumerian times onwards well understood that, if money and manpower were the lifeblood of empire, its nervous system was a good communications network. A text from the third millennium BC records the claim by Shulgi, a king of Ur, to have travelled 200 miles in one day, on a road whose construction he himself had ordered (Casson 1974: 25). Later rulers had servants to do the running for them, in numbers that evidently impressed their neighbours—*angelos*, the Greek word for 'messenger', is itself of Akkadian origin (Cook 1983: 108)—and the maintenance of good communications networks remained a regional preoccupation into Roman times and beyond. Apart from the roads themselves, these networks also comprised way stations at daily, or more frequent, intervals—every 10–15 miles on the Persian 'Royal Road' from Sardis to Susa, and every 25–35 miles on Roman roads—interspersed with smaller relay posts. Equines are much faster than humans in the short term, but they quickly tire and exploiting their potential for rapid communication required some kind of relay system. Using such a system a Babylonian official could cover 120 miles in two days. This is comparable to the 50 or so daily

---

[5] One notorious example of their intelligence function is the help that Venetian merchants gave to the 13th-century Mongol armies in exchange for the latter eliminating Genoese and other commercial rivals from newly conquered territories (Chambers 1988: 24–5). In a later, more benign role, such networks contributed to the struggle against plague by providing civic authorities with advance warning of outbreaks in centres with which they traded (Flinn 1979).

miles maintained by the couriers of the imperial Roman *cursus publicus*, or the 40 to 50 miles covered by royal post riders in sixteenth-century Picardy (Ramsay 1925; Potter 1993: 26), and probably around twice what a private traveller could manage. Much faster rates were possible in a crisis. In AD 69 news of the legions' mutiny reached Rome from the Rhine at a daily rate of over 150 miles, and a fit man using the resources of the *cursus publicus* could cover 200 miles in twenty-four hours at times of pressing need.[6]

The Roman system used a single courier to cover the whole distance to the emperor so that he could be questioned on the contents of his dispatch, but relay riders were much faster. The Mongol and Ottoman systems are credited with daily rates of 200–300 miles. Impressive as these rates are in themselves, they compare dramatically with those achieved by heavy cargoes, or marching armies over comparable distances. They were also very expensive to achieve, requiring substantial investments in infrastructure, animals, and trained personnel. The 300 miles achieved by Mongol couriers in China required some 10,000 posting stations and an estimated minimum of 200,000 horses. In nineteenth-century North America, the Pony Express covered 2,000 miles in less than eight days with a total herd of 400 to 500 animals (Leighton 1972: 18 n. 4). Effective courier networks also needed secure conditions, and this too was expensive. On Minoan Crete, where there was no external threat, the highway from Knossos to the south coast required regular police posts, and the Assyrian network had guard posts at intervals of roughly 6 miles (Casson 1974: 39, 49–51). The maintenance of communications on this scale was a very demanding task requiring the ability to command and co-ordinate resources on a substantial scale. The Roman *cursus publicus* operated in some form down to the very end of the Western Empire,[7] but the barbarian successor states were unable to keep it going, or even to stop local communities ploughing up the roads (Lopez 1956). The task seems also to have been beyond the Byzantines, and the Emperor Justinian was accused by the contemporary commentator Procopius of closing down many posting stations, substituting mules for horses, and boats for land transport, which resulted in a serious deterioration in the service (Leighton 1972: 18–19).

5.1.3. POLITICS, ECONOMICS, AND INVESTMENT

The proliferation of tracks and minor roads that served the needs of low-level traffic reflected local initiative and this necessarily restricted their contribution to larger-scale spatial integration. Major road networks existed in the era of organic economies, but they were generally oriented towards political rather than economic priorities because there were few economic incentives for investment in

---

[6] This journey is credited to the future Emperor Tiberius travelling to the bedside of his dying brother (Ramsay 1925: 63).

[7] Sidonius Apponarius enjoyed its facilities when travelling from southern France to Rome in AD 467. Private usage of this kind, though strictly prohibited, was only one of several abuses that the authorities struggled unsuccessfully to control (Casson 1974: 186–9).

systems of this kind. The underlying problem was rooted in the areal geography of production and consumption. In Wrigley's words, the requirements for

> moving a million tons of coal from pitheads scattered over an area of only a few square miles are quite different from those involved in moving the same weight of grain or timber from an area of several thousands of square miles. The former implies heavy tonnages moving along a small number of routeways, whereas the latter implies the reverse. A heavy investment in improved communications is unlikely to give a good return when the raw materials of industry are organic since the traffic density along any one route is usually low. (Wrigley 1987d: 78–9)

The essence of the problem can be easily grasped if we imagine an agrarian region in which a multiplicity of minor routeways and markets have proliferated in order to serve local needs, enabling cultivators to take their produce to market and goods to be exchanged between local markets. The quality of these 'country roads' is poor, but they are adequate for the short journeys undertaken by local inhabitants. The value to the local community of any journey time that might be saved by substantial improvement is heavily outweighed by the value of the resources they would have to invest in order to obtain it. The network might also provide an acceptable, if not ideal, infrastructure for transport within the region, such as between the various subregional market centres and between these and the main regional centre. The distances between any pair of adjacent centres are rather longer than they would be in a 'rational' centrally planned system of direct links or 'highways', but not greatly so. The existence of multiple paths between centres also compensates to some degree for the poor quality of each one of them individually. Regional users, and other travellers with the benefit of local knowledge, have a good chance of selecting whichever link is currently in the best condition and avoiding any that are completely unusable at any time.

Long-range links with the outside world are, however, a very different matter. The shortest possible route by country roads from the regional centre to its counterpart in an adjacent region, or to the more remote supra-regional metropolis, is much longer than it would be by highway and the cumulative effects of their poor quality on journey times over longer distances is considerable. Moreover, strangers from outside the region are much more likely to get lost, or find themselves stuck on a stretch of road that has deteriorated beyond use. The basic problem is that it is not in the economic interests of local communities to raise the quality of country roads for the benefit of outsiders passing through on them, and still less to build a stretch of highway that might go nowhere near their local market. This is not necessarily the case, however, with other forms of transport infrastructure. The chronology of bridge-building in particular was quite different from that of highway construction, with the medieval period being one of considerable activity. This almost certainly reflected the proliferation of heavy, wheeled vehicles in the countryside, for these often needed wide bridges simply to get from farm to market whereas horsemen, pack trains, or bodies of marching men could manage with fords.

Investment in long-range transport infrastructure could be obtained in one of two ways. The first was to couple supply and demand by charging tolls and investing the proceeds in road-building and maintenance. Tolls of a sort were endemic to the medieval and early modern worlds, but they generally went straight into the pockets of landowners or local rulers and were often little more than legalized extortion. Tolls in the modern sense were levied in eighteenth-century England by the 'Turnpike Trusts' which were private corporate bodies established for the purpose. The Trusts and their roads are credited with major efficiency gains to England's economy (Pawson 1977), but the volume of traffic was almost certainly insufficient to make such schemes workable elsewhere or in earlier periods even where the necessary legal and administrative structures existed.[8]

The alternative to an effective market mechanism was the direction of investment by a central political authority. The spatial structure of organic economies being what it was, it was usually on this basis that large-scale road systems were constructed. Such systems followed a logic that was political and military rather than economic and they served to promote rapid movement of couriers and troops rather than to foster the interests of trade. This was exemplified in the Roman network as we have seen, whilst in the early modern period the much admired Ottoman road network consisted of paired yard-wide tracks allowing the rapid passage of horsemen but of little use to wheeled traffic (Braudel 1972: 284). The royal roads of Bourbon Spain were impressive engineering constructions of little economic value. Linking Madrid with the major cities of the Spanish periphery in long straight lines, they bypassed major provincial centres and had negligible impact on the countryside they traversed (Ringrose 1970: 14).

Substantial investment in transport infrastructure could occur without central direction where large volumes of production or consumption were concentrated at a point.[9] Mines and quarries were one instance of this, and a network of horse-drawn wooden railways developed around England's north-eastern coalfields as early as the seventeenth century. One early eighteenth-century line carried 450,000 tons in a year (Lewis 1997). Major metropolitan centres could produce similar effects in their hinterlands. Some estate owners around late Republican Rome apparently invested in roads across their land, the better to supply the capital's food markets, despite the restricted commercial role generally ascribed to

---

[8] Universal tolls of this kind might enrage local road-users, forced to pay for improvements they had not asked for and did not want, and require considerable force to implement. For a notable British example of anti-toll riots see the case of the so-called 'Rebecca Riots' (Williams 1955).

[9] The subsistence needs of metropolitan centres generated substantial investment in the infrastructure of waterborne trade, but this often required central direction and was complicated by the fact that so many of these centres owed their existence to political rather than economic factors. In Rome, for instance, the Imperial authorities constructed a specialized grain terminal at Puteoli to replace the inadequate facilities of the old port at Ostia, but shippers were reluctant to use it because of the difficulty of obtaining return cargoes from this artificial location (Yeo 1946). The urbanization of the early modern Netherlands by contrast called forth a commercial transport infrastructure in the shape of the passenger canals, or *Trekvaart*, which ran for more than 400 miles at a cost of five million guilders which was raised by municipal authorities (de Vries 1978).

contemporary cross-country transport (Laurence 1998). Nor was the motive always economic. In ancient Greece 'rut roads', incised grooves carved into the rock for vehicle wheels, were constructed around major ritual centres, as they were between Athens and Sparta (Casson 1974: 69–70).

5.2. TOWNS, CITIES, AND SPACE

The land was the productive foundation of organic economies. Their dominant sector was agriculture and the majority of the population lived in the countryside. Towns and cities nonetheless fulfilled essential integrating functions as economic and political structures became more complex and differentiated. These functions bound them into two kinds of spatial system corresponding to the two levels of organization we have already encountered: the areal economy of bulk production and the network-based economy of long-distance exchange. Urban populations relied on their agrarian hinterland for food, and so towns and cities were potential gateways between the two economies. Once cities had outgrown local food resources, new long-range bulk flows emerged together with a supporting apparatus of occupational specialization and a far-reaching potential for regional, and supra-regional, integration. Cities on this scale also required constant immigration in order to grow, or even to maintain their numbers in the face of severe mortality.[10]

5.2.1. URBAN FUNCTIONS AND URBAN SYSTEMS

Urban settlements—towns and cities—are notoriously difficult to define by criteria that are generally valid across time and space because, like human settlements of any kind, their existence has two distinct aspects. The physical aspect of streets, buildings, and population densities coexists with the dynamic functional aspect that is constituted by the inhabitants' relationships and transactions (de Vries 1984; Robson 1973). Towns can be straightforwardly defined in physical terms as relatively dense, nucleated, settlements, with population sizes above a threshold that varies with the context, but geographers and others concerned with the question contend that there are specifically 'urban' functional qualities that evade definition in solely physical terms. This contention raises two questions: what do these qualities consist of in any given context, and what data are required in order to detect them? In practice the answer to the first question resists unequivocal specification and the requisite data are not usually available, so that most studies fall back onto the empirical criterion of population size, allied to some version of 'I know it when I see it' at the conceptual level.

---

[10] Strictly speaking this assertion is demonstrably true only for the early modern period, but there can be little doubt that it also held true in earlier, less well-documented, periods, at least for the larger centres. See Hohenberg and Lees (1985: 74–89), de Vries (1984: 175–98), Landers (1987), and more generally Landers (1993).

Nonetheless, the functional dynamic dimension of 'urbanism' is crucial for any comparative, or long-term, analysis. Towns and cities do not simply pop up at random, or in response to an immanent logic of their own. They develop because living there enables their inhabitants, or the dominant element among them, to achieve their goals in ways that the available alternatives do not. Another way of saying this is that urban settlements always have a function, or functions, with respect to some broader social and economic system within which they are embedded.

These functions are very variable over time and space, but most of them can be incorporated into a small number of categories:

1. Security. A population clustered on a single site is easier to defend, whether by man-made fortifications, the choice of a defensible location such as a hilltop, or both. This may lead farming populations to concentrate in walled settlements the size of small towns, even though these have few, if any, specifically 'urban' functional characteristics.

2. Leisure. Landlords and other *rentiers* have often chosen to consume their surpluses through leisure activities in towns or cities. Where this simply consisted of large-scale eating and drinking, it might not qualify as a specifically 'urban' function, since it could go on just as well in the countryside. A range of other forms of leisure consumption, from artistic patronage through gladiatorial contests to the social events of the London 'Season', clearly do meet this criterion.

3. Specialist services. The wide availability of specialist services is a distinctively urban characteristic. They are extremely variable in nature and range in sophistication from face-to-face marketing of local produce to the conduct of complex financial transactions. Most of them fall into one of two overlapping categories. The first consists of services that are oriented towards the settlement's territorial hinterland and integrate it as a functional economic unit, and the second consists of those oriented towards distant, usually urban, markets.

4. Manufacturing. Manufacturing was often located in the countryside in organic economies, but urban locations were more likely where the processes involved scarce materials or skills. Most manufactured products can be divided, like services, into a category for local, hinterland, consumption and another to be traded in distant markets.

5. Political. Urban centres have often been the foci of political power, fulfilling a range of associate administrative and military functions. These might involve the provision of services to the hinterland's inhabitants or merely keeping up existing power relationships. Such centres operated in one of two contexts. They might be relatively autonomous foci of power, integrating subordinate territorial units in the service of local or regional interests, or they might function as subordinate nodes in an overarching hierarchy of power which execute directives from above. In either case, their functions usually included the extraction of resources from the agrarian economy.

Towns and cities are defined *inter alia* by their inability to exist in isolation. Their functions only make sense in terms of relationships with settlements elsewhere, whether these are dispersed across the surrounding countryside or distantly located on trade routes and other communication networks. Two distinct, but mutually compatible, kinds of system emerge from such relationships.

5.2.1.1. Central place systems

The first kind of system is the subject of geographical 'central place' theory. Systems of this kind consist of a nested hierarchy of spatial integration which arises from the way in which the service, or manufacturing, functions of urban centres co-ordinate the economic activity of their territorial hinterlands (Hohenberg and Lees 1985; Berry 1967). The lower-level units formed by local centre and hinterland are themselves folded into larger entities by the integrative function of centres at the next hierarchical level, the system's upward reach depending on the level of sophistication achieved by the economy. Few but the most primitive lacked some places that were clearly distinct from the generality of rural settlements, even if they only counted as 'urban' on a very generous criterion. Local market centres, perhaps numbering no more than a few hundred inhabitants, integrated production and consumption over a radius of a few hours' journey time. Larger, subregional and regional, centres emerged in more sophisticated economies and provided specialized services to producers over a correspondingly wider area.

Central places of this kind were oriented towards the areal economy of bulk production. As the degree of functional economic integration within and between regions increased and genuine supra-regional economies emerged, so the linkages between centres became stronger and more complex, as did those with the surrounding agrarian economy. This led to a characteristic shift in the distribution of town and city sizes which can be thought of as a spectrum lying between two extremes. At one of these extremes are highly developed economies with sophisticated transport and communication systems (de Vries 1984; Smith 1990) which display a hierarchical spatial organization, with a succession of levels ranging up from localities, through subregions and regions, to the national economy as a whole. The spatial hierarchy is functionally integrated by a similarly nested pattern of economic linkages. Spatial units at each level are integrated by the functions of a town or city of the appropriate magnitude, so that urban hierarchies emerge, paralleling those of districts, regions, and so forth. Integration on this scale results in settlement size distribution fitting the so-called 'rank–size' rule according to which the number of centres in each size class declines in an orderly fashion with increasing hierarchical level. At the other extreme are undeveloped, poorly integrated, economies, where transactions are restricted to short distances. Small local centres abound in such circumstances, but the urban hierarchy is distinctly 'flat-topped' because the regional or subregional economies needed to support its upper levels are absent.

5.2.1.2. *Urban networks*

The nested hierarchies of central place theory form only one kind of urban system, just as the areal economy of bulk production was only one form of spatial economy. Alongside, or superimposed upon it, were long-range high-value exchange networks linking physically remote points of production and consumption along well-defined paths and nodes (Hohenberg and Lees 1985: 46–73). As the volume of long-distance trade ebbed and flowed so these structures crystallized and dissolved. Such a network had emerged in Europe by the second millennium BC. It was held together by small-scale entrepôts which were divorced from the productive activity of the agrarian hinterland and numbered their clients among local elites rather than cultivators (Sherratt 1998). As trading volumes expanded in the classical era, and seaborne bulk trades emerged, some of these centres expanded to take on a wider range of urban functions and to develop into genuine trading cities (Cunliffe 1988). Most were ports in which the needs of shipping and its dependent trades promoted general economic and demographic expansion.

Few of these cities maintained their earlier role through the crises of late antiquity, but a new network of small trading centres or *emporia* appeared with the early medieval revival of long-distance trade. These too were economically divorced from their agrarian hinterlands, existing under the patronage and close scrutiny of political authorities (Hodges 1982: 29–65; Verhulst 1998). They suffered in their turn from the disorders and disruption of trade in the ninth and tenth centuries, but a new network developed as trade revived after AD 1000. Its nodes again lay outside the structure of the local agrarian economy, in the extra-urban fairs that flourished in Champagne and elsewhere on the intersection of north–south and east–west trade routes. Genuine trading cities reappeared with the return of long-distance high-volume trade, first in the Mediterranean and then in northern Europe, providing administrative and financial services as well as a physical location for the exchange of commodities. These functions became increasingly important with the spread of export-oriented rural industry and the regional specialization that this promoted.

5.2.1.3. *Economics, politics, and urban centres*

Urban or 'proto-urban' centres acted as integrating focal points for their hinterlands' agrarian economy, as bases for specialist services, and as nodes on long-range communication networks ranging in scale from minor emporia to large-scale entrepôts with a full range of urban functions. They were also administrative centres and bases for political and military power. The establishment of defended settlements, garrisoned by regular troops or militia, was a common means of establishing control over newly conquered regions or frontiers, particularly where these were thinly populated. Such places were generally small to begin with, and often remained so, but the very largest pre-modern centres owed their magnitude to political or administrative factors rather than narrowly economic ones. Major administrative centres, garrisons, or seats of justice acquired large complements of functionaries and staffs, and the locus of political power acted as a magnet for elites, even if they were not directly involved in its workings. Their wealth, in turn, provided a livelihood for luxury producers and traders, whilst their less affluent followers' subsistence requirements generated demand for agricultural products (Wrigley 1978, 1967).

Political centralization, occurring against a background of weak economic integration and flat-topped urban hierarchies, led to a disproportionate concentration of wealth, power, and population in the capital and the emergence of so-called 'primate' cities which were many times the size of the largest provincial centres (Hohenberg and Lees 1985; de Vries 1984). The leading role of political and administrative functions in this process, and their importance as centres of elite consumption, has meant that large pre-modern cities are often seen as economic parasites that leached off the resources of the countryside and gave little in return. The productive role of most of these centres was certainly very limited, with many of their inhabitants being under- or unemployed (Hopkins 1978), but to see them as necessarily parasitic is to overlook the potentially catalytic role that they could play. Big cities represented a major concentration of demand at a single point and, where the institutional context allowed it, could stimulate output growth through agricultural intensification, regional and occupational specialization, and investment in the means of transport (Wrigley 1978).

5.2.2. URBAN LOGISTICS

Cities developed as a result of regional economic integration or the centralization of political power. The first of these processes provided cities with both an economic rationale, as integrating central places, and a logistical base. Political centralization, by contrast, fostered the growth of primate cities with limited economic functions in the absence of integrated supra-regional markets. In either case, the basic structures of an organic economy made provisioning them difficult. Low agricultural productivity limited the surpluses available to support non-food producers, and transport constraints limited the numbers who could be concentrated at a single point. Big cities were consumers of people as well as food and needed continuing immigration to offset the 'urban penalty' of exceptionally high mortality. These two requirements were supplied in closely related ways. Migrants travelled on the same routes, and sometimes in the same vehicles, as provisions. The organization of urban provisioning also created social networks linking town and country and helped to integrate migrants into urban society.

5.2.2.1. *Provisioning*

The two categories of 'town dweller' and 'non-food-producer' were not quite the same thing. Some towns contained appreciable numbers of people growing their own food, and occupational specialization could develop in the countryside, but the two categories substantially overlapped, and the larger a town or city became, the more its citizens were likely to depend on food grown elsewhere. Assuming that a rural food surplus existed, there were two problems involved in getting the available food to urban consumers. The first problem was 'procurement' or inducing the cultivators to part with their produce and the second was transportation with all the physical and logistical difficulties that this involved. The two issues raised distinct problems, but their solutions were related. Transportation itself required the procurement of resources, and similar combinations of coercion and reward were likely to be applied in both contexts. The scale of major metropolitan centres, with populations running into the hundreds of thousands, fostered logistical possibilities as well as problems. As massive concentrations of demand they offered market opportunities to producers, middlemen, and transport owners where the necessary institutions existed. As centres of political power, their rulers commanded the coercive force to extract resources on a wide geographical scale by non-market means.

The principal transport problems stemmed from the constraints on land haulage which we considered in the last chapter. These alone could raise costs to the point where market mechanisms failed to guarantee the delivery of affordable provisions, necessitating political intervention in the form of subsidy or coercion. The scale of this problem emerges from some simple calculations on variant assumption as to agricultural productivity and haulage efficiency (see Appendix I). The results suggest that, under intermediate assumptions, market mechanisms could probably only support centres of 10,000 to 20,000 people from local resources. Even on optimistic assumptions, the unaided market would be unable to feed a city holding much more than 60,000 people. On the pessimistic assumptions, which are probably quite realistic for many times and places in pre-industrial Europe, non-market means might be needed to provision centres with populations as low as 5,000. On these results it is unlikely that many cities in the 25,000–50,000 size range were able to provision themselves by land, unless resources were mobilized through an economically wasteful exercise of political power.[11]

Calculations of this kind understate the extent of effective dependence on distant production, because they ignore the issues of market stability and the security of supply. The authorities needed to ensure that provisions were available at prices the population could afford, because urban food shortages always threatened political stability and in capital cities they could threaten the position of the ruler, and even his life. Since harvest volumes fluctuated a great deal from year to year in any one region, securing supply required access to the produce of

---

[11] The analysis reported here is restricted to the logistics of urban food supply, but as van der Woude et al. point out, the transport of fuel supplies imposed even greater constraints on urban growth. If Dutch peat deposits had not been readily accessible by water, an estimated 110,000 horses would have been needed to provision the cities with fuel, and their fodder requirements would have accounted for one quarter of the country's land area (van der Woude, de Vries, and Hayami 1990).

more distant regions even if hinterland production sufficed in normal years. Large-scale crop failures were not the only source of concern for urban authorities because market prices could fluctuate out of all proportion to changes in supply volumes. A marginal shortfall, whether actual or potential, could be enough to trigger a crisis, and in practice price stability was best assured by a substantial degree of oversupply. In such circumstances it became a political priority to establish and maintain access to distant grain supplies, even where they contributed only marginally to normal market volumes, and this in turn usually required access to water transport.

Historically, the problem of procurement was solved in three main ways. Resources might be drawn from the countryside by members of the elite: individuals or institutions who had rural estates but based themselves in the city. These might take the form of money rents disbursed in urban luxury markets, or direct transfers from the produce of managed estates. Direct transfers could be significant where large estates were in the hands of absentee landowners, as in late Byzantium or northern Italy in the later Middle Ages (Magdalino 1995; Duby 1972), but neither these nor luxury expenditure sufficed to feed large metropolitan populations in their entirety. This usually required politico-military coercion to extract resources either as tribute or taxation, or else as the produce of state-owned land. Only rarely, before recent times, could large cities 'earn their keep', by providing goods and services to producers elsewhere, or by the profits of long-distance trade.[12]

The 'mode of procurement' question is inseparable from the further question of how city dwellers obtained their livelihood at the individual and household level. Smaller towns served as market centres for rural producers, but the economic role of larger centres was both more complex and ambivalent. Provisioning cities through market exchanges necessitated some kind of 'production for export', whether to an agricultural hinterland or to more distant urban markets. For this to occur it had to be possible to deliver the goods or services to the market, subject to all the constraints we have just considered, but there also had to be a demand for them. Where this existed, and the metropolitan economy was in a position to respond, there was the possibility of a virtuous circle of growth through progressive specialization, in the manner depicted by the classical economists. In practice these conditions were rarely present, and large pre-industrial cities were more often provisioned through rents or politico-military extortion. Many of the inhabitants of such centres survived through the provision of luxury goods and services for the elite. Many more formed an economically inactive lumpenproletariat in a condition of dependence which reached its extreme where, as in old and new Rome, state corn doles were the price of political quiescence. These phenomena underlie the 'parasitism' interpretation of pre-industrial cities' economic role, but even where they were present the sheer

---

[12] Early modern London's reliance on commercial provisioning made it unusual, if not unique, among contemporary capitals (Daunton 1978).

volume of metropolitan consumption played an integrative role and potentially stimulated both innovation and investment.

5.2.2.2. *Migration*

Urbanization was at once a potential route to growth in productivity and a response to actual demographic growth. Cities provided a refuge for surplus members of the rural population, and the volume of their subsistence needs might stimulate production in the hinterland, whilst their growth promoted economic differentiation through the development of specifically 'urban' occupations. Urban proportions generally rose as overall population grew in the 'A' phases of the medieval and early modern demographic cycles and they stagnated or declined in the ensuing 'B' phases. Whereas overall population growth reflected a surplus of births over deaths, urban growth relied heavily on migration. New settlements were, by definition, established by migrants, but once established, the severe mortality of the larger centres meant that they needed continuing immigration if they were to persist, let alone expand. The logistical possibilities and limitations of human movement resembled those of the movement of commodities, but the spatial organization of migration and trade differed in an important respect. Commodity traffic existed on two distinct levels, but the routeways that served them were never physically cut off from each other. Local capillaries fed long-range veins and arteries, and human travellers moved between the two systems in complex patterns that varied over space and time. The low productivity of organic economies itself promoted mobility. Travel was difficult, and often dangerous, but the poverty of the mass of the population and their very lack of possessions freed them from the encumbrances that often held the better-off in place. In the medieval period

> men moved contradictorily between two sets of horizons: the limited horizons of the clearing in which they lived, and the distant horizons of the whole of Christendom, within which anyone could all of a sudden go away from England to Santiago de Compostela or Toledo. (Le Goff 1988: 137)[13]

The spatial organization of early modern migration has been intensively studied, and English systems, in particular, are better understood than their medieval predecessors (Clark and Souden 1987). Large towns and cities were nodes on a network of long-range migration, much of which was associated with poverty. Flows of so-called 'subsistence migrants', beggars and vagabonds supplemented at times by discharged soldiers and deserters, rose and fell with the demographic tide. This contrasted with the movement pattern of the more fortunate and

---

[13] Another distinguished medievalist expressed the same thought in the rather more picturesque words of a fictional creation: 'He [Bilbo] used often to say there was only one road; that it was like a great river: its springs were at every doorstep, and every path was its tributary. "It's a dangerous business, Frodo, going out of your door," he used to say. "You step into your Road, and if you don't keep your feet, there is no knowing where you might be swept off to"' (J. R. R. Tolkien, *The Fellowship of the Ring* (1954), 83).

economically active. This so-called 'betterment migration' was primarily short distance and focused on distinct 'mobility fields' around towns and cities, although supra-regional centres such as Norwich or London recruited apprentices from further afield. A further shift occurred in the century after 1670, as subsistence migration declined and longer-range movement by the better-off increased, much of it associated with leisure consumption. Overall, the relative mobility of England's population contributed powerfully to the country's economic integration and long-term growth. The relatively weak role of the family and inheritance relative to the economic opportunities offered by markets and the 'risk-sharing' role of community-level welfare institutions seems to have made an important contribution to this flexibility. In other circumstances where familial or servile institutions predominated, mobility was more restricted and the progress of spatial integration was impeded as a result (Schofield 1989).

5.3. CONCLUSION

Output growth and political centralization in organic economies had important spatial implications. Both processes involved spatial integration on a regional or supra-regional scale and the emergence of towns and cities as integrating centres, and as such their development, was constrained by the economy's underlying spatial structure. This structure was shaped by the prevalence of local production and consumption, and the predominance of cultivation as a source of raw materials. The result was an areal geography in which most overland bulk transportation took place over short distances at low densities. Long-distance overland trade also existed but was normally confined to low-bulk, high-value commodities. The demand for major road systems suitable for bulk haulage was therefore restricted, and the weakness of administrative and legal institutions made it difficult to translate what demand there was into an investment stream.

Large-scale spatial integration was more often politically than economically driven, and the rulers of large states constructed very effective systems of long-range communication. Some of these incorporated major road systems, but they were oriented primarily to the needs of military commanders. Large-scale state formation in these circumstances often produced capital cities that were very large relative to regional or subregional centres, and provisioning these 'primate' cities was a major political priority and practical problem for their rulers. Security of supply required access to the produce of distant regions and to transport by water. The growth of a large-scale trade in staples stimulated investment in transportation and promoted regional specialization, but market mechanisms had a variable role in metropolitan provisioning. In the ancient world political authorities sometimes assumed direct responsibility for the task and usually exercised close supervision when the trade was in private hands. Where market mechanisms predominated, as they did in early modern London, this encouraged a greater degree of occupational specialization together with the development of financial institutions to support the trade. Long-range geographical linkages developed which in turn fostered the migration on which large cities depended to maintain their numbers. The extent of migration varied with the social and political context. In early modern England spatial integration was promoted by the relative mobility of the population, reflecting the prevalence of free labour and the relative weakness of the family as a welfare institution.

Conclusion

THE NATURE OF the organic economies' resource base affected the levels of productivity of which they were capable, the structure of the societies that depended on them, and the character of their spatial organization. The fundamental constraint was an overwhelming reliance on muscle power and fuel wood as sources of energy. The consequences of this reliance were most severe in metallurgy and other heat-intensive forms of production, but restricted energy inputs kept productivity low throughout the economy. Low productivity in turn restricted the scope for social differentiation and rendered poverty ubiquitous. Mass poverty kept the demand for non-essential goods low and so depressed levels of investment in the technologies that might have boosted productivity. Seasonal and other bottlenecks in production meant that resources were often used inefficiently, and this inefficiency gave scope for political authorities and others to mobilize underemployed man- and animal power in pursuit of major public works and other non-economic projects. Changes in labour productivity in organic economies were heavily affected by levels of population growth. In many low-density ancient and medieval populations productivity may have been depressed by labour shortages, but sustained population growth characteristically led to falling productivity and labour surpluses as well as changes in land use which increased the likelihood of harvest failure.

These phenomena were symptoms of population pressure which included the emergence of a 'surplus' population of landless and under- or wholly unemployed individuals whose fate varied according to the economic and social circumstances of the time. In the medieval and early modern periods they contributed to the development of urban systems which fostered economic growth by providing specialist services as trading centres or as 'central places' which integrated the economies of their agrarian hinterlands. The progress of urbanization in organic economies was constrained by restrictions on the number of non-food-producers who could be supported and by the difficulties of moving bulk cargoes long distances overland. As long as land transport depended on muscle power it was prohibitively expensive to transport staple foods for more than a few days' carriage unless there was an overriding political or military imperative to do so. This meant that large cities needed access to water transport, which was more efficient in energy terms.

The restrictions on land transport also reflected the nature of a transport infrastructure which emerged in response to the geographical dispersion of production and consumption in organic economies. Most commodities moved short distances in low-density flows which provided little economic incentive for investment in road-building. The construction of major long-distance road networks, where it occurred, did so in response to political or military rather than economic priorities. Long-distance trade existed, but it characteristically involved high-value, low-bulk commodities which did not require paved roads, and was largely isolated from the agrarian economy of local production and consumption. One exception to this generalization occurred where metropolitan centres outgrew the resources of their hinterlands and needed to be provisioned from distant sources. The growth of an inter-regional grain trade in order to satisfy this need required the development of large-scale port and shipping facilities which itself stimulated the growth of further occupational specialization.

Urban growth on this scale usually occurred in response to political centralization, rather than purely economic stimuli, and the state had to assume responsibility for provisioning metropolitan centres it had itself created. In early modern north-west Europe, however, cities emerged which had a more dynamic economic role and they were located in the two countries which most fully realized the potential for growth within the confines of the organic economy. These were England and the Dutch Republic, and of these two, it was the Dutch Republic that led Europe in terms of productivity and income per head for much of the period, but in the longer term it stagnated and failed to make the transition to mineral-based factory production before the nineteenth century. The agriculture of the northern Netherlands developed a specialized, commercial, orientation from the close of the Middle Ages, partly because the region's unusual physical geography and exposure to flooding made conventional agricultural subsistence difficult. The Baltic grain trade allowed labour to be transferred from the production of staple foods into higher-productivity occupations in both agricultural and non-agricultural sectors. By the 1580s, and the revolt against Habsburg rule, the provinces of the future Republic had acquired a highly differentiated economy with an advanced division of labour, high productivity, and sophisticated financial and mercantile institutions.

For most of the following century rapid population growth, fostered by substantial immigration, was accompanied by productivity gains of up to 80 per cent above early sixteenth-century levels, and real wages which were to remain Europe's highest until well into the eighteenth century. Growth was fuelled by the accumulation of capital in overseas trade which was supported by a large and highly diversified merchant fleet and allowed massive investment in a range of fixed capital projects. The use of wind-powered machinery and the general efficiency of Dutch mercantile and service institutions greatly reduced costs, but the economy also benefited from cheap non-renewable energy in the form of abundant peat deposits, supplemented by imports of English coal. By the 1670s less than 40 per cent of the labour force was employed in agriculture, and an estimated 42 per cent of the population were living in towns of over 2,500 inhabitants, more than 60 per cent doing so in the province of Holland itself. But from this point stagnation set in, and the Dutch population was one of the few in Europe to experience no appreciable growth in the following century.

High mortality contributed to this stagnation, the 'urban penalty' of elevated mortality among town dwellers being aggravated by the effects of deteriorating groundwater quality on rural mortality in the west of the country, but the key problem was almost certainly a lack of economic opportunities as the Golden Age came to a close and a consequent preventive check which operated through both lower marriage rates and an unfavourable balance of immigration. The ultimate reasons for this are controversial. Wrigley, stressing the importance of energy supplies, implicated rising fuel costs which were brought on by the depletion of readily accessible peat deposits and robbed Dutch manufactured goods of their price advantage, but de Vries and van der Woude find little direct evidence to support this emphasis on energy prices and point to Holland's ability to supplement native energy sources with imports of English coal. Against the vision of a pre-modern economy encountering inevitable limits to growth, they see the Netherlands as confronting 'in sector after sector... the modern problems of profits, employment, market access and costs', and subsequently experiencing a 'modern decline' (de Vries and van der Woude 1997: 698). But on either interpretation, in terms of immediate causes, the Dutch economy was hobbled by the obstinately high production costs which stemmed from the failure to innovate in industrial technology.

It was the early nineteenth-century English economy which first experienced the transforming power of this kind of innovation, but by then the country had already pursued a remarkable economic and demographic trajectory lasting two centuries or more. During this time population roughly quadrupled, but domestic food production more or less kept pace until close to the end of the period, and from the middle of the seventeenth century the country was relatively unaffected by any large-scale subsistence crises. The bases of this achievement were evidently both economic and demographic. Economically, eighteenth-century English agriculture was endowed with a large and high-quality domestic animal stock from which it obtained correspondingly generous inputs of motive power and fertilizer. In addition, the emergence of an integrated national economy from the seventeenth century onwards fostered large-scale regional specialization in agriculture with consequent gains in efficiency.

Urbanization played a very important role as it did in Holland, but the structure of English and Dutch urbanization was very different. The English experience was distinguished by the extraordinary growth of the capital, which by 1700 included some 10 per cent of the country's population and the majority of its town dwellers, and the absence of the tier of large provincial centres common to its continental neighbours. Metropolitan primacy of this kind is conventionally regarded as a symptom of economic backwardness, but in the English case the sheer size of the London market was a vital catalyst to economic modernization, fostering supra-regional integration, occupational specialization, and the development of marketing and credit networks as well as transport and communications. The consequences included a doubling of agricultural labour productivity from the beginning of the sixteenth century (Wrigley 1985b).

In the demographic sphere marriage patterns responded to changing economic circumstances in ways, which allowed the country's demographic regime to function homeostatically and keep overall living standards relatively high. Nonetheless this homeostasis was only partial and by the end of the eighteenth century domestic food production could no longer keep pace with population growth. Although England had displaced Holland at the top of the per capita income tables its demographic expansion was now pressing against the limits of an organic economy. The fact that this pressure eventually resulted not, as Malthus feared, in a collapse of living standards, but rather in an era of continual and unprecedented improvement, reflected England's successful transition to a mineral economy. Recent research suggests that the classical 'industrial revolution' period saw much less economic growth than was once thought, and on this purely quantitative basis the term itself may be an unfortunate one (Crafts 1985).

By contrast, there can be no doubt that the nineteenth-century exploitation of coal as a production and transportation fuel enabled truly revolutionary growth on a scale that transformed both demographic space and demographic regimes in Europe and elsewhere. But coal was already exploited on an appreciable scale before steam power was first applied to manufacturing industry, and in energy terms the transition to a mineral economy had begun before the end of the eighteenth century. Again, it was the scale of the London market that stimulated demand for fuel, whilst the fortuitous location of coalfields near the navigable river Tyne in north-eastern England enabled the demand to be met from this source. Much of this demand was for domestic fuel, the balance being for the traditional energy-intensive industries such as brewing, soap-boiling, or brick-making. Production on the scale needed to supply this trade required ever-deeper mining, running up against the inevitable problems of drainage and ventilation, and it was as pumps that the first steam engines were developed[1]. Similarly the problems of transporting coal from the pits to the docks gave rise to plate ways which had developed into fully fledged horse-drawn railways—boosting the animal's effective traction as much as threefold—before the application of steam traction at the end of the 1820s. By 1800 England consumed a volume of coal with an energy content equivalent to woodlands covering 50–100 per cent of the country's surface area and thereby broke through the fundamental 'hard' limit of the organic economy.

---

[1] In Wrigley's words, the 'beginnings of the new technology of the steam engine and the railway lay in the eighteenth-century coal-mining industry, and one of its chief supports in turn was the large and steadily growing demand for coal afforded by the London coal market' (Wrigley 1967). Eighteenth-century output growth, as Flinn notes, resulted primarily from 'more intensive development of existing areas in combination with deeper mining, and some centripetal expansion as dipping seams were followed outwards, and deeper pits pursued faulted seams' (Flinn 1984: 29). It was this process, and the resulting problems of flooding, that drove the initial development of steam-powered technology.

PART II

Military Technology

Introduction

The deployment of military force represented a commitment of manpower and material resources combined in a manner which depended on the prevailing military technology. Like the technology of civilian production, military technology embodied the three elements of hardware, procedures, and personnel. The hardware in this context consisted of various kinds of offensive and defensive equipment whilst the procedures needed for their effective use ranged from specific weapons-handling skills to general tactics and the broad theoretical 'doctrines' which guided the actions of commanders and their staffs in concrete instances.[1] Most of the personnel who employed the hardware and procedures were common soldiers who did the actual fighting and exercised no authority over anyone else. Above them were the leaders of various grades, many of whom discharged their authority through a display of exemplary courage in the front line rather than by directing operations from further back.[2] A third category consisted of specialists, who might be soldiers or civilians and who operated in the spheres of administration, logistics, engineering, and other support services.

The material resources involved can be divided into two very broad categories. The first category of 'equipment' comprises the supplies, animals, weaponry, and other items committed in support of the troops themselves, whilst the second, which can be termed military 'capital goods', consists primarily of warships, fortifications, and the instruments of siege warfare. Military technology was deployed in three distinct contexts: mobile warfare on land, attacking and defending fortifications, and naval warfare. In each case the development of gunpowder weapons had profound consequences but pre-gunpowder technology was by no means static. The greatest changes occurred in the technology of mobile land warfare, which forms the subject matter of this part's first chapter. The conduct of mobile warfare relied on so-called tactical systems which were interrelated combinations of equipment, tactics, and battlefield organization and were generally defined by their reliance on a particular set of weapons and those who wielded them.[3]

---

[1] Military doctrine, which may be either explicit or implicit, is defined by Dupuy as 'Principles, policies and concepts which are combined into an integrated system for the purpose of governing all components of a military force in combat and assuring consistent, coordinated employment of these components. The origin of doctrine can be experience, or theory, or both' (1984: 9).

[2] See Keegan (1987) for a highly critical review of the role played by exemplary, or 'heroic', leadership in western military history.

[3] The term 'system' in this context refers merely to the existence of interrelated elements functioning as a reasonably coherent whole. It is not intended to imply that these were smoothly functioning, highly co-ordinated, or systematically planned.

The outcome of any given battle might depend on a commander's skill, the terrain, or even the weather, but these 'chances of war' generally evened out in the long term, and the frequency of victory or defeat in encounters between different systems reflected their intrinsic characteristics. Unlike production technologies, whose competitive value can be measured by the absolute criterion of efficiency, the value of competing tactical systems is inherently relative because the requirements for technological superiority depend on the military technology at the disposal of the opposition. No pre-gunpowder system proved able to establish what we shall call a 'global hegemony', the two requirements for which were that the system should be superior to any competing system in all but the most unusual circumstances and that there should be no intrinsic limits to the scale on which it could be implemented. The gunpowder revolution transformed the nature of the relationships between tactical systems, and the 'musket and sabre' system which had emerged by the end of the seventeenth century proved capable of establishing a true global hegemony. The second chapter of this part examines the emergence of this system and examines the reasons for the remarkable period of technological conservatism which ensued.

The third chapter examines the character of military capital goods and the consequences of the gunpowder revolution in naval and siege warfare. Warships and fortifications had common economic characteristics because they were both expensive items which needed specialized skills to design and construct them. The kinds of warfare in which they were employed were at opposite ends of the spectrum operationally, but the coming of firearms transformed both in ways that had a good deal in common. Pre-gunpowder naval operations and tactics were constrained by a number of factors which stemmed ultimately from the reliance on muscle power as a source of energy and greatly restricted the strategic capabilities of naval forces. The strategic role of fortification was also restricted by the limitations of pre-gunpowder technology, although these hampered both attackers and defenders. Garrisons could inflict very little damage on a besieging force, and only very rarely could they block enemy movement, without leaving the shelter of their walls and engaging in open-field battle, but reasonably strong, adequately prepared fortifications usually had to be starved out and this presented major logistical difficulties.

In these circumstances fortifications were almost wholly ineffective at sealing off territory against raiders or an invading army but played a very important role in protecting urban centres and as bases for mobile troops and places of refuge in the countryside. The advent of gunpowder artillery changed this position dramatically. Solidly built ships and fortifications both provided excellent firing platforms for heavy guns whilst also making very good targets. On land, new-style 'artillery fortresses' were constructed which were capable of acting as effective barriers, but were also vulnerable to a well-conducted assault, so that both the cost and the inherent uncertainties of siege warfare increased. At sea a new kind of heavily armed sailing ship emerged whose range, endurance, and destructive power transformed the operational and strategic capacities of naval forces and opened the way to sea power in the modern sense of the term.

CHAPTER SIX

Battlefields before Gunpowder

Military technology incorporated the elements of hardware, procedure, and personnel in the same way as the technology of civilian production, and before the coming of gunpowder it was equally reliant on muscle power as an energy source. The technology of battlefield combat consisted of a succession of interrelated combinations of military hardware and procedures which are conventionally termed 'tactical systems'. These were usually based on the users of one specific type of weaponry, though they might incorporate others in a supporting role, and the principle of specialization operated here as in the civilian economy. The more specialized a tool, the more efficient it will be at an appropriate task and the narrower the range of such tasks will be. Similarly, if two different troop types fought each other using the same tactics, the more specialized of the two was likely to win. Armoured horsemen could ride down unarmoured men who tried to use heavy cavalry tactics, and armoured infantry could disperse bodies of unarmoured foot soldiers if they formed into a compact mass. The more specialized the type, however, the narrower the role and the more any inherent vulnerabilities would come to the surface: unarmoured troops were far more effective at dispersed harassing tactics than were their heavier opponents.

The consequences of military specialization diverged in one very important respect from those seen in economic contexts, reflecting a basic difference between the two kinds of technology. Military and economic technology can both be thought of as having a 'value', but the relationship between the values of competing systems is quite different in each case. The value of a tactical system is intrinsically relative and context dependent, but a productive system's competitive value is determined by its efficiency, and this is an intrinsic characteristic measurable on an absolute scale without reference to the nature of the competition. If system A is more efficient than B, and B more efficient than C, then A will be more efficient than C by definition. This is not true of tactical systems, whose value has no meaning in absolute terms but is determined by the character of the opposition and the setting in which the contest occurs. Values of this kind cannot necessarily be ordered into a single hierarchy in the manner of productive systems. Tactical system A might be superior to B, and system B prevail over C, yet A itself be very vulnerable to C. This pattern of so-called 'non-transitive' relationships was a characteristic feature of pre-gunpowder military technology, and its erosion was one of the most important consequences of the gunpowder revolution.

6.1. MOBILE MILITARY HARDWARE

The ability to fight and win battles was not a sufficient condition for overall military success but in most circumstances it was a necessary one, and victory in battle required killing or disabling enough of the enemy—and putting the survivors in fear of the same—to drive them from the field.[1] Until the twentieth century this could only be achieved by delivering a sufficient quantity of kinetic energy to stun the opponent, break bones, destroy vital organs, or sever major blood vessels. The fundamental problem of pre-gunpowder field and siege combat was therefore the same as it was in the sphere of production: how to make the most effective use of muscle power. Just as in that sphere, there were three possible solutions to the problem: the use of hardware to store and transmit energy, specialization allied to the division of labour, and the exploitation of animal power.

Military technology differed in degree from the technology of civilian life in its much greater use of metals, and so of the energy resources needed to process them. This was partly because metals were more suited to the violent application and deflection of kinetic energy than were organic materials, but it also reflected the power of armed men to appropriate a disproportionate share of scarce resources. In the same way, western military technology, from late antiquity at least, made a disproportionate use of animal power, and particularly the power of horses, which were both valuable and prestigious goods. Indeed the prevalence of mounted fighting among military and social elites may sometimes have been as much an expression of social power and prestige as it was a military expedient. Military demands diverted resources from production and warfare could lead to their systematic destruction, but in the longer term there was the prospect of a more complex relationship between military and productive technology. Military demands might, in principle, lead to the refinement of existing production techniques, or the development of entirely new ones, and this possibility was all the more important in low-productivity economies where mass poverty restricted the level of market-based demand. In practice, however, the technologies of war and peace in organic economies were too different for there to be much prospect of direct transfers between them. Horse-breeding and ironworking are both likely to have benefited, in the long term, from the stimulus of military demand, but in the short term the relative inelasticity of supply meant that the main effect was more likely to be civilian shortages and consequent loss of production.[2]

---

[1] The outcome of battles has generally depended as much on flight as on casualties. As Clifford Rogers argues, 'weapons are as important for their effects on those whom they do not hit as for their effects on the people they do hit. Battles are won more by the psychological effects of weapons than their physical impacts: this is demonstrated simply by the fact that a defeated army rarely suffers even 50 per cent of its numbers in killed or wounded.' (Rogers 1998: 235).

[2] The main economic impact of pre-20th-century military activity, destruction aside, came from the troops' requirement for food and clothing. Where procurement was well organized and underutilized resources existed in the civilian sector, the effect would be beneficial, but the former was rarely the case before the 18th century, and by this time the costs involved were putting a severe strain on the economy (see below, Chapter 8).

Pre-gunpowder military and civilian technologies both had to confront the possibilities and limitations of muscle power as an energy source, but in the military case there were two sides to the problem: how to use such power to best effect against an enemy, and how to stop an enemy from using it against oneself. In each case there were two basic options. Offensively, power could be projected through direct physical contact—using 'shock' weapons—or by using missile weapons from a distance. Similarly, an opponent's blows could be dealt with in one of two ways: by avoiding them through dispersion, concealment, or manoeuvre, or by using external protection—usually body armour—to absorb or deflect the shock. The two options were interrelated, as specialized missile troops could readily avoid enemy blows and required little external protection, whilst those committed to close-in fighting had more need for heavy armour. Just as the palaeontologist Cuvier claimed that an entire animal could be reconstructed from a single vital organ, so the defensive equipment and tactical role of a given troop type were largely determined by the capacities and limitations of their offensive weapons.

6.1.1. ARMOUR

The defensive technology used in mobile warfare consisted mainly of body armour with portable shields as a supplement or substitute.[3] There were three main forms of body armour: organic, mail, and plate. The main sources of organic protection were leather, textiles, and bone or horn.[4] Thick textile or leather jerkins provided some protection against edged weapons or arrows and appear at intervals until the seventeenth century. Organic material was generally less effective than metal armour, but it was also lighter and, above all, much cheaper. Its use was usually restricted to poorer, lower-status troops such as the peasantry of fourteenth-century France whose nickname, 'jacques', derived from the thick jerkins they wore when pressed into battlefield service. Seventeenth-century cavalry troopers, however, often wore 'buff coats' which provided some protection against the growing use of slashing weapons, like the sabre, at a time when armourers were giving up the attempt to produce bulletproof metal armour. Leather was scarcer and so more expensive than textiles in most agricultural societies, but it was widely used among pastoral peoples. Boiled leather, like horn, could make an effective torso protection, or cuirass, and it was the material used for the moulded cuirasses worn by Roman centurions.

---

[3] For the general development of armour and other protective equipment in a military historical, rather than antiquarian, context see Creveld (1991) and O'Connell (1989) *passim*. For Greek hoplite armour see Hanson (1991: 55–88). Roman armour of the late Republic and the Principate is discussed by Goldsworthy (1996: 209–21) and that of later periods by Elton (1996: 110–16) and Southern and Dixon (1996: 91–103). For medieval armour see DeVries (1992: 50–94) and Prestwich (1996: 18–26).

[4] Bone and keratinous scales derived from horses' hooves seem to have been amongst the earliest sources of armoured protection. The Sarmatians are described as using such material and it continued to be widely employed among steppe peoples well into the historical period. This reflected its relative abundance and the scarcity of iron in the region (Christian 1998: 106, 146–80; Maenchen-Helfen 1973: 241–50).

Metallic mail armour provided more protection than organic materials whilst being lighter and suppler than plate. It was widely used by the mounted lancers of the Iranian world and was also adopted by Roman heavy cavalry. Mailed infantry are depicted on monuments from as far back as ancient Egypt and it continued as a common form of infantry protection into the later Middle Ages. Mail armour took a number of different forms although there does not seem to be any evidence of systematic development or improvement over the period. It could be manufactured either from metallic scales or from chain links sewn onto a leather backing. Roman infantry used both at different times, with chain mail becoming the standard form in early medieval Europe. The alternative to mail was rigid, 'plate', armour, which was more resistant than mail and could be shaped to deflect a slashing or glancing blow. Metallic breast plates, or the full cuirass with backplate, were manufactured from the Bronze Age. They were appropriate for troops engaged in loose-formation, close-in fighting or in individual combat which exposed their torsos to blows of this kind. Such armour was used by the Homeric elite and retained by the hoplite spearmen of the classical phalanx but the later close-order pike columns did not usually require this degree of protection, which was often confined to the front ranks if it was used at all.

The cuirass provided an alternative to mail as heavy cavalry armour. Worn by both Macedonians and Romans, it was retained into the nineteenth century by heavier units of European cavalry as a defence against slashing blows like sabre cuts. Other forms of plate armour were also used in the ancient world. The Roman legions of the early Empire were equipped with the *lorica segmentata*, a harness of leather-backed plates that formed a kind of compromise between plate and mail, but extensive plate was generally the horseman's prerogative. The Sassanian Persians fielded cavalry entirely encased in plate armour though their effectiveness is unclear. The Romans may have fielded a few such units, but if so they had apparently disappeared by the early Middle Ages (Coulston 1986).[5] Plate armour re-emerged in the west in the twelfth century, initially as protection for the arms and lower legs. The growing effectiveness of missile weapons led to its progressive extension, and, by the fifteenth century the western heavy cavalryman was encased in a harness of 'full armour' that extended to his mount.

At the same time, these 'men-at-arms', as they are generically termed, began increasingly to adopt a mounted infantry role and dismount on the battlefield to fight on foot. Weighing some 45 to 60 pounds, full armour provided considerable protection at the cost of reduced manoeuvrability. Its weight was substantial but relatively well distributed, falling mainly on the shoulders, and no greater than a modern infantryman's pack (Vale 1981: 184–6; DeVries 1992: 84).[6] Firearms posed

---

[5] Roman sources use the term *Clibanarii* of this Persian 'super-heavy' type. Some Roman units also bore the title *Clibanarii* but their equipment may not have differed from other Roman heavy cavalry (Coulston 1986).

[6] The weight of conventional battlefield armour could become a serious handicap in broken or very muddy terrain, or if men fell on top of each other as at Agincourt (Keegan 1976: 101–4). Very much heavier suits of armour, of 90 lbs or more, were constructed for use in tournaments (DeVries 1992: 84).

the wearers of plate armour a challenge to which there were two opposed responses. One was to increase the weight and complexity of the plate in an attempt to make it bulletproof, whilst the alternative was to accept armour's vulnerability to gunfire and lighten the harness so as to increase mobility. Sixteenth-century armourers had some success in their quest for a bulletproof product (Hall 1997: 147, 177), but in the long run it was the latter course which prevailed.

6.1.2. WEAPONS

Muscle-powered weapons were tools designed to concentrate the greatest possible kinetic energy in the smallest area, usually a point or sharp edge.[7] With only one significant exception, they were developed from prototypes first used in the 'civilian' economy, either for hunting, like the spear and bow, or, like the axe, for materials-processing. As such they were first constructed in stone or wood, but the hardness and malleability of metals makes them a better medium for sharp edges and points, and from the first development of metallurgy the Eurasian world of weapons was one in which metals and, from the first millennium BC, iron played an essential role. These weapons fell into two broad categories: missile or 'fire' weapons employed from a distance, and 'shock' weapons, like swords or spears, that required direct physical contact with the enemy. These can be split into two further categories: longer-range, usually pointed weapons such as spears or pikes, and close-range weapons such as swords or axes which were more often edged. Similarly, an opponent's blows could be dealt with in one of two ways: by avoiding them through dispersion, concealment, or manoeuvre or else by absorbing the shock through the use of external protection which in field combat generally meant body armour.

6.1.2.1. *Shock weapons*

The most familiar, and perhaps the earliest shock weapon is the spear. The basic spear was a relatively generalized implement that could be used in single combat or in a formation, and either as a thrusting weapon or as a missile. As is so often the case, specialization yielded improved performance and from the spear developed both the pike and lance. The pike's greater length made it much more effective when deployed by formed infantry, whether as a defence against cavalry or as an attacking weapon, but its use required a higher level of training, at least for the front-rank fighters, and it was of very little use in open-order fighting. The pike played a central role in both ancient and medieval military systems, and, initially, gained a new lease of life from the spread of firearms. Early handguns took so long to load and fire that pike formations were needed to protect their users against enemy cavalry and the weapon continued to be used into the

---

[7] For general accounts of the development of weaponry see Creveld (1991) and O'Connell (1989). The medieval period is discussed by DeVries (1992).

eighteenth century. The spear was also the principal heavy cavalry weapon. Used as an overarm thrusting weapon in the ancient and early medieval periods, later improvements in horse furniture allowed it to be used in the couched position and encouraged the development of the longer lance. An alternative to elongating the spear was to replace or supplement the pointed tip with a blade. The halberd was one of a number of later medieval 'pole arms' developed on this principle as a response to the offensive power of the armoured man-at-arms. Shorter and wieldier than the pike, the halberd in fact proved itself more effective against pikemen than it did against cavalry.

These distance weapons were preferentially metal headed with a wooden shaft, but edged or pointed close-in weapons were always made of metal where this was available. Short-bladed dagger-like weapons were manufactured in flint, but the true sword awaited bronze-working and is probably the only weapon type developed purely as an instrument of violence against other human beings. The rarity and expense of bronze confined its use to warrior nobility. The readier availability of iron, by contrast, largely accounts for bronze's supersession and the more 'democratic' character of Iron Age warfare. Iron, nonetheless, remained an expensive material to produce and work, and early iron swords were not necessarily superior to the bronze form. The effective use of these edged, slashing weapons required deployment in a loose formation, and they were generally of secondary importance to the spear or pike.

This changed with the appearance of the Roman *gladius*. Unlike the earlier cold-worked iron weapons, this short edged sword was forged of tempered steel, initially derived from high-grade Spanish ores, and became the Roman legionary's primary weapon. As a stabbing weapon it could be wielded efficiently in close-order fighting, whilst its edge was also heavy enough to inflict serious mutilation (Keppie 1984: 34; Dupuy 1984).[8] Later Roman infantry reverted to the longer, heavier *spatha*. This was a slashing weapon and swords on this model predominated in medieval Europe (Elton 1996: 109–10; Southern and Dixon 1996: 103–9; DeVries 1992: 205), whilst in the Islamic world the development of highly carbonized 'Damask steel' enabled a much lighter, edged weapon to be produced. This was the scimitar, long an effective Islamic monopoly and a western metonym for their military power (Braudel 1981: 376–7; Zaky 1979: 206–11). With the advent of firearms, and the refinement of European metallurgy, officers and cavalrymen in particular abandoned the lance for the pistol, adopting lighter pointed swords as secondary armament. The return of the cavalry to a shock role then saw the adoption of the edged sabre as a weapon that inflicted more severely disabling wounds and was better suited to downward blows against foot soldiers. The main alternative to the sword as a close-in weapon was the battle-axe, which was associated particularly with Germanic and Scandinavian warriors. As armoured

---

[8] The impact of the *gladius* was apparently psychological as well as physical. The gruesome injuries inflicted by its slashing blows are said to have seriously demoralized the Macedonian troops who were familiar only with puncture wounds (Anderson 1991: 26–7).

protection became more effective in the course of the high Middle Ages there developed an alternative category of club-like 'crushing' weapons that worked by sheer weight. The most familiar example of these is the mace, whilst a highly specialized late derivative, the war hammer, was developed as an armour-piercing weapon.[9]

6.1.2.2. *Missile weapons*

Early missile weapons also derived from the hunt, and three main forms were used in Eurasian warfare: the throwing spear or javelin, the sling, and the bow. The javelin was a further modification of the basic spear and is best known in the form of the Roman legionary's *pilum*. Legionaries apparently carried two of these, a heavier and a lighter version, and by the early Empire it had been fitted with a soft, untempered iron haft that bent on impact so as to prevent its reuse by an opponent (Goldsworthy 1996: 197–201). Weapons of this kind were usually carried as secondary armament and used in order to disrupt the enemy's ranks prior to shock combat. The remaining categories were more often carried by specialists in support of heavier troops, or as a skirmishing screen.

The sling was a basic energy transmission device, evidently widespread in the Mediterranean world and the Near East. Roman slingers were recruited from the Balearic Islands in the Republican period if not later, and this weapon seems to have represented an ethnic technology whose effective use required considerable skill and training (Goldsworthy 1996: 186). The bow and arrow, by contrast, was ubiquitous, though it too required training to be used effectively. Short-bows, drawn to the chest, were widely used in ancient warfare but they were probably not very dangerous to armoured troops. Early in its development a basic divergence emerged between two models: the wooden 'self-bow' and the 'compound' bow constructed from glued layers of horn and sinew (Heath 1980). The first of these was a European weapon whilst the compound bow was used in Asia and on the steppes. Archery is conventionally presented as a neglected art in classical and medieval Europe with the well-known exception of the Anglo-Welsh longbow. Constructed of yew, this was technically a 'self-compound' weapon, the wood itself being layered in the manner of a compound bow. The longbow, drawn to the ear rather than the chest, developed into an extremely powerful weapon. It had a range of 400 yards and could pierce mail at 200, but it needed great strength and skill to operate (Hardy 1994; DeVries 1992: 37). The crossbow represented an alternative design philosophy, making greater use of mechanical devices and placing less of a physical demand on the operator. Known in the ancient world, its military role then and thereafter is obscure until it re-emerged as a significant weapon in the eleventh century (DeVries 1992: 39–44, 127–8; Alm 1994). By the fourteenth century

---

[9] The mace became a symbol of rulership, evolving into the sceptre, but the widely held belief that it was invented so that clerics could inflict death and injury on the battlefield without shedding blood seems to be without historical foundation (DeVries 1992: 25–8).

the crossbow had acquired a compound construction and a windlass mechanism that allowed it to be drawn in twelve seconds. The final sophistication was a ratchet and cog system, the 'cranequin'. This demanded a minimum of exertion to draw, though the pull was over 1,000 pounds, more than twenty times that of the longbow, and enough to pierce plate armour. This model could, however, manage fewer than two shots a minute, as against five for the windlass version, and more than twice that number for the longbow (DeVries 1992: 42).

6.1.3. ANIMALS

Animals, primarily horses, were as important in European warfare as they were in the civilian economy. They played two main roles. Off the battlefield they provided transport for men, supplies, and military equipment. The technology employed here was essentially that of civilian life with minor adaptations as appropriate, but the second role, as mounts on the battlefield, was purely military. Europeans, like other Eurasian agricultural peoples, responded to the example of the steppe pastoralists in this respect. Horses and other equines were used to draw chariots on Bronze Age battlefields, and some authorities have linked the rise of the chariot to the spread of Indo-European speakers across Eurasia (Christian 1998: 99–107). Certainly, around the middle of the second millennium BC charioteering warrior elites established themselves from Europe's Atlantic coasts to northern China, and as far south as Lower Egypt and the Indus valley. Early in the following millennium steppe dwellers learned how to manage their mounts in combat. Cavalry tactics spread across the steppe, enabling Scythian invaders to break into the lands south of the Caucasus, where they were eventually repulsed by Assyrian forces that adopted cavalry tactics in their turn. Around this time barbarian attacks also forced the rulers of northern China to abandon chariots in favour of cavalry (Barfield 1989: 28–30), and by the time Caesar's troops encountered British charioteers they were a bizarre anachronism.

Away from the steppe, the horse was an expensive item to breed, rear, and train. It also had limited endurance which meant that, for best results, each rider had to have access to more than one mount. Nomad cavalry are known to have used strings of animals on their raids and in larger-scale military operations. Their mounts were light steppe ponies, but the heavier western cavalry required stronger animals. The key development here was the appearance of the so-called 'great horse'. This was bred in south-west Asia by the time of the Parthians and possibly earlier. The growing emphasis on heavy cavalry in medieval military systems led to further specialization through selective breeding. By the high Middle Ages this had culminated in the emergence of a specific variety of great horse to serve as a battlefield mount whilst other less specialized breeds were used on the march and by lighter-armed mounted sergeants. Although the great horse was, apparently, distinct from the carthorse of more recent times, it seems certain that the civilian horse herd benefited from the gains in power obtained in its breeding, with consequent gains in productivity (Hyland 1998, 1999; Ayton 1994*a*).

6.1.4. CONCLUSION

Military hardware was necessarily related to civilian production technology and was bound by many of the same constraints. Scarcity of knowledge, materials, and fuel thus affected the production of weapons and armour just as it did the production of subsistence goods or luxuries. What is less clear is whether, and if so how far, differences in resource endowments or in the knowledge of production processes led to corresponding differences in military power. Iron deposits were accessible throughout the western world, although the Romans thought the material sufficiently scarce in Germany for the export of iron weapons to be worth banning.[10] Whatever military disadvantage this may have imposed on the Germans had evidently been made up by the later Empire, by which time the tribes were generally armed with iron weapons. They gained their triumph over Rome without benefit of armour, however, and it is unlikely that their ancestors were greatly disadvantaged by its absence.

It is also unlikely that, once a given weapon type had emerged, there were many enduring military advantages to be obtained by retaining a monopoly on improvements in design or production techniques, since refinements to existing types could be readily copied. There are two possible exceptions to this generalization. The first is the Roman *gladius*, whose production required a step increase in metallurgical technique, and whose use allowed the legionaries to develop a new, and highly effective, style of fighting. The second is the steppe horse-archers' compound bow. Substantial gains in power, and so in military effectiveness, were evidently obtainable by improvements in design and manufacture, which are hedged around with a certain mystery. Nonetheless, in both cases improved weaponry was a necessary, but not a sufficient condition for enduring military advantage. The effective use of these weapons required specific skills and forms of tactical organization whose development was constrained by political and social structures.

6.2. THE EVOLUTION OF TACTICAL SYSTEMS

The rise and fall of tactical systems depended ultimately on their success or failure in winning battles. This point requires underlining because it goes against the grain of much recent writing in military history. The primacy of battles was once taken for granted—to the point where the subject consisted of little more than battle narratives, and the bigger and more 'decisive' the battle the more it was considered worthy of study[11]—but their role is now more often played down, and there are some very good reasons for this. Siege or manoeuvre, rather than open-field battle, often decided the outcome of campaigns. Hunger and disease claimed

---

[10] In this respect iron differed greatly from the tin that was needed to make bronze. Tin was unevenly distributed geographically and was thus an important trade good. It was inaccessible in Bronze Age Scandinavia where imported bronze weaponry was laboriously copied in flint.

[11] These assumptions are reflected in the title of J. F. C. Fuller's classic two-volume work *The Decisive Battles of the Western World* (1970) and underlie a long-established caricature of military

more lives than combat, in consequence shaping both the conduct and outcome of warfare, and armed forces were social and political, as well as military, institutions and need to be understood as such. The conduct and outcome of battles nonetheless shaped the development and diffusion of tactical systems for a very simple reason. Such systems spread either by conquest or by imitation, the most likely systems to be imitated being those used by successful conquerors, and no army that could not win set-piece battles could carry through a successful conquest if it was opposed by one that had this ability.

Tactical systems were usually defined by their reliance on a particular weapon or troop type, and specialization conferred advantages in this context just as it did in production. A given individual might use more than one tactic for inflicting or avoiding injury but, in practice, specific troop types developed based on the use of an interrelated 'package' of equipment and tactics, generally defined by a principal reliance on a particular type of weapon. Each of these had advantages and disadvantages and imposed particular constraints on their users if they were to be wielded to best effect. The effectiveness of any given class of weapon also depended on those against which it was matched. Soldiers with longer-range shock weapons had the advantage of the first blow, but shorter-range weapons were more wieldy and lethal in close combat, giving their users an advantage if they survived the first blow and got inside their opponent's range. To prevent this happening, troops who relied on spears or pikes were usually deployed in a compact mass, which presented a solid hedge of points towards the enemy. Since this greatly reduced the scope for individual manoeuvre and evasion, a dependence on such weapons was associated with the adoption of body armour and 'heavy' tactics based on weight and direct physical force.[12] Armour protection was even more important for the users of shorter-range weapons, who had to get physically close to their adversaries and so were more exposed to counter-blows. By contrast, missile troops, who could more readily disperse and evade attack by means of 'light' tactics, were much less likely to wear armour which would impede their movements, or to seek physical contact with the enemy.

The appearance of the socket bayonet in the 1690s transformed the previous pattern by creating a combination weapon usable either in shock combat or as a firearm at a distance (Chandler 1994: 82–4). Before this, the nature of the available weaponry meant that military specializations could be defined in terms of three basic oppositions: shock/missile, heavy/light, and mounted/foot. Just as specialization and interdependence are two sides of the coin in the production process,

---

history as a matter of 'ex-brigadiers in tweed jackets' drawing diagrams of how the dragoons outflanked the artillery (Bate 1995). The growing professionalization of the discipline in recent decades has seen a turn to more institutional, and often sociological, analyses of military affairs that have sometimes risked introducing a contrary bias (Bennett 1994; Keegan 1976: 25–61).

[12] The use of very long weapons, such as the pike, reduced the likelihood that their wielders would come within range of enemy blows and thus their need for armour protection. This could be exploited, as it was by the Swiss, to lighten equipment and make the pike formation faster and more manoeuvrable.

so in combat, specialized troops of one kind generally required the presence of others, if only in a subordinate supporting role, if they were to operate at full effectiveness. At its most schematic, a cohesive mass of heavy infantry or cavalry armed with shock weapons could count on sweeping away unsupported light troops, but were themselves vulnerable to missile fire or harassing tactics, particularly in the flank or rear. Infantry was similarly vulnerable to cavalry in these respects. Cavalry in turn could not hold ground or succeed in frontal attacks against properly equipped foot soldiers who kept their nerve and their formation,[13] and they could be fully effective for only a restricted period before their formations lost cohesion and their horses became 'blown'.

By the opening of the Middle Ages the main patterns of relative strength and weakness of the different troop types had already been established and, in an empirical age, practitioners seeking knowledge beyond their own experience looked to the past as a basis for the theoretical understanding of warfare. It was paradoxical that the need for such understanding became all the greater just as technological change threw the relevance of the past and its lessons into doubt. The tactical systems of classical antiquity nonetheless played a shaping role in the tactical and broader military traditions of the western world. This role was well recognized by early modern commanders. Just as new hardware presaged a radical break with the military *longue durée* at the close of the Middle Ages, the study of classical precedents set forth in authorities such as the later Roman author Vegetius acquired a renewed importance in training. In this respect Europe's commanders advanced into modernity with their eyes trained firmly on the ancient world.

6.2.1. INFANTRY SYSTEMS

The ancient world provided two models for infantry-based tactical systems: the spear- or pike-armed phalanx, and the Roman legionary with shield and short-sword. Both of these models re-emerged in the later Middle Ages, after a lengthy period in which horse soldiers predominated, but they were joined by a newcomer which was the English tactical system based on the Anglo-Welsh longbow.

6.2.1.1. *The phalanx*

Ancient Sumerian inscriptions depict armoured spearmen manoeuvring in close-packed columns, but this style of fighting evidently disappeared from the region in later centuries (O'Connell 1989: 35–8). Its documented history begins with the

---

[13] Horses, as animals with a survival instinct, are unwilling to collide with a solid object at speed, or to risk impaling themselves on a line of sharp objects. Hence, for all their physical and psychological shock power, heavy cavalry could not usually break a line of steady, adequately equipped foot soldiers, and a frontal charge would result in a close-quarters mêlée in which the balance of advantage would depend on the arms and equipment of the two sides and could well lie with the infantry.

Greeks, who were the first historical Europeans to develop a regionally hegemonic military system. Literary and archaeological evidence agrees in depicting an earlier Bronze Age system based on warrior nobles who travelled in chariots, dismounting to fight on foot with spears and armour protection (O'Connell 1989: 45–50). In this respect the Greeks resembled other contemporary peoples of Indo-European origin, or those influenced by them, across Eurasia. By the time of the Persian wars, however, Greece had developed a way of fighting, based on the 'hoplite' or heavy infantryman, which was as distinctive as its way of conducting politics (Hanson 1991; Rich and Shippey 1993). Hoplite equipment—helmet, armoured corselet, round shield or *hoplon*, and a thrusting spear some 6 feet long—was a recognizable development of its Bronze Age predecessors, but hoplite tactics represented a radical break with the individualist fighting style of the Homeric heroes.

The hoplite spear was a heavy, clumsy weapon which was of limited value in individual combat or in a loose mêlée against opponents armed with shorter weapons able to get inside its range. Its bearers therefore fought in a closely packed formation, the 'phalanx', some eight to twelve ranks deep. In this formation the hoplite was protected by both his own armour and his right-hand neighbour's overlapping shield, but the phalanx's main protection was the unbroken line of spear points it presented towards its front which kept cavalry, or infantry armed with shorter weapons, out of striking distance. Despite these defensive strengths, however, the tactical function of the phalanx was primarily offensive, because the Greek city states developed a system of drill that allowed a block of spearmen to advance and manoeuvre as a unit without losing their formation (Hanson 1991). The result was a force that proved itself virtually invulnerable to the lighter, less specialized Persian infantry when Greece was invaded at the end of the sixth century. The Persian main force was forced to withdraw, probably for logistical reasons, after the Greeks had sunk their fleet at Salamis Bay, but their occupation corps was crushingly defeated by a numerically inferior hoplite force at Plataea (Burn 1984).

After this debacle the Persians themselves came to rely increasingly on mercenary hoplites as the mainstay of their armed forces. This reliance, and the prevalence of conflict between the Greek states themselves, meant that hoplite actions of the fourth and fifth centuries BC were as often against other hoplites as anyone else. Tactics apparently consisted of forming up and advancing on the enemy, the one sophistication being the late innovation of the so-called 'oblique assault' by the Theban general Epaminondas (Adcock 1957: 14–28). This involved differentially weighting one, advanced, flank at the expense of the other which was held back (or 'refused') and enabled the Thebans to shatter the myth of Spartan invulnerability at the battles of Leuctra and Mantinea. Once the two bodies had closed with each other a pushing match ensued as each side pressed forwards with their shields. At this stage it is likely that fatal casualties were relatively rare, since hoplite armour left few vital areas vulnerable to a spear thrust. The main exposed target was a narrow area of throat, but to hit this an opposing hoplite had to raise his spear up and backwards, which the pressure of the enemy front rank made difficult to achieve without overbalancing (Anderson 1991).

The main casualties were sustained when one or other side gave way and the phalanx broke. Which one it was depended on the relative force exerted by the two formations, and so in part on their relative weight, but psychological factors were also of great importance. When panic hit a column, it broke from the rear ranks, and so the morale—and accordingly the combat effectiveness—of troops engaged at the front depended very much on their faith in the reliability of their comrades behind them whom they could not see. In this respect hoplite tactics embodied a basic contradiction. Their effectiveness depended entirely on that of the phalanx, and thus the cohesion of the mass, but the hoplite helmet effectively deafened and blinkered its wearer, rendering him an isolated individual aware of his comrades only through the physical contact of his neighbours and the pressure of the rear ranks. Hence everything depended on the vigour with which the rear ranks, who could themselves not see what was happening at the front, pressed forwards.[14] Mutual trust and confidence in the outcome were essential to success, and the development of the former, like the repeated drilling that enabled the formation to manoeuvre offensively, has been plausibly linked to participation in the political community of city states. Similarly, the Spartans' edge in this kind of fighting was partly due to superior specialization—the kind of training and experience acquired by those whose lives are dedicated to fighting—rather than to tactical finesse or superior generalship, but was doubtless also influenced by their reputation for invincibility. It is likely that many contests began with the Spartans' opponents half believing themselves already beaten and exerting a faltering pressure, at best, in support of their front rank (Lazenby 1991).

This tactical rigidity reflected the limitations of the spear as a weapon and the inflexible nature of the formation based on it. To retain cohesion the phalanx was condemned to manoeuvre in a single block, which impeded the development of a lower-level unit organization. Such organization as existed on this scale seems to have comprised a series of files each with a front-rank leader, together with a sub-commander who took the rear position, since it was from there that panic spread and the phalanx was likely to break. Unable to manoeuvre in effective sub-units, the fighting ability of the phalanx deteriorated rapidly once its cohesion was shaken, and it had little chance of recovery under these circumstances. This limited its effective operations to open territory but also made it vulnerable to missile-armed light troops who could harass the phalanx from a safe distance, and to flank attacks by more mobile troops especially on its right—shieldless—side. To counter this, light infantry—known from their shields as *peltasts*—appeared in increasing numbers from the mid-fifth century BC onwards. These troops acted as skirmishers, disrupting the enemy line whilst

---

[14] This, at least, is the orthodox view. Goldsworthy dissents, believing that the rear-rankers' role was essentially the passive one of blocking flight from the front line, but he also accepts the central role of collective psychology in hoplite warfare (Goldsworthy 1997).

screening their own, and operated in broken or wooded terrain,[15] but even when supported in this way hoplite armies had a very limited ability to pursue a beaten enemy, scout ahead of a marching column, or forage. Hence later fifth- and fourth-century Greek armies began to feature cavalry in increasing numbers. The increase in the cavalry component of Greek armies may also have led to an increase in casualties since a broken army could now be pursued to a degree impossible for a force of heavy infantry weighed down by their equipment and exhausted by battle.

The Greek system, and the methods of Epaminondas, were further developed in Macedonia by King Philip II, who built the force that his son Alexander led to the conquest of the Persian Empire and eastern neighbours.[16] The basis of the Macedonian system was a new degree of co-ordination between the phalanx and the heavy cavalry which now assumed the principal offensive role on the battlefield. The soldiers of the phalanx itself were further specialized with the adoption of the *sarissa*, a pike some 12 to 13 feet long, and a deeper formation of sixteen ranks. Situated on the right of the line, their function was to pin the enemy's front whilst the 'companions', the right-flank heavy cavalry, delivered the decisive blow. This refinement of the Theban oblique order massed a devastating weight against the enemy's left but ran the risk of a counter-envelopment on the Macedonians' own left flank or a loss of contact between the different elements of their army. Guarding against this required a further range of specialized, lighter cavalry and infantry units to cover the flank that was held back from contact with the enemy. The vulnerable junction between phalanx and heavy cavalry was secured by an elite corps, the *hyspaspes* or 'shield bearers', who were also used for special missions away from set-piece battles (Milns 1971).

The close-order pike formation was eventually displaced by the very different system of the Roman middle Republic, but was revived in the closing centuries of the 'pre-gunpowder' era. Flemish urban militias used pike columns to defeat French heavy cavalry at the battle of Courtrai in 1302 but this first stage in the 'renaissance of infantry' was short-lived, and the outcome was mainly due to the unsuitability of the terrain to heavy cavalry (DeVries 1992). Unsupported in open terrain, the Flemish column displayed all the heavy infantrymen's vulnerability and the verdict of Courtrai was reversed by mounted French chivalry at Mons-en-Pevele and Cassel. Finally the Flemings suffered a crushing defeat at Roosebeke, where their column was enveloped by a flanking cavalry charge whilst frontally engaged by the main body of French men-at-arms fighting on foot. It

---

[15] For a discussion of later Greek tactical developments see Adcock (1957: 14–28). The vulnerability of unsupported hoplites in the latter circumstances was demonstrated at Sphacteria where a force of 120 hoplites surrendered to Athenian peltasts, and although of small scale the psychological shock caused by the debacle was evidently substantial and contributed to the suspension of hostilities at the Peace of Nikias (Kagan 1974).

[16] For an account of Philip's army see *inter alia* Hammond and Griffith (1979: 405–49), Hammond (1989: 100–19), and Hammond (1989: 119–36) for a review of its performance under Alexander. Lane Fox (1974) provides a detailed account of the Alexandrian conquests themselves.

was the infantry of the Swiss communes who found the means to counter this threat and used the pike column to establish a regional military pre-eminence following their victories over Burgundian heavy cavalry (Oman 1991: 233 f.). Like their Greek and Macedonian predecessors, the success of the Swiss lay in their development of a tactical drill which enabled the pike column to attack at considerable speed whilst maintaining its cohesion. The flanks of the columns were covered by an echelon formation supported by light troops using missile weapons that included firearms when these became available.

The spear or pike phalanx enabled the Greeks first to defeat and then to destroy their Persian adversaries, and to establish their rule as far away as northern India and Afghanistan. In the late Middle Ages the Swiss were able to establish their independence and then go on to terrorize their neighbours using a very similar tactical system. Nonetheless, the system failed to establish a global hegemony. This was partly due to its inherent tactical weaknesses. As long as the phalanx retained its close-packed order and was screened in flank and rear by cavalry or light troops, it was essentially invulnerable. Once its ranks were disrupted, or its flanking troops driven off, the inherent clumsiness of the formation and the weapon on which it depended made it very vulnerable to troops in more manoeuvrable formations better armed for close-in fighting. Alexander's victories were based on his ability to co-ordinate the movements of the phalanx with those of several different varieties of cavalry and light troops, but this seems to have been too much for his successors.

The later Macedonian (or 'Hellenistic') rulers neglected light troops and combined arms tactics (Tarn 1930; Bar-Kochva 1976). They relied increasingly on the phalanx as the principal offensive arm and this became correspondingly heavier and more inflexible in order to accomplish its task of breaking the enemy line. In a process of 'super-specialization' the *sarissa* was lengthened to 21 feet so that the weapons of all of the first five ranks projected forward, with the files being more closely packed. The result was lethal under ideal conditions but its vulnerability to disruption or flanking attacks led to a series of crushing defeats at the hands of the Romans.[17] In a similar fashion, the medieval pike column proved itself against heavy cavalry but was much less effective against other infantry armed with shorter weapons such as the halberd. The Swiss themselves had originally relied on this weapon but they had abandoned it after its reach proved inadequate to hold off cavalry attacks. However when an army of Scots pikemen encountered a numerically inferior English force equipped with the 'old-fashioned' halberd at Flodden the greater manoeuvrability of the shorter weapon gave its users a crushing victory (Oman 1987: 314–15). Subsequently, the Swiss pikemen and their imitators proved vulnerable to Spanish infantry using short-swords and shields on the Roman model (Oman 1987: 314–15, 52–6).

---

[17] The Hellenistic phalanx might have had little trouble beating the Romans on flat ground flanked by powerful, well-led cavalry, but as Tarn pithily commented, 'a formation which can only fight under special conditions has ceased to be of much use' (Tarn 1930: 29).

This tactical weakness apart, the system's diffusion was also restricted by inherent characteristics which rendered it in some respects an ethnic technology. Endless drill was required if a pike column was to manoeuvre effectively without losing cohesion, and this was only possible in particular social and political contexts. Furthermore, the phalanx required strong bonds of mutual trust and commitment among its members if it was to be an effective fighting formation. As mentioned above, bonds of this kind were arguably fostered by the egalitarian, participatory style of the Greek political community and were much more difficult to obtain under other circumstances.[18] Phalanx fighting also favoured the development of certain cultural attitudes. As Ferrill puts it, the phalanx was 'more than a tactical formation. It represented a way of life, a code of manliness and morality that was much more deeply engrained in Greeks than in most military societies' (Ferrill 1985). The result was evidently a degree of military conservatism that led to tactical rigidity and a mistrust of styles of fighting, such as archery, which ran against the code. In the later period the Swiss too owed much of their success to sociological factors. The bonds of mutual trust holding their formations together reflected the broader social cohesion fostered by a communal mode of recruitment and based on the particularistic loyalties of kinship and neighbourhood. The system was imitated elsewhere, for instance, by the Scots, as just referred to, and particularly by the German *Landsknecht*. Nonetheless at its most effective it remained a Swiss ethnic technology. Their imitators who came together as adult strangers never achieved quite the same degree of success, and it was not until the sixteenth century that the German *Landsknechts* achieved a major victory against their Swiss models.[19]

6.2.1.2. *The legion*

The Romans established and consolidated their empire using armies built around the heavy infantry legion, which was organized on two successive models. It was the 'manipular' legions of the middle Republic that exploited the rigidity of the Hellenistic system to devastating effect (Keppie 1984). Composed of independent sub-units, or 'maniples', these legions possessed the flexibility and manoeuvrabil-

---

[18] The socio-political bases of Greek hoplite tactics were stressed by Wintringham (Wintringham and Blashford-Snell 1973: 43–4) whilst Oman noted the importance of peer-group solidarity in maintaining discipline among the Swiss (Oman 1987: 71). O'Connell makes similar observations concerning ancient Sumeria (O'Connell 1989: 35–7). Formation tactics of this kind may indeed depend on a certain type of political community, but it would be wrong to romanticize their relationship to 'freedom' as a political ideal—both the Swiss and the Greeks were very effective, and ruthless, mercenaries.

[19] Showalter stresses the important edge given to Swiss infantry units by their communal mode of recruitment: 'the Swiss male, socialised in a structure that enforced compulsory military service from 16 to 60, bound to canton and captain by a network of community-sanctioned oaths, found warfare a ready and acceptable rite of passage into adulthood', whereas a *Landsknecht* company 'was no more than an aggregation of more or less belligerent individuals' in flight from the restrictions of civilian life (Showalter 1993: 425–6). The establishment of regiments as foci of loyalty and units of secondary socialization made up, in the author's view, for some of this lack of intrinsic cohesion.

ity that the phalanx lacked. Each of the thirty maniples numbered 120 to 160 men and was able to fight either as an individual unit or else grouped in close order with the rest of the legion. They were composed of three lines, the *hastati*, *principes*, and *triarii*, together with a screen of light troops, the *velites*. The *triarii* retained the older thrusting spear whilst the first two lines relied on a combination of sword and the heavy Roman throwing spear or *pilum*. The looser formation of the manipular legion allowed the front rank to be relieved at intervals by replacements from the rear (Adcock 1940), and their more flexible organization and close-in weaponry gave the legionaries an overwhelming advantage once the cohesion of the phalanx had been broken.[20]

The manipular legion nonetheless had its weaknesses. One of these, generic to heavy infantry formations, was the vulnerability of the flanks to envelopment by a more mobile enemy. This weakness was exploited to catastrophic effect by the Carthaginian general Hannibal, whose double envelopment of a Roman army at Cannae continued into the twentieth century as the tactical model of this kind of manoeuvre. The only way to counter this was to position a strong guard of cavalry and light troops on each flank. In the early days of the legionary system the legions themselves had included some cavalry troops of this kind, but from the middle Republic onwards the Roman citizen force was largely confined to heavy infantry who relied on allied or subject peoples for the necessary supporting troops.[21]

A second weakness was specific to the manipular formation and represented the obverse of its strength against the phalanx. The formation's very flexibility, based on the arrangement of maniples in a 'chequerboard' formation, exposed it to the risk of being swamped by a looser body of fighters at the charge. This occurred when the legions encountered the barbarian warriors of northern Europe, who relied on the shock of their initial charge, often in a wedge-shaped formation, to break the enemy line before the battle dissolved into a freewheeling mêlée. If this happened, the risk was that the maniples were too small to cope alone, and too widely spaced to help each other. In the century following Rome's victory over Carthage her forces suffered some disastrous reverses at the hands of armies of this kind, and it is likely that the manipular organization was partly to blame. At any rate, as part of a wider programme of military reform, the populist consul Marius suppressed the *velites* and regrouped the maniples into permanent close-order cohorts which were now uniformly armed with the *gladius* and *pilum*.[22] The stabbing power of the *gladius* allowed the legionaries to deploy in a much closer formation than was possible for their Celtic opponents with their

---

[20] This was demonstrated, above all, at the battle of Cynocephelae where the Romans gained victory by peeling off maniples from one wing of their army and launching them at the rear of the phalanx still engaged with the other wing (Keppie 1984: 52–3).

[21] Roman cavalry was originally supplied by the members of the 'middle class' who kept the title of 'equestrians' long after it had ceased to mean anything in practical terms. The cohort legions retained an integral cavalry troop but their role seems to have been one of scouting and dispatch riding rather than battlefield combat (Dixon and Southern 1992: 27–30).

[22] The timing of this reorganization suggests that it was at least partly due to the military crises precipitated by the migration of the Cimbri and Teutones at the end of the 2nd century BC (Todd 1992:

two-handed slashing swords. This is likely to have given the Romans a considerable tactical advantage in sustained fighting, but the close-in style of fighting it imposed also required a high degree of armoured protection by making it much more difficult to avoid enemy blows. This heavy equipment limited their tactical employment and made them more reliant on lightly armed screening troops and cavalry. When Augustus reorganized the army around a core of permanent long-service legions at the end of the civil war he therefore established a regular cavalry and light infantry arm—the *auxilia*—whose numbers appear to have roughly matched those of the legions themselves. Both echelons were stationed in permanent bases close to the frontier.

The cohort legions were effective against northern barbarians in open country, with adequate support from the *auxilia*.[23] Unsupported, or in close country, they remained vulnerable. One manifestation of this was the massacre of Varus' army in the Teutoburger Wald at the hand of Arminius' German tribesmen in AD 9 (Wells 1972; Dyson 1970; Cunliffe 1988: 171–3). In the east, the legions' performance against Iranian cavalry was uneven. The Romans suffered a disastrous defeat at Carrhae in 53 BC, but thereafter the eastern frontier was maintained intact for a substantial period and even advanced at times (Goldsworthy 1996: 61–8; Isaac 1992). Nonetheless, the Augustan system eventually failed to maintain the security of the Empire's borders. A near fatal run of crises in the third century precipitated extensive changes under Diocletian and his successors.

The immediate military problem seems to have been one of strategic mobility, with the frontier legions being simply too cumbersome to meet threats that could now develop very quickly at a series of mutually distant locations. An early response to this problem was the formation of so-called *vexillationes*, which were ad hoc detachments from one or more legions deployed rapidly from quiet areas towards trouble-spots. The post-crisis solution was the division of

---

47–8). This is not, however, the only explanation, and it has its difficulties, as Keppie points out. Rome had already fought invading Gauls, and it was this encounter that led to the adoption of the manipular legion in place of the original phalanx-based model (Keppie 1984). Keppie suggests that the reforms sprang from the fact that the state was now providing equipment at its own expense, which enabled poorer citizens to serve as heavy infantry rather than skirmishers. This would explain the suppression of the *velites* but its relation to the other reforms is less clear. The solution may be a form of path dependency in which the failure of the rigid close-order phalanx led first to the adoption of an open-order system. When this proved inadequate an intermediate solution was adopted. In other words, the cohort was a compromise requiring prior experience of both phalanx and maniple. Alternatively, it has been argued that the cohort organization was just an intrinsically superior system—allowing greater manoeuvrability and tactical flexibility (Goldsworthy 1996)—or an intrinsically inferior system that was forced on the Romans as increasing manpower demands led to a widening of the recruitment net and a decline in troop quality (Dupuy 1984). Given the dearth of evidence, any of these explanations, and doubtless many more, must remain possibilities. The situation is complicated by the fact that the 'reforms' may merely have formalized an already-existing state of affairs since the cohort had already emerged as an ad hoc tactical grouping, just as the maniple apparently continued to exist as a shadowy administrative entity.

[23] There is an extensive literature on the Roman army of this period. For general surveys see *inter alia* Goldsworthy (1996), Le Bohec (1994), Grant (1974), Webster (1985), and the relevant chapters of the *Cambridge Ancient History*.

the whole army into two echelons: a static frontier force, or *limitanei*, and mobile field armies composed of units of *comitatenses*. Under Diocletian there may already have been a permanent field army directly under his personal command,[24] but such a force certainly existed under Constantine. Subsequent events fostered the establishment of a further tier of regional field armies alongside those under the emperors' direct command, and the numbers of *comitatenses* increased in both relative and absolute terms.[25]

The legions of the new field armies were apparently much smaller than the old model, and their tactics and equipment seem to have converged on those of the *auxilia*, a title now borne by a number of elite units. The most distinctive feature, however, of the *comitatenses* was their growing proportion of cavalry. The future Emperor Julian won the battle of Strasbourg, one of very few later Roman battles for which a detailed account survives, with an old-style heavy infantry assault, but the tactical offensive role of Roman infantry seems to have declined subsequently, and especially so after the eastern army was crushingly defeated by Goths at Adrianople. Less armour was worn, and longer-range weapons such as spears and the *spatha* were adopted, which suggests a reduction in the amount of aggressive close-in fighting. After Adrianople the Western Empire, in particular, began to rely increasingly on German troops serving under their own leaders and on the settlement of autonomous communities along the frontier. The *limitanei* nonetheless continued, for some time at least, to constitute a regular, full-time military echelon of sufficiently high quality for units to be upgraded to the mobile armies with the title *pseudo-comitatenses*. However, their static role and remote locations made them tempting targets for cash-strapped governments looking to cut costs, and Justinian eventually reduced them to an unpaid militia role. The main brunt of Byzantine campaigning was borne by heavy cavalry units comprising both lancers and archers, first under the old *comitatenses* organization and then, following the Arab conquests, under the territorial establishment of the *themata* (Haldon 1999; Treadgold 1995).

6.2.1.3. *The longbow*

Archery played an important part in some of the military systems of the ancient Near East.[26] Both the Assyrians and the Persians employed archers on foot,

---

[24] What evidence there is now seems to be against this once widely held view. The main question is whether the term *comitatus* in Diocletianic inscriptions carries its older meaning of a large bodyguard or its later one of a small army (Southern and Dixon 1996: 15–17). Since twenty-two of Diocletian's twenty-four immediate predecessors died violently the Emperor himself might not have grasped the distinction.

[25] The evidence for the later Roman army is scantier than that for the Principate's, but a number of recent studies have begun to remedy historians' neglect of the topic. See Southern and Dixon (1996), Elton (1996), Tomlin (1987), Whitby (2000), and Lee (1998).

[26] For a general review of archery in war see Heath (1980). Roman practice is discussed by Goldsworthy (1996: 183–90). The literature on the English bows and bowmanship is extensive; see *inter alia* Hardy (1994), Bradbury (1992). For the crossbow see Alm (1994) and DeVries (1992: 39–44).

teamed with shield bearers and other heavier defensive troops, but the bow, like other missile weapons, played only a supporting role at most in Greek and Roman armies. Some at least of the Romans' German adversaries made very effective use of archery, and the Vikings also employed the bow extensively. Elsewhere in Europe its early medieval role is obscure and in England it seems to have dropped out of use.[27] This was partly due to the prevalence of cultural codes that stressed the importance of close-contact fighting with all its dangers and which disparaged weapons that could be used from a safe distance. The range and penetrating power of most contemporary missile weapons were also too restricted to confer much military value against mailed troops. This changed in the later Middle Ages. As weapons, crossbows were powerful enough to pose a major threat to armoured cavalry, but their rate of fire was too low for them to dominate the battlefield.

The longbow was less powerful than the developed form of the crossbow, but it made up for this with a much higher rate of fire. The credit for introducing the weapon to England on a large scale is conventionally given to Edward I, whose troops had an early version used against them during their conquest of Wales. Operationally, longbowmen formed a much larger proportion of the total force than was the case with bow-armed troops in other European armies, but they could not fight on their own. They needed the co-ordinated support of a substantial number of medium infantry, the so-called 'foot sergeants' equipped with spears or pole arms, to prevent their being overrun by enemy cavalry or other shock troops, and an echelon of mounted men-at-arms to exploit the damage they wrought to the enemy ranks. Although Anglo-Welsh archers and foot sergeants fought as infantry, from the later fourteenth century it became common for them to be furnished with horses for use on the march.

The English longbow could pierce chain mail but its principal value was against horses.[28] The effect was both physical and psychological and persisted even when the animals themselves were armoured. Cavalry forces faced with substantial bodies of longbowmen learned to counter this by dismounting to fight on foot. They did so, however, at a serious disadvantage, and the combination of archers supported by foot sergeants and men-at-arms brought the English a series of victories against numerically superior French forces in the wars of the fourteenth and fifteenth centuries. The longbow's power was nonetheless bought at a price. All of the lethal kinetic energy concentrated in the arrow's point came from the archer's muscles, and using the longbow effectively required long and constant practice to develop the skill and the strength. In England archery practice was a

[27] The Normans evidently retained their Viking ancestors' interest in the bow, which played a major role at Hastings—although the story of Harold's death from an arrow wound may be a later invention. There is no evidence for English archery in the battle on any substantial scale. An arrow had earlier dispatched the Norse King Harald Bluetooth at Stamford Bridge, but this is thought to have been fired from a hunting weapon borne by one of the local levy (Hardy 1994: 31–4).

[28] The devastating overall impact of massed longbow fire is graphically depicted in Keegan's account of the battle of Agincourt, but the relative importance of the psychological and material damage it inflicted remains controversial (Rogers 1998; Keegan 1976: 78–116; DeVries 1997).

legal obligation, but continental nobilities seem to have been less willing to place a weapon so lethal to armoured horsemen in the hands of commoners (Rogers 1993: 51), whilst their own code of chivalry proscribed the use of such a distance weapon as dishonourable. English archers and Swiss pikemen were both in demand as mercenaries, but, even more than the Swiss pike, the longbow was an ethnic technology over which the English forces retained an effective monopoly.[29]

6.2.2. CAVALRY SYSTEMS

From an early point in the development of Eurasian military specializations a basic divergence occurred between the methods employed in the cultivated regions and in the steppes. This reflected the underlying differences in the economy and general way of life of the two regions. In the steppe zone, horses assumed a central role in warfare and were ridden on the battlefield from around the beginning of the first millennium BC (Christian 1998: 123 f.). In the agricultural zone, infantry warfare was much more important than it was on the steppe, and foot soldiers formed the mainstay of entire military systems. Horses were nonetheless important in this zone too. They served as draught animals, along with mules and oxen, and as a source of mobility for combat troops such as mounted infantry and chariot fighters. The repeated incursions of steppe nomads into the settled lands around their borders meant that agricultural peoples also learned the value of horses as fighting platforms on the battlefield. Cavalry fighting therefore spread to the agricultural zone, particularly in the region of the steppe frontier. The costly nature of horses and of the equipment and training needed to use them effectively on the battlefield meant that in most cases cavalry troops were either adjuncts to the military system or, where they acted as its mainstay, drawn from the elite strata of the society concerned. The period saw two cavalry-based systems rise to a position of regional hegemony. One of these, based on the mobile firepower of the mounted archer, remained confined to the steppe and its borderlands. The steppe was also the cradle of 'shock' cavalry.

6.2.2.1. *The mounted bowman*

The pastoral nomads of the Eurasian steppe posed a recurrent military threat to agricultural societies near, and sometimes far beyond, its frontiers until the gunpowder era.[30] The nomads' military effectiveness rested on their skills in horsemanship and their ability to apply these skills to warfare. They taught the rulers of agrarian states the importance of horseback fighting, although only one

---

[29] By the later 15th century the French monarchy was taking steps to develop an indigenous force of archers, and French longbowmen participated in the closing stages of the Hundred Years War without, however, matching their English enemies in either quality or quantity (Hardy 1994: 124–5).

[30] The pastoralists' threat also reflected the flexibility of their social and political structure. This allowed defeated opponents and others to be readily absorbed into aggressive coalitions, a factor whose importance was recognized by Gibbon; see Ardener (1974: 29–30).

of their two basic cavalry types came to be copied. This was the heavy, shock form, employing lance and armour protection, which seems to have developed first among the Iranian-speaking Sarmatians on the western steppe (Phillips 1965). Lacking stirrups and other 'shock-absorbing' tackle, the heavy cavalrymen of this period used their lances as thrusting weapons. This may have reduced their value as shock troops, but the model was sufficiently effective to be copied elsewhere. Heavy cavalry of this type, the so-called 'cataphract', became the basis of the Persian military system and assumed increasing importance in the later Roman and Byzantine armies (Coulston 1986).

The appearance of the stirrup, probably brought to Europe by the Avars in the sixth century, together with other developments in horse furniture, eventually enabled western Europeans to outperform the nomads and their imitators at shock combat (see DeVries 1992: 95–110 for a review of the controversy on this question). But they were unable to match the second of the two nomad cavalry types. This was the light horse-archer who, supported by armoured lancers, formed the predominant element in the armies of many of the nomad confederations.[31] The mounted archers' compound bow may not, in itself, have posed a great danger to armoured troops but its protracted harassing fire could wear them down, and disrupt their ranks so that they became vulnerable to a charge by the lancers. Moreover, such tactics, particularly when used in conjunction with the tactic of feigned retreat, could provoke all but the most disciplined troops to break ranks and thus fall victim to the light cavalry's ability to rally and counter-charge as well as to the weight of the supporting lancers.

At Carrhae in 53 BC a Parthian army of some 10,000 mounted archers with a small force of lancers destroyed a Roman army four times its size, and they were the one type of force that the armies of the Principate could not be reasonably sure of beating in open-field battle.[32] Mounted archers were, however, vulnerable in two respects. They could be ridden down by heavier cavalry, and their relatively short bows could be outranged by longer infantry weapons. The first of these factors brought the First Crusade its victory at Dorylaeum when one of their columns caught the Turkish horsemen in the flank. This success, however, owed more to luck than good planning, and the Turks soon learned to avoid the Frankish charge. The Third Crusade used the power of the infantry bowman to good effect when it was co-ordinated with foot sergeants and men-at-arms (Bennett 2001), but the forces of feudal Europe found it difficult to maintain either the discipline or organization needed to realize the potential of this style of

---

[31] The horse-archer was the most familiar, and feared, manifestation of nomad military power for medieval Europeans. The relative preponderance of light and heavy cavalry in steppe armies may have varied with the degree of socio-political structure of the entities they served, with the heavier types being characteristic of formations dominated by a semi-sedentary aristocracy (see Christian 1998: 148).

[32] The victory at Carrhae owed much to the logistical organization established by their commander Surenas. This ensured a continuing supply of arrows, of which they are likely to have expended at least 1.5 million (Heath 1980: 42–4). Surenas' abilities were not, however, matched by those of his successors, and the potential Parthian threat to Rome remained unrealized in practice.

fighting. The thirteenth-century Mongol armies comprehensively routed the armies of eastern and central Europe, and had the Mongols not abruptly withdrawn to the steppe it is doubtful if anything but pasture shortages could have saved western Europe from the same fate (Chambers 1988; Christian 1998: 409–11; Oman 1991: 305–35). For all its success, however, the technology of the light horse-archer demanded a degree of horsemanship attainable only through a life spent in the saddle hunting or herding. It remained an ethnic technology effectively confined to the steppe and the areas immediately adjoining it.

6.2.2.2. *The man-at-arms*

The traditional role of heavy cavalry on the battlefield was one of shock troops capable of dealing a devastating blow to the flanks of an enemy formation, or to an army whose ranks had already become disrupted. This role was played to great effect by the heavy cavalry of Alexander and his successors and by the armoured cataphracts of Byzantium and Sassanid Persia. Like their Sarmatian models, however, the effectiveness of these troops was restricted by the limitations of their equipment, and they could use the lance only as a thrusting weapon. This ceased to be true some time in the early medieval centuries when a series of technical innovations appeared including spurs, stirrups, and the high saddle, which allowed the rider to absorb a violent physical shock whilst remaining upright in the saddle. The precise timing of these innovations and the relative contribution of the different elements remain controversial, but there is no doubt that by the middle of the tenth century the ensemble was in place and that it allowed the rider to charge with his lance in the 'couched' position.

This couched position concentrated the entire kinetic energy of charging horse, rider, and armour in the point of the lance itself and yielded a step increase in the potential effectiveness of shock tactics. The resulting impact if the charge struck home was lethal to the target, and probably to the lance as well. The 'man-at-arms', as the new-style horseman came to be called, therefore needed a sword as secondary armament, and some kind of armoured protection for the close-in fighting which would follow.[33] This style of fighting spread across western Europe in the early Middle Ages but the chronology of the process, like that of the underlying technical innovations, is obscure. The tribes who overran northern Gaul, the Franks and Alamanni, fought as foot soldiers, as did most of their Germanic contemporaries. The Gothic nobility, however, had already adopted cavalry fighting by the time they crossed the Danube, and their triumph at Adrianople opened an era of cavalry domination in the Eastern Empire. The key development in the west was the adoption of heavy cavalry by the Franks. Precisely when this occurred and under what circumstances remains

---

[33] 'Man-at-arms' is the conventional generic term for medieval armoured heavy cavalry but is sometimes also used in a narrower sense to distinguish men of less than knightly status from their better-equipped superiors (Prestwich 1996: 12 f.).

controversial, but from Charlemagne's reign at the latest the Frankish elite were required to perform their military service on horseback, and later attempts were made to broaden the social basis of this obligation.

This style of fighting dominated the tactical systems of Charlemagne's successors, and the Frankish model was adopted elsewhere in Latin Christendom, notably by the Scandinavian settlers in Normandy. With time, and particularly from the twelfth century, horse and equipment became heavier as the extent of armoured protection grew. Thus emerged the 'knight in armour', the popular icon of the Middle Ages and all that that term stands for. This iconic status has almost certainly contributed to the fierce divergence of views over the effectiveness of armoured horsemen in the wars of the period, a divergence that makes it all the more important to emphasize both their military predominance and their limitations. The man-at-arms' shock role predominated on the battlefield. He could ride down the lighter, less specialized lancers of the Greek and Islamic worlds and sweep away bodies of foot soldiers if they were disrupted, poorly ordered, or outflanked. Off the battlefield, cavalry was essential for effective reconnaissance, screening, and the pursuit of a beaten enemy. The long-distance strategic mobility of cavalry was not necessarily much greater than that of well-trained and disciplined infantry, but cavalry possessed the ability to travel faster and further over a short period and hence was much more effective at launching or parrying small-scale raids.

Nonetheless, the man-at-arms was far from omnipotent, and the limitations of the military technology he embodied were as important as its potential. If the latter was to be fully realized the man-at-arms could not fight unsupported, and few 'cavalry armies' of the period consisted entirely of horsemen, any more than Second World War Panzer armies consisted entirely of tanks. Heavy cavalry tactics were most effective when the enemy line could be hit with a repeated series of shocks, but horses tire rapidly, and so achieving this result required successive mounted echelons who were best shielded by bodies of infantry whilst recuperating, re-forming, or standing in reserve. Men-at-arms also required attendants to care for their horses and stand ready with replacements, and these may sometimes have equalled the numbers of cavalrymen themselves. Mounted troops were also of little use in securing encampments, in assaults on fortified positions, or in the defence of siege lines. These were cavalry armies in the sense that the cavalry determined both the potential and the limitations of the army as a whole, and the other arms existed to support it, even though men-at-arms themselves might be in a minority.

The limits of heavy cavalry's tactical predominance also need to be stressed, given the lingering influence of an older school of military history whose picture of medieval battlefields is easy to caricature. This was a picture so dominated by mounted men-at-arms that no other arm counted, such infantry as were present being a mere disorganized rabble brushed aside by the opposing cavalry if they had not already been ridden down by their own. In fact, as a number of recent writers have pointed out, this is a serious distortion of the actual relationship between the two arms.[34] Where heavy cavalry on the Frankish model encountered well-armed infantry capable of close-order fighting, such as the Saxons of Charlemagne's day or the Scandinavian raiders of later centuries, the resulting battles were generally very hard fought. There is a simple explanation for this. Unlike the armoured vehicles of the twentieth century, horses are animals, not machines, and are naturally unwilling to collide with hard objects at speed. It was very difficult for cavalry to charge straight into, and so disrupt, a body of suitably armed infantry as long as the latter kept their nerve and their formation, and, in a mêlée with formed infantry, cavalry horses made very vulnerable targets for any weapon with sufficient reach.

Steady infantry could thus generally withstand a frontal charge, and the close-order formation of the Germanic, or Scandinavian, shield wall was relatively secure against flank attack. However, hard fought though the victories gained by Frankish-style cavalry against such troops may have been, they were victories nonetheless, and the period offers very few instances of infantry defeating cavalry at any but the most favourable odds.[35] The reason for this was almost certainly the infantry's dependence on the maintenance of a close-order formation. As long as they did this they could usually hold their position and keep the opposing cavalry at bay, but this in itself was rarely enough to win a battle. Victory required aggressive manoeuvring, and the infantry of this period seem to have found it very difficult to manoeuvre whilst retaining the integrity of their formation. A cavalry force could exploit its mobility to obtain an overwhelming local superiority against the shield wall without the infantry being able to redeploy so as to relieve the threatened sector of their line. Above all, foot soldiers could not exploit a withdrawal by the cavalry, whether real or feigned, without exposing themselves to a potentially devastating counter-attack such as turned the tide at Hastings. Infantry could hold their own against men-at-arms as long as they remained in place, but until they learned to secure their flanks, and advance without losing formation, the decisive offensive role on the battlefield remained with the heavy cavalry.[36] The hegemony of the heavy cavalry was conditional on the kind of opposition they faced, but it was no less real for that.

---

[34] The supremacy of 'feudal' cavalry on pre-14th-century battlefields, asserted by authors including Oman and the German military historian Hans Delbrück early in the 20th century and long unquestioned, has been doubted by more recent authors such as Bachrach and DeVries. For a useful review see Rogers (1993).

[35] Heavy cavalry was most vulnerable, in otherwise favourable conditions, if it attacked undisrupted infantry in a piecemeal fashion without forming up. It seems to have been this that was responsible for the defeat of the Frankish cavalry by Saxon tribesmen at the Weser in 782 (Beeler 1971: 23–4).

[36] Bannockburn is a rare—pre-Swiss—example of a successful assault by a pike formation on heavy cavalry. In this instance the English force was disordered when the attack began and had difficulty deploying due to the confined terrain. At Bannockburn, as in other 'infantry victories' of the period, many of the casualties were actually inflicted by pursuing cavalry whose importance was out of all proportion to their numbers.

6.3. CONCLUSION

Military technology before the gunpowder era depended on the exploitation of human and animal muscle power. The great variety of edged and pointed weapons in use and the pattern of interlocking strengths and weaknesses displayed by their bearers prevented any single enduring hierarchy of superiority from emerging among tactical systems.[37] Like the choices in the 'scissors, paper, stone' game, the relationship between systems was non-transitive. No matter how effective they might be against the generality of opposition, each of them displayed some weakness that could be exploited by at least one other system or possessed features that prevented their being generally adopted. Systems of the latter kind remained ethnic technologies with corresponding constraints on the supply of skilled manpower. The problem of non-transitivity could, in principle, be overcome by intensifying the division of labour and deploying a more flexible combination of troop types capable of overcoming all opposition.

This solution was adopted by some of the most successful powers such as Macedon and Rome, and it underlay the Third Crusade's victory at Arsouf, but it was not cost free. As the variety of troop types fielded increased, so did the problems of co-ordination, with all the demands that this placed on the commanders' skill, and the attendant risk of collapse before a simpler, more robust system. Some systems established regional hegemonies in the sense that their bearers could be reasonably confident of overcoming any other system they habitually came up against unless the circumstances were extremely unfavourable.[38] But all powers, however successful, eventually found themselves bordering a people whom they could not be confident of defeating and with whom they had to coexist, or ran out of specialized troops, or else were overthrown by a power using a different system that could exploit some inherent weakness in their own. The prospect of a globally hegemonic system, a system capable of overcoming any opposition and spreading without limit through conquest or imitation, was unattainable before the emergence of firearms.

---

[37] A similar argument is advanced by O'Connell who sees a cyclical pattern in the succession of pre-gunpowder military technologies (O'Connell 1989: 105–6).

[38] If a power could establish a monopoly over a hegemonic system, as the Romans did, it would normally be guaranteed a corresponding political hegemony. Where a number of competing powers relied on what was essentially the same system, as in the Hellenistic world, the outcomes turned on factors such as leadership, relative numbers, or sheer luck.

CHAPTER SEVEN

The Gunpowder Revolution

The introduction of gunpowder to warfare represented the beginning of the large-scale exploitation of chemical energy by human societies. Gunpowder weapons were prominent offensive arms in all branches of warfare by the middle of the sixteenth century, and fifty years later they enjoyed a near monopoly of this role (Hall 1997; Childs 1982: 105–11; Chandler 1994; Tallett 1992: 21–31). The introduction of firearms to land warfare affected all three mobile arms but the infantry most of all, because it radically shifted the relative power of distance and shock weapons in a historically unprecedented manner. Hitherto distance weapons had rarely made a decisive contribution to victory, and where they had—in the hands of Anglo-Welsh longbowmen or the horsemen of Europe's steppe frontiers—they required so much skill and experience in their use as to make them effectively 'ethnic' weapons, as much symbols of a way of life as a means of fighting.

The appearance of effective handguns in the closing years of the fifteenth century changed this. Infantry formations acquired a potentially decisive firepower, but their intrinsic capabilities remained limited and a tactical combination of all arms was needed to achieve effective results on the battlefields. By the end of the seventeenth century this combination had taken shape with the emergence of the 'musket and sabre' tactical system, which was the first to establish a global hegemony. Once the system had emerged there were almost no changes in weaponry until well into the nineteenth century, probably because the scope for incremental refinements was very limited, whilst radical change offered the prospect of dangerous increases in the destructiveness and cost of war. Increases in army size were left as the one means by which powers could gain an advantage over their rivals, and they were facilitated by contemporary changes in military discipline and organization. The French Revolution led to further quantitative escalation, but military hardware remained almost unchanged until the 1840s, when the preconditions for technological stability broke down, leading to a continuing increase in the destructive power of weaponry.

7.1. THE GUNPOWDER BATTLEFIELD

In two centuries gunpowder altered the battlefield beyond recognition. New troop types, tactics, and organization hierarchies were introduced. Beyond this, the very experience of combat and, eventually, the nature of the 'military virtues' themselves were transformed. The introduction of firearms to the battlefield began a process of development that was both rapid and brutal but was predominantly incremental. No single innovation effected a decisive discontinuity, and some features of late medieval warfare changed slowly if at all,[1] but their cumulative impact marked a radical break with past experience. By the beginning of the eighteenth century a tactical system had come into being that was able to establish a global hegemony in a way that no other system had done before. Based on musketeer battalions numbering a few hundred to a thousand men, supported by cavalry squadrons and muzzle-loading smooth-bore artillery, its operation required tactical organization and discipline on a scale that also allowed much larger forces to be co-ordinated effectively on the battlefield. Once it had emerged, a period of remarkable technological conservatism ensued that lasted well into the nineteenth century.

7.1.1. INFANTRY

The arquebus was the first effective firearm that could readily be used by a foot soldier on the battlefield, and from the 1560s it was superseded by the heavier musket. These weapons, used *en masse*, gave foot soldiers the potential to devastate charging infantry formations, and inflict serious casualties on cavalrymen, before these attackers could bring shock weapons to bear. Early handguns were inferior to the longbow in their performance but needed little training or skill, a more than compensating advantage which enabled them to supersede archery in English military life. The weapons' performance had improved by the seventeenth century, but the basic limitations remained. Contemporary production technology could not make a breach-loading device strong enough to be used with safety, and muzzle-loading a rifled barrel was so difficult that the rate of fire was unacceptably low. Any militarily effective firearm therefore had to be a smooth-bore muzzle-loader firing a loosely fitting ball inaccurately and at relatively long intervals.

These limitations meant that handgunners were initially employed in an auxiliary role to screen the pikemen in their unwieldy square formations, but the relationship between the two arms was reversed by the end of the sixteenth century. The key to the new tactical system was the recognition that the destructive power of handguns, inaccurate and slow firing as they were, was greatly enhanced if larger numbers could be massed and a continuing fire maintained. In the 1590s the Dutch commanders Maurice and William Louis of Nassau developed a way of doing this. It was based on the manoeuvre known as the 'counter-march' whereby the front rank fired a synchronized volley and then retired to the rear, so clearing the way for the second and subsequent ranks to

---

[1] The concept of a 'military revolution' was introduced by Roberts (1995) and subjected to an influential reinterpretation by Parker (1988). For an introduction to the ensuing debate see the contributions to Rogers (1995).

repeat the procedure. The technique enabled troops massed in a ten-deep formation to maintain continuous series of volleys whose destructive force made accurate firing unnecessary (Parker 1988: 19–23; Tallett 1992: 21–8).

The musket's low rate of fire nonetheless remained a potential liability, aggravated by the frequency of misfires in wet weather. A musketeer might have only one chance to load and fire before charging infantry made contact, and cavalrymen who were willing to take casualties during their approach could 'ride down' unsupported arquebusiers or musketeers under favourable circumstances. This vulnerability meant that pikemen had to be used in a supporting role to protect the musketeers. The growing proficiency of the handgunners meant that their ranks could be progressively thinned and the ratio of pike to 'shot' reduced.[2] By the 1630s the Swedes were using a six-deep formation, and by the early eighteenth century—when the socket bayonet effectively abolished the distinction between infantry shock and missile weapons and banished the pike from the battlefield[3]—firing lines were thinned to only three, or even two, ranks.

The key to volley fire was co-ordinated action based on a choreographed sequence of movements, or 'drill', for loading and firing. The essence of drill was that the overall procedure was broken down into a series of stages, with a corresponding word of command for each stage, and set out in illustrated training manuals or drill-books, the first of which was published in 1607. Over time the procedure for loading and firing was simplified, so that by the early eighteenth century the initial forty-two steps had been reduced by almost half (Chandler 1994: 102–3). The initial function of drill may have been simply to prevent the men at the front of a formation from being shot by their rear-rank comrades, but it grew into something much more than this. From the original counter-march there developed a series of 'evolutions' or manoeuvres enabling bodies comprising tens or hundreds of men to deploy and change formation as one unit at a single word of command whilst under fire. The ability to manoeuvre units effectively on the battlefield enabled commanders to co-ordinate larger-scale formations numbering tens of thousands of men in a way that had not previously been possible, but it also had far-reaching implications for the nature of armed forces as organizations and for the lives of the men who served in them.

Sixteenth-century infantry training had consisted of a 'once for all' process, lasting a few weeks, during which the basics of weapons-handling were imparted. Deployment on the battlefield consisted largely of forming square under the

---

[2] This at least is the conventional explanation for the long-term fall in the proportion of pikemen, but Hall believes that the earlier 16th-century decline was due to the temporary displacement of heavy cavalry by pistol-armed *reiters* who posed less of a threat to infantry formations (Hall 1997: 199, 213).

[3] The pike was effectively obsolete by the 1720s but enjoyed a strange afterlife in the imagination of (mainly civilian) military commentators and administrators, particularly those of a republican persuasion. Benjamin Franklin urged its use by the American Continental Army, and in 1792 France's Legislative Assembly got as far as issuing its units with a 'National Pike'; in all cases experience (mainly soldiers') led to the weapon's rapid abandonment. Smaller members of the pole-arm family, such as the halberd, nonetheless proliferated on 18th-century battlefields where they were a convenient means of preventing infantrymen from leaving the firing line.

direction of a sergeant-major assisted by a set of square-root tables (Hall 1997: 186). Seventeenth- and eighteenth-century drill was a very different matter, consisting as it did of a mechanical sequence of movements taught by rote and inculcated by endless repetition. A period of initial training was required to achieve this inculcation, but trained soldiers also had to be kept up to the mark by a daily routine of parade-ground drill. A cadre of drill masters had to be established, and a hierarchy of sub-units with lower-level leaders—sergeants and corporals who were eventually classified as non-commissioned officers or 'NCOs'—was needed to ensure that the drill was properly carried out on the battlefield. At the same time military discipline began to take on a new meaning which was distinct from its older connotations of restraint and self-control in behaviour off the battlefield. In Lynn's words the new tactical system 'united training with discipline in the name of maximising the battlefield assets of manoeuvre and firepower by minutely regulating the actions of the troops... It was not enough to simply practice the practical, mechanical movements of musket loading or pike handling; these actions had to become so automatic and obedience so complete that troops performed their duties regardless of danger, that they suffered and endured without losing their effectiveness or resolution on the battlefield' (Lynn 1997: 525).

7.1.2. CAVALRY

Cavalry remained a force to be reckoned with long after the introduction of gunpowder, but the new weapons confronted them with particular problems.[4] Horsemen always presented larger targets than did foot soldiers, and early firearms were too big and heavy to be conveniently employed on horseback where their matchlock firing mechanism was in any case impracticable.[5] In response to this a range of heavy pistols and carbines—scaled-down versions of infantry weapons—was developed which used the wheel-lock mechanism, but they had a limited range and could not be discharged to any great effect whilst moving.[6] One solution to this problem was the introduction of mounted infantrymen—the 'dragoons' who rode into battle, dismounting to fight on foot—but true cavalry remained essential for the pursuit of a broken enemy and for overrunning disrupted infantry formations. The ancillary functions of screening, foraging, and reconnaissance also required cavalry.

---

[4] For brief surveys of early modern cavalry weapons and tactics see Tallett (1992: 28–31), Hall (1997: 190–200), Hale (1985: 53–6). Wood discusses 16th-century, and Lynn 17th-century, cavalry in French service (Wood 1996: 119–52; Lynn 1997: 489–500).

[5] The matchlock mechanism used a length of slow-burning cord saturated with saltpetre to ignite the charge and appeared around the middle of the 15th century. It was replaced by the familiar flintlock from the later 17th century onwards (Chandler 1994: 75–81; Hall 1997: 95–6).

[6] Wheel-lock pistols appeared in the early 16th century and were used in quantity from the 1540s. The mechanism used a spring-loaded iron disc which required precision engineering and was correspondingly expensive, although the weapons apparently became cheaper over time so that, by the end of the 16th century, they could be had for less than the price of a heavy musket (Hall 1997: 190–3).

A question mark nonetheless hung over the cavalry's future as the decisive shock arm. *Gendarmerie*—heavy cavalry of the late medieval type—persisted more or less unchanged into the later sixteenth century with the addition of pistols to their equipment, but they were joined by the *reiters*, a new medium cavalry type whose pistols were their primary armament. Increasingly *gendarme* and *reiter* converged as the former shed much of their heavy equipment and made greater use of firearms, so that by the beginning of the seventeenth century only Venice preserved an old-style *gendarmerie* (Hale 1985: 55–6). Cavalry tactics underwent a corresponding evolution with the introduction of the *caracole*. This was a kind of rolling pistol barrage delivered from close range and intended to disrupt infantry formations prior to contact. Employed first by the *reiters*, the *caracole* became the primary cavalry tactic by the early seventeenth century. In theory it was a rational and effective solution to the technical problems of using firearms on horseback, but it rarely worked well in practice, and by the middle of the seventeenth century cavalry shock tactics had been reintroduced under Swedish influence.

7.1.3. THE MUSKET AND SABRE SYSTEM

A new tactical system had emerged across much of Europe by the middle of the seventeenth century. It was based on infantry units of volley-firing musketeers protected by pikemen which were flanked by squadrons of sword-armed shock cavalry and supported by mobile field-artillery batteries. By the beginning of the eighteenth century the musket's matchlock firing mechanism had been replaced by the more efficient flintlock. This simplified musketeers' drill whilst the adoption of the socket bayonet let them manage without pikemen, but these were almost the only changes in the system before the end of the eighteenth century, and the only significant hardware innovations before the 1840s. Some of this stability reflected the 'hard' limits that organic economies imposed on ferrous metalworking, but in other cases innovations which were possible were either ignored or implemented very slowly.[7]

This lack of change occurred despite, or perhaps because of, the system's unprecedented success in defeating all the others with which its users came into conflict in or beyond Europe.[8] The French Revolutionary commanders intro-

---

[7] Radical changes in handgun design required the development of an effective breach-loading mechanism which was almost certainly beyond the capacities of 18th-century metallurgy. The introduction of percussion caps also awaited the discovery of fulminate of mercury at the beginning of the 19th century (O'Connell 1989: 191), although it might have been possible to manufacture hollow-based musket balls, and thereby transform the capabilities of muzzle-loaded rifles, before the 1840s. The most obvious instances of technological conservatism concern field artillery, where long delays occurred in the introduction of spherical powder chambers, which allowed substantial reductions in the guns' weight, and in the Swiss technique of precision barrel manufacture which made pieces both more efficient and easier to mass produce (Chandler 1994: 178–9; O'Connell 1989: 158–60).

[8] The main challenge to the musket and sabre system came from the clansmen of the Scottish Highlands whose tactics, a wild charge in wedge-shaped formation, would have been familiar to the legionaries of Caesar's day. They defeated British infantry on a number of occasions, but the latter's

duced some tactical innovations, including infantry shock columns and open-order skirmish formations, but these had little influence on other powers and were partly reversed by Napoleon (Rothenberg 1980: 61–71). Substantial innovation did, however, occur thereafter and was driven by changing hardware. The percussion cap ended the need for priming powder and so speeded up reloading and also ended the problem of misfires in wet weather. Introduced in the 1820s, it only came into use slowly, but the pace of change was revolutionized after 1840 with the invention of a reasonably effective breach-loading mechanism.

The Dreyse breach-loading 'needle gun' was secretly introduced into the Prussian army in 1840 although the army was not fully re-equipped until the 1860s. By then a solution had also been found to the problem of muzzle-loading a rifled barrel at an acceptable rate. The hollow-based Minié bullet could be milled to a substantially smaller diameter than the barrel because it expanded to block the escape of gas when fired. Minié rifled muskets, whose effective range was four times that of a smooth-bore, were introduced into the British army in time for the Crimean War, but the future lay with the breach-loader, whose users could more readily seek cover and load in a prone position. The new weapons' accuracy, range, and rate of fire, reinforced by the appearance of rapid-firing machine guns and explosive artillery shells, rendered old-style close-order fighting suicidal and forced infantry commanders to adopt the looser formation of the skirmish line. The European tactical system of 1914 was nonetheless the recognizable lineal descendant of the musket and sabre system of 1714.

7.2. MILITARY TECHNOLOGY: INNOVATION AND CONSERVATISM

The introduction of firearms represents a radical break in technological development of the kind which we termed in Chapter 3 a 'saltation'. It was not the first such discontinuity in the history of weapons and tactical organization, but it was the most profound and far-reaching in its implications. Military hardware and organization on land and sea were transformed, and the consequences stretched beyond the narrowly military sphere to the economic and financial foundations of the state. The pattern and rate of change in mobile warfare was nonetheless a very uneven one. The first century and a half of the gunpowder battlefield saw incremental refinements in weapons and tactical organization with relatively little change in organization at the higher levels. Once the musket and sabre system stabilized with the introduction of the flintlock and the socket bayonet, there was very little change in tactics and almost none in weaponry until after the fall of Napoleon. Paradoxically, major developments in weapons technology

disciplined fire control eventually proved their nemesis (Parker 1988: 35). Elsewhere in the world troops using the European musket and sabre system or its lineal successors suffered defeats due to factors such as inferior numbers, unfavourable terrain, or poor leadership, but they did not encounter an intrinsically superior tactical system before the 20th century (Black 1990: 55–62; Kiernan 1982: 32–6).

then occurred in a half-century of almost uninterrupted peace. The period of technological stasis nonetheless witnessed substantial growth in armies' numerical strength and organizational sophistication. These had important economic and political consequences, and if we are to understand why they occurred we have first to consider the uneven pace of change in weaponry and tactics.

7.2.1. INNOVATION

We saw earlier that biological metaphors sometimes provide a useful, if partial, insight into the processes underlying technological change. They can be applied in military as well as civilian contexts, but their application presents an additional complexity. The essence of Sewell Wright's 'landscape' model which we encountered in Chapter 3 is that every state of a given system, however we define it, is represented by a point on a surface defined by two dimensions X and Y and also has a 'height' given by its value on the third dimension Z. In Darwinian theory this Z value corresponds to the mean evolutionary 'fitness' of individuals with genetic constitution XY, given by the relative number of reproducing offspring they produce. It corresponds to the system's efficiency in the case of productive technology, and to the level of effectiveness in the military case, but there is an important difference between the way the Z values are determined in the two cases.

7.2.1.1. *Wright's model revisited*

Factors such as the spur of market competition or the desire to minimize effort move economic technology 'uphill' by increasing its efficiency in the same way that directional selection increases Darwinian fitness in biology, but the three-dimensional configuration of the economic landscape does not itself change unless there are substantial shifts in relative input prices. This is true neither of military technology nor, ironically, of the biological systems the model was designed to depict. Biological species have to adapt to environments that include all the other species they interact with as competitor, predator, or prey. It is this which creates the Red Queen problem in nature, because the evolution of one species changes the selective pressures on the others, thereby driving their evolution and altering the pressures acting on that one species. Predation, for instance, often favours the evolution of greater speed and agility on the part of prey species, forcing predators to become faster and more agile to regain their prior level of fitness, and so creating further pressure for speed and agility on the part of the prey. Phyletic evolution in these circumstances is not so much a matter of hill-climbing as of struggling to stay in place on a down escalator.

The 'fitness', or Z value, of military technology is defined in terms of its likely success which, like the success of a predator species, is always relative to the nature of the opposition against which it is matched, and there are many examples of the

Red Queen effect in the history of military technology. As in biological evolution, they result in directional development at a rate depending on the intensity of interactions with a qualitatively stable set of opponents, and often lead to long-term increases in size or weight of the kind that affected medieval heavy cavalry. The eleventh-century Frankish horsemen wore no more protection than many of their ancient predecessors whereas the fifteenth-century man-at-arms was encased in plate armour, a development apparently due to the intervening encounters with increasingly effective missile weapons. The introduction of gunpowder naval artillery ushered in a period of several centuries in which the wooden, sail-powered, man of war became progressively larger, more powerful, and more clearly differentiated from civilian designs. On a shorter time scale, Europe's armies went to war in 1939 equipped with tanks whose guns ranged for the most part between 30 and 50 mm in calibre. By 1945 the standard calibre for a medium tank was at least 75 mm with heavy models reaching 120 mm or more.

Technological evolution, however, is not restricted to directional changes however fast they may occur. It also makes leaps. Darwinians deny that nature ever does this, but nature does display qualitatively diverse forms of organization, and new patterns crop up from time to time in the fossil record. Much neo-Darwinian theorizing has been driven by the problem of reconciling these facts with the assertion that evolution is a continuous process based on unbroken biological descent, and the results have a bearing on the puzzles of technological change. Wright's own solution to the problem started from the recognition that 'adaptive landscapes' are formed by multiple peaks separated by intervening troughs, regions corresponding to maladaptive genetic combinations with low mean fitness. The formation of new species from a smaller number of ancestral ones, or 'speciation', requires these peaks to be progressively colonized, and for this to happen 'colonizing' populations need some means of moving between peaks and crossing the troughs that separate them.

This requirement poses a major theoretical problem because directional selection can only push a population uphill towards the nearest peak. Once this is reached it will be stuck there because any small genetic change will reduce its fitness. A second, higher, peak might be close by, but it will be unattainable because so-called 'stabilizing' natural selection will pin the population at its existing location. The implication of this is that evolution should grind to a halt relatively early in the colonization of new environments as species get 'trapped' and are prevented from evolving towards very different but more adaptive states because the intermediate forms are relatively maladaptive. There would be no problem were the vision of a basically static nature to be acceptable, or if populations were allowed to jump directly between peaks, but neo-Darwinism rejects both of these alternatives, and the central problem for neo-Darwinian evolutionary genetics was to find some means by which populations could move 'downhill' against the gradient of natural selection.

Wright's solution lay in the concepts of 'genetic drift' and the 'founder effect'. These were random, or 'stochastic', gene frequency changes occurring due to restricted population size or the genetic sampling that happens when a small group of colonists splits off from a larger population. Technological evolution is governed by conscious human intentions and systems do not simply reproduce themselves, so the existence of saltations is not in itself a theoretical problem and stochastic change is unlikely. Wright's model is nonetheless relevant because the actual course of radical technological change is very puzzling and is well depicted by the metaphor of adaptive peaks and troughs. This is because whilst technology can 'leap' from one adaptive peak to another without going through intermediate forms, the process is neither easy nor free of risk. It is very difficult, in terms of Wright's metaphor, to determine the precise location of one adaptive peak from the perspective of another. Radical innovation is at best likely to form a leap into the foothills surrounding a neighbouring peak followed by incremental hill-climbing based on learning from experience. But much worse outcomes are possible, and the system may 'land' in a maladaptive trough.

7.2.1.2. *Innovation failure*

There are two ways in which innovation failures of this kind can occur. The first is that the innovation in question may just be misconceived and intrinsically incapable of delivering the desired result, often because it is based on an inappropriate analogy. When cavalry first faced effective gun-armed infantry, the solution appeared to be to arm them in the same way and turn them against the foot soldiers. The result, working by analogy with infantry tactics, was the *caracole*, which failed because cavalrymen were not infantry and had different limitations. The heaviest firearms they could carry were hopelessly outranged by infantry weapons, and performing the *caracole* without disrupting the ranks required a degree of precision virtually unattainable in cavalry manoeuvring. The innovation was not susceptible to incremental refinement because it was basically misconceived. When the Swedes fought the 'conservative' Poles who had kept old-style cavalry tactics, they had to reintroduce the charge, and other powers followed suit.

The tendency to reason by analogy with existing technologies or to extrapolate from older models extended to other cases of innovation failure. A comparable example can be found in warship designers' response to the potential offered by steam power and armour protection. In this instance the availability of a power source freeing vessels from dependence on the wind and allowing them to manoeuvre at will was met by a return to classical models. Nineteenth-century steam-powered ironclads were fitted with rams, a weapon that had graced the oared vessels of antiquity but was almost totally useless in the then prevailing circumstances. Rams are believed to have sent one major enemy vessel to the bottom while sinking more friendly ships in accidental collisions.

The second kind of failure occurred when an intrinsically worthwhile innovation performed badly when first introduced. This might be because the hardware was deficient or because the procedures needed to make it work properly had to be derived from concrete experience. The early history of submarine warfare provides a spectacular instance of this kind of failure in the Confederate vessel the CS *HL Hunley*, which became the first submarine to claim an enemy vessel when it sank the USS *Housatonic* on 17 February 1864 (Schafer 1996: 114–25). Before achieving this, however, it had itself accidentally sunk on five occasions. It was laboriously returned to the surface each time until the stricken *Housatonic* finally dragged it down with all hands. In its brief career the *Hunley* claimed as many as forty Confederate lives—its eponymous creator's among them—only six of which were due to enemy action.

'Hunley cases' sometimes arose when a supporting technology, in this instance the manufacture of watertight seals, was inadequately developed for the system as a whole to work properly. The early history of firearms provides several such instances. The advantages of breach-loading and other rapid-fire devices were readily apparent, but the state of contemporary metallurgy made them more dangerous to their users than to the enemy. The same limitations made the theoretical advantages of rifling unattainable in practice, and firearm designs converged on a single-shot, muzzle-loading, smooth-bore pattern that persisted effectively unchallenged into the nineteenth century. Only the firing mechanisms underwent substantial change.[9]

Hunley cases also occurred when lack of experience in using a new kind of hardware led to seemingly minor design features having disastrous consequences, as occurred in the early development of the bayonet. In its final form this proved a very successful means of combining fire and shock in a single weapon, but this required a socket attachment so the gun could be fired with the bayonet held securely in place. Early models simply tied the blade onto the barrel, but this was insecure and was replaced with a plug attachment. The plug stopped the bayonet falling off, but it also stopped the musket being fired, and a British infantry formation thus equipped was destroyed by charging highlanders at Killiecrankie in 1689 because of their low rate of fire. Shortcomings of this kind could usually be remedied by learning from experience, providing the initial failure was not too disastrous, but it was not always easy to distinguish innovations needing incremental refinement from those which simply had no prospect of success.

Failures of this kind could also arise where new and intrinsically effective technology was misapplied due to inexperience. This was a recurrent problem because appropriate practice usually had to be derived from practical experience given the dearth of robust and applicable scientific theory. Where there was no relevant practical experience it was necessary to reason by analogy or extrapolate from a given model, and it was only too easy to choose the wrong one. This became a serious problem as the pace of change accelerated after 1840 and affected

---

[9] The rifled musket came into use among woodland hunters in parts of continental Europe and north America by the mid-18th century and served as a very effective sharpshooters' weapon in the American Revolutionary War. But its slow rate of fire—only a third that of the smooth-bore—relegated it to a skirmishers' weapon in open-field battles and its contribution to American Independence has been overrated (O'Connell 1989: 171–2; Haythornthwaite 1994: 94–6; Black 1991: 60–5).

the French army in the war of 1870. They possessed an early form of machine gun, the *mitrailleuse*, which should have been very effective against the German troops but made almost no contribution because it was classified as an artillery piece and kept too far back (Howard 1962: 36). In this instance the effects of inexperience were compounded by a secrecy that made it difficult to formulate, test, and transmit an appropriate procedure. In the twentieth century the formulation of effective tank tactics was hampered by recurrent extrapolation from inappropriate cavalry or naval models, possibly encouraged by inter-service rivalries or simple snobbery.

7.2.1.3. *Sources of innovation*

The history of military technology provides many examples of prolonged 'hill-climbing' in which weapons or tactics were progressively refined in the light of experience, usually in the direction of increasing specialization and a growing emphasis on the characteristics which distinguished them from the alternatives. These episodes are relatively easy to explain, but very radical change or the introduction of entirely new systems present greater difficulties because institutionalized 'research' as we understand it was unknown, and there was no robust theoretical foundation on which to develop new technology of any kind. Change of this kind seems usually to have come about by one of two routes. The first was the encounter with some new technology with which an existing system could not cope. These recurred in pre-gunpowder military history, as we argued in the previous chapter, and they could rarely be resolved by incremental refinement. A new technique was required if the power in question was not to collapse.[10]

Many such encounters pitted powers in Europe's politico-military 'core' against those on the 'periphery'. It is noticeable that the core was generally conservative in military terms between the first appearance of heavy infantry and the gunpowder revolution, and most radical innovations emerged on the periphery. The origins of heavy cavalry lie on the Eurasian steppe—as do those of the horse-archers who were later to dispute their control of the battlefield, although this technology was not adopted in settled Europe. The major infantry rivals to this method of fighting also emerged from the economically or politically marginal territories of Scandinavia, Wales, and the Swiss uplands. Into the gunpowder age, the light infantry units who supported the Habsburg musketeer battalions and influenced developments elsewhere were drawn from Croat irregulars on the Empire's Balkan frontier whilst, as we have seen, the Swedish revival of heavy cavalry tactics in the seventeenth century stemmed from their encounter with the Polish lancers. In this respect the crystallization of the 'musket and sabre' system at the end of the seventeenth century represented a major break with past

---

[10] The replacement of the manipular by the cohort legion may be one example of this kind, as was the Swiss adoption of the pike in place of the halberd when confronted with heavy cavalry, but they seem to be relatively rare.

experience, since it was now the core which served as a model, particularly as European powers began to expand overseas. Nonetheless the persistence of light troops in the eighteenth-century Habsburg army and the introduction of rifle units in the British army both bore witness to the influence of the periphery, Balkan in one case and North American in the other (Haythornthwaite 1994: 94–6; Chandler 1994: 70–1).[11]

The second major source of saltations was another kind of technology transfer, analogous to what evolutionary biology terms 'pre-adaptation'. This was the military application of technologies which had been developed for non-military purposes and already tested by experience. In the very longest perspective, this may account for the origins of military technology itself, since it is likely that most early weapons were used in hunting before they were ever turned against human enemies. On a shorter time scale, horses were used as riding or draught animals before they were taken onto the battlefield. Hunting stimulated the development of missile weapons from the sling up to the rifled musket, whose slow rate of fire was offset by the advantages of greater accuracy against targets that were not going to shoot back.

The needs of hunting or stock management also fostered the refinement of 'light' tactics and equipment, whether on horseback or on foot, but heavy tactics and equipment, particularly those of heavy infantry, had no peacetime analogies and were developed for specifically military ends. Transfers could also occur from military to civilian technology, but this was rare. The most likely pre-industrial example is the improvements that selective breeding of warhorse strains may have brought to Europe's agricultural herd. In the industrial period, the precision machinery needed to construct better artillery tubes also led to more efficient pistons, and so allowed more powerful steam engines to be built, but here as elsewhere the military contribution seems to have been primarily the refinement of existing technologies rather than the invention of something wholly new.[12]

7.2.2. CONSERVATISM

Technological innovation offers the prospect of greater success in military affairs no less than in economic affairs, but the history of military innovation is very patchy with many episodes of extreme conservatism. This need not be surprising in itself because innovation is a potentially costly and risky business. Even incremental refinements often require additional investment, and radical change carries the risk of costly and potentially disastrous Hunley failures even if the innovation is basically well conceived. Conservatism also carries risks, however,

---

[11] The concept underlying the Minié ball also seems to have originated on the colonial periphery, since it is said to have been inspired by a form of blowpipe used in south India (O'Connell 1989: 191).

[12] Mokyr is of the opinion that prior to the 20th century 'the needs of military technology seem to have intersected but little with those of civilian production. Innovations in ballistics, the technology of fortification, gunpowder, and military communications had little to contribute to economic welfare' (Mokyr 1990: 184).

because an opponent may spring a technological surprise, thereby gaining a fatal advantage. What is puzzling in this light is the lack of any apparent correlation between the rate of technological change and the incidence or severity of conflict in a given period. Once the musket and sabre system had crystallized almost no changes occurred despite frequent wars between the powers, whilst the decades of peace after Waterloo saw major innovations. One useful way of approaching this paradox is via models derived from the mathematical theory of games.

7.2.2.1. *Games against nature*

Many situations in which decision-makers have to make choices in the presence of uncertainty can be treated as 'games', and the decision for or against innovation is one of these. The essence of the game is that two 'players' each select one from a menu of options and receive a 'payoff' whose value depends on the options that the two have selected. Both players may be conscious decision-makers, or there may be a 'game against nature' with just one player whose payoff depends on the interrelationship between his own choice and the value of an unknown set of variables determined by 'nature'. If we consider the 'decision' to innovate as part of a game against nature, then the benefits of incremental learning from experience are obvious. The payoff from small refinements to an existing system is likely to be small, whether they succeed or fail, but the prospects of success are good until an adaptive peak is approached.

This prospect makes innovation a rational strategy, but once at the peak, where the technology is as good as it can be without radical changes, innovations are increasingly likely to fail and conservatism is the rational option. Radical innovation is a different proposition since the innovator cannot rely on knowledge derived from experience. Innovations based on creative imagination, theory, or extrapolation may lead to costly Hunley cases or be totally misconceived. This provides a rational basis for military conservatism, but it is not one that entirely explains historical experience. At times, as in the eighteenth century, new technology was resisted even though it was demonstrably effective or the likely costs of failure were low. In order to understand the rationality of conservatism in these circumstances we must move to a second class of game based on the interaction of conscious decision-makers.

7.2.2.2. *Prisoner's dilemma*

In two-person games each 'player' chooses from a menu of options and receives a payoff depending on the relationship between the two choices. The character of such games is largely determined by the structure of the 'payoff matrix'. In a 'zero-sum' game the payoffs received by the two players always add up to nought, the outcomes are symmetrical, and one player's gain is necessarily the other's loss, but this need not be the case. In 'positive-sum' games, it is possible for both players to 'win', by some criterion, and in negative-sum games they can both lose. If we think of military success as defined only by the narrow criterion of victory or defeat on the battlefield, then war is necessarily a zero-sum game because a decisive victory for one contestant is necessarily a decisive defeat for the other. This 'agonistic' criterion, as we shall call it, is not, however, the only one on which military effectiveness should be assessed. There is also a broader criterion, which we shall term the 'Clausewitzian' criterion, and which requires armed forces to be effective instruments of policy. Judged on this criterion the relationship between outcomes and payoffs becomes more complicated because military victory is sometimes bought at a crippling economic or political price whilst a doughty loser may actually benefit politically by resisting, even if the resistance is a failure in narrowly military terms. If we want to understand the longer-term payoffs accruing to military innovation we need to keep in mind this wider range of economic and political outcomes.

The so-called 'prisoner's dilemma' game has been widely applied and provides a useful approach to the problem of military innovation. It describes what happens when two collaborators each have to choose co-operative or selfish ('cheating') options without knowing what the other one is going to do. Their information is confined to knowledge of what the other player has done in the past, the distribution of payoff values, and any general expectations they may have about how people characteristically behave. The game has four possible outcomes: both players co-operate, both behave selfishly (or 'cheat'), and one co-operates whilst the other cheats. If both players co-operate they receive a 'reward' (Rd), or a 'punishment' (Pt) if they both cheat, and if one player cheats whilst the other co-operates, the cheat wins the 'prize' (Pz) and the co-operator gets the 'sucker payoff' (Sr). The relationships between payoffs can vary except that the prize is always better than the reward, and the sucker payoff is worse than the punishment; or in formal notation $Pz > Rd > Pt > Sr$.

The 'prisoner's dilemma' is interesting because it shows that selfish behaviour is not necessarily the best means of promoting self-interest. Initially it appears to be in each player's individual interest to cheat, because the worst payoff they can receive is the punishment and they might win the prize, whereas a co-operator can only win the reward and may get landed with the sucker payoff. So both players should cheat if they are behaving rationally, but if they both do this they will each get the punishment and be worse off than if they had co-operated and got the reward. This problem only goes away if the players can be justifiably confident of each other's co-operation, and much of the theoretical interest in prisoner's dilemma focused on how such 'trust' builds up through repeated playing of the game. The likelihood of trust developing is heavily dependent on the relative values of the payoffs, and particularly on the magnitude of $Rd > Pt$ and $Pt > Sr$, which we shall term respectively the levels of 'inducement' and 'danger'.

This logic is readily applicable to circumstances in which comparably armed powers of roughly equal strength repeatedly fight, and each power has to choose whether or not to innovate. Innovation has an economic or political cost while making success in the next war more likely, and vice versa if innovation is rejected. There are three possible outcomes. 'Stasis' occurs if neither innovates. If only one power does so there is a technological 'surprise', and if both innovate there is a technological 'escalation' which leaves the military balance unchanged whilst rendering the next war more costly and destructive for both parties. This corresponds to a prisoner's dilemma in which conservatism represents the co-operative option and innovation a form of cheating. The consequences of stasis represent the reward; the punishment is the cost of escalation, and the prize and sucker payoffs are the consequences of victory or defeat due to a technological 'surprise'.

We shall begin by assuming that the payoffs are the same for both powers and that the magnitude of the inducement (Rd > Pt) is substantial, so both powers are interested in avoiding escalation. The actual outcome depends on the levels of danger (Pt > Sr) and the perceived likelihood of the other power cheating (or 'distrust'). The actual value of the payoffs varies with the length of time needed to counter a technological surprise, relative to the anticipated duration of the 'game' as a whole, and how much damage can be inflicted during that interval. If these quantities are both small then little is to be won or lost by innovation, and conservatism is a relatively safe option—particularly if the calculations are made against a long enough time horizon to allow for short-term losses to be recouped. If the two quantities are larger then much depends on the perceived likelihood of cheating (the inverse of 'trust'). This itself reflects the amount of information the powers obtain about each other's intentions, something that increases with the interaction between them, be this peaceful or violent.

Where reasonably foreseeable innovations are likely to be very destructive, as in the industrial era, then co-operation becomes increasingly risky and the likelihood of technological escalation substantial. But in the musket and sabre period, foreseeable innovations were either minor, or took a long time to introduce, or both, and so their short-term consequences were likely to be small. The costs and benefits of technological surprise were therefore correspondingly low, and Europe's rulers had an interest in avoiding the prospect of escalation which might return them to the destructive horrors of the previous century.[13] The risk of surprise was reduced by the fact that wars were so frequent, which paradoxically promoted trust by letting powers monitor the effectiveness of each other's technologies and verify their conservative propensities. Trust was further promoted by mutual expectations arising from rulers' reciprocal recognition of each other's legitimacy and a shared military culture. This ensured that most wars were fought with limited objectives, and the powers could take a long-term view of costs and benefits because they did not have to face the short-term prospect of total destruction.

---

[13] The likely cost of escalation was increased by the onset of the early modern demographic 'B' phase which made military manpower much more expensive than it had been in the century during which the musket and sabre system first took shape (see below, Chapter 13).

The technological stability of the musket and sabre period had a number of preconditions, one of which was that the rewards of stasis should be roughly equal and acceptable to all parties. This had ceased to be the case by the last years of the French *ancien régime* as the country's history of recurrent defeat led a new generation of military thinkers to despair of victory with existing methods and to contemplate new tactical systems. After the Revolution, the old 'line army' was too depleted for the new leadership to contemplate maintaining stasis if defeat—and possibly their own demise—were to be avoided. The available innovations involved new tactics and military institutions rather than weaponry but they greatly increased the scale of warfare. The movement to mineral economies profoundly altered the payoff matrix, and trust was reduced by the lengthy period of peace. This stopped the powers observing each others' weaponry in action and allowed surprises like the Dreyse needle gun. This represented a kind of directional saltation or 'leap forward' which eliminated the barriers to handgun development and opened up new prospects of incremental development. The danger thereby posed was reinforced by a contemporary revolution in weapons-manufacturing based on the 'American system' of mass production (O'Connell 1989: 192–3; Mokyr 1990: 136–8). This meant, in O'Connell's words, that 'firearms might be changed dramatically and supplied in huge quantities of exact copies in a matter of a few years... Practically overnight an order-of-magnitude shift in the balance of individual firepower might be accomplished' (O'Connell 1989: 193). The level of danger and mistrust both increased as a result and lengthy technological stasis gave way to continuing escalation.

7.3. QUANTITATIVE ESCALATION

The restrictions on production and transport in organic economies limited the numbers of men who could be recruited, assembled, and kept together for any length of time, but alongside this a second set of constraints limited the size of forces that could be controlled effectively on the battlefield. Co-ordinating the movements of a large army presented formidable problems as long as the speed of communications was limited to that of a man on horseback. Solving these problems depended on the development of unit and formation structures with associated staffs. It was their presence or absence that chiefly determined how big an army could be and still function effectively on the battlefield. Organized forces are generally built around basic groupings (or 'units') of anything from a few dozen to as many as a thousand men, which may themselves have been divided into sub-units of varying sizes and combined into permanent or ad hoc 'formations' at successive levels of organization. Since it is a near-universal principle that one leader holds tactical command over any given grouping, a hierarchy of leadership or 'chain of command' corresponds to any given hierarchy of sub-units, units, and formations. The more elaborate a force's chain of command the greater the requirement for experienced and motivated leaders, but the greater also its potential effectiveness provided that effective communication can be maintained between its component parts. The long-term consequence of the gunpowder revolution was to increase both the incentive and the capacity for commanders to deploy larger forces on the battlefield.

7.3.1. ORGANIZATION AND SCALE

A commander's ability to carry out complex manoeuvres, respond to unexpected circumstances, or get his troops off the battlefield in reasonable shape if things came unstuck reflected the effectiveness of the organization above the unit level. Conversely, the resilience of the individual units and their ability to keep together or regroup if disrupted depended more on the sub-unit organization and the number and quality of lower-level leaders. Another way of saying this is that the threshold of 'diminishing returns' to increases in army size depended in different but complementary ways on the effectiveness of these two levels of organization. Where sub-unit organization and the higher chains of command were poorly developed the threshold was correspondingly low. Commanders might even be disadvantaged by excessive numbers where failures of coordination, or flight by part of their force, induced general panic. In these circumstances, beyond a fairly modest threshold, the advantages conferred by greater numbers in high-level warfare could be offset relatively easily by qualitative superiority.

The weakness of unit organization and chains of command revealed itself most clearly in the 'fragility' of poorly organized field armies once things started to go seriously wrong and in the difficulties they experienced in withdrawing from battle in good order, or regrouping after a defeat. Historians' preference for winners over losers is such that relatively little is known about how armies coped with defeat and its immediate consequences. However, those with clear sub-unit structures and a hierarchy of leaders were evidently better able to retain or re-establish some form of order than those that lacked them. Their presence among the Roman armies doubtless explains the successful withdrawal of much of Crassus' army after Carrhae, or the extrication of the army from Persia after Julian's death. Conversely, their absence from barbarian armies and from most of medieval Europe's armies meant that campaigns rarely encompassed more than a single major battle.

This pattern was reinforced by the imbalance of casualties between victors and vanquished (see below, Chapter 14). Few data are available before the eighteenth century but it is generally assumed that, before the era of firearms, casualties, among heavy infantry in particular, were relatively light as long as the formations maintained their cohesion. Losses were mostly sustained once this cohesion was broken and one side had begun to retreat, so the retention of cavalry reserves able to screen or pursue retreating troops was crucially important to the larger-scale outcome.[14] The effective use of such reserves also required the presence of a higher command able to remain 'above the battle' and exercise effective leadership in the confusion of victory or defeat. This seems to have been rare, and the vanquished were likely to be dispersed, suffering heavy casualties relative to the victors. At the same time, the victors often found it hard to organize an effective pursuit beyond the immediate area of the conflict and this meant that single campaigns rarely yielded a politically decisive outcome.

7.3.2. FIREARMS AND TACTICAL ORGANIZATION

The size of effective battlefield armies varied greatly over the long term. In the ancient world, Macedonian and Roman commanders were able to deploy forces of 30,000–40,000 in battle. These numbers were approached again at the height of the medieval and early modern demographic expansion, but in other periods western field armies rarely exceeded the 10,000–20,000 range before the eighteenth century, and they were often smaller. It is unlikely that any medieval commanders who did dispose of numbers much above 15,000 derived any great benefit thereby, but forces of 30,000–40,000 were co-ordinated effectively in some sixteenth- and seventeenth-century battles. The subsequent trend in field army sizes can be seen in Table 7.1, which is based on estimated battle strengths and gives means as well as upper quartiles and deciles (these two statistics are respectively the strengths exceeded by one quarter and one tenth of the figures for each period). The small decline in the mean and upper quartile between the first two periods is difficult to interpret because there is more information for the second period, and this may mean that a larger proportion of relatively small-scale engagements were now being documented, but the rise in the upper decile shows that the biggest armies were getting larger. The eighteenth century shows a noticeable increase in the upper quartile, although there is no appreciable change in the size of the very biggest armies, whilst the Napoleonic period shows

Table 7.1 *Army strengths in battle* (000)

	1619–89	1690–1712	1715–60	1791–1801	1805–15
Mean	23.4	22.3	28.2	30.7	63.6
Upper quartile	30.0	25.0	40.0	45.0	83.0
Upper decile	50.0	56.0	58.7	55.0	120.0
N	63	139	93	131	96

Source: See Appendix II.

[14] The larger-scale consequences of victory on the battlefield depended very much on the degree to which the winning side maintained its discipline. Many victorious commanders saw the prospect of a decisive outcome evaporate because their troops stopped to loot the beaten enemy's camp rather than mount an effective pursuit.

a step increase which is largest at the top of the scale, where 10 per cent of the armies number at least 120,000 men.

This increase in scale was an indirect consequence of gunpowder technology. The new weapons needed new tactics if their destructive potential was to be realized, and these in turn promoted a degree of enhanced tactical organization that fostered increases in the scale and intensity of combat on the battlefield. The tactical organization of both infantry and cavalry in the sixteenth century was built around the company, commanded by a captain, and numbering around a hundred men or so. A number of cavalry companies would be grouped into tactical regiments on the battlefield, whereas infantry companies were formed into much larger blocks of several thousand men. The establishment of permanent infantry regiments comprising around ten companies was begun in France in the mid-sixteenth century, although the composition of these units remained unstable for some decades. The advantage of this development was that it increased the number of leaders and so the scope for maintaining discipline and command control. The complementary development of sub-unit organization in the form of platoons below company level was implemented by Gustavus Adolphus of Sweden. For most of the period, however, the ratio of leaders to fighters remained low and the organizational hierarchy poorly developed. Lacking a strong cadre of lower-level leaders—the subalterns and 'non-commissioned officers' or 'NCOs' of the future—units found it difficult to maintain their cohesion under pressure, or to regroup once cohesion had been lost. At the same time, the lack of an elaborated chain of command rendered armies fragile and prone to rapid dispersal in defeat. Combined with the growing destructive power of firearms, and the uncertainties associated with new weaponry and tactics, this weakness increasingly led commanders to see open-field battles as too dangerous and unpredictable a prospect and to avoid them where possible.

The period from the later seventeenth century saw the growth of an increasingly elaborate hierarchy of organization and command. At the company level, sub-unit organization became more clearly defined, and the number of lower-level leaders increased. Regiments became permanent organizations and were often subdivided into a number of formally established battalions (see Table 7.2).[15] At the same time, higher command structures began to crystallize. The role of general officer was separated from that of regimental commander and army commanders began to be supported by small staffs.[16] One consequence of

---

[15] Most of the figures in the table are for formally authorized company establishments. In practice, the proportion of officers and NCOs is likely to have been higher than this in the latter part of the period because they suffered fewer losses from casualties or desertion than did the common soldiers. In the 16th century, by contrast, some units, at least, had difficulty finding their quota of NCOs (Hale 1985: 50), so the table may understate the actual increase over the period.

[16] It was a common early modern practice for army commanders to hold the command of a specific regiment, or sometimes a company, and to lead this unit into action on the battlefield. The practice was abandoned as chains of command became more elaborate and institutionalized, but some armies continued to appoint ceremonial colonels, with actual command being in the hands of a lieutenant-colonel.

Table 7.2 *Infantry organization*
(a) Authorized company strengths

Elizabethan England (1)	16th-century Spanish (2)	16th-century Dutch (3)	English, 1640s (4)	French fusiliers, 1795 (5)
1 lieutenant	1 captain	1 captain	1 captain	1 captain
2 sergeants	1 ensign	1 lieutenant	1 lieutenant	1 lieutenant
6 corporals	1 sergeant	1 ensign	1 gentleman	1 *sous-lieutenant*
150 privates	10 corporals	2 sergeants	1 ensign	1 sergeant-major
	240 privates	3 squad masters	2 sergeants	5 sergeants
		1 clerk	3 corporals	1 *fourrier*
		1 barber	100 privates	8 corporals
		1 provost		2 drummers
		2 drummers		104 fusiliers
		100 privates		

(b) Actual strengths

France, 1567 (6)	France, 1635 (7)	England, 1640s (4)
5 French companies: 671 men with 25 officers and sergeants (26.8 : 1).	Strength calculated at 3 officers per company of 80–100 'other ranks'	Actual strength of 30 officers and 984 other ranks (32.8 : 1)
18 Italian companies: 1,246 men with 72 officers and sergeants (17.3 : 1).		(Colonel Robert Bennet's infantry regiment, 6 July 1646)

(c) Infantry formations (authorized strength)

Spanish *Tercio*, 1534 (2)	French *Demi-brigade*, 1795 (5)
10 pike companies	Staff:
2 arquebus companies	1 *chef de brigade*, 3 *chefs de bataillons*, 1 quartermaster-treasurer, 2 *adjutants-majeurs*, 3 *surgeons-majeurs*, 3 *adjutants-sous-officiers*, 1 drum-major, 1 drum-corporal, 8 musicians, 3 master-tailors, 3 master-shoemakers
Total: approx. 3,036 men including 24 officers and 132 NCOs	3 battalions, each with 1 grenadier and 8 fusilier companies.
	Total: 3,472 men including 81 officers and 363 NCOs

Sources: (1): Hale (1985); (2): Hall (1997); 't Hart (1993); (4): Carlton (1992); (5): Haythornthwaite (1988); (6): Wood (1996); (7): Parrott (2001).

this was a large increase in the ratio of leaders to ordinary soldiers. By the later eighteenth century the Prussian army had one officer for every twenty-nine men, supplemented by large complements of corporals, sergeants, and other non-commissioned officers which, on O'Connell's estimates, brought the overall cadre of leaders to some 10 per cent of total strength.[17]

The elaboration of regimental and company organization was complemented by the emergence of higher-level formations. This began with the ad hoc brigading of individual regiments on the battlefields of the early eighteenth century, but was formalized in the wake of the French Revolution when infantry regiments were grouped into brigades and divisions with their own supporting troops, services, and staffs.[18] Napoleon went a step further by grouping divisions into a smaller number of *Corps d'Armée* (Elting 1997). These were small-scale armies of 10,000 to 20,000 men which were intended to manoeuvre independently and only converge on the battlefield itself. The French model was copied by other European armies, and divisional and corps organizations became integral parts of the military establishment of continental Europe in the course of the nineteenth century.

7.3.3. SUMMARY

Until the nineteenth century infantry firearms were slowfiring and inaccurate and this required their firing to be co-ordinated if it was to be effective. Achieving this co-ordination in turn required a degree of discipline and tactical organization based on a mechanical 'drill' for loading and firing weapons. This kind of firing drill was distinct from the marching drill needed to manoeuvre units onto and around the battlefield, and the tactical organization needed to make volley fire practicable did not immediately translate into greater unit cohesion or co-ordination. Early gunpowder armies therefore remained fragile in defeat and prone to disorganization in victory, but the use of firearms had already made victory a more costly prize in terms of casualties (see below, Chapter 14). The training and organization required to use them provided the basis for more complex hierarchies and the inculcation of marching and manoeuvre drills, which enabled units to maintain their coherence under pressure and much larger numbers of them to be co-ordinated effectively.

---

[17] The expansion of officer's numbers also provided positions for otherwise unemployed members of the aristocracy and was open to abuse. In France, where this reached grotesque proportions, the officer corps had expanded to over 10% of total strength by the 1770s and was consuming more than half of the total army budget (Childs 1982: 81–2).

[18] The division concept originated in the thinking of *ancien régime* reformers who intended it as a 'miniature army' combining all arms, but in practice divisional organizations were based on either infantry or cavalry. Some artillery divisions were also established in the 20th century alongside the new armoured divisions.

7.4. CONCLUSION: TOWARDS GLOBAL HEGEMONY

The introduction of firearms represented the first large-scale application of chemical energy to a major area of collective human activity. Their adoption on the battlefield was a slower and less dramatic process than that which affected siege warfare but its consequences were, if anything, even more far-reaching. In the long term the advent of portable firearms transformed the relationship between weapons categories, troop types, and entire tactical systems. The consequences of the gunpowder revolution are usually discussed in terms of its effects on siege warfare and in the short term it was here that its consequences were most important, both in a narrowly military sense and as regards the costs of military operations. In a wider perspective, however, the impact on mobile warfare was, if anything, more far-reaching. The close tactical combination of arquebusiers or musketeers with pikemen abolished the distinction between fire and shock weapons at the level of infantry units, and progressive improvements in firearms enabled the proportion of pikes to be reduced until the advent of the socket bayonet gave the individual infantryman a weapon which could be used in either role.

The new infantry formations could hold off cavalry and defeat any other kind of infantry at a distance. Adequately supported they were unbeatable by any other tactical system in all but the most exceptional circumstances. Moreover, training in firearms required no special skill or previous experience. It could be reduced to a drill composed of a series of steps set down in textbooks and instilled through endless repetition. For the first time a clear transitivity—a linear hierarchy of effectiveness—had emerged in the relationship between tactical systems, and there were no barriers to the diffusion of the superior form. The assurance of victory in conflicts between European powers now required either a qualitative refinement of the common system or the attainment of superior numbers.

The seventeenth-century musketeer was still a long way from the despised 'mechanical soldier' of the *ancien régime*, but a watershed had been passed in the individual experience of combat and its social and psychological correlates. Where proficiency in earlier weapon systems had required either individual skill and initiative—approaching artistic 'flair' in some forms of swordsmanship—or else, like the pike phalanx, had relied on the active cohesion of the team, the appearance of drill reduced weapon-handling to a process of rote learning and repetition. The firing line as a collectivity was based neither on individualism nor on solidarity, but on atomistic aggregation. Passively enduring a risk of death or mutilation which his own actions could do nothing to alter, the musketeer could neither give nor receive active support from his neighbours other than by mechanically discharging a sequence of actions whose rationale depended precisely on the absence of any specifically individual contribution.

This change in military culture was promoted by three factors: a growth in the number of lower-level commanders, an increasing emphasis on mechanical drill, and a more elaborate chain of command. Some of these changes were intended to improve discipline and control off the battlefield, but they also enabled larger forces to be used in combat and the state of military technology provided an incentive for this. Contemporary handguns seem to have reached an adaptive peak at which incremental refinement was no longer possible and any substantial improvement in performance required a qualitative innovation. But, as the application of our simple game-theoretic model has suggested, such innovation, or any radical change in military hardware or procedures, was potentially dangerous for Europe's rulers in terms of the destruction and costs that might ensue. This left incremental growth in numbers, and the organizational elaboration underlying it, as the one route by which a power might gain a relative advantage over its opponents. These developments permitted an expansion in the duration and frequency of battles as well as the numbers involved. Defeated forces could now more easily withdraw and re-engage. At the same time the use of massed firearms on the battlefield reduced the imbalance of casualties between victors and vanquished and thus further inhibited pursuit. 'Muscle-power' armies were rarely capable of engaging for more than a matter of hours, and a single battle would often settle a campaign. By contrast, nineteenth-century battles, such as Gettysburg, could extend over several successive days, whilst campaigns such as those around Leipzig and Dresden in 1814, Waterloo the following year, or the 'Seven Days Battles' in the Virginia peninsula during the American Civil War incorporated multiple large-scale engagements in a similar space of time, blurring the very distinction between battles and campaigns.

CHAPTER EIGHT

Military Capital: Oars, Sails, Walls, and Guns

Armed forces need appropriate equipment in order to be effective. Military equipment of any kind represents a certain commitment of capital, but fortifications and warships stand out from other categories because they were potentially much more expensive and required specialized skills to construct and maintain. These two kinds of 'military capital' were the basis of two very different kinds of warfare which nonetheless had a certain amount in common. Fortifications were static and ships were mobile by their very nature, but both siege and naval operations were tightly constrained by logistical considerations and the capacities of both forms of military capital were restricted by the limitations of muscle-powered military technology. The gunpowder revolution consequently transformed both of them in ways that had a surprising amount in common.

The limitations of muscle-powered military technology conferred both advantages and disadvantages on fortifications and their defenders. The principal advantage was that muscle power could not do much damage to strong walls, and it was not hard to build them high enough to stop attackers getting over without great difficulty. Furthermore, attackers could inflict few injuries on the defenders of a well-constructed fortification until they were actually inside it, and so even very powerful fortifications could be held by relatively small garrisons, which made them correspondingly easy to provision against a lengthy siege. On the other hand, there was also very little that the garrison could do to the besiegers without leaving the shelter of their walls and risking open-field combat.

Fortifications, in consequence, played a very important military role but one limited almost entirely to sheltering the civilian or military assets contained within their walls. There was little that their garrisons could do if a powerful intruder chose simply to ignore them and pass on. Naval forces were similarly constrained by the limitations of muscle power. Ships could not do much damage to each other without cannon unless they came into physical contact, and until the eve of the gunpowder era this meant they had to be propelled by oars. This tactical requirement led to operational limitations because oar-powered warships were vulnerable to heavy seas and could not carry enough water for an extended cruise. The strategic role of war fleets was correspondingly limited and consisted mainly of supporting land operations, protecting merchant ships, or intercepting enemy vessels within sight of land. The coming of gunpowder artillery wrought profound changes in all these respects. Oars gave way to sails and the tonnage per crewman rose to a level that gave warships an oceanic range.

War fleets could now operate far out to sea for extended periods and the appearance of specialized scouting vessels meant they could intercept enemy vessels in this environment and thus seek to control areas of open water for the first time. Gunpowder artillery also transformed the role of fortifications. Attackers could now hope to break down the defences with their siege guns, whilst garrisons could bring enough firepower to bear to inflict heavy losses on the besiegers. The consequence was a new balance between the two sides which was unpredictable, bloody, and, like the new warships, very expensive financially. Furthermore, just as ships of the line could control seas and sea-lanes so the new fortification systems could act as barriers to the movement of road-bound siege and baggage trains, which introduced a new element into strategic geography.

8.1. FORTIFICATIONS

The operation of mobile forces was supported or obstructed by fortifications, and manoeuvre warfare was complemented by siege and assault. The technical essence of fortification is simply the erection of a fixed barrier to prevent access to a space. A good choice of site is a great help, and, where possible, fortifications were established on rising ground or hilltops. The materials employed varied with local availability and the technological sophistication of the builders. In North Africa and the Near East mud brick was widely used, whereas in northern Europe earth and timber were the basic materials until the coming of the Romans. Hill forts protected with earthworks and wooden palisades were a defining feature of the so-called La Tène material culture complex associated with historical Celts, who were the principal victims of Rome's western expansion. The Romans themselves used brick as well as stone in their constructions and introduced the use of cement. Their European successors reverted to earth and timber as materials, but by the twelfth century stone structures were reappearing, and stone became the material of choice for fortifications until the appearance of mobile gunpowder artillery forced the adoption of a shock-absorbing earth or brick construction.

The nature and importance of siege warfare varied with the terrain and the economic and political structure of the territory concerned. In the urbanized society of the ancient Mediterranean, cities were major economic and political targets and might serve as military bases, as they did on Rome's eastern frontier. Further north in barbarian Europe there were fewer major fortified centres and prolonged siege warfare was correspondingly less important. The Romans were nonetheless confronted with many Celtic *oppida*, and the suppression of Vercingetorix's Gallic rebellion ended in a siege of massive proportions at Alesia (Planhol and Claval 1994: 19–22; Cunliffe 1988: 121–2). The retrogression of urban life in early medieval Europe necessarily reduced the incidence of major sieges. The period's endemic low-level warfare revolved around the castles that proliferated from the eleventh century, but it characteristically involved small forces that had to remain in place for only a few weeks at most. In the east, Constantinople combined the role of strategic barrier with that of economic and political centre. It was the key to the Empire, and its virtual impregnability largely explains the Empire's remarkable survival. By the fourteenth century cities were again sufficiently important as strategic or economic targets for large-scale sieges to re-emerge as a feature in western European warfare (Bradbury 1992; Corfis and Wolfe 1995) and they assumed an increasingly important role in the early centuries of the gunpowder era.

8.1.1. THE USES OF FORTIFICATION

Permanent fortifications can be split into two categories according to their function. Barrier fortifications were intended to block the passage of an army or raiding force and so seal off a geographical area against incursions from outside. The second kind, 'point' defences, were intended to protect a relatively small enclosed space and can be split into a number of subcategories (Creveld 1991: 27–8).

8.1.1.1. *Barriers*

Barrier defences were rare before the advent of gunpowder weapons, although the agrarian empires of Rome and, especially, China built some on a grand scale. They were usually continuous linear structures, and although they were formidable engineering achievements their military value was questionable. The problem was that, intrinsically, they were not very effective obstacles to anyone who could get hold of a ladder. They were only as effective, militarily speaking, as their garrisons, and in placing these the defender confronted a basic dilemma. Garrison troops had to be posted at short intervals, in forts or towers, if the whole length of the wall was to be covered, but these scattered small detachments were virtually helpless against any but the smallest group of intruders. This was because, lacking firearms, they could only stop attackers getting across the parapet by leaving the shelter of their tower and physically engaging them. An attacking force of any appreciable size could easily achieve a local superiority that would make such action suicidal, whilst small parties could often infiltrate without being seen.

Barrier fortifications, like the Roman walls in northern Britain and elsewhere, could disrupt and delay incursion into the frontier and make it more difficult for intruders to get out again, and they provided fortified bases for the defending troops (Creveld 1991: 27). Many of the structures once identified as barrier fortifications are now thought not to have had a military function, in a narrow sense of the term, but to have been aimed at regulating the movement of goods and people. According to Whittaker, the extensive wall systems built by the

Romans in Libya 'were never military barriers that divided the desert from the sown but were internal controls on shepherds and herdsmen who traditionally traversed them' (Whittaker 1994: 79–81). Other structures, once interpreted as barrier fortifications, have proved on closer examination to be defended communications systems, roads with fortified guard posts and way stations.

More modest but also more effective barriers were possible where a defile, or other natural choke point, could be physically blocked. The Daryal pass through the Caucasus was thus sealed off against nomad incursions by fortifications whose maintenance became a source of dispute between Persians and Byzantines (Isaac 1992: 229–30), but such locations were rare. Even the Alps proved ineffective as a military barrier, their passage often hindered more by hostile tribesmen than by any fixed defences. The advent of gunpowder weapons changed this position substantially. In the course of the sixteenth century a new type of fortification emerged. This was the so-called 'artillery fortress' (see below) whose firepower, together with that of its garrison, could inflict enough damage on a substantial road-bound column to make its passage a hazardous proposition, and whose ability was further enhanced by networks of subsidiary fortifications which were developed around the major centres.

The Dutch Revolt owed its initial survival to the barriers surrounding the provinces of Holland and Zeeland, but these owed as much to the waterlogged terrain as to a chain of fortresses whose co-ordination was hampered by municipal particularism. The first effective barrier fortifications, in the modern sense, were established on the modern Franco-Belgian frontier under Louis XIV and Vauban in the 1690s. Initially intended to screen the countryside against cavalry raids, by the last years of the Spanish Succession War they had developed into a barrier that took the allies three years and 47,000 casualties to break through. Even then, the protection these fortifications afforded the French mobile forces was such that they were able to counter-attack and recoup most of their losses following Marlborough's recall (Duffy 1985: 38–44). For the first time, the prospect emerged of a barrier system capable of blocking access to large areas of territory and effectively sealing off a frontier.

8.1.1.2. *Point defences*

Point defences were much more common and served one or more of three functions: protection for economic or population centres (or 'city walls' for short), refuges, and military bases.

8.1.1.2.1. *City walls*

City walls often had to be adapted to the circumstances of a site that had been chosen for non-military considerations, although settlements established in very insecure terrain, such as piracy-prone coasts, were often located with an eye to defence. They are a familiar feature of the ancient and medieval worlds, but their function was not always first and foremost a military one. In medieval times it could be primarily administrative: a means of enforcing tolls and regulating access. The cities of the Roman east were heavily fortified and served as the basis of frontier defence, but those in the interior were largely undefended before the third-century invasions, when a major programme of fortification was set in train. The division of the Empire was followed by the establishment of new, strategically sited, capitals at Constantinople and Ravenna. Both enjoyed substantial natural defences, but were also heavily fortified.

8.1.1.2.2. *Refuges*

Refuges were the most widely distributed form of point defence and were intended to shelter local people, and whatever movable resources could be gathered there, against frontier raids or more serious incursions. They might be purpose built, often in the form of towers, but could also be adaptations of existing civilian structures such as farmhouses or even churches, as in the Thierache district of north-eastern France. Roman administrative buildings and other non-military installations were also provided with fortifications in some cases although their function is unclear (Isaac 1992: 198–208). The distribution of refuges largely reflected the prevailing levels of insecurity. They were a common feature of threatened frontiers or coastal areas but could also appear in interior regions afflicted by banditry or feuding. Although their primary function might be to provide security and protection for civilians, this does not mean that they were without military significance or some role in a wider scheme of frontier defence. By sheltering crops and animals, as well as people, they could be used to strip the countryside of food supplies and seriously hinder the operations of invading armies as well as smaller bands of raiders.

8.1.1.2.3. *Bases*

Point defences also served as bases for mobile forces, where there was some kind of permanent, or semi-permanent, military establishment. Roman legions and auxiliary units of the early Empire occupied fortified bases conventionally termed 'fortresses' and 'forts' respectively, but the terminology is misleading. The operational role of the troops based there was mobile and aggressive, rather than defensive, and the fortifications—which were not in any case very formidable—were not designed to withstand serious, large-scale assaults but to reduce the risk of surprise attack, restrict access, and, presumably, reduce the incidence of desertion.[1] This changed in the later Empire, such structures becoming less stereotyped in their layout, often smaller, and more heavily defended (Elton

---

[1] Roman armies also constructed distinctive fortified camps whilst on the march. These seem to have had a further military, and psychological, importance as rallying points as well as serving as an intimidating symbol of Roman power (Goldsworthy 1996: 111–13).

1996: 155–74). Walls were thickened and buttressed and frequently provided with firing platforms for artillery. The most obvious interpretation of these changes is that they reflected the deteriorating military situation, and the growing likelihood of serious assault, although this interpretation is not universally accepted.[2]

8.1.1.2.4. *Multi-purpose defences*

These three functions of point defences, namely protection for economic or population centres, refuges, and military bases, are separable, but individual structures might serve more than one of them. Fortified cities acted as military bases in the Roman east and in regions elsewhere under the later Empire, whereas England's thousand-man garrison in fifteenth-century Calais formed a miniature standing army whose importance was quite out of proportion to its numbers (Gillingham 1981: 27–8). Multiple functions were particularly common in areas of high insecurity. The *kastra*, or fortified towns, of late Byzantium fulfilled all three functions whilst acting as instruments of internal control.

As a centre of administration and economic and social life, the kastron performed a variety of functions, one of which was defence. Behind its walls townspeople aided by garrisons defended their homes, and peasants and their animals sought refuge from enemy incursions. Within its walls government officials administered the local soldiery and the supplies needed to provision campaign armies in transit. The typical kastron was a walled hill crowned with a fortified acropolis. There one found the garrison's barracks, stables, administrative offices, occasionally jails, and if need be, a last refuge from invaders who had breached the curtain walls of the town below. The acropolis, or citadel, was also a symbol of authority separating the governmental and military aristocracy from the other urban inhabitants, and as a consequence its walls often served to protect its privileged inhabitants from insurrections mounted by the less privileged population below. (Bartusis 1992: 286)

The most familiar multi-functional structures of the kind exemplified by the *kastron* are the castles of medieval Europe that could serve as both refuge and military base. Initially they served as fortified dwellings for landholders and their armed followers, and as shelters for the local population. Royal castles, or those held by regional magnates, were more specialized as military bases and were often occupied in rotation by feudal tenants under their service obligation. In colonized regions, or in conquest states such as Norman England, such fortifications were intended to dominate and control the surrounding countryside and inhabitants, but they could also generally serve as shelters where the need arose. The early castles consisted of palisaded mounds, topped by wooden structures, with an

---

[2] This view was advanced by Luttwak as part of his case for a systematic policy of 'defence in depth' in the later Empire (Luttwak 1976). Luttwak's arguments have been severely criticized, largely on the grounds that the Empire had no institutional mechanism for formulating and putting into practice a long-term strategy of any kind (Whittaker 1994; Isaac 1992; Mann 1979). For a counter-critique see Wheeler (1993a, 1993b).

adjoining defended enclosure. In the course of the high Middle Ages stone structures became more common and the defences more elaborate.

One important architectural change was the move from square to rounded towers, which were more difficult to undermine, and may have reflected the crusaders' exposure to Roman traditions of military architecture. The later fourteenth and fifteenth centuries saw the development of particularly elaborate defences, perhaps as a response to post-plague manpower constraints, but castle garrisons were always relatively small. Surviving figures for 'castle guard' duties in feudal England are difficult to interpret but suggest garrisons rarely exceeded a few dozen men (Hollister 1965: 140–54; King 1988: 15–19), whilst the garrison of Christendom's greatest medieval fortress, the crusader castle of Krak-des-Chevaliers, probably numbered no more than 150–200 combatants (King 1988: 10).

8.1.2. THE ARTILLERY FORTRESS

In 1494 the French King Charles VIII invaded Italy supported by a siege train of around forty guns. Gunpowder siege artillery was not new in itself. Earlier in the century it had helped prise the English from their last French strongholds (Smith 1994; Hall 1997: 114–23), but the performance of the new cannon easily outclassed the medieval 'bombards' in two respects.[3] They were more powerful, with a range and accuracy equivalent to that of a bombard at least three times their calibre, and they fired iron balls that were both easier to manufacture than the older stone rounds and whose debris was less obstructive to the assault troops. The consequence was one of military history's greatest upsets as Italy's network of fortified places collapsed with unprecedented rapidity; at Monte San Giovanni, a Neapolitan fort which had once withstood a seven-year siege fell to an eight-hour cannonade (Parker 1988: 9–10; Duffy 1979: 7–11).

The new artillery's enhanced mobility was as important as its increased power. Transportable by horse-drawn carriage or wagon—unlike the bombards which had to be carried on unstable ox carts—the guns could now keep up with a campaigning army on the march, and their mobility and intimidating reputation achieved as much for the French cause as did the actual material damage they inflicted (Duffy 1979: 11). This effectively negated the immediate military value of Italy's medieval fortifications. It also set off a rapid process of adaptive change, as a series of what were at first ad hoc engineering improvisations were systematized into a new and very successful system of military architecture.[4] The root of the defender's problem was the large increment in energy resources that gunpowder artillery placed in the hands of the attacker, and the very different demands that

---

[3] The new-style mobile artillery had played a major part in the Castilian conquest of Granada a few years before but apparently without attracting much attention in the wider world (Hall 1997: 123–33).

[4] The standard account of developments in early modern military architecture and siegecraft is Duffy (1979), on which the following account largely depends. For useful brief surveys see Hall (1997: 158–63), Parker (1988: 10–16), Tallett (1992: 32–9). Lynn (1997: 547–93) provides an analysis of the French case.

this placed on fortifications when compared with those of earlier periods. The principal threats then had been an infantry assault coming over the walls, or an attempt to batter down the gates. High walls with strong foundations, deep ditches, and a barbican or other defensive structure for the gates were needed to frustrate such attempts, but the meagre kinetic energy disposed of by muscle-power armies rendered the physical integrity of the walls themselves a secondary problem that could be answered by relatively thin stonework.

Cannon fire presented threats of a radically different kind. Walls now had to absorb substantial energies and take repeated flat-trajectory blows without shattering. Masonry thus gave way to earth as the material of choice, and, in order to strengthen the construction whilst presenting a smaller target, walls were made thicker and lower. Their vulnerability to infantry assault was increased, but here the very technology that created the problem in the first place also presented a solution. From ancient times artillery had enabled garrisons to maintain a demoralizing harassing fire on besiegers, or to break up dense concentrations of assault troops, but well-placed cannon or even small arms fire could deny terrain to a besieger, threaten his own artillery, and inflict serious casualties inside the siege lines themselves. The need to provide a stable firing platform for heavy artillery was a further reason for lowering and thickening fortress walls,[5] but military architects' central concern now became the elimination of 'dead ground', and the provision of all-round, mutually supporting fields of fire in the vicinity of fortifications.

The key to this new geometry of fire was the replacement of rounded medieval structures by the angled 'bastion'. This allowed enfilading fire and was complemented by increasingly complex networks of 'ravelins', and other detached structures or 'outworks', located on the approach to the primary fortifications. These were themselves fitted with angular 're-entrants' and covered ways which provided shelter and jumping-off points for detachments operating outside the walls and further opportunities to bring attacking troops under fire. By the end of the sixteenth century these features were synthesized in the work of the 'New Italian School', a fully elaborated system of military architecture based on the angular ground plan or *trace italienne*, but there was nothing magical about the new system. Its underlying principles were visible in field fortifications improvised within a decade of the fall of Monte San Giovanni, and by the 1520s field works and fortified places had already regained much of their military value.[6]

---

[5] This requirement was painfully demonstrated at the final siege of Constantinople in 1453. The defenders disposed of some heavy guns but they were useless because of the danger that they would literally shake the old Roman walls to pieces (Bartusis 1992: 338).

[6] The architecture of the *trace italienne* has received considerable attention from historians following Parker's claim that its diffusion triggered a general military revolution (Parker 1988). The existence of such a revolution and the causal role, if any, of the new fortification system have both become the subject of controversy (see Rogers 1995 for a selection of views). Parrott has recently questioned the military importance of the 16th-century innovations and argued that some older or rapidly improvised defensive structures were more effective against artillery fire than is generally allowed (Parrott 2000).

8.1.3. ATTACKING FORTIFICATIONS: BLOCKADE AND ASSAULT

A fortified position presented an invader with two options: either to take it or to ignore it and pass by. Unless the fortification was one of the very few that represented an effective physical barrier, the latter was usually easy to achieve before the gun powder era since garrisons lacked the firepower to do serious damage to a column passing in their vicinity. It could, however, be dangerous to leave even small bodies of mobile troops in the rear, and the position might be guarding resources that the invaders needed for subsistence, or which they aimed to seize. Fortifications could be taken by betrayal, blockade, or assault. Defended cities might be vulnerable to treachery particularly if, like Rome, they had a large slave or other subordinate population whose sympathies might lie with an enemy, but this was less often true of refuges or military bases. A successful blockade required sealing off the position from outside help until the garrison was forced to surrender for lack of food or water. Straightforward in principle, this could be difficult to achieve in practice since, if the garrison had been properly provisioned and had an adequate water source, a large besieging force was likely to run out of supplies first. For this reason successful sieges often culminated in an assault once the garrison had been weakened by a protracted blockade, and assault was usually the only option where speed was essential. This meant getting an assault force either through or over the fortifications, and here again a reliance on muscle power imposed serious constraints. These disappeared with the advent of gunpowder artillery, but the logistical constraints on siege warfare became even more pressing.

8.1.3.1. *The limits of muscle power*

Wooden structures were vulnerable to fire, but muscle-power armies could not muster the kinetic energy needed to break through stonework in a short time, and they had great difficulty in doing so at all. A range of muscle-powered siege artillery was developed in the ancient world, using the torsion principle, and the medieval period added the weight-driven trebuchet (DeVries 1996; Landels 1978: 99–132). These, however, required considerable skill and local resources to construct, and, overall, they do not seem to have been very effective. Their psychological effect might be considerable, but their trajectory was probably too high to do serious damage to strong walls, though it allowed them to bombard structures in the interior. Devices of this kind mounted inside fortifications could also be used to harass and disrupt besiegers. An alternative technique was to undermine the walls. Square towers were particularly vulnerable to the removal of cornerstones, but rock foundations or defensive ditches could frustrate such operations. Wooden gates were an obvious weak point and target, but these could be screened by secondary defences and the approaches covered by missile troops.

The remaining option was an 'escalade' or assault over the walls. This required equipment that could range from simple ladders to large mobile towers, or even, in the ancient world, major earthworks in the form of ramps. Escalade was probably the most frequent means of successful assault, and the obvious way to counter it was by building high. The larger and more elaborate the fortification the higher the walls, and military architects usually sought to obstruct the approaches by their choice of site, the construction of secondary defences, or both. A well-sited position could be rendered virtually impregnable against any form of direct assault. This left blockade as the only practicable means of reducing it, and even where assault was eventually successful a preceding blockade was usually required in order to weaken the defenders.

The size of the force required to mount a successful blockade varied with the size of the fortification and its garrison. The larger the force needed, the greater the logistical problems facing the blockaders themselves. An attack on a minor strong point could usually be supplied from local sources unless the countryside had been stripped of food or was inherently unproductive. Detachments on this scale, often small raiding forces, usually lacked much by way of transport or other logistical support, and so would have to move on or go home if supplies ran out before the position was taken. Blockading a major city or other adequately prepared position on a comparable scale was a very different proposition and meant keeping a large force concentrated at one point for an extended period. This posed the greatest logistical challenge ever faced by commanders before the railway age. Meeting it was usually beyond the capacities of barbarian armies, and this gave the defenders of organized states a significant advantage against them. The walled cities of the Western Empire probably owed their preservation at the time of the fifth-century invasions as much to the invaders' logistical inadequacies as to their lack of siege artillery. The clear technological edge retained by the defenders of medieval fortifications, compounded by the increases in army size that accompanied the early modern phase of demographic expansion, meant that blockades and their attendant logistical difficulties became all the more important.

Once a besieging force had eaten all the food and fodder it could bring with it, it had to establish external supply lines or rely on foraging. As set out above, foraging on this scale was essentially an exercise in overland bulk transport, with all the difficulties that this implied. Fodder was particularly difficult to procure in this way, and horses were usually the first casualties of siege warfare. This might not pose immediate military problems, siege lines being the domain of foot soldiers, but it reduced the ability to forage or conduct reconnaissance, and the absence of cavalry or transport animals could be serious when the siege was over and the besieging army, victorious or not, had to move on. In practice, the availability of good pasture could determine the practicability of a siege, but even in favourable circumstances blockading forces were likely to suffer severe shortages. In unfavourable circumstances, or where the defender had had the chance to make extensive preparations, the besiegers were usually the first to run out of supplies. Large forces generally had to rely on external supplies brought by water unless they were operating in highly productive areas that had not been cleared by the defenders.

All this resulted in a substantial asymmetry in favour of the defence. A properly prepared position could be made virtually impregnable with sufficient investment in its construction and provisioning, whereas the attacker confronted a problem of diminishing returns. He had few opportunities for capital investment on his side—the technology simply did not exist to break down major fortifications quickly—and the more manpower he assembled the more likely he was to run out of food. A large force willing to expend the time and effort could usually take local strong points or other minor fortifications without too much difficulty, but this too could consume valuable time and mean that small bodies of troops could wield an influence wholly disproportionate to their numbers. Very large fortified centres generally required an extended siege by substantial forces, and logistical constraints might make this impossible if waterborne supplies were not available.

8.1.3.2. Gunpowder siege warfare

Besieging forces sometimes amounted to tens of thousands in the ancient and medieval worlds, but garrisons were usually small and had little chance to play an active role. The gunpowder revolution changed this. Once military architects had recovered from the first shock of the new weapons they devised effective countermeasures. These dramatically increased the firepower which the defenders could bring to bear and with it the human casualties they could inflict on besieging troops or engineers. In 1522 over 1,000 Swiss assault troops died short of the Imperial trenches at Biccoca—a reverse from which Swiss prestige never recovered—whilst a failed assault on the gates of Maastricht cost Parma's army 2,000 dead in 1578, and at Ostend in 1602 a similar number died in an unsuccessful night attack on a single bastion (Duffy 1979: 86). Losses on this scale, sustained in ill-prepared or otherwise botched operations, sufficed to convince most commanders that they could not hope to storm intact defences over open ground.

Where military architects had had to develop new techniques to counter the power of cannon fire against fortifications, so new systems of siege engineering were needed to offset its destructive power in their defence. They were developed by Spanish and Dutch engineers using large-scale entrenchments which were constructed around an encircling ditch, or 'contra-vallation'. The besiegers worked inwards from this through a series of smaller radial trenches or 'saps' to a position some 30 yards or so from the defences, where a lateral trench and earthwork was built as the base for a final assault. As practised and refined by Spinola and Maurice of Nassau, this technique worked so well that the balance of advantage seemed to have shifted back to the besiegers by the 1630s (Duffy 1979: 100), but it was an advantage bought at a substantial cost.

The new systems of siege-works, which often needed an external 'circumvallation' to ward off relief attempts, demanded the labour of an entire army to construct them. In 1629 when Frederick Henry captured 's-Hertogenbosch from the Spanish he needed 28,000 troops in lines spread around an eleven-hour circumference and supported by 116 cannon (Duffy 1979: 102). Operations of this kind were inevitably time consuming, and the problem was aggravated by the fact that the sapping technique offered only a narrow and constricted avenue of approach to the fortifications. Losses were consequently very high among the men digging the saps, and these so-called 'pioneers' sometimes had to be raised by empressment (Wood 1996: 68, 165–6, 173–5).[7] In addition, the longer the siege the greater was the toll from sickness, desertion, and logistical deficiencies.

The fundamental problem was that new military technology had created increased logistical demands without offering any offsetting innovations on the supply side. Indeed, the problems were exacerbated by the large number of draught animals the new siege trains needed, and supply was not the only difficulty confronting besiegers. The crowded and insanitary conditions of siege camps provided ideal conditions for the spread of infectious disease. This had been the main source of casualties before the spread of gunpowder weapons, but the increase in the scale of forces at this time aggravated problems of sanitation and hygiene, and the incidence of deaths from disease is likely to have increased as a result (see below, Chapter 14, Appendix II). These losses, added to the combat casualties, meant that powerful besieging forces could be seriously depleted in victory and virtually destroyed by failure. Spinola's successful siege of Ostend, whose garrison had access to seaborne communication for most of its duration, lasted over three years, and the Spanish suffered losses running into tens of thousands of men (Duffy 1979: 88–9). Fewer than 5,000 out of 30,000 French troops survived the failure of Francis I's Neapolitan expedition in 1528, and forty years later the French royal army ended the siege of La Rochelle with only a third of its initial strength, having lost around 18,000 men from all causes (Wood 1996: 268–74). Overall, the figures in Table 8.1 suggest that even a successful siege or assault had a one in four chance of costing the attacker at least a quarter or a fifth of his force in casualties.

Table 8.1 *Sieges and assaults: attackers' casualties*

	Casualties		
	Mean	Upper quartile	N
All cases			
1628–1714	20.2	29.0	36
1715–1814	16.2	23.0	27
Attacker successful			
1676–1714	17.1	23.7	30
1715–1812	16.9	20.3	17

Source: See Appendix II.

---

[7] As Wood notes, the low status of pioneers in the French royal army was emphasized by their being the only personnel to be issued uniforms. 'Badging' in this was a mark of stigmatized dependency.

8.1.4. SUMMARY

Fortifications are obstacles whose purpose is to block access to either an area of land or an enclosed space. The first was effectively unattainable before the gunpowder era unless nature co-operated by providing an easily obstructed defile. Garrisons without powerful missile weapons or artillery simply could not patrol a lengthy barrier fortification in sufficient strength to stop attackers crossing it, whether by stealth or open assault. Enclosed 'point defences', by contrast, were ubiquitous. They varied greatly in size, but their function was always to protect some kind of asset whether economic, demographic, or military. The limitations of muscle power made it almost impossible to take substantial fortifications by direct assault as long as they were properly prepared, whilst constraints on transport and agricultural productivity meant that blockading forces often ran out of supplies before the besieged garrison. At the same time, the limitations of muscle-powered weaponry condemned garrisons to an essentially passive role, unless they were prepared to engage the besiegers in open-field combat, and this made smaller numbers preferable so as to ease supply problems.

The appearance of effective siege cannon set off an 'evolutionary race' between the forces of attack and defence, mobility and stasis. It was one whose outcome was always in doubt and is not entirely clear even in retrospect. Whatever balance was eventually attained was inherently unstable. It was also bought at the price of substantial increases in the human and capital costs of fortress warfare, and so of warfare as a whole (see below, Part IV). The balance also differed qualitatively from that prevailing in earlier periods because the new gunpowder weapons aided the two sides in distinct and incommensurable ways. For an attacker, gunpowder siege trains meant that there was no longer, in principle, any such thing as an impregnable fortification. The defender could no longer rely on the success of purely passive defence, but fortifications and their garrisons acquired firearms too, and this allowed them to conduct an active defence. Fortress warfare, in Duffy's words, 'for the first time assumed the character of an equal duel'. The larger perimeters of the new 'artillery fortresses', and the ability of their gun-armed defenders to inflict serious casualties, fostered an increase in the numbers of men on both sides of their walls. Garrisons' strengths now often ran into the thousands (see Table 8.2), and their firepower gave them a new ability to block the passage of large forces encumbered by supply and artillery trains.[8] The result was the appearance of a new kind of fortress warfare, in which the siege of walled cities and other major defensive installations by entire field armies became a matter of routine.

---

[8] The expansion of the road net in parts of western Europe had partly reversed this trend during the 18th century by making it easier for large forces to bypass fortresses (Meyer 2000: 100–2). This allowed a return to more mobile forms of warfare after the French Revolution.

Table 8.2 *Garrison size* (000)

Period	Mean	N
1688–1757	7.7	64
1792–1814	13.4	23

Source: See Appendix II.

8.2. NAVAL WARFARE

Naval and land warfare differed in their strategic and operational principles but the pursuit of both was constrained by the restricted availability of energy. Many of the operational problems and possibilities of naval warfare were the same as those facing peaceful seafarers. Warships exploited wind power as did merchant ships, and the problems presented by naval transport of armed men and supplies differed only in scale from those of trading expeditions. Fighting at sea was a very different matter, however, and its tactical imperatives meant that warship design diverged from that of merchant vessels both before and after the gunpowder revolution. In the earlier period sea fighting revolved around boarding or ramming, and this required precise manoeuvring ability either to establish or avoid physical contact with the enemy. Oar power was the only way to achieve this before the invention of sophisticated fore-and-aft rigging, and even then the wind could be a dangerously unreliable energy source in sea battles. The coming of gunpowder artillery led to a design revolution that dispensed with oars and emphasized firepower, giving warships a range and endurance that introduced a new dimension into naval strategy.

8.2.1. MUSCLE-POWERED NAVAL WARFARE

A series of specialized warships, exemplified by the Greek trireme, emerged in response to the tactical imperatives of muscle-powered sea fighting. Their design sacrificed cargo space for a light hull with a large complement of oarsmen supplemented by sailors and shipboard soldiers or marines (Morrison, Coates, and Rankov 2000; Casson 1971: 77–96). The different models of ship varied chiefly in their size. Hellenistic rulers experimented with very large vessels—some with catamaran hulls—while smaller *dromonds* prevailed in the later Roman and Byzantine periods, but the basic principles governing the design of oar-powered warships did not change (Casson 1971: 97 f.; Pryor 1988: 57–86). The results were extremely labour intensive to operate and this imposed a heavy requirement for food and, more particularly, water. There was very little storage space on board, so frequent resupply was essential, and this seriously restricted their range and endurance away from port.[9] The vessels' low freeboard also made them vulnerable to heavy seas.

---

[9] Guilmartin estimates the daily water consumption of a galley's oarsmen at half a gallon per head and regards two weeks' supply as the 'iron limit' of a galley's storage capacity (Guilmartin 1993: 120).

These operational constraints had important strategic consequences because they meant that fleets could not remain in distant waters for extended periods but had to stay close to their sources of supply. Naval strategy was also shaped by the character of the sea itself. Containing no militarily significant resources, its importance lay in its function as a medium of transport and communications, a medium that was all the more important in an era of muscle-powered land haulage. States whose economy relied on seaborne trading had to secure their shipping routes if they were to survive, but the limitations of naval technology hampered them in this respect. It was very difficult for one fleet to intercept another at sea, and, until the very close of the period, not even the most powerful navy could exclude its opponents from distant waters by remaining 'on station' for an extended period. A state needing to secure its seaborne communications had to do this by physically eliminating its rivals, or by controlling coastlines, narrows, or other choke points. The best way to achieve this was often to establish a presence on land so as to deny bases to enemy fleets or raiders.

Large-scale fleet conflict rarely played more than a very restricted role in warfare as a whole. Where it did impinge on rulers' attempts to establish and maintain control over demographic space it generally occurred in support of operations by land forces. In offensive mode fleets were used to transport troops and equipment, and to keep them supplied once ashore, and they could provide vital logistical support to siege operations. Defending fleets manoeuvred to block such moves, but they were hampered by the difficulty of interception in open water, and combats generally took place in restricted waters close to land, or where the enemy's destination could be predicted in advance. Fleet combat was not, however, the only form of seaborne violence. Much of the naval activity that took place in the ancient and medieval worlds concerned the prosecution or suppression of small-scale raiding.

The intrinsic mobility of seaborne raiders meant that merchant shipping and littoral communities alike found themselves targeted by forces ranging from a single ship to a substantial amphibious contingent. Where extensive networks of seaborne trade existed, 'pirate' attacks of this kind could play an important part in war between organized states. Equally important were raids by coastal barbarian communities on 'civilized' neighbours, or freelance activities by captains who might alternate piracy and peaceful commerce as opportunities arose. Piracy was endemic in the ancient Mediterranean and guarding against it by seaborne means was very difficult (de Souza 1999). In practice, coastal communities had to rely on fixed or mobile land defences or else simply avoid vulnerable locations. The only effective means of pre-emption was to root out the bases from which such attacks were launched. This was rarely practicable given the political fragmentation that prevailed before Roman times, but by the end of the Republic a degree of security had been established across the Mediterranean. The Romans controlled the sea because they controlled its shores, and this control endured until the establishment of a Vandal fleet at Carthage in the fifth century.

The fragmentation of the Mediterranean basin into Christian and Muslim spheres promoted a renewal of seaborne attacks that persisted in one form or another into the nineteenth century. Northern Europe also suffered from the late Roman period onward, the main source of the assaults shifting to the north and east over time. The Low Countries, and especially Frisia, were bases for the attacks on Roman Britain and Gaul (Haywood 1999), whilst Scandinavian raiders—the infamous 'Vikings'—became a serious threat in the ninth century. By the end of the eleventh century, a combination of better military organization in the target zones and the establishment of Christian kingdoms in Scandinavia itself had largely put an end to Viking raids, and Denmark itself became a target for attacks from the eastern Baltic. Barbary corsairs raided Britain's coasts as late as the 1640s (Rogers 1997: 384–5), but the major seaborne threats to northern European states after the Viking Age came from their Christian neighbours.

8.2.2. GUNPOWDER AND SEA POWER

The gunpowder revolution transformed the tactical, operational, and strategic capabilities of naval forces. At the tactical level, the stability of a ship's deck made it an ideal firing platform, and the fact that artillery could be left in place once installed allowed heavy guns to be used at sea with relative ease. The limitations of musclepower were not, however, wholly overcome. As long as cannonballs had to be picked up and loaded by hand the limit on their calibre was set by the capacity of the contemporary human bicep, which turned out to be in the 30- to 40-pound range.[10] Once this limit had been reached greater firepower could only be obtained by adding more guns, which meant lining them up along the sides of the ship in a way that was not possible if oars were going to be used. The result was the emergence of a new kind of warship based on sail power and a broadside artillery layout.

Sail power was widely used in northern sea fighting as early as the thirteenth century, but as boarding became the *coup de grâce* delivered to a vessel already crippled by gunfire the tactical disadvantages of wind power largely disappeared, even in Mediterranean waters. The need to withstand naval artillery also placed a premium on hull strength which ruled out oar power except in restricted waters like the Baltic, where galleys persisted into the eighteenth century (Glete 1992). Sailing ships needed far fewer men relative to their size and so combined cargo space with respectable firepower, which led to a short-term reduction in specialization. Early modern carracks and galleons combined military and commercial functions, but this trend proved short-lived, and the two types diverged in the later seventeenth century. In this period the multi-deck 'ship of the line' emerged, carrying artillery batteries with which no armed merchantman could hope to compete, whilst the Dutch *fluyt* instigated a move to boxier and less warlike merchant vessels.

---

[10] This was discovered by the British during the American Revolutionary War when the rate of fire of their heaviest naval gun batteries, which were 42-pounders, proved unacceptably low because their balls were too heavy for the crews to handle efficiently (Lavery 1992: 21).

Major warship designs that developed after gunpowder themselves diverged into two specialized forms: the ship of the line and the frigate (also termed 'battleships', and 'cruisers'). The latter's main function was to detect enemy battle fleets at sea and act as a screen against probes by enemy vessels of the same type.[11] Frigates were designed for long-distance patrols, but even the largest battleships—mounting over 100 guns—could be designed with a six-month cruising range, which meant that European fleets could now sail thousands of miles and, on arrival, destroy the naval forces of indigenous non-European states even when greatly outnumbered.[12] Their frigates enabled them to detect and intercept shipping in open water whilst their cargo/crew ratios gave them an extended patrolling capacity.[13] The resulting ability to retain substantial naval forces 'on station' in distant water for indefinite periods was a development of historic proportions which laid the basis for the establishment of sea power in the modern sense (Kennedy 1991: 116–19, 168–9; Black 1999: 221 f.).

8.2.3. SUMMARY

The modern concept of 'sea power' is out of place before the era of sail and cannon (Starr 1989). The range and endurance of oar-powered fleets, and their ability to detect an enemy at sea, were too restricted for them to have any realistic prospect of excluding opponents from large areas of open water or protecting lengthy shorelines for an extended period of time.[14] The fact that wooden ships could be replaced relatively quickly also meant that the consequences of victory in a major engagement might be short-lived. As late as the fourteenth century, the major naval victories gained by English fleets over the French yielded only the most short-term protection for Channel shipping and coastal communities.[15] Where 'decisive' battles were won and lost at sea, as they sometimes were in this period, they were important either because they opened or closed a temporary

---

[11] The vital contribution of frigates to the operational and strategic capabilities of contemporary battle fleets can be seen from what happened in their absence. This occurred in the Mediterranean naval campaign of 1798 when Nelson's fleet proved totally unable to intercept, or even locate, the slow-moving transports taking Napoleon's army to Egypt because bad weather had deprived him of his frigate squadron (Lavery 1990; Parkinson 1987: 60–7).

[12] This ability on the part of European interlopers was particularly serious for south Asian powers given the importance of maritime commerce in the region's political economy. See for instance Subrahmanyam (2001).

[13] Fleets that remained at sea for long periods still suffered serious attrition, as much from disease as from shipwreck or weather damage, but the consequent operational limitations were ameliorated by a progressive reduction in crew sickness and mortality from the middle of the 18th century (Haines and Shlomowitz 1998).

[14] Runyan's judgement on 14th-century sea power is equally apposite here. 'Control of the sea', he argues, 'is a meaningful term if limited to a definition which signifies the capacity to continue to move unobstructed by pirates or enemy fleets' (Runyan 1993: 94).

[15] The supposedly 'decisive' English naval victory at Sluys in 1340 was in fact followed by rapid French retaliation. Runyan observes that England's southern coastal ports 'were raided as they had been in the 1330s, and attacks on the routes to Gascony in the Bay of Biscay continued' (Runyan 1993: 94). See also Friel (1994).

'window of opportunity' in support of land operations, or because they broke the loser's will to go on with the struggle.[16] The gunpowder revolution changed this by giving warships a range and endurance that enabled them to remain at sea for long periods and to mount effective blockades in distant waters. As a result, maritime powers could seek to control sea as they might control territory on land.

8.3. CONCLUSION

The gunpowder revolution changed the operational and strategic character of both siege and naval warfare in a way that was qualitatively different from what had gone before and was not true of mobile warfare on land. Its effects were felt first in fortress warfare, where it gave the new mobile siege artillery an overwhelming advantage over medieval-style fortifications. This advantage proved as short-lived as it was dramatic, and within a generation military architects had developed designs that could both absorb the shock of cannon fire and deploy it in the interest of the defence. The competitive evolution of mobile siege trains and the artillery fortress had three main consequences. First, it created a much closer balance between the forces of attack and defence, so that the outcome of an investment became a great deal less predictable than it had been in the days when sieges mostly turned on whether the garrison or the besiegers were the first to run out of food.

At the same time, the enhanced ability of the defenders to inflict casualties on the besiegers meant that large garrisons ceased to be just a logistical liability and acquired a positive military value. By the same token, the higher rates of attrition likely to be sustained by a besieging force provided a rationale for expansion on this side of the equation as well. Finally it changed the character of strategic geography by enabling fortified positions to fulfil a new function. These had previously been confined almost entirely to the role of 'point defences' protecting urban centres, providing refuges for dispersed populations or bases for mobile troops. The firepower of the new fortifications, together with the encumbering trains that armies needed if they were to have any hope of capturing such places, meant that they could block the movement of substantial forces and so act as strategic barriers in a way that had rarely been possible before.

---

[16] Even an expensive victory, such as that of a Greek fleet over Carthage and the Etruscans off the Greek colony of Alalia in c.537 BC, might have this latter effect. Alalia was abandoned after the battle, leaving the south-west Mediterranean in Carthaginian hands and blocking Greek access to the Atlantic, a development with far-reaching consequences (Cunliffe 1988: 17–19). At the other end of the period, even the long-term importance of Britain's naval victory at Trafalgar was less material than psychological. It convinced Napoleon that his sailors could not defeat the royal navy, and though the rebuilt French fleet actually outnumbered its enemy by the end of the war it was ordered to remain in port (Esdaile 1995: 150–3). Conversely, where the will remained intact, a crushing naval defeat might have little long-term effect. The Ottoman sultanate lost two-thirds of its ships at Lepanto in 1571, but Pryor notes that the losses were quickly made up and that the Christian victory 'was arguably of little more than symbolic significance' (Pryor 1988: 177).

Gunpowder weapons also had both operational and strategic consequences at sea. These stemmed from their effects on naval tactics and consequently on the design and construction of warships. The decisive innovation was the invention of the broadside artillery layout which presaged the final victory of sailing ships over galleys. It led to ever-larger and more powerful ships of the line with an oceanic range and endurance and a firepower that could destroy any other kind of wooden ship. With the aid of their fast manoeuvrable frigate squadrons the new battle fleets could also locate and intercept enemy ships at sea. This increased operational flexibility gave naval forces new strategic capabilities. Hitherto these had largely been confined to transporting land forces, protecting other vessels, and intercepting enemy fleets close to land. The new fleets had the potential to deny areas of open water to an enemy for extended periods and by the Napoleonic period this potential was realized. Navies could now hope to control open seas, block shipping lanes, and project sea power on an oceanic scale, just as fortification systems could be designed to seal off entire frontiers. The consequence was a substantial increase in the importance of military capital.

Conclusion

Military technology relied almost entirely on muscle power until the gunpowder revolution allowed the exploitation of chemical energy. The reliance on muscle power was common to naval warfare and to both mobile and siege warfare on land, but its implications were different in the three contexts and the consequences of the gunpowder revolution differed accordingly. The technology of mobile land warfare, like production technology, relied on a variety of energy-transmitting tools, and on animal power to supplement the muscle power of humans. Like production technology, military technology could also be made more effective by greater specialization, and increases in specialization fostered a more developed division of labour. But unlike production technology, more specialized military systems were also potentially more vulnerable because the value of military technology was essentially relative rather than absolute. This relativity reflected the fact that battlefield success depended on being able to overcome a specific opponent employing a specific tactical system, and the tactical systems prevailing before the advent of the gunpowder revolution displayed an interlocking pattern of strengths and weaknesses that prevented a stable global hierarchy from emerging among them.

The few tactical systems which proved capable of beating all those against which they were routinely matched were so skill intensive as to be what we have called 'ethnic technologies' which were incapable of general diffusion. In this respect the spread of handguns heralded a revolutionary break with historical experience, but early models were so inaccurate and slow firing that they required a very specific set of procedures and supporting arms if they were to be used effectively. The requirement was met by the development of the 'musket and sabre' system, which was based on a choreographed drill that enabled infantry formations to deliver a continuous series of synchronized volleys. In its definitive form, which it assumed by the end of the seventeenth century, it proved capable of beating any other military technology, but unlike earlier potentially hegemonic systems, it required no quality of the common soldier beyond endurance and a habit of machine-like obedience. Armies based on this system proliferated across Europe, and eventually the world, and were only displaced by a more sophisticated version of the same technology. The development of drill also laid the foundations for an enhanced degree of tactical co-ordination that underpinned substantial increases in both the scale and duration of battlefield combat, with corresponding increases in numbers of casualties. The technological stability of the musket and sabre system reflected the reluctance of Europe's rulers to contemplate further increases in the destructiveness of combat and the greater costs that this would have entailed.

Naval tactics before the gunpowder age were constrained by the fact that ships had to manoeuvre into physical contact in order to inflict serious physical damage on an enemy. This gave oar power a substantial premium over sail, but oar-powered warships could not carry enough drinking water for a lengthy cruise and so had a very limited range and endurance. This restriction, reinforced by the difficulties of locating ships at sea, effectively prevented fleets from maintaining distant blockades or intercepting each other far from shore. It was not possible to deny large areas of open water to the enemy, and to the extent that there was such a thing as 'sea power' it consisted in the ability to secure passage by the use of escorts or by eliminating enemy bases from neighbouring shores. The gunpowder revolution at sea created an entirely new kind of vessel with unprecedented capacities. The combination of full-rigging and armed broadside artillery batteries gave sailing warships an oceanic range and a hitherto unequalled fighting power. Squadrons of the new battleships supported by faster frigates had the endurance and manoeuvrability to mount distant blockades over long periods and carry European naval dominance across the globe.

Gunpowder artillery also transformed the military role of fortifications, which had long been an important one. The very limited amount of kinetic energy that muscle-powered armies could bring to bear made fortifications very difficult to take by assault, and logistical problems often made them very difficult to take by blockade. Conversely, the relative weakness of long-range weapons meant that garrisons could do little to harm a besieging force or to interfere with one that merely bypassed their walls. The function of fortifications was therefore primarily passive, and they mainly acted as very effective shelters for civilian populations or mobile detachments. The immediate effect of gunpowder siege artillery was a dramatic reduction in the value of fortifications, but military architects quickly established a new balance between attack and defence. It was, however, a balance of a very different kind. The new 'artillery fortresses' and their garrisons were heavily armed and could inflict crippling losses on a poorly led besieging force, but even the strongest of them were vulnerable to a well-conducted assault. The scale of siege warfare therefore increased and its outcome became more uncertain. At the same time, the volume of fire that defenders could now lay down posed serious dangers to the road-bound supply and artillery columns on which gunpowder armies depended. A new strategic geography began to emerge as, for the first time, effective barrier fortifications became a practical proposition.

PART III

Force, Power, and Space

Introduction

The limited availability of energy constrained the development of production and transportation in organic economies, thereby restricting the scope for spatial integration. This restriction affected the exercise of political power as well as the prospects for economic growth. The effective exercise of power requires the ability to exert systematic coercion at a distance from the centre of power and so it too is based on a form of spatial integration. The systematic exercise of coercion requires access to armed force and, since armed force comes at a price, the maintenance of political power requires the ability to extract resources from geographical space. The progression from armed force to sustainable political power encompassed three necessary stages or levels. The first of these was control of a military force strong enough to defeat opposing forces or at least have a good enough prospect of success to deter assaults and overawe potential resistance; the ability to win victories on the battlefield was not enough in itself, however, to make an army into an effective political instrument.

Meeting this second, or 'Clausewitzian', criterion of effectiveness required securing sufficient control over territory to be able to extract resources, whether temporarily or indefinitely, without incurring disproportionate economic or political costs. The requirements for doing this were more complex and not definable simply in terms of the likely opposition. Some of them depended on the aspects of tactical organization and discipline that we considered in Part II, but others were linked to operational and strategic criteria in ways that are examined in the first chapter of this part. The fundamental requirement was to be able to concentrate, manoeuvre, and maintain one's forces in such a way as both to overcome armed opposition and to establish control over the productive resources of the target area. The scope for achieving this, whatever the quality of one's own troops, was limited by one's ability to keep them supplied with food and fodder and so was governed by the familiar constraints of organic economy.

Troops on home ground could be provisioned from pre-positioned stores if the defender was sufficiently well organized, but invaders had to carry their food with them, take it from the surrounding countryside, or establish a supply line to the exterior. The operational capacity of an invading force, and therefore its strategic choice between short-term raiding and prolonged occupation, was heavily dependent on which of these supply options were taken up. An occupation strategy generally required external supply unless decisive victory could be achieved quickly, and this could be very demanding in terms of manpower. Establishing and maintaining occupation was also likely to involve protracted 'low-level' warfare waged by dispersed forces based on local strong points. This form of warfare was extremely destructive and the difficulties of maintaining central control carried a constant risk that it would degenerate into simple banditry.

Once operational military victory had been obtained it had to be transformed into a strategy of resource extraction, and the means by which this was achieved are considered in the second chapter of the section. The long-term systematic extraction of resources requires a form of state organization, and these have existed in a variety of different contexts. The state system which had taken shape in Europe by the end of the seventeenth century was based on a set of structurally equivalent entities which acknowledged reciprocal rights and obligations with respect to each other, but this was historically unusual. In earlier periods organized states often bordered stateless barbarian societies, and their relationships with these and with each other were conditioned by assumptions of hierarchy and cultural difference.

This phenomenon affected strategies of resource extraction, which could take one of two forms. The first was the enforcement of tributary dependence (or simply 'dependence') associated with the short-term or periodic extraction of resources, sometimes on a literally 'hit and run' basis. Enforcing dependence did not require the maintenance of administrative agencies or other continuing forms of engagement with the population in question. It might take the form of simple looting, or accepting bribes to refrain from it, but could also lead to the establishment of more regular formalized tributary relations with local rulers or elites. Since the enforcement of dependence did not require the maintenance of permanent extractive structures it was within the capability of barbarian leaders as well as the rulers of organized states. This was not true of the second form of extraction, which involved the establishment and maintenance of administrative control (or simply 'control'). This form was long term and systemic, involving the levying of taxation in some form. Coercive agencies had to be retained in place and maintain a continuing engagement with the structures of economic and social life in a defined area of physical space. Control in this sense therefore required some form of state organization and establishing it was a two-stage process. The first, 'conquest', stage involved the neutralization of armed opposition and was followed by the establishment of a continuing domination of population and resources sufficient to allow the levying of taxation. The first of these was often easier to achieve in barbarian territories than against organized states, but the second was generally more difficult in these circumstances and could require systematic colonization.

Once control had been established it had to be maintained, and the third chapter of the section considers the problems involved in doing this. There were essentially three tasks: the maintenance of internal control over the population, the defence of frontiers from external attack, and stopping regional governors, commanders, or elites breaking away from the centre. The first of these was made very difficult by the limitations on transport and communications, and internal control was often 'shallow' in the sense that the state's coercive reach was largely confined to major population centres and communication nodes. Frontier defence was also complicated by the limitations on military and transportation technology which were often reinforced by a reluctance to define fixed geographical limits to a state's jurisdiction. Frontiers, as a result, generally formed relatively fluid zones rather than rigid boundary lines. They were also complex sociological entities, especially where organized states bordered barbarian territory, and often harder to defend against recurrent low-level raiding than larger forces waging high-level warfare. The first kind of 'diffused' threat could be extremely destructive to the economic and demographic foundations of frontier society and meeting it usually required decentralizing the structures of command and administration, but this itself increased the danger that the state would disintegrate through a process of regional secession.

CHAPTER NINE

War and the Organic Economy

The conduct of military operations involves the disposition of assets in time and space in the presence of uncertainty. Military assets are deployed in physical space, so as to engage or evade the corresponding assets of an opponent, whether mobile forces or fortified positions, and to seize or defend territorial objectives, however temporarily. Their aim is the achievement of some strategic goal, which itself serves a broader political or economic purpose.[1] Strategy and operations are mutually interrelated because the choice of goals shapes the conduct of operations and the range of practicable goals depends on what is possible operationally. The political and social context of any conflict affected both of these but variations were constrained systematically by the limitations of the military technology which was in use and by the underlying structures of an organic economy. These restricted the ability of military forces to manoeuvre and to obtain adequate supplies. It was, above all, the geography of production, population, and communications—and thus the structure of demographic as much as physical space—that conditioned both the choice of strategic goals and the ways in which they could be achieved.

Demographic space was, as we have seen, structured on two levels. The first level corresponded to the areal distribution of production and consumption of subsistence goods, a distribution oriented around local settlements and markets, interconnected by a mesh of minor routeways. The second corresponded to the punctiform distribution of major political centres, ports, and entrepôts, nodal points on the network of long-distance, mainly luxury, trade routes. At this second level was found 'concentrated' wealth, consisting of rare minerals, artefacts, and other stores of value, or human capital in the form of skilled labour or entrepreneurial ability. Such concentrated wealth was located in cities or other potentially defensible locations that might have a strategic or symbolic value in their own right.[2] Resources at this second level carried a high social and economic

---

[1] Political goals need to be understood broadly in this context. In many cases they consisted of the commander's desire to maintain or advance his domestic political position by gaining glory. One exception to the general rule that military operations had an extra-military goal occurred where they were undertaken simply to keep the troops in condition or to 'blood' new recruits. Drinkwater believes that this was a motive for some Roman campaigns on the Rhine (Drinkwater 1996: 26–8).

[2] Cities might acquire symbolic value because, like Jerusalem, they had a religious significance. In other circumstances, possession of the traditional capital or other centre could lend legitimacy to a contender for power. Rheims, where French kings were traditionally crowned, had such a value during the Hundred Years War.

valuation, but they acquired an immediate military value only in so far as they could be translated into those at the first level, namely manpower and the organic production of the countryside. A militarily significant 'resource' was that of leadership, and the organizational apparatus for formulating and transmitting commands. Its nature varied with context and the degree of socio-political differentiation, but the numbers involved were always small and sometimes consisted of single individuals. The geography of leadership was necessarily punctiform, residing in major cities or fortified centres, or with the army itself. Political and military leadership usually coincided at the higher echelons, and often did so at relatively low echelons, throughout the period under consideration.

Lasting victory could sometimes be attained by striking directly at the enemy leadership, but this was usually only possible where the issue could be decided by physically eliminating a rival, as in dynastic struggles or usurpations. Otherwise, military leaders could usually be replaced, and larger cities were rarely sufficiently integrated into the productive agrarian economy for their loss to represent a seriously damaging blow. Even the capture of the capital was rarely decisive as long as enemy forces retained control of substantial areas of countryside.[3] The fundamental resources of an organic economy, which were those that military forces had to control if they were to cement victory or even sustain themselves, were the areally distributed resources of the countryside. Invaders sought to destroy or seize crops, animals, or capital assets such as mills and, depending on the period and context, to harass, abduct, or massacre populations so as to break the defenders' ability, or will, to resist. The seizure of crops and livestock was often the invaders' only means of subsistence, and so a defender might be equally destructive in order to deny them this. In these circumstances the defender's priority was not territory as such but population and resources. What mattered was demographic rather than physical space, and the configuration of demographic space accordingly shaped both the goals and conduct of military operations.

This configuration created a competition between two overriding but incompatible priorities, namely the concentration and dispersal of force. The priority in destroying the enemy's military assets was to concentrate the greatest force possible at the decisive point. Dispersing one's own troops in the presence of a concentrated enemy was to risk having the separated elements attacked in turn at overwhelming odds and so suffering what is termed 'defeat in detail'. Dispersal, however, was exactly what was needed to control demographic space in organic economies. Settlement and production were broadcast across the landscape, and force had to be dispersed to dominate any significant proportion of the population and the resources on which they depended. Poor transport and

---

[3] In some circumstances the loss of his capital might undermine a ruler's legitimacy in the eyes of his subjects, but it was hardly fatal in itself. Prussian forces, for instance, continued to fight despite the occupation of Berlin during the Seven Years War.

communications exacerbated the problem by increasing the time needed to locate and contact subordinate units and assemble them at a central point. In this respect an important asymmetry existed between attacker and defender. A dispersed invader could achieve little against military targets, and was vulnerable to defeat in detail, but systems of local point defences enabled small bodies of troops to be spread out around settlements and communications centres to great effect. Such installations protected their garrisons against superior numbers, but they also afforded protection for resources—above all food, fodder, and protected stabling for horses—and provided secure bases for mobile troops that could dominate the surrounding countryside.

These systems of local point defences were all the more important given the inability of barrier fortifications to prevent enemy penetration of territory on any substantial scale before the gunpowder revolution, or of mobile forces to form continuous blocking 'fronts' before the twentieth century. Earlier commanders had to counter invasions by manoeuvre. They sought to engage and defeat the enemy in battle, or else to avoid battle in the hope that sickness, lack of supplies, or the end of the campaigning season would do their work for them. In either case they had to accept that the enemy would be able to enter at least a frontier zone, if not the interior of the defended territory itself. Such an enemy might be victorious in the field, but if it could not secure the countryside, at least in part, it would have to withdraw at the end of the season. The most brutal and destructive consequences generally ensued when the invader gained partial control, seizing sufficient strong points to maintain garrisons in a region but not to expel the defenders entirely. Where neither side could clear the other's troops from a given region, or where zones of control bordered each other or interpenetrated, a characteristic form of warfare developed. Known in medieval times as *guerre guerroyante* it was small scale but nonetheless intense and pervasive, usually revolving around the control of local strong points (Ayton and Price 1995; Gillingham 1984; Contamine 1984).

Just as the two-level structure of demographic space created the distinction between high- and low-level traffic, so it fostered the emergence of 'high-level' and 'low-level' warfare. The first was a war of manoeuvre and battle conducted by forces concentrated in thousands or more and oriented towards occupation or major raids. The second was a matter of small-scale raids and ambushes, or the capture and defence of local strong points, waged by dispersed bodies of troops numbering hundreds or less. The basis of the distinction in each case is the superimposition of two distinct levels of spatial organization, and as the relative importance of the two levels shifted in economic life, so did the relative importance of the two levels of warfare. Just as these two levels were distinct but interconnected, so were the two forms of warfare. The ability of large field armies to concentrate and manoeuvre depended on their mastery of the surrounding countryside and its resources, whilst dispersed troops, who could not seek refuge in fortifications, had to concentrate their numbers or risk defeat in detail when an enemy field army approached.

9.1. HIGH-LEVEL WARFARE: FORCE, TIME, AND SPACE

High-level warfare involved the disposition of concentrated force in space and time. Its operational conduct was shaped by the interplay of strategy and logistics. In this context 'strategy' can be thought of as a set of general principles either implicitly or explicitly informing the choice of ends and means in any concrete instance.[4] 'Logistics' represented the practical, context-dependent constraints springing from troops' need for arms, munitions, and the means of subsistence. The dimensions of time and space were intimately related because the area that any force could control varied with the tempo of military operations, and this was ultimately determined by the speed at which troops could be moved. This speed itself depended on the nature of the troops and their equipment, their level of training and discipline, and the relevant terrain and logistical arrangements. The importance of the first three of these factors is self-evident. Other things being equal, cavalry and 'lights' always moved faster than infantry or 'heavies', well-disciplined troops faster than poorly disciplined troops, and all did better on firm surfaces and roads than soft or rough terrain. Well-trained and equipped heavy infantry could march up to 20 miles a day, with cavalry and light troops managing two or three times this daily rate in the short-term, although 20 miles was probably the maximum where horses had to be kept fit for battle.[5] In practice, however, logistical factors often kept movement rates well below their theoretical limits. These factors affected both the speed with which a force could move and its ability to concentrate at a single point. Since these, in turn, set the limits to what it could achieve militarily, logistical factors largely determined the operational feasibility of any given strategic goal.

9.1.1. LOGISTICS AND MOBILITY

The supply needs of pre-gunpowder armies, like those of civilian populations, consisted almost entirely of what the men and animals needed to eat. In one sense this simplified their logistical problems, but it also subjected them to all the constraints that organic economies placed on the production and transport of subsistence goods. In the short-term subsistence 'needs' were flexible to a degree. Mechanical engines require a certain amount of fuel to function. If this is not

---

[4] 'Strategy' before the 19th century rarely consisted of explicit formally articulated goals grounded in theoretical principles, but this does not mean that it was non-existent. As Guilmartin observes: 'In a sense it is...anachronistic to speak of Spanish strategy in the sixteenth century, for few of the historical actors understood or discussed strategy in terms familiar to us. But an implicit strategy is a strategy nonetheless' (Guilmartin 1993: 110–11). This is not to deny that the goals of strategy and its implementation were often guided by political expediency.

[5] As an example of the operational range of raiding cavalry: Robert the Bruce's Scots horsemen are said to have covered 60 to 70 miles in twenty-four hours on some of their raids into England (Hyland 1998: 37). As Bachrach points out, mounted infantry tactics of the kind favoured by Scandinavian and Anglo-Saxon troops gave the greatest operational flexibility. Horses that were not going to be used on the battlefield could move much further and faster on the march, covering up to 300 miles in a week where logistical arrangements permitted it (Bachrach 1985: 724–5).

available they come to a dead stop, but biological 'engines'—human or animal bodies—can continue working for some time on much less than their normal intake, even if their level of performance falls off. The nature of the fuel required was also affected by social and cultural differences which expressed themselves in varying dietary preferences, prohibitions, and 'needs', and could have logistical implications. It is easy enough to calculate rough estimates of what a given force was likely to require, and how the requirement could be met, but actual 'needs' varied with circumstances, as did the military consequences of failing to meet them. Whether an army was willing or able to keep fighting in the face of logistical inadequacy depended on the wider context, as did the implications of declining military effectiveness. This was not an all or nothing question, and outcomes often turned on the issue of which side was better able to cope with partial failure.

9.1.1.1. *The problem*

Food and fodder accounted for nearly all of the consumable supplies required by a body of armed men before the gunpowder revolution. Food was needed for the soldiers themselves and for a variable, sometimes very large, number of non-combatants. Fodder was needed for the soldiers' mounts and for transport animals, most of which were employed in hauling consumable supplies and 'baggage' of all kinds. The more surplus baggage a column accumulated, the more transport animals it needed, and since these also had to eat, further transport might be needed to carry their supplies. The spread of gunpowder weapons increased these requirements by adding powder and ammunition to the list of essential supplies and raising their weight per soldier by as much as 30 per cent. General Grant allowed the northern armies in the American Civil War a quota of five wagons per thousand men for munitions, which was nearly as many as the seven allocated for their subsistence.[6] The new artillery trains meant that more draught animals were needed. The requirements for the heavier artillery pieces (see Table 9.1) meant that the train of around twenty guns supporting the

Table 9.1 *Gun crews and capacities: sixteenth-century French royal army*

Gun	Men	Horses	Powder (*livres*)	Shot (*livres*)
Cannon	90	223	20,000	32,000
Grand culverine	83	141	16,000	15,000
Bastarde	38	93	7,000	12,000
Moyenne	18	37	2,000	5,000

Source: Wood (1996: 158).

[6] Quartermasters in the Union armies allowed 4 lb of supplies per soldier per day. Subsistence accounted for 3 lb of this total and ammunition made up much of the rest (Huston 1966: 215–17).

French royal armies in the 1580s needed over 2,000 personnel and some 1,600 animals to handle it (Wood 1996: 160–1). Heavy siege trains required larger numbers, and in 1708 Marlborough claimed to need 16,000 horses to draw the artillery he was assembling against France (Duffy 1985: 39).[7]

The size of a column's logistical 'tail', and conversely the volume of force supportable by a tail of a given size, depended heavily on its commander's ability to keep non-combatants and unnecessary baggage to a minimum, but the fundamental constant of pre-industrial logistics was the per capita daily ration allowance. Most working adults seem normally to have consumed around 2 pounds of staples daily, supplemented by varying quantities of vegetables and protein in the form of meat, fish, or dairy products. Our evidence for seventeenth- and eighteenth-century rations suggests comparable allowances of one to two pounds of bread, with another pound or so of other food and drink of various kinds. There is no reason to believe that levels were very different in earlier periods although the direct evidence is scanty.[8] Fodder requirements could be met through varying combinations of dry and green fodder and so are more difficult to assess. Horses require at least 20 pounds of food per day. For best performance this should divide equally between grain and fodder. On this basis a day's grazing for a single horse could be met from around 150 square yards of good pasture (Harari 2000: 310). In principle, additional grazing could be used to offset a shortage of grain, although the animal's performance might be impaired. A reliance on grazing also reduced the column's mobility and might expose it to the risk of a surprise attack.[9]

These figures allow rough estimates of the supply needs of a well-organized column's minimum needs. Peddie, for instance, has calculated that an army of six late Republican legions supported by 4,000 auxiliary cavalry would total 43,750 personnel and 13,470 animals for an effective troop strength of just below 35,000. They would consume 79 tons of daily rations of which two-thirds would be

---

[7] Some idea of the additional fodder requirements that this involved can be gained from General Grant's allocation of five fodder wagons for every twenty-five wagons in his army's artillery ammunition train (Huston 1966: 217).

[8] For instance, Cromwell's troops campaigning in Scotland in 1650 received 1–1.5 lb bread and 8–12 oz cheese per day as well as some beer (Edwards 1998: 256). There are some medieval figures which, taken at face value, indicate significantly higher allowances: Prestwich quotes estimates for Edward I's Scottish garrisons 'suggesting that twenty men would need one quarter of wheat a week, and two of malt, along with substantial quantities of meat and fish'. As he continues, like 'much medieval evidence for food consumption, the calorific value of such a diet, at over 5,000, was far in excess of what would be regarded today as appropriate' (Prestwich 1996: 247–8). In fact these totals, like other comparably high figures from medieval and early modern institutions (Harvey 1993: 62–70; Livi-Bacci 1991: 63–4), may include allowances for servants or other non-combatants. When calculating transport requirements it seems reasonably safe to assume a daily consumption of around 3 lb per person.

[9] During the English Civil War, cavalry horses were said to need daily 14 lb of hay, 7 lb of straw, 1 peck of oats, and 0.5 peck of peas (Edwards 1998: 257). A cavalry troop of seventy officers and men would thus have consumed a monthly basic ration of 1.5 tons of bread and 0.75 tons of cheese, whilst the horses would need 13.5 tons of hay, 271 bushels of oats, and 5 bushels of pulses. In practice much of the latter would be met by grazing during campaigns, although as we have seen this might be difficult even where pasture was available.

accounted for by the combat troops and their mounts.[10] A certain number of non-combatant personnel and animals were always needed in order to carry equipment and discharge essential subsistence tasks for the troops in any organized force, and Peddie's calculations assume that no more than this minimum number was present. This may be a realistic assumption for the Roman army of Caesar's day, but in other circumstances commanders often had to deal with much larger numbers than were needed to keep their forces mobile and able to fight. The armies of the ancient world, like those of recent times, were usually organized around minimal groupings of around eight to ten men who would share a tent and cooking utensils and be allocated a servant. A figure of 10 per cent is thus probably the minimum proportion of non-combatants for a heavy infantry force. Cavalry units, however, always needed a much larger proportion of non-combatants to look after the horses and their equipment. This figure may have run as high as one servant per trooper.

The number of transport animals and the logistical demands to which they gave rise were greatly affected by the amount of baggage a column carried with it. Where military and political leadership were combined in the same individual, the camp might have to function as the effective centre of government and so the army would be accompanied by a train of officials with their own servants and possessions—and perhaps even by the treasury. Officers were often drawn from the upper strata, if not actually the elite, of their society, and should they expect to maintain their habitual standard of living on campaign, substantial quantities of 'unnecessary' servants and baggage, including luxuries, could encumber the army.[11] Common soldiers too might be accompanied by companions or even their families. The kind of prolonged fighting that destroyed the structures of a region's civilian life could lead many of the local population to attach themselves to the armies as 'camp followers' of various descriptions, either because no other means of livelihood remained to them or simply for protection. The scale of the overall problem is familiar from ancient and medieval sources but there are some quantitative data from the early modern period. When reinforcements for the Army of Flanders were moved along the 'Spanish Road' from Italy the number of 'mouths' to be fed 'could be almost double the number of actual soldiers... Even in Lombardy, where military life was more closely regimented, between 35 and 40 camp followers were considered appropriate for 200 men' (Parker 1972: 176).

---

[10] This calculation assumes one servant and two-mule cart for each eight-man legionary section, and one additional cart per century. The ration allowance is 3 lb per head for the personnel and 3.5 lb for the animals, and the column has sufficient transport to carry two days' rations (Peddie 1996: 57). See the appendix to Goldsworthy (1996) for a detailed review of what we know concerning Roman logistics under the late Republic and Principate.

[11] The British General Burgoyne complained bitterly of logistical problems but found it necessary to take along thirty cartloads of possessions with him on the march to Saratoga in the American Revolutionary War (Huston 1966: 53). For senior Roman commanders, according to Roth, 'being able to put on an elegant dinner party in the field was a mark of good breeding' (Roth 1999: 57–9).

9.1.1.2. *Solutions*

There were, in principle, four possible solutions to the problem of obtaining food and fodder for a mobile force.[12] First, it might be possible to transport everything needed by vehicle, pack animal, or on the backs of the men themselves. This had obvious advantages but was rarely possible over anything but the shortest distances. Alternatively, supplies could be drawn from pre-arranged depots, markets, or other points along the route. Other circumstances permitting, a force supplied in this way could move more or less uninterrupted as far and fast as muscle power could take it. But such arrangements were practicable only in friendly or at least neutral territory, they required considerable planning, and they restricted the column's operational area to that of a pre-arranged logistical network. A third option was reliance on external depots or other logistical bases. This offered substantial advantages but required the establishment of regular supply lines operated by slow-moving convoys, and so greatly restricted mobility. Finally, troops could 'live off the land' and draw supplies from the area of operations by foraging or some other means. A static force was restricted to the third or fourth options and the practicability of any of them depended on the terrain, the available administrative and transport resources, and the volume of supplies required.

9.1.1.2.1. *Self-sufficiency*

A force able to carry all its own supplies with it constituted a 'flying column' capable, in principle, of manoeuvring independently of any bases and of the conditions in the surrounding countryside, but this logistical solution was very difficult to achieve in practice. In itself, the soldier's 3 pounds of daily rations represented only a modest weight when set against the 60 to 80 pounds that a fit man could carry on his back. An infantryman could carry ten days' rations and still have the capacity for an equivalent weight of personal equipment.[13] The difficulties arose with heavier equipment and fodder. If heavy infantry needed a minimum of one transport animal for six soldiers, a marching column of 10,000 men would need at least 1,350 transport animals. Assuming their green fodder requirements were met by grazing—the availability of which often determined the opening of the campaigning season—ten days' grain supply would amount to 135,000 pounds. Vehicle transport was more efficient but it could also be a lot

---

[12] This typology and much of the argument of this section follows Harari's illuminating analysis of relationships between strategy and logistics in the English campaigns of the 14th century (Harari 2000).

[13] This analysis assumes a force with a strong infantry component, which was true of most European armies even in the feudal period. Cavalry columns could transport their food by pack animal, but substantial numbers were needed if these were to be sufficiently lightly loaded to keep up with troops. English plans for a raid on Stirling in 1298 allowed 300 pack horses for a force of 200 men-at-arms (Hyland 1998: 34). The principal logistical constraint experienced by a force of this kind was the need to obtain grazing for the animals.

slower, particularly in areas with poor surfaces. In good conditions wagons could manage up to 20 miles a day and keep up with marching infantry, but medieval armies often managed only half this and sometimes did no better than 4 or 5 miles daily.[14]

These calculations are very approximate and make no allowance for cavalry or non-combatants but they do suggest that, on this scale, self-sufficiency might be a practical proposition for a sufficiently well-organized and equipped force. The picture is dramatically different if we double the time scale from ten to twenty days. The further ten days' infantry rations would almost certainly have to be carried by additional transport animals who would themselves each consume 200 pounds over the whole interval, which is equivalent to 80 per cent of a pack beast's load. The total requirement for the same 10,000 men would be for a pack train of 11,400 animals, nearly ten times that required to transport the equipment alone, and enough to form a column some 18 miles long. Total grain requirements over the twenty-day period would come to around 1,400 tons, and assembling this at one point so that the column could load up would take 12,600 animal loads in the absence of water transport.

Large numbers of non-combatants and excess baggage often complicated logistical demands, and porterage might be seen as too demeaning for some troops such as aristocratic cavalrymen. In such circumstances it is unlikely that a force of any size could have operated as a flying column for any appreciable period, but if an infantry force was unencumbered by heavy equipment it could, in principle, march a considerable distance without having to draw supplies. The commanders of organized armies sometimes exploited this capacity, under pressure, by jettisoning their equipment and other baggage or leaving it in camp. The above calculation does also suggest that lightly armed foot soldiers, such as the barbarian warbands the Romans faced on the Rhine and upper Danube, had a potential mobility advantage over their more heavily equipped opponents and a corresponding ability to take the field for extended periods. Such peoples seem in practice rarely to have possessed the organization and discipline necessary to realize this potential,[15] but it may be that particularly capable leaders, such as the German Arminius, who were able to establish their authority over a tribal confederation, were also able to discipline their followers sufficiently to take advantage of this logistical 'leanness'. If so, this may have contributed substantially to their successes (Goldsworthy 1996).

---

[14] Edward I's army managed only 4–5 miles daily on the march from Carlisle to Dumfries in 1300 and Edward III's covered less than 6 miles per day from Calais to Rheims in 1359. Both armies had very large trains (Prestwich 1996: 190). By contrast, the 250–300 carts accompanying the Duke of Lancaster's French expedition of 1356 travelled over 120 miles in eight days (Harari 2000: 317). Larger trains are likely to have moved more slowly because of a greater incidence of vehicle breakdown and damage to the roadbed.

[15] Goldsworthy notes that Tacitus singled out one group, the Chatti, for special mention because their warriors carried food with them on their expeditions, the evident implication being that such logistical preparations were very unusual among the contemporary Germans (Goldsworthy 1996: 46–7).

9.1.1.2.2. Depots

A force drawing its supplies from pre-arranged points might be able to manage with relatively little transport capacity if the points were sufficiently close together. It could function as a very effective flying column within the limits of a pre-planned logistical network. Systems of this kind were easiest to organize on home territory, and where troop movements followed regular routes. They might be based on magazines run by the military or civil authorities from which troops would be issued with rations, on privately owned depots, or on officially sanctioned markets. Magazine systems could be operated on the basis of taxes in cash or in kind at home, and a force pursuing an occupation strategy in hostile territory might establish a network of supply dumps supported by local requisitioning or external supply lines. Such 'command-based' systems did not necessarily require a monetary economy, but the use of private depots or markets was only possible once a certain level of economic sophistication had been obtained.

Internal troop movements in seventeenth-century France were facilitated by a system of designated military roads and supply points (or *étapes*) provisioned by local communities or contractors and centrally funded (Lynn 1997: 132–40). Habsburg forces moving along the 'Spanish Road' from Italy to the Low Countries to fight the Dutch rebels were supported by a similar system based, where possible, on contractors who collected and pre-positioned supplies (Parker 1972: 88–95). Under certain conditions supply points could be used to support attacking forces. Alexander's army purchased supplies from local markets in regions where resistance, and loyalty to the Persian regime, had both collapsed (Engels 1978), but more systematic arrangements were also possible. The administrative effort involved might be substantial but so were the potential gains in mobility. These were strikingly demonstrated by Marlborough's advance to Blenheim in 1704. His army covered 250 miles in five weeks with minimal losses from sickness or desertion, whereas the French over the campaign as a whole lost around a third of their effective strength on the march (Chandler 1979: 128–31). The financial cost was equally striking, because supplies had to be purchased and transported at market rates, and as Lynn remarks:[16]

the wonder of Marlborough's march is that the money was at hand. It is worth noting that rather than providing an example of what kind of mobility all armies might have had, the unique character of this advance demonstrated that such a means was really outside the possibility for other armies that lacked the ready cash, and that meant just about everyone else. (Lynn 1993*d*: 18)

A logistical solution of this kind was practicable on a worthwhile scale only for well-organized states on friendly territory or where control had already been secured by a major offensive operation. In such circumstances it allowed a rapid and powerful response to be made to any incursion.

---

[16] Marlborough's achievement nonetheless relied on coercion as well as inducement and left the surrounding countryside in a seriously depleted condition (Creveld 1977: 29–33).

9.1.1.2.3. Supply lines

External supplies could be brought into the area of operations where circumstances permitted, allowing much larger forces to be supported than was possible using local resources alone. Overwhelming force might then be concentrated, even in unproductive areas, and commanders could pursue a strategy of devastation without having to worry about where their own food would come from. Access to external supply was a major asset in protracted operations aimed at establishing full territorial control, but there were three major obstacles to its realization. The first was the familiar one of bulk transport. Land haulage was inefficient and expensive over anything but short distances. In the 1860s it was calculated that a standard Union army supply wagon, drawn by six mules, could carry one day's supplies for 500 men or 125 horses. An army two days' march from its base would need a 'pipeline' of four of these vehicles to ensure daily deliveries. On this basis, around 2,000 wagons and 12,000 mules would be needed to supply an army of 100,000 men with only 16,000 horses. At a distance of three days' march the requirements rose to 3,760 wagons and 22,000 mules.[17]

Operations on this scale might be technically feasible, if the necessary resources were available and political or military priorities enabled economic logic to be set aside, but water transport retained advantages even in these circumstances. It was the only practicable means of moving fodder in the volumes needed by large forces that had exhausted local grazing. A large supply fleet could act as a mobile depot, endowing the force it supported with effective self-sufficiency, but direct waterborne supply was only possible near coasts or navigable waterways. Elsewhere, wagon or pack trains were needed and this posed further operational difficulties. Trains of this kind moved too slowly to be able to overtake even infantry moving at full speed, and so this solution required the mobile troops to remain within limited range of fixed bases or advance very slowly. The trains were also tempting targets, and if the area could not be cleared and secured against hostile forces large numbers of troops might be needed to guard lines of communications and escort convoys. The manpower drain that this represented was all the greater in thinly populated terrain, without clear economic and political centres, and against a defender capable of guerrilla resistance. In the pre-modern period these conditions often prevailed in 'barbarian' lands, and it was probably the need to establish and defend extended supply lines of communication that explains the enormous scale of the Roman forces assembled for some of their campaigns of conquest.[18]

---

[17] These calculations, which were published by the Count of Paris, include the transport of fodder for the convoys' own draught animals (Huston 1966: 216).

[18] In one of the largest of these campaigns the Emperor Tiberius is said to have concentrated ten legions and an equivalent number of supporting troops, or 80,000–100,000 men, to suppress the revolt in Pannonia (Keppie 1984: 166). Forces of at least this size are also credited to the Hellenistic King Antiochus III for his Iranian campaign and the Byzantine Emperor Romanus Diogenes for the Manzikert campaign in 1071. Modern historians have tended to doubt estimates on this scale on the, almost certainly mistaken, assumption that they are intended to represent the active strength of a single field army. They are certainly much too big to be plausible on that basis, but the expeditions in

Water transport was rarely practicable in Germany or elsewhere in central Europe and local supplies were meagre. In Gaul, by contrast, the Romans drew supplies from allied territories and transported them along interconnecting waterways, and territorial control was rapidly established. In the Iberian peninsular, where these advantages were lacking, the process took from Hannibal's time to that of Augustus. Sea routes or inland waterways nonetheless imposed constraints of their own. Their geography necessarily shaped the conduct of operations and mobile forces were tied to shorelines or riverbanks. Fortified positions could sometimes block waterborne troop or supply movements and thereby assumed a vital strategic significance.[19] When the Emperor Charlemagne launched his assault on the Avar khanate at the end of the eighth century, the first stage turned on the fortifications the Avars had established along the river system giving access to their heartland on the middle Danube. These blocked the passage for the supply transports needed to support a major offensive whilst they also shielded the Avar interior against Frankish cavalry raids. As Bowlus argues, 'as long as Avars held forts in lower Austria, most of Trans-danubia and all of the Alföld were effectively out of range for cavalry operating from Bavaria' (Bowlus 1995: 52). The Franks were prevented from exploiting their victories in mobile warfare until these fortifications were captured by a major expedition, supported by infantry, siege equipment, and riverine supply squadrons, in 791. The loss of its frontier defences exposed the Avar interior to Frankish cavalry raids leading to the complete disintegration of the khanate in the years immediately following.

Sea routes were also vulnerable to interruption by bad weather or enemy action. The English reliance on cross-Channel routes to support their armies in fourteenth-century France required a continuing naval effort to keep them open, whilst the loss of the Persian fleet at Salamis seems to have forced the withdrawal of their main force for logistical reasons.[20] External supply on a worthwhile scale was also very expensive, requiring a substantial effort to establish and provision

---

question aimed to clear and occupy remote, thinly populated regions, and the numbers are perfectly credible as sum totals for a main field army, backed up by secondary columns, lines of communication troops and garrisons (for Antiochus see Bar-Kochva 1976: 10 and the Manzikert campaign Friendly 1981).

A more recent, and better documented, example of the manpower demands imposed by extended supply lines comes from the English Civil War, in which one Parliamentary supply train dispatched from London to Gloucester needed over 6,000 escorting troops. The Royalists on the other side suffered badly because their main base at Oxford was on the edge of the heavily contested south midlands region, which exposed their communications to continuous harassment and tied up substantial forces in garrison and escort duty (Edwards 1998: 259).

[19] Suitably located fortified bridges could block river movement as they did at Paris in the early Middle Ages, and the resulting siege of the city by Danish raiders in 885–6 has been seen as a turning point in the development of resistance to their attacks (Oman 1991: 140–8). Subsequently, the appearance of gunpowder shore batteries greatly increased the obstructive power of riverside fortifications.

[20] Commanders were not necessarily beholden to geography for the availability of water transport. Natural waterways could be improved or canals built to supply remote garrisons as they were by the Romans in Britain. Nonetheless, the effort required could be formidable, and such examples are rare, as we saw in Chapter 2.

the relevant bases in the first place. Only a power with access to a substantial geographical area could establish external supply bases, but assembling provisions in the quantities required to make the operation worthwhile was a formidable proposition and required substantial economic and administrative resources. Roman supply trains on the eastern frontier are said to have required several months to assemble (Lee 1989), whilst in 1282, during the supposedly unsophisticated Middle Ages, the English accumulated 23,000 quarters of grain (some 4,600 tons) to support their Welsh campaign. Fourteen years later the Exchequer ordered 63,200 quarters in a single month (Prestwich 1996: 251). The French offensive against the Dutch in 1672 was preceded by the accumulation of sufficient grain for over thirty-six million daily rations (Lynn 1993*c*: 148).

9.1.1.2.4. *Living off the land*

The fourth solution was simply to 'live off the land' by exploiting whatever resources were present in the operational area itself. This solution, or expedient, was the most widely used even if one or more of the others was also adopted in conjunction. Green fodder was nearly always obtained in this way. The state of pasturage was a key factor governing the operations of most armies, and the opening of Europe's campaigning season was traditionally signalled by the availability of ripe grass in the late spring.[21] Barbarians raiding across the Roman frontier habitually took advantage of this by striking in winter when fodder shortages impaired the mobility of defending cavalry (Lee 1993: 98). The ability of a force to support itself by living off the land depended, in the first and last instances, on the volume of its requirements relative to that of the area's resources, and thus the area's level of population and agricultural productivity. It was often a long way from the first to the last instance, however, and there were many intervening contingencies affecting the ability of a force to subsist in this way.

Local resources could be procured in a number of ways, of which the simplest was by foraging along the line of march, or sending out detachments from an encampment or garrison. Foot-bound troops had very limited foraging abilities, but cavalry could easily cover 10 miles on either side of the main axis of advance. On this basis, a daily advance of 10 miles would give them access to around 200 square miles. Containing some 5,000 to 10,000 people, given agricultural Europe's characteristic population densities, such an area should in principle have had little difficulty in furnishing one day's provisions for an army of 40,000 or 50,000. In practice, the time of year and the state of the harvest both affected the availability of local resources. As the season advanced food would become harder

---

[21] From the later 8th century the Frankish military assembly, the 'Marchfield', was held in May when forage was readily available. It may have been moved back from an earlier March date as cavalry increased in importance, though this suggestion has been disputed (Verbruggen 1997: 22; DeVries 1992: 98, 107). Arab geographers had previously analysed pasture growth in Asia Minor with a view to the optimum timing of raids into Byzantine territory (Kaegi 1993: 52).

to find, particularly in areas of low productivity, and an army's ability to subsist by foraging depended heavily on its rate of movement. If it moved too rapidly, effective foraging would become impossible and serious attrition might result. A reliance on foraging consequently reduced mobility, which could suffer still further if supplies were available only as unprocessed grain. The delay involved in milling and baking could be considerable, and troops who were willing or able to consume their staple food as unbaked porridge had an appreciable mobility advantage. Serious difficulties also arose if the rate of movement was too slow to bring the foragers into districts with undepleted resources. Above all a large and static force that tried to live off the land for a protracted period was likely to find itself in a desert of its own making.

The most obvious difficulty confronting foragers was the population's unwillingness to part with food and other resources that might be required. Armed men could usually rely on violence or the threat of it to take what they wanted, but they had to find it first. Food could be hidden or destroyed, and in suitable terrain the inhabitants might simply disappear into hills or forests taking their possessions with them. Guerrilla resistance might be an additional problem in these circumstances. An invader could counter this by the use of terror tactics, but these were inevitably destructive and might only aggravate the logistical problems of a force that had to feed itself from the area concerned. Paying for supplies was a more constructive alternative, but it was also expensive and only practicable where a monetary economy existed. In areas with a functioning administration, the local civilian authorities might themselves be ordered to procure and deliver supplies to the army. This solution was relatively straightforward on home ground, although some payment might be required, but it could also be implemented in hostile territory provided temporary control had been established.

Liaison of this kind between the military and local civilian authorities had advantages for both parties, particularly with ill-disciplined or demoralized troops for whom uncontrolled foraging was an invitation to looting, wastage, and desertion. The prevalence of such conditions in early modern Europe, allied to growing logistical demands, fostered the emergence of the 'contributions' system which was widely used during the Thirty Years War (Lynn 1993a). Civil authorities were required by the invaders to deliver specified quantities of cash and provisions to their forces, resulting in a less destructive and more efficient form of extortion, but one that could still place a crippling burden on the area of operations. Partly in reaction to this, and fearing also the dangers of desertion and of a breakdown of discipline, *ancien régime* commanders avoided living off the land wherever possible. The commanders of the French Revolution's armies, with greater trust in their troops' loyalty, reverted to a reliance on foraging, and this was put on a systematic basis with Napoleon's establishment of separate *Corps d'Armée* (Creveld 1977: 51–5; Lynn 1993d: 23–5).

No matter how systematic or well organized such arrangements might become, they could only deliver the resources that were physically present in the areas concerned. Areas that were much fought over, or simply traversed repeatedly by large forces, could be stripped bare, as they were at times in Germany during the Thirty Years War (Parker 1984: 208–15). This had devastating consequences for the regional economy and could destroy an army that had to rely on it for subsistence. An adroit commander could manipulate this dependence by manoeuvring enemy forces into regions that had already been 'eaten up'. In 1644 an Imperial army withdrawing from Holstein to Bohemia was forced into devastated country and destroyed in this way. Earlier the same winter a French force under Turenne lost up to two-thirds of its strength in an enforced midwinter retreat (Parker 1984: 175).

Invading forces could suffer in a similar fashion if the defenders removed or deliberately destroyed the area's subsistence resources, a tactic that was facilitated by networks of local point defences which could be used to secure animals and harvested crops. Systems of this kind were a common feature of frontier defence although they needed considerable planning and preparation. Even where resources were left in place and undamaged, getting at them could present serious difficulties. Small detachments were always vulnerable to ambush, and dispersing forces in the way required for large-scale foraging could be very dangerous in areas that had not been fully secured. The outcome of a campaign could turn on this. In 1197 the French King Philip Augustus invaded Flanders and achieved early success. The Flemish responded by blocking roads and destroying bridges, so preventing the invaders from bringing in external supplies and forcing them to disperse in order to survive by foraging. In this state they were caught by a series of counter-attacks, launched from the safety of the Flemish fortifications, and forced to make a humiliating peace in order to escape. A similar manoeuvre saved the Frankish position on the Danube at the time of the Slav revolt that followed Charlemagne's death. Heavily defeated in battle and suffering defections, the local loyalists retreated into Dalmatia with its network of strong points. When the pursuing insurgents dispersed to plunder, they launched a series of harassing attacks concentrated on the enemy baggage train, and so avoided their opponents' superior strength. In this way they eventually forced the enemy to withdraw with heavy losses and gained the time necessary for a strong imperial counter-offensive (Bowlus 1995: 62–4).

9.1.1.3. *Success and failure*

The problems of logistics and operational mobility were closely interrelated. In enemy territory a highly mobile force needed either to be self-sufficient or to 'live off the land'. Self-sufficiency, for anything other than a short period, carried its own price in the form of an unwieldy supply train that could itself become a serious liability. Living off the land might offer the best prospects for manoeuvrability, but it was a potentially dangerous option since the necessary supplies might be unavailable or the invader might be prevented from obtaining them. The impact of logistical failure on military effectiveness varied with the context. In principle, rations could simply be reduced for an indefinite period if supplies ran short. Again, in principle, it was better to cut back on food for the troops than to stint on animal fodder. Transport animals and mounts needed to do heavy work and, if their conditions deteriorated, mobility could be dangerously compromised. Cavalry were needed for reconnaissance and screening as late as 1914, and without them a commander was compelled to fight blind.[22] Troops could survive short-term reductions in calorie or protein intake without a serious reduction in their fighting ability if they did not have to march long distances or carry heavy loads. Their susceptibility to disease would not be greatly increased, though hungry men are more likely to become ill from eating rotten or otherwise unsuitable food.

The position in practice, however, was often much more difficult. Food is a social, as well as a biological, good, and cutting rations could lead to desertion or mutiny before it had much physiological effect. The likelihood of this happening depended on the prior morale of the army and its broader context. Early modern European soldiers commonly held their own obligations to have ceased when their commanders failed to feed them, whilst Napoleon's forces, like their Revolutionary predecessors, put up with serious privations for a cause that they believed in. The consequences of deteriorating military effectiveness also depended on the context. From a narrowly military point of view, everything depended on the strength and condition of the opposition, and a hungry and demoralized army might prevail over one in an even worse condition.[23] Such armies were likely, nonetheless, to do terrible damage to the civilian economy, and their victories often came at a disproportionate price.

9.1.2. THE CHOICE OF GOALS

An aggressor targeting a given region had to choose between two basic alternatives. The first was to engage the defender's military assets in the hope of seizing and retaining territorial control. The second was to exploit a temporary, local predominance of force in order to inflict the greatest possible damage on the region's economy and population. On a long term and grand-strategic scale these contrasting military and economic goals were two sides of a single coin. Military assets shield economic resources, whilst the most powerful army would simply 'wither on the vine' without the economic resources it needed to support itself. On the operational scale of a campaigning season that might last only a few weeks a choice had to be made, however, because the spatial structure of organic economies imposed very different operational and logistical requirements on 'occupation' and 'raiding' strategies (Harari 2000).

[22] Arrangements for the supply of fodder broke down during the German advance to the Marne in 1914, leading to a serious deterioration in the mobility of their cavalry and heavy artillery (Creveld 1977: 124–5).
[23] The American forces that triumphed at Yorktown—effectively ending the Revolutionary War—were themselves in a dire condition due to the failure of their logistical system in the southern colonies. Had the British not surrendered ten days before the arrival of a relieving fleet it is doubtful that the siege could have been brought to a successful conclusion (Huston 1966: 83).

9.1.2.1. *Strategic options*

The first requirement for successful occupation was to eliminate the defender's mobile forces and gain control of any major fortified positions that the territory might contain. If the enemy leadership was eliminated in the process then resistance might collapse at this point. Otherwise the invaders had to disperse in order to occupy at least the major population centres and to dominate the countryside on which they depended. Given the restricted size of the forces normally involved, this would mean scattering small detachments across a wide area. A raiding force, by contrast, usually avoided combat with organized bodies of defending troops, and effected only temporary occupation of territorial objectives—at least to begin with. An invasion strategy of simple looting and destruction had a number of advantages. It could be pursued with small forces and so was often the only practical option for commanders with limited manpower such as frontier magnates or the leaders of barbarian warbands. Raiding was also a means by which the mobility advantage of lightly equipped barbarians and similar forces could be exploited to good effect. It could be very profitable, and, especially among barbarian peoples, provided a route to social and political leadership. By a reverse logic, raiding was often the strategy of choice for the armies of organized states campaigning in barbarian territory. Where lands were thinly peopled and lacked clearly defined political or economic centres, an occupation strategy could be enormously expensive in terms of manpower. Mobile forces, by contrast, could sweep large areas of territory, targeting crops, animals, and the local inhabitants. The aim was not so much to inflict lasting economic damage as to undermine the political support of hostile leaders, forcing them to come to terms or risk being deposed by more accommodating rivals (Goldsworthy 1996: 95–100; Elton 1996: 221–7).

The low-level warfare that so often characterized frontier or politically fragmented regions revolved around raids and counter-raids, but raiding was also effective in the high-level warfare mounted by the armies of organized states (Harari 2000). Destroying resources in an opponent's territory was a powerful direct means of pressuring him to give up the struggle, and a ruler unable to protect his subjects' lives and possessions was also likely to be discredited in their eyes. Successful raiding therefore inflicted political as well as material damage by detaching powerful subordinates or provoking popular unrest. On an operational time scale, local devastation deprived the defenders of revenues with which to hire fresh troops, and might deny supplies to a relieving force, but the amount of permanent damage that could be inflicted in one season's raiding should not be exaggerated. One or two crops might be destroyed, but the fertility and future productivity of the land would not be affected. The rural population might be driven away but would usually return, whilst natural increase could normally make good in a relatively short time whatever losses arose from mortality or permanent flight. Livestock and fixed capital might be harder to replace—and the destruction of irrigation systems could be very serious—but inflicting major damage usually required repeated raids over an extended period. Raiding on this scale could destroy an enemy's ability to sustain resistance from regional resources alone. The destruction or removal of crops, livestock, and installations such as barns or mills, together with assaults on the rural population, could wreck a region's economic foundations. Endemic insecurity, particularly where it prevented cultivators from planting or harvesting crops, could lead to flight from the countryside and a failure of the revenue and manpower base needed to sustain military defence. In these circumstances a downward spiral of increasing insecurity and permanent emigration set in that could result in the economic and demographic collapse of entire regions (see below, Chapter 11).

9.1.2.2. *Logistics and strategy*

Logistical and strategic options were closely related. A large raiding force needed to keep moving along its main axis of advance. Unable to establish secure lines of communication and supply, it had to act as a flying column relying on some combination of foraging and self-sufficiency. Forces bent on occupation faced different logistical possibilities and limitations depending on the speed with which they were able to overcome major centres of resistance. If this was achieved quickly then it might be possible to provision the occupying force from local sources but protracted large-scale operations were likely to require support from outside, particularly in unproductive or thinly peopled territories. Unless secure water routes were available, large numbers of vulnerable supply trains would be needed to do this. Defending these would itself require secure territorial control and would possibly extend into areas with little intrinsic economic or strategic value. This was expensive in terms of manpower, and all the more so where there were no major political or economic centres to be taken and occupied. In these circumstances logistical problems dictated an increase rather than a reduction in the scale of forces committed and this was an increase that itself reinforced dependence on external supply. An invader who had once selected an occupation strategy could find logistical constraints locked him into a spiral of increasing commitment.

By the same logic, where an aggressor lacked the means to establish or communicate with external bases, a raiding strategy might be the only strategic option. This could reflect the defenders' continuing ability to cut supply lines, or a lack of resources on the part of the aggressor. The Athenians' control of the sea during the Peloponnesian War stopped their Spartan enemies establishing the logistical basis needed to maintain a protracted siege of their city itself, and the fighting developed into an annual series of large-scale raids into Attica until the Spartans themselves gained a naval victory.[24] Medieval armies generally

---

[24] The Spartans' logistical arrangements are also said to have suffered as a result of their distinctive socio-economic system with its lack of a convertible currency and disdain for commerce. This made it difficult for them to sustain remote operations for any length of time (Roth 1999: 244).

lacked the logistical structures needed to support an occupation strategy and so raiding strategies predominated. The low agricultural productivity and dearth of clear economic or political centres in barbarian territories also hindered the pursuit of occupation strategies, and neighbouring states usually resorted to large-scale raids and punitive expeditions as a means of weakening or coercing the local leadership.

Logistics also constrained operations in ways that owed little to strategic choice, particularly where large forces operated with only rudimentary support. This was often the case in early modern Europe, and attempts to secure regional territorial control under these circumstances could lead to economic damage of a kind that made it impossible for the armies to feed themselves. This was seen during the Thirty Years War, where logistics eventually replaced strategy as the determinant of operations. Troop movements degenerated into a mere 'flight forward' as commanders searched for hitherto untouched areas from which supplies could be drawn. More generally, both foraging parties and supply convoys were chronically vulnerable to guerrilla-style attacks by relatively small numbers of troops. In northern Europe especially, this made it hazardous for an invader to overwinter in a region that had not been cleared of all opposition. Occupation strategies were all the more difficult to achieve if such clearance could not be accomplished in a single campaigning season, and this was a further argument in favour of raiding.

9.1.3. SCALE

The availability of manpower and the resources to support it set limits to the scale of military operations, but some pre-modern states could field very large forces whilst alliances between states yielded a comparable potential in other cases. The larger the political unit, the more resources it should have been able to mobilize for war, and the greater its military power, but organic economies imposed diminishing returns to military investment just as they did in the sphere of production. Even a power with access to troops and equipment of the requisite quality might be unable to translate its economic and demographic superiority into a commensurate military advantage. This was because really large forces were very difficult to supply, co-ordinate, and manoeuvre. Few pre-modern rulers disposed of field armies big enough to have any real difficulty feeding themselves in terrain of the kind that was likely to be militarily important, as long as they kept moving, but keeping moving was critical. Supply difficulties themselves impeded movement by imposing a reliance on foraging or slow-moving convoys and limited the numbers of troops who could be concentrated in a single stationary body.

The most difficult problems usually arose when a force was stationary for an extended period, and they were essentially the same as those of provisioning a large town or city. Compared with the latter, field armies formed relatively short-lived concentrations in any given location and so could take far larger proportions of the available resources on a daily basis. On the other hand, their very impermanence ruled out the development of a permanent transport infrastructure to serve their supply needs. In this respect mobile field armies in Europe benefited relatively little from the coming of railways, although these did affect the conduct of sieges and facilitated the initial concentration and deployment of large forces at strategic railheads.[25] Before this it was very difficult for large armies to remain in one place for a long time unless they could be supplied by water, and this benefited any numerically weak defender able to take evasive action or shelter behind fortifications.

Mobile forces could encounter supply difficulties if foraging was ruled out for disciplinary or other operational reasons. Alternative solutions included the use of civilian contractors or a specialized supply service, but this was more expensive than living off the land and a commander without the necessary funds might be unable to concentrate his manpower effectively. Better discipline or morale could enable correspondingly greater concentrations to be achieved without the expense of a sophisticated logistical apparatus. This was what happened in post-Revolutionary France, whose army commanders could let their troops live off the land without fear of excessive desertion. This ability allowed troop mobilization on such a scale that the resulting armies had to be kept outside the frontiers and fed at the expense of their foreign 'hosts'.

Foraging armies that were too big to be supported along a single line of march could split into parallel columns advancing short distances apart. This procedure was refined by Napoleon who established a series of *Corps d'Armée* which manoeuvred as separate formations converging only on the field of battle, but it was familiar to commanders in much earlier periods. The army of the First Crusade traversed the more desolate regions of Asia Minor in this fashion. Sometimes dispersal worked to the advantage of the army concerned. At Adrianople, returning Gothic foragers caught the Romans in a fortuitous envelopment: while at Dorylaeum the crusader columns converged, as much by luck as by judgement, trapping the Turkish horse-archers between them.[26] Nonetheless, the inherent difficulties of co-ordination and communication made dispersal in the presence of the enemy a very dangerous procedure.

---

[25] Van Creveld believed that railway transport was insufficiently flexible to play a major role in mobile operations during the Franco-Prussian War of 1870–1 or thereafter, whilst conceding that its support was essential for the Prussians' siege of Paris. Railways did, however, make a substantial logistical contribution to northern mobile operations in the American Civil War (Lynn 1993*d*: 14–15; Huston 1966: 199 f.).

[26] Oman's judgement was that 'Dorylaeum can only be called a victory of chance. The Crusaders had deserved defeat by their careless march in two disconnected columns. How utterly unknown the locality of the two divisions was to each other is best shown by the fact that it took five hours for Godfrey's succours to reach Bohemund, though there were only six or seven miles between them' (Oman 1991: 277). France thinks more highly of crusader leadership but concedes that the battle 'was a pell-mell affair with no evidence of overall command' (France 1994: 183). The division into columns was probably enforced on them by the crusaders' logistical difficulties. As Leyser observed, in this, as in other respects, 'subsistence explains far more about the history and success of the First Crusade than any other military or political factor' (Leyser 1994: 95).

The difficulties were partly those of communications technology, the state of the road network and the transmission of information, but they also reflected the problems of co-ordinating separated corps without clear command structures capable of enforcing their leaders' compliance. Such structures depended on a cadre of trained and efficient sub-commanders willing to accept hierarchical subordination. Forming and maintaining such a cadre was expensive, and hierarchical subordination could be difficult to achieve where commanders were members of a political or social elite, jealous of their relative standing. In the early medieval period the Emperor Charlemagne apparently undertook successful multi-corps manoeuvres on a number of occasions (Bowlus 1995: 19–20), but such achievements were rare and the co-ordination of vanguard, rearguard, and main body was usually all, if not more than, could be hoped for.

The increasing sophistication of military organization in the modern period fostered the co-ordination of separated corps in pursuit of a common goal. In principle this promoted the advantages of superior numbers, allowing commanders to undertake operations on more than one front at the same time or to conduct a strategic envelopment with widely separated forces. Again, however, the practicability of such manoeuvres remained questionable as late as the campaigns of 1914, whose outcome was shaped by failures of communications between the Russian armies invading east Prussia, and in the west between, first, the British and the French, and then between the German armies of Bulow and Kluck in front of Paris. Co-ordination between widely separated forces seems to have been rarely attempted, and still more rarely achieved, in the medieval and early modern periods.

9.2. LOW-LEVEL WARFARE: THE CONTROL OF DEMOGRAPHIC SPACE

The goal of high-level warfare was the destruction of enemy forces, the seizure of territory, or the looting and destruction of large swathes of countryside. This put a premium on the concentration of forces in physical space in order to achieve overwhelming local superiority and avoid the risks of defeat in detail. The geography of agrarian resources, however, was one of dispersal, and so securing or resisting lasting control over them required a corresponding dispersal of force. What was true of space was also true of time. Large-scale raids were necessarily short-lived affairs, and logistical difficulties, often reinforced by restricted terms of military service, rendered most manoeuvre campaigns relatively brief. If resistance could not be eliminated in the course of such a campaign, however, the establishment and consolidation of territorial control was likely to require a long-term commitment by forces dispersed across a wide area. So if the distinction between high- and low-level warfare is, spatially, one between concentrated and dispersed force, it is also one between acute and chronic armed conflict.

Chronic armed conflict arose where neither side was able to expel the other from a given territory or where controlled areas bordered, overlapped, or were otherwise liable to continuing incursions from outside. This resulted in endemic small-scale fighting between locally based forces, usually relying on point defences of some kind. The aim was to harass the other side, cut their lines of communications if they had any, and, above all, to seize or destroy crops, livestock, and anything else that could be taken away, whilst resisting the opponents' attempts to do the same. Such warfare characterized the frontier regions of organized states, particularly those bordering barbarian territory or territory in the hands of semi-autonomous magnates.[27] Endemic low-level conflict also arose in prolonged wars between organized states where neither was able to secure a decisive advantage in high-level warfare or willing to abandon the attempt. A number of factors favoured the emergence of such conditions. Low population densities and economic dispersal deprived an invader of targets whose capture might constitute a knock-out blow. Poorly developed systems of transport and communications made it more difficult to secure effective regional control within the length of a campaigning season. This was all the more difficult for poorly organized forces whose commanders might be wary of major engagements because of the difficulty of regrouping after a setback. Difficult terrain, or the existence of numerous point defences, made control much harder to establish, whilst a highly devolved political system increased the likelihood that local resistance would continue even if the central leadership was willing to make concessions.

Most or all of these conditions were found in medieval Europe at one time or another and low-level warfare prevailed as a result. In the words of one authority:

There is one matter on which most medievalists who have written on war agree; medieval warfare revolved essentially around the control of castles and fortified towns, strongpoints with which Western Europe was thickly studded. In these cautious wars of attrition battle was avoided because the outcome was too often unpredictable; far more energy was expended on the pillaging of the countryside—the aim being to destroy an enemy's economic resources and undermine his political credibility—and on the control of fortresses. (Ayton and Price 1995: 7)

The feudal fragmentation of public authority, and the frequency of 'private war' that resulted among magnates and lesser landholders, contributed powerfully to this state of affairs. Such men rarely disposed of enough troops to sustain high-level campaigns, but similar patterns emerged where the rulers of powerful states fought each other. In twenty-five years of campaigning, Richard Lion Heart fought no more than three open-field battles. His French contemporary Philip Augustus fought only one—against his wishes—and his father Henry II of England fought none at all.[28] Most of the fighting that occurred during the

---

[27] Where such conditions prevailed, the demands of endemic conflict often shaped the political and social, as much as the military, institutions of the frontier, as we shall see in the following chapter.

[28] See Gillingham (1984). Gillingham provides an illuminating discussion of the contemporary importance of raiding and devastation which applies equally to high- and low-level warfare.

Hundred Years War also consisted of small-scale local conflicts, interrupted by occasional high-level raiding expeditions. The ability that relatively modest fortifications afforded small bodies of troops to defy much larger forces underpinned a great deal of contemporary low-level warfare, but this type of conflict continued beyond the close of the Middle Ages. It may, indeed, have become more important in the early-modern period as other factors came to bear. The overall size of military establishments rose, and their logistical requirements increased still more. Along with the political developments of the period, this placed a growing premium on extensive territorial control and the dispersal of force that was required to establish this. Certainly, the figures that become available in this period show that large proportions of the total soldiers under arms were distributed in small garrisons.

At the time of the battle of Lützen, in 1632, Sweden's main field army contained only 20,000 of their 150,000 troops, the balance dividing in roughly equal proportions between regional field armies and ninety-eight permanent garrisons. In 1639, around half the strength of Spain's Army of Flanders, some 33,000 men, was distributed in 208 garrisons whose size ranged from a thousand to only ten men (Parker 1988: 40, 1972: 11). The nature of such warfare made it hard for commanders to maintain central control, particularly where discipline was weak and the hierarchy of command poorly developed. Sometimes they did not even try: a study of the French royal army's campaigns in the 1560s concluded that local garrison detachments 'were usually completely abandoned to their own devices and forgotten as the main army moved on'. Whatever problems this created for commanders, they were a great deal worse for local civilians, and the behaviour of such troops was, unsurprisingly, the cause of frequent complaints (Wood 1996: 237).

Chronic and geographically diffuse conflict of this kind can fairly be described as 'low level', but it would be wrong to assume that it was necessarily 'low intensity'. Apart from the damage wrought to civilian society and economy, there is evidence that such fighting was particularly bloody relative to the numbers involved. In an illuminating study, Carlton has compiled a database of casualties from the English Civil Wars broken down by region and by the scale of the engagement in which they were sustained. In total, he identifies 84,830 fatalities in 645 'incidents'. Of these, only 15 per cent occurred in the nine major battles that each claimed a thousand or more lives, whilst nearly half (47 per cent) were sustained in encounters that resulted in under 250 deaths. Carlton also found a negative correlation on a regional level between total combat deaths and the number killed per incident. The three regions with the largest total fatalities (North, West, and Midlands) had an average of 129 killed per incident, and the three with the lowest (Borders, East Anglia, and Wales) had an average of 217 (Carlton 1992: 203–6). As the author concludes, much of the Civil War 'consisted of small-scale, localised fighting, of sudden attacks with minor losses yet all too often fatal results' (Carlton 1992: 207).

The regular forces of organized states often engaged in low-level warfare, but it was in no sense their monopoly. The essence of this kind of fighting was that it did not require a substantial resource base, or any kind of central co-ordination to sustain it. It was well within the means of regional magnates, local lords, or anyone else able to support a small number of armed horsemen and a fortified base. There was a continuum running from local feuding and outright banditry through various forms of irregular and guerrilla operations to systematically conducted small-scale operations by centrally co-ordinated regular troops. The particular danger of protracted conflict on this scale was that the continuum could all too easily become a downward spiral. Even centrally co-ordinated operations could easily degenerate into a pattern of feuding and revenge attacks between opposing detachments, or become enmeshed in vendetta and score-settling between local factions. Where central co-ordination was weak, raiding might easily sink into simple banditry as garrisons slipped increasingly out of command control. The problems were all the worse where logistical and other administrative deficiencies forced local detachments to rely on the surrounding countryside in order to survive. The situation could become critical when the notional superiors of such troops settled their differences and ordered a demobilization. The aftermath of medieval Anglo-French wars all too frequently saw bands of mercenaries, and other former soldiers, seize local strong points from which they terrorized surrounding districts in defiance of any central authority (Jones 1994: 106–8; Contamine 1984: 242–9).

9.3. CONCLUSION

The resource limitations that constrained the productivity levels and spatial structure of organic economies thereby shaped both the strategic goals and the operational conduct of military campaigns. The fact that the productive base of the economy lay in the countryside posed a basic strategic dilemma between the concentration and dispersal of force. The areal geography of agrarian population and resources made dispersal necessary if their sustained domination was to be achieved, but to disperse in the presence of a concentrated enemy force was to court disaster through the process of defeat in detail. One common solution to this dilemma was to forgo sustained domination and adopt a strategy of destructive raiding. This strategy was further encouraged by the difficulty of keeping large bodies of invading troops supplied with food and fodder.

Well-organized forces on home ground could be kept supplied from depots or similar installations, but in enemy territory supplies had to be carried with the column, taken from the surrounding countryside, or brought in by convoys. The first of these options imposed a time limit on the operation and, like the second, meant that the troops had to keep moving. This requirement effectively limited such forces to a raiding strategy, but sustained domination was possible where external supply lines could be established. Supply convoys were, however, so vulnerable that this logistical solution often required, rather than simply facilitated, a strategy of occupation. Occupation strategies could be very demanding in terms of manpower, particularly in thinly peopled unproductive terrain devoid of obvious centres of resistance. In these circumstances, where external supply lines had to be established and secured, logistical difficulties could thus set a lower rather than an upper limit to the size of a sustainable occupying force. Alongside the 'high-level' warfare based on large concentrated forces was a second form involving chronic low-level conflict waged by troops dispersed throughout the countryside. This form, which especially characterized medieval warfare but persisted into the modern era, could be even more destructive than high-level warfare, not least because of the difficulties of enforcing central command control and the all too often realized risk that military operations would degenerate into simple banditry.

CHAPTER TEN

Power and Space I: Expanding Control

The reliance on muscle power prevented any one tactical system from attaining a global hegemony before the gunpowder revolution. It also constrained the operational and strategic uses of military force for as long as the organic economy endured. These constraints had political implications because a ruler who was unable to enforce his will on opponents did not remain a ruler for very long. Access to military force was a necessary condition for political power in any but the shortest term, and the constraints on force were, directly or indirectly, constraints on the maintenance of power. Effective power was always exercised over specific objects in specific places, and so power relationships were intrinsically spatial and the state as an organized structure of power was a spatial phenomenon. Organic economies with their restrictions on production, transportation, and the deployment of military force necessarily constrained the relationship between power and space, but the outcome of this constraint was historically variable.

Europe's political landscape on the threshold of modernity was fragmented and decentralized. Larger, more centralized units emerged as greater energy inputs became available first in warfare and then in the civilian economy. The fact that these developments occurred at the same time might suggest a necessary relationship between organic economies and political fragmentation, but the adoption of a longer historical perspective shows that the suggestion is false because in earlier centuries imperial states controlled large territories and a diversity of peoples in Europe and the Mediterranean basin. The geography of power in any period reflected the interplay of relatively immutable structural constraints—primarily economic, demographic, and logistical—and a diversity of variables that were much more open to change. The outcome of this process varied with historical circumstances and thus with the nature of past outcomes. Expansion of this kind was a two-stage process because the initial conquest had to be followed up by the consolidation of control. The prerequisites for success at these two stages differed, and they made very different demands on the aggressor's political and military resources. They also varied with the target region's degree of political and economic development. Conquest required victory in high-level warfare, and organized states could usually put up a more effective resistance at this stage, but it was more difficult to consolidate control over poor, thinly peopled regions without an institutionalized political structure. The characteristics of the attacking power also affected the outcome. Feudal rulers, with access to limited administrative and financial resources, had more difficulty than the ancient empires in mustering forces that could conquer organized states, but found it correspondingly easier to consolidate control of regions without monetarized economies because they were less reliant on revenues collected in cash.

10.1. THE STATE AND SPACE

The history and geography of political power is very largely the history and geography of states, and so before anything very useful can be said on the subject it is necessary to consider the state as a spatial phenomenon. The 'normal' form of twentieth-century state derived from a system that had emerged in Europe by the later seventeenth century and whose characteristics were unusual in a long-term perspective. This so-called 'modern state' is only one species of a historical genus so diverse that any generally satisfactory all-inclusive definition must be very loose (or in technical terms 'weak'). Any such definition has to embody three distinct elements.[1] The first is that state organization embodies relationships which are distinct from other dimensions of social organization such as kinship and also forms of solidarity like religious or ethnic identity, although they may be legitimized ideologically in terms of metaphors derived from any of these spheres. In addition to this 'specificity of the political', as it can be called, there is also the element of coercion; those who control state organizations thereby gain the ability to impose their will on others, by force if need be. Privileged access to the means of violence and the associated economic resources is an essential constituent of any *de facto* state organization, although its form and extent have varied greatly over space and time, as have the associated *de jure* claims. The third constituent is spatial location. The state's coercive force is exercised over a specific area of physical space, however fuzzily this may be defined.

10.1.1. METAPHORS OF STATE POWER

States are often described as 'large' or 'small', 'strong' or 'weak', depending on the spatial reach of their coercive forces and the degree of control they exert on the structures of the economy or civil society. From this it is a short step to talking of the 'growth of the state' as if this were a purposive, goal-seeking physical entity, or an organism following a developmental process programmed in its genes. To do this is to make two kinds of mistake. The first is to confuse the abstract and the concrete. States are organizations and, as such, they exist in both abstract and

---

[1] This discussion follows Tilly's definition of states as 'coercion-wielding organisations that are distinct from households and kinship groups and exercise clear priority in some respects over all other types of organisations within substantial territories' (Tilly 1990: 1). See also Mann (1986), Krader (1968).

concrete terms. In abstract terms they form patterns of institutionalized role relationships which are ideologically legitimized in cultural representations from myth and ritual to textbooks of political philosophy. Concretely they are manifested in sets of flesh and blood actors who 'play out' roles such as king, minister, or civil servant in specific historical and geographical contexts. State organizations define the relationships between real people with a historical and spatial existence, but they remain patterns of relationships, not concrete objects in themselves. They are abstract, not physical, realities, and to confuse the two is to fall into the error of what is known as 'reification'.

The second error to be avoided is what is known as 'teleology', which in this context refers to the view of state expansion as the natural working out of an intrinsically goal-oriented process. States might get bigger or stronger following decisions deliberately taken to that end, but these were always taken by individuals or groups who had their own ideas, interests, and purposes. They were not taken by a physical being called 'the state'. Decision-makers sometimes strove to expand states for altruistic or self-interested reasons, but expansion also resulted from the pursuit of quite different goals, or from ad hoc responses to the pressure of circumstances.

In the nineteenth and twentieth centuries powerful state bureaucracies proliferated, and with them decision-making cadres whose interests were aligned closely with the growth of state power. Some of these organizations displayed a degree of institutional continuity, and internal dilution of responsibility, that brought them to resemble a kind of collective consciousness on the part of states themselves. In these circumstances reifying and teleological metaphors become increasingly plausible as depictions of the state and its dynamics, but they remain metaphors nonetheless. For the period with which we are concerned they can also be extremely misleading. Policy formation and execution generally rested with individual rulers, surrounded by a coterie of advisers and a restricted social elite, and 'acts of state' resulted from decisions often motivated by considerations of personal power or group interest of a fairly narrow kind. The state itself should be seen, not as a purposive subject, but more as an instrument whose control placed both concrete and symbolic assets at the disposal of those who stood at its head.

10.1.2. CONTROL AND DEPENDENCE

The Treaty of Westphalia, which concluded the Thirty Years War in 1648, is often taken as the point at which early modern Europe's state system crystallized in explicit legal terms (Osiander 1994: 16–89). It was a system of a kind that had not previously existed on the continent, and whose character defined that of the world-spanning system which emerged in the twentieth century. States within this system were defined by realizable claims to sovereignty throughout a specified territory demarcated by unambiguous mutually recognized boundaries. The exercise of sovereignty within these boundaries resided in the assertion of a monopoly of legitimate violence—or 'force'—by the agents of the state, and internationally it implied relationships of formal equality and mutual recognition by other entities similarly defined. States existed within a system of structurally equivalent (or 'homologous') units, central to whose functioning was the conduct of war within a legally defined framework of formal declaration and termination, conducted by armed forces which formed an integral part of the state apparatus or were at least accountable to it. The right to engage in war on these terms, and to make treaties, was the principal manifestation of state sovereignty in international relations.

The relations between states have not always been governed by these principles. The definition of sovereignty in terms of absolute claims over clearly demarcated territories, with the corollary that these be realizable as a condition of legitimacy, and the notion of formal equality between states within a framework of reciprocal rights and duties are historically specific developments. States on any definition have an intimate relationship to physical space, but the nature of this relationship has varied greatly over time, and formal concepts of sovereignty or territoriality are not very useful guides to its long-term functional development. It is more helpful to think in terms of changes in the spatial extent of administrative control. This is the area of geographical space across which rulers could exercise sufficient coercion, whether by the actual or potential use of force, to establish administrative agencies capable of extracting resources on a systematic basis. Administrative control (or simply 'control') in this sense was only one of two forms of spatial power relationship that enabled rulers to extract resources from subordinates. The second, which we can call 'tributary dependence' (or simply 'dependence'), was where rulers were powerful enough to exact tribute but not to establish the agencies needed for systematic resource extraction in the target region. Tributes were arbitrary, and usually irregular, payments often exacted following a raiding strategy which convinced the local leaders that paying up was the lesser of two evils.[2] Administrative control was the hallmark of state organization whereas tributary dependence could also be enforced by successful barbarian leaders; typically it endured just as long as there was a credible threat of renewed raiding.

The spatial extent of control is a phenomenon that requires to be understood in two dimensions, the first of which is 'breadth'. The breadth of control corresponds to the area within a state's frontiers, however these are defined, but on its own it is a potentially very misleading indicator of its true spatial extent. In order to gauge this correctly we also need to consider the second dimension of spatial 'depth', which refers to the spatial reach of the state's coercive agencies within its frontiers. The further this reach extends, the deeper the state's control, and the deeper its control then the greater its geographical extent for a given breadth.[3]

---

[2] Tributes were often paid in kind, including manpower, rather than cash. For a fuller discussion of tribute as a form of revenue see below in Chapter 15.

[3] The geographical depth of control is a *de facto* functional concept that must not be confused with the degree of formal centralization or decentralization of the state's governing institutions. Formal decentralization may be a very effective way of incorporating local elites into the state organization,

Modern concepts of territorial sovereignty imply that the state's coercive reach should extend throughout the area contained within its borders, but such internal ubiquity was rarely feasible before the recent past, as we shall see in the following chapter. At this point we are concerned with the breadth of spatial control and the ways in which it could be expanded.

10.1.3. AGGREGATION AND FRAGMENTATION

Viewing states' political geography in terms of the spatial extent of control naturally returns us to the constraints on military force and its deployment for political purposes. Armed forces long relied on organic sources of energy and raw materials just as much as did the civilian economy and, weaponry apart, this reliance continued for centuries after the gunpowder revolution. This reliance constrained political developments as well as those in production, but it was constraint compatible with a diversity of spatial outcomes. The characteristic scale of states' geographical extent varied enormously with successive movements of fragmentation and aggregation. The last centuries of the pre-Christian west were, broadly speaking, ones of aggregation with only intermittent reversals. Most of south-west Asia and the eastern Mediterranean was unified by the Persian Achaemenid rulers, whose empire was then taken over more or less intact by Alexander of Macedon. The empire fragmented into 'Successor' kingdoms after Alexander's death, but by the middle of the first century BC the Romans had absorbed most of these together with the former Carthaginian trading empire in the west.

The Roman Empire of Tiberius formed a political unit on a scale unprecedented in the west. Bordered on the north by the stateless denizens of what they termed *barbaricum*, and by the Iranian world to the east, its scale proved unsustainable and the following eight centuries saw movements of division that were only temporarily or partially reversed. The empire was split into two halves by the Emperor Diocletian in the late third century and only temporarily reunited before the west collapsed in the fifth century. Italy, most of North Africa, and parts of Spain were recovered by the eastern Emperor Justinian a century later, but Italy was invaded by the Germanic Lombards soon afterwards whilst Arab conquerors overran the Near East, Egypt, and North Africa, which permanently fractured the Mediterranean basin along religious and political fault lines. Meanwhile a movement of aggregation occurred in the west. Frankish kings already ruled most of Gaul and western Germany by Justinian's day, and Charlemagne extended Frankish control across Lombard Italy to Rome, and eastwards to the Elbe and middle Danube, being crowned emperor of the west on Christmas Day 800. Unity died with him as the Empire fragmented into separate French and German states supplemented by numerous autonomous and semi-autonomous

---

and so mobilizing them in pursuit of its own goals, just as the agents of a highly centralized system may, in practice, be relatively powerless away from the capital and major provincial centres.

lordships, and new Christian kingdoms formed in Spain, Scandinavia, and Britain.

Medieval and early modern Europe's fractured political landscape was therefore a historical product and not a timeless corollary of the organic economy. Such economies had supported earlier political units of comparable breadth to those of the industrialized west and still did so in south and east Asia. They set outer limits to the political integration of space and also imposed costs within these limits. In the ancient world the costs seem to have been met on a larger scale than was subsequently the case. We can begin to understand why this was so by considering what was involved in the process of expansion. Expansion required rulers to advance their frontiers against neighbours, and the consequent problems depended very much on the characteristics of the neighbours themselves. These varied enormously, but as a first approximation can be lumped into the broad categories of organized states and stateless 'barbarians'.

The occupants of these categories were heterogeneous but had enough in common, and sufficient differences the one from the other, to represent distinct configurations of threat and opportunity. Stable multi-state systems were a rarity in the west from the rise of the Achaemenids to the death of Charlemagne. Imperial states sometimes maintained a fractious coexistence, as did Rome and its Iranian neighbours, but smaller units were more often drawn into conflicts that ended with all but one being swallowed up. In the early Middle Ages this ceased to be the case, but until then the dynamics of inter-state relations favoured aggregation and the political integration of space. The limits of this process were set by the varying abilities of organized states and their rulers to conquer and control stateless barbarian peoples and by the characteristics of barbarian societies themselves.

10.2. THE STATELESS PEOPLES

The states of early modern Europe were mostly bordered by structural homologues: other states similarly organized and comparably armed. The agrarian empires of earlier centuries were more often ringed by barbarian peoples. This difference was more a consequence than a cause of their greater spatial breadth. Rulers such as those of Rome or successive Chinese dynasties found themselves surrounded by barbarians only when—and because—they had engulfed their 'civilized' competitors. Establishing an empire always involved overcoming neighbouring states and stateless societies, but in the long term, the successful persistence of states on an imperial scale was bound up with their success, or lack of it, in dealing with events on the barbarian periphery. Most of the peoples with whom western rulers had to deal can be grouped into three broad categories: the 'northern barbarians' of antiquity, the early medieval Slavs and cognate peoples in eastern Europe and the Balkans, and thirdly the nomadic peoples who intruded periodically from the steppe and the desert fringes. Dealing with these peoples posed problems that were as much socio-political and ecological as they were narrowly military, and this requires barbarian societies to be understood as such before we can consider the varieties in which they manifested themselves.

10.2.1. BARBARIAN LEADERSHIP AND ECOLOGY

States and stateless societies presented quite different profiles of threat and opportunity to their neighbours. These differences stemmed from political, social, and economic divergences. Politically, states were distinguished by the existence of a formally differentiated structure capable of enforcing a degree of central direction, or at least central co-ordination. Stateless peoples, by definition, had much less in the way of either political centralization or hierarchy. A degree of social hierarchy often existed, with an upper stratum that might be referred to as 'nobles' or even a form of royalty, but this did not necessarily translate into a formal structure of political power or even authority.[4] This absence of central authority might work to the advantage of a neighbouring imperial power by enabling its agents to play off rival leaders or factions. However it also rendered the locus of collective decision-making both potentially unstable and opaque, which made it more difficult for outsiders to predict the outcome of any negotiations they might be involved in and reduced the prospects that an agreement, once negotiated, could be enforced.

The attainment of leadership among such peoples frequently rested on the acquisition of a personal following and a degree of prestige that accrued from conformity to the 'warrior' values of personal courage and military prowess (Cunliffe 1997: 91–110; Goldsworthy 1996: 42–5; Mathews 1989: 314). Where this was the case there was an endemic tendency to conflict and instability, as political rivals strove to outdo each other in the acquisition of loot and social honour in military adventures. A leader's political and social status could also be enhanced by the distribution of valued items to his followers; indeed gift-giving 'generosity' was often a defining characteristic of leadership in such societies. This created a continuing appetite for prestige goods that might be satisfied by raiding or trade and was often exploited by imperial powers as a technique of political manipulation. The result was a strong tendency for barbarian societies to become more hierarchical and centralized on imperial frontiers, with local leaders gaining in wealth and power as they became 'gatekeepers' controlling the influx of such items and distributing them to their followers.

The consequences of competition between barbarian leaders could be all the more unpredictable for their neighbours given the larger-scale social and political structure of such peoples. These often consisted of loose aggregations of bands, or other local units, which recognized ties such as those of kinship or affinity but were capable of snowballing into opportunistic coalitions when the right circumstances

---

[4] See Elton (1996: 15–44) and Goldsworthy (1996: 39–60) for brief reviews of social and political structures among Rome's barbarian opponents. Krader (1968) and Sahlins (1968) provide anthropological perspectives on so-called 'acephalous' societies and early state formation.

arose and effective leadership was present. This was a widespread phenomenon, though particularly noticeable perhaps among pastoral nomads. It meant that, whilst imperial powers could often neutralize their barbarian neighbours by fomenting internal divisions, the emergence of a strong leader, or a period of weakness or division within the empire, could trigger the appearance of a powerful threat at relatively short notice.[5]

Economically, state organizations relied on the production of an agricultural surplus sufficient to allow social hierarchy and occupational specialization (Krader 1968). This might be associated with urban development, but as a rule it involved sedentary cultivation at relatively high population densities. The economic basis of stateless peoples varied, but the division of labour was less developed and population densities were usually low relative to those of states. In Europe subsistence cultivation was widespread, often based on some form of transhumance or periodic movement between different sites, but by the beginning of the Iron Age, the Eurasian steppes were already occupied by nomadic pastoralists. On Europe's northern fringes, in Scandinavia and the Russian forests, hunting and gathering peoples remained throughout the period. The economic and demographic characteristics of what the Romans called *barbaricum* presented would-be conquerors with potentially serious difficulties. Low population densities, high mobility, and the lack of major population centres or agricultural infrastructure deprived an invader of any obvious strategic sites whose capture would destroy the enemy's ability, or willingness, to resist, and could make the logistical support of large forces very difficult.

10.2.2. THE NORTHERN BARBARIANS

The expansion of Roman power in Europe was mainly at the expense of the peoples who are conventionally termed 'Celts'. The question of Celtic origins and ethnic identity, and whether it is indeed legitimate to speak of 'the Celts' as a distinct people, remains controversial, as does their relationship to the languages and cultures that eventually supplanted them (Cunliffe 1997, 1988: 33–7, 80 f.). There is, however, a substantial body of evidence concerning the material culture of the Gauls in particular and about the nature of their social and political life, even if much of this comes from accounts given by their enemies. Gallic society was dominated by a warrior elite of nobles, whose social standing relied on their proficiency in war and feuding, based around the characteristic hilltop forts or *oppida*. Southern Gaul was evidently experiencing the early stages of state formation at the time of the Roman conquest and was a relatively wealthy region with long-established trading links with the Mediterranean world. Further north,

---

[5] Drinkwater's important re-evaluation of the 'German threat' to Rome's Rhine frontier points indirectly to this conclusion. Roman military power was, he believes, more than sufficient to deal with any such threat as long as it was maintained in place. Frankish and Alamannic raids were an opportunistic, and by implication rapid, response to troop withdrawals triggered by insurrection, civil war, or major campaigns on other frontiers (Drinkwater 1996).

where the economy was less productive, hierarchy and centralization were less developed and the conditions of social and political life were more like those in the lands to the east of the Rhine.

The lands to the west of the Rhine were brought under Roman control by the end of the Republic, and the line of the Danube was reached shortly after this. At this time speakers of Germanic languages, who were long established on the north German plain, were spreading to adjacent areas along the Rhine, although it remains unclear how, and how far, this movement had developed.[6] The Romans followed up their conquest of Gaul with an attempt to secure the territory between the Rhine and the Elbe. This was initially successful but was abandoned after the destruction of one Roman army and a subsequent period of indecisive campaigning. The withdrawal of Roman troops was followed by the establishment of Germanic predominance along the Rhine and in Trans-Danubia, whilst Gothic groups moved into southern Russia from which they later moved west against the Roman frontier.

Early Germanic society included an upper stratum of *optimates* and some royal lineages, but was strongly egalitarian and decentralized. The basic social unit was the local canton in whose political life the assembly of free warriors played a key role. By the end of the Western Empire this pattern had undergone radical change in two respects.

The first such change was the emergence of new, inclusive identities, such as Frank and Alamanni in the west and Goth in the east, subsuming the numerous ethnic labels known to earlier writers. Some went on to constitute barbarian successor states in the west, but their status before these events is controversial. It remains unclear whether Franks or Alamanni should be seen as nascent confederacies progressively taking shape through the later Roman period, or whether they merely denoted some sense of shared identity on the part of a conglomeration of local groups without further political or military significance.

A development closely related to the formation of larger ethnic or political units was the emergence of formal kingship and a greater degree of social hierarchy. By the time the Germanic peoples established successor states in the Western Roman Empire, their kings had evidently become effective political rulers with an institutionalized position. This process is more likely to have been a product than a precursor of the barbarian settlements but it is clear that prolonged interaction with the Empire had already made barbarian society more hierarchical than it had once been. Kingship in earlier periods seems to have been a formal office with little actual power and distinct from the role of war leader. The Lombards, who were relative latecomers to the imperial frontier, seem to

---

[6] See Todd (1992) for a general treatment of the early Germans. Studies of specific groups include Christie (1995), James (1988), Heather (1996); for studies of Roman–German relations see Heather (1991), Wolfram (1997), Goffart (1980); for the relationship between 'Gauls' and 'Germans' in the period of the Roman conquest see also Wells (1972: 14–31) and Todd (1987).

have retained many of these 'primitive' Germanic features when they invaded Italy in the sixth century.[7]

10.2.3. SLAVS AND BALTS

The era of Germanic barbarians ended with the establishment of Lombard Italy, but both Germanic and Byzantine states still had to deal with neighbouring stateless peoples. Slav groups moving south appeared on the Danube and were raiding the Balkan interior by the early sixth century. Pressure increased during the reign of Justinian, and the Danube frontier collapsed completely following the murder of the Emperor Maurice. The assault was spearheaded by the Avars, a nomadic people of Asiatic origin established on the Hungarian plain, but it precipitated a large-scale migration into Greece and the Balkans by their Slav subjects. When the Avar siege of Constantinople ended in dismal failure the Slav settlers successfully asserted their autonomy and Byzantine control was restricted to some coastal enclaves (Obolensky 1974: 64 f.).

Slav society in this period was distinguished by its extreme fragmentation (Vana 1983; Bell-Fialkoff 2000; Dolukhanov 1996). Even more than the early Germans, the Slavs lacked political centralization or hierarchy, and where powerful states emerged in the Slav zone they often owed their origin to non-Slav dynasties as in Bulgaria and, above all, Russia. Within the Balkans, the Slavs retained a loose-knit, kinship-based organization without developed political institutions. The *Sklaviniae*, as the Byzantines termed their communities,

> usually possessed a geographical unity and were often centred on river valleys, after which their inhabitants were named...over which Byzantium had lost all effective control but which had acquired no alternative form of central administration. (Obolensky 1974: 82)

The fragmentation of Slav society made it difficult for the Imperial powers to block their raiding or infiltration because the absence of centralized leadership or organization deprived their forces of obvious targets. When Byzantine power revived in the ninth century, and the Imperial forces went over to the offensive, the position was reversed because the absence of any Slav central power now hindered their resistance to co-ordinated assaults. Byzantine control was re-established throughout the Balkan peninsula and Greece was 're-Hellenized'. A similar process occurred in north-eastern Europe in the following centuries when German rulers, aided by the crusading order of the Teutonic Knights, asserted control of lands occupied by Slav and Baltic-speaking peoples. An extensive territory between the Elbe and the Vistula was overrun and colonized although further expansion was blocked by the emergence of organized states in Poland and Lithuania.

---

[7] This at least is the conventional view which is based on contemporary Byzantine accounts but may owe more to their understandably hostile attitude than to ethnographic realities. It is possible that Lombard institutions were already relatively sophisticated at this time (Christie 1995; Collins 1999: 201–2).

10.2.4. THE STEPPE FRONTIER

Europe and the Mediterranean basin experienced recurrent incursions by nomadic pastoral peoples from the Eurasian steppe. This way of life originated there some time in the third millennium BC, and by the time of classical antiquity pastoral nomads dominated the steppe zone from the lower Danube in the west to the northern borders of China (Christian 1998). The early groups, such as those the Greeks knew as Scythians, evidently spoke Indo-European languages and were of so-called 'Caucasian' appearance, having entered the steppe from the west. From classical antiquity, however, phenotypically Mongoloid speakers of languages related to modern Turkish and Mongolian became predominant and the main direction of movement was apparently from the steppe zone towards the settled lands on its borders.[8] Our evidence for the lives of the steppe peoples, other than archaeological evidence of their material culture, comes largely from the written records of their agrarian neighbours, and this makes it difficult to chart the careers of specific groups and their relationships to each other. The defeat and dispersal by Chinese forces of the confederacy they knew as the Hsiung-Nu evidently set in train the events that led to the appearance in the west of the people known there as the Huns, but precisely what relationship, if any, the Hsiung-Nu bore to the Huns themselves, or the Huns to such later occupants of the western steppe as the Bulgars, is very difficult to determine (Maenchen-Helfen 1973).

For most purposes the social, political, and ecological factors uniting these peoples are more important than their ethnic, linguistic, or racial distinctions and it seems clear that the larger groups at least were internally diverse in these latter respects. Pastoral nomadism as an ecological adaptation involved high mobility and a dependence on herds, but pastoral peoples also generally relied on some agricultural products and so on relationships with cultivators, whether as subjects, trading partners, or employers. The social structure of the nomads generally resembled those of the northern barbarians with both being based on small bands allied by ties of kinship, whether real or 'fictive', and going to make up larger entities whose normally very loose identity could be transformed into an effective political and military unit when a strong leader appeared in propitious circumstances. Where this occurred the result could be a snowballing expansion with vanquished peoples recruited as subordinate allies, and confederacies were

---

[8] Biologists use the term 'phenotype' to distinguish the observable characteristics of an organism from its 'genotype' or genetic constitution. By far the largest proportion of the total human genotypic variation occurs within local populations and this means that the traditional racial classification of the human species has little biological meaning (Harrison, Weiner, et al. 1977: 185–6). Contemporary accounts single out apparently Mongoloid or Caucasian phenotypes for particular comment at different points, but this may reflect the tendency of observers to pay disproportionate attention to people who look most unlike themselves, rather than the relative frequency of phenotypes among groups that are likely to have been internally diverse. Chinese chroniclers thus seem to have been particularly impressed by the occurrence of Caucasian features among their nomad enemies and Europeans by Mongoloids. It is noteworthy that Genghis Khan and his descendants are described as blue-eyed with red or blond hair (Maenchen-Helfen 1973: 358–75).

formed capable of dominating huge areas and assuming the characteristics of a nascent state.

The military effectiveness of the nomad horse-archers, and the ties of personal loyalty which bound them to their leader, also enabled them to seize power in neighbouring agricultural lands—whether by invasion or as mercenaries deposing their employers.[9] Pastoralists' reliance on herd animals nonetheless limited such nomads to regions with adequate pasture if they were to retain this way of life. In Europe these were to be found mainly in southern Russia, and this zone was occupied in antiquity by a series of Indo-European-speaking groups, particularly the Scythians and Sarmatians (Phillips 1965). In the later Roman period, Goths established a hegemony until they were displaced by the Huns at the end of the fourth century (Heather 1991; Maenchen-Helfen 1973). There followed a succession of mainly Turkish or Mongol groups, some of whom may have been descendants of the Huns, until the region was conquered, along with northern Russia, by the Mongol khanate in the thirteenth century (Christian 1998: 383 f.).

Despite intermittent hostility, the steppe nomads generally established trading relations with the Greek cities of the Black Sea coast (Rostovtzeff 1922; Tsetskhladze 1998). The lower Danube also acted as a corridor for raiding or migration into the Balkans, but the inhabitants of southern Russia had only a very limited involvement with the rest of Europe until the early modern period. It was the middle Danube plain or the region of modern Hungary that formed the main area of direct confrontation between western and central Europe and peoples of nomadic origin. The Huns established the nucleus of their empire here in the fifth century and the Avars in the sixth. The region's ecology is thought to have curtailed these peoples' ancestral commitment to horse-riding pastoralism as a way of life (Lindner 1981), but they remained a powerful military force and a serious threat to their settled neighbours. The last such group, the Magyars, were crushed militarily in the mid-tenth century, but instead of vanishing from history like their predecessors, they entered the mainstream of European history as rulers of an organized Christian kingdom.

The settled peoples also had to deal with nomadic incursions from the south and south-east. Arab and Berber-speaking nomads on the desert frontiers of North Africa and the Near East had long interacted with agricultural populations in varying combinations of peaceful co-operation and raiding. In Roman times the 'Saracens', as they were collectively known, posed problems of banditry rather than high-level military threats (Whittaker 1994: 213–14, 245–6). Both Romans and Persians used Saracen auxiliaries to mount harassing attacks against their enemies, and this relationship with their imperial neighbours may itself have fostered the growth of larger confederacies and more powerful leaders. The desert-edge peoples seem to have become a more serious military threat as a result, and the Byzantines had already lost some of their newly recovered north

---

[9] This was mainly true of south and south-west Asia. In the east, most nomad dynasties apparently preferred to enforce tributary dependence over Chinese neighbours rather than to attempt territorial conquests (Barfield 1989).

African territories a generation before the seventh-century Arab invasions cost them all the rest together with Syria and Palestine (Isaac 1992: 235 f.).

The establishment of the Arab caliphate led indirectly to another round of encounters between western rulers and peoples of nomadic origin. Dynasties from the steppe north-east of the Iranian plateau had sometimes seized power there and in northern India in antiquity and the early Middle Ages, but successive rulers of the plateau prevented any major incursions to the south-west. From the late tenth century this ceased to be the case. Muslim rulers in south-west Asia increasingly relied on Islamicized Turkish mercenaries who eventually overthrew them and established dynasties of their own, whilst bands of 'Turcoman' nomads infiltrated across the plateau and into the fertile crescent (Bosworth 1968, 1975). Under the leadership of the Seljuk dynasty they participated in the military defeat of Byzantine forces at Manzikert in 1074 and subsequently established themselves on the Anatolian plateau. It was from this base that the Ottoman dynasty created an organized Islamic state on the former territory of Byzantium and regions beyond.

10.2.5. SUMMARY

The formation of the Polish and Lithuanian states effectively closed Europe's barbarian frontier, apart from the far north and the south Russian steppe. Elsewhere the whole continent lay, formally at least, within the borders of organized states, and a process dating back as far as the beginning of Rome's assault on the Cisalpine Gauls had come to an end. A number of generalizations can be made about events over this lengthy period. The first is the long-running stand-off between agriculturalists and pastoral nomads. The pastoral nomads raided the settled lands at intervals, and were able to establish themselves in south Russian and Danube plains, but with the exception of the Mongols in Russia they were unable to effect lasting conquests. They established dynasties in North Africa and the Near East, but this more often followed mercenary revolt than external conquest. The armies of the agrarian states nonetheless found it very difficult to defeat pastoral nomads' mounted bowmen and only established military control over the steppes once gunpowder weapons had become available.

In Europe itself the Romans overcame the Celtic peoples of northern Italy, Gaul, and southern Britain, and with more difficulty the inhabitants of Spain and the Balkans. They were less successful beyond the Rhine and the Danube, but their problems were not simply military in any narrow sense. Roman armies were defeated in Germany, disastrously so at the time of the revolt of Arminius, but they were more often victorious, and when they evacuated Germany they did so as an act of policy, not under the immediate pressure of defeat. Roman armies also won victories in what would become central Scotland but chose not to remain. Gallic and Germanic groups differed amongst themselves, but taken as a whole the principal difference between those who succumbed to Roman rule and those who did not was their prior level of development. Gallic society was more hierarchical, its political life more centralized, and its settlement pattern more nucleated than was the Germans'. But this cannot be the whole of the story. Medieval Slav society resembled ancient Germany more than Gaul but they still succumbed to their Imperial neighbours. In order to understand why this was so we need to examine more closely the prerequisites for successful expansion.

10.3. EXPANSION

Tributary dependence was often enforced by raiding strategies, but the expansion of control usually required occupation. In principle, it was a two-stage process in which an initial conquest was followed up by the second stage of consolidation. Conquest involved high-level warfare aimed at neutralizing the defenders' mobile forces and seizing their major fortifications should they possess any. Defending troops might be neutralized by pinning them within fortifications, but should they offer battle they would have to be decisively defeated and dispersed. The requirements for doing this were essentially relative, but battlefield success was not sufficient in itself to ensure a politically decisive outcome. This required the attacking forces to meet the absolute criteria of mobility, discipline, and organization needed to prevent the enemy regrouping, and to gain control of their bases. These criteria became all the more important once organized resistance had ceased and control had to be consolidated over the new territory's population and resource base. Given the characteristic areal geography of organic economies, this usually meant dispersing them into a large number of small garrisons so as to deter continued resistance and to allow the agencies of administration and resource extraction to be established on a subregional level. Should sporadic local resistance continue, they would also have to wage low-level warfare for an indefinite period.

10.3.1. CONQUEST

A ruler bent on conquest needed field armies that could operate away from home for periods that might run from weeks to years. Assuming the invader won all the battles, the elimination of centrally or regionally organized resistance depended on two main factors. The first was geographical; differences in terrain and things like access to water transport made some regions intrinsically more difficult to conquer than others. Where organized resistance occurred in remote areas, even fairly primitive fortifications posed serious logistical difficulties if they could not be taken quickly. Their potential can be seen in the contrast between Charlemagne's successful attack on the powerful Danubian khanate of the Avars and his subsequent failure against relatively 'backward' Bohemia. On the Danube powerful forces could be assembled and supplied by river and through the old Roman road network of Rhaetia and Pannonia, and protracted siege operations could be pursued. In Bohemia, neither mode of transport was available, and the Franks were unable to benefit from external supply lines or floating magazines. The defenders refused battle and withdrew to their strongholds. The Franks, unable to concentrate the forces needed for a successful siege, then had to withdraw for lack of supplies. They later mounted a series of major raids, but were unable to translate this success into lasting political or military gains (Bowlus 1995).

The second factor was the region's level of economic and political development, and this was often more important. The more developed the target region's economic and political structure the lengthier and more difficult the task of initial conquest was likely to be. Organized states were better able to maintain substantial fortified centres and to field armies with a logistical base that allowed them to manoeuvre strategically and with the necessary organization and discipline to retain cohesion in the face of battlefield defeat. Where population densities were low, and the political structure weakly differentiated, it was more difficult for the inhabitants to sustain high-level warfare, and organized resistance might be negligible to begin with. The institutionalization of political power in organized states also tended to enhance the defender's range of military options, and so the potential effectiveness of the defence, and the elaboration of distinct civil and military leadership positions had the same effect. Where the two were vested in the same personalities, commanders had to consider the domestic political consequences of their strategic or tactical decisions. This could seriously restrict their freedom to pursue the optimum military course. When invaders appeared in great numbers, the 'correct' military response was often to shelter behind fortifications until the attackers ran out of supplies and had to go away. However only a very secure political leader could afford to stand by and watch while his lands were devastated and his dependants massacred.

Internal political divisions, or weaknesses of any kind, could force the hand of a royal commander in a militarily damaging manner. In 1066, Harold Godwinson's premature move against the Norman invaders is likely to have been influenced by his insecure domestic position and the doubtful loyalties of key magnates (Morillo 1996). Similarly, the eastern Roman Emperor Valens's refusal to wait for western aid before the disastrous defeat at Adrianople stemmed from a desire to buttress his position with an unassisted victory (Wolfram 1997: 83–7). Such political considerations weighed on kings and emperors, but they were all the more pressing for the prestige-based leadership of barbarian peoples. Lacking an institutional basis, their power rested on the status brought by victory in battle. This made it hard for them not to fight a destructive invader, even where avoiding battle was desirable from a narrowly military point of view. The revolts against Roman rule in Germany and Gaul both achieved initial success when their leaders refused open battle, but the political cost of this strategy was substantial. Pressure from his peers eventually forced the Gallic leader Vercingetorix to stand and fight with disastrous consequences: his army was annihilated at the siege of Alesia.[10]

---

[10] See Cunliffe (1988: 121–2). Arminius' attempts to withstand the Roman reinvasion in pitched battle were also unsuccessful (Wells 1972: 241–2).

The defeat of an invader in open battle usually ended the invasion there and then unless several armies were involved, but if the defender refused battle or was defeated the wide range of possible outcomes reflected a basic asymmetry between the conditions for successful aggression and resistance. The ability to win battles was a necessary condition for the first but not for the second. The limits to resistance were set by technological, logistical, and other military considerations, but reaching these limits depended on a much wider range of factors whose importance can be seen in the widely different outcomes of military defeat on a comparable scale. The collapse of Visigothic Spain following defeat by Moorish invaders contrasts sharply with the rally and protracted resistance of their Italian neighbours in the face of Byzantine reconquest (Collins 1999: 129–34, 153–61). The robust political foundations of Roman power in Italy, and the Republican institutionalization of military leadership, enabled their forces to sustain a lengthy war of attrition against Carthaginian invaders despite suffering some of the most crushing defeats known to military history in its early stages. Much later, in the Napoleonic period, the Prussian military-political structure effectively collapsed following defeat at Jena whilst the, outwardly much weaker, Habsburgs recovered from a series of such reversals.

This diversity of outcomes reflected a heterogeneous collection of political and other factors which together made up what can be termed 'strategic depth'. They included such things as the loyalty of local elites to the centre and the willingness of the population at large to co-operate with—perhaps to provision or to provide replacement garrisons for—representatives of the old regime once the effectiveness of its coercive apparatus had, at least temporarily, collapsed. The political structure of the 'proto-states' formed by successful barbarian confederacies was particularly vulnerable to military defeat. A dramatic example is provided by the Avars. Their extensive suzerainty over Slav and Germanic peoples was repudiated in the wake of their failure to take Constantinople in 626. This was followed, at the end of the eighth century, by the disintegration of the confederacy itself as its rulers proved helpless in the face of Frankish raids which eventually led to the looting and destruction of their political centre, the so-called 'Ring' (Collins 1998: 95–6). The 790s were marked by civil war, defection, and attacks by newly forming Slav powers rising up against their former masters. Eventually, in 805 the humiliated Khan was forced to request Charlemagne's protection on Imperial territory and:

taking the name Abraham was baptised in the Fischa river and installed as a Frankish client over what remained of the once proud Avars, a people who had dominated the Danubian basin for over two centuries. (Bowlus 1995: 58)[11]

Victory in battle might be achieved by superior numbers, better leadership and tactics, or simple good luck, but successfully conquering all but the strategically 'shallowest' opponent also required forces which could conduct sustained pursuit

---

[11] The Avar collapse was so rapid and total as to spawn a Russian proverb: 'they perished like Avars, and there survives of them neither progeny nor heir'; quoted Ardener (1974: 30).

without getting out of control and could mount a successful siege. Above all, they had to be able to remain in or near the zone of operations until the process had been brought to a successful conclusion. The forces of the agrarian empires were generally able to do this, but their medieval successors found it much more difficult. Charlemagne expanded the Frankish territories with near-annual campaigns under his personal leadership. The main field army drew on the resources of the whole Empire and was mobilized for a period of weeks only. If it succeeded within this period, the victory was exploited by smaller-scale regional forces based on the frontier or the conquered territory itself.[12] Otherwise the Emperor had to bring the army back again the following year or abandon the project.

The conditions of feudal tenure under Charlemagne's successors greatly restricted the liability for distant service away from home and placed obstacles in the way of effective military organization. Armies recruited on this basis often lacked the kind of command structures needed to co-ordinate strategic pursuit and usually held the field for only a few weeks. This made sustained conquest difficult in itself, but the problem was aggravated by the multiplication of effective point defences throughout western and central Europe. Few contemporary rulers could muster the force needed to take such places by storm, or the logistical wherewithal to support a series of successful sieges. Raiding strategies and low-level warfare proliferated as a result, but this rarely provided a basis for territorial conquest and consolidation. The success of the English tactical system brought it tantalizingly close to the successful conquest of France, but this required new structures of military recruitment and maintenance that could keep troops operational for months or years at a time (see below, Chapter 12).

10.3.2. CONSOLIDATION

The demands placed on armed forces by the consolidation phase also varied with the political and economic context but in a different way from those of the initial conquest. Consolidation generally became more difficult the lower a territory's degree of political and economic development. Whereas conquest usually involved manoeuvring concentrated forces in high-level warfare, consolidation required dispersing forces to a variety of duties that might, or might not, involve systematic prosecution of low-level warfare. These detachments had to be kept in place until the required degree of control could safely be exercised by unaided

---

[12] In Bowlus's words, 'Carolingian conquests began with massive invasions of hostile territory, for which troops were summoned from the various Frankish realms. Carolingian pincers converged on enemy forces from several directions, which divided the energies of the defenders and which eased problems of supply. The objective of these operations was to ravish the opponent's territory, to drive him from his fortifications, and to establish strategic strongholds from which Frankish garrisons under the command of margraves could assert effective control over the region. Once these tasks had been accomplished, the men constituting this large array returned to Francia for demobilisation. From fortresses in occupied territory, smaller units (*scarae*) could then periodically be sent out by marcher commanders to reconnoitre and to harass resisters. After a region had been conquered, larger armies were necessary only when rebellions threatened the authority of the margraves' (Bowlus 1995: 19–20).

civilian agencies or, in frontier regions, permanently. Keeping troops away from home, on this time scale, was easier for some military systems than for others. States, like the later Roman Republic and Empire, whose soldiers were paid full-timers had few problems doing this, and might actively prefer to cut costs by supporting units from the resources of conquered territory. Where the state lacked the administrative machinery to extract resources efficiently, or the troops were part-timers with limited service liabilities, it was much more difficult, and both of these conditions prevailed in medieval Europe. Where territorial expansion occurred, as it did in eastern Europe, Spain, and Ireland, as well as in the Levant, it required a system of colonization based on the exchange of land rights for local military service and the establishment of fortified settlements (Bartlett and MacKay 1989).

10.3.2.1. Concentration and dispersal

Consolidation was usually facilitated by a differentiated economic and political structure. Urbanization promoted concentration of population, and higher densities of agricultural production enabled larger forces to be maintained away from the major centres. Conversely, the more dispersed the population the harder it was to consolidate and maintain control, and this was particularly difficult where the mode of subsistence was transhumant or nomadic and based around mobile resources such as cattle herds. Most of Rome's eastern conquests were relatively easy to consolidate, the principal requirement being to occupy and hold the cities. In the Celtic west the initial task was to gain control of the fortified tribal centres or *oppida*. Capturing these was one thing, retaining them was another, and the solution lay in placing and supplying garrisons. Rome was well equipped to undertake this in reasonably productive landscapes of the kind found in much of Gaul and southern Britain.

The logistical problems were greater in poorer, thinly peopled regions elsewhere, but this was not the only difficulty that they posed; their weakly differentiated political structure played an even greater role. The formalized power structure of organized states simplified the task of consolidating control once their military forces had been overcome. It was usually clear, where political roles were institutionalized, just who had to be eliminated, co-opted, or otherwise neutralized in order to pre-empt further resistance. The more rigid, and finely differentiated, the political hierarchy, the more difficult it was for popular leaders to arise once the original elite had surrendered or been removed. Invaders could sometimes hope to take over the whole state apparatus as a going concern simply by eliminating a ruler and his entourage as Alexander tried to do in Persia. By the same token, the more decentralized and egalitarian the structure the more opaque it was to an outsider, the more difficult to judge the potential for continuing large-scale resistance, and the easier for such resistance to coalesce around a charismatic leader.

One consequence of this opacity was to make it harder for imperial conquerors to judge the point at which their forces could safely be dispersed to consolidate control and establish the means of systematic resource extraction. The Romans repeatedly misjudged this point and were badly wrong-footed as a result. Major revolts against Roman rule characteristically occurred in the early stages of consolidation when low-level administrative and, above all, fiscal agencies were being constructed, but higher-level control still depended on networks of partly assimilated aristocratic clients and their supporting factions (Dyson 1970, 1975). Many of these people had looked to the Imperial power to buttress their position in tribal society, but as the demands of the new administration began to threaten the very way of life on which this depended, the Romans found men and women whom they thought they could trust turning against them and assembling large forces with surprising speed.

Revolts of this kind also reflected the mismatch between imperial administrative systems based on cash transactions and barbarian economies that were only weakly, if at all, monetarized. These imperial administrations required revenue in cash or precious metals if conquered territories were to pay their way, but barbarian leaders who handed over valuable prestige goods of this kind risked social humiliation as well as economic hardship and a dangerous loss of status in the eyes of their followers. The consolidation of such regions was, paradoxically, easier for the rulers of less sophisticated feudal polities who could be satisfied with revenue in the form of subsistence goods or service. The former could be obtained by manipulating indigenous notions of gift-giving or 'hospitality', whilst the idiom of feudal lord/follower relations could be used to incorporate co-operative indigenous elements into the new hierarchy in ways that did not compromise their standing in the eyes of their own followers. Lotter has shown how Slavic leaders who became the German Emperor's sworn followers in medieval trans-Elbia gained a status that could be manipulated so as to enhance their position among their peers, something that no one ever achieved by handing over gold to a Roman tax collector (Lotter 1989).

The implication of these observations is that Rome succeeded in Gaul but failed in Germany because the relative centralization of Gallic society provided geographical and political targets that could be picked off in a way that German society did not. Subsequently the very 'backwardness' of feudal society enabled medieval rulers to consolidate control in north-eastern Europe through the salience of personal ties and the limited role of cash transactions in politics and administration. This argument explains a great deal, but it does not explain everything. Rome eventually succeeded, with however much difficulty, in consolidating control over parts of Spain and the Balkans that were more like Germany than southern Gaul, and the Byzantine Imperial authorities eventually reassimilated the Balkan Slavs. This was partly a matter of geography; the regions where consolidation succeeded apparently against the odds were enclaves that were relatively close to imperial bases or accessible by water. This made it easier to mount recurrent raids of the kind that eventually ground down resistance. Roman troops in Germany by contrast were far from their bases in logistically difficult terrain much of which was inaccessible by water and bounded by an open frontier to the east.

10.3.2.2. *Colonization*

The Romans consolidated their conquests through cultural assimilation as well as military force, and the planting of army veterans in colonial settlements played an important part in this process. Roman colonies promoted luxury consumption among the indigenous elite as well as providing manpower for security duties and a 'last ditch' military reserve. They were essentially urban, and therefore rarely found in poor, remote districts, but the colonial settlement of farmers owing military service in exchange for land rights was a widespread solution to the problem of consolidation in thinly peopled areas. It formed the basis of Byzantium's eventual recovery of the Balkan *Sklaviniae* (Obolensky 1974: 106), and was used on the expanding frontiers of medieval Europe. Much of this expansion was undertaken by forces outside the existing state structures, narrowly defined.

The Catholic Church, and the militarized religious orders owing allegiance to it, played a major role in this process. These orders consisted of full-time professional troops, with their own infrastructure of civilian support, able to act outside the framework of secular lordship and establish a permanent presence on conquered land. In the Baltic region the knights of the Teutonic order established what was, in effect, an autonomous state on lands conquered from the pagan Prussians and related peoples (Christiansen 1980). Elsewhere expansion was the work of ad hoc forces recruited from across the boundaries of the feudal domains. The best known of these, the early crusading expeditions to the eastern Mediterranean, were raised under papal sanction and comprised distinct 'national' contingents.[13] Some of them were under royal leadership, but the political entities they established were autonomous and not dependent on any existing lordship.

The ultimate success or failure of these movements depended on their ability to attract a continuing stream of colonists as much as it did on the military prowess of Frankish-style heavy cavalry. This was promoted by the relative mobility of feudal society and the secondary role played by landownership as opposed to landholding. Colonists were also easier to obtain when Europe's population was growing, and so the rhythm of expansion followed the demographic cycle even if it was not demographically driven. The importance of colonization and the role of 'extra-state' forces goes some way to explain the paradoxical contrast between medieval European rulers' success in closing the barbarian frontier and the weakness of any movements of consolidation within the frontier. This contrast, which reversed the pattern of antiquity, was partly due to the fact that 'transnational' colonizing expeditions with papal sanction were much easier to mount against pagan or Muslim targets than against western Christian rulers. William of Normandy's army of 1066 included men from a wide area outside his feudal

---

[13] For general surveys see Smail (1956), Richard (1999), and for the military history Riley-Smith (1999).

domain, but he was unusual in gaining papal support for a purely personal claim to the English throne.[14]

10.3.3. SUMMARY

Successful military expansion depended, in the first instance, on a balance of force in favour of the aggressor. This was a necessary, but not in itself a sufficient, condition for success because the range of likely outcomes was also affected by the terrain, the level of resources, and the degree of economic and political development in the target region. Difficult or unproductive terrain always hampered military operations and this usually acted against the aggressor, but the effect of political and economic development varied according to the stage to which the aggression had progressed. In the early stages, the inhabitants of thinly populated regions with little political organization would be hard put to resist an invasion by powerful, concentrated forces, whereas organized states would be more likely to muster effective opposition. The position was reversed once the first resistance had been overcome and the invading force dispersed to consolidate control, since this was more difficult in the absence of institutionalized political leadership or administrative and fiscal structures in the newly acquired region.

Poor, thinly peopled territories also placed serious logistical difficulties in the way of effective consolidation because of the small numbers of troops that could be supported from local resources. Securing control over such a terrain in the face of continuing local resistance might require substantial forces to be committed for an extended period. Success depended on establishing the infrastructure of low-level warfare in the form of small-scale point defences and the supply system to keep them provisioned. Where the countryside was relatively rich and most of the population co-operative or open to coercion, garrisons might have little difficulty in accumulating the wherewithal to withstand an extended siege. Where neither of these conditions held they needed external provisioning. In the absence of water transport this required supply lines that could be formidably expensive to operate and a substantial manpower commitment to defend them.

There were two ways in which the manpower necessary to consolidate and retain control over conquered territories could be maintained in place. Organized states with full-time professional armies could pay their troops in cash. The marginal costs of territorial expansion undertaken with forces of this kind depended on the nature of the territories concerned. Productive regions, with a monetarized economy and a pre-existing fiscal apparatus, were likely to generate more in revenue than it cost to maintain such additional troops as were needed to garrison them. Barbarian lands were very different, needing large occupation forces and expensive logistical support, whilst yielding little in the way of offsetting

---

[14] Oman saw William 'not as the mere feudal head of the barons of Normandy, but rather as the managing-director of a great joint-stock company for the conquest of England, in which not only his own subjects, but hundreds of adventurers, poor and rich from all parts of Western Europe had taken shares' (Oman 1991: 157).

taxation. The Romans, faced with this dilemma in Germany and the Celtic lands, forced the pace of development by imposing taxation in cash on what were still mostly non-monetary economies. This promised to square the fiscal circle but threatened the position of the tribal elites whose co-operation was still important in the early stages of consolidation (Dyson 1975, 1970). The ensuing revolts were eventually suppressed across most of the region, but in Germany and northern Britain the costs of continuing occupation were eventually deemed to outweigh the benefits.

Rulers without a standing army could maintain troops in conquered territories by assigning them rights over land, produce, or revenues. This might not be too disruptive to the indigenous social and economic life of regions without a monetary economy since it did not require the imposition of regular taxation. In productive lands, where settled agriculture was already practised, military colonists and their followers could be assigned rights over the indigenous cultivators and their produce, as they were in Norman England. Elsewhere, as in Ireland and the lands east of the Elbe, larger numbers of civilian colonists were required to maintain the new order. These colonizing ventures were not themselves driven by population growth, but they did require a sufficiently mobile population of potential colonists with limited prospects in the core territories. This category shrank disproportionately during phases of demographic recession, and at these times the expansion of Europe's frontiers ground to a halt (Bartlett and MacKay 1989; Jiminez 1989).

10.4. CONCLUSION

Political power, whatever else it may be, is also a spatial phenomenon and states are spatial systems. The energy restrictions common to organic economies constrained the political integration of space just as they did its economic integration, but in neither case did they determine the outcome of the process. Medieval Europe's political landscape was fragmented and decentralized, but in earlier periods muscle-power weaponry and organic economies had proved compatible with the emergence of political units on an imperial scale. The relationship between political power and space expressed itself in institutional forms which varied greatly over time, not least because ancient and early medieval states were often bordered by stateless barbarian peoples. From a functional point of view the relationship can best be understood in terms of the spatial extent of control, which is the geographical area over which rulers could exercise sufficient power to extract resources on a systematic basis.

The expansion of control by force should be thought of as a two-stage process requiring successively conquest and consolidation. Conquest required victory in high-level warfare, and organized states were usually better able to resist this than were stateless barbarian peoples. The position was reversed, however, at the second stage of consolidation. The basic problem was the contradiction between the concentration of force needed to secure military victories and the need for dispersal that was imposed by the areal geography of organic economies. The less developed a region's economy, the fewer major settlements and static concentrations of wealth it would possess and the more difficulty an occupying power would have in dominating its population and resources. The decentralized egalitarianism of barbarian societies also made it more difficult for imperial conquerors to pre-empt further resistance by co-opting or eliminating the indigenous power structure.

This contrast underlay the long-term tendency toward spatial aggregation in the ancient world as stronger states eliminated their weaker rivals until the eventual victor's expansion ceased on the barbarian frontier. Some regions of this kind were eventually coerced into submission by repeated raiding, but this required them to be readily accessible to troops operating from well-supplied logistical bases. Rulers in the feudal west rarely had the forces to mount sustained campaigns of conquest or undertake the numerous sieges required by the contemporary proliferation of point defences. It was therefore rare for organized states to conquer each other and the political landscape of the Catholic 'core' remained fragmented, but this was not the case on the periphery. The relative mobility of the feudal warrior class and the overarching structures of the Catholic Church allowed military efforts to be mounted against pagan, infidel, or otherwise heterodox targets on a scale that was often not possible in disputes between Catholic rulers. The medieval assault on Islam eventually failed outside Spain, but much greater success was achieved against the stateless peoples of eastern Europe. Consolidating control in these circumstances depended on a process of colonization whose success was facilitated by population growth and the existence of a politico-military system that was more readily adapted to non-monetarized regional economies than were the more sophisticated systems of antiquity.

CHAPTER ELEVEN

Power and Space II: Maintaining Control

Maintaining control once it had been established required rulers to pre-empt or suppress indigenous revolts, defend their frontiers against external threats, and prevent regional commanders, administrators, or elites breaking away from central control. The degree of military commitment needed to achieve the first of these requirements depended on a range of circumstances and particularly on the degree of accommodation by the conquered population to their new masters. This made it a political and administrative challenge as much as a military one. In practice, successful indigenous uprisings seem to have been rare in the ancient and medieval worlds, once control had been consolidated, and the major dangers posed to a large state consisted of attacks against its frontiers or secession by those who served its rulers in the provinces, particularly frontier provinces.

These two kinds of danger were related to each other, because the most effective means of dealing with the first of them often increased the dangers from the second. The origins of this dilemma lay in the limitations of pre-gunpowder military technology which made it effectively impossible to secure unambiguous linear boundaries in all but the most exceptional circumstances; instead there were frontier zones that were always permeable to some degree. Frontiers were also unstable and ambiguous zones, and the problems encountered in defending them were more than simply military, particularly where organized states bordered stateless barbarian peoples. Under these circumstances the main threats were usually what can be termed 'diffused', endemic low-level infiltration and raiding which was usually opportunistic and lacking in central direction but could be extremely destructive if left unchecked. Threats of this kind could sometimes be dealt with by astute political manipulation and bribery, but such actions could backfire by building up potentially dangerous leaders or coalitions. The military solution incorporated some form of 'defence in depth', but this usually required a substantial degree of decentralization if it was to be effective, and decentralization increased the risks of secession. It was the outcome of just such a process that underlay the fragmented political landscape of medieval Europe.

11.1. FRONTIERS AND THEIR DEFENCE

The complexities of frontier defence reflected the ambiguous and unstable character of frontiers as geographical and sociological entities. The location of frontier zones was often determined by the geographical limits of an imperial state's ability to consolidate its control over barbarian lands with the result that they were economically marginal. Whittaker describes Roman frontiers as settled at the point where the relative risks and rewards of consolidation pushed the marginal cost of further expansion to an unacceptably high level. In his words they were 'ecologically marginal and demographically ambiguous zones' whose location formed a 'compromise between the range of conquest and the economy of rule' (Whittaker 1994). The military geography of frontiers was one of permeable zones, rather than rigid boundary lines, for both ideological and technical reasons, and this favoured decentralized forms of political and military administration. Decentralization was reinforced by the nature of the threats confronting frontier administrations. Although some of these were 'focused', stemming from large-scale invasions by organized forces, more common on ancient and medieval frontiers were the 'diffused' threats represented by endemic, locally directed, low-level incursions. These were very difficult for a highly centralized military or political system to deal with, but left unchecked they could create insecurity on a scale that fatally undermined the social and economic foundations of frontier life.

Frontiers were also complex sociological entities. Where organized states neighboured each other, the devolved authority wielded by frontier commanders or magnates could border on autonomy and render their allegiances ambiguous. Where imperial states bordered stateless societies frontiers became zones of shifting and unstable allegiance of a kind that sometimes shaped collective identities. On the barbarian side, the empire offered material rewards, whether as pay, subsidy, or loot, which enabled successful leaders to build coalitions that sometimes emerged as new ethnic identities or took their place as military units in the imperial order of battle. On the imperial side, intervention in search of loot and the pre-emption of hostile coalitions drew the frontier edge forward into the barbarian zone, just as the settlement or infiltration of barbarians, or unrest among overtaxed provincials, threatened to push it back into the 'settled' zone. The nature of leadership in barbarian societies created a further tendency towards frontier instability. Potential leaders competed to acquire followers through the exemplary display of warrior virtues and the accumulation and distribution of prestige goods, both of which could be advanced by cross-border raiding. Furthermore, where the imperial power paid subsidies to 'friendly' leaders, it enabled them to expand their followings, becoming more powerful and potentially dangerous should they decide that raiding would be more profitable than collaboration.

This was a serious problem because the best way of dealing with frontier threats was to remove them at source. Formal diplomatic channels might achieve this on frontiers between centralized states, but a broader range of methods was required on barbarian frontiers, or wherever central control was weak. The most effective frontier policy was to break up hostile coalitions and establish friendly ones through a combination of bribery, subversion, and 'active defence', but if this went wrong it could create the very dangers it sought to avert. Successful diplomatic manipulation apparently let the Romans manage without frontier troops for a long period in North African Tripolitania, but at a certain point they lost control of the situation, and a coalition including former clients became strong enough to overrun much of the Imperial territory (Whittaker 1994: 143–48). Clients or coalitions whose positions had been too well buttressed could turn against their former friends; barbarian leaders who redistributed imperial subsidies to maintain their domestic position might have to resort to raiding if the incoming stream of wealth dried up. The recruitment of barbarian auxiliaries could be a valuable means of frontier defence, but it too was potentially dangerous since it could foster an awareness of common identity and potential strength among the people concerned[1].

Demography also played a role in fostering instability. Leadership positions are a form of so-called 'positional' goods whose supply cannot be expanded unless the hierarchy itself is restructured in the direction of greater collegiality or through new hierarchies being created. In the absence of any institutionalized hierarchy, barbarian leadership rested on the outcome of competition among peers, and even a marginal rate of population increase could cause what we termed 'Goldstone overpopulation' among the elite stratum (see above, Chapter 2). The problem was that the number of eligible candidates expanded faster than the number of leadership positions because there were, paradoxically, too few people available to constitute followings for the displaced members of the elite. This condition could arise from small changes in mortality or from migration towards the frontier from the outer region of the barbarian periphery. The consequence was intensified competition for followings, leading to raiding and other forms of predatory expansion including the forcible incorporation of neighbouring groups and colonizing expeditions by those unable to achieve leadership status at home.

11.1.1. ZONES AND BOUNDARIES

The spatial limits of pre-modern states generally constituted zones, which were often fluid, rather than unambiguous border lines. This reflected the characteristic ideology of pre-modern state power as well as the limitations of contemporary technology. Modern European states are defined by sharply delineated spatial

---

[1] Dyson suggests that the Romans' concentration of allied contingents had this effect, and helped to precipitate revolt, in Pannonia and elsewhere during the early Empire (Dyson 1970, 1975). In a later period there is a correspondence between the territories of the Franks and Alamanni and the Roman military commands on the lower and upper Rhine, and it is possible that the new entities coalesced through contacts—collaborative as well as hostile—with the respective command staffs (Wolfram 1997: 40–2). See also Lattimore (1962: 115–16).

boundaries as part of a system based on the mutual recognition of sovereignty under conditions of formal equality between states. In earlier periods relations were more often governed by assumptions of hierarchy and difference, and this affected conceptions of political space itself. As Whittaker observes: 'As long as an imperial state has neighbours, the neighbours are necessarily inferior and the state has no frontiers in our sense. That is a conclusion that applies to all early empires' (Whittaker 1994: 66). The Romans, he argues, acknowledged the existence of physical boundaries to the extent of the territory they actually had under their administration at any point in time, but they did not recognize any spatial limits to their authority, a stance which precluded the recognition of neighbouring states' or peoples' rights to permanent independent existence.

Rulers in the medieval west usually acknowledged co-religionist sovereigns as legitimate, though assumptions of suzerainty and subordination often affected their relationships, but elsewhere there was a recurrent perception of 'difference': of a moral and ideological gulf between the self and 'other'. This conditioned relations between ancient Greeks, Romans, and those they perceived as 'barbarians'. It affected relations between medieval Catholic and Orthodox Christians, and between both of these and their Muslim or pagan neighbours. Latin Christendom claimed an inherited sovereignty over Muslim-occupied Palestine, and subsequently over the pagan peoples of north-eastern Europe and elsewhere (Christiansen 1980). Catholics condemned Orthodox Christians as schismatics and they became the eventual victims of the Fourth Crusade, whilst Byzantium itself asserted Imperial authority over its lost territories as well as Russian principalities that had never known Roman administration (Obolensky 1974: 291–4).

The reluctance of rulers to concede spatial limits to their sovereignty made it correspondingly difficult to accept clear linear boundaries, and provided a potential ideological mandate for cross-border raiding. Even where neighbours recognized each other's legitimacy, as they often did in feudal Europe, political geography was complicated by the fact that sovereign claims were more often directed to people and resources, or what we have termed 'demographic space', than to physical space as such. Where lordships bordered each other the result was often a confused overlapping of claims to jurisdiction, revenues, or labour services that defied any simple linear demarcation. These became endemic sources of conflict as the feudal boundaries crystallized into those of early modern national states[2].

The widespread ideological aversion to sharply demarcated boundaries was reinforced by the limitations of contemporary cartographic and military technology. It was very difficult to define and mark boundary lines across open country, and pre-modern map-making skills were of little practical use in

---

[2] Potter has provided an illuminating account of this process on the 16th-century border between France and the Low Countries, where there existed 'a bewildering patchwork of territories subject to various feudal tenures' (Potter 1993: 268). One particular source of confusion here, as in north-western England and elsewhere, was that sovereigns might also be each other's feudal tenants.

resolving disputes. This was particularly true in the featureless terrain of *barbaricum*, but it was also the case in the urbanized Roman east where the limits of Roman and Persian control traced an uncertain path among a network of outposts, forts, and city garrisons (Isaac 1992: 255–7). In principle major rivers made good 'natural' markers, but in practice they were unsuitable boundaries because of their importance as lines of communication and transport, which made it highly desirable to control both banks. The problem may have been conceptual as well as material. Pre-modern maps were characteristically itineraries depicting networks of interconnection between settlements and other places with distinct social, economic, or military significance. It is possible that what geographers term 'mental maps' were similarly constructed and that contemporaries had difficulty in conceptualizing relationships between large blocks of two-dimensional space (Lee 1993: 81–90).

The limitations of muscle-powered military technology meant that linear boundaries were also very difficult if not impossible to defend. Neither natural nor man-made barriers could be relied on except in the rarest of circumstances. River lines were rarely effective defences because a defending force drawn up on the bank could usually be outflanked at the crossing points or fords, which were all the more plentiful before the modern embankment and canalization of many European rivers (Lee 1993: 97). Northern rivers were also liable to freeze during the winter, which became the favourite campaigning season for barbarian invaders, although small boats could be used for infiltration at any time. In addition, both Roman and Persian armies were furnished with bridging equipment (Lee 1993: 96, 100–1). The strategic function of rivers was thus more one of communication than interdiction. Ranges of hills, or even mountains, were also of very limited defensive value except where pierced by the narrowest of defiles and even the Alps were ineffective as a barrier.[3]

11.1.2. THREATS TO FRONTIERS

Frontiers had to be defended against a wide variety of threats that differed in both quality and degree, but for analytical purposes they can usefully be lumped together as either 'focused' or 'diffused'. The two categories correspond broadly to those of high-level and low-level warfare which we encountered earlier. Focused threats consisted of large-scale incursions by forces of substantial size that would generally have clearly defined axes of advance and specific objectives, whether the overthrow of the state itself, the occupation of territory, or the

---

[3] The main strategic advantage such terrain offered to a defender was the possibility of catching an enemy force in a position where it was unable to deploy—the fate which famously befell Charlemagne's rearguard and its commander Count Hruodland at Roncesvalles (Collins 1998: 67–8). Fifty years later another Carolingian army was destroyed by Basques in the same pass, effectively ending Frankish territorial ambitions in the region (Collins 1984: 15). In order to do this, however, the defender needed to have an effective mobile force and to take the initiative. It was no basis for a purely passive defence by a static garrison.

sacking and destruction of settlements. Such threats were more often associated with the forces of organized states, but barbarian groups could also band together in large numbers where circumstances permitted and a suitable opportunity presented itself. The fourth-century frontier of Roman Britain twice collapsed in the face of what contemporaries termed 'conspiracies' but may have been simple opportunism by a series of barbarian neighbours acting independently; the Rhine was crossed *en masse* by a Germanic coalition, or series of coalitions, at the end of 406.[4]

Alongside threats of this kind there was a second category represented by small-scale infiltration in search of targets of opportunity, which might be minor settlements, individual farmsteads, groups of travellers, or even other marauders.[5] Such bands might number no more than a few dozen men or less, but persistent raiding on this scale could create sufficient insecurity to threaten the frontier region's entire military and economic structure. Depending on the perpetrators' mobility such insecurity might reach beyond the frontier into the interior itself. Barbarian peoples usually posed diffused threats of this kind, but they could also arise where the central authority of a neighbouring state exercised only weak control on its frontier, as was often the case on the Anglo-Scottish border before the union of the two crowns. Highly focused and diffused threats represent two ends of a spectrum, and a threat of one kind might transform into the other at short notice. Organized field armies or barbarian aggregations might disperse into much smaller groups, where their goal was raiding rather than permanent conquest, and raiding bands sometimes coalesced into substantial forces if threatened.[6] Most of the threats that frontier commanders and their superiors had to face nonetheless fell fairly clearly into one of these two categories, and it was often the diffuse threats that were the more difficult to deal with.

11.1.2.1. *Focused threats*

Focused threats were most dangerous when posed by an enemy who could base powerful mobile forces close to the frontier and equip them with a well-organized supply service. Forces of this kind might, in principle, be able to penetrate the frontier zone, capturing or destroying local point defences, before the defenders'

---

[4] The 'conspiracy' to invade Britain in AD 367 is described in the near-contemporary writings of Ammianus Marcelinus and its destructive consequences are visible in the archaeological record, but the invasion of AD 360 may have been on an even larger scale (Salway 1981: 361, 373–82). Elton thinks opportunism a more likely explanation than conspiracy and believes 'we should beware of attributing co-operation' where the sources are silent as to named leaders (Elton 1996: 39–41).

[5] One Frankish bandit, Charietto, was so successful in operations of the latter kind in the region around Trier that he was eventually recruited by the Romans and rose to a senior command position (Whittaker 1994: 163–5).

[6] The barbarian 'conspirators' of 367 had evidently dispersed into widely scattered bands by the time Roman relief forces arrived, though it is likely that some, and perhaps many, of the marauders that the latter encountered were themselves Roman deserters. By contrast, the future Emperor Julian's campaign against the Alamanni in northern Gaul precipitated a concentration of some 30,000 or more warriors at Strasbourg (Elton 1996: 255–6).

mobile troops could respond. This threat was all the greater where the defender had to move troops over considerable distances in order to assemble a response. Operations of this kind involved the high-level warfare against centrally organized opposition that brought Rome its eastern territories, that enabled the Byzantines to recover Italy and North Africa, and that led to Charlemagne re-establishing an empire of the west. The states that resulted from this imperial expansion, however, rarely encountered such threats on their own part since it was unusual for them to share borders with other powerful organized states.

The main exception lay in the eastern Mediterranean where Rome's borders met those of the Iranian world. For most of the period in which they coexisted with the Romans the Parthian kings were too weak to mount a coherent challenge without considerable provocation, but their subsequent overthrow by the Persian Sassanid dynasty brought a substantial increase in the perception of threat on the Roman side, if not in reality (Lee 1993: 1–25). In the third century Persian military successes provoked a crisis which contributed to the division of the Roman Empire and the eventual establishment of a new centre closer to the endangered front at the highly defensible site of Constantinople.[7] The city was attacked from the north and west by Avars and by Scandinavian Rus,[8] but it was the eastern frontier which remained the main source of focused threats. The Persians overran much of the Empire early in the seventh century and besieged its capital before being decisively defeated by the Emperor Heraclius (Howard-Johnston 1999).

A generation later the Arab invasions precipitated a near fatal crisis. The Empire lost Syria and Palestine, followed by Egypt and North Africa, and barely held on to Asia Minor. Constantinople was besieged in 674–8 and again in 717–18, but subsequent Arab incursions consisted of regular high-level raids rather than attempts at conquest. The reorganized frontier defences withstood these until a renewed shift in the balance of power enabled eastward expansion in the tenth century. A century later the frontier collapsed entirely under Turkish pressure, but this was more a migration into a politico-military vacuum than an organized invasion (France 1994: 152–5). Further west, the collapse of the Visigothic kingdom in the 710s (Collins 1989) exposed Aquitaine to attacks from Islamic Spain, but this threat had been decisively repulsed by the middle of the eighth century (Collins 1998: 301; Beeler 1971: 11–13). In the absence of standing armies few medieval rulers could maintain powerful forces close to a potential enemy's frontier.

---

[7] The Persians broke into the eastern provinces, reaching the Mediterranean and capturing the Emperor Valerius in AD 260. In the short term the Romans dealt with the crisis by entrusting regional defence to the rulers of Palmyra, a desert-edge entrepôt that they later destroyed (Luttwak 1976: 150–2; Isaac 1992: 220–8). Constantinople—the city of Constantine dedicated in AD 330 on the site of the old Greek city of Byzantium—became the eastern capital by the end of the 4th century but was not necessarily planned as such (Cameron 1993: 63–4).

[8] The Avars and Persians jointly besieged Constantinople in AD 626. The Scandinavian settlers in Russia launched a number of attacks on Constantinople in the 9th and 10th centuries, although their overall relationship with Byzantium was both complex and ambiguous: see Christian (1998: 327–52), Obolensky (1974: 238–63).

Central authorities rarely had to deal with large concentrations of potentially hostile forces maintained right on their frontiers. This gave them, at least in principle, the opportunity to respond to major incursions before the frontier was breached on a substantial scale. The rate at which they could respond depended on four elements. The threat first had to be detected and correctly identified by local commanders, the information then had to be communicated to the centre and an appropriate response formulated, and finally the response had to be delivered to the threatened area. Detecting the threat was generally easier the more sophisticated the enemy's political and military structures. Disputes between organized states usually began with diplomatic exchanges whose deteriorating tone gave some forewarning of war. Above all, the concentration of formed military units, and the assembly of siege or supply trains in populated areas, was more readily detectable than the gathering of warrior bands in remote northern forests. Commanders might try to preserve surprise by crossing the frontier in thinly inhabited regions but this was impracticable if their forces were very large, and Rome was usually able to intercept Parthian or Persian attacks close to the borders provided that it had sufficient troops available. Conversely, on the barbarian frontiers, regional commanders were sometimes overwhelmed by the surprise appearance of hostile coalitions (Lee 1993: 136–9).

The technical problems involved in defending a wide geographical area against focused threats were primarily those of transport and communications. The limitations of muscle-powered traction being what they were, it is here above all that we would expect organic economies to impose severe limits on the defensible breadth of a state, but, in practice, the position was more complex. What mattered was not the absolute speed of communication but the rate of response relative to that at which a given threat could develop. Information could be rapidly transmitted where communications were properly organized and adequate resources were invested in a courier system. Most importantly, mounted couriers could move much more quickly than large bodies of troops, particularly those consisting predominantly of foot soldiers who were reliant on foraging. Formulating a response required information-processing, decision-making, and putting the necessary force together so that it could be dispatched.

The first two of these three requirements need have taken no longer than they did in the early twentieth century, particularly where permanent military staffs were maintained. In any case, the limited range of options available to most rulers, or their subordinates, made them relatively straightforward in most circumstances. The time required to assemble the necessary forces depended on the nature of the political and military system. Where a permanent military establishment existed, as in Rome, it might mean no more than ordering a mobile reserve into action, or concentrating a field army from a number of detached garrisons. Elsewhere, as in feudal Europe, it might require a lengthier process of summoning militia from a wide area, negotiating with allies, or recruiting mercenaries, but major focused threats were rare in such circumstances. The rulers of well-organized states, with standing armies, could counter focused threats by moving central or regional reserves close to the frontier before irreparable damage had been done, provided that the reserves were available.

11.1.2.2. Diffused threats

States capable of maintaining effective standing armies, supported by well-organized logistical services and communications networks, enjoyed substantial advantages over less well-organized neighbours when it came to defence against major incursions. These advantages enabled the agrarian empires to maintain their frontiers for as long as they did, but focused threats of this kind were not the only ones that frontier defences had to deal with. More common, and generally more difficult to deal with, were the diffused threats represented by endemic small-scale raids, often uncoordinated and opportunistic, and aimed at looting and abduction rather than the seizure of territory. The Romans faced such threats on their northern frontiers, but they were particularly associated with coastal regions and those where cultivated lands bordered the steppe or desert edge.

Seaborne raiders could strike without warning and escape with their loot and prisoners before help arrived. Piracy of this kind was an endemic problem in the Mediterranean before the Romans established control over its shores, and it re-emerged with the collapse of Roman control. Further north it became a serious threat in the late Roman period and recurred in the early Middle Ages. The threats originated first from the coasts of Frisia and Jutland and subsequently from Scandinavia, but Denmark itself became a target for Baltic raiders by the twelfth century. Mounted nomads shared the mobility advantages of seaborne raiders and could also band together to mount focused threats. The south Russian and Hungarian steppes provided bases for raids into the cultivated zone, but incursions by small groups of foot-bound raiders were a perennial threat on the Rhine and Danube frontiers.

Contemporaries often characterized attacks of this kind as mere banditry, rather than any kind of recognizable warfare.[9] They can fairly be described as 'small-scale', but their impact should not be minimized. In the long term, very large organized states found diffused threats of this kind a greater danger to the integrity of their frontiers than they did more conventional focused threats. There were two reasons for this. First, in the absence of effective counter measures, endemic raiding could create insecurity on a scale leading to depopulation and the collapse of the economic basis on which frontier defence rested. In a world where most people could carry the majority of their possessions on their backs, it was the right to cultivate a given patch of land that kept the rural population in place. Once this right was rendered forfeit or worthless, for whatever reason, peasant populations could become very mobile. A relatively well-documented

---

[9] See for instance the comments of Ammianus Marcellinus in Whittaker (1994: 159, 173–4). In interpreting such comments it should, however, be borne in mind that 'bandit' (*latro*) was itself an ideological label used as much to deny legitimacy to its objects as to indicate the scale of their activities (Shaw 1984).

early modern example of this dates from the early decades of the Dutch Revolt in the southern Netherlands. In the provinces of Brabant and Flanders, nearly all communities lost an estimated half to two-thirds of their population between 1572 and 1609 (Parker 1975). Sharper falls occurred in the decade of the 1580s, when only 1 per cent of the rural population is thought to have remained continuously on the land, and the area under cultivation fell by 92 per cent.

Precise measurement is impossible in earlier periods for lack of evidence, and this population loss stemmed from the operations of regular armies of substantial size, but it is clear that high-level warfare was not the only form that could have destructive consequences on this scale. Just as there are no 'small wars' for those who lose their lives or loved ones fighting them, so for people whose homes were destroyed and families murdered or enslaved it made little difference whether the perpetrators were numbered in tens of thousands or single figures. The resulting spiral of flight and disintegration impeded effective defence for lack of resources, which promoted further insecurity and demographic collapse. Archaeological evidence for northern Gaul supports contemporary testimony of extensive and lasting depopulation following Alamannic incursions in the fourth century, but more detailed accounts are available concerning the recurrence of the problem on England's north-eastern coastal plain.

In the early decades of Norman rule in England this potentially fertile area was rendered so depopulated and unproductive as a result of raiding from the north-western interior that field armies could only operate with seaborne supply and effective defence was impossible (Kapelle 1979: 226–7). Protection was eventually afforded by military tenants and their castles, established on the landward passes. Once secured, the resources of the coastal plain could sustain a defensive infrastructure of their own, but in a later period the area came under renewed pressure from the north. The problem, and the scale of the potential danger, was described by the Border Commissioners in the mid-sixteenth century:

> In an alert, the inhabitants would abandon their holdings and retreat into England, taking along with them the able-bodied men who would otherwise have been of service in defending the border. It would be long before the husbandry of such an abandoned locality recovered, and in many places the refugees plainly never returned at all. The whole has the appearance of a process of progressive deterioration, which the provision of even a very modest tower could arrest. (Quoted King 1988: 13)

The Border Commissioners put their faith in masonry, and systems of small-scale point defences played a vital role in larger-scale frontier defence. To be effective, however, these also needed garrisons and mobile troops, particularly where settlement was much dispersed. If these were not forthcoming, the result could be a collapse of the entire frontier, as occurred in north-west Anatolia at the end of the thirteenth century. This region had been defended by a Byzantine settler militia, whose members enjoyed land rights and tax exemption in exchange for local military service against Turkish raiders. This system was abolished by the Emperor Michael VIII who, heavily committed in Europe, broke the link between land and service in order to establish a regular salaried force with a wider range of military obligations. Unfortunately the necessary funds were not forthcoming and, left unpaid, the morale of the troops collapsed. Some defected to the Turks, whilst others turned to banditry at the expense of the Byzantine civilians. In the resulting chaos many of the population fled and the region slipped permanently out of Byzantine control (Bartusis 1992: 56–7, 304).

Frontier defences were more often swamped by persistent infiltration than swept away by high-level co-ordinated assault. The Slavs penetrated the Balkan peninsula in this way where the more focused Avar threat had been turned back. The early penetration of Rome's Rhine frontier by Franks and Alamanni must also have taken this form.[10] Diffused threats were all the more difficult to deal with when the enemy lacked an institutionalized political leadership which could be bribed, suborned, or eliminated by military defeat. Both Alamanni and Slavs were amorphous groupings without a tradition of central organization. In Herwig Wolfram's words they 'moved in numerous groups without a monarchical leadership. They clung tenaciously to their common name and took their special names from the occupied lands, the *patriae*' (Wolfram 1997: 47).

Enterprises of this kind could themselves foster the emergence of a leadership based on successful raiding. Such men might gather a substantial following and small 'tribal' entities could snowball into powerful coalitions.[11] This was the second great danger posed by diffused threats; endemic small-scale frontier raids did not stay small scale for very long unless constantly attended to. The social and political structure of barbarian peoples encouraged the formation of opportunistic coalitions around successful war leaders, but frontier magnates in loosely organized states also buttressed their position by such means.[12] Unless rapidly countered, such men might progress, through degrees of autonomy, to a predatory independence at the expense of their neighbours.[13] Guarding against the dangers they represented required an active policy of frontier defence with both military and political components.

---

[10] This at least is the conventional interpretation of events on this frontier (e.g. Whittaker 1994: 156–9); for a sceptical revisionist view see Drinkwater (1996).

[11] The link between socio-political status and successful raiding was found in many other contexts. De Souza remarks of the Archaic Greek world that many 'activities which a status conscious aristocrat would have felt made him worthy of the title *basileus* would seem to his victims to have justified them labelling him a pirate' (de Souza 1999: 22).

[12] In some contexts, as in the Archaic Greek, successful piracy could also be a route to social status and political leadership (de Souza 1999: 17–22).

[13] The permeable boundaries between frontier banditry and dynastic and state formation are demonstrated by the rise of the Parthian Arsacids at the expense of the post-Alexandrian Seleucid rulers in Iran. The dynasty's founder Arsaces, described by the ancient writer Justin as 'a man of dubious origins but proven courage [who was accustomed] to living from robbery and extortion', profited from the Seleucids' internal dissensions and an invasion of their western territory to seize a rugged eastern frontier district at the head of what Justin described as 'a troop of brigands' and establish the fortified base from which his descendants launched themselves to great power status (see Sherwin-White and Kuhrt 1993: 87–90).

11.1.3. STRATEGIES OF FRONTIER DEFENCE

States that covered enough ground to have distinct frontier and core regions could defend themselves against attack by pursuing one of three basic strategies, which Edward Luttwak has termed 'preclusive defence', 'elastic defence', and 'defence in depth' (Luttwak 1976). A preclusive defence was one whose aim was to prevent any incursion from penetrating the frontier zone itself. Since neither artificial nor natural barriers could be relied on to do this, powerful mobile forces had to be stationed close to the outer edge of the frontier in order to intercept invading forces and defeat them in open-field battle. The Romans apparently implemented a policy of this kind under the early Empire but the manpower requirements of such a strategy were potentially enormous as pressures on the frontiers intensified, and it was beyond the resources of later emperors. Such a strategy was, in any case, better suited to dealing with focused than diffused threats. Major incursions could be detected and intercepted relatively easily, whereas small bands of infiltrators could more readily evade the concentrations of force stationed close to the frontier as the strategy required.

Elastic defence was at the opposite pole to preclusive defence. It involved concentrating the available mobile forces in the interior and in such a way as to intercept and destroy the invaders once they had left the inner edge of the frontier zone. The Romans resorted to this approach for a while after their frontiers collapsed during the military and political crises of the third century. Powerful city walls were constructed in the interior, and a mobile striking force was established in northern Italy. The policy was eventually successful, in that control was re-established over nearly all the pre-crisis provinces, but it was very expensive. Rich interior provinces were exposed to attack, while the frontier regions were left unprotected. In fact it is doubtful that elastic defence should be seen as a 'strategy' as such, rather than a desperate expedient forced on a defender whose previous arrangements had collapsed.

The third option, some form of defence in depth, was the only realistic strategy for rulers who wanted to protect their interior provinces but lacked the means to mount a preclusive defence. Defensive systems established on this basis varied greatly, but they were all based on a recognition that the frontier zone as a whole was vulnerable to incursion. The defender then had two tasks: first, to protect the population of the frontier zone and their movable resources, and secondly, to prevent an enemy leaving the inner edge of the frontier in good order. In practice, these were two sides of a coin because the most effective way of disrupting an invading force was to deny it food and fodder while subjecting it to continual harassment. Both tasks required a network of local point defences providing shelter for the local population, their animals, and food stores, and housing small mobile garrisons, whether of regular troops or some form of regional militia. If arrangements of this kind were to work properly they also needed the support of larger mobile forces, either held in reserve behind the frontier, or capable of being assembled at relatively short notice. The nature of the two components, and their relative weight, depended on the resources available to the defender, the terrain, and the nature of the threat. The mobile echelon varied in scale from the regional field armies of the later Roman period to the military households of feudal kings and regional magnates, supplemented by whatever other troops they could assemble when crisis threatened. Frontier point defences too could be anything from isolated towers, fortified dwellings, or other civilian structures, to substantial purpose-built military installations.[14]

These structures, whatever their scale, were not intended to deny passage to large forces. Their garrisons, numbering no more than a few hundreds and possibly less than a dozen, might be capable of trapping and destroying small raiding parties, but they would not be able to engage a substantial invading force directly. Faced with major incursions their task was to serve as refuges and, above all, as supply points in a landscape that would be kept as bare of provisions as possible. By clearing the terrain of food and fodder, and attacking foraging parties where possible, the effect was to delay and disrupt the movement of the invaders. A large force without a supply train would have to move as rapidly as it could—relying on well-defined lines of advance and risking attrition from straggling and lack of supplies—or else slow down to search for provisions, giving the defenders time to bring up their mobile forces. Ideally, these would then engage and destroy the attacking force before it had the opportunity to do much damage. Otherwise, a successful raiding force—encumbered with loot and prisoners—would be vulnerable to ambush by relatively small forces in the defended zone, whilst stragglers and disorganized elements of a defeated force might be annihilated.

There is controversy as to how far the Romans adopted this strategy after the crises of the third century. Luttwak's claim that it was applied systematically across the Empire has drawn criticism, although some critics concede that some frontiers were defended in depth in some periods.[15] Evidence from elsewhere is less controversial. In the fourteenth and fifteenth centuries, according to Contamine:

> at the end of a campaign and once the main army had been dismissed, it was customary to organize the frontiers militarily using a network of garrisons or *establies*. This network could be dense and deep in order to prevent the infiltration or the irruption of enemy forces, who risked being isolated and seeing their line of retreat cut off if they passed through the links of the mesh, or had to capture each fortress one after another with all the delays that such a process implied. (Contamine 1984: 220)

This reflected both the potential and the limitations of contemporary point defences.

---

[14] This does not mean that all such minor structures necessarily formed part of a co-ordinated system. As Hopwood remarks of the Isaurian region of south-east Asia Minor: 'It may be that we are tempted today to posit a "system" of towers whereas those who built them were unaware of anything so organised' (Hopwood 1986: 347). Nonetheless, if they were to guarantee reasonable security against systematic threats, fortification of this kind did have to form part of a wider system.

[15] Critical treatments of Luttwak's arguments include Whittaker (1994), Isaac (1992), and Mann (1979). For a counter-critique and qualified defence of Luttwak see Wheeler (1993a, 1993b).

It will be seen that even small medieval armies were far too strong for the garrisons of the most formidable castles. Any kind of field army could safely bypass a castle (where this was physically possible) both coming and going—provided, of course, that it moved in good order; in case of a hurried and disorderly retreat, the existence of a hostile castle on the road for home raised a number of sinister possibilities. A vigilant garrison could interfere effectively with communications—though these were comparatively unimportant for the relatively small, frugal, and mobile armies of the Middle Ages. Even a little castle could serve to cut off messengers and scattered foraging-parties, and where castles were numerous, whether they were big or small, foraging could be dangerous or impossible. (King 1988: 10)

A force that advanced through a zone defended in this way risked annihilation if it was subsequently defeated and had to retreat.[16]

Defences erected along river systems could act as an effective barrier to large forces relying on water transport. Charlemagne's assault on the Avar khanate turned initially on the fortifications established along the rivers leading into their heartland on the middle Danube. These blocked the supply transports that were needed to support a major offensive and also shielded the Avar interior from Frankish cavalry raids. As Bowlus argues, 'as long as Avars held forts in lower Austria, most of Trans-danubia and all of the Alföld were effectively out of range for cavalry operating from Bavaria' (Bowlus 1995: 52). The Franks were prevented from exploiting their victories in mobile warfare until these fortifications were captured by a major expedition, supported by infantry, siege equipment, and riverine supply squadrons, in 791. The loss of its frontier defences exposed the Avar interior to Frankish cavalry raids, leading as we have seen to the complete disintegration of the khanate in the years immediately following.

11.1.4. SUMMARY

Technological and ideological factors combined to make clearly demarcated political boundaries a rarity before the gunpowder revolution. The frontier zones that took their place were characterized by varying degrees of devolved power and authority and were often areas in which allegiances, and even collective identities, were ill defined and unstable. Hostile or client barbarian groups, local militias, and mobile defensive units mutated into each other, and frontier commanders could achieve autonomous status—or sometimes outlaw status—even on frontiers between organized states. This instability was partly a reflection of the kinds of threat that frontier defences had to deal with. These fell into two main categories. The first, or 'focused' threats, consisted of incursions by substantial organized forces whether aimed at conquest or large-scale raiding.

---

[16] The system of point defences established in southern Germany by the Emperors Henry 'the Builder' and Otto the Great played a central role in halting Magyar raids. A large proportion of the casualties sustained by the Magyar army defeated at the Lechfeld were inflicted by local garrisons in the course of the retreat, particularly at river crossings: see Bachrach (1985: 725–7), Leyser (1982), Oman (1991: 120–5).

Focused threats of this kind posed obvious dangers, but relief forces could be moved long distances to counter them despite the logistical and transport restrictions intrinsic to organic economies. This was possible because mounted couriers could convey information and orders much faster than a marching column could move, and well-organized troops supported by pre-positioned supplies in friendly territory could outdistance a large invading force that had to rely on foraging or supply wagons. Incursions of this kind also took time to prepare and could rarely achieve surprise. The existence of focused threats was rarely enough itself to block the formation of extensive political units providing their rulers disposed of forces that could prevail in high-level warfare.

The second category of 'diffused' threat posed problems of a very different order. These consisted of endemic small-scale raiding by bands acting on their own initiative or under local leaders without any central direction. Attacks of this kind might be militarily insignificant in themselves, but if they were sufficiently frequent the resulting insecurity threatened the foundations of frontier economy and society. Meeting the threat required a network of small-scale strong points to act as refuges for local inhabitants with their property and as bases for mobile detachments to hunt down and destroy intruders. Systems of this kind, deployed in depth over a defensive zone, were also effective against focused threats because they could prevent an invading army living off the land as it advanced and hunt down fugitive survivors in retreat.

11.2. CONTROL AND SECESSION

States in the contemporary world are defined in terms of territory; areas of physical space contained within linear boundaries registered on maps. Their *de facto* legitimacy depends on their ability to exercise effective coercive power throughout this area.[17] As already argued, however, this is a misleading approach to the definition of states and their relationship to physical space before the relatively recent past. The conditions of an organic economy so constrained the practical exercise of political power that 'deep control' of this kind was rarely possible. Effective control was in practice often limited to communications networks, major population centres and their hinterlands, and areas in which troops happened to be stationed. This was a reality which practical policy and ideological representations alike had to accommodate. For most of history the object of control, *de facto* if not *de jure*, was demographic space: what mattered were population, resources, and communication networks and such physical spaces as these occupied, rather than physical space as such. The structures of an organic economy limited the degree to which such control was attainable, even

---

[17] Strictly speaking, in this context the concepts of *de facto* and *de jure* phenomena have only a limited applicability since they assume the mutual recognition of states within an agreed framework of international law which is a historically specific, and recent, development.

for a highly organized state such as Rome. Political and military realities within the frontiers were far removed from the uniform peace and order depicted by imperial ideology. The problem was aggravated by the fact that the disposition of force required to establish control on a subregional basis could itself threaten the relationship between the centre and regional authorities.

11.2.1. THE MAINTENANCE OF CONTROL

The role of military force in the control of settled areas varied with the context. In newly annexed regions, or in 'conquest states' such as early Norman England, it might be substantial. Where the settled population had been sufficiently conciliated or coerced to accept their political masters, no overt military force might be required to control them or to exact resources. Even in these circumstances, however, the proximity of frontiers, vulnerable coastlines, or 'wild' areas of hill or woodland was a potential danger.[18] Some of the threats, given the permeability of frontier defences to small-scale infiltration, might come from outside, but this was by no means always the case. For all its ideological emphasis on the maintenance of ordered peace, Roman rule could not provide security in the countryside. Banditry was endemic and travel dangerous. In the words of one authority, banditry, though perceived as marginal, 'appears as integral to the functioning of imperial society...a phenomenon that impinged on the most mundane aspects of Roman social life' (Shaw 1984: 8).[19] Medieval states struggled to reach even Roman levels of security, usually without success, and French provincial towns suffered bandit attacks even under the *ancien régime* (Anderson 1988: 166, 174).

The endemic prevalence of insecurity resulted from three general problems that were, in turn, rooted in the structure of organic economies. The first reflected the logistical and other constraints that made it almost impossible to maintain a controlling presence in thinly populated areas with difficult terrain. Whatever constitutional or ideological fictions might be maintained, remoter areas of forest, hills, or moorland were prone to slip outside the effective control of central or regional authorities, becoming bases for raids on richer neighbours.

Secondly, the limitations of communications technology made surveillance very difficult away from major towns and cities. It is not surprising that small parties could use local knowledge to evade customs posts and similar official attention by moving on secondary tracks or across country with the benefit of

---

[18] This could necessitate the deployment of appreciable military forces deep in the interior, as in the Roman period around the Pyrenees (Collins 1984: 3–6) and the Isaurian region of south-eastern Asia Minor (Isaac 1992: 75–7; Hopwood 1986).

[19] A character in Steven Saylor's novel *Roman Blood* (London: Robinson, 1997) provides a pithy description of conditions in the late Republic. 'The rich on their way from city and villa and back again travel in retinues with gladiators and bodyguards. The wandering poor travel in bands. Actors go in troupes. Any farmer driving his sheep to market will surround himself with shepherds. But the man who travels alone—so runs that proverb as old as the Etruscans—has a fool for a companion...A man can die on the open road or disappear forever. For the unwary a journey of ten miles may take an unexpected turn that ends in a slave market a thousand miles from home' (p. 145).

local knowledge,[20] but much larger groups could make themselves effectively invisible. In seventeenth-century France the rebel duc d'Épernon crossed the country with a hundred horsemen and a pack train to rescue Marie de' Medici from Blois castle. The journey took a month, during which his party remained undetected 'like a needle in a haystack' (Braudel 1988: 113).

The third problem was the limited scope for occupational differentiation in a low-productivity economy. This meant that rulers simply could not afford sufficient full-time 'security specialists' to enforce control on a continuing basis outside major population centres and communications nodes. Elsewhere they might be able to use troops in areas with permanent garrisons, but otherwise central authorities needed the support of local communities or elites, both of which might have their own reasons for colluding in banditry if they did not actively practise it. At the community level, a permeable boundary existed between passive resistance to taxation and other forms of resource extraction, and active collusion in banditry or open revolt (Shaw 1984). Receiving stolen goods, including livestock or slaves, was always profitable for landowners and other rich provincials whose retainers often outnumbered the local agents of the state. Defensive militias organized by such men in times of civil war or barbarian incursion could be as predatory as the invaders themselves (Wolfram 1997: 48). In medieval England, with an unusual degree of central control by contemporary standards, feudal tenants were prone to banditry when royal authority was disrupted as it was during the reign of King Stephen in the twelfth century (King 1994). Elsewhere in feudal Europe the literary topos of the robber baron reflected a grim reality.

Other causes of insecurity arose from local conditions. Piracy could turn coastal districts into virtual frontiers, and nomads sometimes caused trouble for interior provinces as well as the frontiers. Above all, wherever civil or military power was devolved to men outside the formal structure of the state, on the frontier or elsewhere, shifts in policy or circumstance could turn former instruments of the state into enemies, whether rebels or mere bandits. The interpenetration of imperial and barbarian societies was especially productive of such transitions: auxiliary or allied war leaders became bandits, bandits became rebels, and rebels sometimes kings.[21] The range of problems posed by banditry was very similar to that posed by diffused frontier threats, and so was the range of possible solutions. Just as 'aggressive' and 'defensive' frontier policies could be difficult to distinguish in practice, so it would be a mistake to distinguish too rigidly between internal security and frontier defence. The problems they had to confront often differed more in their geographical location than their nature or scale.

---

[20] Such evasion could itself occur on a large scale. In September 1669 alone, 1800 sheep and cattle were driven across Alston Moor in north-western England to avoid the payment of tolls at the Scottish border (Appleby 1978: 179–80).

[21] Shaw defines Roman banditry as 'a form of political *anachoresis*, leading from its smallest beginnings, over an unbroken trajectory, to its final form: the formation of another state patterned on an existing type' (Shaw 1984: 51).

The object of both aggressors' and defenders' frontier policies was demographic space—settlements, resources, and communications networks—rather than physical space as such. City walls defended major centres and smaller settlements were furnished with towers or other refuges. More sophisticated states provided security for transport and communications. High-level traffic was a perennial target for robbers of whatever kind, but good roads could themselves be put to use by infiltrators and bandits. Roman frontier roads were provided with regular guard posts and fortified way stations, but similar structures could also be found in the interior. As Slav pressure increased in the sixth-century Balkans the road system there was provided with a deep network of fortifications (Obolensky 1974: 68–70), but such systems were not always effective and were in any case beyond the means of most medieval rulers. The hazards of banditry are a recurrent feature of contemporary travellers' accounts.

11.2.2. SECESSION AND FRAGMENTATION

Fortifying large towns and cities, and providing country dwellers with refuges of some kind, presented few practical difficulties as long as the necessary resources were available. Well-organized states could establish defensive, or security, systems for major road networks, and in arid landscapes nomadic movements could be controlled by fortifying wells and cisterns. But it was much more difficult to control the basic productive resources of an organic economy. Unlike mineral deposits or communications nodes, crops and livestock were dispersed across the landscape and could not be secured by fortification alone. Mobile forces were needed. In densely populated, highly productive countryside they could be concentrated in central locations from which substantial populations could be defended or overawed as circumstances required. In less propitious conditions forces had to be dispersed with a multiplication of local detachments and point defences and garrisons. Such arrangements could, ideally, provide 'security in depth', guarding against banditry, rebellion, or infiltration from uncontrolled zones, but the more effective they became in these respects the more they created another problem for central authorities.

Any defensive system effective against threats from outside might serve equally as a base from which regional commanders or magnates could defy the centre. Norman England's network of castles seems to have become as much a liability as an asset to the central authority once the conquest had been consolidated (Hollister 1965: 161–6). The more military resources were devolved to threatened regions, the greater the risk of secession. What was true of regions was true also of smaller geographical units. Effective control in depth depended on systems of dispersed mobile detachments based on local point defences. Their very effectiveness, however, compromised the maintenance of central, or even regional, control over vital garrisons and fortifications. Local commanders, or landowners with an armed following, might pursue their own agendas regardless of higher authority, even if they did not formally secede. At worst, garrisons might revolt and set themselves up as freebooting brigands. Such behaviour was limited in practice by positive and negative sanctions. On the negative side lay the fear of reprisals from the centre, or simply the loss of central support against internal and external threats. On the positive side lay ideologically motivated acceptance of the centre's legitimacy and a perception of the gains that could result from participation in the wider arena furnished by an overarching political structure. The latter was particularly important in the earlier Roman world where, above the long-service centurionate, commanders held office for a period of only a few years and as a stage in the structured public service career known as the *cursus honorum*.

The *cursus honorum* was a Republican institution which was retained under the Principate and incorporated postings to both civil and military offices in different provinces on a trajectory of increasing reward (Keppie 1984: 39–40; Hassall, 2000). Since the senior positions were reserved for members of the senatorial order, it integrated civilian and military institutions on an empire-wide scale and embedded both kinds of institutions in the self-interest of the possessing class. Defiance, where it occurred, was normally the prelude to a bid for power at the centre or the secession of regional 'empires' under the pressure of external threat.[22] The centre continued to suppress these until well into the fifth century, or indeed the sixth if we consider Justinian's conquests in this light. The ordered structure of the *cursus honorum* began to unravel even before the crises of the third century. Military posts were opened to men from a wider range of backgrounds with less experience of political office-holding, but in the aftermath of the crises a more flexible system of promotion was deemed necessary, and military command became a career in itself which was open to men from outside the senatorial order.[23] The extension of this process in the Western Empire's last century saw non-Roman barbarians becoming prominent at all military levels. Command was assumed by men whom the traditional elite were prone to see as outsiders, and whom they were reluctant to accommodate in the structure of government, and the relationship between the central political and military leaderships became increasingly difficult as a result. The most destructive manifestations of this difficulty occurred where senior generals of barbarian, or partly barbarian, origins became powerful enough to be actual or potential military dictators but could not legitimize their position within the constitution by becoming emperor. This led, at best, to the manipulation of puppet emperors

---

[22] The 3rd-century 'Gallic Empire' is the best documented of these entities, and its survival for some fifteen years was probably due in part to a belief that external defence was most effectively organized at a regional level (Drinkwater 1987).

[23] The first manifestation of this tendency was the use of promoted centurions from the equestrian order in place of senatorial office-holders. Credited initially to the Emperor Septimius Severus at the end of the 2nd century, the practice was implemented on a large scale by Gallienus in the middle of the 3rd. In the post-crisis system military command was separated from civilian administration and placed in the hands of senior generals, the *magistri militum*, supported by regional commanders or *duces*. Some commanders were also termed *comes*, which seems to have been a title rather than a specific rank (Hassall 2000: 325–6; Campbell 1984: 407–9; Southern and Dixon 1996: 57–60; Tomlin 1987).

in a manner that discredited the office and, at worst, to a jockeying for power that ended with the violent death of either the general or the emperor.[24]

Provincial elites were much less reluctant to make such accommodations with the centre as the protection offered by the central authority became increasingly ineffective, and the western Imperial structure was supplanted by successor kingdoms founded on a series of accommodations between Romanized landowners, civic authorities, and barbarian war leaders. All but one proved short-lived. By AD 800 the Franks had swallowed up most of their rivals and a new western empire had appeared, but the new structure was unsuited to deal with the endemic diffused threats which developed on a supra-regional scale in the ensuing centuries. They were mounted by Scandinavian and Muslim sea-raiders, and by Magyar horsemen, all of whom possessed the advantages of mobility and external lines of communication. The former were all the more dangerous on account of their external bases and the very limited forewarning of their raids. Against such a threat, the capacity to respond quickly was more important than the capacity to do so in great numbers. A network of strong points capable of sheltering local populations and supporting small mobile forces was more effective than royal hosts that were slow to assemble and could only be in one place at a time. Furnishing a defence of this kind required radical decentralization and a shift of military resources to the local level. This was a military solution that imposed political costs by greatly weakening the centre at the expense of local elites.

The breakdown of central control in the Frankish west was thus part of a broader decentralizing movement at once political and military. Military changes reduced the benefits of loyalty to the centre as well as the potential costs of disobedience. In the new world of endemic diffused threats royal armies were too slow moving and took too long to assemble, and in Duby's words:

the only war chiefs capable of restoring peace were the petty princes in each region. Only they could withstand surprise attacks and call up all able men at the very first alert... In the reality of day to day existence, all prestige and power shifted to the local chiefs, the counts and dukes who became the real heroes of Christian resistance. (Duby 1981: 32–3)

The rewards of participation in Rome's unified political structure encouraged a centripetal orientation among its elites, but these rewards had been underwritten by the overwhelming military power at the disposal of the central authorities. As the effectiveness of this power declined so did the attractiveness of participation at the centre. Local counts and similar figures now enacted their political roles on a local or regional scale, whilst the political culture of feudalism provided a collegial model of rule allowing such men to reject effective central control

---

[24] Two of the most able of the later Western Empire's commanders, Stilicho and Aetius, died in this way as did the promising 5th-century emperor Majorian, who may have been murdered by Aetius' successor Ricimer. Many of the prominent Germans in later Roman service were adherents of the Arian form of Christianity and this may have been an even more important bar to their assuming the Imperial office (I am grateful to my colleague Professor Simon Swain for drawing my attention to this point).

without undermining their own ideological position vis-à-vis their subordinates. Against the Roman ideology of universal sovereignty, sovereignty in the fragmented world of the medieval west was long qualified by overarching ecclesiastical, and sometimes imperial, authority, the ambiguities of feudal tenure, and the particularism of civic or provincial institutions. Rather than exclusive sovereignty over territory, rulers asserted lordship over people and resources within a framework that left spatial boundaries ambiguous or ill defined. Multiple or overlapping jurisdictions complicated the picture, as did the privileges granted to groups such as clerics or privileged 'strangers'.

11.2.3. SUMMARY

The maintenance of control against internal threats needs to be understood as a spatial process in terms of both breadth and depth. The depth of control was constrained by the basic structures of an organic economy. The limits on transport and communications, and the limited number of security specialists supportable in a low-productivity economy, made it very difficult for central or regional authorities to exercise control away from major population centres, garrisons, or communications systems. There seems to have been remarkably little variation in this respect before the modern period, and even Roman rulers exercised only 'shallow' control over most, if not all, of their territory. There was, however, substantial variation in the extent to which central authorities prevented regional subordinates from seceding whether formally or in practice. The rulers of the Roman Republic and the early Empire were remarkably successful in this respect, but secession became an increasing problem in the later Empire and still more so for Charlemagne's successors.

The roots of earlier Roman success were partly institutional; the rotation of office-holders through military and political posts in different provinces seems to have been a very effective way of fostering centripetal tendencies among the elite. This system was largely abandoned in the later Empire, but the subsequent fragmentation also reflected the relationship between scale and effective military power at a time when diffused threats were becoming increasingly dangerous. Large centrally based forces were ill suited to defend against diffuse threats, whereas suitably equipped troops dispersed among local point defences could dominate large areas of countryside. As long as the regular armies of organized states faced each other, or maintained the initiative against barbarian peoples, the advantage tended to lie with the larger and better-organized force. The larger and more highly organized the state, the larger and better organized its army was likely to be, so this favoured aggregation and the emergence of imperial power. Once the ecological and socio-political limits of this kind of warfare were reached, however, the tide turned. The endemic diffuse threats presented by frontier warfare against stateless peoples allowed fewer economies of scale and favoured radical decentralization. The later Empire resisted this tendency in its military organization, but medieval Europe and the Byzantine system of territorial defence based on military districts or *themes* embraced it. Militarily, both east and west survived the early-medieval crisis, but the price was the diminution and fragmentation of central authority in the west and serious political instability in Byzantium.

11.3. CONCLUSION

The spatial extent of a ruler's control was defined by the two dimensions of breadth and depth. Maintaining the breadth of control meant securing the frontiers against external attack and preventing regions inside the frontiers from breaking away. The spatial depth of control reflected the ability of rulers and their provincial subordinates to exercise systematic coercion across the land area contained within their frontiers. 'Deep control', exercised in a more or less homogeneous fashion throughout this area, was very difficult to achieve under the conditions of an organic economy because of the constraints these imposed on transport, communications, and the division of labour. Even highly organized states such as Rome do not seem to have been much more successful in this respect than their less centralized medieval successors. In consequence a pattern of 'shallow' control prevailed, with central authorities having very limited coercive powers away from major population centres, highways, or garrisons.

Rulers do not seem to have varied very much in the spatial depth of control they achieved over the period, but there were enormous differences in breadth, reflecting the differential success of rulers in expanding and maintaining their frontiers. This in turn reflected the different demands that the two phases of frontier expansion, conquest and consolidation, each placed on the forces of organized states and the ways in which these demands varied with the nature of the target region. The requirements for conquest were both relative and absolute. The conquering army had to be stronger, better led, or luckier than the conquered, but it also needed an absolute degree of organization, discipline, and logistical support in order to overcome organized resistance and secure the main centres of government and population. Many armies of the ancient world possessed these abilities and there was a long-term movement of spatial aggregation as stronger states swallowed weaker neighbours until the final victors were ringed by stateless barbarian peoples.

The decentralized egalitarianism of barbarian organization impeded sustained co-ordination in high-level warfare, making the barbarians vulnerable to conquest by the forces of organized states. These same qualities, however, allied to the characteristic ecology of barbarian lands made it much more difficult for imperial conquerors to consolidate control over them, particularly where the imperial administrative system was based on an economy of cash or valuables. Consequently the limits of Roman control, as of other empires, came to rest on the barbarian periphery at a point where the costs of further consolidation exceeded any reasonably foreseeable benefits. The imperial power might exert influence or impose tributary dependence beyond this point, but it had to accept the practical reality of a frontier zone between controlled and uncontrolled territories, however much it might seek to deny this reality in ideological terms.

The limits of muscle-powered transport, communications, and weaponry combined with the prevailing ideologies of rulership to make unambiguous linear boundaries a rarity in the ancient and medieval worlds. Frontiers were zones of interaction, variously peaceful and hostile, and they were often fluid. This was true where organized states neighboured each other, because frontier leaders often had substantial autonomy and potentially ambiguous loyalties, but it was particularly the case on barbarian frontiers. These frontiers were liable to hostile infiltration, unless pre-empted by active policies of manipulation, subsidy, and military action, but such policies created instability in themselves. Successful pre-emptive action against hostile coalitions fostered the temptation to advance the frontier through annexation, whilst economic or political support for client rulers could lead to the emergence of powerful enemies.

Frontiers sometimes had to be defended against invasions by large organized forces with clearly defined objectives, but more often the threat took the form of small-scale opportunistic raiding that lacked any central direction. These two kinds of threat can be termed respectively 'focused' and 'diffused', and both could be countered by systems of local point defences extended in depth and backed by mobile troops. Systems of this kind were effective militarily, but they imposed a political price which could be all the greater where the threat was diffused. It was this as much as anything that hampered the maintenance of control in breadth. As long as imperial powers were expanding or held the initiative on their frontiers, military operations were likely to require concentration of force of a kind that could be directed by the ruler or his close associates, and helped keep centrifugal tendencies to a minimum. The position changed as the initiative shifted away from the empire and its own territory had to be defended against diffused threats. Countering threats of this kind required decentralization and a dispersion of force. The more severe these threats became the more decentralized the physical and administrative structures of frontier defence had to be in order to meet them and the more difficult it was for the central authorities to retain their control. The pressures on the later Roman and Carolingian frontiers instigated a process of just this kind whose effects were intensified as growing insecurity discredited the central authorities in provincial eyes and magnified the incentives to break away. The consequence was the political fragmentation which characterized medieval Europe's political landscape and which the forces of feudal rulers lacked the organizational strength to overcome.

Conclusion

The geography of production and consumption in organic economies restricted the conduct of military operations and the kind of strategic goals that could be pursued. The effect of these restrictions was felt through the logistical difficulties which they created and through a basic strategic dilemma arising from the conflicting needs to concentrate and disperse an invading force. Defending troops had a wider range of logistical options, but invaders had to choose between carrying their supplies with them, living off the surrounding countryside, or maintaining supply lines to the exterior. The first two of these solutions greatly restricted the amount of time a force could spend in a given region and so were better suited to strategies of destructive raiding than to those of indefinite occupation. Unless resistance could be overcome very quickly the pursuit of an occupation strategy was likely to require protracted operations of a kind which would exhaust the food and fodder resources of all but the most productive regions, making external supply essential. Establishing and securing supply lines could, however, be very expensive in terms of manpower, and so forces that relied on them often had to be very big if they were to be adequately supplied. This was, paradoxically, especially true in poor, thinly peopled regions where there was limited scope for living off the land. Large-scale siege operations were also likely to need external supply and this could make them unsustainable in areas without access to water transport.

The establishment of sufficient administrative control to permit the sustained extraction of resources from conquered territory generally required the pursuit of a strategy of systematic occupation. The alternative to establishing control in this sense was the enforcement of tributary dependence, which involved the extraction of payments, in cash or kind, on a less systematic basis in response to the actual or threatened use of force. Raiding strategies were an ideal means of enforcing this kind of dependence, which did not require the continuing presence of the dominant power's troops or administrators. The establishment of control involved the two successive stages of conquest followed by consolidation. The two stages placed very different demands on the forces of the would-be controlling power in ways that varied with the target region's degree of development. A successful conquest required victory in the kind of 'high-level' warfare of manoeuvre and battle waged by concentrated field armies. The forces of organized states were better able to resist this than were those of stateless barbarian peoples, but the position was reversed when forces had to disperse in order to wage the low-level warfare required to consolidate control over the productive resources of an organic economy. The poorer and more thinly populated a region the greater degree of dispersal required and the less benefit the forces of an organized state could derive from their ability to co-ordinate large bodies of troops. Such conditions also made it harder to terminate resistance by occupying key centres or to keep large occupation forces properly supplied.

The progress of large-scale change in the political geography of the ancient world reflected the relative difficulty of consolidating control over the territories of states and stateless peoples. Larger and more powerful states, or those with more effective tactical systems, eventually conquered their rivals and consolidated control over their territory. The result was a long-term pattern of aggregation until the eventual victor, Rome, found itself ringed by barbarian peoples whom it could usually defeat in high-level warfare but over whose lands it could not consolidate control. The medieval west saw a reversal of this pattern. Few rulers could muster forces of the kind needed to conquer organized states, not least because of the protracted sieges that this was likely to require, but feudal social relations facilitated the consolidation of control over stateless regions by allowing local leaders to be incorporated into the structure of power whilst population growth provided a supply of potential colonists to further the process. In consequence, whilst the core regions remained politically fragmented considerable expansion occurred on the periphery.

The maintenance of control once it had been established was a process that requires to be understood in the two dimensions of depth and breadth. The 'depth' of control refers to the ability of rulers to exercise systematic coercion within their frontiers, and in this respect there seems to have been remarkably little variation throughout the period. The constraints imposed by organic economies on transport, communications, and the division of labour meant that even Roman rulers could exercise relatively little systematic coercion away from major population centres or garrisons without the co-operation of local elites. The 'breadth' of control refers to the size of the area within the frontiers, and maintaining this meant defending the frontiers against external threats and preventing or suppressing internal secession. The limitations of pre-gunpowder technology, allied to prevailing ideologies of rulership, meant that frontiers characteristically formed fluid zones rather than linear boundaries. Frontiers faced two kinds of threats. The first of these were the 'focused' threats which consisted of large-scale invasions by concentrated bodies of troops. Threats of this kind were, however, relatively rare, particularly where frontiers were bordered by stateless barbarians.

More common were the 'diffused' threats represented by low-level raiding, lacking in central direction and characteristically opportunistic. Such small-scale incursions did only minor damage in themselves, but if left unchecked they could create insecurity of a kind that threatened the social and economic foundations of frontier defence or trigger the formation of powerful hostile coalitions. Defence against diffused threats required a degree of military and administrative decentralization and the establishment of local defensive systems based on point defences arranged in depth. Arrangements of this kind could be very effective against attacks from outside, but they made it more difficult for rulers to maintain central control, and these difficulties contributed to the origins of medieval Europe's fragmented political landscape.

PART IV

War, Population, and Resources

Introduction

This part is concerned with the costs of war, the factors that influenced them, and how they were met. Military success could bring gains in the form of loot or increased revenue, but before such gains could be realized forces had to be assembled and put in the field and this imposed costs. The actual conduct of operations created further costs, both directly and indirectly. These costs were demographic as well as economic. Demographic costs consisted of population losses that were due mainly to a combination of flight and increased mortality. Economic costs were incurred wherever resources were destroyed or diverted from other possible uses, but not all costs fell on the central treasury in such a way as to deplete the volume of resources available for rulers to commit as they wished. 'Fiscal costs', as we shall term those that did fall in this way, had to be met by taxation or borrowing, and the 'peaky' nature of war-related expenditures made it very difficult to meet them from taxation alone. In the ancient world there was little scope for public borrowing and this acted as a potential cap to military activity. The modern proliferation of credit instruments removed this cap in the short term but brought with it an ever-present danger of over-borrowing and consequent financial crisis.

The first chapter of this part explores the question of how the economic costs of war manifested themselves and how and by whom they were met. Rulers or their subordinates necessarily incurred economic costs in the process of raising, equipping, and fielding troops, but alongside these 'immediate costs' as we shall call them there were also the 'consequential costs' which reflected the military impact on social and economic life and had to be met by the population at large. There was often a trade-off between the two categories because the larger the volume of resources that rulers were prepared to invest in the training, organization, and support of their troops, the more disciplined and less destructive they were likely to be. Fiscal costs formed a very variable proportion of total war-related costs over time and space, and this variation reflected differences in the institutional means by which troops were raised and maintained.

In weakly monetarized economies rulers were often owed military service as one element of the revenues they received in kind. Under these circumstances it was difficult to allocate resources between competing uses and fiscal costs were rarely significant. The rulers of organized states supported by monetary economies could by contrast 'fiscalize' much, if not all, of war's economic costs, at least in principle. In practice however many rulers were either unable or unwilling to do this and resorted to various forms of 'fiscal deflection', or expedients designed to shift the burden away from their treasury and onto other parties, with or without their consent. One method was to replace cash payments with entitlements to goods or services in kind. This reduced costs by eliminating an intervening layer of fiscal administration, but service obligations obtained in this way tended to be inflexible and limited in scope. A common alternative was the devolution of functions onto individuals or groups outside the state's administrative apparatus. Such services were cheaper in fiscal terms, but they led to a reduction in central control that could be politically dangerous and often increased consequential costs because of the damage and disruption that was wrought by the soldiers.

This part's second chapter focuses on changes in the relative military commitment of manpower and capital resources and the factors that lay behind them. These factors can be divided into two groups which are analogous to the supply and demand sides of economic analysis. The 'demand side' is specified by the current military technology and the configuration of politico-military threats and opportunities faced by rulers, whilst on the supply side are the demographic and economic resources available to them. The relative availability of manpower and capital varied with the phases of the demographic cycle, and the military effectiveness obtained by different combinations of the two inputs changed with changes in military technology. For much of the period the two sides of the equation were compatible, in terms of the balance between capital and manpower, and there were limits to the absolute scale of the commitment that could be made within the existing military technology. The gunpowder revolution changed the position by altering the relative returns to investment in military manpower and capital in a way that did not reflect their relative availability and by removing the old constraints on the level of military effectiveness that could be obtained by increases in scale. The forces that resulted from these changes were successful enough in military terms, but they led to an increasing volume of immediate and consequential costs which proved increasingly hard to bear.

Demographic costs featured prominently among the consequential costs and form the subject matter of the third chapter. Regional population losses were mainly due to migration, which was often only temporary and might bring benefits to adjacent areas, but war could also trigger major increases in mortality. These rarely stemmed directly from violence itself but arose instead from the spread of epidemic disease. Disease was also the main cause of death among soldiers themselves, and some civilian epidemics originated from this source. In other cases it was war-related disruption to economic and social life that was responsible and the mechanisms involved were similar to those implicated in subsistence crises. Many such epidemics were small scale and local in their impact, but some very large-scale shifts in mortality seem also to have originated in migration and other forms of movement linked to war and similar phenomena.

Rulers often resorted to entitlements or devolution to reduce their fiscal costs but they obtained the greatest operational and political control over their forces when they paid them regular cash wages from the central treasury. The resulting fiscal costs had to be met from either revenue or borrowing, and the final chapter examines the different ways in which this was achieved and some of the broader consequences of these differences. Tax revenues were not always received in cash. Taxation in kind was common in the ancient and medieval worlds and was retained in some parts of Europe into the eighteenth century. The most basic form of taxation was the payment of tribute, which sometimes bordered on simple plunder, but organized states generally relied on enumerated taxes, payable per head or per household, taxes on economic transactions, or taxes on wealth. Wealth taxes were politically difficult to levy where land, the main form of wealth in organic economies, was in the hands of powerful elites. Transaction taxes on sales or the movement of goods were more commonly implemented as expenditure rose beyond the income of the royal estates that were the financial mainstay of rulers in feudal Europe.

The difficulties with direct taxation were one manifestation of the broader problem of taxing the wealth of an organic economy. Another was the high cost of the administration that was involved. As in the military case, many rulers were unable or unwilling to meet such costs and devolved the task to local elites or so-called 'tax farmers' with results that were frequently inefficient, unjust, or both. The consequent financial and political repercussions aggravated the need for borrowing. In medieval Europe this was undertaken by rulers on their own account, but the early modern period saw the growth of public credit secured on taxes or other assets. This imposed a double penalty on states with a weak or unreliable revenue base. Not only did they have to borrow larger sums but their creditors demanded higher interest payments to offset the risk of default. Conversely, fiscally strong states like England or Holland could borrow cheaply and with relative ease. The growing size and cost of European armies in the gunpowder era led to large increases in the scale of borrowing, particularly as rulers reacted against the practice of devolution and met more of the costs of war in fiscal terms. The resulting forces were effective political instruments but the continental powers' fiscal system proved too weak a foundation for the military superstructures that were built upon it, and even England faced a grave fiscal crisis that was averted by a new fiscal regime of a kind that only an incipient mineral economy could have sustained.

CHAPTER TWELVE

The Cost of War: Manpower and Resources

Rulers who wanted to keep themselves in power needed access to force and this meant recruiting and maintaining sufficient quantities of men with the requisite skills and equipment. Properly trained and equipped forces usually represented only a very small fraction of the relevant adult male population, and absolute shortages of manpower were rare except in the immediate aftermath of a major defeat. Even states such as Carthage whose citizen body was relatively small could field large numbers of foreign mercenaries provided it could afford to pay them. The primary constraints on recruitment were therefore economic and financial, rather than demographic in a narrow sense, and included the costs necessarily incurred by removing men from the productive labour force. The problems involved in maintaining an army were, at the most general level, just one more manifestation of the basic question dogging organic economies: how to promote occupational specialization and the division of labour against a background of low productivity. They were aggravated in this instance because the specialists were armed men, well able to take what they wanted from civilian society and even to usurp political power.

Resolving the problems required committing material resources and this implied the existence of costs that had to be met in some form by someone. How and by whom they were met depended on the institutional forms through which recruitment was undertaken. These varied enormously in time and space but most of them were based on one or more of four underlying principles which we shall refer to as compulsion, the vocational principle, entitlement, and devolution. Within this framework resources were allocated to raise, maintain, and equip troops. This did not necessarily involve cash payments, but market transactions of this kind are a useful starting point from which to analyse costs. The costs can be split into two categories, immediate and consequential, of which the immediate costs were the direct costs of raising, maintaining, and equipping troops. These increased with increasing standards of training, organization, and equipment, but they also rose with levels of labour productivity in the civilian economy. In this respect, economic growth made war more expensive although military capital goods, such as fortifications and warships, were likely to get cheaper—like for like—with increasing productivity.

War also imposed consequential costs through its destructive impact on civilian life and the economy. There was a relationship between these two categories because the impact of war was all the greater where troops were poorly paid, organized, and disciplined. The prevalence of these conditions reflected rulers' unwillingness or inability to bear the direct costs of warfare, and in particular to maintain not just the troops themselves but also a supporting logistical and administrative apparatus. Rulers had to do the first if they wanted any kind of army at all, but few were willing or able to do the second. Instead they devised a range of institutional expedients that enabled administrative and other costs to be evaded or passed on to third parties. Many of these were highly effective in furnishing troops that could win battlefield victories and so meet the agonistic criterion of military effectiveness, but they were much less so on the Clausewitzian criterion which requires armed forces to be effective instruments of policy. In deflecting costs from their treasuries, rulers also gave up a potentially dangerous degree of administrative and political control over their armed forces. The costs rulers evaded or passed on did not simply vanish but reappeared in other forms, often as consequential costs paid by the civilian population through the general prevalence of looting and indiscipline.

12.1. MODES OF RECRUITMENT

The material foundation of any ruler's fighting capacity was control over resources, in cash or in kind, but building on that foundation required sufficient quantities of manpower to be recruited and furnished with the requisite skills and equipment. There were many ways in which this task could be undertaken. Historians have often attempted to classify them in terms of different 'military systems', but the term 'system' is potentially misleading in this context and needs to be treated with care. The means employed to raise and maintain troops rarely formed coherent integrated wholes, designed for the purpose and systematically implemented. Rulers often used quite different methods in different parts of their domain or to raise different troop types. Typically they were more or less desperate ad hoc expedients, resorted to for want of anything better, but even in quieter times military institutions were also social and political institutions and their forms bore the imprint of social and political interests in addition to the weight of the past and the constraints of geography and economics.

Most of Europe's rulers, from the later Roman Empire to the *ancien régime*, found themselves having to make do with military arrangements that were almost certainly other than what they would have wished, from either a military or a political viewpoint. In these circumstances it is not very helpful to try to classify mutually distinct systems of recruitment in the way we did tactical systems, but we can recognize a number of recurrent features. Apart from the payment of cash wages, most of the expedients that were adopted for recruiting and maintaining troops involved some form, or combination, of four general principles that can be loosely termed 'compulsion', 'entitlement', 'vocational', and 'devolutionary'.

12.1.1. GENERAL COMPULSION

The simplest and probably the oldest solution to the recruitment problem was to compel the entire (male) population to take up arms to defend themselves and their dependants. Europeans inherited the idea of a universal obligation to some kind of military service from their Iron Age past, but progressive social and economic differentiation made its realization impractical in all but the most acute emergencies, since a differentiated economy required at least some people to remain at work whilst others fought. The growth of military specialization and its concomitant skills also meant that an increasing amount of time had to be spent in training, and so specialized military personnel had to be maintained by the produce of other people's labour.

When general levies were enforced they usually yielded untrained troops with very limited obligations for service, like the early modern territorial militias. The principle of general obligation nonetheless continued to legitimize more restricted forms of compulsion, and most eighteenth-century armies fell back on some kind of ad hoc conscription when the number of volunteers proved inadequate. In the words of one authority, it 'usually produced the worst types of soldiers—vagabonds, criminals, the mentally ill and the socially undesirable' (Childs 1982: 45). The basic problem was that few states had the administrative means to register those eligible for service and make an appropriate selection.[1] The task was therefore devolved to local landowners or community bodies who used it as a way of getting rid of people they did not want. Even under the pressure of French invasion, when Russian nobles 'gave' their serfs to the army in 1812 they continued 'to use military service as a way of ridding themselves of the lazy, the incompetent, and the troublesome' (Esdaile 1995: 254). A more sophisticated form of compulsion based on population registration was implemented by Prussia in the 1730s. This 'cantonal' system as it was called established a link between each military unit and a specific household grouping from which conscripts were selected. Some four million men were drafted by this means over the seventy-year period in which the system operated (Childs 1982: 52–6).[2]

The French authorities had manipulated traditional militia obligations to draft conscripts into regular units throughout the eighteenth century (Lynn 1997: 380–93; Forrest 1989: 9–12), but the scale of compulsion increased massively

---

[1] Even where the administrative potential existed local and other interests could block the implementation of a rational system of compulsory service. In England compulsion, though of only marginal significance for army recruitment, was the main means of recruitment to the wartime navy. Legal liability was restricted to those in seagoing or riverine occupations, but political opposition prevented these men from being registered and so no rational system of selection could be implemented. Conscription was enforced by 'press gangs' at the point of a club, using criteria such as whether men had tar on their hands. At best brutal, inefficient, and arbitrary, the process was also subject to many abuses with numerous landsmen being illegally forced on board ship (Lavery 1990: 120–3; Anderson 1988: 126).

[2] Successful as the cantonal system was by the standards of its time, it did not free the Prussian army from a heavy reliance on foreign mercenaries. Territorial recruitment did, however, convey further military benefits by providing units with an additional degree of coherence (Childs 1982: 52–4).

after the Revolution. The mass levies of 1793 furnished the new Republic with an army of at least three-quarters of a million men (Forrest 1989: 20–36), and in 1798 a regular system of conscription was introduced in time to provide the manpower for Napoleon's armies. The new system was based on registration by age classes. The members of each class were liable for service at the age of 20 and the required proportion was selected by ballot (Forrest 1989: 34–42). In relatively peaceful years some 78,000 men were taken, but much larger numbers could be drafted by drawing on younger classes and reballoting classes from previous years. In the crisis of 1813 some 800,000 Frenchmen were conscripted, including many under-age adolescents or 'Marie-Louises', and Napoleon was able to replace the half-million or so casualties from the previous year's Russian campaign more easily than he could the horses which had been lost (Esdaile 1995: 52, 268–76). In all, more than 40 per cent of French males born in the years 1790–5 are thought to have served in Napoleon's army (Houdaille 1972).

12.1.2. ENTITLEMENTS

An alternative to compulsion was the imposition of specific obligations in exchange for some bundle of socially underwritten rights. An early form of this, which could shade into the compulsion principle, was the duty of military service as a condition of enfranchisement in the body politic. The armies of the Greek city states, and of the Roman Republic for most of its existence, were raised on this basis, with differential obligations being imposed according to wealth or political status. This principle was readily suited to small political units with a representative or participatory political system, and it re-emerged in the civic militias of the medieval urban communes. The principle had the virtue of simplicity, since it avoided the need to collect and redistribute resources in the form of taxation, and it could be a very effective source of motivated soldiers who were fighting for their civic rights, their lands, or their hearth and home. Its principal weakness, which it shared with the compulsion principle, was that citizen militiamen were normally part-time soldiers. This restricted the amount of training they could do and imposed limitations on the duration and geographical scope of the service they could be called upon to undertake. Some states who recruited on this basis were very successful militarily and, like the Roman Republic, grew to control large areas of territory. In such cases the original citizen militia gave way to an army based on full-time soldiers serving for extended periods (Keppie 1984: 32–4).

12.1.3. THE VOCATIONAL PRINCIPLE

Military service was both a livelihood and a basis of social identity for full-time long-service soldiers, at least whilst they were in service. This concentration of military participation among specialists who relied on it for their place in society, the 'vocational' principle, was almost the only means by which agricultural or urban populations could support specialized military skills.[3] This support could be forthcoming in either or both of two forms. One form was the payment of a money wage, either to the regular soldiers of a standing army or, more often in the ancient and medieval worlds, to members of a floating population of mercenaries who were hired for specific periods or campaigns. The alternative was the allocation of entitlements to land, produce, or the labour services of cultivators.[4] Entitlements of this kind were widely used, even in societies with a monetarized economy, and were not confined to the support of full-time military specialists. Settlements of farmer-soldiers were widely used in frontier defence and formed the basis of the Byzantine *theme* system established in the aftermath of the Arab conquests (Treadgold 1995: 98–109; Haldon 1999: 74–85).

In other cases landholdings were grouped into larger units, each of which owed the service of an armed man. This organization, practised from pre-Conquest England to eighteenth-century Sweden, allowed troops to serve for longer and further afield than could farmer-soldier militias, but it might still restrict the opportunities for military specialization and skill formation. These were best promoted where fighting men were allocated entitlements to produce, or to the labour of cultivators. Arrangements of this kind existed in the ancient world, particularly in Sparta,[5] but they are best known from their medieval form. The origins of western European 'feudalism' remain the subject of controversy as does the appropriateness of the term itself (DeVries 1992: 95–110; Contamine 1984: 179–84; Reynolds 1994), but it is clear that at least by the end of the eleventh century the region's rulers derived most of their effective troops from the service of sworn followers, and their retainers, in exchange for grants of land. In these circumstances, as was often the case where the vocational and entitlement principles were combined, the recipients came to form a social elite, whether hereditary or not, with a common sense of identity and a cultural code built around war. The combination formed a very successful basis for the recruitment of highly skilled and motivated troops and was widespread in the pre-industrial world. This was not least because it confined the most effective means of violence to those who had the strongest interest in maintaining the existing order of

---

[3] One alternative found in some non-European societies such as the east African Masai was a form of 'age-set' organization which tied military service to a specific stage in the male life-cycle: see Spencer (1965). Ironically, this 'tribal' system was adopted by most continental armies in the heyday of European imperialism.

[4] The concept of 'entitlements' in the sense used here represents the allocation of legally enforceable rights to goods or services by a political authority and so is distinct both from the market-based 'exchange entitlements' discussed by Sen (1981) and from the payment of wages in kind through administrative channels. Wage payments establish a qualitatively different relationship between the beneficiary and the administrative organs of the state from that implied by entitlements, although the distinction may sometimes be a fuzzy one in practice.

[5] The 'spartiates', as the state's full citizens were known, were essentially a militarized ruling class supported by the labour of 'helots' who greatly outnumbered them. Helots were state property but could marry and own property and their position was generally closer to that of medieval villeins, or bonded sharecroppers, than to chattel slaves (Cartledge 1979: 160–95).

things. From the rulers' point of view such arrangements were not entirely satisfactory. Possession of a secure landed base, especially if hereditary, gave the military elite a potentially dangerous degree of independence from their political superiors. Service owed in exchange for land, like other forms of territorial recruitment, also tended to be hedged about with restrictions, making it difficult to raise troops for protracted campaigns far from home.

One way round this problem was to pay cash wages in exchange for service, either for a specific campaign or for membership of a permanent standing force. This was the most flexible arrangement from the ruler's point of view, but implementing it required access to a cash income and so to an economy that was, at least in part, monetarized. Some of the agrarian empires, notably Rome and at times Byzantium, could afford large standing armies of paid full-timers, but the medieval successor kingdoms rarely managed to maintain more than a few royal guards and key garrisons on this basis. When paid troops were needed, they relied heavily on men raised specifically for the occasion, who might be drawn from the feudal service pool under special arrangements or else be foreign mercenaries owing no specific loyalty or obligation beyond their contract of employment. The low productivity of organic economies placed two major obstacles in the way of raising and maintaining a standing army. The first obstacle was the expense of supporting large numbers of economically unproductive soldiers on a permanent basis, but organizations of this kind also required a civilian bureaucracy to raise and administer the resources needed to support them and this too was a major burden. The burden was aggravated by the fact that the equipment, shelter, and provisioning of permanent units was usually a care of the state, and so standing armies made qualitatively different demands on its administrative apparatus from those made by troops serving only for specific campaigns.

12.1.4. DEVOLUTION

Mercenaries, like troops raised on the entitlement principle, usually provided their own equipment and looked after themselves when not on active service, substantially lowering the 'administrative overhead'. Nonetheless, procuring and organizing such troops in the time available itself required a substantial cadre of civilian and military officials if mercenaries were to be signed up as individuals. Faced with these problems, most rulers devolved responsibility onto individuals acting, in varying degrees, outside the framework of whatever formal administrative structure their state possessed. This 'devolutionary' principle took many forms, but most can be grouped into one of four loose categories.[6] The first was reliance on men from outside the domestic political or social structure, who were able to deliver units *en bloc* under their own commanders and with their own

---

[6] The concept of 'devolution' as employed here owes much to Thompson's analysis of Habsburg Spain (1976). The term 'military devolution' is also employed by Parker (1988: 64–7).

organization and equipment. In the ancient world, this commonly involved war leaders and their followers from the barbarian periphery. The later Roman Republic raised its cavalry and light troops in this way, and the phenomenon re-emerged in the later Roman Empire. Germanic federate troops formed an increasingly important element in the Imperial armies of the late fourth and fifth centuries and their leaders took on a close, but ambivalent, association with the formal structures of the state. The medieval Islamic world saw a similar process, with 'native' Arab troops increasingly displaced by Turkic bands, under their own leaders.

The late medieval and early modern Christian world saw the rise of an international market for military manpower. Mercenary networks developed that could furnish large numbers of trained and experienced troops, but it was difficult and time consuming for rulers and their officials to tap into them directly or to organize units from pools of individual recruits. The gap was filled by the emergence of a class of 'military brokers': men who could supply ready organized and equipped units on a scale ranging from a few dozen soldiers to an entire army (Anderson 1988: 33–55). Such men exploited a range of contacts, usually based on previous military experience, and it was just a step from this to the maintenance of semi-permanent military units of the kind that appeared in the later Middle Ages. The reliance on outsiders could be reduced by using regional magnates, or lower-level provincial figures, to raise forces in the areas under their influence. Under the conditions of feudal tenure such men, in their role as 'tenants-in-chief', were required to bring a retinue of armed subtenants to the royal host.

These arrangements later took on a contractual form, with magnates manipulating their regional networks of kinship, affinity, or clientage to obtain a stipulated number of troops. Although these arrangements involved cash payments, rulers were often able to exploit residual notions of feudal obligation, or social honour, in order to obtain service more cheaply than they might from outsiders. Such men might also be less dangerous politically, if also less competent militarily, than were large-scale brokers. Another way of exploiting territorial allegiances was to devolve responsibility for recruitment onto local communities or civic officials. In the absence of an effective centralized bureaucracy this was the only realistic means of enforcing compulsory service, for anything other than local defence, on the general population of large states. Some rulers tried to do this, but their attempts rarely yielded anything other than a collection of people their communities wanted to get rid of. In England 'Commissions of Array' were introduced to enforce recruitment during the reign of Edward I. They were retained into the early modern period, but without adequate administrative resources the commissioners had to rely on lower-level officials or communities, and the system has been described as 'a means of collecting together the weak, the imbecile, and the outsiders of village society' (Prestwich 1996: 124).

Another form of devolution occurred where men holding official positions as administrators or commanders had to use their own private resources in order to get the job done. Devolution of this kind persisted into the eighteenth century and coexisted with the growth of formal bureaucratic structures. The resources involved were social as well as financial. Medieval and early modern commanders with formal commissions often had to use networks of personal contacts to raise units varying in size from companies to entire regiments or even larger contingents. Such men also had to dip into their own pockets in many cases, and they usually expected something in return. The armies of the late Roman Republic were partly financed in this way since the state treasury could no longer afford the sums that were required. The fabulously wealthy Crassus raised an entire army from his private resources in order to suppress the Spartacus slave revolt, but Caesar also contributed personally to the financing of his Gallic campaigns. This investment yielded returns in the form of political power, based on glory and the army's loyalty, as well as a share of the loot. In other cases they were less tangible. The Spanish Habsburgs tapped their magnates' wealth, as well as their leadership abilities and social networks. The magnates gained prestige, and sometimes influence, by commanding their own troops for the crown, but the financial cost could be ruinous. The reappearance of standing armies in *ancien régime* Europe was associated with this form of devolution. In many cases regiments were the virtual property of their colonel who was responsible for paying, equipping, and supplying them in return for capitation payments from the central authorities (Childs 1982: 29). This system avoided the administrative costs of a centralized logistical bureaucracy, but the numerous opportunities for misappropriation meant that few regimental commanders lost money in the process.

12.2. IMMEDIATE COSTS

The immediate costs of military activities can be divided for convenience into three categories: (i) 'troop costs', which are the costs of raising, training, and equipping soldiers and maintaining them in an adequate condition; (ii) 'operational costs', which are the further costs of fielding a force given that it has been raised and equipped, and; (iii) 'capital costs' which are the additional costs of establishing and maintaining 'military capital' such as fortifications and warships. These three kinds of costs were not necessarily paid in cash or by the rulers themselves. In weakly monetarized economies troops were unlikely to be paid cash wages and elsewhere cash wages might be supplemented or replaced by employing the range of obligations and entitlements which we considered previously. It is, however, analytically convenient in most cases to begin by treating military costs as if they were incurred through cash purchases in markets, including labour markets, because this has the advantage of making costs transparent and commensurable with one another. It therefore makes a valuable point of departure from which we can consider the effects of different kinds of departure from the assumption of market purchase.

12.2.1. TROOP COSTS

Troop costs can be further broken down into two main components. The first of these is the 'basic wage' which is what is needed to get men into the army from civilian life and to provide for their subsistence. Where the state purchases military service in a market it is in the same position as any other employer, and the army has to pay the 'going rate', at least in principle. Basic wage costs therefore vary with the state of the civilian labour market and the relative attractiveness of military, as opposed to civilian, employment. The second component of troop costs represents the costs incurred in rendering the troops militarily effective. Some of these 'quality costs' as we shall call them are incurred through the higher wages paid in exchange for increased skill and responsibility, and others represent the costs of weaponry, equipment, and other facilities needed to boost troop quality. Quality costs of this kind depend more on narrowly military considerations than do the basic wage costs.

12.2.1.1. Basic wage costs

For the army to attract recruits in a free labour market, military service must be marginally more attractive than the most desirable civilian employment available to potential soldiers. The basic wage cost, which is the cost of inducing a man to volunteer of his own free will, can accordingly be split into two components: the 'comparator element', and the 'military premium'. The comparator element represents the wage level accruing to the potential recruits' most remunerative alternative employment, and for simplicity we shall take it to include the costs of basic subsistence.[7] The prevailing poverty and underemployment endemic to organic economies kept this component fairly low, as long as the demands of recruitment did not expand too far up the socio-economic scale. The military premium is the second component of basic wage costs and represents the additional payment needed to attract men away from civilian employment. Its level was set by a wide range of factors reflecting both the material circumstances of military life and the nature of civilian society and culture. Where both of these components were concerned there existed a potentially perverse relationship between economic growth and the available level of military power. Raising and equipping troops required resources, and one way of obtaining these was to increase the productivity of labour through economic growth. Increases in productivity, however, also made civilian labour a more valuable commodity, which increased the comparator element of the basic wage and made soldiers more expensive. Since soldiering was itself an economically unproductive activity,

---

[7] Strictly speaking the comparator element relates to civilian incomes rather than simply wages, and so is affected by changing levels of employment, hours worked, and so forth. In practice, however, whilst wage data are scarce, income data are virtually non-existent before the recent past, and economic theory predicts that movements in the two should be very closely related; for a discussion see Schwarz (1985).

these increased troop costs could not be offset by any increases in the value of their activity.

One way around this problem was to recruit soldiers from less productive regions elsewhere or from relatively unproductive sectors of the domestic economy, and recruiting from the barbarian periphery, or from other undeveloped frontier zones, was common in the ancient and medieval worlds. In the early modern period, impoverished uplands, the urban lumpenproletariat, and the population of the economically dislocated war zone itself provided a disproportionate number of recruits (Tallett 1992: 90–2). Similarly, in disturbed circumstances the army might offer greater security than civilian life, and the military premium would be correspondingly low, but such conditions were not conducive to economic growth, which was more likely to occur in conditions of order and security. These conditions, however, were likely to increase the level of the military premium, as did the growth of a richer and more diversified civilian society. Conversely, in a warrior culture, where fighting was seen as intrinsically desirable, the premium would be lower and possibly even negative—which was something that provided a further incentive to recruit from the barbarian periphery.

12.2.1.2. *Quality costs*

Basic wage costs were incurred simply by recruiting and maintaining manpower, but turning these men into effective soldiers incurred a second tranche of costs. These 'quality costs' reflected the fact that military employers, like their civilian counterparts, had to pay more for men with greater skills, experience, or responsibility. They also had to pay if they wanted access to specialized equipment. The figures in Table 12.1 are chosen to represent as wide a chronological range as possible and show the sort of wage differentials that could arise.[8] From a military point of view overall quality costs of this kind can be split into two subcategories which we shall call 'skills costs' and 'organization costs'. Skills costs were incurred in boosting an individual's military abilities whilst organization costs were incurred by measures that improved the quality of units and higher-level formations as a whole and allowed larger numbers of men to be deployed to good effect.

12.2.1.2.1. *Skills costs*

Improvements in soldiers' military effectiveness could be obtained through greater training and experience or by the provision of better equipment. Each of these imposed its own costs.

---

[8] The early modern wage figures are difficult to interpret. Actual pay was so irregular as to make the official rates something of an accounting fiction, but they do give some indication of how much different categories of soldier were thought to be worth. Since the authorities made much greater efforts to provide the pay for veteran and other high-quality units the actual premium attaching to troop quality may have been higher than appears from the official figures. (I am grateful to Dr David Parrott for bringing this point to my attention.)

Table 12.1 *Some military wage differentials*

(a)

Augustan Rome Source (1) Base: 100 = 900 *sestertii* per annum		England, Richard I Source (2) Base: 100 = 2 pence daily	
Rank	Index	Rank	Index
Chief centurion (*Primus pilus*)	6,000	Knight	600
Senior centurion (*Primus ordo*)	3,000	Mounted sergeant with hauberk	300
Legionary centurion	1,500	Mounted sergeant	200
Legionary infantry	100		
Auxiliary centurion	417	Foot sergeant	100
Auxiliary infantryman	83		

(b)

England, Edward I Source (2) Base: 100 = 2 pence daily		French royal army, 1560s[a] Source (3) Base: 100 = 7 *livres* monthly	
Rank	Index	Rank	Index
		Gendarmes	
		Captain	2,614
Banneret	2,400	Lieutenant	1,257
Knight	1,200	Ensign	957
Mounted sergeant	600	Man-at-arms	471
Light cavalry	300	'Archer'	243
Infantry	100	Infantry	
		Captain	1,514
		Lieutenant	800
		Ensign	514
		Sergeant	286
		Lanspessade	171
		Corseleted pikeman	114
		Pike/arquebus	100

Table 12.1 *Some military wage differentials (Continued)*
(c)

France, early 1600s Source (6) Base: 100 = 10 *livres* monthly		France, early 1700s Source (6) Base: 100 = 5 *sols* daily	
Rank	Index	Rank	Index
Cavalry captain	4,125	Cavalry captain	2,000
Cavalry lieutenant	2,625	Cavalry lieutenant	1,000
Infantry captain	1,250	Infantry captain	800
Infantry lieutenant	500	Infantry lieutenant	400
Infantryman	100	Infantry sergeant	200
		Infantry fusilier	100

(d)

French Napoleonic infantry[b] Source (4) Base: 100 = 30 centimes daily		British Napoleonic infantry[c] Source (5) Base: 100 = 1 shilling daily	
Rank	Index	Rank	Index
Marshal	37,033		
Général de division	13,900		
Général de brigade	9,267	Lieutenant colonel	1,892
Colonel	4,633	Major	1,408
Chef de bataillon	3,333	Captain	942
Captain	2,223	Lieutenant	467
Lieutenant	1,157	Ensign	367
Sous-lieutenant	1,000	Sergeant	156
Sergeant-major	267	Corporal	119
Sergeant	207	Private	100
Corporal	150		
Fusilier	100		
Old Guard, private	387		

[a] Infantry pay rates are those of Brissac's company; *gendarme* rates are for a standard company of thirty 'lances'. The *lanspessade* rate was used to reward higher-quality troops. See Wood (1996: 88–9, 134–5).
[b] Fusiliers received additional monthly pay of 1 franc after ten years' service and 1.5 francs after fifteen years (Elting 1997: 582).
[c] The lieutenant colonel's rate is calculated for the commander of a standard ten-company battalion.
Sources: (1): Speidel (1992); (2): Prestwich (1996); (3): Wood (1996); (4): Haythornthwaite (1994); (5): Elting (1997); (6): Lynn (1997).

12.2.1.2.1.1. Training

Different forms of military technology and methods of organization and recruitment created different opportunities and demands where training was concerned. Some pre-gunpowder weapons systems were effectively ethnic technologies and required more skill and experience than could be imparted through formal training. In these cases skilled men were usually recruited as combat-ready 'mercenaries' or retained on the entitlement principle. In the latter case training was usually the responsibility of the individual, or sometimes of the community, and the results were very variable.[9] Where armies were raised and subsequently disbanded for specific campaigns, there was rarely either the time or money to undertake basic training before fighting began. Commanders therefore relied on recruiting at least some men with prior training and experience, and under these circumstances, training costs were met by the higher wages such veterans could command.

Standing armies could train new recruits from scratch. We know very little about training procedures in the pre-gunpowder era, but most of it will have taken place once recruits had joined their units. Since the men already in the ranks needed constant training to keep them up to the mark, the marginal cost of training a new recruit with an existing unit was correspondingly low. It was, however, much more difficult and expensive to create a large number of new units in a short period because, in order to be effective, such units had to be built around cadres of experienced men. It was therefore preferable to run down unit strengths in time of peace as the Romans seem to have done, rather than disband or amalgamate entire units. Since many of the soldier's skills could only be learnt from experience, combat veterans were a valuable commodity and commanded higher wages in many standing armies.

The spread of infantry firearms led to major changes in the nature of foot soldiers' fighting skills and the means by which they were transmitted. Whereas previously, in Hall's words, many military skills 'were taught as part of civilian life...In the sixteenth century, by contrast, rulers preparing for war sought to recruit men who possessed no martial skills whatsoever' (Hall 1997: 234). Smooth-bore muskets were slow firing, inaccurate, and unwieldy weapons. Unlike pistols or the hunting rifle, they had little non-military value and so recruits were taught musketry from scratch on the assumption that they were unfamiliar with the weapon. The basics could be taught relatively quickly, and in Hall's judgement 'masses of untrained men could be made into competent soldiers in 6 months or less' (Hall 1997: 148).

The development of the Dutch drill made training more mechanical and further reduced any element of skill that might be involved. The process intensified as drill was extended from the exercise of weapons-handling to tactical manoeuvre, but the results were paradoxical. Infantry soldiering was thoroughly 'deskilled', becoming a mechanical process of mindless obedience to commands, and yet training metamorphosed into a semi-permanent condition as drill was institutionalized in the soldiers' daily routine. In the process training costs were

---

[9] Skill with horse and sword was a conventional accomplishment for gentlemen in many pre-industrial western societies, making it relatively easy to raise capable cavalrymen. The existence of widespread skill with hunting weapons also made it possible to raise effective light infantry from certain regions without the need for investment in specialized training.

swallowed up in the general increase in expenditure required to maintain standing armies as these developed into 'self-perpetuating training institutions, drilling raw recruits until they became quite different from their former selves, that is, until they became soldiers' (McNeill 1983: 138). As soldiers remained with their units, receiving pay, for increasing periods, the amount spent on them necessarily grew and the veteran was increasingly valued, not for what he could do, but for what he had become or what his training had made him, which was a well-drilled cog in a machine that required only unthinking obedience.[10]

12.2.1.2.1.2. *Equipment*

Military equipment costs were mainly accounted for by weaponry, armour, and horses, with expendable munitions being added in the gunpowder era. These costs were met in various ways. Troops raised on the entitlement principle usually had to provide their own equipment, which meant that cavalry or heavy infantry service was restricted to the wealthier and this imposed a limit on the numbers of troops available. Standing armies more often issued equipment to their troops— sometimes making an offsetting deduction from pay—or paid allowances for equipment purchase, and under these circumstances some or all of the costs fell directly on the state treasury. Where armies were raised only for specific campaigns, this arrangement was rarely practical and the troops came ready equipped, but those with more expensive equipment generally commanded higher wages.

Heavy cavalry equipment was particularly expensive because horses and iron were two of the most valuable commodities in organic economies, and warhorses were generally more costly than those used in farming or haulage. There are few data from the ancient world, but a sample of 500 warhorse values from third-century BC Athens reported by Spence yields a median (or middle value in rank order) of 600 drachmas (Spence 1993: 275–6). This is twice what the author describes as the 'minimum price of a decent horse' and more than enough to purchase two years' supply of grain for a six-person household. By the late fourth century AD Roman cavalry recruits were apparently given 7 *solidi* to buy their horse, when the official value of an ox was only 3 *solidi* and 5 *solidi* would purchase 200 *modii* (approximately 1.3 tons) of seed corn (Elton 1996: 122).

The relative value of warhorses seems to have risen substantially in the early Middle Ages. In the middle of the eighth century, the Frankish Ripuarian Law valued a warhorse at 12 *solidi*, which was six times the value of an ox and four times that of a good mare (Verbruggen 1997: 23). The horseman's armour and weapons were valued at a further 33 *solidi*, lending credence to Bachrach's claim

---

[10] The valuation placed on veterans is illustrated by the advice of Maurice de Saxe, the 18th-century French military commander and theorist, against unnecessarily 'losing rashly a single grenadier: he has been twenty years in the making' (quoted Jones 1995: 156). By contrast, the 11 *livres* per head that Marshal Belle-Isle paid to redeem prisoners of war in 1758 valued their experience at only about six weeks' pay per man, but Belle-Isle may have been very short of money (Forrest 1989: 8).

that the output of twelve agricultural workers was required to meet the cost of supporting a single mounted warrior in that period (Bachrach 1985: 750). Further increases occurred in later centuries, at least at the top end of the range, and may have reflected the effects of selective breeding on the most sought-after strains. In 1297 Geraard de Moor, lord of Wessegem, had seven warhorses with an average value of over 130 *livres*, which was more than ten times the price of a 'good horse' in local markets (Verbruggen 1997: 26). A similar differential existed between the values of warhorses and the mounted archers' humble nags in later fourteenth-century English armies (Ayton 1999, 1994*a*). The trend towards greater armoured protection increased the costs of medieval heavy cavalry equipment, although the effect of this is likely to have been partly offset by the progress in the technology of iron working.[11] Armour was nonetheless expensive. A late twelfth-century English mail shirt could cost £1, which was the equivalent of four months' wages for a foot soldier, whilst the £2 that Edward III paid for a helmet in the later fourteenth century would have paid an infantryman for six months. Wood estimates that a full coat of plate armour for a man-at-arms cost £100 in sixteenth-century France, equal to half the cost of a warhorse and more than twelve months' wages for a pikeman (Wood 1996: 136, 88).

Medieval infantry equipment was much cheaper since these men usually wore little if any armour.[12] In 1300 some Yorkshire villages paid 5 shillings per man to equip the infantry complement they were required to raise (Prestwich 1996). This was equivalent to a month's pay for the soldiers concerned. Where heavier infantry were raised their equipment was more expensive. A planned force of this kind in early fourteenth-century England involved a cost of £1 per man, and Verbruggen estimates the cost of equipping contemporary Flemish bourgeois militiamen at more than half a year's wages for an artisan (Verbruggen 1997: 170). Infantry weapons were often relatively cheap. The cost of a large crossbow in late thirteenth-century England ran from 5 to 7 shillings, which was some two to three weeks' pay for a crossbowman. A good-quality fourteenth-century longbow cost only 1*s*. 6*d*., which was less than a fortnight's pay for an infantryman (Hardy 1994: 44). Infantry firearms were relatively more expensive, but they were still cheap by the standards of cavalry equipment. In the later seventeenth century French muskets cost between 6 and 10 *livres*, some four to six weeks' pay for a musketeer (Lynn 1997).

---

[11] Where armaments or munitions were produced as a seasonal by-employment, as in parts of early modern Spain (Thompson 1995: 288–9), economic growth would tend to increase costs as labour was more fully utilized in the workers' primary activity, forcing the purchaser to switch to specialist arms producers and bear the full cost of their product.

[12] There seem, unfortunately, to be no data on the cost of heavy infantry equipment in the ancient world, but it was clearly substantial because many citizen militiamen in the earlier Roman Republic and the Greek city states—who had to provide their own equipment—were unable to afford it and had to serve as lighter infantry or non-combatant auxiliaries. Elton puts the cost of equipping a 4th-century Roman infantryman at 6 *solidi* as against 13 for a cavalryman (Elton 1996: 124).

12.2.1.2.2. Organization costs

Troops' military effectiveness reflected their training and equipment, but it could be further enhanced by better organization, which imposed its own costs. Their effect was to enable larger bodies of troops to be concentrated and deployed to greater effect rather than to boost the fighting quality of the individuals, and they fall loosely into two categories. The first area of cost refers to what is currently termed 'command control', which is the ability of commanders to maintain the co-ordination and cohesion of their units on the battlefield. Some tactical systems required a relatively sophisticated sub-unit structure in order to function at all. Most could benefit from the development of higher-level organization which enabled an army's component formations to be better co-ordinated. More and better training could usually improve co-ordination at all levels, but there was also a need to increase the ratio of leaders to fighters. The more sub-units and higher formations there were, the more officers of varying grades were required. Such men usually performed better if they were provided with subordinates, and all of these commanded higher pay than could a common soldier.

The second area of costs related to discipline. More sophisticated unit organization usually improved the troops' fighting ability, but it did not necessarily make them better disciplined off the battlefield, or more effective as political instruments. Improvements could be obtained in these areas by investment in military administration. Better supply and other services, the provision of uniforms, and the maintenance of military police and associated infrastructure such as barrack blocks were all likely to reduce desertion and make troops more disciplined and amenable to political direction.[13] Measures of this kind, which were widely implemented in the armies of eighteenth-century Europe, carried direct 'discipline costs' in the form of additional wages and construction and maintenance expenditure, although they might yield some limited savings through reduced desertion. But as military life became more tightly disciplined and 'regimented', service in the ranks also became a less desirable alternative to civilian employment.[14] The level of the military premium therefore rose, bringing a further increase in troop costs which was often met by a resort to compulsion.

12.2.2. OPERATIONAL COSTS

The concept of operational costs refers to the additional, or so-called 'marginal', cost of actually putting an army into the field once it had been raised, equipped, and trained. The scale and incidence of these costs differed greatly between forces of different kinds and particularly standing armies and those specially raised for a

[13] As Jones argues, barracks acted as 'a kind of discipline factory'; they were to be found in more than 300 French towns by 1741 and by 1775 they housed some 200,000 men (Jones 1995: 162).
[14] For a review of this 'military reformation' (Hale's term for the 16th century but more appropriate as a description of this period) see Childs (1982), Anderson (1988: esp. 99–135), and for France Jones (1995).

specific campaign. Troops serving in campaign armies would normally be recruited at active service rates, and transport was needed simply to assemble the force in the first place, so that it was rarely much more expensive to send it into action than to keep it standing idle in need of food and shelter. Standing armies offered a very different prospect. Their troops had to be paid whether they were fighting or not, but they often received additional 'campaign pay' or allowances on active service, and additional costs were incurred because of the need to transport supplies and equipment.[15] Transport costs could also be incurred simply by peacetime movement of units within friendly territory, without any actual fighting. On the other hand, an offensive campaign offered the prospect of plunder and the possibility of feeding the troops at the enemy's expense by 'living off the land'. These gains could more than offset the operational costs of brief raids and plundering expeditions, but it is unlikely that protracted campaigns on a large scale ever yielded much profit unless they resulted in substantial territorial conquests.

One particularly important source of operational costs was the conduct of major siege operations.[16] These had two main components, the first of which was the cost of feeding and supplying the troops.[17] Even if food was requisitioned from the surrounding countryside without payment, it had to be transported to the site of operations and this might require a substantial commitment of resources where large numbers of men were involved for a protracted period. The building of trenches and other siege-works was also an expensive process. In some seventeenth-century instances up to 20,000 civilian labourers were conscripted for the purposes. Even if such labourers were forced to work without pay they still had to be fed at the besiegers' expense, but from the early modern period it became customary to pay wages of as much as a florin a day. Few figures are available for the cost of major sieges, but the siege of La Rochelle in 1627–8 is estimated to have cost as much as forty million *livres*, which was the equivalent of some seventy to eighty million days' pay for an unskilled labourer (Anderson 1988: 41, 140–1).

---

[15] Data on operational costs are hard to come by. In a rare example from the ancient world, Treadgold puts the operational cost of the Romans' unsuccessful attack on Vandal Carthage, as defined here, at around four million *nomismata*. This was evidently a huge enterprise and one whose failure left 'the west almost helpless and the east weakened for a generation' (Treadgold 1995: 190).

[16] Operational costs were also very important in naval warfare because ships' crews had to be fully provisioned since they could not live off the land. Thompson puts victualling costs at one third of the total operating expenses of Habsburg Spain's sailing fleet and 40% of the galley fleet's. The cost of rations was approximately equal to the wage bill (Thompson 1995: 284).

[17] Munitions could also be an appreciable element of total operational costs in major sieges, where hundreds, or even thousands, of artillery rounds might be discharged per day at a unit cost, in the 17th-century, equivalent to an infantryman's monthly wage (Tallett 1992: 170). The cost of firing a contemporary 40-lb Spanish naval cannon was equivalent to two months' pay, and munitions accounted for some 7.5% of the total naval expenses bill (Thompson 1995).

12.2.3. CAPITAL COSTS

Productivity gains in the civilian economy generally reduced the cost of producing military 'capital goods', such as fortifications, shipping, or heavy equipment, by making the process more efficient. This effect could, however, be offset by the fact that growth in the civilian use of labour was likely to reduce the pool of under- or unemployed workers available for military projects at low cost. The existence of such a pool means that calculations based on the number of man-hours particular projects may have required are not necessarily reliable guides to the actual burden they placed on the productive economy. There are, in any case, very few data available on the cost of fortifications for the pre-modern period,[18] although substantial construction programmes were embarked on in the Roman period, particularly in the later Empire. Much of the labour involved appears to have been provided by members of full-time, regular military units, so that the actual cost of this may have consisted of materials.

The gunpowder revolution led to the development of a new kind of fortification, the so-called artillery fortress. Earthwork fortifications proved an effective counter to cannon fire but they were troublesome to maintain in peacetime, and the sixteenth century saw a return to masonry as the material of choice for permanent structures (Duffy 1979). The new-style defences were extremely costly and their construction had to be borne as a fiscal cost. The building of a single bastion at Rome cost 44,000 ducats, whilst the fortifications at Antwerp—which consisted of 4.5 miles of walls with nine bastions—cost one million florins. Between 1529 and 1572 26 miles of new defences, including four citadels and twelve circuits of walls, were built across the Netherlands at a cost of ten million florins (Parker 1988). The revolt against Spanish rule led to more construction, and the expenditure of the Dutch Estates on fortifications rose from 100,000 florins in 1596 to 500,000 florins in 1606, compared with 600,000 florins spent on the field army in the latter year (Duffy 1979: 82). In the 1680s Vauban's plan to fortify the frontier of France absorbed an annual average of 8.5 million livres and accounted at times for 10 per cent of total expenditure (Anderson 1988: 88; Meyer 2000: 101).[19]

---

[18] Bachrach has attempted to cost the 10th-century tower at Langeais in terms of the number of man-days of work needed to build it, which he puts at around 83,000 or the equivalent of two years of work by 140 men. During this period they would, he estimates, consume the surplus output of around 480 cultivators. Since this surplus would otherwise have supported only 100 heavy cavalry, the fortification was, he concludes, extremely cost-effective (Bachrach 1984). The £11,500 which Richard I spent on the fortification of Château-Gaillard over two years in the 1190s would, by contrast, have paid the wages of more than 300 knights at contemporary rates for 104 weeks (Gillingham 1984: 90; Prestwich 1996: 17).

[19] These fortification costs were substantial in absolute terms but they totalled much less than the military wages bill of the major powers and could usually be staged over a lengthy period which made them manageable (Thompson 1995). The real problems arose for city states and other minor powers, such as Siena, who over-invested in fortification as a substitute for the maintenance of mobile units. Siena lost its independence when it could not afford to garrison its ruinously expensive defences, and other minor rulers also found the new fortifications to be more of an economic and strategic liability than an asset (Parrott 2000).

The construction of warships also involved substantial capital costs. Medieval and early modern rulers often hired merchant vessels, which needed only minimal conversion, for the duration of hostilities, but growing specialization made this increasingly difficult, and 'standing navies' of purpose-built warships emerged from the later sixteenth century. The Spanish fleet of this period is estimated to have cost some 30 ducats per ton to construct, and a comparable amount to furnish with artillery, giving it a capital value of around a million ducats (Thompson 1995). On this basis each ship cost about six months' pay for a thousand infantrymen, whilst in 1789 a British 38-gun frigate cost £20,830, approximately equal to twelve months' pay for the same number of men at contemporary rates, and a 74-gun battleship cost £43,820 (Lavery 1990: 47). Once afloat, these vessels might require annual maintenance expenditure equivalent to some 25 per cent of their construction costs (Gardiner 1992).

12.3. FISCAL DEFLECTION AND CONSEQUENTIAL COSTS

Rulers who wanted to mount an effective military effort had to commit properly trained and equipped manpower, whether their subjects' or that of foreign mercenaries, and this required a corresponding commitment of material resources. This commitment of resources was required in order to meet what we have termed the 'immediate costs' of war, but there was also a second category of 'consequential costs' which reflected the damage sustained by the civilian economy, whether directly or indirectly. Immediate and consequential costs all consumed resources and had to be met by someone, but they were not necessarily all met by rulers themselves, even in the first instance. Some fell on their subjects in the war zone, on the troops themselves, or on enemy troops and civilians. Immediate and consequential costs were also interchangeable to some degree. Rulers often used a variety of expedients to reduce the immediate costs of warfare to their own treasuries, but the consequence of this was a reduction in the degree of military discipline and in the control that rulers could exercise over their commanders and soldiers. This in turn led to an increase in the consequential costs that had to be shouldered by civilians and sometimes by the troops themselves.

12.3.1. CONSEQUENTIAL COSTS

War inflicted 'consequential' costs primarily through the population losses and material damage it wrought in the area of operations, or in areas where troops concentrated or manoeuvred in the absence of any fighting. More sophisticated economies also suffered losses to shipping or through the disruption of trade. The scale and nature of the damage done varied with circumstances. At one extreme the entire structure of a regional economy might collapse, bringing with it the wholesale displacement of population. This was particularly likely on exposed frontiers, but material damage to houses, crops, and agrarian capital often occurred on a more widespread, if less drastic, scale. Such damage is difficult to translate into monetary values given the dearth of documentary evidence and such values have, in any case, little meaning in economies that were not themselves monetarized. Variations in the character and extent of consequential costs reflected a wide variety of factors, but they can be roughly grouped into four main categories.

12.3.1.1. Ravaging

The deliberate ravaging of enemy territory was a common tactic, particularly in raiding expeditions. Destruction of this kind, deliberately inflicted by order of the army commanders or their subordinates, might be intended to weaken the enemy's ability or will to resist, to enrich the invader's treasury, or to reward the troops in lieu of pay. The logistical constraints on war in organic economies made destructive raiding an attractive strategic option as we have seen, but defenders also used 'scorched earth' tactics in order to deny the invader access to loot or the means of subsistence. Similar measures were employed when dealing with internal rebellion, either to deprive the rebel forces of subsistence, or in reprisal against their civilian sympathizers. Deliberate destruction fell from favour, as an invasion tactic, from the later seventeenth century, but it never disappeared. French commanders systematically devastated the Rhineland Palatinate in the 1680s (Childs 1982: 151–2) and Marlborough ordered some 400 Bavarian villages to be burned in the campaign of 1704. A century and a half later devastation featured significantly in the closing stages of the American Civil War as Sherman's army traversed the Confederacy's agricultural heartland. The extent of the damage that could be inflicted on regional economies is difficult to assess. The most serious consequences usually stemmed from lengthy periods of endemic insecurity, but the condition of late eleventh-century Yorkshire gives an indication of how much damage could be inflicted by one episode of systematic devastation. The effects of the Norman 'harrying' after the regional uprising of 1069 were visible seventeen years later in 'what was still nearly an empty land... and oxen were as rare as men' (Kapelle 1979: 162).[20]

12.3.1.2. Subsistence

The second category of costs reflected the supply needs of troops who were living off the land. They varied with the size of the force, its length of stay, and the

---

[20] The evidence of Domesday Book suggests that population densities were some two to three times lower than in comparable areas further south. As Kapelle notes, the harrying 'displaced thousands of peasants by destroying their livestock, agricultural implements and winter food supply... and set in motion a population movement that reached the Midlands and ultimately even Scotland. The object of this migration was to find food and probably the chance to sell themselves into slavery' (Kapelle 1979: 169).

relevant institutional arrangements or lack of them. The first two of these factors set the minimum amount of resources that the region had to supply, but much larger amounts might actually be taken, depending on the efficiency of the requisitioning arrangements. The effects on regional economies also depended on their level of agrarian production and the timing of the demands in the agricultural cycle, whilst the net costs they incurred could be substantially reduced if supplies were paid for in cash. The later seventeenth century saw growing attempts to mitigate the costs inflicted on rural economies from this source, including arrangements for reciprocal tax waivers in border regions, so that local inhabitants might set the value of produce handed over to invaders against the revenue demands of their own rulers (Gutmann 1980: 62–6).

12.3.1.3. Indiscipline

Failures of discipline also imposed costs on the civilian economy and population. These overlap with the previous categories since they arose from looting and destruction, whether by hostile or 'friendly' troops, and from the seizure of excessive quantities of supplies. In this instance, however, the behaviour was neither instigated nor sanctioned by their commanders, and it could run seriously contrary to their interests. Damage of this kind could turn a potentially sympathetic civilian population against the perpetrators or could compromise the role of an area as a logistical base. Unpaid troops were especially prone to this form of behaviour, particularly if they were mercenaries, and some of the most notorious early modern atrocities including the sack of Rome by unpaid German mercenaries in 1527 and of Antwerp by Spanish mutineers fifty years later arose in this way.

Much of the damage wrought on rural economies during the wars of the seventeenth century, and in France during the Hundred Years War, can be traced to lack of discipline among the troops and failures of control by army commanders. These did not necessarily end with the cessation of hostilities. When poorly disciplined troops were demobilized they might take to banditry on a substantial scale, or, in extreme instances, usurp the political position of their former employers. This was particularly so with mercenaries hired under their own leaders. As in other respects, the excesses of the seventeenth century triggered a reaction. The troops of the *ancien régime* armies, more regularly paid and effectively policed, had less need and fewer opportunities for looting.[21] French

---

[21] The close link between pay and discipline was captured by the 17th-century writer who observed that 'one could not hang those whom one did not pay' (Tallett 1992: 123). Irregular and inadequate pay remained a problem in the 18th century, but the situation was much better than it had been 100 years before and governments' growing administrative control over pay, exemplified by the appearance of pay books, ended many of the worst abuses by colonel-proprietors and others (Anderson 1988: 107–10). The spread of the pay book was accompanied by the noose and the lash as discipline became more severe (Childs 1982: 67–70). Frederick the Great may have been extreme in his wish that Prussian soldiers should fear their officers more than the enemy, but there can be no doubt that discipline in this period was generally based on fear (Chandler 1994: 106).

army discipline was loosened after the Revolution and remained relatively lax under Napoleon, which may have led to an increase in violence against civilians (Rothenberg 1980: 134; Best 1982: 75–6, 104–5; Esdaile 1995: 110–11, 279–80). The worst atrocities of the seventeenth century resulted from the general breakdown of discipline that often occurred when cities fell after a lengthy siege, and this problem too re-emerged after 1789.[22]

12.3.1.4. *Economic disruption*

The final, and most diverse, category of costs were those imposed by general disruption resulting from military operations. These varied greatly with circumstances, and were often heaviest where the social and economic structure was most differentiated and its elements most interdependent. Trading centres were vulnerable to disruption in their immediate hinterland but could also suffer from interruptions of economic activity in distant regions. War could interrupt the supply of raw materials, close markets to manufactured goods, or increase costs by diverting trade onto more expensive routes. In eighteenth-century England, wartime conditions often forced the substitution of land haulage for coastal shipping with a consequent increase in costs, as well as creating a general economic depression (Ashton 1959). The flight of refugees disrupted production in the countryside, but death or flight could also destroy the networks of trusted agents and middlemen which underpinned long-distance trade and credit arrangements (Hoffman 1996: 203).

12.3.2. FISCAL DEFLECTION

The costs of raising, maintaining, and fielding armed forces varied with economic and military circumstances. How and by whom these costs were met also varied. In our earlier analysis we assumed that what we termed the immediate costs of war were met as wages or other cash payments which were disbursed by central authorities in open markets. Where this was the case the relevant costs necessarily fell on the central treasury, even if they were subsequently recouped from the resources of enemy territory, but as we have seen rulers could obtain military manpower in many ways other than by paying market wages. In weakly monetarized economies some or all of the costs were often met through the allocation of entitlements, but even where rulers enjoyed cash revenues the immediate costs

---

[22] Eighteenth-century commanders ameliorated this problem with a formal code of conduct that allowed besieged garrisons to surrender honourably at an early stage; only if the town fell to assault should defenders be executed and the attacking troops let loose on the civilian population. In 1705 Louis XIV reinforced this trend by permitting his officers to surrender after their walls had sustained a minor breach and one assault had been repelled—hitherto one major breach and multiple assaults had been required. The Revolutionaries showed their contempt for such niceties early on by guillotining a commander and his wife who had surrendered prematurely, and sieges were increasingly protracted to their inevitable and very brutal conclusion (Rothenberg 1980: 222–3; Best 1982: 101–2; Childs 1991: 139–40; O'Connell 1989: 161–2).

of war could be passed on to third parties, met in other ways, or simply evaded. This phenomenon, which we shall term 'fiscal deflection', took many forms, but the consequence was generally to reduce the degree of political or operational control that rulers could exercise over their troops and this often led to a substantial increase in consequential costs.

The operational costs of aggressive war could be reduced or eliminated by feeding the troops at the enemy's expense, and a successful plundering expedition might even turn in a profit, but there remained the problem of meeting troop and capital costs. Military service could be obtained in exchange for entitlements to land or other resources in kind, even in a monetary economy. Entitlements of this kind were evidently used in the later Roman period, at least for the support of frontier troops, and they were reintroduced into Sweden in the later seventeenth century. The use of entitlements in such circumstances reduced the burden on the treasury by eliminating the administrative costs of raising and disbursing revenue, but they imposed costs of their own in the form of limited service obligations and other operational rigidities. The allocation of large amounts of land or other resources to provincial commanders or magnates also carried potential political dangers.

Compulsion provided an alternative to entitlement in some circumstances. General levies were of little military value in themselves, but the principle could be invoked to justify selective compulsion at below the 'true' basic wage cost, whilst conquerors rarely needed any justification to impose obligations on their subject peoples. The need for compulsion arose where the basic wage, as we defined it, was higher than rulers were willing or able to pay, and the available entitlements were inadequate. This happened on a large scale in the later Roman Empire where forced recruitment seems to have been widespread under Diocletian and his immediate successors. It re-emerged to a lesser degree in *ancien régime* Europe, particularly in France, where military expansion under Louis XIV was accompanied by substantial cuts in the real value of soldiers' wages at a time when civilian wages were rising (Allen 2001; Lynn 1997: 148–9). The consequent failure of voluntary recruitment led the authorities to exploit militia service obligations as a form of *de facto* conscription to the regular army.

The expansion of the eighteenth-century Prussian army also relied in part on conscription, but compulsion was not a very effective solution to the problem of excessive troop costs and it was rarely the primary means of recruitment. Rounding up forced recruits and stopping them from deserting once they had reached their units required a coercive apparatus which was itself expensive to establish and maintain. Few states had the administrative means to force large numbers of men into the ranks on a systematic basis and the task had to be devolved to local communities or elites. The resulting drafts usually consisted of the men whom their neighbours or social superiors wished to be rid of and these were rarely high-quality troops. Compulsion only became a practicable basis for recruiting large numbers of troops of adequate quality in the nineteenth century, when rulers disposed of substantially greater administrative resources than had their early modern predecessors.[23] Before this skilled soldiers had to be induced to enlist, or raw recruits had to be trained and disciplined at their new employer's expense.

An alternative means of deflecting troop costs from the central treasury was simply to default on wage payments. Late or non-existent pay was an almost universal feature of early modern military life, and the scale of the problem is such as to make it effectively impossible to calculate how much the soldiers of any contemporary army received from their paymasters even where we have detailed knowledge of the wages to which they were entitled. Default of this kind reduced the burden on a ruler's treasury but just like defaulting on debt it had serious longer-term consequences. Unpaid troops, particularly mercenaries, characteristically made up the shortfall in their incomes by extensive plundering. Default was therefore a means of converting rulers' immediate troop costs into consequential costs for the inhabitants of the regions concerned, but it also reduced an army's military effectiveness. Unpaid troops were prone to desertion and mutiny, whilst excessive plundering could damage the war effort by destroying logistically important resources and undermining a ruler's political support.

Neither compulsion nor default provided an adequate alternative to meeting quality costs in cash. Skills could not be created by force and considerable efforts seem to have been made to pay the most experienced units on a reasonably regular basis. Quality costs could, however, be deflected wholly or in part, through the principle of devolution. The frequency with which this principle recurs in military affairs throughout the period is largely explained by the prospects it offered for passing on both skill and organization costs. A degree of devolution was virtually universal. Even in organized states with standing armies, recruiters supplemented their official powers by exploiting personal networks and allegiances, whether local or based on past campaigns. Where the principle was highly developed, soldiers' principal loyalty was to their immediate commander rather than to the ruler or to the state he headed. Depending on the circumstances these might be barbarian war leaders, regional magnates, or military brokers at any level from company commander to entrepreneurial general. What united these otherwise diverse figures was their access to recruiting channels based on such social assets as affinity or clientage networks, local or ethnic solidarities, or the power of personal reputation.

All of these assets existed outside either the impersonal cash nexus of the market, or the bureaucratic apparatus of the state. By devolving military responsibility to men who could exploit them, rulers could avoid the need to meet some, or all, of their troop costs in fiscal terms. Recruiting troops from the barbarian periphery was cheap for reasons that we have already encountered. It was very

---

[23] There are some limited exceptions to this generalization of which the most important occurred where relevant skills existed in civilian life, as in the case of naval recruitment. The British navy in particular relied on 'impressing' experienced sailors from the merchant marine in time of war. Captured soldiers might also be conscripted by their captors, as the Romans often did with conquered barbarians.

inefficient for the state to train up raw units and disband them after a single campaign, and very expensive to keep them on foot in peacetime. Mercenaries, by contrast, could offer military effectiveness cheaply because they had the prospect of lengthy periods of near continuous employment. They did not have to recover the value of their training and experience in a relatively short period, but most rulers had to rely on brokers to recruit such men in the time required. Military brokers offered the prospect of raising experienced, equipped, and ready-organized troops under competent commanders, without paying the fiscal costs of an extensive recruitment apparatus or a standing army. Reliance on brokers was, however, a dangerous procedure. The Roman elite lost their military, and eventually their political, leadership in the west through devolution to the leaders of Germanic warbands. Early modern mercenary commanders rarely assumed political power on any substantial scale—though Wallenstein may have come close—but their troops were poorly disciplined off the battlefield and inflicted substantial consequential costs on their employers' subjects and their property.

12.4. CONCLUSION

Preparing and waging war consumed resources directly and through the damage it inflicted on civilian life and property. Equipment and military capital goods had to be built, maintained, and replaced. Animals had to be procured and fed, and the troops themselves had to be paid or otherwise rewarded. The costs of raising and maintaining troops depended on a range of factors. Experience, skill, and greater responsibility commanded premiums as they did in the civilian economy, but in other respects the determinants of military and civilian reward diverged. Soldiering by its nature involved violence and exposure to danger and so imposed a potential 'disutility' whose reality varied with the social context. Where civilian society offered a valued prospect of safety and a settled life, recruitment required an offsetting 'military premium' if men were not to be forced into the army against their will. Conversely, where warrior values prevailed, or civilian society was itself insecure and dangerous, the conditions of military life might be a positive attraction. In other circumstances voluntary recruits had to be offered at least as big a reward as they would obtain in civilian life, and since soldiers were economically unproductive this made for a perverse relationship between troop costs and economic growth. This, together with the problem of the military premium, made barbarian and other peripheral regions extremely attractive as recruiting grounds.

Recruitment was undertaken by a variety of institutional means, and rewards could take many forms beyond cash payment, but most of the alternatives came with strings attached in the form of geographical or time limits to the service that was owed. The payment of wages gave commanders a degree of flexibility that made it an intrinsically desirable basis for recruitment providing that the necessary funds could be obtained. Throughout the period rulers tried to lessen the burden on the central treasury by devolving administrative and other responsibilities, with their associated costs, to officials acting in a private capacity or to figures altogether outside the administrative apparatus. Devolution of this kind reduced fiscal costs, but it did so by converting or passing them on, not by eliminating them. Ultimately the costs had to be met in some form and by someone. Pre-existing units recruited with their own leaders had greater bargaining power vis-à-vis their employers and might set themselves up as independent agents, or even seize power in the state by deposing their nominal employers. Smaller-scale military brokers presented fewer political risks but enjoyed all the advantages of middlemen in an opaque market and often provided shoddy goods at inflated prices. Devolution to magnates sometimes cemented political alliances to a ruler's benefit, or concentrated military force in the hands of existing allies, but it carried the risk of defection and the possibility that a politically indispensable ally might prove an indifferent or worse commander. Entrusting military power to foreign, or barbarian, mercenary leaders might enhance a ruler's personal security, where political leadership was a monopoly of the native elite, but if this monopoly could not be enforced in practice it could result in the wholesale displacement of that elite.

The practical consequences of the devolutionary principle show that in military affairs, if not in the history of economic growth, there were indeed no free lunches.[24] Training, equipping, and administering effective fighting units imposed costs of a kind that states based on organic economies had great difficulty in meeting. The difficulties did not have to be insuperable, at least in the short term, as was demonstrated in *ancien régime* Europe, but they were serious. Devolution offered the prospect of avoiding them by passing responsibility outside the state apparatus, but there was still a cost that had to be met, and how it was paid and by whom depended on the nature of the devolution question. Devolution to magnates enabled political capital, whether symbolic or more concrete, to be realized in military form if these men could be induced to shoulder part of the financial burdens, but some of the costs reverted to the state in the form of reduced military effectiveness and increased political risk. Reliance on mercenary commanders externalized the costs of recruitment and training, but likewise carried political risks. It also rendered the military market more opaque by reducing rulers' ability to influence or predict the quality and quantity of troops that they would eventually find at their disposal.

---

[24] Thompson makes this point very effectively with reference to Habsburg Spain where, he argues, the 'Military Revolution was from the financial point of view a redeployment of the costs of war between society and the state, a transfer between the social and the public accounts. The cost of "feudal" warfare of the sort that was still so important in the Conquest of Granada was a charge on the economy levied directly through the social system; the cost of war in the Military Revolution was a charge on the economy levied by the state through the fiscal system. Government budgets, therefore, inevitably, exaggerate the costliness of war in the age of the Military Revolution compared with "feudal" war... But government budgets also *understate* the cost of war, for the unaccounted social costs of war in this period did not disappear; they were simply levied in a different way' (Thompson 1995: 289).

Devolution enabled training, equipment, and organization costs to be passed on to military entrepreneurs, or other figures who could meet them more cheaply than could the state apparatus, even where such a thing existed and was equal to the task. The resulting forces were often very effective on the battlefield. But devolution provided no answer to the problem of discipline costs. Off the battlefield, barbarian warbands and mercenary units with their own commanders were notoriously prone to looting and other forms of indiscipline. In addition, many rulers, particularly in early modern Europe, either could not or would not meet the organization costs needed to provide their troops with regular and effective pay and supplies. When they were not forthcoming the troops recouped them from the inhabitants of the war zone in the form of loot. Like discipline costs, these unmet organization costs simply became consequential costs laid on the civilian population. Mercenary rapacity and the suffering of civilians were measures of the failure, or inability, of rulers to bear the immediate costs of their military ambitions.

CHAPTER THIRTEEN

Population, Power, and Technology

The components of armed force are technology, manpower, and economic resources of various kinds. Committing manpower and economic resources to war requires diverting them from the productive economy. Men actively bearing arms are not available for productive work, and even in peacetime their military role may withdraw them from the productive economy to varying degrees.[1] Raising troops from the domestic population therefore involves an additional cost in terms of production forgone, and it is a cost whose level rises with the level of labour productivity per capita. The volume of resources available for military purposes, however, rises with the level of total production, and since population growth affected these two quantities in different ways, so the economically optimal combination of army size and investment per soldier varied between the phases of the demographic cycle in organic economies.

This economically optimal combination was of course simply the one that the civilian economy was best suited to provide. There was no guarantee that it would provide an optimal level of military effectiveness, or even one that was acceptable in the prevailing circumstances. Optimal military effectiveness required the commitment of manpower and resources in ratios that varied with military technology and the nature of the opposition rather than that of the civilian economy or the demographic cycle.[2] In practice, military demand generally 'trumped' economic supply because rulers usually decided what forces they required according to the criteria of security or military ambition and only worried about what they could afford when the money began to run out. The degree of 'fit' that existed between actual patterns of military resource and manpower investment and those

---

[1] Where troops served for cash wages in monetarized economies much of the value of lost production would actually be met through the military wage bill, although the lost production might still deplete the revenue base. Recruiting foreign mercenaries was one way of avoiding the latter problem but mercenaries still had to be paid, and for the most part their wages derived ultimately from the labour of the domestic population. Total troop strengths therefore reflect the general burden the latter had to bear, and the proportionate relationship between the two indicates a ruler's ability to extract military force from a given demographic base.

[2] 'Military effectiveness' in this context, as throughout the chapter, refers to effectiveness on the narrowly military, or 'agonistic', criterion which simply requires an army to be able to beat its opponents rather than to serve as an effective political instrument.

predicted from any theoretical model of population and economy is therefore a historical question that can only be resolved from evidence.

The available evidence is, unfortunately, relatively scanty and of poor quality. It is difficult to quantify investment, even in principle, in economies that were only weakly monetarized. Even where cash transactions were widespread the available data rarely allow precise measurement, but it is nonetheless possible in both cases to form some impression of likely trends from what we know of changes in military equipment and the prevalence of military capital goods. The position is much simpler in principle on the manpower side, but there are still formidable practical difficulties. Different societies had very different systems for recruiting and maintaining troops, and few have left accurate records, but again there is enough information to allow a rough impression of changing force levels and their relationship to population trends over lengthy periods.

The results suggest that actual changes in the level of investment and manpower commitment to military goals conformed broadly to the theoretical expectation for much of the period, but there are at least two episodes in which this conformity seems to have broken down. The first of these, in the later Roman period, is very poorly documented but circumstances apparently forced an expansion in numbers that ran against the trend of the demographic cycle and beyond what the economy could support in any form compatible with the existing political structure. The gunpowder revolution ushered in a second period in which military demands diverged from what the demographic conjuncture was best suited to offer. The new military technology altered the relationship between scale, investment, and military effectiveness so as to demand increased investment per soldier at a time when economic logic favoured large cheap armies and subsequently to favour quantitative expansion at a time when manpower was relatively expensive.

13.1. MILITARY MANPOWER AND INVESTMENT: A MODEL

The concrete relationships between population growth and the commitment of manpower and resources to war are complex, but as is often the case a schematic abstraction can help elucidate their salient features. The French demographic economist Alfred Sauvy constructed a form of optimum population model which does this very well. It is based on the classical population model which we have already encountered (see above, Chapter 2) and incorporates the assumptions of diminishing marginal returns to labour and the existence of a 'subsistence minimum' level of output that workers need to consume in order to function efficiently. If they do not receive this level their output declines, but everything above it is available for the pursuit of what Sauvy calls 'power' and defines in a very general sense as any *collective aim* which may or may not take the form of armament' (Sauvy 1969: 51).

The volume of available power is therefore equivalent to the total volume of output after the necessary deductions for the workers' subsistence. This volume of power increases with population growth, even as marginal and average productivity decline, until marginal productivity falls to the subsistence minimum at a point corresponding to P(p) in Fig. 13.1. This point represents the 'power optimum' population size because any additional workers will need to consume more than they can produce and so deplete the volume of available power. The fact that P(p) lies where it does on the horizontal axis is a matter of some importance because it is substantially above the point where *average* output, and thus average living standards, reach their peak. This reveals a basic conflict of demographic interest between rulers and ruled, inasmuch as the latter have an interest in a higher standard of living and the former in a larger volume of power.[3]

P(p) represents the population size that maximizes total output net of subsistence requirements, but it makes no allowance for the recruitment of soldiers. The 'military optimum' population size, defined as the population size that maximizes military force, is therefore given by the expression:

$$P(mil) = P(p) + N(s)$$

where N(s) is the army size that maximizes military power given the prevailing military technology and the volume of resources available. The army draws on these resources in two ways. Soldiers need to consume a certain minimum level of resources which is assumed to equal the subsistence minimum of civilian workers. Resources are also needed for 'investment' in the various additional troop and capital costs that we considered in the previous chapter. Since the volume of available power is fixed there is a necessary trade-off between what goes to the soldiers' subsistence and what is available for investment. If investment is increased then less will be available for subsistence and so armies will be smaller but better trained and equipped.

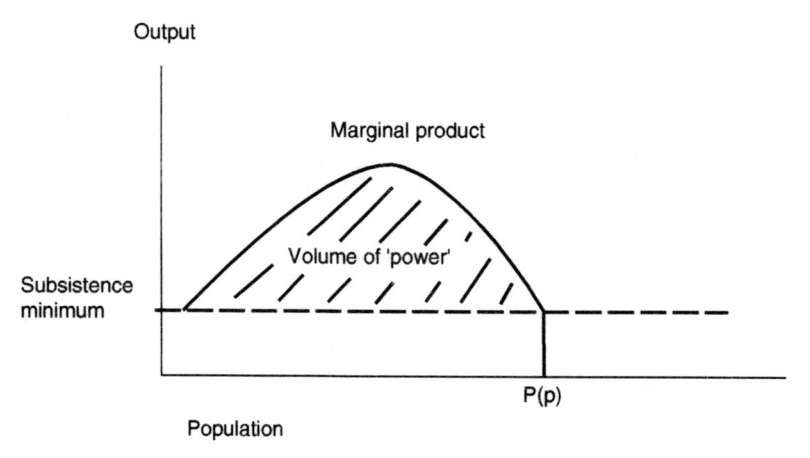

FIG. 13.1. Sauvy's model of the 'power optimum' population.
Source: Based on Sauvy (1969: fig. 18).

---

[3] Another way of expressing this is Lindegren's comment that, for early modern rulers, poverty was 'a resource' (Lindegren 2000).

The problem of determining N(s) is therefore one of finding the optimum allocation of power between military subsistence and investment, or the best balance of troop quantity and quality. Sauvy assumed that the optimum level of investment per soldier, termed K^, was fixed by the prevailing military technology and was capable of being known. K^ ranges between theoretical limits of infinity and zero. In a science fiction world of robotic weapon systems human soldiers would be redundant so N(s) would be zero, K^ infinite, and P(mil) would equal P(p). At the other extreme is a hypothetical 'technology free' world where disorganized bands of untrained men fight each other barehanded. In this case there are no opportunities for military investment, so K^ is zero and the entire output of the economy is devoted to the production of subsistence resources. P(mil) now approaches P(max), which is the greatest number the economy can support with living standards at the subsistence minimum. In reality K^ will always be finite and greater than zero, so P(mil) will be smaller than P(max), implying that overpopulation always has the potential to impede military as well as economic effectiveness.

Sauvy's intention was to find the population size yielding the maximum military force for a given technology, but in practice we usually want to approach the problem from the other direction because rulers could not fix the size of their population, though they might seek to influence it. The model's main interest lies in what it tells us about the likely effects of population change on relative troop strengths and levels of investment per soldier. This can be determined quite easily if we make the simplifying assumptions that the population is closed and that relative wage levels allocate males of military age either to the labour force or to the army. Where population size is greater than P(p) the position is quite straightforward. Marginal productivity is below the subsistence minimum so no extra workers will be hired and any more adult males will have to join the army or starve. Beyond this point soldiers can therefore be recruited at a wage equal to the subsistence minimum, and their numbers will increase relative to population size,[4] but the volume of 'power' remains unchanged and so this subsistence is deducted from the share going to investment. We should therefore expect to see ever-larger armies with progressively lower standards of training and equipment as population growth proceeds.

The position is similar where population size is below the point of declining marginal productivity and classical underpopulation prevails. Each additional soldier recruited now depresses marginal productivity further, so the 'comparator element' of the military wage falls. Recruitment therefore becomes cheaper as the army gets bigger, but there are fewer and fewer resources available for investment in training and equipment. Circumstances of this kind are likely to have prevailed in many barbarian societies, but things are very different when population size is

---

[4] For simplicity we treat subsistence costs as part of the wage. If the authorities issued food, clothing, and accommodation in kind they would, in theory, be able to recruit without having to pay any wages at all once population size exceeded P(p). The additional adult males are in fact analogous to the hearth model's 'marginal' population whose disproportionate growth was highlighted in Chapter 2.

in the region of diminishing marginal returns below P(p). In this case, every additional soldier recruited now depletes the productive population and reduces the volume of power available. The market alone will retain the whole male population in the productive economy, and so military recruiters will either have to outmatch relatively high civilian wages or use coercion. Since military recruitment reduces the size of the labour force things can only get worse, because marginal productivity will rise, increasing both civilian wages and the costs of recruiting and retaining troops. This imposes a potentially severe constraint on growth in troop numbers, but since productivity remains high there will be a relative abundance of resources available for investment, so we would expect to find small high-quality armies as a result.

The model's predictions can be expressed very simply. Manpower can be recruited cheaply when the marginal productivity of labour falls below subsistence requirements, but there will be a growing scarcity of resources for investment in troop quality. The position is similar when marginal productivity is rising, but manpower will be expensive and investment relatively easy to procure when population is in the 'comfort zone' between the two. If procurement strategies followed this simple 'supply-side' logic quality and relative quantity should be traded off as marginal productivity varied between demographic peaks and troughs, but even in these schematic terms we can identify a number of factors that might stop this happening. In particular, the classical model assigns a driving role to wages and marginal productivity that may be inappropriate for pre-industrial economies with weakly developed labour markets. In peasant economies the maintenance of the family farm labour force might, as we saw earlier, assume a priority capable of overriding strict market calculations and cause labour to be retained beyond the point where marginal productivity fell below subsistence. Military recruitment would then require coercion or premium payments even though population size was above P(p).

It might also be desirable from a narrowly military point of view to retain some of the surplus men in the productive economy, since there they will produce at least some of their own subsistence and so free resources for investment in a smaller but qualitatively superior army. The practicability of this would depend on institutional factors outside the scope of the model, but it would be relatively straightforward where the state controlled large agricultural estates and workshops. In other circumstances, however, military expansion provided an attractive solution to the problems posed to rulers by an underemployed surplus population, as well as an attractive avenue of escape from such a condition for the ruled themselves. The effects of quantitative expansion on overall military effectiveness were very hard to gauge at the margin, and so a deliberate restriction of army size was potentially risky if the opponent was not doing the same. Indeed the pressure is more likely to have been to do the opposite under these circumstances, and try to make up for deficient quality with greater quantity. This is because, if total investment remains constant, a given proportionate change in army size has a smaller absolute effect on the level of investment per soldier where this is already low than it does when it is high. In other words, when manpower is abundant and the quality of training and equipment is already mediocre there is relatively little to be lost by expanding numbers or to be gained by cutting back.

13.2. MANPOWER COMMITMENTS

The schematic model set out in the previous section predicts that the relative size of armed forces should change with changing demographic conditions. It is difficult to determine how far this prediction is borne out in historical experience. This is due partly to the dearth of surviving evidence, but it also reflects the fact that reality is much more complex than the simplified abstraction embodied in the model discussed above. Quantitatively speaking, military manpower commitments varied greatly in both absolute and relative terms, but the nature of the commitment also varied, and if we are to understand the demographic burden imposed by war-related activities, we have to deal with questions of definition as well as measurement. The obvious distinction is that between states that maintained standing armies in peacetime and those that relied on forces raised for specific campaigns (or 'campaign armies'). Many ancient states maintained standing armies, and in modern times they have become one of the defining characteristics of state organization. In principle it is relatively straightforward to measure manpower commitments where such forces exist. We need only multiply the established strength of each type of unit by the numbers of such units in the army's order of battle. The reality is more complicated, because actual strengths often fell substantially below authorized 'paper' strengths, particularly in peacetime, and even regular soldiers in permanent units might spend some of their peacetime hours in civilian occupations, as they did, for example, in eighteenth-century Prussia (Showalter 1996: 23–4). The man-hours withdrawn from the productive economy might therefore be far fewer than would appear at first sight.

Peacetime standing armies were often expanded substantially in wartime, when numbers fluctuated with attrition from disease, desertion, or combat losses. Even where accurate figures exist for the opening of a campaign they can therefore be unreliable guides to subsequent strengths. Such figures are nonetheless valuable for a number of reasons. They indicate the levels of recruitment that were undertaken prior to active operations, and they set a base threshold to the numbers experiencing service at some point in their life. They also throw light on the financial burden that the authorities had to shoulder. Where units were raised for specific campaigns, particularly in the early modern period, a large fraction of troop costs might consist of bounties and other recruitment expenses that were paid 'up front' and were unrelated to the actual duration of a man's service (Parrott 2001: 339–40; Anderson 1988: 121; Lynn 1997: 351–4). In addition, subordinate commanders often appropriated pay and allowances for 'paper' soldiers, who had died, deserted, or never existed in the first place, and so the shortfall in effective numbers did not always reduce the pay bill proportionately.

In the medieval west campaign armies were the rule, and it is correspondingly more difficult to gauge the manpower levels. Peacetime commitments were low, but not necessarily zero even without a formal military establishment. Most rulers kept some men more or less permanently under arms, if only as household guards, and peacetime garrisons were usually maintained at key strong points. Exposed frontiers often had *de facto* permanent military establishments under the command of regional magnates. Behind these usually very small forces was a much larger echelon composed of men whose liability to serve at need kept them outside the peacetime productive economy. The extent of this commitment is measurable in theory, but in practice the necessary data do not exist. Actual wartime levels can be gauged in some cases with varying degrees of accuracy. Such reasonably robust figures as exist usually refer to the initial strength of the main campaign armies and are likely to reflect high estimates of manpower peaks. This limits but does not negate their value as indicators of long-term trends. Peak to peak comparisons are a perfectly valid means of tracking such trends in time series that also display shorter-term fluctuations, providing that we remain clear on what precisely it is that is being measured.

13.2.1. ROME AND BYZANTIUM

The Emperor Augustus reorganized Roman military and political institutions following his victory over Mark Antony in 31 BC which concluded the civil wars of the late Republic. Many of the troops that had fought them were stood down and the remainder drafted into a standing force of long-service professionals. At the same time the previous more or less ad hoc arrangements for raising cavalry and light troops from allied or conquered peoples were replaced by a permanent force of regularly organized and equipped units, the *auxilia*. This is the earliest point at which we can form a reasonably reliable estimate of the overall establishment of a western standing army, and forms a natural starting point for any survey of changing force levels. Initially standing at twenty-eight, the legionary establishment rose to the equivalent of thirty-five by c. AD 235 on the eve of the third-century political and military crises (Treadgold 1995: 45). At full strength, with 5,500 men per legion and a matching number in the *auxilia*, the total forces available at the two dates would have come to around 310,000 and 385,000, equivalent to some 0.7 and 0.8 per cent of the total population.[5] Actual numbers are, of course, a different matter. They doubtless fluctuated over time as they did in later periods, but the paper totals indicate the scale of the manpower targets that the authorities aimed at, and serious attempts do seem to have been made to bring units up to strength before major campaigns (Elton 1996: 153–4, 227–8).

---

[5] The Augustan legions comprised ten cohorts. Nine of these numbered 480 men, whilst the first, for at least some of the period, was apparently double strength. The *auxilia* order of battle is not known in detail, but it is generally assumed that the two echelons were of approximately equal size. McEvedy's population total of forty-six million for c. AD 200 is used for both dates (McEvedy and Jones 1978: 21).

The temporary collapse of Roman arms in the third century precipitated far-reaching military and political changes. The reforms of Diocletian and his successors in the later Empire, or 'Dominate', produced a more complex and variegated military establishment, many aspects of which remain obscure. The main source of documentary information is the *Notitia Dignitatum*, a list of official positions in the civilian and military administration whose surviving folios derive from different periods in the western and eastern halves of the Empire (Goodburn and Bartholomew 1976; Mann 1991). The western sections date from the fifth century, by which time much of the army there had been destroyed, but the eastern material derives from the eve of the great invasions in the 390s. If the reconstruction they allow is accurate, the eastern armies are likely to have numbered a little over 300,000 men, about a third of them in the field armies, and the remainder in the frontier force.[6] The contemporary western establishment was probably about the same size.

The western army disappeared with the Empire it served in the course of the fifth century, but the Eastern, or 'Byzantine', Empire survived, in one form or another, until the fifteenth century. Treadgold has produced a series of estimates of eastern troop strengths from 284 until the 1020s, when the regular, native, army of Byzantium began to disintegrate. Their interpretation is complicated by the fact that the sixth-century frontier troops had to supplement their military wages from other sources in order to survive, and the territorial forces of the later military districts, or *themes*, relied on income from military lands. The totals for these 'part-time' troops, as Treadgold calls them, have been arbitrarily discounted by a half in order to arrive at the 'full-time equivalent' percentages in the right-hand column of Table 13.1. This may be too large a discount since thematic troops constituted the army's main echelon for much of the period. Certainly the early eleventh-century army was a heavier burden than the Empire could support. A substantial reduction ensued, followed by military disaster at Turkish hands in the 1070s. The later Byzantine Empire proved surprisingly resilient, but the old military establishment was never restored and the emperors relied increasingly on fluctuating numbers of foreign mercenaries and an increasingly desperate series of ad hoc military expedients (Bartusis 1992).

13.2.2. THE MEDIEVAL WEST

The armies of the medieval west consisted mainly of feudal levies supplemented or supplanted by mercenaries raised for specific campaigns, with very small numbers of men retained permanently under arms in time of peace. Such figures as we have therefore relate to the size of specific campaign armies, and reasonably reliable estimates are notoriously hard to come by. Few seem to have exceeded

---

[6] This reconstruction is derived from Treadgold (1995: 45–9). Elton observes simply that the Roman army of AD 350–425 'was at least 300,000 and may have been 600,000 strong' (Elton 1996: 128), though elsewhere (p. 120) he regards 450,000 as a 'reasonable' estimate of the paper establishment.

Table 13.1 *Estimated east Roman and Byzantine troop strengths*

Year	Population (millions)	Full-time soldiers Absolute	% pop.	Part-time soldiers Absolute	% pop.	Total % pop.
284	19.0	253,000	1.3			1.3
305	19.0	311,000	1.6			1.6
395	16.5	335,000	2.0	—		2.0
518	19.5	95,300	0.5	206,000[a]	1.1	1.1
540	26.0	145,300	0.6	229,000[a]	0.9	1.1
565	19.5	150,030	0.8	229,000[a]	1.2	1.4
641	10.5	109,000	1.0	20,000[b]	0.2	1.1
775	7.0	18,400	0.3	100,100[c]	1.4	1.0
842	8.0	24,400	0.3	130,200[c]	1.6	1.1
959	9.0	29,200	0.3	150,200[c]	1.7	1.2
1025	12.0	43,200	0.4	240,000[c]	2.0	1.4

[a] Includes frontier troops and oarsmen.
[b] Includes oarsmen.
[c] Includes thematic troops and oarsmen.

Source: Treadgold (1995).

10,000 before the thirteenth century, and many were much smaller.[7] In some regions, chiefly those where the lands of Christian rulers bordered Muslim or pagan territories, their troops were supported by those of the crusading orders, technically monks or their lay affiliates, who were available to fight in royal armies. Charlemagne may have been able to raise as many as 100,000 troops across his Empire. This would correspond to about 1 per cent of a population that probably totalled around ten million people (Pounds 1973: 182–4; Contamine 1984: 25–6), but it is difficult to relate such evidence as we have on changing troop strengths to the economic and demographic base of continental rulers because of the period's shifting and fragmented political geography.

England, by contrast, experienced few changes in its territorial boundaries after c.1000, and major breakdowns of central control were rare.[8] The English evidence is therefore of particular interest and allows rough orders of magnitude to be tracked at intervals from the eve of the Norman Conquest. At this point, the kingdom's forces consisted of a small elite of 'huscarls', who were permanently retained in the households of the king and regional magnates, backed by a main echelon of reasonably well-equipped warriors recruited through tenurial or territorial quotas. The men of this 'select fyrd' were liable for general service when needed and may

---

[7] The army of the First Crusade, at the end of the 11th century, was clearly much bigger than this but was drawn from a wide area of west and central Europe. Its numbers have often been put at some 30,000, but Bachrach has recently given credence to the contemporary figure of 100,000 (Bachrach 1999).

[8] England's northern border assumed its present form in the course of the 12th century as Cumbria was gained and north-eastern territory conceded to Scotland. The shifting dominion of the English crown outside England itself does not greatly affect this analysis, with the partial exception of Wales which did serve as an important reservoir of military manpower in the later Middle Ages.

have been supported by a third echelon, the 'great fyrd', consisting of a general levy of the inhabitants of threatened districts. The institutional basis of select fyrd service remains controversial, but surviving documentary evidence from Berkshire reveals that there one man was required for each five 'hides' of tenanted land (Hollister 1962: 80–1). This should have yielded around 500 men, equivalent to some 8 per cent of the Domesday enumeration, or perhaps 1.5 per cent of the total population. If this relatively large percentage were applied to the country as a whole it would yield a theoretical total of at least 20,000 to 30,000 for the select fyrd alone. The evidence from the campaigns of 1066, however, suggests that no more than 15,000 men in all marched in defence of the kingdom.[9]

In principle the Anglo-Norman military organization was built around the heavy cavalry provided by the king's lay and ecclesiastical tenants under their feudal service obligation or *servitia debitum*. Again in principle, this should have furnished the king with around 5,000 knights, backed by a service obligation of some kind on the free peasantry. If the latter corresponded to the old select fyrd obligation, then the forces theoretically available should have been very powerful and a correspondingly heavy burden on the country's productive economy. The scanty evidence for the two post-Conquest centuries is, however, sufficient to demonstrate that nothing like these force levels were available in practice. For most of the period, English kings disposed of small numbers of men, and the feudal host had only a limited operational role. Major lay tenants served in person, but they often did so with only a few followers and commuted much of their service obligation (whose actual level was often a source of dispute) to cash payments which the king used to hire mercenaries. Similarly, whilst 'native' English troops evidently lent militarily important support to the early Anglo-Norman kings, by the twelfth century whatever remained of the old select fyrd had dwindled to insignificance with the progressive erosion of the numbers and standing of the free peasantry on which it depended.

The knights actually serving at any time seem to have numbered only in the hundreds, and it is doubtful if the kings of this period disposed of more than a few thousand men in practice. These levels contrast sharply with those attained in the years c.1290–1360, a period for which relatively good data survive in the form of central payroll accounts (Prince 1931; Prestwich 1996). These show a dramatic expansion, most of which is accounted for by the better-documented infantry. The Welsh wars of Edward I saw peak totals over 15,000 in the 1277/8 campaign, and more than 30,000 in November 1294—equivalent to around 0.6 per cent of the contemporary English population (Dyer 1989: 4). In 1298 the Falkirk campaign amassed over 25,000 infantry and an estimated 4,000 heavy cavalry. Numbers declined substantially in the closing, debt-ridden years of the reign,

---

[9] This assertion is based simply on the conventional range of estimates for the strength of the English army at Hastings and the contemporary claim that Harold had brought only half his strength with him. As such, it does not allow for the northern army which was defeated by the Danes and so may be on the low side. On the other hand the claim that Harold had left half his force behind may well be an exaggeration. For some views of the battle and campaign see Morillo (1996).

but 15,000 infantry are thought to have been mobilized for Edward II's Bannockburn campaign and around 20,000 in 1322. The numbers of men fielded in continental campaigns were generally lower, affected as they were by the costs of sea transport. Nonetheless, armies of around 10,000 men were assembled for the campaigns of 1346/7 and 1359/60, and at least 25,000 men—perhaps more than 30,000—were concentrated for the Calais siege in 1347. Thereafter there was a clear overall decline in the size of English armies. Richard II is said to have taken 14,000 men to Scotland in 1385, but the French expeditions of the 1370s were in the range 4,000–6,000 (Ayton 1994b: 29). Some 10,000 men were assembled for French campaigns in 1415, 1417, and 1475,[10] but most fifteenth-century expeditions numbered fewer than 5,000 men, and in 1433 total English manpower in France was put at between 7,000 and 8,000.

13.2.3. THE MODERN PERIOD

The modern period in Europe saw the reappearance of regular, standing armies. The quantity and quality of documentary sources were transformed in consequence, and this makes it much easier to gauge the scale of military forces. Many more or less well-founded estimates exist, but interpretative difficulties remain, and they are particularly troublesome for the sixteenth and seventeenth centuries when military administration was less developed, discipline more lax, and the volume of surviving records generally smaller than they were later to become. The figures for this period need therefore to be treated with particular caution, but the long-term trend is not in doubt. Numbers rose substantially in the three centuries after 1490, although the increase was neither regular nor consistent. There were two waves of growth which, short-term reversals aside, were separated by an interval of stagnation or declining numbers between the latter phase of the Thirty Years War and the early campaigns of Louis XIV. The two waves correspond very roughly to the 'A' and 'B' phases of the early modern demographic cycle and for convenience we shall refer to them as the 'Habsburg century' and the 'Bourbon century' after their leading dynastic protagonists. The wars that followed the overthrow of the French Bourbons saw a new phase of expansion.

13.2.3.1. *The Habsburg century*

The scale of military manpower had already begun to increase before the Dutch Revolt against Spain initiated a new cycle of conflict in the 1560s.[11] It is difficult to

---

[10] Curry provides figures for expeditions to northern France in thirty-one years over the period 1415–50 (Curry 1994: 44–6). In no year after 1417 were more than 8,000 men dispatched, and this number was approached only in what the author terms the 'crisis' years of 1430 and 1436. In only twelve of the remaining twenty-seven years were the numbers in the 2,500–4,999 range, and in ten of them they fell below 1,000.

[11] For data on troop strengths in this period see Anderson (1988: 36–8), Hale (1985: 62–3), Tallett (1992: 4–13). Lynn (1997: 32–64) and Parrott (2001: 164–222) provide detailed studies of French troop strengths in the 17th century. The strength of the Dutch army is discussed by 't Hart (1995: 43–5).

date the beginning of the process with any certainty, and some expansion had already occurred in Spain before 1500. The numbers fielded are thought to have risen from 16,000–26,000 to 60,000 in the 1480s during the conquest of Granada, but Parker places the crucial developments in the 1530s. The Habsburg Emperor Charles V raised some 60,000 men in northern Italy in 1536–7, and within twenty years his forces had a payroll strength of 150,000. The Spanish Habsburgs, following the division of Charles's domain, marshalled much smaller forces at first, but the defence of their extensive possessions forced a continuing expansion. By the 1620s Philip IV could claim command of 300,000 men.[12] In France, wartime paper establishments rose from 41,000 in 1515 to at least 69,000 thirty years later and 80,000 by 1567–8.

The military establishment voted for by the Dutch Estates-General (known as the 'standing army') increased from 21,000 in 1588 to 32,000 by the late 1690s and more than 60,000 at the suspension of hostilities in 1609. When war returned twelve years later numbers were increased to 55,000, from the peacetime level of 30,000, and eventually to 75,000. Many paper soldiers marched in this host, but the establishment totals exclude numerous auxiliaries, mercenaries, and other short-term hirelings, who brought the actual payroll figure close to an unprecedented 130,000 men by 1629. Sweden emerged as a major power under Gustavus Adolphus in the early seventeenth century. Its army, which had numbered around 15,000 a century before, rose to include some 40,000 'native' troops by the 1630s, but German and other mercenaries brought the total force to a peak that may have reached 120,000 men.

The French monarchy, reconstructing after a period of civil war, may also have fielded over 100,000 men at times in the 1630s when it intervened in the Thirty Years War. On the other side of the Channel England established a large militia of doubtful quality in the mid-sixteenth century. The country remained predominantly unmilitarized in other respects although the seventeenth century saw periods of substantial military effort. Some 50,000 men were recruited for the debacles at Cadiz and La Rochelle in the 1620s, and an estimated 110,000 men were under arms within a year of the outbreak of civil war in the 1640s. At its close the victorious Republic retained a peacetime establishment of 34,000 men, although Parliament was informed in 1654 that there were actually 53,000 armed men throughout Great Britain.

This first phase of expansion had already reached its limit before the Thirty Years War concluded in 1648. The Dutch army wound down in the last years of the conflict with Spain. This was partly because it had less fighting to do, but the Spanish crown also seems to have controlled fewer troops at the end of the war in 1648 than it had in 1600. A widely quoted estimate credits Wallenstein, the Imperialist general, with as many as 150,000 troops in Germany around 1630.

---

[12] Thompson suggests simply that 'for perhaps two decades from the later 1620s the number of soldiers in Spanish service may again have reached, and perhaps gone beyond, the levels of 1552' (Thompson 1995: 283–4).

Eighteen years later the Imperialist total was less than half this, and their enemies, including both the Swedish and French armies, mustered no more than 140,000 in all (Parker 1984: 191). France retained powerful forces for the duration of the war and after the conclusion of peace, but its military effort of the 1630s was not matched for another generation.

13.2.3.2. *The Bourbon century*

The tempo of growth in the second phase differed between different regions of Europe and the dramatis personae also changed over time (see Table 13.2).[13] In the north and west it was the early decades that saw the greatest expansion. Louis XIV mobilized as many as 250,000 men for his attack on the Dutch in 1672 and actual strengths peaked at around 340,000 during the War of the League of Augsburg (1688–97). Thereafter the trend was downwards, and the 1690s peak was not approached again until the Seven Years War. The British army establishment

Table 13.2 Total troop strengths (000)

	Austria	Britain	France	The Netherlands	Prussia	Russia	Sweden	Spain
1690	50[a]			73[a]	30[e]	90[a]	90[c]	
1695		88[g]	340[f]					
1703								13[h]
1710	100[a]		255[f]	100[a]	39[a]	220[a]	110[c]	80[d]
1712		145[g]						
1725						215[c]		
1740	108[a]		160[a]		83[a]			
1746		78[g]						
1756	201[a]		330[a]	40[a]	143[a]	330[a]		
1762		121[g]						
1778	200[a]				160[a]			
1782		132[g]						
1786					194[b]			
1789		156[a]				500[a]		

Sources:
[a] Childs (1982: 42).
[b] Black (1990: 7).
[c] Anderson (1988: 84).
[d] Black (1990: 30).
[e] Tallet (1992: 8).
[f] Lynn (1997: 55).
[g] Floud, Wachter, and Gregory (1990: table 2.1 (figures for army establishment; 1782 effective strength 89,000)).
[h] Anderson (1988: 110).

[13] For discussions of changing European army sizes over this period see Childs (1982: 28–57) and Anderson (1988: 82–94). Brewer (1989: 29–42) considers British army and naval strengths, and Lynn (1997: 32–64) provides a detailed discussion of the French army up to 1715.

also peaked relatively early and it was not till the last decade of the eighteenth century that the 1712 total was surpassed.[14] The Netherlands and Sweden ceased to be major powers by the end of the eighteenth century, but both fielded powerful armies in its opening decades. The Dutch military establishment remained over 100,000 through the Spanish Succession War, a substantially larger number than the corresponding figure at the height of the struggle with Spain. Sweden also mobilized larger native forces for the Great Northern War (1700–21) than it had under Gustavus Adolphus.

Habsburg Spain went into military eclipse after 1660, but re-emerged under the Bourbons after 1700 as a second-rank power with around 80,000 troops. Elsewhere the main phase of expansion came later. The Austrian Habsburgs had broadened their territorial base at Turkish expense by 1720 when their army had a paper strength of 165,000. It rose to 200,000 in 1756 and 307,000 in 1783. Black accepts actual totals below 75,000 in 1733, around 108,000 in 1740, and 171,000 in 1775 (Black 1990: 91). New powers emerged on Europe's perimeter. The Prussian establishment doubled from 40,000 to 80,000 over the reign of Frederick William I (1713–40), and rose further from 143,000 to 260,000 in the course of the Seven Years War (1756–63). The Russian army, already 200,000 strong by 1720, more than doubled over the remainder of the century.

These totals predominantly represent peak wartime strengths, but the period also saw the proliferation of peacetime standing armies based around permanent regiments with an increasing degree of internal organization. Permanent forces were not completely new to post-classical Europe. In France their origin can be traced back to the *bandes d'ordonnances*, which were heavy cavalry units set up at the end of the Hundred Years War along with an archery militia, followed shortly by the establishment of a small standing force of infantry and cavalry. Units of this kind had, however, been no more than the nucleus of a war-fighting force, whilst the later seventeenth century saw the retention of substantial numbers of peacetime troops—some 25,000 by the Habsburg emperor and over 100,000 in France (Lynn 1997: 48–55). By the eighteenth century the continental peacetime establishments were generally equivalent to at least 25–50 per cent of wartime levels, supplemented by large militias of varying quality. Even in Britain, peacetime troop strengths rose in a so-called 'ratchet' pattern through the wars of the eighteenth century, with numbers expanding at the outbreak of hostilities and then remaining above their previous levels when peace returned. Britain's peacetime troops were, moreover, full-time soldiers, whereas continental powers sometimes released substantial numbers of men for civilian occupations whilst retaining them, nominally, on the peacetime strength.

---

[14] Figures for actual British strengths do not become available until the 1770s. Childs (1982: table 1, p. 42) gives larger figures for 1778 than 1710 (100,000 and 75,000 respectively), but the official effective strength for 1778 is only 53,302 and Jones defends a payroll strength for 1710 (including foreign troops in British service) of around 120,000 (Jones 1988). The trend in naval establishment figures, which are only available from 1715, differed from that of the army, with substantial growth occurring later in the century from a relatively low base.

13.2.3.3. After the Revolution

The overthrow of the French Bourbons led to large increases in the size of western European armies. The 1793 levies gave France itself an army of at least three-quarters of a million men. Ten years later Napoleon's army had less than half this number, but over 600,000 men were available in 1812 (some of them conscripted from annexed territories outside France itself) and an even larger number were mobilized the following year.[15] The size of the British forces also rose to an 1814 peak of over 420,000 men in the army, navy, and marines.[16] Spain too managed to field a much larger army, numbering some 150,000 men, to confront the French invasion of 1807 (Esdaile 1995: 40). Elsewhere, such increases in size as occurred seem to have been on a much smaller scale. Esdaile (p. 269) gives peak 1813 strengths as 270,000 for the Prussians, 296,000 for the Russians, and 250,000 for the Austrians;[17] the Swedes fielded no more than 50,000.

13.2.4. THE LONG TERM

The dearth of quantitative evidence and the changing structure of military institutions make it impossible to track long-term shifts in military manpower and investment with any precision, but some broad outlines are nonetheless discernible. At the opening of the period we have surveyed, Rome's standing army had a paper strength that was probably a little under 1 per cent of the early Empire population. By the early fourth century this proportion had apparently doubled in the eastern half, and it may have reached 2 per cent across the Empire by the 390s. Thereafter changes in both land area and military structures, and general uncertainty as to population totals, make the apparent trends difficult to interpret. Accepting Treadgold's population estimates and arbitrarily discounting his total 'part-time' soldiers by 50 per cent produces percentages that fluctuate between 1.0 and 1.4 with no clear pattern. The undiscounted percentages are naturally higher, rising to around 2 per cent in the period of recovery after AD 840, and an unsustainable 2.4 per cent early in the eleventh century.

The medieval west was relatively unmilitarized by late Roman and Byzantine standards. It had no standing armies, and if the forces gathered for specific campaigns are any guide, the number of reasonably well-trained and equipped fighting men was very small in relation to the population. The total military

---

[15] Esdaile indicates that the 1813 levy, which totalled 840,000 men, was almost wholly met, whilst Bonney cites an 1813 mobilization total of 1.1 million including non-French draftees (Bonney 1995c: 387; Esdaile 1995: 286).

[16] The total comprised 302,000 in the army and 126,000 in the navy and marines (Floud, Wachter, and Gregory 1990: tables 2.2 and 2.6). Comparable numbers were enrolled in part-time militia and volunteer units (Cookson 1997).

[17] Rothenberg gives larger totals for the Austrians. He credits them at the beginning of the campaign with '300,000 combat troops and a grand total of 480,000, raised by the winter of 1813 to 500,000' (Rothenberg 1980: 173). The Russians had also raised a militia force of 223,000 men to resist the French invasion in 1812 (Esdaile 1995: 254).

manpower of Charlemagne's Empire may have proportionately equalled, or even exceeded, that of the Principate, but his campaign armies seem never to have exceeded about 20,000 men (Contamine 1984: 25–6). The English sources provide evidence for a relative growth in peak manpower commitments as population expanded. Population probably doubled between c.1125 and c.1325, but the size of the larger campaign armies evidently rose by much more than this. No twelfth-century English army is likely to have reached the 10,000 mark, but several forces in the 15,000 to 30,000 range were raised in the years of demographic high tide from the reign of Edward I to the Black Death.[18] Thereafter, population probably fell by about half and remained at this level for much of the fifteenth century, but army sizes seem to have fallen disproportionately.

The first phase of modern expansion, which we termed the 'Habsburg century', is difficult to document quantitatively because the military organization and administration retained many medieval characteristics. Armies were often raised and disbanded campaign by campaign, and numbers fluctuated substantially. The figures for this period therefore represent peak estimates rather than the establishment totals available for ancient and more recent times, but such as they are they leave no doubt that peak commitments rose by much more than total population in the century or so after 1470. We are on firmer ground for the second phase, which we have called the 'Bourbon century'. Force totals can also be related to population size in some instances, although we should bear in mind that many countries fielded a large proportion of foreign mercenaries.

The results again emphasize the high levels of manpower commitment in the decades around 1700. French troop strengths were equivalent to some 1.5 per cent of the population in the 1690s, compared with only 1.3 per cent in the Seven Years War and lower levels in the intervening period. Britain's military establishment in 1712 equalled some 1.7 per cent of population, which was also higher than anything before the 1790s.[19] Some other states had very large percentages; both Sweden and the Dutch Republic fielded armies equal to more than 5 per cent of their population at this time but played little role in the century's later military history. The army totals for Russia and Spain are both equivalent to a little over 1 per cent of population, and Russia's military expansion more or less matched its population growth. The French Revolutionary and Napoleonic Wars saw substantial proportionate increases in manpower commitments. The French armies of 1793 were equal to at least 2.5 per cent of the country's population, from which—unlike Napoleon's troops—they were almost entirely derived. Britain's

---

[18] At this time an army of 25,000 men would have equalled some 0.4–0.6% of England's population—by comparison, Charlemagne's 20,000 probably represented about 0.2% of his Empire's population. Here, as throughout the early modern and *ancien régime* periods, the employment of variable, but often large, numbers of foreign mercenaries means that a force equivalent to a given percentage of the domestic population was not necessarily drawn from it in that proportion.

[19] Comparable percentages are obtained if we take the peak military establishment and naval effectives (given by Rodger 1986: 149) for the Seven Years War or the peak effectives for the American War in the 1780s. Since the 1712 figure relates only to the army, however, it seems safe to conclude that the overall commitment was greater at this point.

1814 peak of 420,000 full-time soldiers and sailors corresponded to around 2.2 per cent of its population.

13.2.4.1. Theory and evidence

This pattern is broadly consistent with the expectations of the Sauvy model over the millennium or so that separates the end of Roman rule in western Europe from the beginning of the sixteenth century. There can be little doubt that the fall in population was associated with a disproportionate fall in early medieval troop strengths. The model also predicts contemporary increases in the resources available for investment per soldier and the shift to heavy cavalry in the Frankish kingdoms involved corresponding growth in investment on a substantial scale.[20] The position in England at this time is obscure. Late pre-Conquest manpower levels may have been unusually high, but numbers fell substantially in the ensuing century along with the introduction of more resource intensive heavy cavalry. The demographic peak coincided with very large campaign armies, but they had a high proportion of poorly trained and equipped infantry who did not perform well on the battlefield (Prestwich 1996). Men-at-arms' equipment became heavier and more expensive, but their declining relative numbers seem certain to have offset this and to have reduced the overall level of investment per soldier.

The post-plague century saw the expected reversal of these trends. Troop numbers shrank disproportionately, but they were better trained and equipped and there can be little doubt that levels of investment rose. Men-at-arms constituted as much as a half of late fourteenth-century, and a quarter of early fifteenth-century, English armies, and the development of full plate armour increased the cost of their equipment correspondingly. At the same time, the infantry component was transformed, consisting now of highly trained archers who came equipped as mounted infantry off the battlefield.[21] This lengthy period was apparently one in which the quantity and quality of armed force were, on the whole, balanced in such a way as to accommodate changing levels of population and marginal productivity. These factors did not drive military changes any more than rulers necessarily lived, or fought, within their means. Military methods were preserved or altered in response to military success or failure, and overspending was always possible as long as credit was available, but the military technologies of this period do seem to have allowed acceptable, if not optimal, combinations of quality and quantity to be found within the envelope of sustainable possibilities offered by the state of the demographic cycle.

---

[20] This expectation is based on the assumption that the marginal productivity of labour rose at this time. Such an increase cannot be proved, but it is consistent with what is known of the period's agricultural developments.

[21] There can be little doubt that the additional cost of these developments more than offset the decline in the quality of the men-at-arms' warhorses which Ayton has detected in this period (Ayton 1994a: 209–24).

This was not the case in the periods that preceded and followed. We cannot determine the exact size of Rome's third- or fourth-century army with any confidence, but it was clearly getting bigger at a time when the population had stopped growing and was probably in decline. This expansion was presumably forced on the Empire's rulers by their deteriorating military situation, but it was unsustainable and culminated in disaster. The greater costs of additional cavalry and fixed defences were partly offset by the lightening of infantry equipment, so the trend in investment per soldier is obscure. What is clear is that more was being demanded of the fiscal system, and the productive economy on which it rested, than either was capable of meeting. Standards of discipline and infantry training apparently declined, and much of the increased cost was met by fiscal deflection. Recruits were obtained by coercion, and cash wages were supplemented or replaced by entitlements in kind. Even more damagingly, the institutional meshing of state and army that had been so important in establishing Roman power began to come apart. Civilian rulers increasingly lost effective control of the army to military commanders who eventually took political power, either as effective dictators within the formal structure of Imperial government or as rulers of successor kingdoms outside it. The east's economic recovery, allied perhaps to better financial management, enabled the process to be reversed in the fifth century as the greater availability of cash bound the army more closely within the fiscal and administrative structures of the state and allowed civilian control to be reasserted.

The experience of the centuries following the gunpowder revolution was very different, and it differed between the phases of demographic expansion and stagnation. The first of these phases petered out around the central decades of the seventeenth century and saw substantial increases in military manpower which have been the focus of much debate among historians. In the perspective of the long term and the Sauvy model they do not, however, seem particularly remarkable. What was remarkable was that, whilst total manpower expanded, costs per man rose rather than fell in the latter decades of the Habsburg century. The spread of handguns probably lowered unit costs to begin with by reducing the proportion of cavalry and substituting cheaper arquebusiers and *reiters* for heavily equipped pikemen and *gendarmes*, but these cost reductions had run their course by the later sixteenth century and some of them were reversed whilst the proportion of officers and NCOs helped to raise unit costs by as much as 40 per cent (Thompson 1995: 280–2).

Costs per man rose still more in the Bourbon century as pay became more regular and reliable and the volume of organization and discipline costs increased, but there was also a quantitative expansion despite the fact that the demographic cycle was holding civilian wage costs reasonably steady if not actually increasing them. The spread of gunpowder weapons was ultimately responsible for this departure from the long-term relationship between economic and demographic circumstances on the one hand and the balance of military manpower and resource inputs on the other, but the influence of the new technology acted through more than one channel, and in order to understand how this occurred we need to look more closely at the determinants of military effectiveness.

13.3. MANPOWER, INVESTMENT, AND EFFECTIVENESS

The effect of changing troop strengths and investment on military effectiveness depends on the prior level of the variables themselves and the nature of the prevailing military technology. We can investigate the relationships involved by returning to the terminology of Sauvy's model and representing military effectiveness as a single variable (M).[22] We shall also assume that military investment occurs in either or both of two forms corresponding to the troop quality costs that we considered in the last chapter. These two forms are 'skills investment' that boosts the fighting power of individual soldiers 'man for man', and 'organization investment' which allows larger bodies of men to be concentrated and deployed to greater military effect. Their per capita levels are denoted respectively by K(skill) and K(org)[23] such that total investment is given by:

$$K = K(skill) + K(org)$$

For any given value of K(skill) the effectiveness of a force will rise as it gets bigger, at least to begin with. At a certain point, however, diminishing returns will set in just as they do in economic life, and eventually the curve may even turn down as further increases in size (or N(s)) actually reduce the force's effectiveness. An increase in K(skill) will increase the value of M at any level of N(s) by raising troop quality, but better trained troops are also likely to be more amenable to battlefield discipline, less liable to panic, and better able to communicate with each other in combat. Investment in individual troop quality is therefore likely to confer a secondary benefit by facilitating the effective use of large numbers. Hence, as K(skill) increases, so the curve of M plotted against increase N(s) will also remain steeper for longer.

These relationships are set out in Fig. 13.2. Fig. 13.2(a) plots values of M with respect to N(s) for troops varying in quality from grades I to IV. The resulting trade-offs between quality and quantity are expressed in Fig. 13.2(b) as a matrix of notional values of M for forces of grades I–IV in four increasing size categories A–D. On the assumptions embodied in this model ('assumptions A') it is evident

---

[22] One of the assumptions of this analysis is that there is a single, stable hierarchy of relative effectiveness between forces of different kinds which, as we saw in Chapter 6, was not the case on a large-scale basis before the gunpowder revolution. It is, however, a reasonably realistic assumption if we consider the relative strengths of armies over a restricted area of space and time.

[23] The elements of K(org) are not, strictly speaking, quite the same as the organization costs considered in the last chapter since we are not concerned here with discipline costs off the battlefield and are including some forms of military capital such as logistical installations or fortifications that allow larger forces to be concentrated and deployed effectively. There is, however, a very large degree of overlap between the two categories.

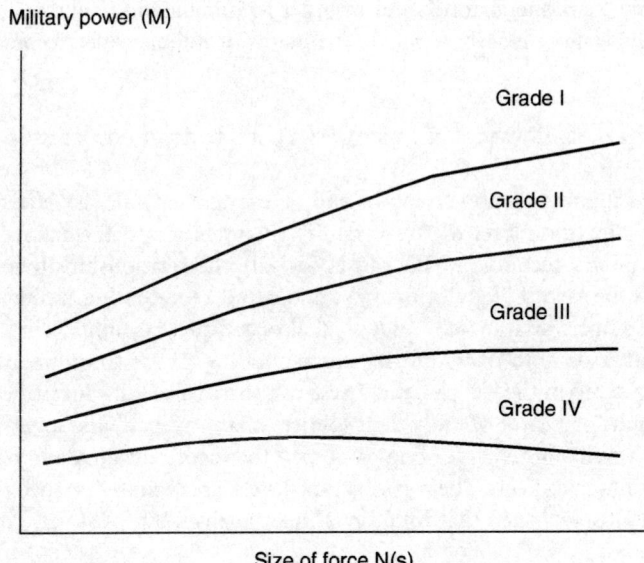

[Graph: Military power (M) vs Size of force N(s), showing four curves labeled Grade I, Grade II, Grade III, Grade IV from top to bottom]

	Force size category			
	A	B	C	D
Grade I	16	20	23	25
Grade II	14	17	19	20
Grade III	12	14	15	15
Grade IV	10	11	11	10

FIG. 13.2. Military power as a function of force size and troop quality (on assumptions [A])
(a) Effectiveness curves.
(b) Values of M for forces of quality grades I–IV and size categories A–D (A<B<C<D)

that there are limits to the military power which size alone can bestow on poor-quality forces. The early onset of diminishing and negative returns on lines III and IV means that high values of M can only be obtained by good-quality troops, regardless of numbers. In particular, intermediate-sized forces of grades I and II cannot be outmatched by those of grades III or IV however big they may be. There are therefore limits to overall growth in the scale of warfare. As population increases troop numbers will expand, but once past the power optimum population size, troop quality will be reduced by a growing shortage of resources for training and equipment, until eventually no more gains in M can be obtained.

Conversely, at lower levels of population the attainable troop quality will be higher, but increases in scale will be limited by the scarcity of manpower. Hence it will be in the long-term interests of rulers to strive for increased quality, since it is this which affords the readiest route to immediate increases in military power whilst retaining the option of future quantitative expansion should manpower become available.

The shapes of curves I–IV are based on plausible assumptions, but they are not the only ones possible. The return to increased N(s) may change because of new military technology or because of greater organization investment. In model terms, the effect will be to move the points of diminishing and negative returns further to the right of the curve. Figure 13.3, for instance, depicts one possible relationship between the regular forces of the agrarian empire and those of its 'barbarian' neighbours. Here relative power varies with absolute scale. Where both forces are small the barbarians' warrior virtues and sheer brute ferocity give them the edge, but their advantage falls off rapidly as the size of the forces increases and the benefits of the regulars' superior organization and support services begin to tell. It is this which underlies the phenomenon Luttwak terms—in the jargon of twentieth-century strategic theory—'escalation dominance', the phenomenon by which the scales shifted increasingly in favour of the imperial power as the scale of the conflict increased (Luttwak 1976: 41–2). In this case too, however, there is a ceiling to the potential increases in scale. A point is reached at which the barbarians' marginal returns fall to zero whilst the imperial advantage eventually becomes so overwhelming as to remove any motive for further escalation.

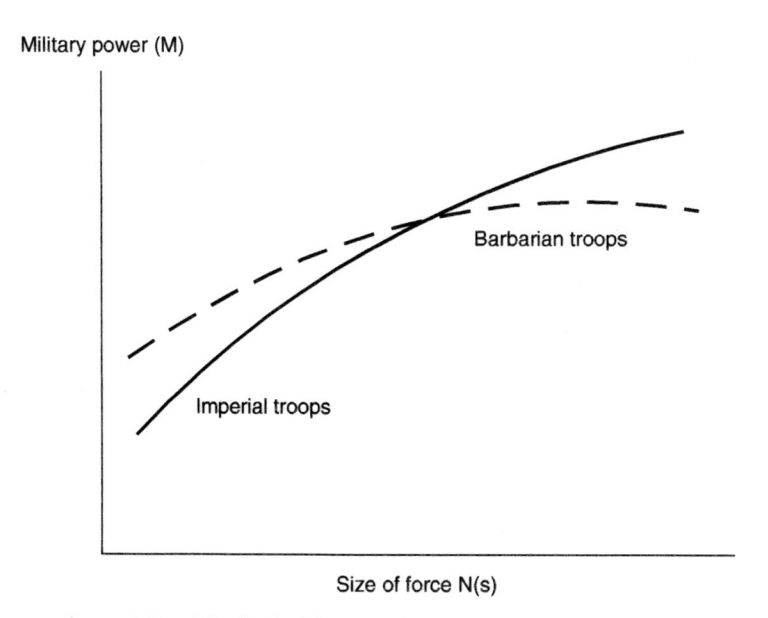

FIG. 13.3. 'Imperial' and 'barbarian' forces: military power and escalation dominance

This simple model shows how increased investment per soldier can move a force to a higher 'effectiveness curve', delay the point at which the curve begins to flatten out, or both, but constraints remain even where sufficient resources are available. Investment is potentially liable to diminishing returns, and the scope for it to occur at all depends on what the available technology will allow. As circumstances change, therefore, there is likely to be pressure for different kinds of technological innovation. When population is below $P(p)$ and manpower is expensive, this will be aimed at innovations that improve the returns to skills investment in 'man for man' troop quality and thus increase the vertical separation of the curves. As population rises above the optimum, and resources become scarce, attention will shift to the shape of the curves and innovations allowing the effective use of larger numbers of poorly trained and equipped troops. The aim here, in model terms, is to boost returns to organization investment so that the point at which the effectiveness curve begins to flatten can be 'right-shifted' more cheaply.

One possible outcome of this process is a set of curves shaped as they are in Fig. 13.4. In this instance ('assumptions B') it is assumed that technological changes, or possibly a step increase in organization investment, allow a much larger number of poor-quality troops to be deployed to reasonable effect. The advantages of better quality persist at any given army size, but the shape of the curves for grades III and IV is now much closer to those of I and II, and the point of negative returns has been eliminated. Under these circumstances there is no longer any theoretical limit to the military power that can be obtained by fielding greater numbers at lower

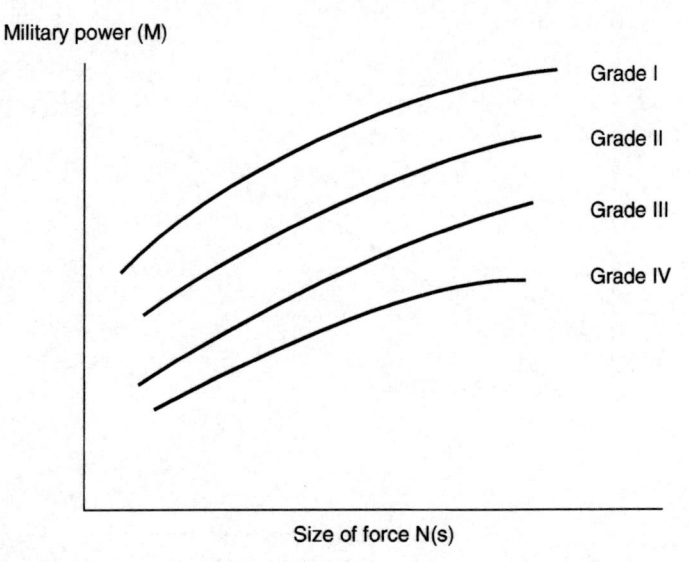

FIG. 13.4. Military power as a function of force size and troop quality (on assumptions (B))

levels of per capita investment.[24] In principle, high-quality forces of any size can now be overwhelmed by larger bodies of inferior troops. There is in fact no level, of either quality or quantity, at which a force is not vulnerable to being outmatched in this way. As long as manpower is available the way is therefore open for unlimited quantitative escalation as contending powers seek to overwhelm each other by mobilizing larger and larger forces.

The gunpowder revolution initiated a process of just this kind in early modern Europe. Smooth-bore muzzle-loaders had to be fired in volleys if they were to be effective primary weapons on European battlefields,[25] and this made a choreographed drill essential to stop soldiers on the same side shooting each other by accident. A by-product of this technique, and of the organization needed to inculcate it, was the extension of drill from weapons-handling to a method of synchronized manoeuvre which enabled commanders to co-ordinate large bodies of infantry much more effectively than had previously been possible. At the same time the mechanical nature of infantry weapons-handling limited the scope for individual qualitative improvement through 'skill investment'. Once the common soldier had been taught to load, fire, march in step, and about turn when ordered to do so there was little more that training or experience could achieve other than to keep him steady and obedient in the firing line.

More time and money was invested in infantry training from the later seventeenth century, but the aim of the training was to render men passive, obedient cogs in a larger machine on and off the battlefield rather than to foster individual-level skill.[26] The bulk of this training expenditure therefore represented what we have termed an 'organization cost', and it went along with more sophisticated unit organization, support services, and chains of command, all of which allowed the deployment of larger forces to good effect. In terms of our model, European military systems moved from the family of curves set out in Fig. 13.2 to something more like those in Fig. 13.4, and once the new tactical organization was in place substantial gains in overall effectiveness could most readily be obtained by quantitative expansion.[27]

---

[24] It is assumed here that any indirect, or structural, investment is essentially fixed and so does not vary with the size of the force.

[25] Some non-European peoples adopted muskets without using volley fire. This occurred where, as in parts of Africa and north America, warfare was oriented more towards establishing which side was stronger, or to taking captives, rather than to inflicting large numbers of casualties in the European manner (Parker 1991).

[26] Hall argues that infantry soldiering was effectively 'proletarianized' after the 16th century and the career soldier's hallmark became the ability to 'live within the ranks of a unit, to submit to the harshness, occasional brutality and constant alienation of a soldier's life' (Hall 1997: 234–5). Much of the quality of passive endurance on the battlefield that was so valued by commanders is likely to have resulted from experience under fire rather than on the parade ground. It was this which made veteran soldiers such a valuable commodity and helped to limit the quality gains which could be realized through investment in training.

[27] This is not to deny that well-trained and experienced troops could defeat larger numbers who lacked these advantages; that they could is demonstrated by the victories of outnumbered British forces against European-trained native armies in India (Parker 1988: 134–6). But the qualities in question could not be obtained simply on the exercise ground no matter how much money was

13.4. CONCLUSION

The process of raising, maintaining, and deploying military force required the commitment of men and resources. Men committed in this way were not available for economic production and the scale of recruitment was normally limited by the costs that sprang from this rather than by the physical availability of manpower itself. The restricted ability of organic economies to make productive use of an expanding labour force shifted the relative costs of procuring manpower and resources for military use. The costs of procuring manpower fell with declining labour productivity, but this also made it harder to obtain resources for training and equipping a large force. Where labour productivity was high it was correspondingly expensive to withdraw men from civilian employment, but there was a relative abundance of resources available for military investment. If recruitment were governed by 'supply-side' criteria alone we should therefore expect the demographic 'A' phase to witness disproportionate growth in army size accompanied by qualitative deterioration with the 'B' phase dominated by forces that were much smaller but much better trained and equipped.

Supply-side factors were not, however, the only ones affecting the size and composition of armed forces. The scale of a ruler's ambitions, the threats that he faced, and the ability of the prevailing military technology to make good use of additional manpower or investment were at least as important, and usually more so in the short term. The available data, fragmentary and approximate as they are, suggest nonetheless that military quality and quantity changed broadly in line with the predictions of the supply-side model during the thousand years or so between the fall of the Western Empire and the gunpowder revolution. Before this the crises of the third and fourth centuries apparently forced an expansion in Roman army size that ran against the demographic tide and proved too much for the economy to support within the old institutional framework. The gunpowder revolution introduced a discontinuity of a different kind. Army size grew in the ensuing century but possibly not by any more than could be explained by population growth. What could not be explained in this way was the apparent rise in costs per soldier.

For maritime powers, and particularly Spain, the biggest burden was the appearance of specialized warships based on broadside artillery. On land, the increase in costs due to gunpowder artillery trains and fortresses may have been relatively modest, but the fact that it occurred at all was historically unusual and ran against the grain of economic and demographic circumstances. A further

---

spent in training, and there is likely to have been an early point of diminishing returns to such investment. Strong motivation could, moreover, make up for lack of experience, as the British discovered when they encountered the untrained American Revolutionary infantry at Bunker Hill in 1775. This 'undisciplined rabble', as they were contemptuously derided by the British commander before the battle, inflicted 42% casualties on their opponents, who afterwards described them as 'fighting like veterans' (Black 1991: 75–9).

source of rising per capita expenditure was the increased number of lower-level leaders who were needed to operate the new gunpowder-based infantry tactics. These tactics, and the drill systems on which they depended, themselves changed the relationship between army size and military effectiveness. Much larger forces could now be deployed to good effect on the battlefield, which greatly reduced the extent of diminishing returns to scale and made it much more difficult to compensate for a numerical disadvantage by fielding better-quality troops. Quantitative expansion therefore continued through the 'B' phase of the demographic cycle when population growth slowed or ceased altogether, whilst the search for means to deploy these larger forces effectively, and to enhance their Clausewitzian effectiveness, brought further increases in discipline and organization costs.

CHAPTER FOURTEEN

The Cost of War: Mortality and Population Loss

War imposed economic costs through the destruction of resources and their diversion to non-productive ends. It also imposed demographic costs in the form of relative or absolute population losses due to forced emigration, increased mortality, and lower fertility resulting from the loss of actual or potential marriage partners.[1] The relative importance of these three demographic components of population varies with the geographical and chronological scale adopted. The importance of mortality relative to migration increases as we move from localities, through subnational regions, to entire countries or continents. The effects of migration can also be reversed relatively quickly, as can nuptiality effects as women adapt to a loss of potential spouses by choosing from a wider geographical or age range. Migration from a war zone may also benefit neighbouring regions and sometimes open new opportunities to the individuals concerned. Mortality, by contrast, imposes losses which are absolute and irreversible for those who are touched by them, even if some demographic ground may be recovered by immigration or increased fertility. This gives mortality a unique status among the components of population loss.

There have been a number of attempts made to estimate the lives lost in wars from classical times onwards, but the necessary data only become available in the course of the nineteenth century.[2] Rather than seek overall totals for the deaths resulting from earlier wars, whether directly or indirectly, we shall try to understand the ways in which military operations affected mortality, and the factors

---

[1] 'Absolute population loss' refers to an actual decline in population whereas a 'relative population loss' is a shortfall in numbers relative to what would have been expected given normal rates of population growth. The calculation of relative losses therefore requires some assumption and extrapolation even if all the relevant data are available, but this does not make them any less real or significant in the long-term demographic evolution of a population.

[2] Most of the calculations that have been made start from estimates of battle deaths and assume a uniform relationship between these and total war-related mortality. In practice, however, this relationship varied greatly in times and space, and figures such as those presented by Sorokin (1937), whilst they might have some value as general indices of warfare's 'intensity', should not be taken at face value. It is sometimes possible to assess the extent of population loss in areas afflicted by warfare, but translating this into an estimate of deaths due to the war requires knowledge of the relative contribution of emigration and mortality and of the likely course of mortality had peace prevailed. It is rarely possible to specify either of these two pieces of information with any great confidence.

which aggravated or ameliorated their impact, on the basis of the material available for the post-medieval period. The relationship between war and mortality was transformed between 1860 and 1945 as the emergence of a scientifically informed preventive medicine, followed much later by effective treatments, broke the earlier links between resistance and prior exposure to infection.[3] At the same time, the scale of warfare in Europe also underwent a qualitative transformation. In the war of 1914–18, the numbers involved, the duration of their exposure to combat, and the accompanying dislocation of the civilian economies were such as to take the demographic impact of warfare out of the range of previous experience. The wars of 1939–45 added a further destructive dimension in the direct exposure of civilian populations to weapons of industrialized warfare.

The numbers of wartime civilian deaths due directly to enemy action before the twentieth century were, by contrast, small, and combat was in most cases only a secondary source of mortality among the troops themselves. War might increase mortality substantially, but it did so primarily through its effect on patterns of infectious disease, and most of the additional deaths arose indirectly through its impact on civilian economic and social life. The impact of war on a population's mortality can be thought of in terms of a stone thrown into still water. Successive circles spread outward. At the centre are battle deaths—combat deaths in major engagements—with other combat deaths, in small-scale engagements and skirmishes, just beyond these. In the next ring are the 'surplus' non-combat deaths among the military which represent deaths from infectious disease in excess of those expected among an equivalent population of peacetime civilians. Beyond these are civilian deaths themselves. In the first instance there are civilian deaths directly due to military activity in the zone of operations, whether through violence of soldiers against civilians or, at a slightly further remove, brought on by the disruption of regional economies as a result of military operations. In the final, and most permeable, circle are deaths due to war-induced epidemics which may spread far beyond the limits of the zone of operations itself.

14.1. MILITARY DEATHS

There are few tolerably reliable figures available for loss of life among soldiers before the very end of the eighteenth century, and even where they exist the calculation of mortality rates is often hampered by a lack of accurate data on the size of the forces to which they refer.[4] The scale of military mortality is therefore difficult to judge before the relatively recent past, but two features emerge clearly

---

[3] This link had been previously broken only in the case of smallpox for which vaccination was available from the early 19th century.

[4] The main sources used here for war-related deaths are the volumes published by the Clarendon Press in 1916 and 1923 under the auspices of the Carnegie Endowment for International Peace and the general editorship of Harald Westergaard. Bodart (1916) and Dumas and Vedel-Peterson (1923) are primarily concerned with military casualties whilst Prinzing (1916) provides an encyclopaedic, and somewhat depressing, catalogue of war-related epidemics.

from the figures in Table 14.1. The first is the contrast in overall mortality between the earlier and later parts of the period. The figure for total British mortality 1793–1815 is difficult to interpret because it includes large numbers of men based in the home islands, but setting this aside the annualized rates up to 1856 are roughly in the range 135–200 per thousand,[5] with the earlier Swedish estimate being much higher. After this year, with the exception of the brief but intense Six Weeks War of 1866, they fall in the range 40–80 per thousand. Alongside this overall decline in mortality, a second striking feature of the table is the long-term importance of disease as a cause of wartime death, and the dramatic decline in its toll after 1900. With the exception of the 1859 French invasion of Italy and the Prusso-Danish War of 1864, disease accounts for the majority of wartime military deaths until the twentieth century, and it is often responsible for 70 per cent or more.[6]

14.1.1. COMBAT DEATHS

The figures for overall war deaths among servicemen can be used to provide estimates of total combat deaths—those killed in action or died of wounds—and the associated measures of risk (see Table 14.2). The annualized rates for the Napoleonic and Crimean Wars are generally in the range of ten to forty per thousand with the Russian Crimean figure being substantially larger. The rates for the wars of national unification in the years 1859–71 are generally fifty per thousand or above with the Austrian losses in the Six Weeks War of 1866 being much larger. There are almost no data on total deaths in combat before the eve of the nineteenth century, but there are some estimates for casualties in specific battles.

Battle casualties before the gunpowder era are largely a matter of speculation, but contemporary accounts suggest that, at least where armoured troops were involved, they remained fairly light as long as the troops maintained formation, and that substantial losses generally occurred only when a force broke and was systematically pursued. Krentz estimates that, in seventeen hoplite battles from 472 to 371 BC, the winners lost 5 per cent on average and the losers 14 per cent (Krentz 1985).[7] In some relatively well-documented encounters the disproportion

---

[5] The annualized rates were calculated by adjusting the observed total deaths in proportion to the duration of the hostilities that produced them and dividing by the average troop strength quoted in the source. Technically speaking, rates of this kind render data for differing durations directly comparable but it should be borne in mind that, from a substantive point of view, it is difficult to compare figures from a short campaign dominated by nearly continuous fighting with those from a long war in which nothing very much happened for extended periods.

[6] The Russo-Japanese War serves as a natural end point for this analysis because it was the first major war fought in a temperate environment between two 'conventional' armies after germ theory had been formulated and applied to the practice of hygiene and sanitation. The low level of disease deaths is all the more noteworthy given the important role of trench warfare in the conflict. By contrast, casualties in the Spanish-American War of 1898 were affected by the epidemiological hazards of its tropical theatre, and Britain's South African War (1898–1902) was a guerrilla conflict in its later stages.

[7] The scarcity of Greek cavalry limited the opportunities for pursuit and kept losses relatively low, but Krentz makes the important point that they would not necessarily have seemed low to contemporaries; 'in the small world of the Greek polis, the death of even five percent of the hoplites sent out to fight would seem a significant loss' (Krentz 1985: 20).

Table 14.1 *Total wartime troop losses*

Army	Absolute	% of strength	Annualized (per 000)	Combat	Disease	Note	Source
Swedish, 1620–1719	—	—	250.0	12.0	88.0	(5)	(6)
British, 1793–1815	143,808	—	56.2	18.7	81.3		(2)
Peninsular campaign, 1810–14	35,630	55.4	162.3	30.8	69.2		(2)
						(1)	(3)
French, 1803–15	870,000	—	145.0	22.4	77.6	(2)	
Russian, 1854–6	129,349	32.3	194.1	31.4	68.6		(4)
French, 1854–6	95,615	30.9	185.7	21.2	78.8		(4)
British, 1854–6	22,182	22.7	136.4	20.7	79.3		(4)
French, 1859	7,538	4.3	79.4	72.9	27.1		(1)
Danish, 1864	2,933	4.2	56.0	76.5	23.5	(3)	(1)
Prussian, 1864	1,048	2.1	28.0	70.4	29.6		(1)
US, 1861–5	359,618	—	73.1	30.6	69.4		(5)
Confederacy, 1861–2	55,478			44.0	56.0		(5)
Austrian, 1866	27,825	6.8	589.0	31.9	68.1	(4)	(1)
Prussian, 1866	10,877	2.5	217.7	37.6	62.4		(1)
German, 1870–1	40,745	4.5	78.4	30.6	69.4		(4)
Russian, 1877–8	103,754	12.6	53.6	21.6	78.4		(4)
Russian, 1904–5	43,586	6.5	38.8	72.2	27.8		(4)
Japanese, 1904–5	86,004	13.2	72.2	68.4	31.6		(4)

Notes:
1. The calculated mortality assumes an average strength of 500,000 French troops.
2. The breakdown of combat and disease deaths is taken from Houdaille's table IV which is based on the statements in his sample military records. In addition, an estimated 370,000 French soldiers disappeared from the records, and Houdaille estimates that, of these, 149,000 perished. The proportion of combat deaths among these may well have exceeded that among the men whose fate is known, but against this should be set an estimated 246,000 non-returning prisoners very many of whom are likely to have died of disease.
3. Combat deaths include 808 classified as 'missing probably killed'.
4. +12,361 missing.
5. The dates in the table represent the period for which data are available. The estimates are based on Lindegren's assessment of a 25% annual mortality among the main Swedish field army during the Thirty Years War and an estimated life expectancy of three to four years for a common soldier during the subsequent 'Great War of the North'. He breaks down total wartime military deaths as 10% field actions, 5% sieges, 10% deaths among prisoners, and 75% from 'the normal hardships of war'; the breakdown given in the table is based on the ratio of deaths in the first and last of these categories. Some of the latter may have occurred in low-level combat but these are likely to have been outweighed by disease deaths among prisoners which have not been included.

Sources: (1): Dumas and Vedel-Peterson (1923); (2): Hodge (1857); (3): Houdaille (1972); (4): Kozlovski (1912); (5): Livermore 1957: 8–9; (6): Lindegren (2000).

Table 14.2 *Total combat deaths (killed in action and died of wounds)*

	Combat deaths	
Army	% of strength	Annualized per 000
Swedish, 1620–1719	—	30.0
British:		
Total 1793–1815		10.5
Peninsular campaign, 1810–14	17.1	50.0
French, 1803–15	—	32.5
Russian, 1854–6	10.1	60.9
French, 1854–6	6.6	39.4
British, 1854–6	4.7	28.2
French, 1859	3.1	57.9
Danish, 1864	2.8	42.8
Prussian, 1864	1.5	19.7
US, 1861–5	—	22.4
Austrian, 1866	2.2	187.9
Prussian, 1866	0.9	81.9
German, 1870–1	1.4	24.0
Russian, 1877–8	2.7	11.6
Russian, 1904–5	4.7	28.0
Japanese, 1904–5	9.0	49.4

Sources: See Table 14.1.

was apparently much greater, with the victors emerging relatively unscathed despite a great deal of hard fighting. At Strasbourg in AD 357 the Romans are said to have lost only 247 dead after considerable hard fighting. Deaths among the defeated Alamanni, however, are estimated at 6,000–8,000, many of whom were drowned in the Rhine which blocked their escape, whilst the Romans were able to recover and treat the wounded from their own side (Elton 1996). At Agincourt the English are said to have lost less than a hundred dead against as many as 6,000 French (Oman 1991: 383).

This position evidently changed with the shift to firearms, and the gap between losers' and victors' casualties narrowed substantially. A database of battle casualty statistics by twenty-five-year periods from the seventeenth to the late nineteenth century shows average casualties on the losing side running between an eighth and a third of the total (see Table 14.3).[8] The highest figure is for the second quarter of the seventeenth century. This is the period for which there are fewest

---

[8] It is not possible to specify precisely what proportion of total combat deaths were inflicted in major battles, as opposed to the undocumented skirmishes of low-level warfare, but it appears to have been much higher in the Napoleonic period than it was in the 17th-century British conflicts studied by Carlton (see above, Chapter 9). Bodart used data on officer casualties to estimate the total killed and wounded in the armies of France and its allies during the period 1805–15 (Bodart 1916: 128 f.). A comparison of these numbers with the figures for larger battles and sieges tabulated in Appendix II suggests that nearly 40% of the total casualties were sustained in the forty-seven engagements that

Table 14.3 *Battle casualties by period*

Period	Winner Mean casualties (%)	Upper quartile (%)	N	Loser Mean casualties (%)	Total losses (%)	N
1619–58	13.5	18.5	19	25.5	38.8	25
1674–1719	9.8	15.0	92	23.4	33.0	87
1734–60	11.9	16.7	43	19.7	26.0	43
1790–1801	7.2	10.0	63	12.3	26.7	76
1805–15	14.0	19.5	48	17.7	23.0	48

Note: N = number of battles in each period.
Sources: See Appendix II.

reliable data and so the implied level of casualties needs to be treated with caution. It may nonetheless be close to the truth and reflect the fragility of contemporary armies, their consequent tendency to disperse when defeated, and the vulnerability of the fugitives to the pursuing victors. In the century after 1675 casualties generally average around 25 per cent, with a noticeably lower figure in the period 1725–49. In the century after 1775 the figure falls again to around 15 per cent. Casualties on the winning side also fluctuate, with the majority of values lying between 10 and 15 per cent, but in this case there is no evident pattern over time. The ratio of losers' to victors' casualties tends to fall from a value of between two and four in most periods before 1725 to around 1.5 in most of the subsequent periods.

14.1.2. DEATHS FROM DISEASE

The high level of disease mortality among troops was partly due to the logistical problems of supply and transport which meant that they were frequently badly fed and exposed to rotten or otherwise contaminated food and water. Beyond the operational stresses of active service, however, the institutional conditions of military life itself, with the concentration of men in unhygienic camps or barracks, promoted the maintenance and transmission of infection, as can be seen from the mortality of troops in peacetime or away from the major theatres of conflict. According to Lindegren, Finnish urban garrisons on the Baltic coast suffered an annual mortality of 37.3 per thousand in the years 1662–74, which is likely to have been double the level of the civilians around them (Lindegren 2000:

---

claimed at least 1,000 casualties each. Just under half of these 'battle casualties'—and slightly under a fifth of the total—were sustained in the eight battles which each saw more than 20,000 killed. A third of the total was sustained in the four battles of Leipzig, Borodino, Wagram, and Waterloo. The proportion of 'major battle' deaths was lowest in 1808, 1810, and 1811—years in which the casualty totals are dominated by the fighting in Spain—and highest in 1807, 1813, and 1815.

143 n. 15).[9] Houdaille's study of three French regiments in the years 1782–93 found that, taking account of age structure and eliminating combat deaths, there were twice as many deaths as would have been expected in the general population, whilst a group of coastguard companies had a 40 per cent excess over the period 1803–14 (Houdaille 1977). Disease mortality among troops in Britain reached 18.4 per thousand in the years 1801–5, and was apparently running at 15.9 in the 1850s (Hodge 1857: 160). These levels are likely to have been some 50 to a 100 per cent above those prevailing in the civilian population.[10]

A more dramatic illustration of the dangers of confinement is given by the level of mortality among prisoners of war. At Vilna in 1813, typhus claimed the lives of 25,000 French prisoners out of the 30,000 that were in Russian hands (Dumas and Vedel-Peterson 1923: 39). In the relatively well-documented American Civil War, deaths among prisoners ran at 291 and 121 per thousand in the south and north respectively. The increase in the scale of warfare from the later eighteenth century exacerbated the problems of hygiene and sanitation that accompanied the prolonged concentration of troops, and this had particularly serious consequences for siege warfare since garrisons might now be numbered in the tens of thousands. At Mantua an Austrian garrison of 30,000 lost over 10,000 dead, the great majority from disease, in an eight-month siege in 1796–7, whilst in 1813 at the siege of Danzig 43.8 per cent of the 35,900-strong French garrison died of disease.

The level of disease mortality, and still more the prevalence of sickness, cannot be measured with any accuracy before the nineteenth century. Even qualitative evidence can be difficult to interpret since descriptions of armies being 'devastated' or 'melting away' as a result of disease rarely distinguish the effects of mortality from those of temporary incapacity or even desertion due to the resulting demoralization and indiscipline. What is clear, however, is that infectious disease could reduce the short-term combat effectiveness of armies to virtually zero and that it was an ever-present threat. The overall casualty figures in Table 14.1 can also be used to obtain estimates of disease mortality deaths on the same basis as those from combat (see Table 14.4). The figures for the earlier part of the period generally range between 100 and 150 per thousand with a substantially higher figure for the early modern Swedish army. The rates for the latter part of the period are noticeably lower although the annualized figures for the Six Weeks War are severe, exceptionally so for the Austrians. As armies became more highly organized and disciplined they took on the character of 'total institutions' in which obedience to regulations, including sanitary regulations, could be readily enforced (Goffman 1968). This meant that as military and naval medicine developed so barracks and particularly ships could be treated as

---

[9] In this instance the soldiers are likely to have been drawn primarily from small-scale rural settlements and so their mortality was almost certainly aggravated by a lack of prior exposure, and therefore immunological resistance, to urban disease environments.

[10] According to the Registrar-General's third English life table covering the years 1838–54 the age-specific mortality rate for males in the age range 20–30 years was 9.1 per thousand (Wrigley and Schofield 1981: 709). Adult mortality is likely to have been somewhat higher during the years 1793–1815.

Table 14.4 *Estimates of wartime disease mortality among troops*

	Disease deaths	
Army	% strength	Annualized per 000
Swedish, 1620–1719	—	220.0
British:		
Total, 1793–1815	—	45.7
Peninsular campaign, 1810–14	38.3	112.3
French, 1803–15	—	112.5
Russian, 1854–6	22.2	133.2
French, 1854–6	24.3	146.3
British, 1854–6	18.0	108.2
French, 1859	1.2	21.5
Danish, 1864	1.0	13.2
Prussian, 1864	0.6	8.3
US, 1861–5	—	50.7
Austrian, 1866	4.6	401.1
Prussian, 1866	1.6	135.8
German, 1870–1	3.1	54.4
Russian, 1877–8	9.9	42.0
Russian, 1904–5	1.8	10.8
Japanese, 1904–5	4.2	22.8

Sources: See Table 14.1.

'natural laboratories', and the success of many of the resulting methods for avoiding exposure to infection was manifest in a substantial reduction in deaths from disease.

The specific diseases responsible for any given level of mortality are notoriously difficult to identify from historical accounts, and particularly from those pre-dating present-day disease categories, most of which are nineteenth century in origin. It seems safe to conclude, however, that most of the diseases responsible for excess military mortality were epidemic infections, rather than endemic conditions such as respiratory tuberculosis which could be of greater significance as civilian causes of death, and it is often possible to classify them according to their mode of transmission. The most important categories were those of water- and food-borne disease, disease transmitted by arthropod vectors such as lice and mosquitoes, and airborne disease.[11]

14.1.2.1. *Water- and food-borne diseases*

Troops concentrated in camps, or during sieges, were often crowded together at high densities with inadequate hygiene and sanitation, the effects of which might

---

[11] Sexually transmitted diseases have also been a major problem for military medicine, but they have not been a significant cause of death among serving soldiers.

be reinforced by exposure to tainted food. These were ideal conditions for the spread of water- and food-borne diseases, and outbreaks of dysentery—which can arise from infection by a variety of micro-organisms—were a common result. They were particularly likely where troops were concentrated at a single point for an extended period, but could also strike at mobile forces such as the English army in the Agincourt campaign. Contemporary accounts suggest that dysentery and related conditions were a familiar accompaniment of military operations, and that they could have a substantial impact on armies' combat effectiveness, as they apparently did on the Prussians at Valmy in the first stages of the French Revolutionary War. It is much more difficult to assess what influence, if any, these conditions had on overall military mortality and it is likely that their primary effect was to weaken victims and so make them more vulnerable to any other epidemics that might be raging at the time.

The growing scale of warfare after 1790 brought with it denser aggregations of troops and an increase in exposure to this group of conditions, particularly where mobile campaigns gave way to positional warfare. At the same time, the progress of urbanization in nineteenth-century Europe increased the prevalence of waterborne disease and particularly typhoid, which was responsible for a very large proportion of disease deaths in nineteenth-century armies. The Austro-Prussian War of 1866 coincided with one of the period's recurrent cholera outbreaks, which caused a high level of disease mortality. In the Prussian army cholera killed a larger number of men than were killed in action or died of wounds.[12] The prevalence of cholera and typhoid was a very accurate indicator of inadequate sanitary conditions, and a growing understanding of the mechanisms of infection helped promote major improvement in this respect from the 1870s onwards. Mortality from this group of causes declined correspondingly and by the time of the Russo-Japanese War combat deaths substantially outnumbered deaths from disease.

14.1.2.2. *Arthropod vector disease*

The main killing conditions carried by arthropod vectors were bubonic plague, malaria, and typhus. Plague, which was the most deadly epidemic disease in the historical record, arises from exposure to the bacillus *Yersinia pestis*. This normally infects rodents and is spread by their parasitic fleas. In Europe the black rat (*Rattus rattus*) is thought to have been principally implicated, and the standard biomedical model assumes that epidemics began with an outbreak, or 'epizootic', among the rat population. The subsequent collapse in rat numbers forced the 'homeless' fleas to transfer to human hosts taking the bacilli with them.[13] Humans were then infected by rat flea bites, although the disease may also have

---

[12] 4,529 as against 4,008 according to Prinzing (1916: 186).

[13] For some discussions of plague epidemiology in a historical context see, among others, Benedictow (1987), Slack (1985: 3–21), and Bray (1996).

been spread from person to person by the human flea *Pulex irritans*.[14] Plague had disappeared from northern and western Europe by the 1680s, and from eastern Europe by the end of the eighteenth century, so there are very few reliable data on its incidence among troops.

When plague broke out in cities, however, it could kill between 25 and 40 per cent of the inhabitants, and there is no reason to doubt that it could be as destructive among large troop concentrations. Contemporary accounts describe plague as having 'almost entirely exterminated' the Swedish and Imperialist armies campaigning in Silesia in 1633, and to have killed 'most' of a Spanish army of 20,000 men sheltering in the Alpine foothills the following winter (Prinzing 1916: 47; Parker 1984: 132). In a better-documented Balkan outbreak in 1828–9, plague was largely responsible for the deaths of at least 50,000 out of some 68,000 Russian troops fighting the Turks in the Balkans (Dumas and Vedel-Peterson 1923: 40–1).

Malaria, which was spread by mosquitoes, was also potentially a very serious problem, but it was one restricted to distinct 'malarial' regions which were usually low-lying and waterlogged. The scope for effective protection was very limited before the malarial mosquito's reproductive cycle was elucidated, but Roman writers were already aware of the health risks associated with marshy terrain and recommended that it be avoided. In 1809 the British expedition to Walcheran in the Scheldt estuary was devastated by malaria,[15] and the disease caused many deaths in the American Civil War, but its main impact was felt in tropical campaigns outside Europe. The eventual identification of the mosquito's role as a vector allowed effective preventive measures to be developed, first through the use of defensive measures such as nets and then through assaults on the mosquito vectors themselves through the use of insecticides.

The third of the major arthropod vector diseases, typhus fever, arises from infection by a micro-organism belonging to the category known as *rickettsia* (Zinsser 1935). These pathogens can be spread by a number of vectors, but epidemic typhus is transmitted through the bites inflicted by the body louse. Lice are arthropod vectors like fleas and mosquitoes, but the epidemiology of typhus differs from those of malaria or plague because lice remain in close proximity to the human body, generally in clothing. Transmission of the disease usually required close physical contact with an infected individual or item of clothing, although it might also be caught from dust contaminated with louse faeces. Typhus and other closely related conditions spread easily among

---

[14] The pneumonic form of plague occurred where the lungs were infected. Pneumonic plague, which was an airborne condition with nearly 100% case fatality, is thought to have contributed significantly to the impact of the Justinianic plague and the 14th-century Black Death, but it does not seem to have played a major role in early modern plague epidemics.

[15] Dumas (Dumas and Vedel-Peterson 1923: 37) quotes a rate of 346.9 per thousand for disease mortality among the British troops (compared with 16.7 deaths per thousand due to enemy action). Survivors of the expedition—which initially numbered 40,000 men—were so prone to relapses that Wellington requested that no more be sent to his Peninsular army (Haythornthwaite 1988: 134, 236–7).

overcrowded institutional populations with poor hygiene, giving rise to common sobriquets such as 'jail fever', 'camp fever', or 'ship fever'.

The early history of typhus is obscure, and the epidemic form may have arisen in central Europe during the wars of the sixteenth century. The condition was certainly a significant cause of death amongst sixteenth- and seventeenth-century armies. It seems to have receded during the wars of the *ancien régime* but it returned as a major scourge in the armies of the French Revolutionary and Napoleonic Wars. Subsequently it declined in importance, and it was conspicuously absent from the Franco-Prussian War even in besieged Paris, only re-emerging as a substantial cause of death in the Serbian army of the First World War and in the Russian Civil War. The reduction in typhus mortality reflected an improvement in hygiene and general cleanliness, and particularly improvements in the cleanliness of clothing.

14.1.2.3. Airborne diseases

Airborne diseases were not susceptible to the hygienic and sanitary measures that brought conditions like typhus and dysentery under control. The airborne category comprises a wide range of conditions, including some like respiratory tuberculosis which could account for a large share of overall mortality, but the most readily identifiable disease historically speaking was smallpox, and this was also the disease which posed the greatest short-term threat. Smallpox was an unusual disease because it was passed directly from person to person without immune carriers, animal vectors, or reservoirs—though it could be spread by infected clothes or bedding—and survivors of the infection were effectively immune for life. It was therefore the epidemiological model for the so-called 'crowd diseases' and the prevalence of adult smallpox mortality was the inverse of that among children; where the disease was universal in childhood it was unknown among adults, and where substantial numbers of children escaped infection its incidence at older ages was correspondingly higher.

Smallpox emerged as a demographically significant cause of death in Europe from the later seventeenth century, and its population dynamics were radically altered by the introduction of vaccination at the end of the eighteenth century. Before this time there was a very high incidence of the disease among children. Swedish data indicate that it was effectively a universal childhood disease in that country, and even though a proportion of England's rural population escaped infection before adulthood, most European armies will have contained relatively small numbers of susceptible individuals. This changed with the spread of vaccination in the course of the nineteenth century because, unlike exposure to 'natural' smallpox, the immunity conferred by vaccination was only temporary. Initially vaccination led to a major reduction in smallpox deaths which is strikingly visible in the Swedish data (Sköld 1996), but as the prevalence of infection declined in subsequent decades the practice of revaccination was neglected, and there was a corresponding build-up in the numbers of susceptible adults.

The consequence was a major smallpox epidemic which broke out first among the French troops in the Franco-Prussian War of 1870. It then spread from French prisoners to civilians throughout Germany and subsequently through Europe as a whole. Military service provided a means of enforcing revaccination, and this was practised in the Prussian army from the 1830s and in the French army, but apparently less rigorously, from 1857. The incidence of smallpox in the Prussian field army during the war was very low, although it was higher among the troops of the static reserve who had a lower priority for revaccination.[16] On the French side adequate data are lacking, but it is clear that the mass mobilization which followed the collapse of the old Imperial army caused a crisis, as a large proportion of those called to the colours lacked protection against the disease and there was no time to vaccinate them. In Paris, where many of the new regiments were concentrated, nearly 7 per cent of the garrison contracted smallpox during the siege. Of the more than 370,000 prisoners taken to Germany, 3.8 per cent became infected of whom 13.8 per cent died. The course of the epidemic among the prisoners was checked by wholesale vaccination, but by then the disease had already entered the German civilian population.

14.1.3. THE IMPACT OF MILITARY MORTALITY

Military deaths were almost always concentrated among younger adult males whose normal mortality rates were relatively low. Such deaths might therefore increase mortality levels in these age groups substantially, but they were unlikely to have a major effect on overall population mortality because the proportion of males surviving childhood to reach military age was rarely above one half and was often much smaller.[17] In nineteenth-century France, for instance, the relative movement of male and female mortality in the 15–24-year age group is clearly marked by the impact of warfare. Male excess mortality rose substantially in the 1840s and 1850s, reflecting the wars in Algeria and the Crimea, and also in 1871 after the Franco-Prussian War, but only the truly massive mortality of the 1812–14 campaigns was translated into a major fall in relative life expectancy at birth (Meslé and Vallin 1989). British troop losses in the Revolutionary and Napoleonic Wars also had very little relative direct demographic impact. Total war-related

---

[16] On Prinzing's figures the incidence among the two echelons was of the order of five and eleven per thousand respectively. It should be noted that the rate quoted in the text (1916: 207) for the incidence among the field army does not agree with either the absolute numbers or the author's argument and is clearly erroneous. Here, as in a number of other cases where similar discrepancies arise, the value given is that calculated from the absolute numbers.

[17] This phenomenon can be demonstrated using the actuarial method of life table analysis. Suppose, for instance, that 10% of all adult males aged 20–39 were to die in a single year in a population whose life table was that estimated for France in 1740–9 (Vallin 1991: table 3.3). The 'period' age-specific death rate for that year would be multiplied approximately sevenfold, but life expectancy at birth (e_0) would be reduced by barely a year, from 24.75 years to 23.7, and life expectancy at age 20 (e_{20}) would fall from 34.2 years to 31.8. The impact increases as normal mortality declines. If the life table were that of France in 1877–81 ($e_0 = 42.1$), the period age-specific rate would rise tenfold, e_0 would fall by two years, and 3.2 years would be lost from e_{20}.

deaths among British-born men in the army and royal navy averaged some 6,000 per year over the period 1793–1815, a level equivalent to less than 3 per cent of annual deaths in England alone (Hodge 1857, 1856).

Lindegren estimates that half a million Swedish and Finnish soldiers died in wars during the years 1620–1719 (Lindegren 2000). As a proportion of the general population this mortality only exceeded an annual level of six per thousand in the decade 1700–9, and in only four other decades did it exceed four per thousand, but the effect on adult male mortality was substantial. It is likely that 30 per cent of males who survived to the age of 20 in this period died as soldiers. Lindegren puts military deaths among the Castilians as 300,000 out of a total of 6 million over the years 1618–59, or around 1.3 per thousand of population per year, which implies that 10 per cent of all adult males died as soldiers. Houdaille estimates that, of the roughly 1.8 million Frenchmen in the birth cohorts 1790–5 who reached the age of 20, 45 per cent served with the colours and 20 per cent died during the campaigns of the later Empire (Houdaille 1970). Military losses on the scale experienced by Sweden for a full century had long-term demographic effects, not least because they seriously reduced women's marriage chances and thus their fertility,[18] but generally speaking the main demographic impact of war was felt through its effects on civilians.

14.2. CIVILIAN DEATHS

Warfare could trigger civilian mortality crises among civilians, but these could also result from the presence or movement of troops through a region without any actual fighting. The scarcity of demographic data makes it impossible to measure the resulting movements in national mortality before the nineteenth century, but figures from the 1860s and 1870s show what could result. The Six Weeks War of 1866 increased the Austrian annual death rate by nearly 40 per cent to 40.8 per thousand, whilst following the Franco-Prussian War the French death rate rose by 50 per cent of its short-term average to 35.1 per thousand. In Scandinavia, where demographic statistics are available for a longer period, the impact of the Russian invasion of Finland in 1808–9 is visible in a doubling of the death rate to around sixty per thousand in each of the two years. Parish registers can provide some evidence on short-run movements in local mortality for the centuries immediately preceding civil registration, but before this it is rarely possible to gauge even relative increases and the impact of military crises has to be approached through estimates of overall population loss. This combines the effects of mortality, fertility, and migration, and usually has to be estimated indirectly through changes in the numbers of households, land-use patterns, or

---

[18] Lindegren argues that the effects of male war losses of up to 25% could be offset by changes in marriage behaviour—as they apparently were in France after the First World War (Henry 1966)—but that beyond this level these adaptive mechanisms broke down and fertility fell as a result.

rural taxation. In most cases emigration was chiefly responsible for population loss, although mortality increases could also be substantial and epidemics of infectious disease played the principal role.

Civilian deaths resulting directly from combat or other military operations are unlikely to have made a major contribution to excess mortality before the twentieth century, when bombardment by high explosive or powerful incendiary charges led to increasing numbers of casualties. In the absence of such weapons the main sources of direct civilian mortality were personal 'face-to-face' violence inflicted by enemy troops, hardship induced by the destruction of buildings and other installations, and the destruction or removal of subsistence resources by friend or foe. Violence sometimes occurred in the form of deliberate, systematic massacres of civilians, but the extent of these is uncertain. Contemporary accounts speak of widespread massacres accompanying nomad and other 'barbarian' incursions into settled regions, but they are often difficult to verify and we should apply the same caveats regarding likely exaggeration that the demographers Watkins and Menken have identified in comparable accounts of famine mortality (Watkins and Menken 1985).

The ability of pre-industrial armies to inflict civilian casualties was limited given the absence of high explosives or automatic weapons and the ability of local inhabitants to take refuge in wooded or hilly terrain, or in specially constructed refuges. Substantial massacres could occur, however, in densely populated and deforested terrain where effective concealment was made difficult, or where urban centres fell to siege or assault. In these circumstances massacres might be ordered by victorious commanders as a reprisal to punish prolonged resistance, although they were more often a result of spontaneous outbreaks of violence by victorious troops. In this respect the decline or suppression of slavery as an institution removed an important disincentive to massacre. In other circumstances civilian casualties arose during the looting or destruction of rural resources, but there is no evidence to suggest that this had a major effect on overall mortality.[19]

Rural devastation was an important form of economic warfare in the ancient and medieval periods although its impact on mortality is very difficult to ascertain. Protracted conflict in a given region could lead to substantial depopulation through death or flight, and entire regional economies could virtually collapse where peasants were unable to sow crops and large tracts passed temporarily out of cultivation. Such circumstances, or simply the presence of major troop concentrations, could lead to large-scale subsistence crises, but these do not seem to have triggered major mortality crises in themselves. Empirical studies of mortality crises and a priori reasoning from present-day clinical data both lead to the conclusion that substantial mortality, even under conditions of major food shortage, required the outbreak of epidemic disease.

---

[19] Even during the Thirty Years War in Germany, Outram concludes that violent 'deaths of civilians perpetrated directly by the military appear to have been quite insignificant' (Outram 2001: 157).

14.2.1. EPIDEMIC DISEASE

The nature of medieval and early modern armies and their interactions with civilians meant that transmission of infection between the two was virtually inevitable. Armies could transfer infection from one region to another or diffuse infections afflicting the troops themselves. The disruption caused to civilian life by the military presence in the form of short-term migration and overcrowding also promoted the spread of epidemics. In the Russo-Swedish War of 1808–9, for instance, Russian troops were quartered on households in the Baltic Åland islands and the resulting epidemic trebled mortality levels even though there was almost no actual fighting (Mielke and Pitkanen 1989). The conditions chiefly responsible for epidemic crises on this scale were those in the vector- and airborne categories.

Military operations were responsible for epidemics of both bubonic plague and typhus among civilian populations. The passage of armies with their attendant carts, rats, and fleas was highly conducive to the transmission of the plague bacillus. One French army of 6,000 men, sent from La Rochelle in the 1620s to intervene in the War of Mantuan Succession, has been blamed for an outbreak which killed over a million people throughout northern Italy (Prinzing 1916: 74–5; Ladurie 1981*b*: 14). Transmission could occur through contact with infected articles, so that civilians were infected as they looted abandoned camps, as happened at Nuremberg in 1632, or stripped the dead on battlefields (Prinzing 1916: 53), and military hospitals, casualty stations, and the movement of prisoners posed further hazards. Armies contributed to the spread of plague from the time it first reappeared in fourteenth-century Europe at the siege of Caffa, but the phenomenon is best documented for the later sixteenth and seventeenth centuries when plague mortality seems to have become more severe. More important than any specific route of transmission were the general conditions of wartime disruption induced by the movement of poorly disciplined and provisioned armies with a large mercenary component. These conditions forced the flight of civilian populations into overcrowded towns and other places of refuge, allowing infection to diffuse and frustrating the implementation of effective countermeasures.[20]

Typhus fever could also spread from soldiers to civilians and was responsible for serious mortality crises in seventeenth-century Germany (Outram 2001; Zinsser 1935; Bray 1996: 135–53). The vector in question, the body louse, remained in clothing, and the major avenue of transmission was close physical contact, but

---

[20] Outram concludes his illuminating survey of the effects of the Thirty Years War on civilian mortality with the following apt judgement: 'It is the wanton destruction of the peasants' means of livelihood and their frequent flight from their fields that explains how the 15 million people of Germany were unable to support armies of perhaps 210,000 (less than 2 per cent of their number) without repeated episodes of starvation. It is flight from violence and atrocity and the conditions they endured in their places of refuge that explain the exceptionally high mortality from epidemic disease' (Outram 2001: 181). He particularly notes the difficulties that commanders had in disciplining mercenary units and the importance of the consequent disorders in promoting civilian flight.

this included contact with the clothing of the recently deceased, and civilian epidemics sometimes resulted from the looting of battlefields or abandoned campsites. In other cases, and probably of greater general importance, epidemic crises were due to the breakdown of hygienic conditions in overcrowded places of refuge. War-induced typhus epidemics seem to have declined in their incidence and severity from the later seventeenth century, though they never disappeared, but they returned dramatically with the onset of the French Revolutionary War and were a general accompaniment to the Napoleonic Wars.

The Austerlitz campaign in 1805 brought a dramatic increase in civilian mortality which was largely attributable to typhus. The disease broke out as a serious epidemic among troops on both sides during the Russian campaign and was subsequently spread by the retreating French and the advancing Russians. Conditions in military hospitals and clearing stations were appalling and contact with attendants and other staff there promoted the spread of the disease among the civilian population. The following year Napoleon raised a fresh army and returned to Germany for a campaign that focused on Saxony. The movement of wounded and prisoners led to epidemic crises in both Leipzig and Dresden and thereafter typhus was spread further westwards by the advancing allies. In the later wars of the nineteenth century the incidence of civilian typhus remained at a low level.

Airborne infections are, with the important exception of smallpox, harder to identify from historical accounts than are either plague or typhus, since their symptoms are often ill defined and can arise from infection by a number of different micro-organisms. The Antonine 'plague' in the second-century Roman Empire, which may have triggered a major increase in mortality, was possibly due to an airborne infection brought back by troops returning from the eastern frontier, but the most likely pre-eighteenth-century instance of an airborne epidemic spread by troops is that of the English 'sweating sickness'. This was an influenza-like condition which appeared shortly after the victory of Henry Tudor over Richard III in 1485 and was probably introduced by his Flemish mercenaries. Serious killing epidemics recurred well into the sixteenth century before the disease disappeared almost as suddenly as it had first appeared (Prinzing 1916: 18–19).

Smallpox emerged as a significant cause of death in eighteenth-century Europe, and in England at least there are instances of local epidemics attributable to troop movements. The failure to implement revaccination in the middle decades of the nineteenth century led to a build-up in the numbers of adult susceptibles as we have seen, and the disease was already undergoing some resurgence on a local scale in France in the winter of 1869–70. The defeat of the old long-service professional French army in the early campaigns of 1870 led to the collapse of Louis Napoleon's imperial regime and a mass mobilization by the government of the new Republic. Large numbers of immunologically unprotected young men were concentrated in the newly raised regiments and moved across the country to the zone of operations. In the process smallpox became established among the army and the general population. In Germany the epidemic was communicated from prisoners to civilians directly and through the sale of infected articles. In the words of the German Health Report:

> The dissemination of the disease, which broke out simultaneously in various parts of Germany, was helped along in numerous ways. From the lazarets and from prisons it was communicated by nurses and guards, and by working men and tradesmen, to the civil population and to the local garrison, and from there it spread from place to place, often considerable distances, by the moving population itself, not infrequently by marching troops, and by the removal of prisoners from one place of detention to another. (quoted Prinzing 1916: 213)

Overall the smallpox epidemic was responsible for at least 170,000 deaths across Germany in 1871–2 with the north and east suffering more heavily due to the lower incidence of pre-war vaccination. The epidemic also spread across western and central Europe.

14.2.2. SIEGES

The worst circumstances for civilians generally arose in connection with sieges. Any kind of prolonged troop concentration raised logistical and sanitary problems which posed a potential threat to the well-being of the surrounding civilian population, and so suffering could occur on both sides of the siege lines. The worst impact, however, was usually felt by the populations of besieged towns and cities. This arose from a number of factors, some of which varied over time but many of which were intrinsic to siege warfare itself and so represented historical constants. By their very nature siege conditions produced shortages of food, water, and fuel of a severity varying with geographical location and the extent of the preparations which the defenders had been able to make. Commanders generally responded to these by rationing essential commodities with priority being given to the garrison and 'essential' civilian workers. Conditions in besieged towns were often exacerbated by a prior influx of civilians from the surrounding countryside, or even further afield, on the approach of an enemy force. In the face of this, attempts were often made to conserve supplies by controlling the numbers of civilians and expelling refugees or non-essential citizens. Since the besiegers might refuse to let such people pass their lines, their fate was often grim.

Shortages of food, water, fuel, and living space—often aggravated by the destruction of buildings—provided ideal circumstances for the spread of pathogens, particularly those responsible for water- and food- and vector-borne infections. The occurrence of epidemics under these circumstances is attested from classical times, and Thucydides' account of 'plague' in Athens during the Peloponnesian War furnished later authors with a literary model for the depiction of many subsequent epidemics. Unfortunately, the salience of Thucydides' text makes the evidential status of later accounts difficult to assess. It is likely that some, at least, represent the deployment of a conventional literary figure rather than historically accurate narrative. Levels of war-related epidemic disease in the ancient and medieval worlds are correspondingly obscure, but both the incidence and severity of outbreaks seem to have increased as a result of early modern changes in the conduct of warfare. The overall scale of military forces increased and sieges grew in length and frequency. The growing organizational sophistication of field armies in the eighteenth and nineteenth centuries added a further dimension to siege warfare. Their greater resilience meant that defeated armies, rather than being dispersed, might disengage and seek refuge from pursuit in fortified towns or cities. Such places might thus find themselves sheltering forces which were much larger than was required to form an effective garrison, or for which accommodation existed, and which might outnumber the pre-siege population many times.

The consequences of this for the civilian population could be catastrophic, as can be seen in a number of instances assembled by Prinzing from the closing stages of the Napoleonic Wars when fugitive French corps, and other elements, were besieged in German towns and cities. Danzig, with a population of 40,000, many of whom had fled before the siege, was held by a garrison 36,000 strong when the siege began in January 1813. Civilian deaths ran at 200–300 a week through February and March and these, together with the expulsion of indigent civilians, many of whom died of starvation as the Russian besiegers refused to let them pass, reduced the population to some 16,000 by November. Surrender negotiations then allowed the passage of typhus from the besiegers to the city, and registered civilian deaths in December alone totalled 473 not allowing for unregistered deaths of paupers. Overall, Prinzing quotes a figure of 5,592 for civilian deaths for the siege as a whole, equivalent to some 14 per cent of the pre-siege population. Mortality on this scale within a besieged city meant that effective disposal of the dead became impossible, and disease was further spread by the large numbers of unburied corpses. Torgau, with a civilian population of 5,000, witnessed some 30,000 deaths in the four months it was besieged in 1813–14. Among these casualties were 678 civilians, which was equivalent to an annualized civilian death rate of over 400 per thousand. At Mayence typhus had already become established before the opening of the siege in November 1813 as a result of the passage of the *Grande Armée*'s field ambulances. Between November and April 17,000 to 18,000 of the 30,000-man garrison died together with 2,445 of the approximately 24,500 civilian inhabitants—equivalent to an annualized civilian death rate of some 200 per thousand; all the gravediggers died, leaving thousands of bodies in heaps awaiting burial.

In the preceding instances a large proportion of the deaths was evidently due to typhus. In this respect the Franco-Prussian War represented a major departure from historical experience, since typhus seems to have been unknown among either troops or civilians. The war was also distinguished by a siege on a hitherto unprecedented scale. Paris, a city containing around two million people including 246,000 troops, was besieged for twenty-eight weeks (September 1870–March 1871). During this period the death rate tripled relative to the same period twelve months before and was equivalent to an annualized rate of seventy-two per thousand. The autumn months saw the climax of the smallpox epidemic, affecting particularly the unvaccinated provincial troops of the *gardes mobiles*, but the onset of winter saw a major increase in deaths from bronchitis and pneumonia. Metz, where an Imperial field army of over 100,000 men had taken refuge, also underwent a prolonged siege and, in 1870, suffered 3,174 civilian deaths as against a normal annual average of 1,200 (Dumas and Vedel-Peterson 1923: 12). The villages surrounding Metz also suffered a tripling of their normal mortality during the siege as the concentration of besieging troops led to pollution of the water supplies and a consequent outbreak of typhoid and dysentery (Prinzing 1916: 190–1).

14.2.3. THE SCALE OF CIVILIAN MORTALITY

The available evidence indicates that war-induced, or at least war-related, population crises had a major supra-regional impact on parts of early modern Europe. Northern France may have lost as much as 20 per cent of its people in the period of civil war and invasion between 1580 and 1600 (Benedict 1985). This loss, however, pales into insignificance beside Germany's experience during the Thirty Years War when population fell from some 15–16 million to around 10 million, mostly as a result of mortality crises (Outram 2001; Stier and von Hippel 1996). There is insufficient evidence to attempt a global assessment of what larger consequences stemmed from war-induced population crises elsewhere or in earlier periods which would, in any case, lie beyond the scope of this volume, but it is possible to make some general observations. The limited destructive power of pre-industrial military technology restricted the direct toll that it could inflict on civilian lives, but the economic disruption caused by war or large-scale troop movements, and their potential for transmitting epidemic disease, could trigger major mortality crises. It is difficult to determine how often, and on what scale, this potential was realized. Very large regional population losses certainly occurred but recovery could be very rapid, and it is difficult to determine how far the devastation described by contemporaries in the worst-affected regions, and for which documentation sometimes survives, should be taken as an indicator of conditions over a wider area, or whether it was an essentially localized phenomenon. A great deal depended on the relative roles of mortality and emigration. Migratory losses were more readily reversed than those due to mortality and might also generate offsetting gains elsewhere in a way that was not possible where mortality was responsible.

The speed of recovery was affected by the broader demographic conjuncture and the state of surrounding regions since this largely determined the availability of potential immigrants, and by the duration of the crisis itself. Where this was brief the demographic effects were often brief as well, but protracted crises could damage the foundations of a region's economic and social life as capital assets were destroyed, arable land reverted to overgrown waste, and skills were lost due to death or migration. The worst results ensued where persisting insecurity prevented cultivators from planting crops with any confidence that they would be able to harvest them. Where these conditions prevailed, as they did in some frontier regions of the ancient and medieval worlds and in parts of central Europe during the seventeenth century, the result could be a self-perpetuating downward spiral in which the remaining inhabitants were forced to become soldiers or bandits in order to survive.

A region's own socio-economic characteristics had a major effect on its ability to withstand military crises. Regions with more complex, differentiated economies were usually more resilient than were poorly endowed or overpopulated 'marginal' regions whose poverty deprived their inhabitants of a shock-absorbing buffer of accumulated resources and reduced their subsequent attractiveness to potential immigrants. This may explain why the crises of the Thirty Years War turned Alsace-Lorraine's earlier demographic growth into long-term stagnation whilst population levels in the much fought over Basse-Meuse around Liège and Maastricht proved resilient (Gutmann 1980; Dupâquier 1988a: 200–1). Regions with relatively sophisticated economies could, however, suffer long-term damage if the crisis was sufficiently severe or protracted to disrupt the higher-level spatial integration on which they depended. The mercantile and industrial cities of southern Germany and the Rhineland suffered in this way in the aftermath of the Thirty Years War which destroyed long-range economic linkages and led to a persisting 'regionalization' of the German economy.[21]

14.3. CONCLUSION

The effects of war on mortality can be thought of as a series of concentric circles spreading outward from the battlefield itself to civilian society in regions beyond the war zone. There is very little reliable information on levels of battlefield mortality before the eighteenth century, but what there is supports the a priori argument that casualties before the gunpowder revolution tended to be much heavier on the losing side than among the victors and that their absolute levels depended on the effectiveness of the pursuit. The advent of gunpowder weapons is likely to have increased casualty levels overall, and produced a more even distribution of losses. These tendencies were reinforced as improvements in tactical organization and discipline led to increases in the scale and duration of major set-piece battles. The major cause of death among armies nonetheless

---

[21] Stier and von Hippel quote Lütge's judgement to the effect that the longer-term damage inflicted by the war was less material than 'the breaking apart—often a violent tearing apart—of domestic and international economic relationships, which in most cases were impossible to put back together again'. The consequences were still visible in the German urban network of 1800, which was dominated by ports and administrative centres at the expense of the old mercantile and industrial centres (Stier and von Hippel 1996: 242; François 1990).

continued, even in wartime, to be infectious disease, mortality from which ran substantially above normal civilian levels until the end of the nineteenth century.

Poor living conditions in camps and barracks were responsible for these excess deaths, as on ships, but these institutional settings also provided an opportunity for the enforcement of hygienic and sanitary measures. The substantial decline in disease mortality at the end of the nineteenth century was due to measures of this kind which were aided by progress in the scientific understanding of disease. The latter was not, however, an essential prerequisite for the implementation of better hygienic and sanitary standards and for improvements in the general living conditions of military personnel. Measures of this kind had already been implemented in the course of the eighteenth century as rulers assumed greater administrative responsibility for their armed forces. The level of excess military disease mortality seems to have declined somewhat as a result, but the Revolutionary and Napoleonic periods may have seen a reversal of the trend.

The level of military mortality did not have any appreciable impact on overall population levels although it increased adult male mortality substantially in some cases. The demographic effects of war were felt through its effects on civilian populations. In most cases these are very difficult to assess, although it is clear that in the short term they could be very great on a regional level. The speed of regional recovery depended on the relative contribution of migration and mortality to the loss of population, the availability of potential immigrants, and the attractiveness of the region to them. In most cases forced emigration played the major role and recovery is likely to have been rapid once the immediate crisis was past. Military occupation or the passage of troops could, however, trigger substantial mortality increases—for which epidemic disease was almost entirely responsible—and prolonged military crises sometimes inflicted lasting economic damage which impeded demographic recovery. Even where demographic recovery was relatively rapid, however, major mortality crises deprived the survivors of neighbours and loved ones who could not be replaced and inflicted a deep trauma on those who lived through them.

CHAPTER FIFTEEN

Spending, Taxing, and Borrowing

War imposed costs. The expedients adopted to meet these costs and the degree of success they attained shaped both the conduct of war and the development or retrogression of the state apparatus. The concept of cost implies the loss or forgoing of anything that is of value, and not all the costs imposed by war were straightforwardly economic. Some took the form of 'disutilities', such as emotional damage through the loss of loved ones or reductions in quality of life that could not be evaluated in material terms. Nor can all material costs be lumped together because not all of them fell on the shoulders of rulers in such a way as to deplete the resources they had available for other purposes. Those costs that did fall in this way, which we have called 'fiscal costs', had to be met from the proceeds of taxation, broadly defined, or by borrowing. The various forms of taxation can be divided into three general categories. The first, arbitrary payments or 'tribute', could be levied by a public authority, foreign aggressor, or threatening neighbour, and a thin line divided it from simple plunder. The second category, domain taxation, consisted of income in cash or kind derived from the rulers' estates or other property directly owned by the public authority. Revenue of this kind featured prominently in the ancient empires and was the fiscal mainstay of feudal Europe, but it was relatively inelastic and proved inadequate to the demands of medieval military expenditure. The inadequacies of domain revenue stimulated the re-emergence of the third category, public taxation, whose seemingly inexorable rise is the *leitmotif* of modern fiscal history.

Public taxation was levied on goods or transactions, in cash or kind, either directly by state officials or through some form of devolution. As in the case of military recruitment, cash and state administration provided the most efficient and flexible options, but they were difficult to implement in the context of an organic economy where cash might be a rarity and the overhead costs of direct administration too much to bear. Even where rulers could tap the resources of the real economy effectively it was difficult to fund wars from this source alone because, where peacetime military budgets were nugatory, the onset of hostilities ratcheted up expenditure by much more than taxation could be increased in the short term. This made some form of borrowing almost unavoidable.

Public credit was poorly developed in the ancient world, and prolonged excesses of expenditure over revenue were usually met by running down accumulated stocks of precious metals and other valuable items. When these stocks ran out expenditure had to be cut to match revenue, unless the treasury had been refilled with the profits of conquest in the meantime, and the result was a characteristic stop-start pattern of military activity. Medieval rulers borrowed money on their own account, but increasing demand led to the proliferation of debt secured on taxes and other public assets. Where this grew too burdensome, as in Habsburg Spain, the entire fiscal structure of the state could be compromised, but countries that combined efficient financial management with a robust revenue base, like England and Holland, successfully funded global expansion by this means. The rise of public credit removed the cap that their limited revenues had previously placed on rulers' expenditure. This enabled them to fund a larger share of their military costs from the central treasury and the consequential costs of war fell as a result. But borrowing also removed an important check to excessive ambition and provided only cloudy and confused signals as to what military commitments were affordable in the long term. The last decades of the organic economy in Europe were ones of recurrent financial crisis as rulers struggled to meet the costs of earlier borrowing.

15.1. REVENUE

The energy constraints common to organic economies meant that state agencies could usually exercise only a spatially shallow control and they were also very restricted in their capacity to engage with the wider structures of economy and society. The limit on the numbers of non-food-producers who could be supported imposed a corresponding limit on the size of the administrative apparatus which rarely did more than sustain itself and the coercive forces of the state by extracting resources from land and people. Sometimes the receipts from taxation barely exceeded the coercive and administrative costs sustained in extracting it. The category of 'taxation' broadly defined embraces any form of systematic resource extraction and can be subdivided into three major groupings: 'public taxation', which was levied on the population at large or on specific elements within it; 'domain revenue', which was garnered from assets controlled directly by the ruler and did not require a general public obligation to support his financial outgoings; and 'tribute', which was commonly imposed on their subordinates by the barbarian elites of stateless societies but might also be employed by the rulers of organized states.

Taxation could be imposed in cash or in kind. Taxes in kind involved the rendering of either goods or services. Labour in agriculture, or construction on projects, were the most common service obligations, although, in some respects, military service owed in exchange for entitlements to domain resources might also be treated as a form of taxation in kind. Levying revenue in kind had the advantage of simplicity and did not require the existence of a cash economy. This could be important where imperial powers sought to tap resources on the periphery, but in more economically sophisticated 'core' areas coinage could also be hard to come by. Money taxes were then a cause of hardship and potential unrest, particularly where the value of coin was manipulated by the central power.

Taxation in kind was useful for obtaining unskilled labour and meeting the subsistence needs of local officials, garrisons, or, as in early medieval Europe, of an itinerant court. It might also provoke less resistance in circumstances where the payment of taxes was a mark of subservience or unfree status, since it could be represented as gift-giving, or 'hospitality' (Poulson 1995: 104–7).

Taxation in kind suffered from the drawback that it was relatively inflexible and there was no guarantee that the resources it yielded would be in the form and location that the authorities required. Moreover fiscal costs, such as the salaries of senior officials, usually had to be met in cash, and marketing tax goods created inefficiencies that were avoided where taxes were paid in cash to begin with. The Roman authorities provisioned their metropolitan centres largely with grain procured in kind, and tax grain was also used to provision the army. A substantial proportion of taxation under the Principate was levied in cash, however, and the shift towards taxation in kind after the crises of the third century reflected the general disruption that these had wrought and the consequences of the repeated currency debasements that accompanied them. As the situation improved money taxes became more important, among them a tax in gold that was apparently designed to force hoarded bullion back into circulation (Cameron 1993: 6). The role of money was greatly reduced during the economic retrogression that followed the end of the Western Empire, and the successor kingdoms of the early Middle Ages relied heavily on taxation in kind. From the twelfth century, at least, the economies of western Europe became increasingly 'remonetarized', and there was a corresponding movement to commute existing taxes in kind and introduce wholly new taxes payable in cash. Money taxes' inherent flexibility made them the usual mode of choice for taxing powers, and taxpayers often found them less irksome than labour service. Substantial quantities of revenue nonetheless continued to be collected in kind, even in eighteenth-century Europe, chiefly in heavily garrisoned or economically backward regions (Bonney 1995b: 464–6).

15.1.1. TRIBUTES

Tributes, arbitrary payments levied by dominant figures on their subordinates, were a common feature of early state organization, and stateless barbarian societies. They needed no administrative apparatus, nor even a permanent presence in the territory concerned; intimidation and a readiness to inflict reprisals for non-payment would suffice. Many early imperial formations were based on tributary relations, for they were very flexible, and there were hazy boundaries between the levying of tribute, bribery, and plundering.[1] All that was required for

---

[1] This phenomenon is exemplified in the 'taxing rounds' conducted by the princes of early medieval Russia who are described by Franklin as 'itinerant *rentiers*'. One of them, Vladimir Monomak, claimed to have made eighty-three 'great journeys' on most of which 'he was a kind of roving enforcer: collecting tribute, assisting or confronting troubled or troublesome cousins' (Franklin 1996: 123–4, 195). As local circumstances allowed these men extracted resources from their subjects and neighbours by coercion, trade, or the provision of defence against raiding nomads.

the levying power, be it a central authority or an aggressive neighbour, was to enter a territory in question and wreak sufficient damage to convince the local elite that paying up was the lesser of two evils, and often a mere threat would suffice. Payments usually then continued, on a more or less regular basis, until such time as the subordinates tried their hand at defiance, and the cycle either resumed or was broken by a successful revolt. Where an imperial power used this technique, life in the subordinate territories might continue unaffected by their notional incorporation into the overarching political unit. One characteristic of such payments was that the parties could endow the transaction with different, and possibly opposed, meanings. The rulers of organized states often paid barbarian leaders to refrain from raiding, or to act against neighbouring groups or rival pretenders. The recipients might treat the payment as tribute, betokening a form of submission, and thereby gain status in the eyes of their peers or subordinates, whilst the donors regarded the transaction as gift-giving or payment for services rendered. Useful as short-term expedients, such payments were potentially dangerous in the longer term since they could consolidate potentially hostile coalitions and furnish an ideological basis for their aggression. Conversely, tributes levied by hostile forces on the periphery could stimulate the development of fiscal systems by forcing subordinate rulers to raise funds by taxation. This happened in Anglo-Saxon England where the Danegeldt, first levied to pay off the Vikings, was retained thereafter as a form of public taxation, and subsequently in the Russian principalities after the Mongol conquests.

15.1.2. DOMAIN TAXATION

The category of domain taxation incorporates cash revenue, labour, or produce obtained in respect of assets held directly by the taxing power. Agricultural land was most commonly the source of such revenue, but it was the usual means too of exploiting mineral deposits for a ruler's benefit, and domain taxes could also be drawn from state-owned workshops or from assets such as forests and fisheries. Roman Imperial estates were an important source of revenue, particularly tax grain, but domain taxation really came into its own in medieval Europe where domains were, in principle, supposed to provide the entirety of royal income. The advantage of domain revenue was that it could be raised through administrative channels that were required in any case for purposes of estate management. This made domain revenue relatively easy to collect and it was well suited to the maintenance of local officials and their staffs. The existence of a royal 'private income' gave rulers the ability to act independently of representative bodies, but there were relatively narrow limits to how much could be obtained in this way from agricultural lands. The fiscal costs of war had clearly surpassed these limits by the later Middle Ages, and rulers needed public taxation to meet them.

The expectation that 'the king should live of his own' remained a powerful one nonetheless, and the story of Christian Europe's political evolution is often told in terms of how that expectation was variously met, evaded, or defied. By the early modern period public taxation was an integral feature of revenue systems across Europe, and many domain assets had been alienated, but domain taxes did not disappear. The inclusion of mineral rights as part of the royal domain could yield substantial, and sometimes spectacular, sums. The Castilian crown exploited the New World silver deposits on this basis and the resulting revenues formed the mainstay of Spanish public finance. Elsewhere domain revenues played a much smaller role, if any, with the significant exception of Prussia, where it remained the major element of the kingdom's revenue throughout the reign of Frederick the Great.

15.1.3. PUBLIC TAXATION

The long-term development of European fiscal structures, from the early medieval period to that of the *ancien régime*, is conventionally seen in terms of the progressive replacement of domain revenue by public taxation as the mainstay of governmental income. The transition from the so-called 'Domain State' to the 'Tax State' was a process in which the reliance on domain revenues, intermittently supplemented by 'extraordinary' taxes granted to the king in times of crisis, gave way to a system based on regular public taxation and the acceptance of a general obligation to contribute to state expenditure. As this happened, the volume of public taxation increased relative to domain revenue, but it also became a regular feature of state administration that could be collected without the need for specific, ad hoc authorization from representative bodies. Public taxation, if it was to be most effective, had to be directed at the major sources of wealth and income, but both the power structure and the limited administrative resources of pre-nineteenth-century states made this difficult. In practice, public taxation was usually directed at the resources that were easiest to tax, rather than the most intrinsically valuable.

For public taxes to be levied at all several things had to happen. The resources liable to taxation had to be properly assessed, the appropriate revenue had to be collected, and, if it was not to be locally consumed, the revenue then had to be transmitted to some central point. For this to be done effectively it was necessary to have a body of relatively competent and uncorrupt agents, operating in physical security and with access to the necessary transport and communications. Most forms of regular taxation also required a system of accounting and record-keeping. These were difficult requirements to meet in the context of an organic economy, and they help to explain why taxation in kind persisted, even in monetarized economies.

15.1.3.1. *Modes of collection*

There were three possible ways of organizing the collection of tax, whether in cash or kind: administrative collection, farming, or repartition. Administrative collection involved officials acting on behalf of the central authority, and responsible directly to it or to its provincial delegates. In principle it allowed substantial central control over how much tax was paid, and by whom. In practice it suffered from two disadvantages. It needed a specialized administrative apparatus of a kind that was beyond the means of many rulers who had neither the trained manpower nor the funds to pay for it. Furthermore, in anything less than ideal conditions, the centre could not know the yield of a given tax in advance. Where corruption or insecurity prevailed this could fall well short of expectations. The Romans collected some revenues administratively in some periods (Goldsmith 1987), but even they had to fall back on other means at times. Most rulers, before the eighteenth century, relied on one of the two other alternatives.

'Tax-farming' was a form of devolution in which the public authority sold its tax-gathering rights to an individual, or syndicate, who kept what they collected in exchange for an advance payment. The method had a number of advantages and was commonly used from the time of the Romans to the period of the *ancien régime*. Its principal benefit was that it delivered an assured sum 'up front', without the need to maintain a cadre of trained personnel at public expense. Tax farms, like the trading monopolies they closely resembled, were also valuable political assets that could be used to reward powerful individuals for their loyalty, or other services, or tie their interests to those of the state. The difficulty with tax-farming was that it was generally unpopular, sometimes dangerously so, and was notoriously open to abuse. The farmers' profits could also be seen as an element of revenue forgone by the central authority.

The main alternative to farming was repartition, in which responsibility was devolved to governing authorities, or elites, in the various provinces, cities, or other geographical units. Each was allocated a tax quota and made responsible for distributing the liability, and collecting the appropriate revenue, within its jurisdiction. In this way central government avoided the need to establish its own fiscal bureaucracy without the odium that could result from a reliance on farming. In principle, repartitional taxation was also likely to be more efficient since the assessments were carried out by authorities who knew the region and its inhabitants, and who would be less prone to abuses than farmers or their agents, since they had to live with the consequences of their actions and with the people on whom they imposed taxation. In practice, however, the distribution of tax liabilities under systems of this kind was rarely imposed on an equitable basis. Landowners and other wealthy groups, from amongst whom local or regional decision-makers were drawn, often got off lightly at the expense of poorer groups excluded from power. In these circumstances it could be difficult for the central authority to tap the wealth of the regions, or to lighten the tax burden on the poorest when times were hard, since the benefits of any quota reductions might be appropriated by the rich. Where regular taxation was imposed in this way for an extended period the result could be the shrinkage of the tax base and the progressive immiseration of those who made it up.

15.1.3.2. *Forms of public taxation*

The forms in which public taxation was imposed and the resource on which it was imposed both varied greatly, but most public taxation fell into one of four general categories.[2]

15.1.3.2.1. *Enumerated taxes*

Enumerated taxes were taxes that were levied on the basis of a count of taxable units. Usually these units were either people, in the case of poll taxes, or else households in the case of hearth taxes. This form of taxation was commonly resorted to in late medieval and early modern Europe when an extraordinary injection of revenue was required, and it was frequently the fiscal mainstay of agrarian empires. An attempt was usually made to vary liabilities according to wealth, for instance, by exempting the poorest or by taxing households according to the number of hearths, but in essence the method depended simply on counting the relevant units. Enumerated taxation, unlike tribute, was not completely arbitrary in its incidence, and it required some kind of assessment. It did not, however, require the maintenance of a permanent fiscal bureaucracy, an administrative presence in the territory concerned, or any detailed knowledge of its economic structure.

15.1.3.2.2. *Indirect taxes*

Indirect taxation tapped economic 'flows': the movement or exchange of goods and the provision of services. Taxes of this sort can be divided into two main categories. The first are 'boundary taxes' or taxes levied on the physical movement of goods across demarcation lines of some kind, whether international borders or those of internal fiscal districts. The second category consists of 'transaction taxes', which are those levied where goods changed hands or services were provided. The origins of boundary taxation antedate those of organized territorial states and can be seen in the efforts of barbarian leaders to buttress their position by controlling the supply and distribution of prestige goods in favour of their followers. Imports and exports were both taxed in medieval Europe, and internal tolls proliferated, to become a common cause of complaint in reformist writing of the *ancien régime*. Tolls were also levied on bridges, waterways, and at choke points, such as the Baltic Sound, in a manner that often overlapped with domain taxation, or simple robbery. The motive of boundary taxation could be protectionist as well as fiscal, and it was often used to discriminate against 'foreign' merchants and their products.

The commonest transaction taxes were the sales taxes levied by municipal authorities, or administered by them on behalf of the central authority. Taxes of

---

[2] This classification is mainly based on Tilly (1990: 87), but differs in treating 'enumerated' taxes such as poll taxes as a category distinct from 'tribute'.

this kind met much of the increased fiscal demands of Europe's rulers from the later Middle Ages. A variant form was the sale, or grant, of monopoly rights to the distribution of taxed commodities. This could be very remunerative but generated resentment where purchase was enforced, or the commodity was essential, as in the notorious case of the French salt *gabelle*. Transaction taxes had to be collected over an extended period, if not indefinitely, and this could make them expensive to administer, unlike enumerated taxes with their potential for a 'hit and run' levy. Nonetheless, they had both fiscal and political advantages. Fiscally, they were a means of tapping economic activity, and could be imposed on an *ad valorem* basis. Most of the relevant transactions took place in municipalities that already possessed regulatory institutions, and these could be pressed into service to administer the tax. Above all, transaction taxes did not require the assessment of elite wealth, with all the intrusion and political dangers that this involved.

15.1.3.2.3. Direct taxes

Direct taxes on economic assets, or 'stocks', were in principle easier to administer than indirect taxes. They were concerned with tangible, physical assets that could be assessed at intervals, rather than with movement or transactions that needed continuous monitoring. In organic economies, moreover, the principal form of wealth was land, and this was not something that could be readily concealed. Nonetheless, there were serious obstacles to the effective use of direct taxation. Some of these were practical. Much wealth was in the form of luxury goods and stores of value such as bullion or gems and as such it was readily portable and easy to conceal. The main difficulties were political. Effective direct taxation required knowledge of land values, and ownership of land was linked to prestige and power. Carrying out the required assessments meant intruding into the affairs of a privileged elite, whether on a national, regional, or local basis. Even the English land tax, in existence from 1692, had reverted to a fixed levy bearing little relationship to actual values by the end of the eighteenth century. In France, the Napoleonic assessment was not completed until 1850 and was then already out of date (Bonney 1995*b*: 483–4). The efforts of city states to tax mercantile wealth ran into similar difficulties. One of the most sophisticated and best known, the Florentine *catasto* of 1427, involved a remarkably comprehensive survey of wealth and income which has proved a boon to later historians. As a fiscal instrument, however, it was unsuccessful and short-lived (Bonney 1995*b*: 476–7).

15.1.3.2.4. Income taxes

Regular taxes on incomes were potentially a very valuable form of revenue, but they were also the most difficult and demanding to administer. Rents and other income derived from stocks were taxed, in effect, by direct taxation on the levied assets themselves, but income taxes in the modern sense of direct taxation on individuals emerged only at the close of the period with which we are concerned, and then only in the most advanced economies (Bonney 1995b: 485–8). There were two difficulties. If income taxes were to be worthwhile the economy had to be not just highly monetarized but also 'commercialized', with large volumes of salaries, professional fees, or wages at a level much in excess of subsistence requirements. The assessment and collection of the tax also required a substantial administrative apparatus and a formidable body of record-keeping. This was both expensive and intrusive, and its operation had to be acceptable to a substantial body of opinion for a protracted period. The Dutch Republic, for all its wealth and institutional sophistication, proved unable to institute a workable tax of this kind (de Vries and van der Woude 1997: 107), and it was left to England to play the pioneering role when threatened with foreign invasion and imminent financial collapse at the end of the 1790s.[3] Income tax became law in 1799, but was then abolished on the return of peace with the destruction of all relevant records.

15.2. WAR, FISCAL COSTS, AND PUBLIC CREDIT

The recruitment, maintenance, and deployment of armed force consumed resources and so imposed costs which could be met in a number of different ways. The principles of compulsion, entitlement, and devolution as defined above provided alternatives to meeting the full costs of war as what we have called 'fiscal costs'. Few if any rulers were able to manage entirely without these alternatives, but they imposed military rigidities, political dangers, or consequential costs of a kind that could be avoided where troops were recruited in exchange for cash payments from the central treasury. The existence of fiscal costs requires that resources should be inter-convertible for different ends—so the economy, to all intents and purposes, must be at least partly monetarized—and that the political system should possess some kind of central mechanism for resource allocation and appropriation.[4]

These requirements were met by some states in the ancient world, and both cash economies and central treasuries re-emerged in later medieval Europe. This made it possible to 'fiscalize' military costs, but the obvious disadvantage of doing this was that rulers then needed cash incomes on a scale that was not required where troops were obtained in other ways. Such incomes could be obtained in one of two ways: either by compulsion, in the form of taxation; or by inducement, in the form of credit. The ancient world had little in the way of public credit

---

[3] As O'Brien notes: 'Only the armies of revolutionary France and the probable collapse of public credit prompted the political classes to accept a policy which translated into law their oft-proclaimed principle that Englishmen should contribute to the needs of the state in accordance with their abilities to pay.' Lax administration reduced yields in the early years, but 'from 1808–16 it made massive contributions to the war effort' (O'Brien 1988: 22).

[4] Something very similar to fiscal-like costs could in principle exist outside the context of an exchange economy. Trees cut down to build a fort would not, for example, be available for shipbuilding, but in practice it is doubtful if many such instances occurred without a certain degree of economic exchange having already developed.

facilities, and fiscal costs had to be met from current or accumulated revenue eked out by whatever could be extracted from the treasure hoards of wealthy individuals, temples, or other institutions. This set an effective limit to how much could be spent on the army or fleet, and when circumstances demanded expenditure above this limit the consequence was a fiscal crisis with far-reaching political and military consequences. The re-emergence of cash economies was accompanied by an expansion of credit in ever more sophisticated forms. This removed the old limits to military commitment by allowing rulers to spend substantially in excess of revenue in the short or medium term. Nonetheless credit was itself expensive and the costs had to be met eventually out of the limited productive resources of an organic economy. The long-term consequence of excessive military commitment was another round of fiscal and political crises.

15.2.1. WAR AND FISCAL COSTS

The data that are needed to estimate fiscal costs are very hard to come by before the early modern period, and even where they exist, it is difficult to make long-term comparisons because this requires a common standard against which fiscal costs can be set. Standards of this kind are very hard to define in a generally applicable fashion, but one approach is to try to define the total value of overall production in an economy. On this basis Goldsmith has estimated military and naval expenditure at around 7 per cent of Athenian national product in the fifth century BC and somewhat over 2 per cent in early Imperial Rome (Goldsmith 1987).[5] These levels can be compared with the more than 15 per cent of British national income devoted directly to military and naval expenditure in the last years of the war with Napoleon,[6] but the comparison has little meaning because, apart from the highly speculative nature of the ancient estimates, the nineteenth-century British economy was generating a far larger volume of resources surplus to subsistence needs.

Another possible source of a common standard is the level of household subsistence needs or basic incomes. On this basis Athens's annual military expenditure equalled the expenditure of 9,000 to 10,000 households, which was probably around 17 per cent of the contemporary total households.[7] Augustus' military expenditure may have equalled the subsistence consumption of 620,000

---

[5] Interpretation of Athenian expenditure is complicated by the fact that half of the amount was contributed by the city's subordinate allies in the Delian League. Wealthy citizens were also directly responsible for the support of warships which may have added 100 talents to the estimated annual state military expenditure of 350 talents.

[6] In 1814–15 expenditure on the army, navy, and ordnance accounted for 64.5% of a United Kingdom total which may have been a quarter of contemporary gross national product. Debt charges, which were mostly due to the war, accounted for another quarter of expenditure, and large sums were also disbursed to Britain's continental allies (Bonney 1995c: 379–82; Mitchell 1962: 396).

[7] One talent was worth 6,000 drachmas. Goldsmith estimates annual expenditure for a four-person household at 200–40 drachmas and accepts a figure of 55,000 for total households (Goldsmith 1987: 16–18).

urban households or of 2–2.5 per cent of the Empire's population.[8] Treadgold estimates mid-fifth-century Byzantine military expenditure at 5.4 million *numismata* annually at a time when minimal household subsistence income was around 10 *numismata* (Treadgold 1995: 156 and table 12). If this is correct, then the military was consuming the equivalent of 540,000 household incomes, which was probably some 10–15 per cent of the contemporary total.[9]

The preceding calculations can convey some impression of the weight that military expenditure imposed on the 'real' economy of production and consumption, but they remain difficult to interpret in economies where most households were engaged in subsistence production and made few if any cash purchases. We are on surer ground when we come to relate military expenditure to the overall total since, whatever problems there may be with the data, we are at least comparing like with like. Analyses of this kind can be undertaken at intervals from the classical era onwards, and the dominant role of military expenditure is starkly apparent at least from the later Roman period. Goldsmith estimates military expenditure as 54–71 per cent of total expenditure under Augustus. The military proportion may have fallen to around a third of the total by the middle of the second century, but it had risen to some 80 per cent by the time of the Emperor Diocletian (Duncan-Jones 1978; MacMullen 1984), and in the surviving eastern half of the Empire military expenditure seems to have remained at 60 to 70 per cent of the total for most of the period up to the early eleventh century (Treadgold 1995: 198).

Calculations of this kind can be undertaken for the major European states from the fifteenth century onwards and they clearly demonstrate the crucial role played by military expenditure in the growth of taxation and public finance generally. Körner puts the average proportion of expenditure devoted to war in the major European states at 40, 27, 46, and 54 per cent for each of the four centuries 1400–1800 (Körner 1995: 416), but there are two reasons why these percentages understate the true importance of military expenditure. The first reason is that long-term averages mean little in themselves because expenditure fluctuated greatly between peacetime troughs and wartime peaks. It was the magnitude of the peaks which 'drove' the development of fiscal systems and some of them were very large indeed: in England three-quarters of total expenditure was devoted to war in the years 1598–1603 (Bean 1973: 216), whilst in the closing decades of the seventeenth century France spent 76 per cent, Denmark 88 per cent, and Austria 93 per cent of its expenditure on war (Körner 1995: 411). In 1705 Russia's war with Sweden consumed 96 per cent of its total expenditure (Bonney 1995c: 331).

---

[8] Goldsmith quotes a figure of 700 *sestertii* (HS) for a 'modest' level of household expenditure in urban Italy, but believes this to have been above the Imperial average. He estimates annual output per head throughout the empire at HS 350–400. The median estimate of annual military expenditure (including veterans' discharge bonuses) is HS 435 million (Goldsmith 1987: 34–59).

[9] It would be the equivalent of 12% of households if the population was eighteen million, as it may have been, and average household size was four persons.

The proportion of revenue spent directly on armies and navies also fails to capture the full fiscal burden of early modern war because a large proportion of it was met in the first instance by borrowing. In one extreme instance, war-related expenditure consumed over 75 per cent of the Spanish Habsburgs' overall total in 1572–6 but actually equalled 150 per cent of total revenues (Bean 1973: 217). Borrowing on anything like the scale implied by these figures generated further costs which ultimately had to be met from taxation, and the costs of debt servicing came to form a substantial proportion of total expenditure in many states. The Castilian crown allocated only 20 per cent of its expenditure directly to war during the second half of the seventeenth century, but a further 40 per cent was consumed by the debts run up in earlier military adventures (Körner 1995: 409). In Britain some 60 per cent of peacetime expenditure from 1688 to 1815, and nearly 90 per cent of wartime expenditure, was accounted for by the army, the navy, and the debt taken together (Körner 1995: 414 n. 43). The modern fiscal history of war is therefore inextricably bound up with the development of public credit.

15.2.2. BORROWING

The low productivity of organic economies necessarily limited the volume of resources that could be devoted to war, but this was not the only reason why rulers found it so difficult to fund wars' fiscal costs out of their normal revenue. No matter how strong the revenue base might be, the time profiles of revenue and expenditure streams were radically different. War expenditure was by its nature 'peaky'. Major campaigns like those mounted by the French in 1536–7 consumed more than the kingdom's total revenue for the period (Bean 1973: 217), and even where powerful standing armies existed, the outbreak of war usually brought some expansion in numbers, imposed operational costs, and often increased capital expenditure. Normal taxation could be increased and extraordinary taxes imposed to cover some of the excess, but there were economic and political limits on how much could be achieved in this way, particularly as war-related disruption often shrank the revenue base of more sophisticated economies. The gap had to be made up by borrowing, if it was to be made up at all.

In the ancient world there were few credit facilities available to either public or private borrowers. Public authorities drew on gifts, or forced loans, from wealthy individuals or institutions. The latter, however, were as much a form of taxation as of credit and the former often involved the devolution of military authority, and so evaded rather than covered fiscal costs. Most current deficits were met through a cycle of hoarding and de-hoarding; state expenditure was run below revenue for extended periods, and the assets accumulated, usually in coins or unminted precious metals, were disbursed to meet exceptional expenditure. Other public institutions, particularly temples, also accumulated substantial stores of valuable objects that could be used to meet exceptional expenditure. The sums involved could be very large; the 6,000 talents held in the Athenian treasury on the eve of the Spartan wars was equivalent to an estimated 22 per cent of national wealth. It was supplemented by an unquantifiable accumulation of treasure in the temple of Athena which was also expended to fund the unsuccessful war effort. In the fourth century AD when the Roman Emperor converted to Christianity and stripped the pagan temples of their treasure, the quantity seized was sufficient to help re-establish an Imperial gold currency.

The growing importance of cash transactions, in both civilian and military spheres, meant that war-related fiscal costs had returned as a problem for rulers by the thirteenth century. The difficulties were aggravated by prevailing attitudes to revenue-raising. In normal circumstances rulers were expected to manage on inelastic domain income, sometimes supplemented by modest levels of regular public taxation. Extraordinary taxes could be imposed in support of war, but this often required the assent of representative bodies which imposed political costs and could be dangerous, particularly where the war lacked popular support. These difficulties were partly offset by the rise of international merchant capital and the merchant-banking networks that this underpinned in the more advanced regions of western Europe, particularly northern Italy. In England, the fiscal costs of Edward I's campaigns rose to twice the level of normal revenue in the last years of the thirteenth century, and the gap was met by Italian merchant bankers (Ormrod 1995: 125). Borrowing of this kind remained, however, some way from modern notions of public credit. It generally involved personal transactions by the ruler, and the debts could be difficult to recover if he died. Edward's Tuscan creditors were ruined when, in 1307, he died owing more than £300,000 of unpayable debts. Both English and French monarchs ran up very large debts during the Hundred Years War, and Edward III's over-borrowing triggered a second wave of Italian banking failures in the 1340s (Körner 1995: 509). This borrowing was short term and secured on specific revenues or domain assets. The procedure was expensive and risked alienating much of the ruler's revenue base. Scandinavia's lack of mercantile development forced rulers to pledge domain income. By 1340 the practice had brought Denmark effectively under foreign rule, whilst in Sweden the area directly under royal control shrank to the equivalent of a single county (Poulson 1995: 113–16).

Large-scale public indebtedness seems to have been the exception rather than the rule before the late fifteenth century, but this changed with the growing scale of war-related fiscal costs. The principle of public taxation was increasingly accepted in the course of the early modern period, however grudgingly, but funding the new scale of expenditure from taxation alone would have required levels that could not be met by organic economies, however much public support existed in principle. Borrowing was the only alternative. It offered the prospect of spreading additional revenue requirements over an extended period of post-war prosperity, but it also offered a means of raising funds far beyond anything peacetime taxation could ever possibly redeem. The biggest casualties of this process were the Spanish Habsburgs, who, New World silver notwithstanding, sank into an ever-deeper morass of military commitment, borrowing, and fiscal alienation allied to the entrenchment of social and regional privilege (Thompson 1976; Gelabert 1999). At the same time, the growing sophistication of contemporary financial institutions offered a tantalizing prospect of ameliorating, if not actually solving, the indebtedness problem. Compared with the older short-term, redeemable debt, the new long-term credit instruments, such as annuities, attracted relatively light servicing costs (Körner 1995: 521 f.). They also deferred repayment for an extended if not indefinite period, provided creditors could be brought to accept the consolidation of their existing loans in this form. The Spanish monarchy used its political assets by means of coercion, defaults, and technical bankruptcy to achieve this. In the short term they were largely successful but the process inflicted grave damage on royal credit, and the later seventeenth century saw recurrent crises and endemic financial weakness.

This experience contrasts dramatically with that of two other powers whose fiscal strength allowed them to tap the potential of the new credit instruments. The first was Madrid's own rebellious subjects in the Netherlands. The Dutch financed their independence war out of long-term debt, floated domestically and funded from regular taxation (de Vries and van der Woude 1997: 113–29). Apparently the first public authority to achieve this, they benefited twice over from the wealth and commercial sophistication of their domestic economy. This economy, principally that of the province of Holland, furnished both the market for government bonds and the secure revenue base needed to fund them. The result was a stream of loan income, at rates of interest less than half that paid by the authorities in France or England, which funded the successful independence struggle against Spain, but in the long run the system made Dutch capital excessively reliant on government bonds and contributed to the country's eighteenth-century economic stagnation (de Vries and van der Woude 1997: 696).

The English adapted Dutch methods in order to finance their wars with France from the later seventeenth century (O'Brien 1988; Brewer 1989). The basis of the system was a shift from long-term to permanent debt, with the Bank of England issuing non-redeemable bonds funded from a highly lucrative system of indirect taxation. As England's overseas empire expanded, largely at the expense of France, the ensuing century saw a corresponding growth in public debt. The French, by contrast, managed their debt relatively well as long as their army was doing badly. Indebtedness fell for much of the century, and it was calculated as late as 1762 that total French tax revenues still exceeded those of England by 40 per cent (Körner 1995: 116; Bonney 1995c: 336). But French debt was more costly to service, partly because past defaults necessitated a risk premium, and its unreformable fiscal system was less able to tap the wealth of the real economy.

These handicaps were compounded by Louis XVI's refusal to contemplate further defaults, and the borrowing undertaken to support the American Revolution began a chain of events that by 1789 had exhausted the French crown's credit (Bonney 1995c: 342 f.). The consequent need for extraordinary taxation forced the summoning of the Estates-General with fatal consequences for the monarch and his regime. The Revolutionary leadership set aside many of the

Bourbon taxes, so that taxation met only 13 per cent of revenue in the years 1790–5, and covered the deficit by issuing the *assignats*, a paper currency supposedly secured on confiscated Church lands. *Assignats* accounted for more than 80 per cent of French revenue in the first years of the Revolution, but their supply was grossly overexpanded and by 1796 they were worth less than 1 per cent of face value (Bonney 1995c: 349–51).

The Revolutionary regime resolved the crisis by coercion. At home maximum prices were enforced along with compulsory military service whilst in the conquered territories—where most of the French servicemen soon found themselves—resources were obtained through requisition and the enforced circulation of depreciated *assignats*. Napoleon abandoned paper currency but retained the policies of domestic conscription and foreign exploitation. France's ability to sustain a military effort on this basis ground down its continental adversaries' financial systems just as much as it did their armies, and by the mid-1790s both Austria and Prussia already depended on British finance to maintain their resistance (Bonney 1995c). Britain disbursed some 10 per cent of its wartime revenue in foreign subsidies as well as maintaining armed forces equivalent to over 4 per cent of its population. This was possible because of the country's underlying economic strength but it also required a fundamental change in financial policy. Earlier wars were financed out of borrowing funded from higher taxes, but this time the strain was too great and by 1798 the spectre loomed of a collapse in public credit like that which had destroyed the Bourbons. Unlike them, however, the British ministers obtained tax increases on a scale that not only saved public credit but made it possible to fund military expenditure directly from revenue. Tax returns yielded over 60 per cent of the government's additional wartime income. In the process their real value more than trebled, making Britain the most heavily taxed European nation (Bonney 1995c: 380–5; O'Brien 1988).

15.2.3. WAR AND FISCAL CRISIS

The long-term story of how manpower and resources were converted into military force is conventionally told in terms of changes in the scale of military establishments and in their costs. Important as these were, a crucial role was also played by changes in how the costs were met, in what form, and by whom. The very limited availability of public credit in the ancient world meant that fiscal costs had initially to be met from current revenue, or from de-hoarding where this was possible, even if a campaign eventually turned in a net profit. This set relatively rigid limits to the volume of fiscal costs that a state could sustain, which led in turn to a characteristic 'stop-start' pattern with the treasury surpluses accumulated during quiet times being expended in episodes of military activism or official *largesse*. It also meant that, where states had to sustain long periods of warfare, the result was likely to be a fiscal crisis unless the burden of costs could be shifted away from the public treasury.

A crisis of this kind developed in the last years of the Roman Republic as the troops became increasingly dependent on their commanders for the pay and land grants which the state treasury promised but could no longer provide. The personal dependence of their troops enabled men like Caesar and his rivals to act as virtual warlords and become the eventual gravediggers of the Republic. The guiding principle of Augustus' military system was to eliminate the soldiers' personal dependence on anyone save their emperor by integrating the army as closely as possible into the administrative structures of the state. A necessary corollary of this policy was that military costs should be met from the central treasury, and as long as this was possible on a regular basis the army of the Principate was as effective a political instrument and war-fighting machine as any army has ever been.

The roots of the political and military crises afflicting Rome in the third century AD were doubtless deep and complex, but the immediate precipitating factor seems to have been a fiscal crisis. Successive increases in army pay compounded by general Imperial extravagance emptied the treasury, and by the time the Emperor Caracalla was assassinated in AD 217 there was no longer enough money to pay the army on a regular basis.[10] As in the later Republic the troops turned to their commanders to provide them with what the formal structures of the state had failed to provide, but now they did so by supporting Imperial claimants in exchange for bounty payments and loot. This pattern of 'payment by usurpation' was virtually institutionalized as successive debasements wiped out the value of regular army pay, making the troops increasingly dependent on the special bounties—or 'donatives'—paid at the accession of each new emperor.

Order was eventually restored by Diocletian and his successors, but the later emperors had to support an expanding military force from a damaged and declining economic base in a world where Roman military supremacy was no longer assured. Constantine gave imperial finances a valuable boost by stripping the pagan temples, but this was no long-term substitute for an adequate revenue base (Cameron 1993: 53, 115). Troop costs were reduced by coercive recruitment, with an inevitable decline in quality, and deflected from the treasury by the use of entitlements in a manner that compromised the flexibility of the frontier units. The military crises that followed the Romans' defeat at Adrianople were met by a resort to devolution as the Western Empire became increasingly dependent on Germanic 'federate' troops whose leaders eventually became the rulers of successor kingdoms.

The survival of the Eastern Empire was partly a matter of strategic geography, and the availability of the west as a softer target, but the eastern economy was also wealthier and reviving. This greater real wealth was combined with good man-

---

[10] Caracalla's father, the Emperor Septimius Severus, allegedly gave the deathbed advice to 'enrich the soldiers and ignore the rest'. The new emperor evidently took this advice to heart and increased army pay beyond the treasury's ability to sustain it. When cautioned against extravagance he is said to have pointed to his sword with the words, 'the money will not run out as long as we have this' (Campbell 1984: 175, 195).

agement and a successful currency reform under the Emperor Athanasius which enabled the process of devolution to be reversed. The key to this process was the availability of sufficient money to 'refiscalize' military costs by paying the troops regular wages, and integrate the army into the formal administrative and command structures of the state. Federate troops remained important, but the revival of regular units enabled civilian emperors to exercise effective military control on a scale that had eluded many of their western predecessors (Whitby 2000). At the same time, cautious foreign and military policies allowed a treasury surplus to be built up which subsequently financed the reconquest of Italy and North Africa under Justinian.

An extended period of stable peace and good management might have allowed consolidation of Justinian's conquests and the re-emergence of a Mediterranean empire, but plague and renewed pressure from the north prevented this. The frontier troops were allowed to languish unpaid, but field army strengths apparently remained unchanged despite the Empire's greatly reduced revenue base, and the inevitable consequence was a renewed crisis when the money ran out under the unfortunate Emperor Maurice.[11] As in the third century, the troops turned to a usurper to provide them with what the legitimate authorities could not, and the ensuing civil war triggered a series of crises culminating in the Arab invasions and the establishment of a military system based on landed entitlements. Money nonetheless continued to play an important role in taxation and eventually a sufficient surplus was built up to establish the salaried, centrally controlled, military units that spearheaded the tenth century's territorial reconquests (Treadgold 1995).

The re-emergence of monetary economies in western Europe was followed by an expansion of credit on a scale unknown in the ancient world. The availability of borrowing, initially in the form of rulers' personal indebtedness and then as a charge on the public treasury, enabled rulers to shoulder a much larger volume of fiscal costs, and entitlements gave way to cash as the main instrument of military recruitment. But credit also lifted the older fiscal disciplines and made it possible for expenditure to outrun revenue on a continuing basis as long as money was available to service the debt and fresh loans could be raised. Borrowing therefore expanded with the scale of warfare across the Habsburg century, leading to an unsustainable growth in the costs of debt servicing and recurrent financial crises.

In practice the major powers were able to survive the consequences of default and raise new loans, since private borrowers were an even more hazardous prospect, but the resulting risk premiums drove up costs even further. In consequence much of the increase in military costs had to be met by what we have termed fiscal deflation, and in particular by devolution. Training and organization costs

---

[11] Maurice is said 'to have found the treasuries empty, as if swept by a broom' and was forced to adopt a policy of retrenchment, leading to increasing resentment among the soldiers who complained they could not 'endure to be ruled by a shopkeeper' (Whitby 1988: 18–19). The last straw seems to have been Maurice's attempt to cut supply costs by overwintering the army in barbarian territory north of the Danube.

were devolved to military brokers, who could do the job more efficiently, and discipline costs were largely ignored. The system 'worked' in so far as it produced armies that could win battles and occupy territory, but it generated consequential costs on a scale that emptied military victory of much political or economic gain. In reaction to this, the ensuing 'Bourbon century' saw rulers assume responsibility for the training, organization, and discipline of their troops as the army was integrated into the formal structures of state administration.

This 'Augustan' policy reduced the consequential costs of war and made armies more effective instruments of policy, but it also made them a much heavier burden on the treasury. As the volume of fiscal costs grew beyond what could be funded from revenue, public indebtedness expanded to fill the gap, until this also became too costly for the revenue base to sustain, and the *ancien régime* financial systems went into crisis. The Dutch, still struggling in the aftermath of their seventeenth-century borrowing, were the initial casualties, but Bourbon France was the first major regime to fall and within a few years of the Revolution most of the major continental states had either collapsed financially or were being propped up by British subsidies. Britain's war effort was aided by its underlying economic strength and the relative efficiency of its fiscal system, but it too had overreached itself by the end of the 1790s when the traditional reliance on borrowing no longer sufficed to stave off crisis. The vital margin between success and collapse was covered by the income tax which generated sufficient income to save the nation's credit and allowed part of the effort to be funded directly from taxation. On the French side successive regimes relied on ideological zeal, followed by compulsion when zeal subsided, to raise an army of unprecedented size at much less than the 'market rate' and pursue a policy of predatory expansion. The profits, in the form of loot, indemnities, and the manipulation of devalued *assignats* as occupation currency, sufficed to keep France afloat financially for as long as its armies were victorious.[12]

15.3. CONCLUSION

The low productivity of organic economies created two problems for rulers who wanted to support military or other governmental activity. The first problem was the physical scarcity of resources above what was needed for their people's material survival. This scarcity set absolute, or 'hard', limits to the numbers of non-producers who could be supported, and therefore to the growth of special-

---

[12] Borrowing was not the only means of bridging the gap between revenue and expenditure. Printing money was an alternative, and a number of 18th-century states introduced paper currencies. Persuading their subjects to accept pieces of paper in exchange for 'real' money was an attractive solution to governments' financial difficulties, but few of them knew where to stop. The failure to keep note issues in line with the assets on which they were based meant that most currencies depreciated disastrously and degenerated into something between public borrowing and institutional fraud (Bonney 1995*c*: 364–5, 1995*b*: 463–71).

ized military or administrative institutions, but there was a second problem which meant that such limits were rarely if ever reached. This problem was that the coercive and administrative apparatus of the state was too weak for rulers to appropriate whatever surpluses were physically available, and the origins of this weakness lay in the fact that rulers did not have enough resources to support a strong state apparatus.

There were a number of ways of sidestepping, if not of breaking, this vicious circle. One way was to levy tribute on subordinate peoples, a process that was often little more than taxation by terrorism. The enforcement of tributary dependence could be cheaply accomplished, but the yield was rarely reliable enough to satisfy the needs of an organized state. A more effective solution was to transfer resources directly from producers to military or governmental specialists without channelling them through an intermediate bureaucracy. Taxation in kind, and domain taxation in any form, both went some way towards doing this, but they were inflexible fiscal instruments. Taxation in kind was only really effective where it furnished goods or services that were needed in the same region that provided them, and the yields of domain taxation were too rigid to cover wartime peaks in expenditure. Revenues of this kind might be appropriate for regional military forces or administrators, particularly where they were rewarded with entitlements and their distribution followed the geography of production, but they were ill suited to support centralized bureaucracies or mobile forces who were paid money wages.

Forces of the latter kind needed the support of regular public taxation paid in cash, and it was revenue of this kind that underpinned the military system of the early Roman Empire. This system, established by Augustus, was historically unusual in the degree to which it integrated the military and civilian administration and bore its costs as charges on the central treasury. For as long as revenue and expenditure remained in long-term balance it was very successful, but by the early third century they no longer did so and the Empire was plunged into a general crisis. Political and military order was eventually restored but the Empire was never again able to rely entirely on a regular, volunteer army paid wholly in cash from the central treasury.

Domain taxes and taxes in kind were not the only ways of raising resources without an expensive fiscal administration. Borrowing offered rulers a means of obtaining the resources that they lacked the political or administrative wherewithal to extract by compulsion. In the short term it provided a cheap and politically uncomplicated supply of money, and one that was much more elastic than revenue, but in the longer term it was expensive and it was dangerously easy to over-borrow. The growing importance of public credit from the later Middle Ages therefore went along with the growth of public taxation, much of which was needed to pay the costs of earlier borrowing and nearly all of which was ultimately driven by the mounting fiscal costs of war. The result was a new kind of vicious spiral in which fiscal weakness led to an unsustainable level of debt that led in turn to defaults and further increases in the cost of borrowing. The economic and fiscal strength of the Dutch Republic enabled it to borrow in a manner that avoided this spiral, until the Dutch overextended themselves in the struggle against Louis XIV,[13] but no other early modern continental power could match their achievement and they were condemned to wage war in ways that moderated its immediate fiscal costs but magnified the consequential economic and political damage that was wrought.

In the aftermath of the Habsburg century the European powers returned to something like the Augustan system of regular military units incorporated into the apparatus of the state and paid, clothed, and housed at the expense of the central treasury. The armies of the *ancien régime* were effective political instruments but they were too expensive to be financed out of revenue. The growing sophistication of Europe's financial systems made the expansion of public debt a more orderly process than it had been in the preceding century, but in the long run this only postponed the final day of reckoning. When that day came the Bourbons' Revolutionary heirs faced foreign invasion, a devastated treasury, and a royal army that was melting away. Their solution was a military system founded on an unprecedented scale of compulsion and a logistical system that transferred resources directly from producers to soldiers—as long as they were located outside France. Britain followed the continental powers into fiscal crisis, but resolved it with a new kind of taxation that no purely organic economy had ever sustained on such a scale. The European conflict accordingly resolved itself into a struggle between two very different military-fiscal regimes: one of them founded on the economic and administrative resources of an emerging mineral economy and the other on coercion at home and the exploitation of conquests abroad. In their different ways each of them offered a window on the future.

---

[13] Van de Woude and de Vries describe the 200 million guilders of loan finance which the Republic raised between 1690 and 1713 as a 'public gamble' whose failure 'established the basic contours of the eighteenth century economy' (de Vries and van der Woude 1997: 680).

Conclusion

The structure of organic economies placed two obstacles in the way of rulers who wanted to convert the manpower and material resources at their disposal into armed force. The first was the prevalence of absolute scarcity. Low productivity per worker limited the availability of manpower by restricting the numbers of non-producers who could be supported. In particularly backward economies the prevalence of seasonal under-employment meant that large numbers of men might be available at certain times of the year, and the pool of potential recruits also increased disproportionately once population grew beyond a certain point and the marginal returns to labour began to decline. Lower productivity, however, meant a greater scarcity of material resources, and western military technology made extensive use of two of the most valuable of these: animal power and ferrous metals.

The prevalence of absolute scarcity created a second kind of problem which was the one more often encountered in practice by the rulers of organized states. This problem resulted from the fact that low-productivity economies could not support many people who were not engaged in food production and, in particular, they could not sustain large numbers of full-time administrative and military specialists. Few rulers therefore had access to the kind of administrative and coercive apparatus which was needed if those surpluses which were physically available were to be appropriated and committed to military or governmental purposes in the most efficient fashion. In these circumstances a downward spiral of inadequate revenue and political weakness was unavoidable unless some means could be found of extracting and deploying resources without the need for an intervening fiscal bureaucracy.

There were two main ways in which this could be done. The first was to transfer goods or services directly from agricultural producers to specialist consumers. There was little alternative to this if military or administrative functions were to be discharged in the absence of a cash economy, but taxes could be collected in kind and service rewarded with what we have called 'entitlements' even where money played an important part in economic life. This method was straightforward administratively, but it was also cumbersome and inflexible in practice. Troops rewarded with entitlements usually served only for fixed periods, or within a limited range of home, and the method was best suited to the needs of static garrison or frontier troops and subregional or peripatetic administrators. The alternative to direct transfer of resources was the devolution of fiscal or military functions responsibility to individuals outside the formal apparatus of the state, or who could use their own resources to supplement those formally attaching to their office.

Devolution of this kind was a recurrent phenomenon throughout the era of organic economies. European states 'farmed' taxes, or devolved their administration to local elites, well into the modern period, and the prevalence of this kind of fiscal devolution exemplifies a basic dilemma of rulers who lacked the initial resources to establish systems of resources extraction that were both efficient and politically uncontentious. Farming could yield regular, predetermined amounts without the need for a fiscal bureaucracy and provided a means of rewarding support from magnates or other important figures close to the centres of power. But farmers creamed off a substantial margin that might otherwise have gone to the treasury and often generated a dangerous degree of popular hatred. Devolution to local elites, through methods such as repartitional taxation, created fewer political problems than did farming but practically guaranteed that the tax regime would bear lightly on those with the greatest wealth. The devolution of military functions to men such as barbarian warlords, regional magnates, or mercenary brokers might yield militarily effective troops who were cheaper than regular units raised, supplied, and commanded by salaried officers of the state. But if devolution lowered fiscal costs it imposed a range of consequential costs by weakening the ruler's control over his troops and their commanders.

The long-term development of western military-fiscal arrangements amply demonstrates both the attractiveness and the dangers of these expedients. Following the collapse of the Roman Republic, the Emperor Augustus established a system which was remarkable in its avoidance of either entitlements or devolution. Salaried office-holders recruited, trained, equipped, and commanded soldiers paid in cash out of taxes whose administration was increasingly transferred from farmers to state officials. By the third century, however, the fiscal costs of these arrangements proved too great for the public treasury to sustain. The Augustan system unravelled and gave way to a series of expedients that placed a growing importance on devolution and transactions in kind.

Control of the Empire's western territories eventually passed to barbarian war leaders who received military service in exchange for landed entitlements as the monetary economy contracted dramatically. Its subsequent revival saw cash transactions assume an increasing role in military and administrative affairs, but the tradition that domain taxation should suffice for a ruler's needs kept the fiscal apparatus of most medieval states weak amid an enduring hostility to the idea of public taxation. The growing availability of credit provided rulers with an alternative short-term means of financing war, but it was an expensive one and in the longer term they had to expand their tax income to repay past debts or risk alienating much of their revenue base.

The early modern period saw public credit became institutionalized as it expanded to meet increases in the costs of war due both to the greater scale of armed forces and to a rise in costs per man. The reasons for the increases in scale remain controversial. They may have included technological or political changes, but it is also possible that the process was driven by population growth through its effects on the supply of recruits. The increases in costs per man, however, were clearly due to gunpowder technology and ran against the logic of the demographic conjuncture. Whatever its causes may have been, the increase in military costs was too much for the treasuries of the major powers to bear. Only Holland managed to use its underlying economic strength to finance war out of tax-funded borrowing without provoking a crippling financial crisis. The system worked well during the struggle against Spain, but the heavier burden of war with Bourbon France proved too much for it and lasting damage seems to have been wrought to the economy. Fiscal weakness elsewhere compelled rulers to make extensive use of military devolution and this led to severe consequential costs that were demographic as well as material. The subsequent reaction saw *ancien régime* Europe return to something like the Augustan system in which permanent military institutions were closely integrated into the administrative and fiscal structures of the state.

Eighteenth-century armies were better supplied, organized, and disciplined than their predecessors, and the consequential costs of war fell as a result, but the burden of immediate fiscal costs again proved unsustainable in spite of the growing sophistication of banking and public credit. England provides a partial exception to this generalization since it successfully adapted Dutch methods, backed by a system of indirect taxation better able to tap the economy's real wealth than were those of continental Europe. The struggle against Revolutionary France nonetheless brought its credit close to collapse, but the country's economy proved strong enough to support tax increases on a scale that contributed directly to its war effort whilst floating successive anti-French coalitions. In France itself the Revolution led to a new military system which looked both forwards and backwards. It looked forwards in its exploitation of ideological zeal backed by large-scale compulsion as a means of recruitment, but the loosening of discipline and the policy of making war pay for war looked back to an earlier era of more destructive warfare.

CHAPTER SIXTEEN

Conclusion

In the preceding chapters we have tried to trace the consequences of a reliance on organic sources of raw materials and energy for the economic and political life of pre-industrial western societies and particularly for the process of spatial integration. Spatial integration was fundamental to the development of more complex and differentiated structures in both the economic and political spheres. Economic growth in pre-industrial economies was best promoted by specialization and the division of labour, and this in turn was bound up with the formation of regional and supra-regional markets. The maintenance of political power, which is manifested in state organization, requires the ability to exercise coercion at a geographical distance from the centre of power, and so it too is a spatial phenomenon. The military sphere has loomed large in the discussion because it is this which formed the mechanism linking political and economic life. Gaining and keeping political power for any length of time required access to armed force, whilst maintaining such force required control of economic resources. Safeguarding and extending such control was consequently the principal employment of both force and power.

There were two particularly important features of the resource base in pre-industrial economies, or 'organic economies' as we have called them. The first was the low level of energy availability and the second was the role played by the produce of the land as the ultimate source of nearly all raw material and energy inputs. They made it very difficult to effect large short-term increases in the volume of inputs and created a potential for serious long-term conflicts over different demands, particularly between food crops and other uses. They also imposed a distinctive 'areal' pattern on the spatial organization of production. Low energy availability restricted output across the board, but especially in heat-intensive sectors such as metalworking, and made heavy land transport very inefficient. This inefficiency, allied to the areal geography of production, imposed a corresponding pattern of dispersal on the geography of consumption and thus of population.

These two features of organic economies imposed heavy and restrictive costs on the societies that depended on them and limited the resources that they had available to meet such costs. The result was a set of constraints on the development of collective life which ensured that all such societies would have a great deal in common. Labour productivity, and therefore living standards, were very low compared with those in industrialized or 'mineral' economies. The endemic poverty which ensued dictated that the bulk of consumption should consist of goods necessary for material survival and the great majority of the population should be food-producers, whilst the inefficiency of land haulage meant that they would have to live in the countryside. As a population grew, more and more labour had to be devoted to growing food, but the scarcity of other factors of production meant that this labour became increasingly inefficient so that productivity fell and living standards deteriorated further.

The reliance on organic resources imposed structural constraints which limited what could be achieved in the sphere of production. Since political power depended ultimately on access to economic resources, the limits on economic life were also limits on the elaboration of power, but in both the political and economic instances these limits fell into two categories. The first category comprised what we have termed the absolute or 'hard' limits. These were the limits of what was physically possible given the resource base of an organic economy and the technology used to exploit it, but such limits were rarely if ever reached in either political or economic life. The reason for this was that the structural constraints which limited the potential for what could be achieved in organic economies also limited the degree to which this potential could be realized.

In the economic sphere, once markets had come into being, the problem lay in the failure of demand that necessarily followed from the fact that most people were too poor to purchase anything but subsistence commodities. There was consequently very little incentive to invest in more efficient methods of production, or to clear the 'bottlenecks' that prevented the available factors of production and in particular labour from being fully utilized. Politically the problem was that for rulers to appropriate resources they required access to an effective means of coercion, and they needed an effective administrative system if it was to be done in a systematic and efficient manner. But systematic coercion and administration both required a state apparatus that was itself expensive to establish and maintain, and most rulers lacked the resources to do this. In consequence a kind of low-level equilibrium trap or vicious circle was established in which rulers lacked the wherewithal to appropriate the surplus resources which were physically available. In many cases taxation required the active co-operation of elite groups whose interest lay in ensuring that the burden fell as lightly as possible on the country's real wealth.

The extent of the 'soft limits' as we have called them reflected the organization of economic and political life and the degree to which it realized the potential offered by the resource base and the technology used to exploit it. These soft limits acted as limits by determining what economic or political actors could achieve in the short term, but in the longer term, unlike the hard limits, they could be pushed back without the need for thoroughgoing transformation in the technology of resource exploitation. This 'extension of the possible' came about primarily through spatial integration and for most of the period the factors driving it were political rather than economic. Large-scale economic integration occurred at times through the development of 'high-level' traffic flows, but these were generally confined to traffic in luxury goods for the elite and were often manipulated by rulers to buttress and extend their power. The demand for luxuries was too weak in itself to fuel a powerful integrative movement, whilst mass subsistence commodities were too bulky to generate spontaneous inter-regional trade in an age of muscle-powered transportation.

The constraints and inefficiencies endemic to organic economies set limits to what rulers could achieve in the long term, but in the short term they also created opportunities. Man- and animal power was chronically underutilized and so could often be obtained 'below cost' in pursuit of collective, and essentially political, projects such as warfare. Military success could lead to the political integration of space and thereby foster economic integration by enriching the elite, and so boosting the long-distance luxury trades. Expansion might also become self-sustaining as resources were mobilized for war, leading to territorial conquests and the exploitation of new resources for further expansion. Where large states emerged in this way a second kind of economic integration occurred as political centralization fostered the growth of metropolitan power centres whose provisioning required an inter-regional grain trade. The 'primacy of the political' did not however come about merely by default.

Military expansion might eventually be a self-sustaining process, but to set it in motion resources had first to be mobilized by either coercion or inducement. This initial 'pump-priming' process presented great difficulties for rulers without access to a powerful state apparatus. In Rome, the momentum was provided by a series of defensive and pre-emptive campaigns waged by a citizen militia that was founded on the traditional obligation of free men to defend their community. Military success brought neighbouring territorial conquests whose resources furnished the Republic with the kind of long-service force that was needed to wage protracted campaigns far from home. The system broke down when the army grew too large to be maintained from readily available public resources and the first loyalty of the troops shifted from the state to the commanders on whom their material well-being had come to depend. When the Emperor Augustus emerged victorious from the ensuing civil wars he used his victory to reduce the size of the army and to integrate it into a state apparatus whose servants owed obedience to superior office, rather than to the person of the office-holder. This achievement was possible because economic and fiscal conditions enabled soldier and bureaucrat alike to be paid in cash from a public purse whose strings were firmly held by the Emperor.

The spatial extent of the Roman state was defined less by the limits of the legionaries' ability to defeat barbarians in battle, than by the cost of consolidating control over barbarian territories relative to the resources that could be extracted from them. Its spatial extent was unprecedented but this itself imposed heavy burdens. Demographically, large-scale spatial integration promoted the spread of pathogens to hitherto unexposed populations, triggering unpredictable and potentially destructive epidemic waves, whilst the formation of densely populated primate cities produced large increases in endemic mortality. As population stagnated, if it did not actually decline, so did production. At the same time military costs mounted, driven in large part by the problem of defending porous frontier zones against persistent low-level infiltration and larger-scale attacks by the opportunistic coalitions that materialized whenever the defenders' attention was distracted.

The imbalance between revenue and expenditure eventually emptied the treasury and although the Empire's territorial integrity was restored following the crises of the third century, its economic health and Augustan institutions were not. Military and civilian offices were separated, and as the Empire's revenue base shrank the role of cash transactions was reduced. The latter process was partially reversed, but fresh military and political crises in the later fourth century imposed burdens which the Western Empire's fiscal system could not meet and so initiated a process of military devolution that culminated in the disappearance of the central authority. The east's greater fiscal strength enabled this process to be reversed and civilian authority reasserted, but a combination of overextension, demographic collapse, and external assault precipitated a new crisis from which a much reduced Empire eventually emerged with a military system that, like that of the post-Roman west, was based on landed entitlements rather than cash payments.

Money played such a small role in the early medieval economy of the former Western Empire that landed entitlements were the only realistic basis on which military service could be obtained, but they were no basis on which to construct a powerful administrative apparatus. As the monetary economy revived, western Europe's rulers consequently found themselves without the means to impose large-scale public taxation. They remained fiscally weak, with military systems that resembled those of the early Middle Ages more than they did those of Imperial Rome. Lacking standing armies, or a sophisticated logistical apparatus, the west's medieval rulers had great difficulty in sustaining the kind of campaign that was needed to establish territorial control in the face of organized opposition, particularly given the advantage that contemporary fortifications conferred on the defender. In the political core territories this led to a style of warfare based on short-term raiding rather than sustained occupation, but the military opposition of stateless peoples on the European periphery was much easier to overcome, and a military system based on landed entitlements lent itself well to the colonization of such areas at a time when population growth provided a ready supply of colonists. In consequence, considerable expansion occurred on the periphery whilst the core remained politically fragmented.

Europe's medieval rulers lacked the means to appropriate large shares of their economies' surplus resources and build powerful state organizations, but contemporary economic development offered an alternative means of funding their activities. The rise of public credit, initially funded from the profits of the long-distance luxury trades, provided a means of 'pump-priming' for rulers whose access to agrarian wealth was largely confined to their royal domains. In principle, armies raised on borrowed money could make a profit by conquering territory and seizing resources in excess of the costs involved in acquiring them. This possibility became all the more important as the spread of gunpowder weapons—the first great energy revolution in human affairs—increased the military returns to investment in greater numbers of troops and made it more difficult to make up for deficient quantity with greater quality, but in what we have called the 'Habsburg century' the actual consequence was a downward spiral of destruction and indebtedness.

The fundamental problem was that, even on borrowed money, Europe's rulers could not or would not pay the organization and discipline costs that were needed to make armed forces effective political instruments. Instead they devolved responsibility to military brokers who provided relatively cheap, militarily competent, but very poorly controlled forces whose operations were destructive in both economic and demographic terms. Much of the cost of war was effectively passed on to the population through loss of life and property, but so much damage was inflicted that rulers derived scant profit from any victories they obtained. The reaction, during the ensuing Bourbon century, was a closer integration of armies into the state apparatus and a corresponding increase in central control.

Armies became less destructive but they also became a lot more expensive to maintain and their immediate costs could only be met by borrowing on a scale that even the Dutch Republic proved unable to fund without sustaining serious economic and political damage. In the Netherlands as elsewhere in continental Europe the long-term consequence was fiscal crisis, and the period ended with a protracted conflict between two distinct systems of resource appropriation. In Revolutionary France the pump was primed by a mixture of ideological zeal and coercion which initiated a process of predatory foreign expansion in which war was made to pay for war without the need for substantial borrowing. By contrast, Britain's victorious military and diplomatic effort was underpinned by greatly expanded borrowing funded from a new kind of fiscal system.

It was a system which realized to an unparalleled degree the economy's potential to sustain military and political power, but it was no longer the potential of an organic economy. With Britain's triumph the era of organic economies which has been the subject of this book approached its close. Wood and muscle gave way to coal and iron, and these in turn to oil and steel. High explosives took the place of gunpowder before chemical energy yielded to nuclear as the final arbiter of human conflict. The history of population, production, and power continued and continues, but this volume has reached its conclusion.

APPENDIX I

Metropolitan Provisioning: Economic and Administrative Maxima

THE PRINCIPAL TECHNICAL obstacles to metropolitan provisioning lay in the physical limitations of muscle-powered transport over land. At the root of the problem was the relationship, analysed by Von Thünen, between the daily fodder requirements of working animals and the capacity of the load which they could carry or draw. Some simple calculations should suffice to demonstrate the implications that this relationship had for the provisioning of a large population concentrated at a point. For simplicity's sake we shall assume that each city dweller requires 3 daily pounds of 'grain' and that transport animals need 20 pounds each and can move 10 miles in a day. Three pounds is rather more than normal daily grain consumption, but is likely to have been somewhat below the total requirement for agricultural products overall. The figures for transport animals probably approximate to a realistic norm. In order to show the range of plausible outcomes we make two sets of assumptions for the energetic efficiency of transport and the availability of grain surpluses in the hinterland. These are as follows:

Surplus:

Case I—we assume that the rural population has a density of 80 per square mile and that agriculture can support a further 'urban' population equal to 20 per cent of the rural total.

Case II—assumptions as I, but we assume figures of 40 per square mile and 10 per cent.

In each case it is assumed that 3 pounds of provisions must be transported per day to support one urban dweller

Transport:

Case A—assumes a load capacity of 600 lb per animal.
Case B—assumes a load capacity of 300 lb per animal

In each case we assume a sustainable rate of 10 miles' transport per day and that animals require the equivalent of 20 pounds of grain daily.

The figures in the table results show the size of the population that can be supported as the provisioning radius moves out an increasing number of days' journey from the point.[1] We assume that, on average, each wagon travels from a point in the middle of the daily 'ring' and measure the costs of transport entirely in terms of grain consumed by animals. This ignores labour and capital costs, and so in this respect is over-optimistic, but it also discounts the possibility of back-hauls and so loads total metropolitan transport costs onto

---

[1] We have assumed that staple commodities are available throughout the hinterland, whereas, in fact the zone immediately surrounding is more likely to have been given over to the production of perishable dairy and horticultural commodities.

food supply more than is entirely justified. The size of the animal herd required is calculated, in the first instance, from the number of animals required in the 'pipeline' to supply the point population. We also need to take account of the arrangements required to provision the draught animals. In practice these could not be fed from their own loads, but if they were all provisioned along the wayside the inner rings would be stripped clean by teams travelling further afield. We therefore assume that further draught animals are required sufficient to move half the grain 'fuel' one daily journey.

The 'administrative maximum' (or Max(admin))—that is the absolute maximum that the technology will support, once economic logic is set aside and costs ignored—can be determined directly from the calculations. It is the geographical radius beyond which the animals' fodder requirements exceed their load capacity. It is more difficult to determine the economically sustainable maximum (or Max(econ)). In a free market, provisioning would expand geographically until the costs of procuring the marginal unit of subsistence exceeded the price premium urban consumers were prepared to pay. But this is not a realistic model criterion in the context of provisioning large towns or cities before the nineteenth century. In these cases provisioning was regulated, if not subsidized, by the authorities. Where subsidies are paid the maximum population may be anywhere up to Max(admin), but we can construct a simple model on the basis that the authorities purchase grain from middlemen, paying them their transport costs, and resell it on the urban market at a standard price. On the basis of such 'cross-subsidy', and ignoring other costs, provisioning will expand until the average transport cost equals the urban premium. This extent of this premium cannot be determined, but it seems unlikely to have been more than 20 per cent. Hence the maximum economic size for 'point' populations provisioned on this basis will be as in the table below (Max(admin) values bracketed):

A	66,400 (370,780)	IA	16,60 (90,450)
IA	16,800 (90,380)	IB	4,200 (20,350)

These calculations are too schematic, and the underlying assumptions too arbitrary, for the results to be worth much consideration in terms of their absolute values, but they should serve as reasonable indicators of orders of magnitude. As such they suggest that, under intermediate assumptions, centres of 10,000 to 20,000 people could be supported from local resources on an 'economic' basis, but this ceased to be possible as population grew much over 60,000, even on the most optimistic assumptions. Moreover on the most pessimistic assumptions, which are probably quite realistic for many times and places in pre-industrial Europe, 'extra-economic' means may be needed to provision centres in the 5,000 range. Of equal significance, however, is the range of values resulting from variant assumptions. The differences between cases (I) and (II), high and low volumes of agricultural surplus, are just what we would expect, but changes in the energetic efficiency of transport have disproportionate effects. Doubling the animals' load capacity quadruples the size of the population that can be supported. This is because the additional resources made available are proportional to the square of the extra distance travelled. The value for population at the Max(admin) point is in each case some five times the 'economic' maximum and exceeds 20,000 even under the most pessimistic assumptions (IIB), a divergence which indicates the scope of politically driven resources mobilization.

APPENDIX II

Army Strengths and Casualties

TABLE II. 1a. Losers

Battle	Year	Strength (000)[a]	Casualties (%)	Others (%)	Source
Neuhausel	1621	12.0	25.0		(1)
Wiesloch	1622	17.0	11.8		(1)
Breitenfeld	1631	34.0	23.5	11.8	(1)
Lützen	1632	25.0	20.0		(1)
Rain am Lech	1632	27.0	11.1		(1)
Oldendorf	1633	15.0	46.7	20.0	(1)
Leignitz	1634	12.0	33.3	3.3	(1)
Wattweiler	1634	6.0	25.0	8.3	(1)
Wittstock	1636	30.0	33.3	26.7	(1)
Fontarabia	1638	−9.0	33.0		(1)
Rheinfelden	1638	4.0	17.5	57.5	(1)
Wittenweir	1638	17.0	11.8	8.2	(1)
Thionville	1639	20.0	33.0	15.0	(1)
La Marfée	1641	11.0	41.0	27.0	(1)
Breitenfeld	1642	30.0	33.3	16.7	(1)
Honnecourt	1642	−9.0	20.0	25.0	(1)
Kempen	1642	9.0	44.4	33.3	(1)
Schweidnitz	1642	18.0	16.7	6.7	(1)
Tuttlingen	1643	18.0	16.0	22.0	(1)
Freiburg	1644	16.0	25.0		(1)
Allersheim	1645	16.0	25.0	12.5	(1)
Jankau	1645	16.0	25.0	28.1	(1)
Mergentheim	1645	11.0	14.0	18.0	(1)
Zusmarshausen	1648	10.0	18.0	2.0	(1)
Valenciennes	1656	−9.0	8.0	16.0	(1)
Ensisheim	1674	32.0	12.5		(1)
Mülhausen	1674	5.0	6.0	18.0	(1)
Seneffe	1674	70.0	12.3	7.7	(1)
Sinsheim	1674	7.5	33.3		(1)
Altenheim	1675	−9.0	29.0		(1)
Consarbrück	1675	−9.0	18.0	17.0	(1)

(*continues*)

TABLE II. 1a. (*continued*)

Türkheim	1675	30.0	3.0	8.3	(1)
Fleurus	1690	38.0	28.9	21.1	(1)
Kachanik	1690	3.5	71.4		(1)
Staffarda	1690	18.0	15.6	6.7	(1)
The Boyne	1690	23.0	6.5	0.0	(2)
Tohany	1690	4.0	25.0	50.0	(1)
Aughrim	1691	25.0	17.6	0.0	(2)
Leuze	1691	12.0	12.5	3.3	(1)
Steenkerke	1692	63.0	10.5	2.2	(1)
Marsaglia	1693	36.0	25.0	5.6	(1)
Neerwinden	1693	50.0	24.0	4.0	(1)
Toroella	1694	20.0	17.5	11.0	(2)
Lugos	1695	8.0	62.5		(1)
Olaschin	1696	50.0	10.0		(1)
Narva	1700	60.0	33.3	0.0	(2)
Carpi	1701	38.0	0.9	0.4	(2)
Chiari	1701	38.0	9.5	0.5	(2)
Kasaritsch	1701	8.0	12.5	0.0	(2)
Riga	1701	20.0	14.0	0.0	(2)
Cremona	1702	8.0	10.0	5.0	(2)
Erestfer	1702	5.0	28.0	8.0	(2)
Friedlingen	1702	14.0	20.7	0.0	(2)
Hummelshof	1702	4.0	30.0	10.0	(2)
Kletschow	1702	22.0	9.1	8.6	(2)
Luzzara	1702	30.0	11.7	0.0	(2)
Nimwegen	1702	23.0	1.7	1.3	(2)
S. Vittoria	1702	2.8	21.4	14.3	(2)
Eckenren	1703	15.0	16.7	5.3	(2)
Höchstädt	1703	18.0	25.0	0.0	(2)
Pultusk	1703	12.0	16.7	0.0	(2)
Schagarin	1703	8.7	34.5	0.0	(2)
Sieghardin	1703	10.0	25.0	0.0	(2)
Speyer	1703	20.0	20.0	10.0	(2)
Steckene	1703	2.5	28.0	0.0	(2)
Blenheim	1704	56.0	35.7	25.0	(2)
Castelnuovo	1704	1.0	0.0	90.0	(2)
Eisenstadt	1704	10.0	20.0	0.0	(2)
Pata	1704	12.0	33.3	0.0	(2)
Punitz	1704	9.0	22.2	0.0	(2)
Raab	1704	7.4	37.8	0.0	(2)
Schellenburg	1704	11.0	36.4	0.0	(2)
Schmöllnitz	1704	2.4	66.7	0.0	(2)
Tyrnau	1704	20.0	10.0	0.0	(2)
Cassano	1705	24.0	16.7	2.1	(2)

(*continues*)

TABLE II. 1a. (*continued*)

			Losses		
Battle	Year	Strength (000)[a]	Casualties (%)	Others (%)	Source
Gemauerthof	1705	20.0	25.0	0.0	(2)
Zsibó	1705	24.0	25.0	0.0	(2)
Calcinate	1706	19.0	15.8	0.0	(2)
Castiglione	1706	10.0	15.0	25.0	(2)
Fraustadt	1706	18.0	27.8	44.4	(2)
Kalisch	1706	12.0	11.7	21.7	(2)
Ramillies	1706	60.0	20.0	10.0	(2)
Turin	1706	60.0	5.0	10.0	(2)
Almanza	1707	15.0	26.7	20.0	(2)
Dobroje	1708	6.0	50.0	0.0	(2)
Golontschin	1708	33.0	2.7	1.8	(2)
Hondschoote	1708	1.2	16.7	83.3	(2)
Oudenarde	1708	80.0	8.4	10.3	(2)
Propoisk	1708	13.0	38.5	7.7	(2)
Trentschin	1708	16.0	37.5	3.1	(2)
Wynendael	1708	22.0	11.4	2.3	(2)
Malplaquet	1709	80.0	11.3	3.8	(2)
Poltava	1709	21.5	31.6	13.0	(2)
Rumersheim	1709	7.0	37.1	0.0	(2)
Almenara	1710	22.0	6.8	1.4	(2)
Brihuega	1710	4.0	15.0	85.0	(2)
Helsingborg	1710	11.0	36.4	18.2	(2)
Saragossa	1710	20.0	25.0	25.0	(2)
Villaviciosa	1710	13.6	22.1	14.7	(2)
Faltschi-on-the Pruth	1711	40.0	5.3	2.3	(2)
Nagy-Majeteny	1711	10.0	100.0	0.0	(2)
Tortosa	1711	2.0	45.0	30.0	(2)
Denain	1712	10.0	23.0	41.0	(2)
Gadebusch	1712	12.0	33.3	16.7	(2)
Rugen	1715	5.0	50.0	0.0	(2)
Sheriffmuir	1715	10.0	0.0	0.0	(2)
Storkyo	1715	5.0	60.0	0.0	(2)
Carlowitz	1716	3.0	23.3	0.0	(2)
Kissoda	1716	70.0	5.7	0.0	(2)
Peterwardein	1716	60.0	10.0	0.0	(2)
Belgrade	1717	150.0	10.0	3.3	(2)
Milazzo	1718	6.0	25.0	5.0	(2)
Francaville	1719	10.0	31.0	0.0	(2)
Bitonto	1734	6.2	16.1	0.0	(2)

(*continues*)

TABLE **II. 1a.** (*continued*)

Guastalla	1734	27.0	21.1	0.4	(2)
Parma	1734	37.0	16.2	0.0	(2)
San Bendetto	1734	40.0	17.8	0.0	(2)
Ostrovica	1737	4.5	15.6	0.0	(2)
Grocka	1738	40.0	13.0	1.0	(2)
Kornia	1738	17.0	11.8	0.0	(2)
Mehadia III	1738	20.0	25.0	0.0	(2)
Stawutschene	1738	100.0	2.0	0.0	(2)
Mollwitz	1741	16.6	18.1	9.0	(2)
Wilmanstrand	1741	5.0	50.0	30.0	(2)
Chotusitz	1742	28.0	10.7	11.8	(2)
Scharding	1742	7.0	2.1	7.1	(2)
Campo Santo	1743	11.0	14.5	3.6	(2)
Dettingen	1743	26.0	10.8	4.6	(2)
Bellino	1744	6.0	18.3	6.7	(2)
Coni	1744	25.0	14.4	3.6	(2)
Velletri I	1744	1.0	100.0	0.0	(2)
Velletri II	1744	16.0	8.8	0.6	(2)
Weissenburg	1744	10.0	6.5	4.5	(2)
Bassignano	1745	30.0	3.3	5.0	(2)
Fontenoy	1745	50.0	18.0	6.0	(2)
Hennersdorf	1745	5.5	9.1	16.4	(2)
Hohenfriedburg	1745	58.7	14.7	8.7	(2)
Kesselsdorf	1745	31.0	12.3	21.6	(2)
Pfaffenhofen	1745	7.0	34.3	0.0	(2)
Prestonpans	1745	2.2	13.6	68.2	(2)
Soor	1745	39.3	11.5	7.6	(2)
Culloden	1746	5.4	18.6	10.3	(2)
Falkirk	1746	8.0	5.0	5.0	(2)
Lobositz	1756	34.5	8.3		(3)
Prague	1756	62.0	14.4	7.3	(3)
Breslau	1757	28.0	22.7	0.0	(3)
Gross-Jägersdorf	1757	25.6	17.7	0.0	(3)
Kolin	1757	32.0	43.0	0.0	(3)
Leuthen	1757	65.0	15.4	18.5	(3)
Rossbach	1757	41.1	24.7	0.0	(3)
Hochkirch	1758	31.0	29.3	0.0	(3)
Zorndorf	1758	43.3	42.7	0.0	(3)
Kay	1759	28.0	29.6	0.0	(3)
Kunersdorf	1759	50.9	37.5	0.0	(3)
Liegnitz	1760	66.0	12.9	0.0	(3)
Torgau	1760	53.4	16.3	13.1	(3)
Jemappes	1792	13.2	7.6	3.8	(4)
Valmy	1792	35.0	0.6	0.0	(4)

(*continues*)

TABLE II. 1a. (continued)

Battle	Year	Strength (000)[a]	Losses Casualties (%)	Losses Others (%)	Source
Famars	1793	−9.0	11.0		(1)
Hondschoote	1793	16.0	10.0	8.8	(4)
Kaiserslautern	1793	−9.0	8.0	2.0	(1)
Neerwinden	1793	41.0	7.3	2.4	(4)
Wattignies	1793	30.0	8.3	1.7	(4)
Aldenhaven	1794	77.0	3.9	1.0	(1)
Fleurus	1794	46.0	10.9	0.0	(1)
Sprimont	1794	18.0	8.3	5.6	(1)
Tourcoing	1794	74.0	5.4	2.0	(4)
Tournai	1794	45.0	12.2	1.1	(4)
Warsaw	1794	28.0	28.6	0.0	(4)
Loano	1795	18.0	16.7	22.2	(1)
Mayence	1795	33.0	9.1	5.5	(4)
Quiberon	1795	17.0	10.0	38.2	(4)
Altenkirchen	1796	14.0	7.1	10.7	(1)
Amberg	1796	34.0	3.5	2.4	(4)
Arcola	1796	24.0	9.2	16.7	(4)
Bassano I	1796	16.0	3.8	12.5	(1)
Biberach	1796	23.0	1.3	17.4	(1)
Castiglioni	1796	30.0	10.0	0.0	(4)
Lodi	1796	9.5	4.2	17.9	(4)
Lonato	1796	15.0	20.0	0.0	(4)
Malsch	1796	45.0	2.9	2.9	(1)
Maritime Alps I	1796	28.0	5.0	15.0	(1)
Mondovi	1796	13.0	12.3	0.0	(4)
Montenotte	1796	4.5	18.3	37.2	(4)
Neresheim	1796	48.0	2.3	1.9	(4)
San Giorgio	1796	14.0	7.1	10.7	(1)
Würzburg	1796	30.0	6.7	3.3	(4)
Diersheim	1797	34.0	7.9	5.9	(1)
Heddesdorf	1797	30.0	3.3	13.3	(1)
La Favorita	1797	16.0	8.1	54.4	(1)
Rivoli	1797	28.0	14.3	28.6	(4)
Tarvis	1797	8.0	12.5	43.8	(1)
Mt. Tabor	1798	26.0	23.1		(1)
Pyramids	1798	60.0	3.3	0.0	(4)
Aboukir II	1799	18.0	66.7		(1)
Amsteg	1799	4.4	9.1	40.9	(1)
Bergen	1799	−9.0	9.5	9.0	(1)
Cassano	1799	−9.0	14.3	25.0	(1)

(continues)

TABLE II. 1a. (continued)

Castricum	1799	−9.0	7.5	5.0	(1)
Chur	1799	3.4	5.0	83.2	(1)
Feldkirch	1799	−9.0	25.0	0.0	(1)
Frauenfeld	1799	10.0	22.0	30.0	(1)
Genola	1799	−9.0	23.0	27.0	(1)
Heliopolis	1799	50.0	20.0		(1)
Linth R.	1799	10.0	15.0	35.0	(1)
Magnano	1799	41.0	8.5	11.0	(4)
Maienfeld I	1799	2.2	22.0	50.0	(1)
Maienfeld II	1799	8.0	7.5	24.5	(1)
Modena	1799	6.0	12.5	27.5	(1)
Nauders	1799	6.0	8.3	25.0	(1)
Novi	1799	35.0	20.0	11.4	(4)
Ostrach	1799	−9.0	18.0	3.0	(1)
Pastrengo	1799	8.8	22.7	17.0	(1)
San Giuliano	1799	8.0	12.5	16.3	(1)
Stockach	1799	38.0	5.3	5.3	(4)
Tauffers	1799	6.5	15.4	61.5	(1)
Trebbia	1799	33.0	28.8	21.2	(4)
Verona	1799	−9.0	9.0	6.0	(1)
Zurich I	1799	45.0	2.9	0.7	(4)
Zurich II	1799	23.0	26.1	8.7	(4)
Aboukir	1800	10.0	30.0	5.0	(4)
Biberach	1800	20.0	6.3	13.8	(1)
Engen	1800	72.0	4.2	5.6	(1)
Hochstadt	1800	10.0	10.0	30.0	(1)
Hohenlinden	1800	55.0	10.0	15.5	(4)
Marengo	1800	31.0	22.6	12.9	(1)
Maritime Alps III	1800	17.0	11.8	47.1	(1)
Mincio	1800	50.0	8.2	8.6	(4)
Montebello	1800	16.0	13.1	13.8	(1)
Mosskirch	1800	48.0	5.0	3.3	(1)
Stockach	1800	72.0	4.2	5.6	(4)
Canopus	1801	10.0	30.0	0.5	(1)
Austerlitz	1805	83.0	16.0	20.0	(1)
Caldiero	1805	46.0	13.7	3.7	(4)
Auerstädt	1806	50.0	20.0	6.0	(1)
Jena	1806	54.0	22.0	28.0	(1)
Maida	1806	4.3	39.5		(4)
Pultusk	1806	44.0	8.0		(4)
Eylau	1807	83.0	28.0	4.0	(1)
Friedland	1807	61.0	33.0		(1)
Heilsburg	1807	95.0	11.0		(1)
Bailen	1808	22.0	9.4		(4)

(continues)

TABLE II. 1a. (*continued*)

			Losses		
Battle	Year	Strength (000)[a]	Casualties (%)	Others (%)	Source
Vimiero	1808	13.0	11.5	2.3	(4)
Aspern	1809	66.0	35.0	3.0	(1)
Corunna	1809	20.0	7.5		(4)
Eckmuhl	1809	74.0	8.1	6.8	(4)
Ocano	1809	33.0	6.0		(1)
Ratisbon	1809	47.0	4.3	12.8	(4)
Talavera	1809	47.0	15.0		(1)
Wagram	1809	130.0	20.0	9.0	(1)
Busaco	1810	58.0	8.0		(1)
Albuera	1811	23.0	35.0		(1)
Fuentes de Oñoro	1811	45.0	6.0		(4)
Beresina	1812	87.0	9.0	2.0	(1)
Borodino	1812	122.0	43.0		(1)
Krasnoi	1812	90.0	6.0		(1)
Malo Jaroslawez	1812	24.0	33.0		(1)
Polotzk	1812	22.0	27.0		(1)
Salamanca	1812	42.0	24.0	17.0	(1)
Smolensk	1812	30.0	20.0		(4)
Bautzen	1813	97.0	11.0		(1)
Bidassoa	1813	14.0	7.9	4.3	(4)
Dennewitz	1813	80.0	18.0	2.0	(1)
Dresden	1813	200.0	8.0	12.0	(1)
Hanau	1813	40.0	12.5	12.5	(4)
Katzbach	1813	60.0	13.0	30.0	(1)
Kulm	1813	37.0	24.0	22.0	(1)
Leipzig	1813	175.0	29.0	9.0	(1)
Lützen	1813	93.0	17.0		(1)
Nivelle	1813	18.0	17.8	7.2	(4)
Pyrenees	1813	60.0	19.0	7.0	(1)
Vitoria	1813	60.0	10.0		(1)
Brienne	1814	30.0	10.0		(4)
Craonne	1814	23.0	22.0		(1)
La Rothière	1814	41.0	7.3	7.3	(4)
Paris	1814	42.0	17.0	3.0	(1)
Toulouse	1814	32.0	13.0		(1)
Ligny	1815	84.0	14.0	11.0	(1)
Quatre-Bras	1815	32.0	16.0	2.0	(1)
Waterloo	1815	72.0	42.0	17.0	(1)

[a] −9.0 indicates 'unknown'.

Sources: (1): Bodart (1916: *passim*); (2): Chandler (1994: app. 2); (3): Duffy (1974: app. 1); (4): Rothenberg (1980: app. 1).

TABLE II. 1b. Winners

Battle	Year	Strength (000)[a]	Casualties (%)	Source
Zablat	1619	3.0	16.7	(1)
Weissen Berg	1620	28.0	5.4	(1)
Hochst	1622	26.0	7.7	(1)
Wimpfen	1622	20.0	25.0	(1)
Stadtlohn	1623	28.0	3.6	(1)
Dessau Bridge	1626	16.0	6.3	(1)
Lutter am Barenberge	1626	17.0	11.8	(1)
Nuremberg	1632	60.0	2.5	(1)
Nördlingen	1634	35.0	5.7	(1)
Ratisbon	1634	30.0	26.7	(1)
Avein	1635	34.0	9.0	(1)
Leucate	1637	−9.0	25.0	(1)
Rheinfelden	1638	−9.0	8.0	(1)
Wittenweir	1638	14.0	12.0	(1)
Thionville	1639	14.0	10.0	(1)
Casale	1640	−9.0	20.0	(1)
La Marfée	1641	10.0	10.0	(1)
Kempen	1642	7.5	5.0	(1)
Rocroi	1643	23.0	17.0	(1)
Tuttlingen	1643	22.0	4.5	(1)
Freiburg	1644	20.0	40.0	(1)
Allersheim	1645	−9.0	33.0	(1)
Mergentheim	1645	10.0	7.0	(1)
Lens	1648	−9.0	28.0	(1)
Zusmarshausen	1648	−9.0	10.0	(1)
Rethel	1650	−9.0	9.0	(1)
Arras	1654	−9.0	7.0	(1)
Dunkirk	1658	−9.0	13.0	(1)
Ensisheim	1674	−9.0	11.0	(1)
Seneffe	1674	50.0	12.0	(1)
Sinsheim	1674	−9.0	15.0	(1)
Altenheim	1675	22.0	13.6	(1)
Consarbrück	1675	17.0	6.5	(1)
Mont Cassel	1677	30.0	15.0	(1)
Saint Denis	1678	40.0	10.0	(1)
Bisamberg	1683	13.0	10.0	(1)
Kahlenberg	1683	76.0	6.6	(1)
Parkany	1683	28.0	3.6	(1)
Hamszabeg	1684	10.0	4.0	(1)
Waitzen	1684	32.0	0.9	(1)
Gran	1685	60.0	1.0	(1)
Buda	1686	50.0	1.0	(1)
Harsány	1687	50.0	4.0	(1)

(continues)

TABLE II. 1b. (continued)

Battle	Year	Strength (000)[a]	Casualties (%)	Source
Derwent	1688	3.0	10.0	(1)
Batodschina	1689	18.0	2.2	(1)
Kostanjnica	1689	20.0	1.0	(1)
Nish	1689	17.0	2.4	(1)
Fleurus	1690	50.0	12.0	(1)
Staffarda	1690	−9.0	17.0	(1)
The Boyne	1690	35.0	5.7	(2)
Aughrim	1691	18.0	15.0	(2)
Slankamen	1691	50.0	16.0	(1)
Steenkerke	1692	57.0	12.0	(1)
Landen	1693	80.0	11.3	(2)
Marsaglia	1693	−9.0	8.0	(1)
Neerwinden	1693	80.0	15.0	(1)
Toroella	1694	26.0	5.0	(2)
Zenta	1697	50.0	4.2	(1)
Narva	1700	10.0	20.0	(2)
Carpi	1701	22.0	0.5	(2)
Chiari	1701	22.0	0.9	(2)
Kasaritsch	1701	6.0	13.3	(2)
Riga	1701	8.0	15.0	(2)
Cremona	1702	10.0	15.0	(2)
Erestfer	1702	12.0	10.0	(2)
Friedlingen	1702	17.0	15.9	(2)
Hummelshof	1702	15.0	9.3	(2)
Kletschow	1702	17.0	6.5	(2)
Luzzara	1702	25.0	10.8	(2)
Nimwegen	1702	25.0	0.8	(2)
S. Vittoria	1702	4.0	5.0	(2)
Eckenren	1703	19.0	12.1	(2)
Höchstädt	1703	23.0	6.5	(2)
Pultusk	1703	2.0	30.0	(2)
Schagarin	1703	1.3	15.4	(2)
Sieghardin	1703	12.0	4.2	(2)
Speyer	1703	8.0	50.0	(2)
Steckene	1703	7.0	18.6	(2)
Blenheim	1704	52.0	23.1	(2)
Castelnuovo	1704	10.0	15.0	(2)
Eisenstadt	1704	4.4	0.0	(2)
Pata	1704	3.0	3.3	(2)
Punitz	1704	6.5	15.4	(2)
Raab	1704	3.6	5.6	(2)
Schellenburg	1704	25.0	24.0	(2)
Schmöllnitz	1704	10.0	4.0	(2)

(continues)

TABLE II. 1b. (*continued*)

Tyrnau	1704	7.0	7.1	(2)
Cassano	1705	22.0	13.6	(2)
Gemauerthof	1705	7.0	14.3	(2)
Zsibó	1705	13.0	4.6	(2)
Calcinate	1706	41.0	1.2	(2)
Castiglione	1706	15.0	6.7	(2)
Fraustadt	1706	12.0	16.7	(2)
Kalisch	1706	36.0	2.8	(2)
Ramillies	1706	62.0	5.8	(2)
Turin	1706	35.0	8.6	(2)
Almanza	1707	30.0	6.7	(2)
Dobroje	1708	12.0	16.7	(2)
Golontschin	1708	7.0	22.9	(2)
Hondschoote	1708	3.0	6.7	(2)
Oudenarde	1708	80.0	5.0	(2)
Propoisk	1708	17.0	23.5	(2)
Trentschin	1708	10.0	5.0	(2)
Wynendael	1708	11.0	9.1	(2)
Malplaquet	1709	110.0	21.8	(2)
Poltava	1709	80.0	1.6	(2)
Rumersheim	1709	6.0	6.7	(2)
Almenara	1710	24.0	1.7	(2)
Brihuega	1710	12.0	12.5	(2)
Helsingborg	1710	14.0	21.4	(2)
Saragossa	1710	22.0	7.3	(2)
Villaviciosa	1710	21.0	19.0	(2)
Faltschi-on-the Pruth	1711	260.0	2.7	(2)
Nagy-Majeteny	1711	6.0	0.0	(2)
Tortosa	1711	3.0	0.0	(2)
Denain	1712	24.0	8.8	(2)
Gadebusch	1712	14.0	12.1	(2)
Rugen	1715	22.0	2.3	(2)
Sheriffmuir	1715	3.3	0.0	(2)
Storkyo	1715	18.0	2.8	(2)
Carlowitz	1716	10.0	10.0	(2)
Kissoda	1716	16.0	0.0	(2)
Peterwardein	1716	63.0	7.1	(2)
Belgrade	1717	50.0	10.8	(2)
Milazzo	1718	9.3	16.1	(2)
Francaville	1719	29.0	6.9	(2)
Bitonto	1734	16.0	5.0	(2)
Guastalla	1734	40.0	14.8	(2)
Parma	1734	53.0	7.5	(2)
San Bendetto	1734	20.0	4.5	(2)

(*continues*)

TABLE II. 1b. (*continued*)

Battle	Year	Strength (000)[a]	Casualties (%)	Source
Ostrovica	1737	5.0	0.0	(2)
Grocka	1738	80.0	10.0	(2)
Kornia	1738	40.0	3.3	(2)
Mehadia III	1738	10.0	10.0	(2)
Stawutschene	1738	30.0	0.3	(2)
Mollwitz	1741	23.4	16.7	(2)
Wilmanstrand	1741	10.0	30.0	(2)
Chotusitz	1742	28.0	15.0	(2)
Scharding	1742	4.0	25.0	(2)
Campo Santo	1743	13.0	24.6	(2)
Dettingen	1743	35.0	5.9	(2)
Bellino	1744	24.0	12.5	(2)
Coni	1744	26.0	15.4	(2)
Velletri I	1744	5.0	0.0	(2)
Velletri II	1744	24.0	5.8	(2)
Weissenburg	1744	40.0	3.8	(2)
Bassignano	1745	50.0	2.0	(2)
Fontenoy	1745	60.0	9.3	(2)
Hennersdorf	1745	8.5	1.4	(2)
Hohenfriedburg	1745	58.5	8.2	(2)
Kesselsdorf	1745	30.0	17.0	(2)
Pfaffenhofen	1745	10.0	8.0	(2)
Prestonpans	1745	2.45	4.5	(2)
Soor	1745	22.5	16.4	(2)
Culloden	1746	9.0	3.3	(2)
Falkirk	1746	8.0	1.9	(2)
Lobositz	1756	29.0	10.0	(3)
Prague	1756	31.2	21.3	(3)
Breslau	1757	84.0	7.0	(3)
Gross-Jägersdorf	1757	72.5	7.2	(3)
Kolin	1757	44.0	20.5	(3)
Leuthen	1757	33.0	35.1	(3)
Rossbach	1757	22.0	2.5	(3)
Hochkirch	1758	80.0	9.5	(3)
Zorndorf	1758	36.0	35.5	(3)
Kay	1759	40.0	12.0	(3)
Kunersdorf	1759	59.5	26.1	(3)
Liegnitz	1760	30.0	11.3	(3)
Torgau	1760	50.0	33.3	(3)
Jemappes	1792	45.0	4.4	(4)
Valmy	1792	59.0	0.5	(4)
Famars	1793	53.1	2.0	(1)
Hondschoote	1793	24.0	12.5	(4)

(*continues*)

TABLE II. 1b. (continued)

Kaiserslautern	1793	−9.0	3.5	(1)
Neerwinden	1793	43.0	6.0	(4)
Pellenberg	1793	38.0	2.4	(1)
Wattignies	1793	45.0	11.1	(4)
Weissenburg	1793	43.0	4.2	(1)
Cateau	1794	90.0	1.7	(1)
Catillon	1794	60.0	1.7	(1)
Erquellines	1794	28.0	2.5	(1)
Fleurus	1794	−9.0	6.0	(1)
Gosselies	1794	28.0	3.6	(1)
Grandreng	1794	22.5	12.4	(1)
Tourcoing	1794	70.0	4.3	(4)
Tournai	1794	50.0	6.0	(4)
Warsaw	1794	22.0	18.2	(4)
Lambusart	1795	41.0	7.3	(1)
Loano	1795	−9.0	10.0	(1)
Mannheim	1795	27.0	2.6	(1)
Mayence	1795	36.0	4.4	(4)
Quiberon	1795	13.0	3.8	(4)
Amberg	1796	46.0	1.1	(4)
Arcola	1796	20.0	17.5	(4)
Bassano II	1796	28.0	10.0	(1)
Caldiero	1796	26.0	5.0	(1)
Castiglioni	1796	30.0	5.0	(4)
Emmendingen	1796	28.0	3.6	(1)
Lodi	1796	17.5	5.1	(4)
Lonato	1796	20.0	10.0	(4)
Mainz	1796	36.0	4.4	(1)
Millesimo	1796	9.0	7.8	(4)
Mondovi	1796	17.5	3.4	(4)
Montenotte	1796	10.0	8.8	(4)
Neresheim	1796	50.0	2.4	(4)
Schliengen	1796	36.0	2.2	(1)
Würzburg	1796	44.0	2.7	(4)
Kehl	1797	40.0	12.0	(1)
Rivoli	1797	22.0	10.0	(4)
Mt. Tabor	1798	4.0	12.5	(1)
Pyramids	1798	23.0	1.3	(4)
Aboukir II	1799	6.0	18.3	(1)
Bergen	1799	−9.0	4.5	(1)
Cap Mantua	1799	32.0	6.6	(1)
Cassano	1799	52.0	7.3	(1)
Castricum	1799	−9.0	5.0	(1)
Feldkirch	1799	7.5	12.0	(1)

(continues)

TABLE II. 1b. (continued)

Battle	Year	Strength (000)[a]	Casualties (%)	Source
Legnago	1799	23.0	3.0	(1)
Linth R.	1799	−9.0	5.0	(1)
Magnano	1799	46.0	8.7	(4)
Mannheim	1799	30.0	4.3	(1)
Novi	1799	50.0	14.0	(4)
Ostrach	1799	50.0	3.1	(1)
Remus	1799	18.0	7.8	(1)
San Giuliano	1799	−9.0	7.0	(1)
Stockach	1799	46.0	6.3	(4)
Trebbia	1799	37.0	13.5	(4)
Verona	1799	−9.0	10.0	(1)
Winterthur	1799	15.0	6.7	(1)
Zurich I	1799	55.0	4.0	(4)
Zurich II	1799	33.5	11.9	(4)
Aboukir	1800	12.0	12.5	(4)
Ampfing	1800	37.0	5.4	(1)
Biberach	1800	−9.0	9.0	(1)
Engen	1800	−9.0	3.6	(1)
Hohenlinden	1800	55.0	4.5	(4)
Marengo	1800	28.0	23.2	(1)
Maritime Alps II	1800	30.0	16.7	(1)
Mincio	1800	66.0	6.1	(4)
Montebello	1800	−9.0	25.0	(1)
Mosskirch	1800	−9.0	5.7	(1)
Stockach	1800	84.0	3.6	(4)
Canopus	1801	12.0	12.5	(1)
Austerlitz	1805	65.0	15.0	(1)
Caldiero	1805	49.0	11.6	(4)
Auerstädt	1806	27.0	26.0	(1)
Jena	1806	96.0	6.0	(1)
Maida	1806	4.8	6.3	(4)
Pultusk	1806	26.0	12.7	(4)
Eylau	1807	75.0	31.0	(1)
Friedland	1807	87.0	14.0	(1)
Heilsburg	1807	65.0	19.0	(1)
Bailen	1808	32.0	3.1	(4)
Vimiero	1808	19.0	3.9	(4)
Aspern	1809	99.0	22.0	(1)
Corunna	1809	15.0	0.6	(4)
Eckmuhl	1809	66.0	4.5	(4)
Ocano	1809	50.0	8.0	(1)
Ratisbon	1809	72.0	2.8	(4)
Talavera	1809	54.0	11.0	(1)

(continues)

TABLE II. 1b. (continued)

Wagram	1809	160.0	21.0	(1)
Busaco	1810	32.0	4.0	(1)
Albuera	1811	32.0	22.0	(1)
Fuentes de Oñoro	1811	35.0	4.3	(4)
Beresina	1812	33.0	30.0	(1)
Borodino	1812	124.0	34.0	(1)
Krasnoi	1812	50.0	20.0	(1)
Malo Jaroslawez	1812	24.0	33.0	(1)
Polotzk	1812	34.0	18.0	(1)
Salamanca	1812	46.0	11.0	(1)
Smolensk	1812	45.0	22.2	(4)
Bautzen	1813	167.0	13.0	(1)
Bidassoa	1813	32.0	5.0	(4)
Dennewitz	1813	70.0	12.0	(1)
Dresden	1813	100.0	12.0	(1)
Hanau	1813	60.0	10.0	(4)
Katzbach	1813	80.0	5.0	(1)
Kulm	1813	103.0	11.0	(1)
Leipzig	1813	325.0	23.0	(1)
Lützen	1813	144.0	14.0	(1)
Nivelle	1813	45.0	11.8	(4)
Pyrenees	1813	55.0	15.0	(1)
Vitoria	1813	90.0	6.0	(1)
Brienne	1814	36.0	8.3	(4)
Craonne	1814	23.0	25.0	(1)
La Rothière	1814	80.0	7.5	(4)
Paris	1814	100.0	9.0	(1)
Toulouse	1814	60.0	11.0	(1)
Ligny	1815	71.0	16.0	(1)
Quatre-Bras	1815	21.0	19.0	(1)
Waterloo	1815	120.0	19.0	(1)

[a] −9.0 indicates 'unknown'.
Sources: As Table II. 1a.

TABLE II. 2a. Sieges and assaults: attacking army strengths and casualties

Siege	Year	Strength (000)	Casualties (%)	Outcome (S=success, F=failure)	Source
Stralsund	1628	24.0	50.0	F	(1)
Philippsburg	1676	60.0	16.7	S	(3)
Buda	1684	34.0	50.0	F	(1)
Buda	1686	60.0	33.3	S	(1)
Belgrade	1688	53.0	2.5	S	(2)
Mainz	1689	60.0	8.3	S	(3)

(continues)

TABLE II. 2a. (continued)

Siege	Year	Strength (000)	Casualties (%)	Outcome (S=success, F=failure)	Source
Bonn	1689	30.0	13.3	S	(3)
Namur	1692	46.0	6.5	S	(3)
Belgrade	1693	30.0	26.7	F	(3)
Namur	1695	80.0	22.5	S	(1)
Ath	1697	52.0	0.4	S	(2)
Barcelona	1697	32.0	31.3	S	(3)
Kaiserswert	1702	38.0	23.7	S	(3)
Ruremonde	1702	25.0	0.4	S	(2)
Trarbach	1704	20.0	5.0	S	(2)
Landau	1704	30.0	16.7	S	(3)
Verrua	1704/5	30.0	40.0	S	(1)
Bonn	1705	40.0	1.5	S	(2)
Badajoz	1705	22.0	4.5	F	(2)
Ostend	1706	20.0	8.0	S	(2)
Menin	1706	30.0	8.7	S	(3)
Turin	1706	36.0	38.9	F	(1)
Toulon	1707	38.0	26.3	F	(1)
Lille	1708	35.0	45.7	S	(1)
Tournai	1709	40.0	13.5	S	(3)
Béthune	1710	31.0	9.7	S	(3)
Aire	1710	28.0	25.0	S	(3)
Douai	1710	60.0	13.3	S	(3)
Bouchain	1711	30.0	16.0	S	(3)
Barcelona	1712	20.0	2.0	S	(2)
Le Quesnoy	1712	18.0	16.7	S	(3)
Landau	1713	20.0	50.0	S	(1)
Barcelona	1713/14	30.0	66.7	S	(1)
Stralsund	1715	70.0	14.3	S	(1)
Temesvar	1716	45.0	10.0	F	(1)
Belgrade	1717	100.0	20.0	S	(3)
Messina	1719	18.0	28.9	S	(1)
Philippsburg	1734	117.0	8.5	S	(3)
Banjaluka	1737	13.0	7.7	F	(1)
Oczakov	1737	60.0	6.7	S	(2)
Prague	1744	80.0	0.6	S	(3)
Freiburg	1744	30.0	53.3	S	(2)
Ostend	1745	55.0	3.6	S	(1)
Schweidnitz	1761	14.0	12.1	S	(2)
Dunkirk	1792	10.0	10.0	S	(2)
Valenciennes	1793	24.0	7.5	S	(2)
Mainz	1793	43.0	7.0	S	(2)
Dunkirk	1793	37.0	5.4	F	(3)

(continues)

TABLE II. 2a. (continued)

Acre	1799	12.0	16.7	F	(2)
Mantua	1799	32.0	6.6	S	(2)
Genoa	1800	24.0	10.4	F	(2)
Gaeta	1806	12.0	8.3	F	(2)
Kolberg	1807	14.0	35.7	F	(2)
Saragossa	1808	15.0	23.3	F	(3)
Gerona	1809	18.0	83.3	S	(3)
Saragossa	1809	50.0	24.0	S	(1)
Ciudad Rodrigo	1812	36.0	3.6	S	(1)
Burgos	1812	32.0	7.2	F	(2)
Badajoz	1812	51.0	16.7	S	(2)
Hamburg	1814	56.0	25.0	F	(3)

Sources: (1): Bodart (1916: *passim*); (2): Chandler (1994: app. 3); (3): Rothenberg (1980: app. 2).

TABLE II. 2b. Sieges and assaults: garrison strengths

Siege	Year	Strength (000)	Outcome (S=success, F=failure)	Source
Vienna	1683	16.0	S	(1)
Belgrade	1688	8.3	F	(2)
Philippsburg	1688	2.0	F	(1)
Mainz	1689	8.0	F	(2)
Loss Belgrade	1690	5.0	F	(1)
Nissa	1690	4.0	F	(2)
Mons	1691	4.8	F	(2)
Namur	1692	8.3	F	(2)
Namur	1695	13.0	F	(2)
Barcelona	1697	16.0	F	(2)
Ath	1697	3.7	F	(2)
Riga	1700	6.0	S	(2)
Guastalla	1702	2.2	F	(2)
Luttich	1702	8.0	F	(2)
Ruremonde	1702	2.4	F	(2)
Landau	1703	5.6	F	(1)
Trarbach	1704	0.6	F	(2)
Landau	1704	5.0	F	(2)
Verrua	1704/5	7.3	F	(2)
Gibraltar	1704/5	20.0	F	(2)
Barcelona	1705	5.8	F	(2)
Bonn	1705	3.6	F	(2)
Badajoz	1705	1.0	S	(2)
Ostend	1706	5.0	F	(2)
Menin	1706	5.5	F	(2)

(*continues*)

TABLE II. 2b. (*continued*)

Siege	Year	Strength (000)	Outcome (S=success, F=failure)	Source
Dendermonde	1706	4.0	F	(2)
Turin	1706	10.5	S	(2)
Lérida	1707	2.5	F	(2)
Toulon	1707	9.0	S	(2)
Lille	1708	16.0	F	(2)
Tournai	1709	7.0	F	(2)
Pultava	1709	4.0	S	(2)
Douai	1710	8.0	F	(2)
Bouchain	1711	5.0	F	(2)
Marchiennes	1712	7.0	F	(1)
Bouchain	1712	2.0	F	(2)
Douai	1712	3.2	F	(1)
Landrecies	1712	5.0	S	(2)
Gerona	1712/13	9.0	S	(2)
Landau	1713	7.0	F	(2)
Freiburg	1713	9.3	F	(1)
Barcelona	1713/14	16.0	F	(5)
Stralsund	1715	12.0	F	(5)
Corfu	1716	6.0	S	(5)
Temesvar	1716	18.0	S	(5)
Belgrade	1717	30.0	F	(5)
Messina	1719	4.0	F	(5)
Novara	1734	1.3	F	(5)
Philippsburg	1734	4.5	F	(5)
Oczakov	1737	22.0	F	(5)
Banjaluka	1737	5.0	S	(5)
Choczin	1738	1.0	F	(5)
Orsava	1738	2.0	S	(5)
Helsingfors	1742	15.0	F	(5)
Prague	1744	14.9	F	(5)
Freiburg	1744	7.0	F	(5)
Kosel	1745	2.3	F	(5)
Louisbourg	1745	3.0	F	(5)
Tournai	1745	6.0	F	(5)
Ostend	1745	4.0	F	(5)
Breslau	1757	17.0	F	(1)
Schweidnitz	1758	8.0	F	(1)
Olmutz	1758	7.5	S	(1)
Schweidnitz	1762	12.5	F	(1)
Mayence	1792	2.9	F	(6)
Longwy	1792	6.0	F	(6)
Dunkirk	1792	21.0	F	(6)

(*continues*)

TABLE II. 2b. (continued)

Charleroi	1794	3.0	F	(6)
Mantua	1797	28.0	F	(6)
Acre	1799	12.0	S	(6)
Genoa	1800	12.0	S	(6)
Magdeburg	1806	24.0	F	(6)
Kustrin	1806	2.4	F	(6)
Stettin	1806	5.3	F	(6)
Gaeta	1806	4.0	S	(6)
Kolberg	1807	6.0	S	(6)
Saragossa	1808	13.0	S	(6)
Gerona	1809	9.0	F	(6)
Saragossa	1809	30.0	F	(6)
Badajoz	1812	5.0	F	(6)
Ciudad Rodrigo	1812	2.0	F	(6)
Riga	1812	21.0	S	(6)
Burgos	1812	2.0	S	(6)
Danzig	1813	36.0	F	(6)
Hamburg	1814	40.0	S	(6)
Magdeburg	1814	20.0	F	(6)
Huningen	1815	3.0	S	(6)

Sources: As Table II. 2a.

References

ABEL, W. A. (1980). *Agricultural Fluctuations in Europe: From the Thirteenth to the Twentieth Centuries.* London: Methuen.

ABULAFIA, D. (1987). 'Africa, Asia and the Trade of Medieval Europe', in M. M. Postan and E. Miller (eds.), *The Cambridge Economic History of Europe*, ii: *Trade and Industry in the Middle Ages.* Cambridge: Cambridge University Press: 614–90.

ADCOCK, F. E. (1940). *The Roman Art of War under the Republic.* Cambridge, Mass.: Harvard University Press.

—— (1957). *The Greek and Macedonian Art of War.* Berkeley and Los Angeles: University of California Press.

ALLEN, P. (1979). 'The Justinianic Plague', *Byzantion*, 49: 5–20.

ALLEN, R. C. (2001). 'The Great Divergence in European Wages and Prices from the Middle Ages to the First World War', *Explorations in Economic History*, 38: 411–47.

ALM, J. (1994). *European Crossbows: A Survey.* London: Royal Armouries Museum.

ANDERSON, J. K. (1991). 'Hoplite Weapons and Offensive Arms', in V. D. Hanson (ed.), *Hoplites: The Classical Greek Battle Experience.* London: Routledge: 15–37.

ANDERSON, M. S. (1988). *War and Society in the Europe of the Old Regime, 1618–1781.* London: Fontana.

APPLEBY, A. B. (1973). 'Disease or Famine? Mortality in Cumberland and Westmoreland, 1580–1640', *Economic History Review*, 26: 403–31.

—— (1978). *Famine in Tudor and Stuart England.* Liverpool: Liverpool University Press.

ARDENER, E. (1974). 'Social Anthropology and Population', in H. B. Parry (ed.), *Population and its Problems: A Plain Man's Guide.* Oxford: Clarendon Press: 25–50.

ARNOLD, D. (1988). *Famine: Social Crisis and Historical Change.* Oxford: Basil Blackwell.

ASHTON, T. S. (1959). *Economic Fluctuations in England 1700–1800.* Oxford: Clarendon Press.

AYTON, A. (1994a). *Knights and Warhorses: Military Service and the English Aristocracy Under Edward III.* Woodbridge: Boydell.

—— (1994b). 'English Armies in the Fourteenth Century', in A. Curry and M. Hughes (eds.), *Arms, Armies and Fortifications in the Hundred Years War.* Woodbridge: Boydell Press: 21–38.

—— (1999). 'Arms, Armour, and Horses', in M. Keen (ed.), *Medieval Warfare: A History.* Oxford: Oxford University Press: 186–208.

—— and PRICE, J. L. (1995). 'Introduction: The Military Revolution from a Medieval Perspective', in A. Ayton and J. L. Price (eds.), *The Medieval Military Revolution.* London: Tauris Academic Studies: 1–22.

BACHRACH, B. S. (1984). 'The Cost of Castle Building: The Case of the Tower at Langeais, 992–994', in K. Reyerson and F. Powe (eds.), *The Medieval Castle: Romance and Reality.* Dubuque, Ia.: Kendall/Hunt: 46–62.

—— (1985). 'Animals and Warfare in Early Medieval Europe', *L'uomo di fronte al mondo animale nell'alto medioevo: Settimane* 31: 707–64.

—— (1999). 'The Siege of Antioch: A Study in Military Demography', *War in History,* 6 (2): 127–46.

BAIROCH, P. (1990). 'The Impact of Crop Yields, Agricultural Productivity and Transport Costs on Urban Growth between 1800 and 1910', in A. van der Woude, J. de Vries, and A. Hayami (eds.), *Urbanization in History.* Oxford: Clarendon Press: 134–51.

BARFIELD, T. J. (1989). *The Perilous Frontier.* Cambridge, Mass.: Blackwell.

BAR-KOCHVA, B. (1976). *The Seleucid Army: Organization and Tactics in the Great Campaigns.* Cambridge: Cambridge University Press.

BARTLETT, R., and MACKAY, A. (eds.) (1989). *Medieval Frontier Societies.* Oxford: Clarendon Press.

BARTUSIS, M. C. (1992). *The Late Byzantine Army: Arms and Society 1204–1453.* Philadelphia: University of Pennsylvania Press.

BATE, J. (1995). Review of Gillian Russell, *Theatres of War* (1995): 'The Image of Military History—Tweedy Brigadiers', *Times Literary Supplement:* 7.

BATH, B. H. S. V. (1963). *Agrarian History of Western Europe.* London: Edward Arnold.

BEAN, R. (1973). 'War and the Birth of the Nation State', *Journal of Economic History,* 33: 203–31.

BEATTIE, J. M. (1986). *Crime and the Courts in England 1660–1800.* Oxford: Clarendon Press.

BEELER, J. (1971). *Warfare in Feudal Europe 730–1200.* London: Cornell University Press.

BELL-FIALKOFF, A. (2000). 'The Slavs', in A. Bell-Fialkoff, *The Role of Migration in the History of the Eurasian Steppe.* London: Macmillan: 133–49.

BENDER, B. (1975). *Farming in Prehistory.* London: John Baker.

BENEDICT, P. (1985). 'Civil War and Natural Disaster in Northern France', in P. Clark (ed.), *The European Crisis of the 1590s: Essays in Comparative History.* London: George Allen & Unwin: 84–105.

BENEDICTOW, O. J. (1987). 'Morbidity in Historical Plague Epidemics', *Population Studies,* 41: 401–31.

BENNETT, M. (1994). 'The Development of Battle Tactics in the Hundred Years War', in A. Curry and M. Hughes (eds.), *Arms, Armies and Fortifications in the Hundred Years War.* Woodbridge: Boydell Press: 1–20.

—— (2001). 'The Crusaders' "Fighting March" Revisited', *War in History,* 8 (1): 1–18.

BERNARD, J. (1972). 'Trade and Finance in the Middle Ages 900–1500', in C. M. Cipolla (ed.), *The Fontana Economic History of Europe: The Middle Ages.* London: Fontana: 274–338.

BERRY, B. (1967). *Geography of Market Centres and Retail Distribution.* Englewood Cliffs, NJ: Prentice-Hall.

BEST, G. (1982). *War and Society in Revolutionary Europe.* London: Fontana.

BIRABEN, J.-N. (1979). 'Essai sur l'évolution du nombre des hommes', *Population,* 34: 13–25.

—— and GOFF, J. L. (1969). 'La Peste du Haut Moyen-Âge', *Annales:* 1484–510.

BLACK, J. (1990). *A Military Revolution? Military Change and European Society 1550–1800,* London: Macmillan.

—— (1991). *War for America: The Fight for Independence 1775–1783.* London: Allen Sutton Press.

—— (1999). *Britain as a Military Power, 1688–1815.* London: UCL Press.

BLAUT, J. (1961). 'Space and Process', *Professional Geographer,* 13: 1–7.

BLOCH, M. (1967). 'The Advent and Triumph of the Watermill', in M. Bloch, *Land and Work in Medieval Europe.* London: Routledge & Kegan Paul: 136–68.

BOAK, A. E. R. (1955). *Manpower Shortage and the Fall of the Roman Empire in the West.* Ann Arbor: Oxford University Press.
BODART, G. (1916). *Losses of Life in Modern Wars, 1683–1916.* Oxford: Clarendon Press.
BOIS, G. (1984). *The Crisis of Feudalism: Economy and Society in Eastern Normandy c.1300–1500.* Cambridge: Cambridge University Press.
BONNEY, R. (ed.) (1995a). *Economic Systems and State Finance.* The Origins of the Modern State in Europe. Oxford: European Science Foundation, Clarendon Press.
—— (1995b). 'Revenue', in R. Bonney (ed.), *Economic Systems and State Finance.* Oxford: European Science Foundation, Clarendon Press: 423–505.
—— (1995c). 'The Eighteenth Century II: The Struggle for Great Power Status and the End of the Old Financial Regime', in R. Bonney (ed.), *Economic Systems and State Finance.* Oxford: European Science Foundation, Clarendon Press: 315–89.
BOSERUP, E. (1965). *The Conditions of Agricultural Growth.* London: George Allen & Unwin.
—— (1981). *Population and Technology.* Oxford: Basil Blackwell.
BOSWELL, J. (1950). *Boswell's London Journal 1762–1763* ed. F. A. Pottle. London: Heinemann.
BOSWORTH, C. E. (1968). 'The Political and Dynastic History of the Iranian World (AD 1000–1217)', in J. A. Boyle (ed.), *The Cambridge History of Iran,* v: *The Saljuq and Mongol Periods.* Cambridge: Cambridge University Press: 1–202.
—— (1975). 'The Early Ghaznavids', in R. N. Frye (ed.), *The Cambridge History of Iran,* iv: *The Period from the Arab Invasion to the Saljuqs.* Cambridge: Cambridge University Press: 162–97.
BOWDEN, P. J. (1962). *The Wool Trade in Tudor and Stuart England.* London: Macmillan.
—— (1967). 'Agricultural Prices, Farm Profits and Rents', in J. Thirsk (ed.), *Agrarian History of England and Wales.* Cambridge: Cambridge University Press: iv. 593–65.
BOWLUS, C. R. (1995). *Franks, Moravians and Magyars: The Struggle for the Middle Danube, 788–907.* Philadelphia: University of Pennsylvania Press.
BOYLE, J. A. (ed.) (1968). *The Cambridge History of Iran,* v: *The Saljuq and Mongol Periods.* Cambridge: Cambridge University Press.
BRADBURY, J. (1992). *The Medieval Archer.* Woodbridge: Boydell & Brewer.
BRADY, N. (1997). 'The Gothic Barn of England: Icon of Prestige and Authority', in E. B. Smith and M. Wolfe (eds.), *Technology and Resource Use in Medieval Europe: Cathedrals, Mills and Mines.* Aldershot: Ashgate: 76–105.
BRAUDEL, F. (1972). *The Mediterranean and the Mediterranean World in the Age of Philip II.* London: Collins.
—— (1980). *History and the Social Sciences: The Longue Duree.* London: Weidenfeld & Nicolson.
—— (1981). *The Structures of Everyday Life: The Limits of the Possible.* London: Collins.
—— (1982). *The Wheels of Commerce.* London: Collins.
—— (1988). *The Identity of France: History and Environment.* London: Collins.
—— (1990). *The Identity of France: People and Production.* London: Collins.
BRAY, R. S. (1996). *Armies of Pestilence: The Effects of Pandemics on History.* Cambridge: Lutterworth Press.
BRESCHI, M., and BACCI, M. L. (1997). 'Month of Birth as a Factor in Children's Survival', in A. Bideau, B. Desjardins, and H. P. Brignolo (eds.), *Infant and Child Mortality in the Past.* Oxford: Oxford University Press: 157–73.

BREWER, J. (1989). *The Sinews of Power: War, Money and the English State, 1688–1783.* London: Unwin Hyman.
BRUNT, P. (1987). 'Labour', in J. Wacher (ed.), *The Roman World.* London: Routledge. ii. 701–16.
BULLIET, R. (1975). *The Camel and the Wheel.* Cambridge, Mass.: Harvard University Press.
BURFORD, A. (1960). 'Heavy Transport in Classical Antiquity', *Economic History Review,* 13: 1–19.
BURN, A. R. (1984). *Persia and the Greeks: The Defence of the West, c.546–478 B.C.* London: Duckworth.
CAMERON, A. (1993). *The Later Roman Empire,* AD 284–430. London: Fontana.
CAMPBELL, B. M. S. (1983a). 'Agricultural Progress in Medieval England: Some Evidence from Eastern Norfolk', *Economic History Review,* 36: 26–46.
—— (1983b). 'Arable Productivity in Medieval England: Some Evidence from Norfolk', *Journal of Economic History,* 43: 379–404.
—— (ed.) (1991). *Before the Black Death: Studies in the Crisis of the Early Fourteenth Century.* Manchester: Manchester University Press.
—— GALLOWAY, J. A., et al. (1993). *A Medieval Capital and its Grain Supply: Agrarian Production and Distribution in the London Region c.1300.* London: Historical Geography Research Group.
—— and OVERTON, M. (eds.) (1991). *Land, Labour and Livestock: Historical Studies of European Agricultural Productivity.* Manchester: Manchester University Press.
—— (1984). *The Emperor and the Roman Army, 31 BC–AD 235.* Oxford: Clarendon Press.
CARLTON, C. (1992). *Going to the Wars: The Experience of the British Civil Wars, 1638–1651.* London: Routledge.
CARTLEDGE, P. (1979). *Sparta and Lakonia: A Regional History 1300–362 BC.* London: Routledge.
CARUS-WILSON, E. (1987). 'The Woollen Industry', in M. M. Postan and E. Miller (eds.), *The Cambridge Economic History of Europe,* ii: *Trade and Industry in the Middle Ages.* Cambridge: Cambridge University Press: 614–90.
CASSON, L. (1971). *Ships and Seamanship in the Ancient World.* Princeton: Princeton University Press.
—— (1974). *Travel in the Ancient World.* London: George Allen & Unwin.
CHAMBERS, J. (1988). *The Devil's Horsemen: The Mongol Invasion of Europe.* London: Cassell.
CHAMBERS, J. D. (1972). *Population, Economy and Society in Pre-industrial England.* Oxford: Oxford University Press.
CHANDLER, D. (1979). *Marlborough as Military Commander.* London: Batsford.
—— (1994). *The Art of Warfare in the Age of Marlborough.* London: Batsford.
CHAPPELLE, H. I. (1968). *The Search for Speed under Sail, 1700–1855.* London: George Allen & Unwin.
CHARBONNEAU, H., and LAROSE, A. (eds.) (1979). *The Great Mortalities: Methodological Studies of Demographic Crises in the Past.* Liège: Ordina Editions.
CHARTRES, J. (1977a). 'Road Carrying in England in the Seventeenth Century: Myth and Reality', *Economic History Review,* 30: 73–94.
—— (1977b). *Internal Trade in England, 1500–1700.* London: Macmillan.
CHESNAIS, J.-C. (1992). *The Demographic Transition: Stages, Patterns and Economic Interpretations.* Oxford: Clarendon Press.

CHILDS, J. (1982). *Armies and Warfare in Europe 1648–1789*. Manchester: Manchester University Press.
—— (1991). *The Nine Years War and the British Army*. Manchester: Manchester University Press.
CHRISTIAN, D. (1998). *A History of Russia, Central Asia and Mongolia*, i: *Inner Eurasia from Prehistory to the Mongol Empire*. Oxford: Blackwell.
CHRISTIANSEN, E. (1980). *The Northern Crusades: The Baltic and the Catholic Frontier 1100–1525*. London: Macmillan.
CHRISTIE, N. (1995). *The Lombards: The Ancient Langobards*. Oxford: Blackwell.
CIPOLLA, C. (1965). *Guns, Sails, and Empires: Technological Innovation and the Early Phases of European Expansion, 1400–1700*. Manhattan, Kan.: Sunflower University Press.
—— (1976). *Before the Industrial Revolution: European Society and Economy, 1000–1700*. London: Methuen.
CLARK, C. (1967). *Population Growth and Land Use*. London: Macmillan.
CLARK, P., and SOUDEN, D. (eds.) (1987). *Migration and Society in Early Modern England*. London: Hutchinson.
CLAY, C. G. A. (1984). *Economic Expansion and Social Change: England 1500–1700*. Cambridge: Cambridge University Press.
COALE, A. J., and DEMENY, P. G. (1966). *Regional Life Tables and Stable Populations* (2nd edn.). London: Academic Press.
COLEMAN, D., and SCHOFIELD, R. (eds.) (1986). *The State of Population Theory: Forward from Malthus*. Oxford: Blackwell.
COLLINS, R. (1984). 'The Basques in Aquitaine and Navarre: Problems of Frontier Government', in J. Gillingham and J. C. Holt (eds.), *War and Government in the Middle Ages*. Bury St Edmunds: Boydell Press: 3–17.
—— (1989). *The Arab Conquest of Spain 710–797*. Oxford: Blackwell.
—— (1998). *Charlemagne*. Basingstoke: Macmillan.
—— (1999). *Early Medieval Europe, 300–1000*. Basingstoke: Palgrave.
CONTAMINE, P. (1984). *War in the Middle Ages*. Oxford: Basil Blackwell.
COOK, J. M. (1983). *The Persian Empire*. London: J. M. Dent.
COOKSON, J. E. (1997). *The British Armed Nation*. Oxford: Clarendon Press.
CORCORAN, S. (2000). *The Empire of the Tetrarchs: Imperial Pronouncements and Government AD 284–324*. Oxford: Clarendon Press.
CORFIS, I. A., and WOLFE, M. (eds.) (1995). *The Medieval City under Siege*. Woodbridge: Boydell Press.
COTTERILL, J. (1993). 'Saxon Raiding and the Role of the Late Roman Coastal Forts of Britain', *Britannia*, 24: 227–39.
COTTRELL, W. F. (1955). *Energy and Society: The Relation between Energy, Social Change and Economic Development*. New York: McGraw Hill.
COULSTON, J. C. (1986). 'Roman, Parthian and Sassanid Tactical Developments', in P. Freeman and D. Kennedy (eds.), *The Defence of the Roman and Byzantine East*. Oxford: BAR: 59–75.
CRAFTS, N. F. R. (1985). *British Economic Growth during the Industrial Revolution*. Oxford: Clarendon Press.
CREVELD, M. VAN (1977). *Supplying War*. Cambridge: Cambridge University Press.
—— (1991). *Technology and War*. New York: Free Press.

CROSBY, A. W. (1972). *The Columbian Exchange: Biological and Cultural Consequences of 1492*. Westport, Conn.: Greenwood Press.

CUNLIFFE, B. (1988). *Greeks, Romans and Barbarians*. London: Guild Publishing.

—— (1997). *The Ancient Celts*. Oxford: Oxford University Press.

CURRY, A. (1994). 'English Armies in the Fifteenth Century', in A. Curry and M. Hughes (eds.), *Arms, Armies and Fortifications in the Hundred Years War*. Woodbridge: Boydell Press: 39–68.

DAUNTON, M. J. (1978). 'Towns and Economic Growth in Eighteenth Century England', in P. Abrams and E. A. Wrigley (eds.), *Towns in Societies*. Cambridge: Cambridge University Press: 245–78.

DAVIS, R. (1962). *The Rise of the English Shipping Industry in the Seventeenth and Eighteenth Centuries*. London: Macmillan.

DE SOUZA, P. (1999). *Piracy in the Graeco-Roman World*. Cambridge: Cambridge University Press.

DE VRIES, J. (1976). *The Economy of Europe in an Age of Crisis, 1600–1750*. Cambridge: Cambridge University Press.

—— (1978). 'Barges and Capitalism: Passenger Transport in the Dutch Economy', *A A G Bijdragen*, 21: 33–398.

—— (1984). *European Urbanisation 1500–1800*. London: Methuen.

—— (1985). 'The Population and Economy of the Pre-industrial Netherlands', *Journal of Interdisciplinary History*, 15: 661–82.

—— and VAN DER WOUDE, A. (1997). *The First Modern Economy: Success, Failure, and Perseverance of the Dutch Economy, 1500–1815*. Cambridge: Cambridge University Press.

DEVRIES, K. (1992). *Medieval Military Technology*. Peterborough, Ontario: Broadview Press.

—— (1996). *Infantry Warfare in the 14th Century*. Woodbridge: Boydell & Brewer.

—— (1997). 'Catapults are not Atomic Bombs: Towards a Redefinition of "Effectiveness" in Premodern Military Technology', *War in History*, 4: 454–70.

DINARDO, R. L., and BAY, A. (1988). 'Horse-Drawn Transport in the German Army', *Journal of Contemporary History*, 23: 129–42.

DIXON, K. R., and SOUTHERN, P. (1992). *The Roman Cavalry*. London: Batsford.

DOBSON, M. J. (1997). *Contours of Death and Disease in Early Modern England*. Cambridge: Cambridge University Press.

—— (1989). 'Mortality Gradients and Disease Exchanges: Comparisons from Old England and Colonial America', *Social History of Medicine*, 2 (3): 259–98.

DOLUKHANOV, P. M. (1996). *The Early Slavs: Eastern Europe from the Initial Settlement to the Kievan Rus*. London: Longmans.

DOUGLAS, M. (1966). 'Population Control in Primitive Groups', *British Journal of Sociology*, 17: 263–73.

DRINKWATER, J. F. (1987). *The Gallic Empire: Separatism and Continuity in the North-Western Provinces of the Roman Empire, A.D. 260–274*. Stuttgart: Franz Steiner.

—— (1996). 'The "Germanic Threat on the Rhine Frontier": A Romano-Gallic Artefact?', in R. W. Mathisen and H. S. Sivan (eds.), *Shifting Frontiers in Late Antiquity*. Aldershot: Variorum: 20–30.

DUBY, G. (1968). *Rural Economy and Country Life in the Medieval West*. Columbia, SC: University of South Carolina Press.

—— (1972). 'Medieval Agriculture', in C. M. Cipolla (ed.), *The Fontana Economic History of Europe: The Middle Ages*. London: Fontana: 175–220.

DUBY, G. (1981). *The Age of the Cathedrals: Art and Society, 980–1420*. London: Croom Helm.
DUFFY, C. (1974). *The Army of Frederick the Great*. Newton Abbot: David & Charles.
—— (1979). *Siege Warfare: The Fortress in the Early Modern World 1494–1660*. London: Routledge & Kegan Paul.
—— (1985). *The Fortress in the Age of Vauban and Frederick the Great 1660–1789*. London: Routledge & Kegan Paul.
DUMAS, S., and VEDEL-PETERSON, K. O. (1923). *Losses of Life Caused by War*. Oxford: Clarendon Press.
DUNCAN-JONES, R. (1974). *The Economy of the Roman Empire: Quantitative Studies*. Cambridge: Cambridge University Press.
—— (1978). 'Pay and Numbers in Diocletian's Army', *Chiron*, 8: 541–60.
DUPÂQUIER, J. (ed.) (1988a). *Histoire de la population française*, ii: *De la Renaissance à 1789*. Paris: Quadrige/Presses Universitaires de France.
—— (ed.) (1988b). *Histoire de la population française*, i: *Des origines à la renaissance*. Paris: Quadrige/Presses Universitaires de France.
—— (1988c). 'La Peuplade', in J. Dupâquier (ed.), *Histoire de la population française*, ii: *De la Renaissance à 1789*. Paris: Quadrige/Presses Universitaires de France: 68–81.
—— (1988d). 'L'Autorégulation de la population française (XVIe–XVIIIe siècle')', in J. Dupâquier (ed.), *Histoire de la population française*, ii: *De la Renaissance à 1789*. Paris: Quadrige/Presses Universitaires de France: 413–36.
—— (1989). 'Demographic Crises and Subsistence Crises in France, 1650–1789', in J. Walter and R. S. Schofield (eds.), *Famine, Disease and the Social Order in Early Modern Society*. Cambridge: Cambridge University Press: 189–200.
—— FAUVE-CHAMOUX, A., and GREBERICK, E. (eds.) (1983). *Malthus Past and Present*. London: Academic Press.
DUPUY, T. (1984). *The Evolution of Weapons and Warfare*. London: Jane's.
DURAND, J. (1967). 'The Modern Expansion of World Population', *Proceedings of the American Philosophical Society*, 111 (3): 136–59.
—— (1977). 'Historical Estimates of World Population: An Evaluation', *Population and Development Review*, 3: 253–96.
DYER, C. (1989). *Standards of Living in the Later Middle Ages: Social Change in England, c.1200–1520*. Cambridge: Cambridge University Press.
DYOS, H. J., and ALDCROFT, D. H. (1974). *British Transport: An Economic Survey from the Seventeenth to the Twentieth Century*. Harmondsworth: Penguin.
DYSON, L. (1970). 'Native Revolts in the Roman Empire', *Historia*, 20: 239–74.
—— (1975). 'Native Revolt Patterns in the Roman Empire', *Aufstieg und Niedergang der römischen Welt*, 2 (3): 138–75.
EDWARDS, P. (1998). 'Logistics and Supply', in J. Kenyan and J. Ohlmeyer (eds.), *The Civil Wars: A Military History of England, Scotland, and Ireland, 1638–1660*. Oxford: Oxford University Press: 272–305.
ELTING, J. R. (1997). *Swords around a Throne: Napoleon's Grande Armée*. London: Phoenix Giant.
ELTON, H. (1996). *Warfare in Roman Europe AD 350–425*. Oxford: Clarendon Press.
ENGELS, D. W. (1978). *Alexander the Great and the Logistics of the Macedonian Army*. London: University of California Press.
ESDAILE, C. (1995). *The Wars of Napoleon*. London: Longmans.

FERRILL, A. (1985). *The Origins of War: From the Stone Age to Alexander the Great.* London: Thames & Hudson.
FINLEY, M. I. (1958). Review of A. E. R. Boak, *Manpower Shortage and the Fall of the Roman Empire. Journal of Roman Studies,* 48: 157–64.
FLINN, M. W. (1979). 'Plague in Europe and the Mediterranean Countries', *Journal of European Economic History,* 8: 131–48.
—— (1981). *The European Demographic System 1500–1820.* Brighton: Harvester.
—— (1984). *The History of the British Coal Industry,* ii: *1700–1830: The Industrial Revolution.* Oxford: Clarendon Press.
FLOUD, R., WACHTER, K., and GREGORY, A. (1990). *Height, Health and History: Nutritional Status in the United Kingdom, 1750–1980.* Cambridge: Cambridge University Press.
FOGEL, R. W. (1992). 'Second Thoughts on the European Escape from Hunger: Famines, Chronic Malnutrition and Mortality Rates', in S. R. Osmani (ed.), *Nutrition and Poverty* Oxford: Clarendon Press: 243–86.
FORBES, R. J. (1957). 'Metallurgy', in C. J. Singer, E. J. Holmyard, A. R. Hall, and T. I. Williams (eds.), *A History of Technology,* iii: *From the Renaissance to the Industrial Revolution, c.1500–c.1750.* Oxford: Clarendon Press: 27–71.
FORREST, A. (1989). *Conscripts and Deserters: The Army and French Society during the Revolution and Empire.* Oxford: Oxford University Press.
FRANCE, J. (1994). *Victory in the East: A Military History of the First Crusade.* Cambridge: Cambridge University Press.
FRANÇOIS, E. (1990). 'The German Urban Network between the Sixteenth and Eighteenth Centuries: Cultural and Demographic Indicators', in A. van der Woude, J. de Vries, and A. Hayami (eds.), *Urbanization in History.* Oxford: Clarendon Press: 84–100.
FRANKLIN, S. (1996). *The Emergence of Rus.* London: Longman.
FRIEL, I. (1994). 'Winds of Change? Ships and the Hundred Years War', in A. Curry and M. Hughes (eds.), *Arms, Armies and Fortifications in the Hundred Years War.* Woodbridge: Boydell Press: 183–93.
FRIENDLY, A. (1981). *The Dreadful Day: The Battle of Manzikert, 1071.* London: Hutchinson.
FRIER, B. W. (2000). 'Demography', in A. K. Bowman, P. Garnsey, and D. Rathbone (eds.), *The Cambridge Ancient History,* xi: *The High Empire.* Cambridge: Cambridge University Press: 787–816.
FRYE, R. N. (ed.) (1975). *The Cambridge History of Iran,* iv: *The Period from the Arab Invasion to the Saljuqs.* Cambridge: Cambridge University Press.
FULLER, J. F. C. (1970). *The Decisive Battles of the Western World, and their Influence upon History.* London: Paladin.
GALLOWAY, P. R. (1986). 'Long Term Fluctuations in Climate and Population in the Preindustrial Era', *Population and Development Review,* 12: 1–24.
—— (1988). 'Basic Patterns in Annual Variations in Fertility, Nuptiality, Mortality and Prices in Pre-industrial Europe', *Population Studies,* 42: 275–304.
GARDINER, R. (1992). 'Design and Construction', in R. Gardiner (ed.), *The Line of Battle: The Sailing Warship, 1650–1840.* London: Conway Maritime Press: 116–24.
GARNSEY, P. (1983). 'Grain for Rome', in P. Garnsey, K. Hopkins, and C. R. Whittaker (eds.), *Trade in the Ancient Economy.* London: Chatto & Windus: 118–30.
—— (1988). *Famine and Food Supply in the Ancient World: Responses to Risk and Crisis.* Cambridge: Cambridge University Press.

GELABERT, J. (1999). 'Castile, 1504–1808', in R. Bonney (ed.), *The Rise of the Fiscal State in Europe c. 1200–1815*. Oxford: Oxford University Press: 201–41.

GILLIAM, J. F. (1961). 'The Plague under Marcus Aurelius', *American Journal of Philology*, 82: 224–51.

GILLINGHAM, J. (1981). *The Wars of the Roses: Peace and Conflict in Fifteenth-Century England*. London: Weidenfeld & Nicolson.

—— (1984). 'Richard I and the Science of War in the Middle Ages', in J. Gillingham and J. C. Holt (eds.), *War and Government in the Middle Ages*. Bury St Edmunds: Boydell Press: 78–91.

GLASS, D. V. (1965). 'Two Papers on Gregory King', in D. V. Glass and D. E. C. Eversley (eds.), *Population in History: Essays in Historical Demography*. London: Edward Arnold: 159–220.

GLETE, J. (1992). 'The Oared Warship', in R. Gardiner (ed.), *The Line of Battle: The Sailing Warship, 1650–1840*. London: Conway Maritime Press: 98–105.

GOFFART, W. (1980). 'Barbarians and Romans: Techniques of Accommodation'. Princeton: Princeton University Press.

GOFFMAN, E. (1968). *Asylums*. Harmondsworth: Penguin.

GOLDSMITH, R. W. (1987). *Premodern Financial Systems: A Historical Comparative Study*. Cambridge: Cambridge University Press.

GOLDSTONE, J. (1986). 'The Demographic Revolution: A Re-examination', *Population Studies*, 40: 5–33.

—— (1991). *Revolution and Rebellion in the Early Modern World*. Berkeley and Los Angeles: University of California Press.

GOLDSWORTHY, A. K. (1996). *The Roman Army at War, 100 BC–AD 200*. Oxford: Clarendon Press.

—— (1997). 'The *Othismos*, Myths and Heresies: The Nature of Hoplite Warfare', *War in History*, 4 (1): 1–26.

GOODBURN, R., and BARTHOLOMEW, P. (eds.) (1976). *Aspects of the Notitia Dignitatum*. Oxford: British Archaeological Reports.

GOODY, J. (1977). *The Domestication of the Savage Mind*. Cambridge: Cambridge University Press.

GOUBERT, P. (1960). *Beauvais et le Beauvaisis de 1600 à 1730*, 2 vols. Paris: SEVPEN.

GRANT, M. (1974). *The Army of the Caesars*. London: Weidenfeld & Nicolson.

GREENE, K. (1986). *The Archaeology of the Roman Economy*. Berkeley and Los Angeles: University of California Press.

—— (2000). 'Technological Innovation and Economic Progress in the Ancient World: M. I. Finley Re-considered', *Economic History Review*, 53 (1): 29–59.

GRIGG, D. (1980). *Population Growth and Agrarian Change*. Cambridge: Cambridge University Press.

—— (1992). *The Transformation of Agriculture in the West*. Oxford: Blackwell.

GUILMARTIN, J. F. (1993). 'The Logistics of Warfare at Sea in the Sixteenth Century: The Spanish Perspective', in J. A. Lynn (ed.), *Feeding Mars: Logistics in Western Warfare from the Middle Ages to the Present*. Boulder, Colo.: Westview: 109–36.

GUTMANN, M. P. (1980). *War and Rural Life in the Early Modern Low Countries*. Princeton: Princeton University Press.

HAINES, R., and SHLOMOWITZ, R. (1998). 'Explaining the Modern Mortality Decline: What Can we Learn from Sea Voyages?', *Social History of Medicine*, 11 (1): 1–13.

HAJNAL, J. (1965). 'European Marriage Patterns in Perspective', in D. V. Glass and D. E. C. Eversley (eds.), *Population in History: Essays in Historical Demography*. London: Edward Arnold: 101–47.

—— (1983). 'Two Kinds of Pre-industrial Household Formation System', in R. Wall, J. Robin, and P. Laslett (eds.), *Family Forms in Historic Europe*. Cambridge: Cambridge University Press: 65–104.

HALDON, J. (1999). *Warfare, State and Society in the Byzantine World 565–1204*. London: UCL Press.

HALE, J. R. (1985). *War and Society in Renaissance Europe*. London: Fontana.

HALL, B. (1997). *Weapons and Warfare in Renaissance Europe*. Baltimore: Johns Hopkins University Press.

HAMMOND, N. G. L. (1989). *The Macedonian State: The Origins, Institutions and History*. Oxford: Clarendon Press.

—— and GRIFFITH, G. T. (1979). *A History of Macedonia*, ii: *550–336*. Oxford: Clarendon Press.

HANSON, V. D. (ed.) (1991). *Hoplites: The Classical Greek Battle Experience*. London: Routledge.

HARARI, Y. N. (2000). 'Strategy and Supply in Fourteenth-Century Western European Invasion Campaigns', *Military History*, 64: 279–334.

HARDY, R. (1994). *Longbow: A Social and Military History*. New York: Bois d'Arc Press.

HÄRKE, H. (1994). Review of S. McGrail, *Maritime Celts, Frisians and Saxons* (1990) and J. Haywood, *Dark Age Naval Power* (1999), *Britannia*, 25: 329–31.

HARRIS, W. V. (1980). 'Toward a Study of the Roman Slave Trade', in J. H. D'Arms and E. C. Knopf (eds.), *The Seaborne Commerce of Ancient Rome: Studies in Archaeology and History*. Rome: American Academy in Rome: 117–40.

—— (2000). 'Trade', in A. K. Bowman, P. Garnsey, and D. Rathbone (eds.), *The Cambridge Ancient History*, xi: *The High Empire*. Cambridge: Cambridge University Press: 710–40.

HARRISON, G. A., WEINER, J. S., et al. (1977). *Human Biology: An Introduction to Human Evolution, Variation, Growth, and Ecology* (2nd edn.). Oxford: Oxford University Press.

HARVEY, B. (1993). *Living and Dying in England 1100–1540: The Monastic Experience*. Oxford: Clarendon Press.

HASSALL, M. (2000). 'The Army', in A. K. Bowman, P. Garnsey, and D. Rathbone (eds.), *The Cambridge Ancient History*, xi: *The High Empire*. Cambridge: Cambridge University Press: 320–43.

HASSAN, F. A. (1981). *Demographic Archeology*. London: Academic Press.

HATCHER, J. (1977). *Plague, Population and the English Economy 1348–1530*. London: Macmillan.

—— and BAILEY, M. (2001). *Modelling the Middle Ages: The History and Theory of England's Economic Development*. Oxford: Oxford University Press.

HAYTHORNTHWAITE, P. J. (1988). *Napoleon's Military Machine*. Tunbridge Wells: Spellmount.

—— (1994). *The Armies of Wellington*. London: Arms and Armour Press.

HAYWOOD, J. (1999). *Dark Age Naval Power*. Hockwood-cum-Wilton: Anglo-Saxon Books.

HEATH, E. G. (1980). *Archery: A Military History*. London: Osprey.

HEATHER, P. (1991). *Goths and Romans 332–489*. Oxford: Clarendon Press.

—— (1996). *The Goths*. Oxford: Blackwell.

HELLEINER, K. (1967). 'The Population of Europe from the Black Death to the Eve of the Vital Revolution', in E. E. Rich and C. H. Wilson (eds.), *The Cambridge Economic History of Europe*, iv. Cambridge: Cambridge University Press: 1–95.

HENDY, M. F. (1985). *Studies in the Byzantine Monetary Economy, c. 300–1450*. Cambridge: Cambridge University Press.

HENRY, L. (1966). 'Perturbations de la nuptialité résultant de la guerre 1914–1918', *Population*.

HILL, D. R. (1984). *A History of Engineering in Ancient and Medieval Times*. London: Croom Helm.

HINDE, A. (1998). *Demographic Methods*. Leeds: Arnold.

HODDER, I. (1990). *The Domestication of Europe*. Oxford: Basil Blackwell.

—— and HASSALL, M. (1971). 'The Non-random Spacing of Romano-British Walled Towns', *Man*, 6: 391–407.

HODGE, W. B. (1856). 'On Mortality Arising from Naval Operations', *Assurance and Journal of the Institute of Actuaries*: 254–77.

—— (1857). 'On Mortality Arising from Military Operations', *Assurance and Journal of the Institute of Actuaries*, 6: 80–90, 151–217, 275–85.

HODGES, R. (1982). *Dark Age Economics: The Origins of Towns and Trade AD 600–1000*. London: Duckworth.

—— and WHITEHOUSE, D. (1983). *Mohammed, Charlemagne and the Origins of Europe*. London: Duckworth.

HOFFMAN, P. T. (1996). *Growth in a Traditional Society: The French Countryside, 1450–1815*. Princeton: Princeton University Press.

HOHENBERG, P. M., and LEES, L. H. (1985). *The Making of Urban Europe*. Cambridge, Mass.: Harvard University Press.

HOLLINGSWORTH, T. H. (1976). *Historical Demography*. Cambridge: Cambridge University Press.

HOLLISTER, C. W. (1962). *Anglo-Saxon Military Institutions*. Oxford: Clarendon Press.

—— (1965). *The Military Organization of Norman England*. Oxford: Clarendon Press.

HOLT, R. (1997). 'Mechanization and the English Medieval Economy', in E. B. Smith and M. Wolfe (eds.), *Technology and Resource Use in Medieval Europe: Cathedrals, Mills and Mines*. Aldershot: Ashgate: 139–57.

HOPKINS, K. (1978). 'Economic Growth and Towns in Classical Antiquity', in P. Abrams and E. A. Wrigley (eds.), *Towns in Societies: Essays in Economic History and Historical Sociology*. Cambridge: Cambridge University Press: 35–77.

HOPWOOD, K. (1986). 'Towers, Territory and Terror: How the East was Held', in P. Freeman and D. Kennedy (eds.), *The Defence of the Roman and Byzantine East*. Oxford: BAR: 243–56.

HORDEN, P., and PURCELL, N. (2000). *The Corrupting Sea: A Study of Mediterranean History*. Oxford: Basil Blackwell.

HOUDAILLE, J. (1970). 'Le Problème des pertes de guerre', *Revue d'histoire moderne et contemporaine*, 17: 339–58.

—— (1972). 'Pertes de l'armée de terre sous le premier Empire, d'après les registres matricules', *Population*, 27 (1): 27–50.

—— (1977). 'La Mortalité (hors combat) des militaires français à la fin du XVIIIème siècle et au début du XIXème siècle', *Population*, special issue: 481–97.

HOUSTON, R. A. (1992). *The Population History of Britain and Ireland*. London: Macmillan.

HOWARD, M. (1962). *The Franco-Prussian War: The German Invasion of France 1870–1871*. London: Rupert Hart-Davis.

HOWARD-JOHNSTON, J. (1999). 'Heraclius' Persian Campaigns and the Revival of the East Roman Empire, 622–630', *War in History*, 6 (1): 1–44.
HOWELL, N. (1976). 'Towards a Uniformitarian Theory of Palaeodemography', in R. H. Ward and K. M. Weiss (eds.), *The Demographic Evolution of Human Populations*. London: Academic Press: 25–40.
HUSTON, J. A. (1966). *The Sinews of War: Army Logistics 1775–1953*. Washington: Office of Military History.
HYLAND, A. (1998). *The Warhorse, 1250–1600*. Stroud: Sutton.
—— (1999). *The Horse in the Middle Ages*. Stroud: Sutton.
ISAAC, B. (1992). *The Limits of Empire: The Roman Army in the East*. Oxford: Clarendon Press.
JAMES, E. (1988). *The Franks*. Oxford: Blackwell.
JIMINEZ, M. G. (1989). 'Frontier and Settlement in the Kingdom of Castile (1085–1350)', in R. Bartlett and A. MacKay (eds.), *Medieval Frontier Societies*. Oxford: Clarendon Press: 49–74.
JOHANSSON, S. R. and C. M. Mosk (1987). 'Exposure, resistance and life expectancy: disease and death during the economic development of Japan, 1900–1960.' *Population Studies* 41: 207–36.
JONES, C. (1995). 'The Military Revolution and the Professionalisation of the French Army under the Ancien Regime', in C. J. Rogers (ed.), *The Military Revolution Debate: Readings in the Military Transformation of Early Modern Europe*. Boulder, Colo.: Westview: 149–67.
JONES, D. W. (1988). *War and Economy in the Age of William III and Marlborough*. Oxford: Blackwell.
JONES, M. (1994). 'War and Fourteenth-Century France', in A. Curry and M. Hughes (eds.), *Arms, Armour and Fortifications in the Hundred Years War*. Woodbridge: Boydell Press: 103–20.
JORDAN, W. C. (1996). *The Great Famine: Northern Europe in the Early Fourteenth Century*. Princeton: Princeton University Press.
KAEGI, W. E. (1993). 'Byzantine Logistics', in J. A. Lynn (ed.), *Feeding Mars: Logistics in Western Warfare from the Middle Ages to the Present*. Boulder, Colo.: Westview: 39–55.
—— (1992). *Byzantium and the Early Islamic Conquests*. Cambridge: Cambridge University Press.
KAGAN, D. (1974). *The Archidamian War*. Ithaca, NY: Cornell University Press.
KAPELLE, W. E. (1979). *The Norman Conquest of the North: The Region and its Transformation, 1000–1135*. London: Croom Helm.
KEEGAN, J. (1976). *The Face of Battle*. London: Cape.
—— (1987). *The Mask of Command*. London: Cape.
KELLENBENZ, H. (1974). 'Technology in the Age of the Scientific Revolution 1500–1700', in C. M. Cipolla (ed.), *The Fontana Economic History of Europe: The Sixteenth and Seventeenth Centuries*. London: Fontana: 177–272.
KENNEDY, P. (1991). *The Rise and Fall of British Naval Mastery*. London: Fontana.
KEPPIE, L. (1984). *The Making of the Roman Army*. London: Batsford.
KIERNAN, V. G. (1982). *European Empires from Conquest to Collapse*. London: Fontana.
KING, D. J. C. (1988). *The Castle in England and Wales: An Interpretative History*, London: Croom Helm.
KING, E. (ed.) (1994). *The Anarchy of King Stephen's Reign*. Oxford: Clarendon Press.
KNODEL, J. (1988). *Demographic Behavior in the Past*. Cambridge: Cambridge University Press.

KNODEL, J. and VAN DE WALLE, E. (1979). 'Lessons from the Past: Policy Implications of Historical Fertility Studies', *Population and Development Review*, 5: 217–45.

KÖRNER, M. (1995). 'Public Credit', in R. Bonney (ed.), *Economic Systems and State Finance*. Oxford: European Science Foundation, Clarendon Press: 507–38.

KOZLOVSKI, N. (1912). 'Statistical Data Concerning the Losses of the Russian Army from Sickness and Wounds in the War against Japan', *Journal of the Royal Army Medical Corps*, 18: 330–46.

KRADER, L. (1968). *Formation of the State*. Englewood Cliffs, NJ: Prentice-Hall.

KRAUSE, J. T. (1959). 'Some Neglected Factors in the English Industrial Revolution', *Journal of Economic History*, 19: 528–40.

KRENTZ, P. (1985). 'Casualties in Hoplite Battles', *Greek, Roman and Byzantine Studies*, 26: 13–20.

KRIEDTE, P., MEDICK, H., and SCHLUMBOHM, J. (eds.) (1981). *Industrialization before Industrialization. Studies in Modern Capitalism*. Cambridge: Cambridge University Press.

KUNITZ, S. J. (1983). 'Speculations on the European Mortality Decline', *Economic History Review*, 2nd ser. 36: 349–64.

—— (1987). 'Making a Long Story Short: A Note on Men's Heights and Mortality in England from the First through the Nineteenth Centuries', *Medical History*, 31: 269–80.

KUSSMAUL, A. (1990). *A General View of the Rural Economy of England, 1538–1840*. Cambridge: Cambridge University Press.

LADURIE, E. L. R. (1979). 'Amenorrhea in Time of Famine', in E. L. R. Ladurie, *The Territory of the Historian*. Brighton: Harvester: 255–71.

—— (1981a). 'A Concept: The Unification of the World by Disease (Fourteenth to Seventeenth Centuries)', in E. L. R. Ladurie, *The Mind and Method of the Historian*. Brighton: Harvester: 28–83.

—— (1981b). 'History that Stands Still', in E. L. R. Ladurie, *The Mind and Method of the Historian*. Brighton: Harvester: 1–27.

LANDELS, J. G. (1978). *Engineering in the Ancient World*. London: Chatto & Windus.

LANDERS, J. (1987). 'Mortality and Metropolis: The Case of London 1675–1825', *Population Studies*, 41: 59–76.

—— (1990a). 'Age-Patterns of Mortality in C18 London: A Test of the "high Potential" Model', *Social History of Medicine*, 3: 27–60.

—— (1990b). 'Fertility Decline and Birth Spacing among London Quakers', in J. Landers and V. Reynolds, *Fertility and Resources*. Cambridge: Cambridge University Press: 92–117.

—— (1993). *Death and the Metropolis: Studies in the Demographic History of London 1670–1830*. Cambridge: Cambridge University Press.

—— (1995). 'Stopping, Spacing and Starting: The Regulation of Fertility in Historical Populations', in R. I. M. Dunbar (ed.), *Human Reproductive Decisions: Biological and Social Perspectives*. London: Macmillan: 180–206.

—— and MOUZAS, A. J. (1988). 'Burial Seasonality and Causes of Death in London 1670–1819', *Population Studies*, 42: 59–83.

LANDES, D. S. (1983). *Revolution in Time: Clocks and the Making of the Modern World*. Cambridge, Mass.: Harvard University Press.

LANE, F. C. (1963). 'The Economic Meaning of the Invention of the Compass', *American Historical Review*, 68: 605–17.

LANE FOX, R. (1974). *Alexander the Great.* London: Allen Lane.
LANGDON, J. (1984). 'Horse Hauling: A Revolution in Vehicle Transport in Twelfth and Thirteenth Century England', *Past and Present,* 103: 37–66.
—— (1986). *Horses, Oxen and Technological Innovation.* Cambridge: Cambridge University Press.
LASLETT, P. (ed.) (1973). *The Earliest Classics.* Pioneers of Demography. Farnborough: Gregg.
—— (1985). 'Gregory King, Robert Malthus and the Origins of English Social Realism', *Population Studies,* 49: 351–62.
LATTIMORE, O. (1962). *Studies in Frontier History.* London: Oxford University Press.
LAURENCE, R. (1998). 'Land Transport in Roman Italy: Costs, Practice and the Economy', in H. Parkins and C. Smith (eds.), *Trade, Traders and the Ancient City.* London: Routledge: 129–48.
LAVERY, B. (1990). *Nelson's Navy: The Ships, Men and Organisation, 1793–1815.* London: Conway Maritime Press.
—— (1992). 'The Ship of the Line', in R. Gardiner (ed.), *The Line of Battle: The Sailing Warship, 1650–1840.* London: Conway Maritime Press: 11–26.
LAZENBY, J. (1991). 'The Killing Zone', in D. Hanson (ed.), *Hoplites: The Classical Greek Battle Experience.* London: Routledge: 87–109.
LE BOHEC, Y. (1994). *The Imperial Roman Army.* London: Batsford.
LEE, A. D. (1989). 'Campaign Preparations in Late Roman-Persian Warfare', in D. H. French and C. S. Lightfoot (eds.), *The Eastern Frontier of the Roman Empire.* Oxford: BAR: 257–65.
—— (1993). *Information and Frontiers: Roman Foreign Relations in Late Antiquity.* Cambridge: Cambridge University Press.
—— (1998). 'The Army', in A. Cameron and P. Garnsey (ed.), *The Cambridge Ancient History,* xiii: *The Late Empire A. D. 337–425.* Cambridge: Cambridge University Press: 211–37.
LEE, R. B., and DE VORE, I. (eds.) (1986). *Man the Hunter.* Chicago: Aldine.
LEE, R. D. (1973). 'Population in Pre-industrial England: An Econometric Analysis', *Quarterly Journal of Economics,* 87: 581–607.
—— (1977). 'Methods and Models for Analyzing Historical Series of Births, Deaths and Marriages', in R. D. Lee (ed.), *Population Patterns in the Past.* New York: Academic Press: 337–70.
—— (1986). 'Malthus and Boserup: A Dynamic Synthesis', in D. Coleman and R. S. Schofield (eds.), *The State of Population Theory.* Oxford: Basil Blackwell: 96–130.
LE GOFF, J. (1988). *Medieval Civilisation.* Oxford: Basil Blackwell.
LEIGHTON, A. C. (1972). *Transport and Communication in Early Medieval Europe.* Newton Abbot: David & Charles.
LEVINE, D. (1977). *Family Formation in an Age of Nascent Capitalism.* London: Academic Press.
LEWIS, M. (1997). 'Wooden Railways', in J. Simmons and G. Biddle (eds.), *The Oxford Companion to British Railway History.* Oxford: Oxford University Press: 567–8.
LEYSER, K. (1982). 'The Battle at the Lech, 955: A Study in Medieval Warfare', in K. Leyser, *Medieval Germany and its Neighbours, 900–1250.* London: Hambledon Press: 43–67.
—— (1994). 'Money and Supplies on the First Crusade', in T. Reuter (ed.), *Communications and Power in Medieval Europe.* London: Hambledon Press: 77–95.

LINDEGREN, J. (2000). 'Men, Money and Means', in P. Contamine (ed.), *The Origins of the Modern State in Europe*. Oxford: European Science Foundation, Clarendon Press: 129–62.

LINDNER, R. P. (1981). 'Nomadism, Horses and Huns', *Past and Present*, 92: 1–19.

LITTMAN, R. J., and LITTMAN, M. L. (1973). 'Galen and the Antonine Plague', *American Journal of Philology*, 94: 243–54.

LIVERMORE, T. L. (1957). *Numbers and Losses in the Civil War in America, 1861–1865*. Bloomington: Indiana University Press.

LIVI-BACCI, M. (1977). *Two Centuries of Italian Fertility*. Princeton: Princeton University Press.

—— (1978). *La Société italienne devant les crises de mortalité*. Florence: Dipartiments statistico.

—— (1991). *Population and Nutrition: An Essay on European Demographic History*. Cambridge: Cambridge University Press.

—— (1999). *The Population of Europe*. Oxford: Blackwell.

LOPEZ, R. S. (1956). 'The Evolution of Land Transport in the Middle Ages', *Past and Present*, 19: 17–19.

LOTTER, F. (1989). 'The Crusading Idea and the Conquest of the Region East of the Elbe', in R. Bartlett and A. MacKay (eds.), *Medieval Frontier Societies*. Oxford: Clarendon Press: 267–306.

LUTTWAK, E. N. (1976). *The Grand Strategy of the Roman Empire*. Baltimore: Johns Hopkins University Press.

LYNN, J. A. (1993a). 'How War Fed War: The Tax of Violence and Contributions during the Grand Siècle', *Journal of Modern History*, 65: 283–310.

—— (ed.) (1993b). *Feeding Mars: Logistics in Western Warfare from the Middle Ages to the Present*. Boulder, Colo.: Westview.

—— (1993c). 'Foods, Funds and Fortresses: Resource Mobilization and Positional Warfare in the Campaigns of Louis XIV', in J. A. Lynn (ed.), *Feeding Mars: Logistics in Western Warfare from the Middle Ages to the Present*. Boulder, Colo.: Westview: 137–59.

—— (1993d). 'The History of Logistics and Supplying War', in J. A. Lynn (ed.), *Feeding Mars: Logistics in Western Warfare from the Middle Ages to the Present*. Boulder: Colo.: 9–27.

—— (1997). *Giant of the Grand Siècle: The French Army 1610–1715*. Cambridge: Cambridge University Press.

MCEVEDY, C., and JONES, R. (1978). *Atlas of World Population History*. Harmondsworth: Penguin.

MACMULLEN, R. (1984). 'The Roman Emperors' Army Costs', *Latomus*, 43: 571–80.

MCNEILL, W. H. (1977). *Plagues and Peoples*. Oxford: Basil Blackwell.

—— (1983). *The Pursuit of Power*. Oxford: Basil Blackwell.

MACZAK, A. (1994). *Travel in Early Modern Europe*. Cambridge: Polity Press.

MADDICOTT, J. R. (1997). 'Plague in Seventh Century England', *Past and Present*, 156: 7–54.

MAENCHEN-HELFEN, O. J. (1973). *The World of the Huns*. Berkeley and Los Angeles: University of California Press.

MAGDALINO, P. (1995). 'The Grain Supply of Constantinople, Ninth–Twelfth Centuries', in C. Mango and G. Dagron (eds.), *Constantinople and its Hinterland*. Aldershot: Variorum: 35–47.

MALTHUS, T. R. (1970). *An Essay on the Principle of Population: and, A Summary View of the Principle of Population.* Harmondsworth: Penguin.
—— (1989). *An Essay on the Principle of Population: or, A View of its Past and Present Effects on Human Happiness; with an Inquiry into our Prospects Respecting the Future Removal or Mitigation of the Evils which it Occasions.* Cambridge: Cambridge University Press.
MANN, J. C. (1979). Review of E. N. Luttwak, *The Grand Strategy of the Roman Empire* (1976): 'Power, Force and the Frontiers of the Empire', *Journal of Roman Studies*, 69: 175–83.
—— (1991). 'The Notitia Dignitatum: Dating and Survival', *Britannia*, 22: 215–19.
MANN, M. (1986). *The Sources of Social Power,* i: *A History of Power from the Beginning to A.D 1760.* Cambridge: Cambridge University Press.
MARK, R. (1997). 'Technological Innovation in High Gothic Architecture', in E. B. Smith and M. Wolfe (eds.), *Technology and Resource Use in Medieval Europe: Cathedrals, Mills and Mines.* Aldershot: Ashgate: 11–25.
MASSCHAELE, J. (1993). 'Transport Costs in Medieval England', *Economic History Review*, 46 (2): 266–79.
MATHEWS, J. (1989). *The Roman Empire of Ammianus Marcellinus.* London: Duckworth.
MENARD, R. R. (1991). 'Transport Costs and Long-Range Trade, 1300–1800: Was There a European "Transport Revolution" in the Early Modern Era?', in J. D. Tracy (ed.), *The Political Economy of Merchant Empires: State Power and World Trade 1350–1750.* Cambridge: Cambridge University Press: 228–75.
MENKEN, J., TRUSSELL, J., and WATKINS, S. (1981). 'The Nutrition–Fertility Link: An Evaluation of the Evidence', *Journal of Interdisciplinary History*, 11: 425–44.
MESLÉ, F., and VALLIN, J. (1989). 'Reconstitution de tables annuelles de mortalité pour la France au XIXe siècle', *Population*, 44 (6): 1121–58.
MEYER, J. (2000). 'States, Roads, Armies and the Organisation of Space', in P. Contamine (ed.), *The Origins of the Modern State in Europe.* Oxford: European Science Foundation, Clarendon Press: 99–128.
MIELKE, J. H., and PITKANEN, K. J. (1989). 'War Demography: The Impact of the 1808–9 War on the Civilian Population of Åland, Finland', *European Journal of Population*, 5: 373–98.
MILNS, R. D. (1971). 'The Hyspaspists of Alexander III: Some Problems', *Historia*, 20: 186–95.
MITCHELL, B. R. and DEANE, P. (1962). *Abstract of British Historical Statistics.* Cambridge: Cambridge University Press.
MOKYR, J. (1990). *The Lever of Riches: Technological Creativity and Economic Progress.* New York: Oxford University Press.
MORILLO, S. (1996). *The Battle of Hastings: Sources and Interpretations.* Woodbridge: Boydell Press.
MORRISON, J. S., COATES, J. F., and RANKOV, B. (2000). *The Athenian Trireme.* Cambridge: Cambridge University Press.
MOSKOFF, W. (1990). *The Bread of Affliction: The Food Supply in the USSR during World War II.* Cambridge: Cambridge University Press.
MUMFORD, L. (1946). *Technics and Civilization.* London: Routledge.
NAISH, G. B. P. (1957). 'Ships and Shipbuilding', in C. J. Singer, E. J. Holmyard, A. R. Hall, and T. I. Williams (eds.), *A History of Technology,* iii: *From the Renaissance to the Industrial Revolution, c.1500–c.1750.* Oxford: Clarendon Press: 471–500.

NORTH, D. C. (1991). 'Institutions, Transaction Costs, and the Rise of Merchant Empires', in J. D. Tracy (ed.), *The Political Economy of Merchant Empires: State Power and World Trade 1350–1750*. Cambridge: Cambridge University Press: 22–40.
OBOLENSKY, D. (1974). *The Byzantine Commonwealth, Eastern Europe 500–1453*. London: Sphere.
O'BRIEN, P. (1988). 'The Political Economy of British Taxation, 1660–1815', *Economic History Review*, 2nd ser. 41: 1–32.
O'CONNELL, R. L. (1989). *Of Arms and Men*. New York: Oxford University Press.
OGILVIE, S. (1993). 'Proto-industrialization in Europe', *Continuity and Change*: 159–79.
OHLIN, G. (1961). 'Mortality, Marriage and Growth in Pre-industrial Populations', *Population Studies*, 14: 190–7.
OMAN, S. C. (1987). *The Art of War in the Sixteenth Century*. London: Greenhill Books.
—— (1991). *The Art of War in the Middle Ages*, ii: 1278–1485 AD. London: Greenhill Books.
ORMROD, W. M. (1995). 'The West European Monarchies in the Later Middle Ages', in R. Bonney (ed.), *Economic Systems and State Finance*. Oxford: European Science Foundation, Clarendon Press: 123–60.
OSIANDER, A. (1994). *The States System of Europe*. Oxford: Clarendon Press.
OUTRAM, Q. (2001). 'The Socio-economic Relations of Warfare and the Military Mortality Crises of the Thirty Years' War', *Medical History*, 45: 151–84.
OVERTON, M. (1996). *Agricultural Revolution in England: The Transformation of the Agrarian Economy 1500–1850*. Cambridge: Cambridge University Press.
PARKER, G. (1972). *The Army of Flanders and the Spanish Road 1567–1659*. Cambridge: Cambridge University Press.
—— (1974). 'The Emergence of Modern Finance in Europe 1500–1730', in C. M. Cipolla (ed.), *The Fontana Economic History of Europe: The Sixteenth and Seventeenth Centuries*. London, Fontana: 527–94.
—— (1975). 'War and Economic Change: The Economic Costs of the Dutch Revolt', in J. M. Winter (ed.), *War and Economic Development*. Cambridge: Cambridge University Press: 49–71.
—— (1984). *The Thirty Years War*. London: Routledge & Kegan Paul.
—— (1988). *The Military Revolution*. Cambridge: Cambridge University Press.
—— (1991). 'Europe and the Wider World, 1500–1700: The Military Balance', in J. D. Tracy (ed.), *The Political Economy of Merchant Empires: State Power and World Trade 1350–1750*. Cambridge: Cambridge University Press: 161–95.
PARKIN, T. G. (1992). *Demography and Roman Society*. Baltimore: Johns Hopkins University Press.
PARKINSON, C. N. (1987). *Britannia Rules: The Classic Age of Naval History 1793–1815*. Gloucester: Sutton.
PARROTT, D. (2000). 'The Utility of Fortifications in Early Modern Europe: Italian Princes and their Citadels', *War in History*, 7 (2): 127–53.
—— (2001). *Richelieu's Army: War, Government and Society in France, 1624–42*. Cambridge: Cambridge University Press.
PARRY, J. H. (1967). 'Transport and Trade Routes', in E. E. Rich and C. H. Wilson (ed.), *The Economies of Expanding Europe in the 16th and 17th Centuries*. Cambridge: Cambridge University Press: iii. 155–219.
—— (1974). *The Discovery of the Sea*. London: Weidenfeld & Nicolson.

PASSMORE, R., and DURNIN, J. V. G. (1955). 'Human Energy Consumption Expenditure', *Physiological Review*, 35: 801–39.
PATLAGEAN, E. (1969). 'Limitation de la fécondité à Byzance', *Annales*, 6: 1353–69.
—— (1977). *Pauvreté économique et pauvreté sociale à Byzance (4e–7e siècles)*. Paris: Mouton.
PEDDIE, J. (1996). *The Roman War Machine*. Stroud: Sutton.
PERJÉS, G. (1970). 'Army Provisioning, Logistics and Strategy in the Second Half of the Seventeenth Century', *Acta Historica*, 16: 1–51.
PFISTER, C. (1996). 'The Population of Late Medieval and Early Modern Germany', in B. Scribner (ed.), *Germany: A New Social and Economic History*, i: *1460–1630*. London: Arnold: 33–62.
PHILLIPS, E. D. (1965). *Royal Hordes: Nomad Peoples of the Steppes*. London: Thames & Hudson.
PLANHOL, X. DE and CLAVAL, P. (1994). *An Historical Geography of France*. Cambridge: Cambridge University Press.
POST, J. D. (1985). *Food Shortage, Climatic Variability and Epidemic Disease in Pre-industrial Europe: The Mortality Peak of the Early 1740s*. Ithaca, NY: Cornell University Press.
—— (1990). 'Nutritional Status and Mortality in Eighteenth-Century Europe', in L. Newman (ed.), *Hunger in History: Food Shortage, Poverty, and Deprivation*. Oxford: Basil Blackwell: 241–80.
POTTER, D. (1993). *War and Government in the French Provinces: Picardy 1470–1560*. Cambridge: Cambridge University Press.
POULSON, B. (1995). 'Kingdoms on the Periphery of Europe: The Case of Medieval and Early Modern Scandinavia', in R. Bonney (ed.), *Economic Systems and State Finance*. Oxford: European Science Foundation, Clarendon Press: 101–22.
POUNDS, N. J. G. (1973). *An Historical Geography of Europe 450 BC–AD 1330*. Cambridge: Cambridge University Press.
—— (1979). *An Historical Geography of Europe 1500–1804*. Cambridge: Cambridge University Press.
—— (1994). *An Economic History of Medieval Europe*. London: Longman.
POWER, E. (1969). *The Wool Trade in English Medieval History: Being the Ford Lectures*. London: Oxford University Press.
PRESTON, S. H. (1976). *Mortality Patterns in National Populations*. New York: Academic Press.
PRESTWICH, M. (1996). *Armies and Warfare in the Middle Ages: The English Experience*. New Haven: Yale University Press.
PRINCE, A. E. (1931). 'The Strength of English Armies in the Reign of Edward III', *English Historical Review*, 46: 353–71.
PRINZING, F. (1916). *Epidemics Resulting from Wars*. Oxford: Clarendon Press.
PRYOR, J. H. (1988). *Geography, Technology, and War: Studies in the Maritime History of the Mediterranean 649–1571*. Cambridge: Cambridge University Press.
RAMSAY, A. M. (1925). 'The Speed of the Roman Imperial Post', *Journal of Roman Studies*, 15: 60–74.
RAZI, Z. (1980). *Life, Marriage and Death in a Medieval Parish: Economy, Society and Demography in Halesowen 1270–1400*. Cambridge: Cambridge University Press.
RAZZELL, P. E. (1974). '"An Interpretation of the Modern Rise of Population in Europe"—a Critique', *Population Studies*, 28: 5–17.

REYNOLDS, S. (1994). *Fiefs and Vassals*. Oxford: Oxford University Press.
RICH, J., and SHIPPEY, G. (eds.) (1993). *War and Society in the Greek World*. London: Routledge.
RICHARD, J. (1999). *The Crusades c. 1071–1291*. Cambridge: Cambridge University Press.
RICKMAN, G. (1980). *The Corn Supply of Ancient Rome*. Oxford: Oxford University Press.
RILEY-SMITH, J. S. C. (1999). *The Oxford History of the Crusades*. Oxford: Oxford University Press.
RINGROSE, D. (1970). *Transportation and Economic Stagnation in Spain, 1750–1850*. Durham, NC: Duke University Press.
ROBERTS, M. (1995). 'The Military Revolution', in C. J. Rogers (ed.), *The Military Revolution Debate: Readings in the Military Transformation of Early Modern Europe*. Boulder, Colo.: Westview: 13–35.
ROBSON, B. T. (1973). *Urban Growth: An Approach*. London: Methuen.
RODGER, N. A. M. (1986). *The Wooden World: An Anatomy of the Georgian Navy*. London: Collins.
ROGERS, C. J. (1993). 'The Military Revolutions of the Hundred Years War', *Journal of Military History*, 57: 241–78.
—— (ed.) (1995). *The Military Revolution Debate: Readings in the Military Transformation of Early Modern Europe*. Boulder, Colo.: Westview.
—— (1998). 'The Efficacy of the English Longbow: A Reply to Kelly DeVries', *War in History*, 5 (2): 233–42.
ROGERS, N. A. M. (1997). *The Safeguard of the Sea: A Naval History of Britain*. London: HarperCollins.
ROSSABI, M. (1993). 'The "Decline" of the Central Asian Caravan Trade', in J. D. Tracy (ed.), *The Rise of Merchant Empires: Long-Distance Trade in the Early Modern World 1350–1750*. Cambridge: Cambridge University Press: 351–70.
ROSTOVTZEV, M. I. (1922). *Iranians and Greeks in South Russia*. Oxford: Clarendon Press.
ROTH, J. (1999). *The Logistics of the Roman Army at War (264 B.C.–A.D. 235)*. Leiden: Brill.
ROTHENBERG, G. E. (1980). *The Art of Warfare in the Age of Napoleon*. Bloomington: Indiana University Press.
RUNYAN, T. J. (1993). 'Naval Logistics in the Late Middle Ages: The Example of the Hundred Years War', in J. A. Lynn (ed.), *Feeding Mars: Logistics in Western Warfare from the Middle Ages to the Present*. Boulder, Colo.: Westview: 79–100.
RUSSELL, J. C. (1972). 'Population in Europe 500–1500', in C. M. Cipolla (ed.), *The Fontana Economic History of Europe: The Middle Ages*. London: Fontana: 25–70.
SACK, R. D. (1980). *Conceptions of Space in Social Thought*. London: Macmillan.
SAHLINS, M. D. (1968). *Tribesmen*. Englewood Cliffs, NJ: Prentice-Hall.
—— (1972). *Stone Age Economics*. Chicago: Aldine-Atherton.
SALLARES, R. (1991). *The Ecology of the Ancient Greek World*. London: Duckworth.
SALWAY, P. (1981). *Roman Britain*. Oxford: Oxford University Press.
SARRIS, P. (2002). 'The Justinianic Plague', *Continuity and Change*: 169–82.
SAUVY, A. (1969). *General Theory of Population*. London: Weidenfeld & Nicolson.
SCHAFER, L. S. (1996). *Confederate Underwater Warfare: An Illustrated History*. London: McFarland.
SCHOFIELD, R. S. (1989). 'Family Structure, Demographic Behaviour and Economic Growth', in J. Walter and R. S. Schofield (eds.), *Famine, Disease and the Social Order in Early Modern Society*. Cambridge: Cambridge University Press: 279–304.

—— REHER, D., and BIDEAU, A. (eds.) (1991). *The Decline of Mortality in Europe.* Oxford: Oxford University Press.

SCHWARZ, L. D. (1985). 'The Standard of Living in the Long Run: London, 1700–1860', *Economic History Review*, 2nd ser. 38: 24–41.

—— (1992). *London in the Age of Industrialisation: Economy and Society in the Capital, 1700–1850.* Cambridge: Cambridge University Press.

SCOTT SMITH, D. (1977). 'A Homeostatic Demographic Regime: Patterns in West European Family Reconstitution Studies', in R. D. Lee (ed.), *Population Patterns in the Past.* New York: Academic Press: 19–51.

SEN, A. (1981). *Poverty and Famines: An Essay on Entitlement and Deprivation.* Oxford: Clarendon.

SHAW, B. D. (1984). 'Bandits in the Roman Empire', *Past and Present* 105: 3–52.

SHERRATT, A. (1998). 'The Human Geography of Europe: A Prehistoric Perspective', in R. A. Butlin and R. A. Dodgshon (eds.), *An Historical Geography of Europe.* Oxford: Clarendon Press: 1–25.

SHERWIN-WHITE, S., and KUHRT, A. (1993). *From Samarkhand to Sardis: A New Approach to the Seleucid Empire.* London: Duckworth.

SHOWALTER, D. E. (1993). 'Caste, Skill and Training: The Evolution of Cohesion in European Armies from the Middle Ages to the Sixteenth Century', *Journal of Military History*, 57: 407–30.

—— (1996). *The Wars of Frederick the Great.* London: Longmans.

SIMON, J. (1977). *The Economics of Population Growth.* Princeton: Princeton University Press.

SINGER, C. J., HOLMYARD, E. J., HALL, A. R., and WILLIAMS, T. I. (eds.) (1956). *A History of Technology*, ii: *The Mediterranean Civilizations and the Middle Ages, c.700 B.C. to A.D. 1500.* Oxford: Clarendon Press.

———— et al. (eds.) (1957). *A History of Technology*, iii: *From the Renaissance to the Industrial Revolution, c.1500–c.1750.* Oxford: Clarendon Press.

SKIPP, V. (1978). *Crisis and Development: An Ecological Study of the Forest of Arden, 1570–1674.* Cambridge: Cambridge University Press.

SKÖLD, P. (1996). *The Two Faces of Smallpox: A Disease and its Prevention in Nineteenth-Century Sweden.* Umeå: The Demographic Data Base.

SLACK, P. (1985). *The Impact of Plague in Tudor and Stuart England.* London: Routledge & Kegan Paul.

SMAIL, R. C. (1956). *Crusading Warfare (1097–1193).* Cambridge: Cambridge University Press.

SMITH, C. A. (1990). 'Types of City-Size Distribution: A Comparative Analysis', in A. van Der Woude, J. de Vries, and A. Hayami (eds.), *Urbanization in History.* Oxford: Clarendon Press: 20–42.

SMITH, C. S., and FORBES, R. J. (1956). 'Metallurgy and Assaying', in C. J. Singer, E. J. Holmyard, A. R. Hall, and T. I. Williams (eds.), *A History of Technology*, ii: *The Mediterranean Civilizations and the Middle Ages, c.700 B.C. to A.D. 1500.* Oxford: Clarendon Press: 27–71.

SMITH, R. D. (1994). 'Artillery and the Hundred Years War: Myth and Interpretation', in A. Curry and M. Hughes (eds.), *Arms, Armies and Fortifications in the Hundred Years War.* Woodbridge: Boydell Press: 151–60.

SMITH, R. M. (1981). 'Fertility, Economy and Household Formation in England over Three Centuries', *Population and Development Review*, 7: 595–622.

SMITH, R. M. (1991). 'Demographic Developments in Rural England, 1300–48: A Survey', in B. M. S. Campbell (ed.), *Before the Black Death: Studies in the Crisis of the Early Fourteenth Century*. Manchester: Manchester University Press: 25–77.

SNODGRASS, A. M. (1983). 'Heavy Freight in Archaic Greece', in P. Garnsey, K. Hopkins, and C. R. Whittaker (eds.), *Trade in the Ancient Economy*. London: Chatto & Windus: 16–26.

SOROKIN, P. A. (1937). *Social and Cultural Dynamics*. New York: Bedminster.

SOUTHERN, P., and DIXON, K. R. (1996). *The Late Roman Army*. London: Batsford.

SPEIDEL, M. A. (1992). 'Roman Army Pay Scales', *Journal of Roman Studies*, 82: 87–106.

SPENCE, I. G. (1993). *The Cavalry of Classical Greece: A Social and Military History*. Oxford: Clarendon Press.

SPENCER, P. (1965). *The Samburu: A Study of Gerontocracy in a Nomadic Tribe*. London: Routledge.

SPUFFORD, M. (1974). *Contrasting Communities: English Villagers in the Sixteenth and Seventeenth Centuries*. Cambridge: Cambridge University Press.

SPUFFORD, P. (1987). 'Coinage and Currency', in M. M. Postan and E. Miller (eds.), *The Cambridge Economic History of Europe*, ii: *Trade and Industry in the Middle Ages*. Cambridge: Cambridge University Press: 788–873.

SQUATRITI, P. (1997). '"Advent and Conquests" of the Water Mill in Italy', in E. B. Smith and M. Wolfe (eds.), *Technology and Resource Use in Medieval Europe: Cathedrals, Mills and Mines*. Aldershot: Ashgate: 136–68.

STARR, C. G. (1989). *The Influence of Sea Power on Ancient History*. Oxford: Oxford University Press.

STENTON, F. (1936). 'The Road System of Medieval England', *Economic History Review*, 7: 1–21.

STIER, B., and VON HIPPEL, W. (1996). 'War, Economy and Society', in S. Ogilvie (ed.), *Germany: A New Social and Economic History*, ii: *1630–1800*. London: Arnold: 233–62.

STRADLING, R. A. (1984). 'Spain's Military Failure and the Supply of Horses, 1600–1660', *History*, June: 208–21.

SUBRAHMANYAM, S. (2001). *Penumbral Visions: Making Politics in Early Modern South India*. Ann Arbor: University of Michigan Press.

SYMONS, L., and WHITE, C. (eds.) (1972). *Russian Transport: An Historical and Geographical Survey*. London: Bell.

TALLETT, F. (1992). *War and Society in Early Modern Europe, 1495–1715*. London: Routledge.

TARN, W. W. (1930). *Hellenistic Military & Naval Developments*. London: Cambridge University Press.

'T HART, M. (1993). *The Making of a Bourgeois State: War, Politics and Finance during the Dutch Revolt*. Manchester: Manchester University Press.

—— (1995). 'The emergence and consolidation of the "tax State". II: The Seventeenth Century', in R. Bonney (ed.), *Economic Systems and State Finance*. Oxford: European Science Foundation, Clarendon Press: 281–93.

THOMPSON, I. A. A. (1976). *War and Government in Habsburg Spain*. London: Athlone.

—— (1995). '"Money, Money and Yet More Money!" Finance the Fiscal-State and the Military Revolution', in C. J. Rogers (ed.), *The Military Revolution Debate: Readings in the Military Transformation of Early Modern Europe*. Boulder, Colo.: Westview: 273–98.

TILLY, C. (1990). *Coercion, Capital and European States, AD 990–1990*. Oxford: Basil Blackwell.
TODD, M. (1987). *The Northern Barbarians*. Oxford: Basil Blackwell.
—— (1992). *The Early Germans*. Oxford: Basil Blackwell.
TOMLIN, R. (1987). 'The Army of the Late Empire', in J. Wacher (ed.), *The Roman World*. London: Routledge: i. 107–120.
TRACY, J. D. (ed.) (1993). *The Rise of Merchant Empires: Long-Distance Trade in the Early Modern World 1350–1750*. Cambridge: Cambridge University Press.
TREADGOLD, W. (1995). *Byzantium and its Army, 284–1081*. Stanford, Calif.: Stanford University Press.
TSETSKHLADZE, G. R. (1998). 'Trade on the Black Sea in the Archaic and Classical Periods: Some Observations', in H. Parkins and C. Smith (eds.), *Trade, Traders and the Ancient City*. London: Routledge: 52–74.
TYLECOTE, R. F. (1992). *A History of Metallurgy*. London: Institute of Materials.
UNGER, R. W. (1978). *Dutch Shipbuilding before 1800: Ships and Guilds*. Assen: Van Gorcum.
—— (1980). *The Ship in the Medieval Economy 600–1600*. London: Croom Helm.
—— (1984). 'Energy Sources for the Dutch Golden Age: Peat, Wind and Coal', *Research in Economic History*, 9: 221–53.
USHER, A. P. (1954). *A History of Mechanical Inventions*. Cambridge, Mass.: Harvard University Press.
VALE, M. (1981). *War and Chivalry*. London: Duckworth.
VALLIN, J. (1991). 'Mortality in Europe from 1720 to 1914: Long-Term Trends and Changes in Patterns by Age and Sex', In R. S. Schofield, D. Reher, and A. Bideau (eds.), *The Decline of Mortality in Europe*. Oxford: Oxford University Press: 38–67.
VANA, Z. (1983). *The World of the Ancient Slavs*. London: Orbis.
VAN DER WOUDE, A., DE VRIES, J., and HAYAMI, A. (1990). 'Introduction', in A. van der Woude, J. de Vries, and A. Hayami (eds.), *Urbanization in History*. Oxford: Clarendon Press: 1–19.
VAN POPPEL, F. (1989). 'Urban–Rural Differences versus Regional Differences in Demographic Behaviour in the Netherlands 1850–1960', *Journal of Urban History*, 15: 363–98.
VERBRUGGEN, J. F. (1997). *The Art of War in Western Europe during the Middle Ages, from the Eighth Century to 1340*. Woodbridge: Boydell Press.
VERHULST, A. (1998). 'Towns and Trade, 400–1500', in R. A. Butlin and R. A. Dodgshon (eds.), *An Historical Geography of Europe*. Oxford: Clarendon Press: 100–14.
VOTH, H. -J. (1998). 'Time and Work in Eighteenth-Century London', *Journal of Economic History*, 58(1): 29–57.
—— (2000). *Time and Work in England 1750–1830*. Oxford: Clarendon Press.
WALTER, J., and SCHOFIELD, R. (1989a). 'Famine, Disease and Crisis Mortality in Early Modern Society', in J. Walter and R. S. Schofield (eds.), *Famine, Disease and the Social Order in Early Modern Society*. Cambridge: Cambridge University Press: 1–73.
—— —— (1989b). *Famine, Disease and the Social Order in Early Modern Society*. Cambridge: Cambridge University Press.
WARD-PERKINS, B. (2000a). 'Land, Labour and Settlement', in A. Cameron, B. Ward-Perkins, and M. Whitby (eds.), *The Cambridge Ancient History*, xiv: *Late Antiquity: Empire and Successors, A.D. 425–600*. Cambridge: Cambridge University Press: 315–45.

WARD-PERKINS, B. (2000b). 'Specialist Production and Exchange', in A. Cameron, B. Ward-Perkins, and M. Whitby (eds.), *The Cambridge Ancient History*, xiv: *Late Antiquity: Empire and Successors, A.D. 425–600*. Cambridge: Cambridge University Press: 346–91.

WATKINS, S. C., and MENKEN, J. (1985). 'Famines in Historical Perspective', *Population and Development Review*, 11: 165–70.

WEBSTER, G. (1985). *The Roman Imperial Army in the First and Second Centuries*. London: Black.

WEIR, D. (1984). 'Rather Never than Late: Celibacy and Age at Marriage in English Cohort Fertility, 1541–1871', *Journal of Family History*, 44: 27–47.

WELLS, C. M. (1972). *The German Policy of Augustus*. Oxford: Clarendon Press.

WHEELER, E. L. (1993a). 'The Mirage of Roman Strategy: Part I', *Journal of Military History*, 57(1): 7–42.

—— (1993b). 'The Mirage of Roman Strategy: Part II', *Journal of Military History*, 57(2): 215–40.

WHITBY, M. (1988). *The Emperor Maurice and his Historian: Theophylact Simocatta on Persian and Balkan Warfare*. Oxford: Clarendon Press.

—— (1998). 'The Grain Trade of Athens in the Fourth Century BC', in H. Parkins and C. Smith (eds.), *Trade, Traders and the Ancient City*. London: Routledge: 102–28.

—— (2000). 'The Army', in A. Cameron, B. Ward-Perkins, and M. Whitby (eds.), *The Cambridge Ancient History*, xiv: *Late Antiquity: Empire and Successors, A.D. 425–600*. Cambridge: Cambridge University Press: 288–314.

WHITE, K. D. (1963). 'Wheat Farming in Roman Times', *Antiquity*, 37: 207–12.

—— (1965). 'The Productivity of Labour in Roman Agriculture', *Antiquity*, 39: 102–7.

—— (1970). *Roman Farming*. London: Thames & Hudson.

—— (1984). *Greek and Roman Technology*. Ithaca, NY: Cornell University Press.

WHITE, L. J. (1962). *Medieval Technology and Social Change*. Oxford: Oxford University Press.

—— (1972). 'The Expansion of Technology 500–1500', in C. M. Cipolla (ed.), *History of Europe: The Middle Ages*. London: Fontana: 143–74.

WHITTAKER, C. R. (1982). 'Labour Supply in the Late Roman Empire', *Opus*, 1: 171–9.

—— (1994). *Frontiers of the Roman Empire: A Social and Economic Study*. Baltimore: Johns Hopkins University Press.

WHITTAKER, C. W., and GARNSEY, P. (1998). 'Rural Life in the Later Roman Empire', in A. Cameron and P. Garnsey (eds.), *The Cambridge Ancient History*, xiii: *The Late Empire, A.D. 337–425*. Cambridge: Cambridge University Press: 277–311.

WHITTLE, A. W. R. (1985). *Neolithic Europe: A Survey*. Cambridge: Cambridge University Press.

WILLIAMS, D. (1955). *The Rebecca Riots: A Study in Agrarian Discontent*. Cardiff: University of Wales Press.

WINCH, D. (1987). *Malthus*. Oxford: Oxford University Press.

WINTRINGHAM, T., and BLASHFORD-SNELL, J. N. (1973). *Weapons and Tactics*. Harmondsworth: Pelican Books.

WOLFRAM, H. (1997). *The Roman Empire and its Germanic Peoples*. London: University of California Press.

WOOD, J. B. (1996). *The King's Army: Warfare, Soldiers, and Society during the Wars of Religion in France, 1562–1576*. Cambridge, Cambridge University Press.

Woods, R., and Williams, N. (1995). 'Must the Gap Widen before it can be Narrowed? Long-Term Trends in Social Class Mortality Differentials', *Continuity and Change*, 10(1): 105–37.

Wrigley, E. A. (1967). 'A Simple Model of London's Importance in Changing English Society and Economy 1650–1750', *Past and Present*, 37: 44–70.

—— (1969). *Population and History*. London: Weidenfeld & Nicolson, World University Library.

—— (1973). 'The Process of Modernization and the Industrial Revolution in England', *Journal of Interdisciplinary History*, 3: 225–59.

—— (1978). 'Parasite or Stimulus: The Town in a Pre-industrial Economy', in P. Abrams and E. A. Wrigley (eds.), *Towns in Societies: Essays in Economic History and Historical Sociology*. Cambridge: Cambridge University Press: 295–309.

—— (1983). 'Malthus's Model of a Pre-industrial Economy', in J. Dupâquier, A. Fauve-Chamoux, and F. Grebenik (eds.), *Malthus Past and Present*. London: Academic Press: 111–24.

—— (1985*a*). 'The Fall of Marital Fertility in Nineteenth-Century France: Exemplar or Exception?', *European Journal of Population*, 1: 31–60, 141–77.

—— (1985*b*). 'Urban Growth and Agricultural Change: England and the Continent in the Early Modern Period', *Journal of Interdisciplinary History*, 15: 683–728.

—— (1986). 'Elegance and experience: Malthus at the Bar of History', in D. Coleman and R. Schofield (eds.), *The State of Population Theory*. Oxford: Basil Blackwell: 46–64.

—— (1987*a*). 'No Death without Birth: The Implications of English Mortality in the Early Modern Period', in R. Porter and A. Wear (eds.), *Problems and Methods in the History of Medicine*. Beckenham: Croom Helm: 133–50.

—— (1987*b*). 'The Classical Economists and the Industrial Revolution', in E. A. Wrigley, *People, Cities and Wealth*. Oxford: Basil Blackwell: 21–4.

—— (1987*c*). *People, Cities and Wealth*. Oxford: Basil Blackwell.

—— (1987*d*). 'The Supply of Raw Materials in the Industrial Revolution', in E. A. Wrigley, *People, Cities and Wealth*. Oxford: Basil Blackwell: 75–91.

—— (1988). *Continuity, Chance and Change: The Character of the Industrial Revolution in England*. Cambridge: Cambridge University Press.

—— (1989). 'Some Reflections on Corn Yields and Prices in Pre-industrial Economies', in J. Walter and R. Schofield (eds.), *Famine, Disease and the Social Order in Early Modern Society*. Cambridge: Cambridge University Press: 235–78.

—— (1993). 'Reflections on the History of Energy Supply, Living Standards and Economic Growth', *Australian Economic History Review*, 33: 2–31.

—— Davies, R. S., et al. (1997). *English Population History from Family Reconstitution 1580–1837*. Cambridge: Cambridge University Press.

—— and Schofield, R. S. (1981). *The Population History of England 1541–1871: A Reconstruction*. London: Edward Arnold.

Yeates, R. (2001). *Longitude*. London: Council for Museums, Archives and Libraries.

Yeo, C. A. (1946). 'Land and Sea Transportation in Imperial Italy', *Transactions and Proceedings of the American Philological Society*, 77: 221–44.

Zaky, A. R. (1979). 'Medieval Arab Arms', in R. Elgood (ed.), *Islamic Arms and Armour*. London: Scolar Press: 202–12.

Zinsser, H. (1935). *Rats, Lice and History*. London: Routledge.

Index

absolute population loss 334, 334n. 1
administrative collection (of taxes) 359–60
administrative control 12, 244–7, 251, 379
  military resources 267–8, 283, 287, 297, 307
  Roman 268, 370–1, 373
  and tributary dependence 200, 230, 271–2, 273
  see also political power; state
aggregation and fragmentation 231–2
agricultural productivity:
  harvest failure 57, 58–60
  nomadic peoples 4–5, 232, 237–8, 239
  population dynamics 35–6, 40, 44–5, 60–3, 347
  regional variations 101–2, 104
  seasonal variations 4–5
  and the state 234, 244
  technological innovation 48–52, 53–7, 63, 70–1
  and trade 99
  transport costs 88, 89table, 93
  see also production
airborne diseases 344–5, 348, 349
Alamanni 235, 260, 338
Alexander the Great (of Macedon) 140, 141, 149, 211, 231, 244
American Civil War 206, 217n. 23, 301, 340, 343
ancient world:
  ancient demographic cycle 3, 20, 21–3
  armies 138, 144–5, 169, 208, 285, 288
  communications networks 105–6
  fortifications 177, 178
  military power 329, 329fig.
  plague 21–3, 29, 349, 350–1
  political control 228, 268, 274, 370
  shipping 73n. 1, 74, 76, 189
  spatial integration 1
  tactical systems 37–40, 141, 142–6, 148
  taxation and fiscal costs 355, 363–4, 369–70
  trade in 8, 102, 103–4, 117
  see also Greeks; Rome
Anglo-Welsh longbow 137, 146, 243
animals 2, 50, 54, 55–6, 58, 71
  herd animals 237, 238, 244
  metropolitan provisioning 383–5
  and military technology 9, 9n. 1, 134, 152, 164, 187
  and transport 72–3, 81–3, 83table, 89, 91–3
  use in warfare 206–7, 208, 209, 210, 212, 217
  see also fodder; horse power
Antonine 'plague' 29, 349
Appleby, Andrew 34
archery 145–7, 147–9, 325

steppe horse-archers 134, 135, 163, 238
armies 168–73, 170table, 172 table, 314–27, 380
  ancient world 138, 144–5, 169, 208, 285, 288
  and epidemic disease 348
  feudal 243, 249, 257, 316–19
  local militia 257, 259–60, 266, 285, 286, 304
  organization 208, 297, 315–31
  professional (paid) 244, 247, 370–1, 376
  recruitment 283–9, 312–13, 370
  standing 258, 294–5, 298, 314–15, 319, 322
  strength, and size 224, 312, 313–25
  strengths and casualties 386–403tables
  see also battles; manpower; mortality; warfare; warfare costs
armour 129–31, 136, 296, 325
arquebus 154
arthropod vector disease 30, 342–4, 348
artillery, naval 76, 160, 176–7, 191, 194, 332
artillery fortresses 179, 182–3, 193, 196, 299, 332
artillery, gunpowder 176–7, 182–3, 189, 191, 194
artillery trains 206–7, 332
assignats 369
asymptotic growth 47, 47n. 1
Augustus 144, 315, 370, 380
  military expenditure 364–5, 373, 376
Austria 322, 323n. 17, 346, 365
'autonomous death rate' 32
auxilia 144, 315
Avars 236, 238
  attacked by Franks 213, 240, 242, 242n. 11, 263
Ayton, A. and Price, J. L. 223q.

Bachrach, B. S. 295–6, 299n. 18
baggage 206–8, 210
Balts 236
barbarians 200, 210, 218, 232, 245, 248
  leadership 8, 233–6, 251, 260, 376
  as mercenary leaders 251, 288, 291, 305, 307
  power and effectiveness 4–5, 329, 329fig., 347
  tributes 357–8
barley 54, 57
barrier fortifications 178–9, 188, 299
bases (point defences) 180–1
bastions 183, 299
Bath, B. H. S. V. 59
battles:
  ancient 138, 144, 145
  Anglo-French 146, 146n. 27, n. 28, 192, 211, 225, 338
  army strengths 170, 170 table

battles: (*cont*):
  Arsouf 152
  Bannockburn 151n. 36, 319
  Carrhae 144, 148, 148n. 32, 169
  casualties 224, 336–9, 338table, 339table, 386–98tables
  Courtrai 140
  Flodden 141
  Killiecrankie 162
  naval 192–3, 193n. 16
  outcomes 128n. 1
  pre-gunpowder 204, 223–4, 241–2, 242–3, 336, 353
  tactical systems 135–6
  use of gunpowder 153–4, 171, 175, 338–9
  see also armies; manpower; mortality; warfare; warfare costs
birth rates 19, 26–7, 28, 38, 45
Black Death 24, 324, 343n. 14
  see also plague
blockade and assault 184–7
borrowing 12, 355–6, 366–9, 371, 373
Boswell, James 84
boundaries 250, 251, 252–4, 272, 361
'boundary taxes' 361
'Bourbon century' 319, 321–2, 324, 326, 372, 382
Bowlus, C. R. 213q., 243n. 12q.
Braudel, Fernand 2, 50, 52, 76q., 79, 94, 99
breech-loading mechanism 157n. 7, 158
brewing 63
bridges 107, 213n. 13
Britain:
  military strength 321–2, 322n. 14, 323, 324
  war and fiscal costs 12, 364, 364n. 6, 366, 369, 372, 374, 382
  wartime mortality rates 336, 340, 345–6
  see also England
building materials 177, 184, 299
  for military architecture 178, 181–2, 183
bulk production 111
bulk transport 7, 86, 87, 87–8table, 89table
  long-distance 102, 119, 212
burial registers 30
Byzantium 236, 238–9, 365, 370–1, 380
  military strength 259–60, 286, 316, 317table

camels 81
'campaign armies' 314, 315, 319, 325
campaigning season 214, 214n. 21, 220, 223, 254
Campbell, B. M. S. and Overton, M. 57q.
canals 85–6, 95, 108n. 9
cannon 182–3, 184, 186, 188, 191
capital costs and resources 280, 289
  see also military capital
caracole 157, 161
Carlton, C. 224
carracks 78, 191
'carvel' building 77

cash economies 12, 355, 363–4, 366–7, 371–2, 373, 376–7
castles 181–2, 223, 263
casualties, military 169–70, 175, 186, 187, 187table, 224, 335–46
  see also mortality
Catholic Church 246, 249
cavalry 134, 137, 137n. 13, 146, 147–51, 163
  cost of equipment 295, 325, 326
  Greek 140
  mobility of 205, 205n. 5, 217
  Roman 143n. 21, 144, 145
  twentieth century 9, 9n. 1
  use of firearms 156–7
  see also horses
Celts 177, 234, 239, 244
censuses 20, 27
central place systems 111
ceramic manufacture 63
chariots 134
Charlemagne, Emperor 231, 256, 317, 324
  campaigns 213, 222, 240, 243, 263
  see also Franks
Charles V, Emperor 320
chemical energy *see* gunpowder
Chesapeake Bay 33–4
Childs, J. 284q.
China 106, 178, 237
cholera 342
cities:
  Celtic tribal centres 177, 234, 244
  fortified 180, 181, 184, 185, 188, 223
  growth of 98, 99, 103, 108n. 9, 109–17, 121
  political centralization 18, 380
  strategic value 177, 202, 202n. 2, 203
  taxation and fiscal costs 362
  war, epidemics, and mortality rates 33, 343, 350–2, 353
city walls 179–80, 267
classical model 36–9, 37table, 43, 44–5, 44n. 13
climate and weather 4–5, 54, 86
'clinker' building 77
clock making 66
coal 3, 50–1, 107, 120, 122, 122n. 1
colonization 244, 246–7, 248
combat deaths 336–9, 338table, 339table
comitatenses 145, 145n. 24
command structures, military 171–3, 268, 297
commitments 10, 314–27
commodity prices 38
communications *see* information; sea routes; supply lines; transport and communications
communities:
  local in frontier regions 258–9, 266, 274
  local, and tax collection 360
  military recruitment in 284, 288, 304
  small-scale and villages 4, 43–4

INDEX

companies (military) 171, 173
compass 79–80
compulsory recruitment 282, 283, 284–5, 304, 370
concentration and dispersal 244–5
conquest 240–3, 244, 246, 248, 271, 273
conscription 12, 284–5, 304
'consequential costs' 279, 300–3
consolidation 243–7, 248–9
Constantinople 178, 236, 242, 256, 256n. 8
consumer expenditure 47
Contamine, P. 262q.
control:
   decentralized 251, 267–8, 271–2, 273
   of frontiers 250, 251–65, 267, 270, 271–2
   maintenance of 7–8, 265–7, 274
   of military resources 283, 287, 297
   and secession 250, 264–71
   see also administrative control; military power; political power; state
copper production in organic economies 65
'core-periphery' relations 8
Corps d'Armée 173, 215, 221
costs:
   military 167, 167n. 13, 176–96, 215, 325–6, 380
   military wages 290–1, 292–3tables, 304, 305, 309n. 1, *see also* wages
   transport 73, 85, 86–96, 87–8table, 89table, 92table
   of war *see* warfare costs
'counter-march' (Dutch drill) 154–5, 294
countryside, strategic value of 203–4, 217–20, 225, 347
couriers 105–6, 257, 264
credit facilities 366, 368, 371
   public credit 10, 355, 356, 373–4, 376, 380
Creveld, M. van 221n. 25
Crimean War 336
'crisis' theory 29–31, 46
crop production 53–5, 58–60, 61, 62, 71
   new crops 35, 54
   transport costs 88, 89table
   and warfare 353
   see also harvest failure
crossbows 146, 296
'crowd diseases' 31, 35n. 10, 344–5
crusades 148, 152, 221, 249, 253
cultivation *see* agricultural productivity
cultural assimilation 246
currency 64, 366–7, 369, 372n. 12
cursus honorum 268, 370, 373, 381
cursus publicus 106

'Damask steel' 70, 70n. 17
Danegeldt 358
Danzig, siege of 340, 351
Darwinian theory 159–61
   neo-Darwinian theory 68–9, 160

de Vries, Jan 4, 40, 121, 374n. 13
deaths, civilian, and warfare 280, 334, 346–54
   see also mortality
debt 368–9
decision-making 233
'deep control' 271
'defeat in detail' 203, 225
'defence in depth' 261
defences:
   barrier fortifications 178–9, 188, 299
   frontiers 200–1, 250, 251–64
   point defences 178, 179–82, 188, 193, 204, 247
   sieges 186
deflection, fiscal 300, 303–6, 326, 371
demographic costs 279, 280, 300–3, 334–5, 346, 354
demographic cycles 19, 20–6, 57, 246, 319, 324, 332
   see also population dynamics
demographic space 5–6, 17, 203–4, 222–5
   and frontier control 253–4, 264–5, 267, 270, 271–2
   see also spatial integration and organization
dependence 229–31
   tributary 200, 230, 230n. 2, 240, 245, 273, 281
depopulation 22, 24, 119, 223, 259, 347
depots (military) 209, 211, 225
devolution 282, 283, 287–9
   fiscal costs 305–6, 307–8, 371–2, 375–6, 377
diet *see* food
'diffused' threats 251, 254–5, 264, 272, 274
Diocletian 145, 365, 370
direct taxes 362
discipline, military 156, 169, 170n. 14, 221, 297
   drill 142, 154–6, 173, 174, 294–5, 331
   and indiscipline 302–3, 308, 326, 372
   sanitary regulations 340–1
disease:
   deaths from 33, 343, 350–2, 353
   and demographic change 21–2, 23, 24, 335, 347, 354
   epidemiological regimes 31–5
   and military operations 135–6, 187, 280
   and mortality rates 28, 29–35, 45–6, 135–6, 343, 350–2, 353
   and naval warfare 192n. 13
   wartime mortality rates 280, 335, 336, 339–45, 341table, 348–52, 354
Dobson, Mary 33
domain taxation/revenue 355, 356, 358, 373, 376
'dragoons' 156
draught haulage *see* haulage
Dreyse 'needle gun' 158, 168
drill, military 142, 154–6, 173, 174, 294–5, 331
Duby, G. 57q., 269q.
Duffy, C. 188q.
Durand, J. 34–5

Dutch Republic:
  canals (Trekvaart) 85n. 10, 95, 108n. 9
  depopulation 259
  fortifications 299
  military techniques 154–5, 179, 186–7
  taxation and fiscal costs 363, 368, 372, 374, 377
  urban mortality rate 121
  urbanisation 40–1, 50, 120
  water power 52
Dutch Revolt 179, 186, 259, 299, 319, 322
dysentery 342

early modern period, demographic cycle 3, 20, 24–5, 319, 352
Eastern Empire *see* Byzantium
ecological model 42–4, 45, 233–6
economic factors:
  cash economies 12, 355, 363–4, 366–7, 371–2, 373, 376–7
  disease and mortality 35, 352–3
  economic integration 11
  and military goals 217, 219, 241, 247
  and pre-industrial population 35–45
  state organizations 234
  urban centres 112–13, 115–16
  see also agricultural productivity; production; warfare costs
effectiveness, military 327–31, 333
'elastic defence' 261
emigration *see* migration
employment:
  city dwellers 115
  non-agricultural 40–1, 42
  and troop costs 290–1
  see also labour force
emporia (trading centres) 112
energy:
  chemical (gunpowder) 2–3, 153, 173
  and productivity 6, 7, 11, 47n. 2, 48, 48table, 70
  restrictions and spatial systems 2, 5–6, 227, 248, 378
  sources of 2, 50–2, 119, 120
  and warship design 161–2
  see also animals; horse power; muscle power; oars and oar power; resources; sails and sailpower; water power; wind power
engineering 66–7
England:
  Civil War 207n. 9, 213n. 18, 224
  disease and mortality rates 32, 33–4, 46
  economy and population dynamics 35, 37, 41–2, 42table
  frontier control 259, 265, 267
  industrialisation 121–2
  military strength 288, 317–19, 320, 324
  military tactics (longbow) 137, 146, 243
  'new husbandry' 57
  taxation and fiscal costs 358, 362, 365, 367
  taxation and fiscal success 10, 363, 368, 377
  troop costs 292–3table
  'Turnpike Trusts' 108
  urban migration 116–17
  see also Britain
entitlements 282, 283, 295
  entitlement principle 285
  and warfare costs 304, 356, 373, 375
entrepôts 104–5, 112
enumerated taxes 361, 362
Epaminondas 138, 140
epidemic disease *see* disease
equipment (military) 295–7, 325–6
  see also armour; horses; weapons
'escalade' 184–5
'escalation dominance' 329, 329fig.
Esdaile, C. 323, 323n. 15
'ethnic' technologies 2, 70, 149, 152, 153, 195, 293
  see also Anglo-Welsh longbow; steppe horse-archers
expansion 149, 240–8, 380
expenditure *see* costs; warfare costs
exploration, voyages of 35
extraction *see* resource extraction

family-based structures 39–40, 42, 117, 118
Ferrill, A. 142q.
ferrous metal *see* metal production
fertility 3, 19, 22n. 4, 27–8, 334
  see also birth rates
feudalism:
  military obligations 286–7, 288, 316–19, 356
  military strength 243, 249, 257
  political power 223, 228, 243, 245, 266, 269
  social relations 246–7, 274
financial institutions 12, 105, 118, 367, 368
firearms 153–75, 294, 296
  see also names of firearms
First World War 9, 9n. 1
'fiscal costs' 10, 279, 355, 363–72, 376, 382
fiscal deflection 300, 303–6, 326, 371
fiscal systems 281, 376–7, 382
Flanders 140, 216
Flinn, M. W. 122n. 1
fluyts 78, 191
fly-borne diseases 30, 342–4, 348
'flying column' 209
'focused' threats 254, 255–8, 263–4, 272, 274
fodder:
  crop production 55, 58
  metropolitan provisioning 383–5
  and military operations 185, 205–6, 207, 207n. 7, n. 9, 209, 212, 214, 217
  and transport costs 17–18, 91, 93
Fogel, R. W. 32n. 9
food:
  diet and agricultural productivity 43–4, 47–8, 57

prices and population growth 38, 46
resources and urban growth 109, 113–16, 119, 122, 383–5
shortages 350
trade 103–4
food supplies (military) 180, 199, 209–10, 217
 living off the land 203, 209, 214–16, 264, 298, 301–2
 naval supplies 189, 189n. 9
 sieges 184, 185
 subsistence 'needs' and rations 205–6, 207–10, 207n. 8
food- and water-borne diseases 341–2, 350
foraging 209, 214–15
forge *see* metal production
fortifications 176, 177–89, 196
 artillery fortresses 179, 182–3, 193, 196, 299, 332
 blockade and assault 184–7
 Celtic tribal centres 234, 244
 earthworks 299
 frontier control 259, 261–3, 262n. 14, 267
fragmentation 231–2, 267–70
France:
 bandes d'ordonnances 322
 Corps d'Armée 173, 215, 221
 costs of war 292–3table, 302–3, 303n. 22
 financial collapse 10, 12, 372, 377
 fortifications 299
 military conscription 12, 284–5, 304
 military strength 206table, 320, 321, 323, 324
 military tactics 157–8, 168, 173, 182
 mortality rates 345–6, 349
 road networks 101, 211
 taxation and fiscal costs 362, 365, 368–9, 372, 374, 382
 village communities 43–4
Franco-Prussian War 345, 346, 351
Franks 231, 235, 241, 263
 cavalry 149–50, 151, 160, 213, 246
French Revolutionary Wars 324, 342, 344, 349
frigates (cruisers) 192, 192n. 11, 194, 196
frontiers 4, 200–1, 223, 246, 353
 control of 250, 251–65, 267, 270, 271–2
 the steppe frontier 232, 234, 237–9
fuel 2, 7, 50, 114n. 11, 119, 122
functions, urban 109, 110–11

galleons 78, 191
games theory 165–8, 175
garrisons 188, 189table, 224, 401–3table
Gauls 234–5, 239–40, 241, 245
gendarmerie 157, 326
geographical space *see* spatial integration
German Health Report 350q.
Germanic peoples 149, 234–6, 239–40, 245, 370
gladius 135, 143–4
goals:
 military 202, 205, 217–20
 political 229
Godwinson, Harold 241
Goldsmith, R. W. 364, 365
'Goldstone overpopulation' 45, 252
Goldsworthy 138n. 14
Goubert, Pierre 43–4
grain:
 grain trade 103–4, 120, 380
 metropolitan provisioning 383–5
 tax grain 357, 358
 transport costs 91, 92table
Greeks 138–40, 189, 219, 364, 366–7
guerre guerroyante 204
guerrillas 215, 220
Guilmartin, J. F. 189n. 9, 205n. 4
gunpowder 153–75, 380
 army size and costs 280, 326, 332
 effect on military technology 8–10, 179, 182–3, 195
 gunpowder artillery 176–7, 182–3, 189, 191, 194, 332
 military supplies 206–7, 206table
 and military training 294
 and naval warfare 189, 191–2, 193, 196
 new military technology 188, 299, 310, 331
 pre-gunpowder technology 127–52
 pre-gunpowder warfare 205–6, 336, 347, 353
 and siege warfare 182, 183, 186–7, 188, 196, 298n. 17
 and war casualties 338–9
Gustavus Adolphus, of Sweden 171, 320, 322

'Habsburg century' 319–21, 324, 326, 371, 380
Halesowen 44
Hall, B. 294q., 331n. 26
Hannibal 143
harness (horse) 56, 82
Hartley, L. P. 1q.
harvest failure 34, 43–4, 57, 58–60, 115
 regional 101, 104
 see also crop production
haulage 4, 7, 81, 82–3, 89n. 15, 91–4
 costs of 17–18, 93, 114, 378–9
 military 206–7, 212
hearth model 39–42, 41table, 42table, 44, 45
hearth taxes 361
heavy cavalry 149–51, 151n. 35, 163, 295
'heirship' 39–40
herd animals 237, 238, 244
'high-level traffic' 99–100, 101–5, 112, 379–80
high-level warfare 204, 205–22, 226, 227, 243, 259
high-value, low-bulk goods *see* luxury goods
hoarded wealth 355–6, 357, 362, 366, 369
Hodge, W. B. 340, 346
holidays 4
Holland *see* Dutch Republic
hoplites 138–9, 142n. 18, 336
horse-archers 134, 135, 147–8, 149, 163, 238, 324

horse furniture 82, 148, 149
horse mills 52n. 7
horses:
  couriers 105–6, 257, 264
  and military technology 134, 135, 137n. 13, 146, 147–51, 164
  in organic economies 52n. 7, 56, 58
  and transport 72, 81, 82, 83–4, 108
  see also cavalry
'hospitality' (gift-giving) 233, 245, 357, 358, 366
hospitals, military 348, 349
Houdaille, J. 340, 346
hulls (ship) 75–8
Hundred Years War 224, 367
'Hunley cases' 162, 164, 165
Huns 237, 238
hunting 164
hydraulic engineering 64
hygiene and sanitation 340–1, 342, 349, 350, 354
hyspaspes ('shield bearers') 140

ideology, and morale 142, 217, 372, 382
immigration *see* migration
income taxes 362–3, 372
indirect taxes 361–2
industrial production and technology 50–2, 63–7, 121–2
  industrial revolution 1, 10–11
  military 'pre-adaptation' 164, 167
infant mortality rates 30, 33
infantry 137–47, 150–1, 171, 172table, 174, 205
  costs 296, 325, 331
  use of firearms 153, 154–6, 163–4
infectious disease *see* disease
information 2, 69–70, 97, 98, 101, 105–6
  military communications 222–3, 264, 265–6
  see also transport and communications
infrastructure 18, 44, 99–109, 117, 120, 188n. 8
inland waterways and transport 4, 72, 73, 84–6, 108n. 9
  transport costs 89, 95, 96–7, 114n. 11, 119
innovation *see* technological innovation
investment:
  military 309–14, 311fig., 325–31
  transport infrastructure 18, 106–9
iron production 3, 7, 51, 64n. 13, 65–6, 135, 135n. 10

journey times and costs 4, 5, 79, 80table, 86–96, 92table
  inland waterways 4, 86
  land transport 83–4, 83table
Justinian 231, 236, 268, 371

kastra 181
King, D. J. C. 263q.
King, G. 42
knights 150, 246, 318

knowledge transmission 2, 69–70
Körner, M. 365
Krentz, P. 336
Kunitz, S. J. 34

labour force:
  agricultural productivity 2, 4, 61–2, 71, 234, 313
  authorities' use of 12, 22, 94, 119, 187, 298–9, 380
  classical model 36–7, 44, 44n. 13
  ecological model 43–4
  and migration 117, 118
  service obligations 356–7
  ships' crews 76, 79n. 8
  shortages and surpluses 4, 17, 22, 119, 182, 313
  specialist services and non-producers 2, 11, 110, 118, 356, 372–3
  and transport costs 73, 85, 93–4
  see also employment; manpower
Ladurie, Leroy 47, 47n. 1
land transport 17–18, 73–4, 81–4, 88–9, 96
  control of goods 73, 178–9, 361
  trade in luxury goods 102–3
  urban provisioning 114
land use 6, 53–7, 378
landownership and landholding 246, 248, 259–60, 286–7, 362
'landscape' model 68–9, 159–61
Landsknecht 142, 142n. 19
Le Goff, J. 83, 84q., 100–1q., 116q.
leadership:
  barbarian 8, 233–6, 251, 260, 376
  and frontier control 251, 252, 263, 266
  military 203, 241, 268–70, 297
  military, lower-level 171, 222, 326, 333
  Roman 268–70, 370–1
  see also names of leaders; rulers
legion 142–5
leisure 110
life expectancy 28, 29, 32
light infantry *see* infantry
limits, 'hard' and 'soft' 11–12, 379
Lindgren, J. 339, 346, 346n. 18
Livi-Bacci 48
'living off the land' 203, 209, 214–16, 264, 298, 301–2
living standards 31–4, 350–1, 354, 378–9
local and minor roads 106–7
locks (inland waterways) 85, 86
logistics (military) 205–17, 219–20, 273
Lombards 235–6
London 33, 121, 122
long-distance trade 101–5, 112, 120
long-distance transport 7, 98–9, 101–6, 108, 119, 212
longbows 137, 145–7, 296
'longships' (galleys) 74–5
longue durée 2, 3, 8, 10

Lotter, F. 245
Louis XIV, of France 304, 319, 321, 368
'low-level' traffic 7, 10, 18, 98–9, 99–101
low-level warfare 199–200, 204, 218, 222–6, 243
Luttwak, Edward 181n. 2, 261, 262, 329
luxury goods (high-value, low-bulk goods) 97, 98, 99, 102–3, 112
  taxation and fiscal costs 362
  trade in 8, 103, 120, 246, 380, 381
  urban production 115
Lynn, J. A. 156q., 211q.

Macedonia 140, 141
machine gun 163
McNeill, William 35, 35n. 10
Maczak, A. 84q.
magnates 260, 288, 305, 307
Magyars 238
malaria 342, 343
Malthus 20, 20n. 1, 36n. 11, 38, 122
maniple 142–3, 143n. 22
manoeuvres, military 154–6, 169–70, 294–5, 331
manpower, military 22, 94, 167n. 13, 168–73, 268–9, 314–27
  and conquests 244, 246, 273
  frontier control 257, 258, 259–60, 261–2, 266
  full- and part-time soldiers 244, 285–7, 317table
  gun crews 206table
  investment in 309–14, 311fig., 325–31
  leadership 203, 222, 241, 260, 268–70, 297, 333
  mercenaries 147, 239, 282, 286, 287–9, 294, 302
  military service duty 259, 279, 285, 304, 356, 380
  mobile forces 177, 180, 205, 218, 261–2, 267
  non-combatants 208, 210
  paid in cash 247, 281, 286, 287, 289, 376
  paid in cash (Roman) 244, 370–1, 380
  quantity and quality 312, 314–23, 317table, 321table, 327–31, 328fig., 330fig.
  recruitment 282, 283–9
  religious orders 246, 317
  resources and population dynamics 309–33
  resources and supplies 202–17, 247, 273
  troop costs 289, 290–7, 292–3tables, 303–6, 309n. 1, 314, 325–6, 370
  unpaid 302n. 21, 305
  see also armies; battles; mortality; muscle power; warfare; warfare costs
manufacturing 63, 66–7, 110, 168
maps 253–4
marine insurance 96, 97
market centres 100, 101–2, 104, 107, 115
  military use of 209, 211
Marlborough, John Churchill, 1st Duke of 207, 211, 301
marriage 19, 27, 28, 38, 45, 46, 122
  and warfare 334, 346

massacres 347
matchlock mechanism 156n. 5
mathematical games theory 165–8, 175
Maurice of Nassau 154, 186
medical treatment 340–1, 348
medieval demographic cycle 3, 20, 23–4
medieval west:
  military strength 315, 316–19, 323–4
  military technology 127–52
  political space 253, 274
  taxation and fiscal costs 355, 356, 357, 358–9, 376, 380
  warfare 223–4, 226
men-at-arms 146, 149–51, 149n. 33, 160, 325
mercenary commanders 287, 288–9, 305, 307–8
mercenary soldiers 147, 239, 282, 286, 287–9, 294, 302
merchant bankers 367
metal production 7, 50, 51, 63–4, 64n. 13, 65–6, 71
  and military technology 2–3, 51, 135, 135n. 10, 157, 162
  and trade 103
metropolitan centres see cities
metropolitan provisioning 383–5
migration 3, 4, 26–7, 120
  urban 109, 113, 116–17, 118
  and war 280, 301n. 20, 334, 347, 348, 352
mileage costs 86, 87–91
military architecture 177, 178, 181–2, 183, 299
  siege engineering 186–7, 298
military brokers 288, 305, 306, 307, 372, 376, 382
military capital 176–96, 289
  fortifications 177–89
  naval warfare 161–2, 189–93
military power:
  investment and effectiveness 327–33, 328fig., 329fig., 330fig
  and political power 9–10, 227–8, 231, 238, 241, 244–9, 326
  and production 135, 225, 273, 290–2
  and spatial integration 199, 202–5, 227–32
  use of labour force 12, 22, 94, 187, 298–9
  see also warfare
military technology 125–99
  mobile forces 177, 180, 205, 218, 261–2, 267
  mobile military hardware 128–35, 174, 182–3, 193
  and political power 152, 152n. 38, 167, 199, 202, 238
  size of forces 168–73, 185
  tactical systems 135–52, 153–8, 171–3, 184–7, 297, 333
  technological innovation 153–8, 157n. 7, 158–68, 175
  transport infrastructure 108, 117, 188n. 8
  use of metals 2–3, 51, 135, 135n. 10, 157, 162
millet 54, 57
mineral economies 1, 3, 122, 168, 358, 359

mines and mining 64–5, 108
Minié rifled muskets 158, 164n. 11
missile weapons 1, 133–4, 136, 145–7
   cannon 182–3, 184, 186, 188, 191
mobile forces 177, 180, 205, 218, 261–2, 267
mobile military hardware 128–35, 174, 182–3, 193
mobility (military) 205–17, 219–20
models:
   'landscape' model 68–9, 159–61
   pre-industrial population 35–45
modern period 20, 26, 319–23
   early modern demographic cycle 3, 20, 24–5, 319, 352
'modern state' 228
Mokyr, J. 49, 51n. 6, 164n. 12
money *see* cash economies
Mongols 106, 149, 238, 239
monopoly rights 362
morale, military 139, 142, 217, 221
mortality:
   civilian deaths and war 280, 334, 346–54
   and disease 28, 29–35, 45–6, 135–6, 343, 350–2, 353
   military casualties 169–70, 175, 186, 187, 187table, 224, 335–46
   and population dynamics 3, 19, 24, 26–7, 38, 45
   urban in Dutch Republic 121
multi-purpose defences 181–2
Mumford, L. 64, 67q.
muscle power:
   military technology 9, 152, 176, 184–6, 188, 196
   naval warfare 189–91, 191n. 10
   and productivity 17, 58, 63, 380
   as a source of energy 2, 52, 119
   and transport 73–4, 86, 96
'musket and sabre' system 153–4, 157–8, 163–4, 168
muskets 154, 155, 157, 158, 294, 296, 331n. 25

Napoleon:
   army size 285, 323, 349
   military organization 158, 173, 215, 221, 303, 369
Napoleonic Wars 324, 336, 344, 349, 351
natural increase 26–7, 218
naval supplies 189, 189n. 9
naval warfare 161–2, 176–7, 189–93, 332
navigation (shipping) 78–81
NCOs (non-commissioned officers) 171, 326
neo-Darwinian theory 68–9, 160
Netherlands *see* Dutch Republic
networks *see* information; roads; sea routes; traffic; transport and communications
New England 33–4
nomadic peoples 4–5, 214, 232, 237–8, 239, 244, 267
non-producers and specialist services 2, 11, 110, 118, 356, 372–3

Norman conquest 146n. 27, 241, 259, 265, 267, 301, 318
'northern barbarians' 232, 234–6
nuptiality 19, 22n. 4, 27–8
nutrition and mortality 31–2, 34, 45

oars and oar power 74–5, 176–7, 189, 192
Obolensky, D. 236q.
O'Brien, P. 363n. 3
occupation, military 199, 217, 219, 225–6, 240, 273
ocean-going vessels 77, 79–80, 95
   see also sea transport
O'Connell, R. L. 168q.
Oman, S. C. 247n. 14q.
oppida 177, 234, 244
organic economy 1, 2, 202–26, 378
Ottoman dynasty 239
Ottoman road system 106, 108
over- and underpopulation 40, 44–5, 60–3, 347
oxen 56, 58, 81, 82

pack carriage 17–18, 81–3, 210, 212
Paris, siege of 350–1
parish registers 24, 346
Parker, G. 320
passenger transport 82, 84
pastoral nomads 4–5, 214, 232, 237–8, 239, 244, 267
peacetime military commitments 314, 315, 322
peat 50, 120
Peddie, J. 207, 208
peltasts 139
Persians 138, 148, 231, 256
phalanx 137–42
phenotype 237n. 8
Philip II of Macedonia 140
phyletic evolution 68, 69, 159, 164
pike and pikemen 140, 141, 147, 151n. 36, 155n. 2, n. 3
   and use of firearms 154–5, 326
pilum 143
piracy 190–1, 266
plague:
   ancient world 21–3, 29, 349, 350–1
   bubonic plague 23, 24, 30, 32, 342–3, 348
Pliny 65
ploughs, ploughland 53, 55
point defences 178, 179–82, 188, 193, 204, 247
   frontier control 259, 261, 263n. 16
political power:
   and dependence 229–31
   feudal 223, 228, 243, 245, 266, 269
   local and regional 267–8, 274
   and military power 9–10, 227–8, 231, 238, 241, 244–9, 326
   and military technology 152, 152n. 38, 167, 199, 202, 238
political integration 11
and resources 379

Roman 231, 234–5, 238, 239, 245, 248
  and state organization 244, 378
  and trade routes 103, 104, 202
  and transport infrastructure 108–9
  urban functions 110, 112–13, 117
  and urbanization 99, 120
  use of labour force 12, 22, 94, 119
  see also administrative control; cities; state
political space 253
poll taxes 361
population dynamics:
  and agricultural productivity 35–6, 40, 44–5, 60–3, 347
  cycles of growth 3–5, 19, 20–6, 57, 246, 324
  demographic costs 279, 280, 300–3
  depopulation 22, 24, 119, 223, 259, 347
  low density population 234, 241, 244, 247, 265, 273
  military resources and manpower 309–33
  population growth 3–4, 18, 35–6, 120, 122
  pre-industrial models 35–45
  stateless peoples 232–40, 248
  vital processes and regimes 3, 26–35
  and warfare 334–54
  see also migration and immigration
ports 104, 112, 120
Potter, D. 84q., 253n. 2
poverty 2, 17, 19, 61, 100, 119, 375
power *see* animals; energy; horses; military power; muscle power; political power; water power; wind power
"power optimum" population 311, 311fig.
precious metals 64, 65
  stocks of 355–6, 357, 362, 366, 369
'preclusive defence' 261
printing 66, 66n. 14, 67, 67n. 15
Prinzing, F. 350q., 351
'prisoner's dilemma' 165–8
prisoners of war 340
production:
  low, and poverty 2, 17, 19, 61, 100, 119, 375
  and military power 135, 225, 273, 290–2
  and military service 309–10, 312–13, 332
  output and risk 53, 54, 61–2, 71
  subsistence and luxury goods 98, 99, 103–4, 115
  traffic and trade 100, 101, 111
  and transport costs 93–4, 97
  see also agricultural productivity; industrial production
Prussian army 304, 322, 323, 342, 345
public credit 10, 355, 356, 373–4, 376, 380
public taxation 356, 359–63, 367, 373–4
public works 91, 93, 119

quality costs (military) 291–9

raiding 199, 217, 218–19, 225, 273, 380
  banditry 238, 258, 265
  costs of 301, 308, 347
  cross-border 253, 255, 258, 260, 262, 269
  and expansion 240, 249
  raiding cavalry 205n. 5
  seaborne raiders 190–1, 258, 269
railways 108, 221, 221n. 25
rations *see* food supplies (military)
ravaging 301, 302, 347
raw materials 2, 7, 103, 375, 378
Razi, Z. vi 44, 44q.
recorded data (registers/censuses) 20, 23–4, 27, 30, 35, 346
  military 310, 335
recruitment (military) 36, 282, 283–9, 304, 312–13, 370
'Red Queen' phenomenon 36, 49, 53, 57, 159
refuges 180
regiments 171, 173
regional market centres 17, 100, 101–2, 104, 107, 115, 378
reiters 155n. 2, 157, 326
relative population loss 334, 334n. 1
religions and political space 253
religious orders, military 246, 317
repartition 359, 360
resources:
  capital resources 280, 289
  cost of war 279–308, 355–6, 372–3
  and frontier control 262
  manpower and population dynamics 309–33
  metropolitan provisioning 383–5
  military infrastructure 176–96
  military supplies 135, 199–200, 202–3, 204, 205–17, 220–1
  raw materials 2, 7, 103, 375, 378
  resource extraction 200
  and urban growth 109, 113–16, 119, 122
  see also energy; food; food supplies; taxation
respiratory diseases 29, 34, 344, 352
revenue *see* taxation
rigging (ship) 75, 189
Ringrose, David 91–3
river transport 85, 86
rivers, as barriers 254, 263
roads 82–3, 99–100, 100–1, 100n. 2
  communications and information 105–6, 117, 222
  economics of infrastructure 106–9, 120
  frontier control 267
  and military operations 188q.
  see also transport and communications
Rogers, C. 128n. 1
Rome:
  armies 257, 315–16, 323, 370
  emperors 370–1, *see also* names of emperors
  engineering 64
  fortifications 177, 178
  frontier control 251, 253, 261, 267

Rome: (cont):
  military campaigns 212n. 18, 213, 244, 289
  military strength 317table, 323, 326, 332, 376, 380
  military technology 135, 142–5, 148, 169, 180, 180n. 1
  political power 231, 234–5, 238, 239, 245, 248
  population in Italy 21
  provincial control 268–70
  public service career (cursus honorum) 268, 370, 373, 381
  roads 82–3
  shipping 73n. 1, 76–7
  trade in luxury goods 102
  transport costs 88–9
  troop costs 289, 292table, 304, 306, 338, 370, 373
  war, taxation and fiscal costs 357, 364–5, 370, 373, 376
  see also ancient world
rotation (crop production) 53–4, 55
Rothenberg, G. E. 323n. 17
'roundships' 74, 75
routes see roads; sea routes; transport and communications
rulers:
  civilian, and military power 7–8, 274, 312, 326, 332
  taxation and fiscal costs 355, 358, 367, 375–6
  see also leadership; names of rulers; state
Runyan, T. J. 192n. 14, n. 15
Russia 238, 239, 322, 323, 324

Sack, R. D. 5q.
sails and sailpower 74, 75, 191
saltation 68, 69, 158, 164, 168
sanitation and hygiene 340–1, 342, 349, 350, 354
Saracens 238
sarissa 140, 141
Sarmatians 148, 238
Sauvy, Alfred (Sauvy model) 310–12, 311fig., 325, 326, 327
Scandinavia 346, 367
sea routes, control of 190, 192–3, 194, 213
sea transport 72, 73, 74–80, 87, 95, 97
  naval 189, 190
  and trade 104, 120, 190
  see also vessels
seasonal variations 3–5, 29–30, 375
secession 250, 264–71
'security in depth' 267
security measures:
  communications networks 106, 266
  frontiers 266, 267
  trade routes 102–3
  transport costs and journey time 95–6
  urban functions 110
seed–yield ratios 58–60, 59table, 61–2, 71

'select fyrd' 317–18
Sewall Wright 'landscape' model 68, 159–61
'ship of the line' (battleship) 191, 192, 194, 196
ships and ship building 69n. 16, 72, 73, 74–8
  military and naval technology 160, 161, 189–92, 300
shock weapons 131–3, 136–7, 148, 174
siege warfare 135, 174, 176, 177–88, 187table
  costs of 298, 298n. 17
  mortality rates 340, 350–2
  sieges and assaults 399–403tables
  use of gunpowder 182, 183, 186–7, 188, 196, 196, 298n. 17
Six Weeks War 336, 340, 346
skills, military 286, 291, 292–3table, 294, 305, 327, 331
  steppe horsemen 135, 147–8, 149
  see also training, military
slave trade 103, 347
Slavs 232, 236, 260
smallpox 22, 30, 33, 344–5, 349, 352
social structures:
  barbarian 8, 233–4, 235, 237–8, 245, 248
  demographic factors 6, 252
  feudal 246–7, 274
  hierarchies 229, 268–9
socio-economic factors:
  and agricultural production 43, 56, 353
  cultural assimilation 246
  and military technology 142, 142n. 18, n. 19, 202
  'strategic depth' 242
  and warfare 279, 353
socket bayonet 136, 155, 157, 162
sovereignty 230, 231, 270
space see demographic space; spatial integration and organization
Spain:
  animals and transport costs 93
  Dutch revolt 179, 186, 259, 299, 319, 322
  Habsburg military strength 322, 366
  maritime strength 332
  military technology 186–7
  road networks 101, 108, 211
  taxation and fiscal costs 359, 367–8
Spanish Succession War 179, 322
spatial integration and organization 1, 5–6, 378, 379
  and state power 199, 202–5, 227–32, 248
  towns and cities 109–17
  trade and economic growth 11, 98, 99
  travel distance, time and cost 4, 90–1
  see also demographic space
specialist services and non-producers 2, 11, 110, 118, 356, 372–3
Spence, I. G. 295
Spinola, Amrogio di Filippo, marqués de Los Balbases 186, 187

state 10, 199, 202–5, 227–32, 248
  aggregation and fragmentation 231–2
  and agricultural productivity 234, 244
  and dependence 229–31
  expansion 240–8, 380
  fiscal administration 355, 356, 359, 363, 366–9, 370–1
  frontier control 251, 257, 272
  military administration and control 258, 372, 373, 382
  organization and administration 244, 375–6, 378, 379
  stateless peoples 232–40, 248, 357–8, 380
  see also administrative control; barbarians; political power
steam power 74, 161
steppe frontier 232, 234, 237–9
steppe horse-archers 134, 135, 147–8, 149, 163, 238
stirrup 148, 149
stone (building material) 177, 183, 299
'strategic depth' 242
strategies, military 202, 205, 217–20, 225, 261–3, 273
submarine warfare 162
subsistence:
  failure 36–7, 43–4, 347
  goods 7, 98, 99, 103–4
  migrants 116–17
  'subsistence minimum' 310
  warfare costs 301–2
supply lines 199, 209, 211, 212–14, 219, 220–1, 225
  colonized areas 247, 273
'supply-side' 332
'sweating sickness' 349
Sweden 224, 320, 322, 324, 346, 367
Swiss pikemen 141, 147

tactical systems (military) 135–52, 153–8, 171–3, 184–7, 297, 333
'tax-farming' 359, 360, 376
taxation 245, 248, 279, 281, 355–6, 375–6, 379
  borrowing 355–6, 366–8, 371, 373
  cash payment 356–7, 366–7, 373
  military service duty 259, 279, 285, 304, 356, 380 *see also* entitlements
  payment in kind 280, 356–7, 373
  revenue 245, 247–8, 356–63
technological innovation:
  and agriculture 48–52, 53–7, 63, 70–1
  invention and output 2, 67–70, 71, 330
  military technology 153–8, 157n. 7, 158–68, 175
  power and population 309–14
  transport technology 73–86
technology, definitions of 49
Teutonic order 246
textiles 66, 103
themes 286, 316
Thirty Years War 215–16, 220, 229, 320

and demographic change 319, 352, 353
Thompson, I. A. A. 307n. 24
threats (to frontiers) 254, 254–60, 263–4, 272, 274
Thucydides 350
Tiberius 231
time frontiers 4, 5, 79, 80table, 83–4, 83table, 86–96, 92table
TMFR (Total Marital Fertility Rate) 27
tolls 108, 108n. 8, 180, 361
tools 54, 63, 66–7
towers 182, 183, 267
towns *see* cities
trade:
  control of movement of goods 73, 178–9, 361
  'core-periphery' relations 8
  cost of land haulage 17–18, 93, 114, 378–9
  costs of war 303, 367
  long-distance 101–5, 112, 120
  networks 11
  seaborne 104, 120, 190
  steppe nomads 238
  time and cost 4, 86–96, 87–8table, 89table, 92table
  and traffic 18, 98–118, 379–80
  and water transportation 72, 74, 76, 78–9, 108n. 8
trade routes 102–3, 104, 202
traffic:
  infrastructure 99–109
  towns, cities and space 109–17
  and trade 18, 98–118, 379–80
training, military 139, 222, 282, 284
  cost of 293–5, 297, 331
  see also discipline, military; drill, military; skills
'transaction taxes' 361, 362
transport and communications 17–18, 72–122
  costs 73, 85, 86–96, 87–8table, 89table, 92table
  and frontier control 254, 257, 264, 265
  long-distance 7, 98–9, 101–6, 108, 119, 212
  'low-level' traffic 7, 10, 18, 98–9, 99–101
  military 168–9, 179, 200–1, 203–4, 206–10, 222–3
  military costs 298
  time frontiers 4, 5, 79, 80table, 83–4, 83table, 86–96, 92table
  towns, cities and space 109–17
  traffic infrastructure 99–109
  see also information; roads; sea routes; supply lines; travel distance
travel distance, time and cost 4, 5, 90–1
Treadgold, W. 315, 316, 323, 365
Westphalia, Treaty of 229
Trekvaart 85n. 10, 95, 108n. 9
tributary dependence 200, 230, 230n. 2, 240, 245, 273, 281
tributes 355, 356, 357–8, 373

troop costs 289, 290–7, 292–3tables, 303–6, 309n. 1, 314, 325–6, 370
troop strengths 312, 314–23, 317table, 321table, 327–31
troop types 137–51
    see also manpower
'Turnpike Trusts' 108
typhus fever 340, 342, 343–4, 348, 350

urban centres 112–13
urban functions 109, 110–11
urban networks 112
urban populations 40–1, 41table, 120–1
urbanization 98, 99, 109–17, 119–21, 342

vaccination 344–5, 349–50
van der Woude, A. 4, 121, 374n. 13
vehicles 72–3, 82, 134, 206–7, 209–10
Verbruggen, J. F. 296
vessels:
    inland waterways 84–5
    sea-going 74–8, 79–80
    warships 161–2, 189–92, 300
    see also sea transport
vexillationes 144
Vikings 191
villages 43–4
vital processes and regimes 3, 26–35
vocational principle 282, 283, 285–7
'Von Thünen problem' 88, 93, 383

wages:
    levels and population dynamics 37, 312–13
    troop costs 290–1, 292–3tables, 304, 305, 309n. 1, 370
    troops paid in cash 247, 281, 286, 287, 289, 376
    troops paid in cash (Roman) 244, 370–1, 380
Wallenstein, Albrecht Herzog von 306, 320
walls, defensive 178–9, 184–5, 299
war fleets 177
War of the League of Augsburg 321
warfare 8–10, 202–26
    combat deaths 336–9, 338table, 339table
    deaths from disease 335, 336, 339–45, 341table, 348–52, 354
    goals and strategy 202, 205, 217–20, 225, 261–3, 273
    high-level 204, 205–22, 226, 227, 243, 259
    logistics and mobility 205–17, 219–20, 273
    low-level 199–200, 204, 218, 222–6, 243
    mortality and disease 35, 135–6, 187, 280, 336

scale of operations 220–2
see also armies; battles; manpower; military technology; mortality; warfare costs
warfare costs 10, 279–308, 334–54, 355–74, 376–7, 380, 382
    consequential costs 279, 300–3
    fiscal costs 10, 279, 355, 363–72, 376–7, 382
    fiscal deflection 300, 303–6, 326, 371
    immediate 279, 289–99
    military deaths 186, 224, 335–46
    operational 289, 297–9
    recruitment 282, 283–9, 306, 370
    troop costs 289, 290–7, 292–3tables, 303–6, 309n. 1, 314, 376
    see also manpower; military technology; mortality; warfare
warhorses see horses
warships 161–2, 189–92, 300
    broadside artillery 160, 176–7, 194, 332
water power 51–2, 65–6, 71
water transport 185, 186, 212, 213, 213n. 20, 263, 273
    and trade 72, 74, 76, 78–9, 108{n. 8}
    see also inland waterways; sea transport
water- and food-borne diseases 341–2, 350
Watkins, S. C. and Menken, J. 347
weapons 131–4, 135, 136–7, 136n. 12, 145–7, 152, 174
    firearms 153–75, 294, 296
    introduction of gunpowder 9, 179, 182–3, 188, 206–7, 206table
    technological 'pre-adaptation' 164, 167
    see also names of weapons e. g. longbow; musket
weather and climate 4–5, 54, 86
west see medieval west
wheat 54, 92table
wheel-lock mechanism 156, 156n. 6
Whittaker, C. R. 178–9q., 251q., 253q.
William of Normandy 246–7, 247n. 14
wind power 51–2, 71, 72, 120, 189, 191
Wolfram, Herwig 260q.
wood 66, 75–8, 177, 184, 192
    fuel wood 2, 50, 119
Wood, J. B. 296
wool 103
Wright, Sewall 68, 159–61
Wrigley, A. E. 1, 2, 41–2, 60, 62, 107q., 121, 122n. 1

yield ratios 58–60, 59table, 61–2, 71

zones (frontier) 250, 251, 252–4